D0898049

Petrochemicals:
The Rise of an Industry

Petrochemicals
THE RISE OF AN INDUSTRY

Peter H. Spitz

WILEY

JOHN WILEY & SONS
New York • Chichester • Brisbane • Toronto • Singapore

Jacket. *Background:* Courtesy of Bayer AG at Leverkuesen, West Germany, which operates some of the most modern chemical plants, but has preserved many years of industrial architecture and design that reveal traces of its past.

Inset: Union Carbide and Shell Chemical, two companies that made important early contributions to the development of the petrochemical industry, have collaborated in polypropylene technology. The picture shows a plant at Seadrift, Texas.

Copyright © 1988 by John Wiley & Sons, Inc.

All rights reserved. Published simultaneously in Canada.

Library of Congress Cataloging in Publication Data:
Spitz, Peter H.
 Petrochemicals: the rise of an industry.

 Includes indexes.
 1. Petroleum chemicals industry—History.
 2. Petroleum chemicals—History. I. Title.
 HD9579.C32S65 1988   338.4'7661804   87-23019
 ISBN 0-471-85985-0

Printed in the United States of America

10 9 8 7 6 5 4 3 2 1

This history of the petrochemical industry is dedicated to the memory of Professor Glenn Bennett, who taught chemistry and physics at Germantown Friends School in Philadelphia for many years. Mr. Bennett was one of those inspiring teachers who can shape people's lives. He endowed me with a lifelong interest in chemistry and in the application of chemistry to industrial processes.

Foreword*

It's almost fifty years since I entered the freshman class in chemical engineering at Oregon State University in the fall of 1938. That was just about the time that the word "petrochemicals" entered the vocabulary of chemical engineers. The industry has grown since that time from a few pockets of competence scattered around the world into a massive force responsible for about ten percent of the gross national product of the industrial countries. Its processes and products impact the lives of billions of people in both developed and undeveloped nations, almost always in useful ways, frequently in unseen ways, sometimes in dramatic and lifesaving ways, very rarely in damaging ways.

Petrochemicals: The Rise of an Industry paints an interesting and thought-provoking mosaic of interconnected scientific, engineering and economic achievements over the course of the past century. Those of us in the chemical engineering profession, beginners and veterans alike, will profit from some reflection on these achievements and on the character and abilities of the individuals who made them possible. In the early days of the chemical industry, persistent and creative scientists and engineers with an appreciation of economic realities built the industry.

*By Robert W. Lundeen, formerly chairman, Dow Chemical Company.

Today, successors of those pioneers with many of the same talents are required to lead the industry into its future.

As a young researcher in the early 1950s, it was my privilege to have had as a counselor and role model a European scientist of the old school, Dr. Wilhem Hirschkind. He had been a graduate student of Fritz Haber's at the Technische Hochschule of Karlsruhe during the early years of this century, when Haber was doing his research work in ammonia synthesis. Hirschkind carried with him to this country strong views about professional integrity and about the broader responsibilities of those of us in the chemical business to our profession and to society. Of equal importance, he believed and demonstrated in his own work that any significant advance in chemical production practice must be based on solid scientific understanding and carefully done research. And to this day, I vividly remember a comment he made to me in his office at Pittsburg, California, one afternoon almost forty years ago: "Any otherwise well-qualified individual who aspires to a position of business leadership and high professional achievement must also be a gentleman!" Great advice then; great advice now.

I give this personal anecdote space in this foreword because it says something significant about the character of the people who were the builders of our industry. Character and breadth are even more essential qualities for today's petrochemical leaders. The industry lives in an unforgiving environment with the long-established requirement for making sound technical and economic judgments, but with even greater pressure for making sensible and sensitive judgments in a whole variety of sociopolitical issues, e.g., balance of constituency interests, political risk assessments, ethical standards, public policy development, constituency communications. Professional competence, self-confidence, personal integrity, and intellectual breadth—those are the qualities that today's leaders must bring to the job.

The petrochemical industry began an aggressive migration from the United States to a variety of seemingly attractive foreign production and market opportunities in the late 1950s. Its accomplishments in Europe are well documented, and American companies stand there today as formidable competitors in a sophisticated market. Perhaps less well appreciated is the transfer of petrochemical technology and management skills from the large industrial nations to the less developed and/or smaller countries in Latin America and Asia. In those countries, the impact of the transfer was relatively larger, because what was brought was generally of a much higher standard than what had been developed locally up to that time. Transfer of technology and management skills was of obvious value, but the companies brought something else of equal or greater value ... opportunity. Until foreign investors, frequently but not exclusively from the United States, introduced their advanced technology and built their factories, job opportunities for technically trained and ambitious young people were distinctly limited. Local petrochemical investments enabled talented young men and women to work at home rather than being forced to emigrate to capitalize on their skills.

Even less appreciated is the fact that in many instances American petrochemical investors in less-developed countries set the standards for environmental protection and worker safety. (It is of course popular in some sectors of our society today and was even more popular a few years ago to "bash" the chemical industry for its sins of omission in environmental matters. The industry was not perfect, to be sure, but in the great majority of cases it acted responsibly on the basis of information available at the time.) In most less-developed countries, environmental standards were completely absent or elementary at best when American petrochemical investment began in the late 1950s and early 1960s. Having no national guidelines, companies normally applied their U. S. standards. Those company standards frequently provided a foundation for the local authorities to get started on their own environmental programs. The same can be said of worker safety: the gap between local and U.S. safety standards was probably even greater than in environmental matters. I was always very proud of Dow Chemical's policy (and I paraphrase): With respect to worker safety and environmental protection we will apply the stricter of either our own or the national standard.

I dwell on the foregoing, because I believe a strong case can be made that the petrochemical business is a very useful business, useful not only in economic terms but in social terms. Its products, its opportunities, and its standards are now part of many societies that didn't even know the term "petrochemicals" twenty-five years ago. The industry's impact on the standard of living, personal health, and economic opportunities for people around the world is pervasive and positive.

Looking back on a forty-year career in the business, it seems to me that the driving forces in world petrochemical developments are three: (1) advances in the physical sciences, (2) opportunities for economic gain, and (3) changes in the global social and political movement. In the "olden days", i.e., when I began my professional career, advances in physical sciences and opportunities for economic gain were the recognized driving forces. Little if any recognition was given to changes in the global sociopolitical environment. Today, industrial leaders who fail to develop awareness of and competence in dealing with the impact of these latter forces on their enterprises will not be leaders for long. In saying this, I am reinforcing what Peter Spitz says in his excellent concluding paragraphs on the future. He cogently sums up the whole issue in one sentence "One way or the other, the future is up to the industry's current and future management." Quality management does make a difference, a huge difference. The premier managements in the industry have prepared themselves by building reserves, both financial and human, to withstand hard times brought on by forces outside their control and, more importantly, to capture opportunities when they present themselves. Failure to build such reserves is as lethal in the long term as failure to do research or to provide quality products on a continuing basis.

Management of petrochemical enterprises must now be viewed in global rather than national or regional terms. Individual national markets and national policies are receding in significance. It is the complex simultaneous global equations of supply and demand, relative economic strength, political equilibria, military power, ideological fervor, and the relentless advance of scientific knowledge that are the major determinants of the future of the petrochemical business. Those who involve themselves in the mastery of these equations have in prospect as challenging, exciting, and personally rewarding careers as any of us who had our career in the first half-century of the petrochemical age.

ROBERT W. LUNDEEN

Pebble Beach, California, March 1987

Preface

The petrochemical industry is unique in that it experienced an unusually rapid transition from its birth in the early 1920s to what many people called "maturity" by the mid-1970s. Between 1940 and 1960, it became one of the largest industry sectors, providing an astounding variety of chemical intermediates used for the manufacture of plastics, fibers, synthetic rubber, and many other end products. The petrochemical industry was to a large extent "made in America," because it was in the United States that an unusual combination of circumstances existed at a certain point in time: an abundance of inexpensive gaseous and liquid petroleum feedstocks, suitable technology, a large market, and an incentive for rapid development, occasioned by military needs in World War II. This was followed by a consumer-oriented boom that developed when the war was over.

Much of the technology, of course, came from Europe and particularly from Germany, which had built up a formidable chemical industry over a 100-year period. But the German chemical industry was based on coal. And it was largely built by chemists, before chemical engineering became a separate discipline. Chemical engineers in the United States, and later in many other countries, were primarily responsible for the success of the new petrochemical industry.

This book is written for people interested in the origins of the petrochemical industry, in its technology, in some of the personalities who founded this industry and made it grow, and in the development of the business aspects of a new industry. It was a magnificent achievement and deserves being remembered at a time when the chemical industry is under a cloud, due to a history of benign neglect of the environment and, at times, a lack of sensitivity to health hazards caused by some of its products. It is no longer a glamor industry, since the production of commodity chemicals, as bulk petrochemicals are now often called, became a relatively unprofitable business. Many producers of these materials have now diversified into other fields. But to those of us who remain involved in the petrochemicals business, many challenges still remain: new polymers, "breakthrough" processes with novel catalysts, lower production costs through energy savings, etc. A mature industry doesn't have to be dull! And is it really *mature*?

Parts of this book will seem like a course in industrial chemistry. I must admit that was, in fact, part of my intention. The curricula of many chemical engineering departments in universities no longer feature industrial chemistry courses, concentrating instead on the more theoretical aspects of chemical engineering (transport phenomena, computer applications to complex physical chemistry problems, etc.). This has apparently been justified on the basis that students will develop a practical knowledge of manufacturing operations when they enter industry. But, as a result, many of these graduates will not go into the chemical industry, because they have not been exposed to the challenges and excitement this industry can evoke. Perhaps, by reading this book, some students will have a better opportunity to appreciate this, while learning about the origins of the modern organic chemical industry. Some of them may, in the future, experience the excitement of participating in the process whereby a new synthesis that at first produced just a few grams of material is transformed into a plant producing 100 million pounds per year.

Although I did not have a well-developed thesis when I started to write, it became evident that a number of conclusions could be drawn from the historical growth of the industry I was examining. Several themes suggested themselves and they became more firmly established, as the work progressed.

The first is that technology keeps advancing in an inexorable manner, certainly to the benefit of mankind, sometimes to the considerable benefit of the inventor, but not always to the expected financial gain to the firm or firms employing the new technology. Companies in the petrochemical industry derived meaningful profits from inventing a new technology only if it was really unique and they could maintain control over it through the use of the patent system. That this is more difficult than expected, in many cases, must come as a surprise to many people. Many times it is easier than one might think to get around patents. At other times, the patent is not really broad enough to dominate. Many of the technological developments made in the petrochemical industry were not enough of a "breakthrough" to provide major entry barriers for competitors. And where inventions were made by engineering firms eager to sign up licensees, there was no reason to expect anything but a free-for-all, as new entrants to the industry lined up to purchase the new technology.

The second theme is that an industry can undergo a total transformation when its raw materials base changes. It didn't matter that coal, alcohol, crude oil, or natural gas could all be transformed into many of the same organic chemicals. The important thing was that this could be done most inexpensively from feedstocks derived from petroleum or from the natural gas discovered by companies drilling for oil. When these materials became abundantly available, coal and alcohol chemistry was no longer economically viable for the production of commodity organic chemicals. Regardless of the fact that Europe's chemical industry was for a long time more advanced than that in the United States, the future of organic chemicals was going to be related to petroleum, not coal, as soon as companies such as Union Carbide, Standard Oil (New Jersey), Shell, and Dow turned their attention to the production of petrochemicals.

European chemists in the 1800s and 1900s had concentrated on synthesizing molecules from available coal-derived feedstocks, which largely involved aromatic chemicals. They therefore largely neglected industrial aliphatic chemistry. Alcohol-based chemicals did become of some importance in the years between World War I and the 1930s. Then U.S. oil and chemical companies recognized the value of reactive petroleum-derived hydrocarbons and not only came up with a number of industrially significant processes for aliphatic chemicals, but also found out how to make the originally coal tar-derived chemicals more inexpensively and in much larger quantities. The fact that European know-how greatly helped in this effort is an important sidelight.

The third theme relates to the conditions under which business has been conducted in the chemical industry over time. Before the war, the number of producers of each chemical was small, there was relatively little real competition as we know it today and, in fact, there existed a system of cartels and "clubs" that made the production of chemicals (and a number of other products) sort of a gentleman's game. This was often illegal, but governments tended to look the other way for a number of reasons, some vaguely associated with "national security." After the war, this system became obsolete, replaced with an industry so competitive as to deny reasonable profits to many of its participants much of the time. It seems, however, that the pendulum may have swung too far the other way. It is partly swinging back now, as the number of industry participants is being reduced through a restructuring program and profitability is again on the rise.

This brings me to the fourth theme, the one I had the most trouble with. It is closely related to the other three, namely: How could it be that an industry that fostered so much innovation, produced so many desirable consumer products, and was characterized by such remarkable growth over such a short period of time turned out to be so unprofitable for so many of its participants? Could the companies engaging in this industry have played the game differently, to reap greater advantage from the technological magic they created? Was the petrochemical industry unique in fumbling away a large part of its potential profits and, if so, what were the circumstances that caused this to happen? Some of the answers to these questions suggested themselves during my work, but other parts of the question remain unclear. While some of the methodological business analyses derived with current strategic planning theory (matrices, growth/maturity charts, etc.) have validity, a comprehensive answer is certainly more complicated. The history of the petrochemical industry needs to be studied in greater detail so that future managers engaged in rapidly growing industries can learn the appropriate lessons.

One point kept coming back to me, as I focused on what had transpired over the 40 years or so during which these events took place (a period that started when I was in grammar school in Austria, where I was born): It had all happened so rapidly! I now know that when I first heard my father play Caruso and Gigli opera records on a gramophone that said "His Master's Voice" (then the RCA symbol), these records had been made of phenol–formaldehyde plastic or hard rubber—not from vinyl resins. PVC (polyvinyl chloride) had not yet been invented. The records were blank on one side and, of course, they turned at 78 revolutions per minute. At the time, it seemed miraculous to me that you could hear the voice of an opera star in your own home.

Nylon came to my attention when I was going to high school in Philadelphia and a friend of my parents showed us a pair of "nylons" he was bringing home to his wife. He was in the stockings business, a customer of DuPont. When war broke out, there was gasoline rationing (we had "A" coupons—the lowest priority) and everybody looked for old tires to be recycled for shredding and rubber recovery. Then, when we received gas masks in Army basic training, we were told that this was one of the uses for this recycled rubber. Rubber was in very short supply and the synthetic rubber development program took a long time to start making a contribution.

Plastics were around in the 1930s, but they really burst on the scene in the late 1940s. Polyethylene and polystyrene were unknown to consumers before that time, but then all sorts of molded and extruded articles started to appear. We learned that the clear and rigid objects were made of methyl methacrylate (Lucite or Plexiglas), acetate or polystyrene, and the flexible articles, of vinyl resins or polyethylene. A little later, the Bakelite telephone earpieces (heavy, black, and conical) started being replaced with headsets made of lighter plastics that had more pleasing colors. At some point, it became obvious that the industry that was making these materials had come a long way over a very short time.

After my discharge from the Signal Corps, I returned to college. MIT used to send about ten percent of its chemical engineering graduates to Standard Oil Development Company (a Standard Oil of New Jersey affiliate), and this is where Professors Lewis and Gilliland suggested I should apply. When I joined Esso Engineering in 1949, all of the so-called "Four Horsemen" (Standard Oil technical executives) who had invented fluid cat cracking were still with the company. I now feel that there couldn't have been a better place to start my career.

In 1956, I accepted an offer from Scientific Design Company and was fortunate to have been in responsible positions there when many of that company's petrochemical process "breakthroughs" were made. In the mid-1960s, I left to start Chem Systems.

One problem that presented itself in writing this book related to the varied audience I felt I was addressing. A considerable part of the subject matter is necessarily highly technical and beyond the reasonable knowledge of a reader without any chemical background, who might nevertheless be interested in this book from a historical or business standpoint. On the other hand, highly trained industry people will feel that I am elaborating the obvious. I thought about putting some of the information in "boxes" that could either be read or skipped, but then realized that I would have to decide whether these boxes should contain the simpler or the more complicated material. Unwilling to judge who would be the main readers, I decided not to use this technique. I have, however, included an appendix with a list of some of the more important technical terms used in the text, so that the lay reader can perhaps follow the subject matter in some of the chapters in a more informed manner. Some readers may also want to skip ahead here and there, if progress becomes too slow or, in other cases, if the text becomes too technical for a few paragraphs.

Another problem I encountered was in the organization of the material and in its presentation to the reader. It was immediately obvious that a totally chronological development would be wildly confusing, since so many different strands of product families, technologies, and historical company development would then somehow have to be brought along in parallel. This would require a great deal of jumping back and forth, which would cause major problems in following the development of any one subject. On the other hand, there had to be a certain sense of historical development in the organization of the material; otherwise I would have to keep returning to a much earlier period each time a new subject was commenced. Actually, either of these techniques make for a rather dry narrative style and I had already decided that I would try and make the book interesting and readable rather than a scholarly historical work. I had neither the time nor the ambition to write a book with the dimensions of Haynes' *American Chemical Industry* (published in 1946 in five volumes). I leave this task to others, hoping that this will also soon be done.

It seemed obvious to me that I would start with the German chemical industry and trace its development through World War II. My early research confirmed that many of the products that later became the most important "petrochemicals" were first made in Germany between 1900 and 1930, but from feedstocks other than petroleum (see Table A.1). During the later years of this period, the companies comprising I.G. Farbenindustrie, the vast German

TABLE A.1   Historical Dates for the First Commercial
Production of Some Important Organic Chemicals

Chemical	Producer	Year (Approx.)
Phenol	F. Raschig (Germany); Hoffmann-LaRoche (Switzerland)	1901
Carbon tetrachloride	Griesheim-Elektron (Germany)	1903
Trichloroethylene	Wacker (Germany)	1908
Ethylene	Griesheim-Elektron (Germany)	1913
Ammonia*	BASF (Germany)	1913
Acetic acid	Wacker (Germany)	1916
Ethylene Oxide	BASF (Germany)	1916
Acetaldehyde	Hoechst (Germany)	1916
Acetone	Hoechst (Germany); Weitzman (U.K.); Standard Oil of N.J. (U.S.)	1917
Vinyl acetate	Shawinigan Chemicals (Canada)	1920
Methanol	BASF (Germany)	1923
Butanol	BASF (Germany)	1923
Vinyl chloride	Wacker (Germany)	1930

*Not an organic chemical.

chemical combine, came close to dominating much of the chemical industry as the world then knew it. They also provided the Nazi government with some of its most critical war materials. Perhaps for these reasons I found it interesting to start Chapter 1 with the victorious Allies' inspection tours of some of the I.G. Farben plants and then to use flashbacks to develop a number of chemical themes. Chapter 1 sets the technical tone of the book, including an appreciation of coal chemistry, which is later contrasted against the production of many of the same chemicals from petroleum feedstocks.

Chapter 2 describes the beginning of the petrochemical industry and here I found it useful to describe the accomplishments of four companies I considered major contributors in this effort: Union Carbide, Dow Chemical, Standard Oil (N.J.), and Shell. Chapters 3 and 4 then show how the outstanding contributions of the United States refining industry during World War II really put the petrochemical industry on the map. In the course of describing how this was done, it was possible to show how commercialization of the more sophisticated petroleum refining technology also happened to create petrochemical feedstocks. It seemed particularly important to focus on the development of catalytic cracking, catalytic reforming, and aromatics extraction technology—in other words, on the refinery processes that make ethylene, propylene, butadiene, benzene, toluene, and the xylenes.

World War II represents an important dividing line, not only between coal and oil chemistry, but also in the way that companies conducted business. Before the war, there was a cartel mentality. After the war, the chemical industry became highly competitive. Since I had, from the start, intended to deal in later chapters with some of the business problems of the industry, I wanted to cover the conduct of chemical industry business before and after World War II in sufficient detail to allow some conclusions to be formulated at the end. I also found my research on cartels interesting and wanted to share some of it with readers of the book. Thus, Chapter 5 on prewar cartels and clubs.

Now, I could shift the narrative to the phenomenal growth of the industry in the postwar period, from the late 1940s to the late 1960s, mainly involving the development of plastics and synthetic fibers (Chapters 6 and 7), from their inception to the point where the industry started its explosive growth. Then I explain, in Chapter 8, how the sort of technical monopoly that a small number of firms had established over the production of certain key chemicals was broken through the dissemination of production technology by engineering firms and by some of the companies themselves. This allowed the addition of new capacity as fast or faster than the increase in demand for its products increased, a process that can now be seen to have started industry down the slippery slope.

Chapter 9 on international developments has two main themes: first, the efforts by U.S. firms to benefit internationally from their advantageous position in the new, originally largely U.S., industry and second the European and Japanese response to this effort.

By the late 1960s, a number of patterns had been established. It had become obvious that in spite of the industry's hugely successful development of technologies and products to serve continually expanding markets, the manufacture of commodity chemicals was becoming a considerably less profitable business than before. I decided to select one product, vinyl chloride monomer, used for the production of PVC resins, to illustrate how and why this happened (Chapter 9). And then I showed in Chapter 11 on "Large Plants" how a number of operating companies and engineering contractors crowned the technological achievements of the industry through the development of truly outstanding low-cost processes for ethylene, ammonia, and several other chemicals, only to recognize that even these developments would only add to the industry's profitability problems.

Conceivably, I could have concluded the book at this point. However, I wanted to address the question of how the events of the 1970s, involving energy and feedstock economics, the construction of chemical plants by the oil-rich nations, and the slowdown in product demand growth changed a number of things and might, in the future, influence the further development of the industry. For this reason, I decided to add Chapter 12, "Discontinuities and Uncertainties," and then attempted to arrive at some conclusions (Chapter 13).

It is impossible in a book of this kind to provide adequate background information on many of the technical, economic, and market issues concerning the industry. A number of books would serve as good references on this subject including *Petrochemical Manufacturing & Marketing Guide, Volumes I & II,* by Robert B. Stobaugh, Jr., Gulf Publishing Company, Houston, Texas, 1966; *Industrial Organic Chemicals In Perspective, Parts I and II,* by Harold A. Wittcoff and Bryan G. Reuben, John Wiley & Sons, New York, New York, 1980; *Trends in Petrochemical Technology, The Impact of the Energy Crisis,* by Arthur M. Brownstein, Petroleum Publishing Company, Tulsa, Oklahoma, 1976; *Kirk-Othmer Encyclopedia,* John Wiley-Interscience, New York, New York; and *The Chemical Plant: From Process Selection to Commercial Operation,* edited by Ralph Laudau, Reinhold Publishing Company, New York, New York, 1966.

Writing this book has been both an exciting and humbling experience. Certainly, I did not realize at the start how many hours of research would be required for every hour spent at the word processor and how difficult it would be to write a book in short bursts in the evening, on weekends, or on business trips. When traveling, I would try to visit libraries in such cities as Washington, Houston, London, Duesseldorf and Zurich. There, I would look for additional reference books or for useful articles in chemical industry trade publications, going back as far as the 1930s. I also wrote to companies for corporate biographies and to people in the industry for verification of specific issues, and I interviewed a number of industry participants in the United States, Europe and Japan, who I felt might be able to add valuable recollections and insights. In my research, one thing, in particular, kept me on course. I found no book that covered the history of this interesting industry in a reasonably comprehensive manner. This was confirmed in my discussions with industry people. Everybody felt that this story had to be written before many of the people who grew up with the industry would no longer be around.

There were many exciting moments, such as the time I discovered that the records of the inspection teams visiting the German plants after the war were still available in the Military Section of the National Archives in Washington, D.C., stacked in dusty boxes there and in a warehouse on the Washington Beltway. Or when I realized that one of my sometime golfing partners, Dick Willstatter was, in fact, the nephew of the famous German chemist, Prof. Richard Willstatter, who received the Nobel prize for his work on plant pigments, including chlorophyll. And certainly the most dramatic point came when my friend, Dr. Dieter Ambros, who heads the chemical division of the German firm of Henkel, arranged a long meeting in Mannheim with his 86-year-old father, Dr. Otto Ambros, who had been a key member of the I.G. Vorstand during the war and who had spearheaded the development of the German Buna-S synthetic rubber program. These experiences became important milestones along the way.

I feel certain that other books on this subject will appear before too long. When history, technology, business and geopolitics intersect, the results can be fascinating. This book is written as a homage to the industry in which my colleagues and I have spent most of our working life.

PETER H. SPITZ

Scarsdale, New York
December 1987.

Acknowledgments

This expresses my thanks to a number of people who have helped me in various ways with this book. Many of their names are listed under the heading of "Personal Communications" in the chapter footnotes. Aimison Jonnard, Bob Stobaugh, Joe Bower, Richard Foster, Jim Mathis, Don Burke, Attilio Bisio, Bob Purvin, Ralph Laudau, Hal Sorgenti, Don Thompson, Peter Sherwood, Val Haensel, Jim Carr, Bill Hettinger, Carolyn Corwin, Max Appl, Ray Waters, Akiro Mazume, and Yasuji Torii reviewed chapters or chapter sections and gave me the benefit of their comments and suggestions. I would also like to thank reviewers from DuPont, Dow, Union Carbide, Exxon, Shell, Universal Oil Products, Imperial Chemical Industries, Amoco, BASF and several other companies for furnishing helpful comments. At Chem Systems, Bert Struth, Marshall Frank, Harold Wittcoff and Roger Longley helped me by commenting on certain subject areas. Martin Sherwin, who once headed up Chem Systems' research laboratory and is now a research executive at W.R. Grace & Company, also reviewed many parts of the book from a technical standpoint.

My research work was greatly facilitated through the efforts of Maryann Grandy and Ellen Faccioli in Chem Systems' Tarrytown office information center and of Hilary Nunn, who has the corresponding responsibilities in Chem Systems' London office. Much of my research was carried out with the help of the Chemists Club Library in New York and here I wish to thank Elsie Lim and Mildred Hunt for their efforts in my behalf.

My former sister-in-law, Dr. Judy Spitz, now living in Toronto, and Barbara Stern, an editor at Chem Systems, assisted with editing and proofreading—no small task, when a first-time author is involved. Pat McCurdy, Alec Jordan, Ben Luberoff, Gabe Perle, and Henry Graff were helpful with aspects involving publication.

At Wiley, I received great cooperation from Jim Smith, Joel Bell, and Diana Cisek.

Special thanks are due to my secretary and executive assistant, Jane Curley, for her unflagging dedication in transforming my drafts on "floppy discs" into a final manuscript. Given my propensity to rewrite sections more times than Jane wishes to remember, I can only say that the book would have been impossible without her devotion to the cause. Lynn Murray also helped.

Last, but not least, I am deeply appreciative to Hilda and I hereby express my gratitude for making it possible for me to spend so much time away from normal home pursuits and chores. If she had not taken firm charge of our domestic life, the results would be hard to contemplate. But she came through with flying colors!

P.H.S.

Contents

Petrochemicals:
The Rise of an Industry

1 / The German Chemical Industry: Chemicals from Coal

Although the petrochemical industry is an American phenomenon, created by oil and chemical companies in the United States in the 1930s and early 1940s, the technical origins of this industry are found just as much in Europe as in the United States. While American chemical engineers successfully created this new industry in time for the Allies to build a massive number of plants for the production of high octane blending components, synthetic rubber, and critical plastic materials, the shadow of advanced German technical know-how was often in the background. There was, however, a critical difference between these two industries, located on opposing continents. Whereas the United States could use as raw materials an almost unlimited supply of Gulf Coast petroleum and natural gas, the German tanks ran on synthetic gasoline made by I.G. Farbenindustrie's chemical factories from coal, and on tires also produced from coal in synthetic rubber plants built a number of years before the United States entered the war.

It was, therefore, hardly surprising that when the war was over, U.S. companies immediately prevailed on the government to dispatch numerous groups of experienced chemical executives—many still in uniform—to learn how the German industry had been so successful in supporting the country's war effort. Also, from a more academic standpoint, there was intense interest in seeing how far German research had proceeded in a number of key areas of organic chemistry. Chemists from both sides of the conflict had obviously been out of touch with the other side's inventions and technical progress.

The Allied inspection groups were not disappointed, as will become clear later in this chapter. But my discussions with some of the executives who participated in these inspection trips brought out another side of the story. Looking at the ruins of this mighty chemical industry, with its historical ties to Germany's coke ovens and steel mills, the officers could not help but feel that they were witnessing the end of a phase of industrial history.

To understand the origins of the petrochemical industry, it is necessary to start in Germany, where modern industrial chemistry began.

ALLIED TEAMS CONDUCT TECHNICAL AUDIT

On April 17, 1945, a joint United States-Canadian military team, comprised of officers selected for their chemical industry background, left London for Krefeld, Germany, a town located near Duesseldorf in the Ruhr, the heart of Germany's chemical industry. The next morning, they proceeded by truck to Task Force Headquarters at Herten (Kreis Recklinghausen) and immediately continued on to Marl, the site of Chemische Werke Huels, a sprawling installation forming part of I.G. Farbenindustrie, up to then the world's largest combine of chemical manufacturing companies and a key contributor to the German war effort. The I.G. Farben cartel had been established in 1925 through the combination of Germany's largest chemical firms, including Badische Anilin and Soda Fabrik (BASF), Farbwerke Hoechst, and Farbenfabriken Bayer, which also had holdings in a number of other firms, including Chemische Werke Huels. Bunawerke Huels, which produced Buna-S synthetic rubber, had been designated C.I.O.S.* "Black List" Target No. 22.6 by the Allies, because this plant was the second largest German installation for the manufacture of tire

---

*Combined Intelligence Objectives Subcommittee, a joint operation conducted by United States, Canadian, and British military and civilian authorities after the conclusion of the war. The reports published by these groups later also became known as the F.I.A.T. documents.

rubber for Hitler's Wehrmacht (1). Buna-S type rubbers are based on styrene and butadiene and have many, though not all, of the important characteristics of natural rubber.

In the 1930s, German research on synthetic rubbers was well ahead of that in the United States, so that when the supply of natural rubber from the Malay Peninsula was shut off from the Allies due to the Japanese occupation and from the Germans due to the Allies' control of the sea lanes, Germany was in a far better state of preparation. The Allied inspection team knew that the two large Buna rubber plants of Huels in the Ruhr and at Schkopau, in what is now East Germany, had a combined capacity of well over 100,000 tons per year, with another plant located at Ludwigshafen, near the town of Mannheim on the Rhine.

The Ruhr region (*Ruhrgebiet,* in German) is often considered the cradle of large-scale heavy organic chemicals manufacture, linked as it is to the largest iron and coke oven operation in Europe. Of the two types of coal found in this area, the higher-grade bituminous variety (*Steinkohle,* in German) occurs in relatively narrow seams, which have become progressively more expensive to mine. Lower-grade lignite, called *Braunkohle,* occurs in large surface deposits in the southern part of the Ruhr, sometimes actually under sections of towns such as Wesseling near Cologne, which must be periodically rebuilt as the coal mining drag line advances and housing foundations collapse. Lignite and coal were, of course, used not only by industry, but also by utilities such as Union Rheinische Braunkohle A.G., which had, for a long time, produced a large part of the power and steam in the region and had also established a chemical subsidiary, based on coal gasification, well before the war. Chemische Werke Huels used coal as a raw material to make synthetic rubber.

The heavy concentration of coke ovens, coal-burning power generating plants, and chemical factories had long made the Ruhr well known for the choking fumes and mists encountered throughout the region, particularly during the winter months. Before the war, and for sometime thereafter, at a time when environmental control had not yet become a major issue, the Ruhr was redolent with a large variety of chemical odors and was also known for its impenetrable smogs, caused by a combination of nitric and sulphuric acid droplets, flue gas ash particles, coke oven vent gases, and other pollutants. I have vivid memories of driving in fog and winter rain from Duesseldorf to Dortmund, Duisburg, and Essen, passing smaller towns with picturesque names like Wanne-Eickel, Castrop-Rauxel, or Oberhausen-Sterkrade, when it was often necessary to slow down to 20 kilometers per hour or less to avoid going off the road and into fields dominated by huge hyperbolic cooling towers, eerie structures housing blast furnaces, and ghostly remote distillation towers. Even today, the Ruhr is still an important province for chemicals manufacture, but the advent of petrochemicals has pushed coal into the background as a raw material.

At the time the Allied teams were inspecting the captured plants, industrial activity in the Ruhr had almost come to a standstill, with many plants manned by skeleton crews. At some plants, all of the managers had left or fled, while in others both management and technical people were willing and sometimes eager to cooperate in answering questions.

The military team found that Bunawerke Huels had been started up in August 1940 and was actually kept in operation through March 29, 1945, the day before its occupation by the United States Ninth Army. It had employed 7,000 workers, including 95 Ph.D. chemists and 150 mechanical engineers. During the war, it had been subjected to several bombing attacks at different times, the most serious on June 22, 1943, when the main acetylene gas holder received a direct hit, leaving the plant out of operation for two months. Partial production had then resumed, with acetaldehyde, an intermediate in the so-called four-step process used to make butadiene, shipped in from the nearby Knapsack plant.* By 1944, Bunawerke Huels actually reached its highest wartime capacity. In early 1945, production had again declined substantially, when raids succeeded in destroying large parts of coal hydrogenation plants located at Gelsenkirchen and Scholven, which had been supplying cracked hydrocarbon gases to Huels. After that, only natural gas from the small German gas fields near the Dutch border remained available as a raw material source (1).

The C.I.O.S. team was familiar with the production processes used for making Buna-S rubber, since the United States and Canada had eventually succeeded in bringing somewhat similar plants on stream during the middle of the war. A crash program, headed by Bernard Baruch, had been set up by President Roosevelt

---

*A number of routes have been developed over the years to produce the diolefin butadiene. In Germany, the four-step process via acetaldehyde was the primary route, though others (including a two-step route via butynediol) were also developed.

to develop technology and build plants for the production of synthetic rubber, desperately needed for the trucks, planes, and tanks of the Allied forces. The Buna-S technology was actually known to a number of U.S. scientists, since Standard Oil of New Jersey (now Exxon Corporation) had in the late 1920s, set up a technology exchange agreement with the I.G. Farben combine. However, neither styrene nor butadiene had been made in the United States in any appreciable quantities before the war, when synthetic rubber had been limited to specialties and plastics to cellulosics and thermosets. It was, therefore, of the utmost importance for the team to note in detail the manufacturing techniques employed at Huels. According to the team's records, the inspection resulted in the shipment of three C.I.O.S. bags of documents as well as several drums to the Secretariat in London. The drums contained 200 kilograms of ethylbenzene dehydrogenation catalyst for testing and comparison with catalysts in use by Dow and other U.S. and Canadian styrene producers. The documents gave a complete description of the development of Buna-S technology, the design and construction of the plant, its manufacturing cost and a record of the plant's operation throughout the war.*

The main findings of the C.I.O.S. team were of great interest to chemical operating companies outside Germany, for they showed that Bunawerke Huels had relied on a number of different schemes for producing the two key synthetic rubber components. Ethylene, required for the production of styrene, was actually available from four sources: as a by-product of electric arc cracking of hydrocarbons, by hydrogenation of acetylene, via recovery from coke oven gas, and via dehydration of ethyl alcohol. The latter had sufficient impurities in the form of ethers to be unsuitable for the benzene alkylation step that leads to styrene and was, therefore, primarily employed for ethylene oxide manufacture. Production of acetylene for conversion to ethylene (a styrene intermediate) and acetaldehyde was the key to Bunawerke Huels' manufacturing scheme.

Development of acetylene manufacture, and acetylene chemistry in general, had been a key aspect of German chemical industry development in the 1920s and 1930s. The French chemist

---

*Most of this material was furnished by Dr. Paul Baumann, deputy managing director of the plant, who had a record as an eminent researcher before his assumption of managerial duties.

Berthelot had found as early as 1863 that acetylene was formed when methane gas was passed across an electric arc. Another French researcher, Moissan, demonstrated in 1892 that acetylene is made by hydrolizing calcium carbide, which he produced from high temperature processing of coal-limestone mixtures, using an electric furnace. Early uses for acetylene were for gas lamps and, later, for oxygen welding. But it soon became evident that acetylene was an ideal chemical feedstock for a tremendous variety of products, including solvents, pharmaceuticals, dyes, plastics, and rubberlike materials. By 1934, world production of calcium carbide had reached 3 million tons, with 600,000 tons made in Germany alone.

German industrial chemists felt, however, that an electric arc process could also become an important contributor to their country's acetylene supplies. Intensive work on producing acetylene in this manner had therefore been initiated by BASF at Oppau near Ludwigshafen, initially using coke oven gases and later methane as a feedstock. Between 1925 and 1928, quartz-lined arcing chambers had increased in size from 1 to 500 kilowatt power input. However, acetylene yields remained too low—in the range of 5–6 percent—to be commercially viable. Dr. Baumann, initially a member of BASF's Ammonia Laboratory and later transferred to Huels, had been the man responsible for developing a commercially successful arc process in the early 1930s. Close study of the thermodynamics of acetylene formation led him to modify the arc chamber system such that the feedstock gases were subjected to the extremely short residence time of 1/1000 second at 1300°C, followed immediately by quenching. This led to a doubling of yields to achieve an acetylene concentration of up to 18 percent in the gases leaving the arc.

In the mid-1930s, the cooperation between I.G. Farben and Standard Oil Company (New Jersey) was extended to this field and led to a commercial process. Dr. Baumann's excellent command of English stemmed, in part, from his five years at Esso's Baton Rouge refinery, where an arc installation had been built under his direction, with acetylene used for the production of 300 tons per year of acetic acid. Huels had started arc production of acetylene shortly after Dr. Baumann's return to Germany.

German operating capacities for acetylene during the war were very substantial, though actual production rates were subject to periodic bombings. By 1942, the calcium carbide plants at Huels,

Schkopau, and Knapsack were supplemented by a number of arc process installations at Huels and elsewhere, fed with coke oven gas fractions as well as with natural gas from Germany's limited gas fields. Bunawerke Huels had 15 sets of arcs, with mercury rectifiers operating at 1000 volts, a power consumption of 7000 kilowatt-hours (KWH) and a gas input of 2800 cubic meters per hour. By-products from the arc process included ethylene, hydrogen, and carbon black. The team noted that arc process acetylene was produced for 30 Reichmarks (RM) per 100 kilograms, based on a power cost of 1.5 pfennig per kilowatt-hour and a gas cost of 1.5 RM per million BTU(1). Though these costs were perhaps higher than the cost of raw materials and utilities of corresponding U.S. plants making synthetic rubber, the important fact to the Germans was that these costs were manageable and that they had, in effect, established "autarky" (i.e., raw materials independence) in the production of critical war materials, such as synthetic rubber and aviation gasoline, before embarking on a *blitzkrieg* against the Allies in 1939.

At Huels, much of the acetylene was converted to acetaldehyde using a mercury-sulfuric acid catalyst. The acetaldehyde underwent aldol condensation in the presence of potassium hydroxide, followed by hydrogenation to butylene glycol over a copper-chrome catalyst. Dehydration to butadiene was accomplished using a phosphate catalyst on coke support. Styrene was produced by a process that is employed to the present time: purified coke-oven benzene was alkylated in liquid phase with $AlCl_3$ catalyst, and the ethylbenzene dehydrogenated over zinc oxide. Diethylbenzene was separated as a by-product and used as aviation blending stock for the Luftwaffe.

Just before the start of the war, Dr. Walter Reppe at Schkopau had developed a butadiene process based on acetylene and formaldehyde, that amounted to a two-step instead of the more usual four-step process. However, this technology never became important—only a small fraction of Germany Buna production came via this route by 1944 (approximately 2000 tons per month). At that time, total German Buna production capacity was 117,000 tons per year.

The inspection team learned that Bunawerke Huels had made four types of Buna-S on a commercial scale, whereas the other Buna rubber works at Schkopau and Ludwigshafen only produced two types. Considerably more information was obtained while

covering German research work on still other routes to butadiene
and on various rubber modifiers as well as latices, lacquers, etc.
Research work had been at a high level throughout the war and
had continued almost to the end.

The U.S. team, headed by John Fennebresque, left Marl on April
24th for visits to Schkopau and Leverkuesen. Shortly thereafter,
the group dissolved and its members returned to civilian life. Much
later, Fennebresque was to head up Mobil Chemical during that
company's major drive into petrochemicals, after an earlier career
with Monsanto and Celanese.

Fennebresque's team was only one of many sent by the C.I.O.S.
to Germany just before and immediately after cessation of hostilities, because the Allies were well aware of the advanced state
of German chemical research and development. Another C.I.O.S.
team, headed up by John M. DeBell, toured a large number of German plants and eventually submitted a report, later published as
a book (2). The degree of detail covered in this book was generally much greater than in most of the C.I.O.S. or B.I.O.S.* reports.
However, many of these reports provided a very good overview
of industrial chemical technology in use at the captured plants.
These reports were eventually published in the United States and
United Kingdom and served as a prime source of information on
the state of the German chemical industry up to the end of World
War II. The information contained in the DeBell report included
not only various process details, but also a considerable amount
of analysis and editorial comment.

DeBell's group was particularly interested in styrene and
polystyrene production. Figure 1.1 is a flowsheet taken from the
DeBell report depicting the styrene unit at Schkopau, which had
a capacity of 1700 tons/month, based on 15 dehydrogenation furnaces (2). Since much of the ethylene at this plant was produced
from acetylene, the DeBell team spent a considerable amount of
time with Dr. Wulff, a key figure in German chemical industry advances before and during the war. Dr. Wulff proved very helpful
in understanding the process schemes employed at the Schkopau
plant. Later, he became known in the United States as the inventor of the Wulff acetylene and ethylene process, which achieved
some success after the technology was acquired by Union Car-

---

*British Intelligence Objectives Subcommittee (similar to C.I.O.S. but involving
only British members).

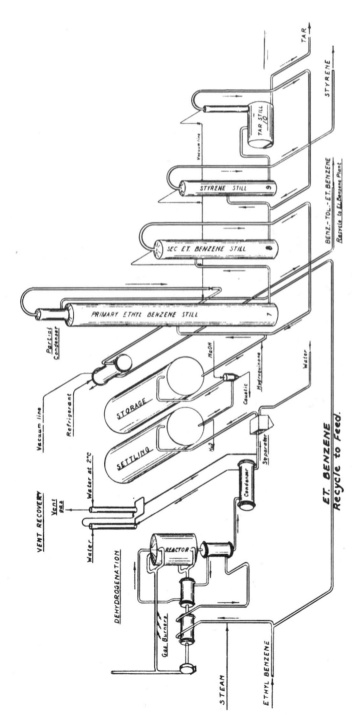

Figure 1.1 Styrene unit at Schkopau. (*Source:* J.M. DeBell, W.C. Goggin, Walter E. Gloor, *German Plastics Practice*, DeBell and Richardson, Springfield, MA, 1946.)

bide. Plants were built by Marathon in Burghausen, Germany, and by Union Carbide in Brazil. Nevertheless, the Wulff process could never compete successfully with the steam cracking process for making ethylene, due to the latter's lower fixed cost and valuable by-products.

Careful study of the Schkopau plant's manufacturing history indicated that German styrene technology had been commercialized somewhat earlier than in the United States. Just before the war, Dow had attempted to get the U.S. government to support construction of a 10,000 ton per year styrene plant in joint venture with the Goodyear Tire and Rubber Company, but this proposal had been rejected. Some styrene was then being produced with Dow catalyst in the United States, but high production rates were not achieved until the synthetic rubber program was in full swing.

The DeBell report also provided much detail on German research in low density polyethylene during the war. Although ICI had obtained the basic patents on this material during its pioneering work in the 1930s, BASF, whose scientists had been shown through the ICI plant just before the war* had been rapidly catching up, producing two grades of material at Ludwigshafen and Gendorf. These polyethylene plants were based on polymerization at 300 atmospheres, with oxygen as catalyst. High-molecular-weight low-density polyethylene was used primarily as insulation in high frequency cable and for the production of films. Although by the end of the war, the Germans still lagged their British counterparts in the state of polyethylene technology, they had accomplished a great deal in four years.

The DeBell group also inspected a BASF plant at Oppau with a production capacity of 400 tons per month of polyisobutylene, tradenamed Oppanol B, a material used as a lubricating oil additive (2). Isobutylene monomer was based on the catalytic dehydration of isobutanol, produced under high pressure from hydrogen and carbon monoxide. This reaction, and related schemes known under the general heading of "synthesis gas chemistry," had been, as DeBell and his team knew, exhaustively studied by German chemists well before it became of interest to researchers in the United States. German leadership in many areas of industrial organic chemistry had, in fact, caused Standard Oil of New Jersey

*Dr. Otto Ambros, personal communication.

to set up the technology exchange agreements with I.G. Farben in the late 1920s.

The Standard Oil-I.G. Farben relationship, of which the Fennebresque and DeBell teams were well aware, had started in 1925 when several directors of BASF invited Jersey directors to Germany to view the status of coal hydrogenation work. German technology resulted in the successful conversion of powdered coal under high pressures and temperatures and a hydrogen atmosphere into a liquid closely resembling crude oil. Frank A. Howard, president of Standard Oil Development Company, wrote to Jersey President Teagle in April 1926, that "(he) was plunged into a world of research and development on a gigantic scale such as (he) had never seen" (3, p. 47). Jersey's interest was actually not so much in coal hydrogenation but in converting very heavy crudes into lighter materials—a prophetic view of the future, as it now turns out, taken at a time when such modern refinery processes as hydrocracking and deasphalting were unknown, although experiments along these lines had been carried out in German research laboratories. In 1927, Jersey and I.G. Farben reached an agreement whereby the U.S. company would build a 40,000-ton-per-year heavy oil hydrogenation plant, using the BASF patents but without paying a royalty. They also identified several other areas of research cooperation, including acetylene production via electric arc processing, which had involved the work of Dr. Baumann at Baton Rouge. The companies also agreed to exchange information in other areas, to share royalties from potential future licensees using the jointly developed technology, and to abide under a number of other provisions. It was also agreed, somewhat later, that I.G. Farben's main interest was to be in chemicals and Jersey's in fuel products, thus leading to further refinements in their contractual arrangements, with the companies exerting respectively greater influence in their major area of interest.

In 1932, I.G. Farben informed Jersey that its researchers had succeeded in polymerizing isobutylene with boron fluoride to a tough, resilient plastic resembling rubber, though it had not been able to produce a vulcanized product. Standard Oil took over this research work with great enthusiasm, resulting in the butyl rubber process,* based on further development work by R.M.

---

*Used to make tire inner tubes—no longer required in modern automobile tires.

Thomas and W.J. Sparks. The key, it eventually turned out, was the incorporation of small amounts of conjugated diene materials such as butadiene, and later isoprene, which made vulcanization possible through cross-linking with isobutylene. Jersey made this discovery in 1937 and so informed I.G. Farben under its agreement. A series of production difficulties kept both BASF and Jersey from commercializing butyl rubber until after the war. DeBell's team was primarily interested in the status of polybutylene production at Oppau, but other teams also visited the Oppau works to obtain information on the preparation of the isobutylene monomer. They found that the isobutanol required as a feedstock had largely been shipped in from Leuna (now in East Germany), which was a main center for hydrogenation and synthesis gas research.

After the visit to Oppau, DeBell and his team traveled to a number of other plastics and plastic monomer plants. Their comprehensive C.I.O.S. report led to the publication of DeBell's book, with even more details. DeBell's report *German Plastics Practice* was widely studied. The publicity received through publication of this report contributed to the success of DeBell and Richardson, Inc., one of the first plastics consulting firms, which played an important supporting role in a number of plastics industry developments in the United States during the 1950s and 1960s.

Dr. Baumann was intensively interviewed by another C.I.O.S. team that included Gordon Cain, then working for Freeport Sulphur Company, and Nick Carter of DuPont. This team had been charged with the responsibility of studying the state of acetylene chemistry in Germany, which was far more advanced than in other countries. The group was in Germany for more than six months, visiting many installations and talking with a number of German research and production executives. Cain, who later became general manager of Conoco Chemicals and then a successful financial entrepreneur, recently recounted his team's experiences with personalities such as Baumann, Karl Ziegler, and Dr. Hans Sachsse, the inventor of the flame cracking process, which produced acetylene as well as synthesis gas via partial oxidation. Cain generally found the Germans friendly and forthcoming, except for Sachsse, whom he characterized as an "unreconstructed German." He remembers that in briefings with Sachsse held in Ludwigshafen, which was in the French Occupation Zone, he frequently had to bring in a French officer to remind Sachsse that the Allies won the war and that better cooperation was therefore expected.* Sachsse did eventually provide much of the information.

Many of the teams worked out of the Hoechst offices near Griesheim, where most of the I.G. Farben records had been kept or where they had later been transferred. From there, the teams branched out to visit various plants in different occupied zones, including some plants in Berlin and in the Russian Zone (later to become East Germany). As a representative of Freeport Sulphur Company, an important focus of Cain's interest were the installations that produced elemental sulphur from hydrogen sulphide by partial oxidation. This was an early application of what later became known as the Claus process, which was later extensively applied on a worldwide basis to produce sulphur from refinery gases and from natural gas deposits containing hydrogen sulphide.

Many other American chemical engineers, including numerous research executives, visited German chemicals plants as members of C.I.O.S. teams. One of these group members was Vladimir (Val) Haensel, later destined to play a key role in the development of catalytic reforming at Universal Oil Products Company. In a number of reports (4), Haensel and his group described what they had seen in plants at Leuna (now in East Germany), where many of the more advanced German hydrocarbon conversion processes had been installed.

- In a hydroforming plant rated at 7500 tons per day feed rate, naphtha, with a clear motor octane of 58.5, was reformed over a molybdenum-on-aluminum catalyst to obtain a gasoline with a motor octane rating of 80. One of the charge stocks so reformed was *hydrogasoline* made from brown coal (lignite). On-stream time for the reaction was 100 hours, followed by a regeneration cycle of 25 hours.

- An experimental "cat cracker" was inspected, which used the moving-bed principle to transport silica-alumina catalyst between the reactor and regenerator vessels. No plant of this type was built during the war and there was no indication that fluid catalytic cracking (see Chapter 3) was ever considered.

- An alkylation plant had been in operation at Merseburg (Leuna Works), producing about 900 barrels per day of finished

*Gordon Cain, personal communication.

high-octane alkylate. As in the United States, sulfuric acid was used as the catalyst to alkylate propylene-butylene mixtures with isobutane. In many respects, this unit looked very much like those built in the United States during the war, although the C.I.O.S. report did not speculate whether alkylation technology was developed in Germany or copied from information obtained in some manner from the Allied side. Figure 1.2, drawn by one of the team members, depicts the German installation.

The advanced state that German chemical research had reached by the end of the war was highlighted by another C.I.O.S. inspection team that visited the Ruhrchemie complex at Oberhausen-Holten (5). Based on Otto Roelen's work at Ruhrchemie prior to 1938, production of oxo alcohols had been planned through the establishment of a company just before the outbreak of hostilities, with shares split among Ruhrchemie, I.G. Farben, and Henkel, the largest detergent producer in Europe. The process was based on reacting olefins, obtained from Ruhrchemie's Fischer Tropsch plant, with carbon monoxide and hydrogen at 150 atmospheres. The olefins ranged from ethylene and propylene to a C_{11} to C_{17} fraction, giving products that included lower aldehydes and ketones, as well as higher alcohols in the detergent range, which accounted for Henkel's interest. The reaction system to be used in this plant employed modern shell-and-tube design and became the model upon which many such Oxo plants were built in the United States, Europe and Japan after the war (see Fig. 1.3). The CO/H_2 mixture was produced in a Winkler coal gasifier, which, as it later turned out, was one of the three relatively advanced gasifiers considered in the 1970s for the U.S. synthetic fuels program. Construction of a 12,000 ton per year plant had been started in 1942, but the project had a low priority, so that the unit actually never went into operation. As it turned out, the Ruhrchemie Fischer-Tropsch plant had been badly damaged by bombing, and it had therefore been proposed to produce the olefins on site by cracking available stocks of Fischer-Tropsch $C_{20}+$-C_{40} fractions in a Dubbs-type cracking furnace. The C.I.O.S. team only found out about the existence of the Oxo plant after intensive questioning of the Ruhrchemie staff, who were at first very secretive, but who broke down when they realized that other German chemists in Ludwigshafen and Wolfen had revealed the existence of this plant.

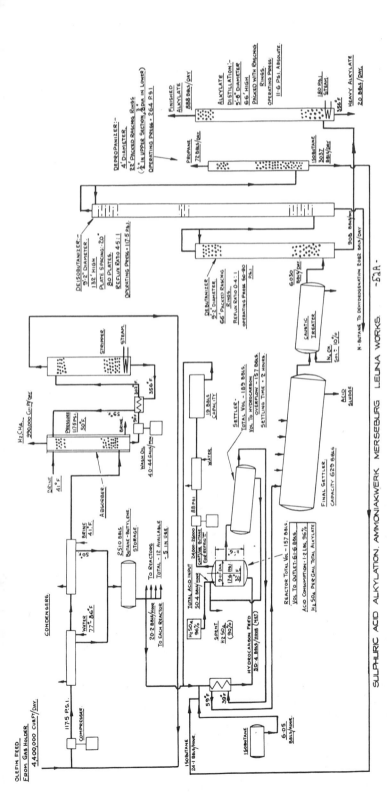

Figure 1.2 Sulphuric acid alkylation, Ammoniakwerk Merseburg, Leuna Works. (*Source:* C.I.O.S.—Report SHAEF General Staff, G-2 RG 331 Entry, 13 D, Box 93, Washington, DC. National Archives.)

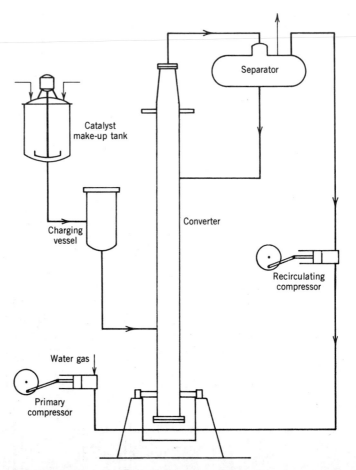

Figure 1.3 Diagram of oxo unit, Oberhausen—Holten. (*Source:* C.I.O.S.—Report SHAEF, G-2, APO 13.)

After inspecting the Oxo installation, the group traveled to Ludwigshafen to observe the only plant in Germany built for the production of hydrogen cyanide. While this chemical had an infamous history as a lethal intermediate for Zyklon B, used in the gas chambers at Auschwitz, one of its main uses was for making methyl methacrylate, a polymer that had been produced before the war by DuPont, Rohm, and Haas, and ICI. The three-step process used in this plant involved the reaction of methanol with carbon monoxide to methyl formate, production of formamide by reaction with ammonia, followed by dehydration to hydrocyanic acid (HCN). This reaction sequence had already been used in plants outside Germany but, as in all other plant inspections by B.I.O.S. and C.I.O.S. teams, the catalysts, reactions conditions, equipment specifications, and the plant operating and maintenance records were carefully noted. All teams were instructed to learn as much as possible about the state of knowledge of Germany's chemical industry, which had achieved so many successes over the period 1870 to 1940, based on the emphasis that its chemists had placed on upgrading the by-products of the country's highly developed coal and steel industry.

The German chemical industry was held in awe for a period extending from the late 1800s through World War II. Since that time, it has been possible to gain a real perspective of the accomplishments of this industry, while at the same time recognizing that many of its achievements were based on the discoveries of British, French, Russian, American, and other chemists. These issues have been examined by other authors, with different conclusions regarding, for example, the real amount of innovation contributed by the German firms. However that may be, there seems little disagreement on the fact that the I.G. Farben companies excelled in the production and marketing of organic chemicals over the period in question. This occurred partly because of the country's needs for self-sufficiency and export trade and partly because, during much of this period, the German government strongly supported its chemical industry.

RISE OF THE ORGANIC CHEMICAL INDUSTRY: DYESTUFFS CAME FIRST

German and British chemists had in the mid-1800s discovered the many chemical uses of the various gaseous and liquid products of their coke oven operations. While many countries were still using these organic compounds as fuel for their iron and steel industries, or in street lamps, German chemists were already well along in converting coke oven by-products into chemicals of various kinds.

It is significant that the names of all three of the major firms making up the I.G. Farben cartel (Badische Anilin und Sodafabrik, Farbwerke Hoechst, and Farbenfabriken Bayer) are associated with the manufacture of synthetic dyestuffs, although it is not generally known that the dyestuff industry's origins actually were in England, and that Britain was first in developing a coal tar industry. Coal tar and coke oven gases had been used to produce chemicals as early as 1817 in Lancashire, England. By 1834, a large tar distillery was in operation in Manchester, associated with an adjacent town gas works that produced additional coal tar. In 1842, coal tar naphtha was distilled with a mixture of sulphuric acid and potassium nitrate by John Leigh, who determined the presence of nitrobenzene, an intermediate for aniline. In 1851, picric acid, used for silk dying, was synthesized from phenol, recovered from coal tar (6). Shortly thereafter, a process was also developed to make phenol synthetically from coal tar benzene, using dilute alkali.

The Industrial Revolution, which originated in Britain, created a large demand for textile dyes and mordants, at that time comprising only natural materials, which were largely imported. British industrialists soon recognized the possibility that future shortages of these key materials could halt the progress of the local textile industry. And this led to the discovery of the first synthetic dye—but, as so often happens when important discoveries are made, this was the result of research in an entirely different area. Queen Victoria's Prince Consort Albert had brought over from Germany the great chemist A. W. von Hoffman to teach at the Royal College of Chemistry in London. One of his pupils, William Henry Perkin (for whom the Perkin Medal* was eventually named), was working on a synthesis for aniline, since he felt that he could use this chemical to make quinine, thus breaking a Dutch monopoly for that substance. This work was not progressing well. At one point, for reasons he could not explain at a later time, he dropped a piece of silk into a tarry substance he had derived from aniline. When he drew out the cloth the next morning, it was stained a deep purple—the famous "Perkin Mauve" as it was called later. Perkin built a factory in the Midlands in the 1860s to manufacture the new synthetic dye. Over the following 10 years, a number of different aniline dyes were synthesized in England and France, included magenta, violet imperial, Bleu de Lyons, and aniline black (7, pp. 64–68).

---

*The Perkin Medal is still awarded by the Society of Chemical Industry to honor outstanding contributors in the field of industrial chemistry.

German chemists, including Heinrich Caro (later chief chemist at BASF), Otto Witt, Peter Griess, and others came to Britain to lend the benefit of their organic chemical experience to the synthesis of new dyes. German chemical firms were not as yet engaged in this business area, but research work in Germany was also accelerating. In an important breakthrough, Perkin in England and Carl Graebe, Adolph von Baeyer, and Carl Liebermann at Leverkuesen identified alizarin, the key ingredient in one of the most important natural dyes, Turkey red madder, as an anthracene derivative. They all came up with the same synthesis, based on anthraquinone sulfonic acid, using a pressure fusion process. The German patent application in 1869 beat Perkin's to the patent office by one day! Perkin then modified his synthesis slightly to avoid infringement and built the first small alizarin plant. Bayer's much larger plant went into operation two years later in 1875, producing at the rate of 100,000 kilograms per year. This seemed to be a major turning point, for it soon became apparent to Perkin and other British dyestuffs makers that the Germans were now determined to take the initiative in dyestuffs manufacture and to risk capital funds not available to the same extent in England. Also, German chemists returning from England were coming up with many new dyes, largely based on azo synthesis. Caro, now back at BASF, discovered methylene blue in 1876 and patented the synthesis a year later. Hoechst challenged the patent, claiming prior art, but now BASF hired Professor August Kekulé, discoverer of the structure of benzene, to help win its case. Hoechst went into production of dyestuffs in 1878, making scarlet red from disulfonic acids produced from beta-naphthol and diazotized amines. Carl Duisberg, later to become the first chairman of I. G. Farben, also made key contributions in dyestuff chemistry with the synthesis of such materials as benzopurpurin, a red vat dye based on o-toluidine. This work was accomplished at Farbenfabriken vorm. Friedrich Bayer and Co. A.G. at Elberfeld in the early 1880s.

The fact that several large German firms were vying for leadership in organic chemistry breakthroughs—at that time largely related to dyestuffs and pharmaceuticals—provided a great spur for industrial development. The competition between BASF and Hoechst to develop an economic synthesis for indigo was particularly keen. The correct formula for this important blue dye had been correctly identified for the first time by Adolph von Bayer in 1883. This pointed toward naphthalene as a feedstock, though at first a number of other routes were researched. Both BASF and Hoechst acquired a Swiss patent for indigo dyes based on phenylglycine, usually made from aniline and chloroacetic acid. However, the phenylglycine-based synthesis encountered major difficulties, which led BASF to consider phenylglycine-o-carboxylic acid as an alternate intermediate to indigo. This compound could be obtained from anthranilic acid, derived in three steps from naphthalene. Soon thereafter (in 1897), a practical, economic manufacturing process had been found to make this important dye. And since naphthalene is considerably more abundant in coke oven tars and liquids than benzene—from which aniline is produced—there was now a favorable raw material condition for producing indigo. Synthetic indigo spelled the doom of the natural product, just as synthetic alizarin had replaced the cultivation of madder root. Heinrich Brunk and Carl Glaser, who supervised the research, were later elevated to the board of BASF as a result of this important work.

Continued vigorous competition among the large German firms was a key factor in the many advances made in organic chemical synthesis in the late 1800s and the first third of the Twentieth Century. But, as Peter Morris has pointed out, the experience gained in the development of indigo had broader implications.

"... There were three lessons to be drawn. Firstly, chemical research was perceived to be essential to the successful future of a company, but also slow to mature and expensive. Secondly, the synthetic product was often more expensive than the natural alternative in the initial stages, but continuous improvement of the process, to make the synthetic both cheaper and also to give it improved characteristics, allowed it to succeed eventually. The third lesson was that competition between the German firms could be fatal to all" (8).

The synthesis of indigo dye had an important separate implication for the development of Germany's organic intermediates industry, because the process required an inexpensive method to make phthalic anhydride. This chemical is made by a reaction that opens up one of the two double rings in naphthalene to produce a reactive organic acid anhydride. Chromic acid worked as a naphthalene oxidant, but a synthesis based on this reactant was costly and had led to the use of fuming sulfuric instead of chromic acid. BASF did produce phthalic anhydride in this manner in the 1880s but the yield was poor—no better than 15 percent. But in

1891, in one of those famous accidents of history, a thermometer broke in the phthalic anhydride reaction vessel, spilling mercury into the fluid. To the surprise of Eugen Sapper, the chemist working on this project, the mercury proved to be a perfect "catalyst" (though the meaning of this term was still not completely understood), with the result that phthalic yield was sharply increased.

The production of phthalic anhydride with mercury catalyst at BASF in the early 1890s has frequently been considered as the birth of organic chemical catalysis. The liquid phase process, using acid, was employed until World War II, when H.D. Gibbs and C. Conover at the U.S. Department of Agriculture found that naphthalene could be oxidized in the vapor phase, using vanadium pentoxide as a catalyst. Improved versions of this same technology have been in use since that time, with BASF developing the most efficient route of this kind in the 1970s.

Phthalic anhydride was a natural intermediate to consider for the manufacture of dyestuffs and other intermediates, since it is based on naphthalene, one of the most important products separated from coal tar. Such coal tar chemicals also include benzene, toluene, xylene, phenol, cresol, anthracene, pyridine, and many other organics, present in smaller quantities. Benzene could be converted to aniline and anthracene to anthraquinone, both important dye intermediates.

Substantial amounts of ammonia are also present in coke oven gases. These were traditionally recovered in a washing operation with sulphuric acid, whereby ammonium sulphate crystals were crystallized from the wash liquor.

The rising demand for sulphuric acid for fertilizers, explosives, and dyestuffs manufacture had led BASF, just before the turn of the century, to develop and commercialize an entirely new vapor-phase process for the production of this most important product derived from sulphur (once also known as brimstone).

The history of sulphuric acid manufacture is an interesting case study in how technology breakthroughs transcend international borders, spurred partly by local needs, while also providing a poignant reminder of the relative importance of different kinds of industries in three countries, all of which required sulphuric acid. The earliest technology, known as the lead chamber process, was developed by John Roebuck and Samuel Garbett in Birmingham, England, in 1746 in direct consequence of the calico cloth printers' rapidly rising need for sulphuric acid for use before and after the dye treatment. The original raw materials were sulphur and Chilean saltpeter, which yielded nitric acid, used to catalyze the oxidation of sulphur dioxide with air. An important drawback of this route was the release of oxides of nitrogen into the atmosphere, causing noxious fumes to pollute close-by residential areas. Many such plants were built throughout Europe, however, including several in the wine regions of the Loire Valley, where copper sulphate (produced from sulphuric acid) was used for the spraying of vineyards after a philloxera epidemic had destroyed most of the vines. A French chemist, Joseph-Louis Gay-Lussac, whose name remains associated with a number of physical chemistry advances, was requested to study the sulphuric acid process to determine whether the pollution problem caused by nitric oxide fumes could be eliminated. As a result, he was able to improve the process during that time by installing the first commercial absorption system—known as the *cascade absorbante* (9). This was a coke-packed tower in which the nitrogen oxides were absorbed and recirculated in a sulphuric acid stream fed to the top of the tower. His solution to the atmospheric pollution problem had one drawback, however. The acid stream flowing down the *cascade absorbante* was substantially diluted by the water vapors absorbed along with the nitrogen oxides. A few years later, in 1810, John Glover in England conceived of the idea of installing a second tower, where the nitrogen oxides and water could be stripped from the dilute acid, using hot sulphurous gases from the lead chamber, returning the vapor stream to the main oxidation system. In this stripping tower, the acid was also reconcentrated back to a strength of 82 percent. This modification became the basis of the standard lead chamber process used for a century thereafter, which is shown on Figure 1.4 (10, p. 797–798).

It remained to be seen how sulphuric acid could be produced without the use of nitric acid. The origins of such a direct process were also in England, but now it was German chemists who came up with the practical solution. Sir Humphrey Davy had suggested, in 1817, that platinum might be used to accelerate the oxidation of sulphur dioxide to sulphur trioxide, but no practical use had been made of this concept, since it was found that gaseous impurities quickly "poisoned" this catalyst. In the mid-1800s, iron oxides were shown to be resistant to poisons, but they had much lower activity. In 1898, Wilhelm Ostwald and Rudolph Knietsch at BASF, charged with developing an improved sulfuric acid pro-

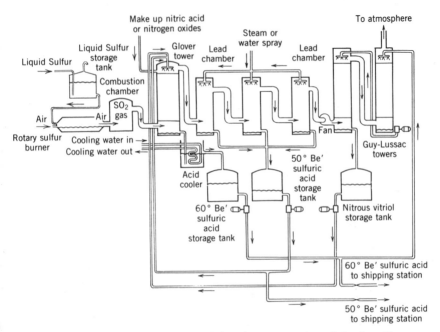

Figure 1.4 Schematic flow diagram of chamber process for sulphuric acid manufacture. (*Source:* Texasgulf, Inc.)

cess to serve the dyestuffs industry, succeeded in commercializing a vapor-phase route that became known as the "contact" process. (*Kontakt* is the German word for "catalyst.") Iron oxide was used in the first stage and platinum in the second. Producing very pure acid, this process was considered one of the other key advances in the history of industrial inorganic chemistry, greatly enhancing the reputation of BASF.

Rudolph Knietsch, the company's leading chemist at that time, used what many now feel was the first application of reaction system design on the process that oxidizes sulfur dioxide with air (11, p. 517). His diagrams, preserved to this day, show an amazing understanding of the interaction between reaction velocity and equilibrium (Fig. 1.5). He also invented the tube bundle reactor design, which used the hot reaction mixture flowing outside the tubes for preheat.

These advances and others, made just before the turn of the century, were significant in the development of more sophisticated

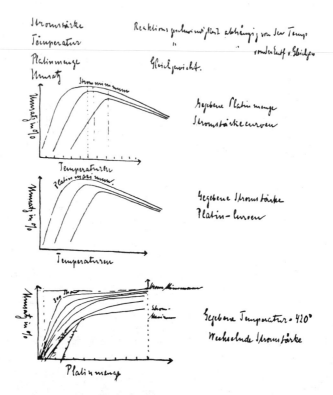

Figure 1.5 Knietsch's original diagrams of SO₃ catalysis. *(Source:* K. Schoene-mann, Chemical Engineering in Germany, In *History of Chemical Engineering,* William F. Furter, ed., Advances in Chemistry Series 190, American Chemical Society, Washington, DC, 1980, p. 254.)

theory and of the larger, more versatile equipment that would be needed for the next stage of industry development.

CATALYSIS BRINGS A NEW DIMENSION

Germany had recognized earlier than other countries that the demand for some chemicals would rise faster than their availability—directly or indirectly—from the coke ovens. Thus, by the turn of the twentieth century, it had become evident that while world supplies of phosphates and potash (the other two key plant growth materials) were amply available in natural form in many parts of the world, the amount of ammonia available from coke oven operations was already becoming insufficient for the world's agricultural needs. Moreover, ammonia could also be useful for the manufacture of nitrate explosives, thus further limiting the amount available for food production. Nitrates in the form of salt-peter came to Germany from as far away as Chile, which would be a problem in case of war. In 1905, Gustav von Bruening, son of the co-founder of Hoechst, established a team under the direction of Martin Rohmer to study the synthesis of ammonia and nitric acid. The latter process proved easier to develop. Research by Frederick Kuhlmann in France as early as 1839 had shown that platinum catalyzed the reaction of ammonia with oxygen to make nitrogen oxides. These results were now confirmed and extended by Professor Ostwald, who later received a Nobel prize for his work, which also included the catalytic process for sulfuric acid production. The first commercial plant was placed in operation at Bochum, Germany, in 1906, making 300 kilograms of nitric acid per day.

Ammonia synthesis proved more elusive, however, though two processes had become available to make synthetic fertilizers. In 1898, F. Rothe, an assistant to Dr. Adolf Frank and Dr. Caro, had found that calcium cyanamid was formed when nitrogen was passed over calcium carbide at 1000°C (12, p. 304). The cyanamid could be used directly as a fertilizer or treated with superheated steam to release ammonia. For the first time, a synthetic nitrogen source had been found that was independent of coke oven operations. However, the process was expensive, depending as it did on the use of electric power as an energy source. It therefore took some time for this technology to come into commercial use.

The first successful fixation of nitrogen on an industrial scale was accomplished by Kristian Birkeland and Samuel Eyde, two Norwegians who had studied the observations made by Sir Henry Cavendish. Cavendish had analyzed the gases leaving an electric arc chamber and had found that oxides of nitrogen had formed in the discharge. In 1903, a Norwegian plant used cheap hydro-electric power to make nitric oxide from the nitrogen and oxygen in the air. Combined with more oxygen and absorbed in water, it gave nitric acid. A synthetic fertilizer was then produced by reacting the nitric acid with limestone, the resulting calcium nitrate being sold under the name of Norwegian saltpeter. (This product remained on the market until 1928, when its production finally became uneconomical.)

Then, the important breakthrough came. In 1908, Fritz Haber, working at the Technische Hochschule in Karlsruhe, conducted his famous experiment where he "fixed" atmospheric nitrogen through the catalytic conversion of hydrogen and nitrogen at 500–600°C and 100–200 atmospheres.

The developments leading up to this discovery can be fairly well documented. Joseph Priestley had discovered the composition of ammonia in 1774. During the following century, a number of chemists attempted its synthesis without success, primarily due to a lack of knowledge of physical chemistry. Greater understanding of chemical equilibria and the mass action principle, largely through the work of Jacobus Van't Hoff and Henri Le Chatelier, finally led to the conclusion that an increase in pressure would favor the combination of four molecules (three hydrogen and one nitrogen) to form two molecules of ammonia (12, p. 266). Le Chatelier, who largely studied the reactions of carbon monoxide, carbon dioxide and coke (i.e., the so-called "Boudard equilibrium") had tried to make ammonia, but without success. Haber particularly recognized the role of reaction kinetics in equilibrium reactions and correctly visualized a recycle process with low yields per pass, withdrawal of the product from the reaction loop and the favorable action of a catalyst.

Born in Breslau, Haber received an education in chemistry and soon developed a strong interest in industrial applications. In 1893, he began to study the decomposition of organic compounds at high temperatures, a process called pyrolysis. In this early work, he was able to correct the famous French chemist Berthelot's fairly arbitrary generalizations in this area. He then turned his attention to electrochemistry, including the "voltage" of chemical reactions. In the course of this work, he wrote a book on energy relationships in gas reactions.

At the turn of the century, Haber and Professor Walther Nernst, one of the most eminent chemists of his day, started working on the ammonia problem. Nernst actually produced some ammonia at 75 atmospheres and 800–1000°C. However, when he suggested this synthesis to the director of the Hoechst plant at Griesheim, it was turned down as being impractical, due to the high pressures and temperatures involved. Haber recognized the desirability of lowering the reaction temperature since the equilibrium would become more favorable. In an attempt to allow operating under less severe temperature conditions, Haber eventually tried a number of rare earth catalysts. Finally, he discovered osmium, a substance that was far superior to anything tried before and that gave sensational results. Uranium was found to be similarly effective. At this point, however, the process was still at the bench scale. Looking ahead to the commercial application of this technology, Haber foresaw the need to maintain the reaction system at high pressure in a circulating mode since any other scheme would be hopelessly uneconomical. Accordingly, he patented a process reflecting such a scheme and incorporating a rare earth catalyst. This system became the forerunner of today's ammonia synthesis, though at that point the process used a prohibitively expensive catalyst.

Soon thereafter, at the suggestion of Karl Engler, a great authority on chemical technology, BASF acquired the patents to this process. The company entrusted the development of a practical commercial approach to Carl Bosch, then a young industrial chemist. Bosch had both a chemical and a mechanical engineering background, having graduated from Leipzig University in 1898. He joined BASF immediately after graduation and commenced working on ammonia synthesis soon thereafter. In cooperation with Alwin Mittasch, later chief chemist at BASF and eventually known as "the Father of Catalysis" at that company, Bosch set out to develop the high pressure apparatus necessary for building such plants, eventually resulting in the famous Haber-Bosch process. A key aspect of this development was the substitution of iron for the rare-earth catalysts used in Haber's first experiments, allegedly after 20,000 systematic trials of different catalytic materials by Mittasch. The eventual catalyst, not very different from that in use today, was magnetite (iron oxide) with a few percent aluminum and a small amount of potassium.

To allow large-scale production, Bosch and his co-workers also developed a commercial shift gas process to produce the required hydrogen from carbon monoxide and steam. One of Bosch's significant achievements was the design, for the first time, of a practical high pressure reactor. And here he had to solve a major problem. The high strength carbon steel used for the tubes was attacked by the hydrogen, producing pores and cracks that caused rapid failure at the 200 atmosphere pressures employed. Bosch solved the problem by using an ingenious design, where an inner annulus made of low strength, low carbon steel was in contact with the reactants and an outer tube fabricated of high strength steel was used to contain the pressure. The outer tube had a series of small holes, which allowed hydrogen leaking through the inner tube to be dissipated harmlessly to the atmosphere.

By 1913, the first plant was under construction by BASF at Oppau, barely in time to serve German needs during the war. It had a capacity of 4000 tons per year, operating at 200 atmospheres and 500°C. Within a short time, another ammonia plant was in operation at BASF's Merseburg plant near Leipzig. Five more were soon thereafter built in the Ruhr, operated respectively by Hibernia, Victor, Ruhrchemie, Scholven, and Stickstoffwerke Ewald.

Haber's contract with BASF paid him a royalty of one pfennig for each kilogram of ammonia, which eventually made him a multimillionaire. He became a controversial figure because, during the 1914–1918 war, he was active in the development of poison gases, actually supervising the use of chlorine gas at the battle of Ypres. One of Germany's most famous chemists and Nobel Prize winners, Richard Willstatter, at first refused to work on the poison gas project but was ordered to do so by Haber, who had received an army rank. Haber's wife pleaded with him to discontinue his activities in this sphere, but to no avail. When she failed to convince him, she committed suicide and this episode became a "cause celèbre." When Haber received the Nobel prize for chemistry in 1918 for his work on ammonia synthesis and "high pressure technology for chemistry" in general, the award was widely protested, due to his wartime activities with poison gases.

In the early 1920s, Haber resumed his otherwise distinguished career, taking a major lead in rebuilding German chemical research by assembling a brilliant group of scientists at the Kaiser Wilhelm Institute in Dahlen. His wide knowledge and insights helped to make the Institute a center of inspired research, where Haber became a guiding light to a younger group of researchers. Then, after Hitler came to power, Haber's Jewish ancestry came to light. Haber had, in fact, long ago become a Protestant, believing that anti-Semitism was hampering his career, but his blood was not "pure" by Nazi standards. In failing health by 1933, he left Germany and traveled to Switzerland and England, where the British chemist and Zionist Chaim Weitzmann offered him a position with a newly established research institute in Palestine

tine. Haber never went there, however, and died shortly thereafter from pituitary gland disfunction and angina pectoris. He donated his library to the new university. The Kaiser Wilhelm Institute's memorial service for Haber, organized by Carl Bosch, who had been named chairman of the Institute's governing board in 1935, was attended by most of the renowned scientists in Germany, in spite of being denounced in advance by Hitler. The ceremony honoring Haber became a legendary event in the annals of the world's scientific community.

The uncoupling of the production of ammonia from the supply available in coke oven gas was a milestone. It established the principle that countries should consider alternate raw materials—requiring new process technologies—to meet end product demand, thus becoming independent of the supply of a single feedstock available in limited quantity.

The development of the Haber-Bosch process for synthetic ammonia remains one of the most important achievements in the history of chemical process development. In 1913, when the first such plant came on stream, the world consumption of nitrogen-based fertilizers and explosives was 720,000 tons, expressed as nitrogen (N). Essentially all of this material came either from Chile in the form of saltpeter or from coke oven gases. By 1929, world consumption had increased to 2,140,000 tons divided as follows (13):

Chilean saltpeter	23.8%
Coke oven ammonia	19.9%
Arc process	1.0%
Calcium cyanamid	11.9%
Synthetic ammonia	43.0%

Between 1913, when the Oppau ammonia plant first went on stream and the late 1920s, by which time synthetic ammonia had become the most important source of nitrogen, many improvements were made in various sections of the flowsheet. Among these, the development of a large-scale coke gasifier, the CO shift conversion, and an improved CO_2 scrubbing system were perhaps of greatest importance. A process flow diagram of the Haber-Bosch process as it operated around 1929 is shown in Figure 1.6.

The creation of a domestic nitrogen industry in Germany made the country much less dependent on supplies of Chilean and other important nitrates for agricultural and munitions industries. More-

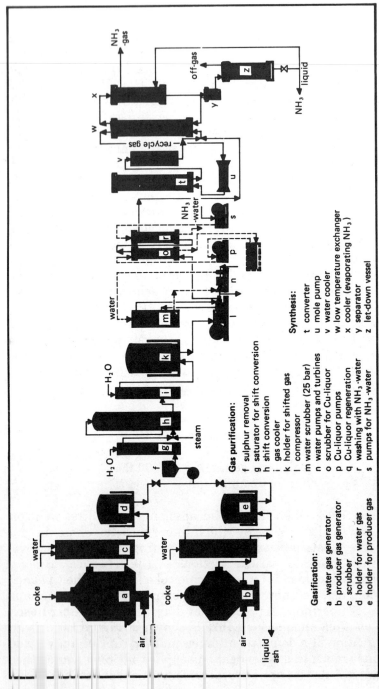

Figure 1.6 Simplified process flow diagram of the Haber-Bosch process. (*Source:* Dr. Max Appl, A brief history of ammonia production from the early days to the present. Figure reproduced from BASF Information August 1974 and also published in *Nitrogen,* March/April 1976.)

Gasification:

a water gas generator
b producer gas generator
c scrubber
d holder for water gas
e holder for producer gas

Gas purification:

f sulphur removal
g saturator for shift conversion
h shift conversion
i gas cooler
k holder for shifted gas
l compressor
m water scrubber (25 bar)
n water pumps and turbines
o scrubber for Cu-liquor
p Cu-liquor pumps
q Cu-liquor regeneration
r washing with NH$_3$-water
s pumps for NH$_3$-water

Synthesis:

t converter
u mole pump
v water cooler
w low temperature exchanger
x cooler (evaporating NH$_3$)
y separator
z let-down vessel

over, it provided a strong link between its military machine and its chemical industry, as embodied in the I.G. cartel, which played such an important role in Germany's rise to world power status in the 1930s and 1940s.

THE BIRTH OF I.G. FARBENINDUSTRIE

The origins of the I.G. cartel date back to World War I—probably to the aftermath of the Battle of the Somme. This engagement had been planned for some time by Marshall Joseph Joffre, then heading the Allied Forces. French troops had been decimated at Verdun, but Joffre convinced Sir Douglas Haig, the British commander, to again throw the entire weight of the Allied forces against the Germans, dug in along the Somme River. The main burden of this campaign was for the first time borne by the British forces, a battle of attrition that lasted from July to November. British losses amounted to 420,000, French casualties were 200,000, while Germany left 670,000 dead in the field. Neither side gained in this poorly conceived engagement, which resulted in Joffre being relieved of his command. However, when the staggering toll of casualties became known, it resulted in a major setback to the German war spirit. For the first time, serious questions were raised whether the war could be won, with 450,000 German soldiers previously lost at Verdun and the British showing a degree of fighting ability and determination not originally expected by the Kaiser. German industrialists, in particular, became apprehensive about what would happen at the conclusion of a war they might after all lose, with all the unfavorable commercial implications this suggested.

In the early 1900s, Carl Duisberg, one of the most important figures at Bayer, had already attempted to rally leaders of the largest German firms to join up in a "Common Interest of the German Dyestuffs Industry." Duisberg had traveled to the United States, where he became acquainted with such "trusts" as Standard Oil, and those in the iron, steel, and glass industries. He became convinced of the merits of such an arrangement for the German dyestuffs industry and set about trying to establish a German trust company. In this, he only succeeded in part. In 1904, in cooperation with BASF's chairman von Brunck, Duisberg was able to line up a dyestuffs group containing BASF, Bayer, and AGFA, which agreed to cooperate on sales, research, and some other areas.

The combine was called "Interessengemeinshaft" ("community of interests"), from which the letters IG were later taken. However, Hoechst, Cassella, and Kalle set up a competing trust, as these firms were concerned about the other group's intention to become more active in the pharmaceutical as well as dyestuffs industries (13).

Now, in early 1917, sobered executives of BASF, Bayer, and Hoechst were joined by directors of the other three companies as well as Griesheim-Elektron to establish an association known as "Interessengemeinschaft der Deutschen Teerfarbenfabriken," the precursor of I.G. Farbenindustrie. In many respects, BASF took a leading role in this combination, with Carl Bosch, known by the world for the Haber-Bosch ammonia process, slated to become the motivating force thereafter. At this point, however, the companies were still operating as independent entities and some areas (e.g., nitrogen fixation, calcium carbide, and electrolytic metals reduction) remained outside the profit sharing scheme.

After the cessation of hostilities in 1918, the Allied powers agreed on steps to destroy for a long time to come Germany's capacity to make war. The stiff terms of the Treaty of Versailles included not only seizure of many plants and all patents, but also the payment of heavy reparations for war damages, with substantial amounts to be paid in the form of dyestuffs and chemicals. Such influential military leaders as Field Marshal Ferdinand Foch of France and Sir Henry Wilson of England also insisted on demolishing the German plants that had made poison gas and nitrate explosives. Carl Bosch frantically tried to modify and soften these provisions, at first meeting with little success. Soon after the treaty was signed, however, Bosch was able to convince the French official in charge of I.G.'s confiscated dyestuffs plants to start negotiations that would soften the terms of the treaty, which would have resulted in razing some of BASF's prize units. The deal negotiated between Bosch and M. Frossard, a top executive of one of the leading French dyestuffs firms, called for the I.G. to go into partnership with the French government to exploit the French dyestuffs market. In return, the I.G. would regain a half interest in the dyestuffs plants, while the I.G. plants marked for destruction, which were largely in the French occupation zone, would be spared. At first, the French General Staff bitterly opposed this scheme, which would make France a partner with its traditional enemy. Eventually, it relented, however, under the condition that

I.G. Farben would share all know-how in ammonia and nitrate production with the French military and help build equivalent modern plants in France. Bosch readily agreed to this, thus saving the fate of the plants he had built before the war, and particularly the Oppau unit, his crowning achievement, resulting from his historic cooperation with Fritz Haber.

Loss of the war had placed German industry in a very weak position in the early 1920s, with foreign companies taking business away from the I.G. concerns. Bosch soon recognized that the association form of organization that had been agreed upon in 1916 would not be suitable for the difficult period ahead. He saw that a complete amalgamation of Germany's heavy and organic chemical industry would be needed to compete with French, Italian, British, and American firms. On December 9, 1925, he succeeded in merging seven of the largest German companies into BASF, with the new entity entitled I.G. Farbenindustrie Aktiengesellschaft (13). Duisberg was named chairman of the supervisory board and Bosch became head of the board of directors (Vorstand). The new I.G. combine's ranks now included many of the outstanding inventors of their time including Fritz Klatte (vinyl chloride), Bosch and Haber (ammonia synthesis), Alwin Mittasch (methanol) and Paul Duden (acetylene chemistry). Later, disciplinary committees (i.e., relating to the "disciplines" of chemistry involved) were formed to coordinate I.G. Farben's research activities. These included Otto Ambros (R&D director at BASF), Heinrich Hopff (plastics and intermediates), Otto Bayer (R&D director at Leverkuesen), and George Kranzlein (director of the alizarin laboratory at Hoechst).

The interests of the entire German chemical industry had now truly been combined and united under the leadership of Carl Bosch. The German public, and foreign investors as well, recognized the potential of the new firm, and bid the value of its shares up to triple the offering price. Fritz ter Meer, primarily a scientist but also a member of the new I.G. board, was quoted as prophesying that "the opening of hitherto unknown chemicals fields was the motif of the new combine" (13). However, the I.G. had more prosaic, commercial goals. It soon gained control of Germany's munitions industry through investment in such firms as Dynamit A.G., Rheinische-Westfaelische Sprengstoff, and others. It established foreign sales and manufacturing subsidiaries, including the American I.G. Company, and even attempted to buy a substantial interest in the large French chemical firm of Kuhlmann, though this thrust was quickly blocked through concerted action by the French Chamber of Deputies. In the aftermath of this attempted coup, however, I.G. Farben and Kuhlmann executives agreed on the establishment of a cartel involving sales of explosives, fertilizers, and other products, and calling for price fixing, exchange of technical information, and division of markets. Eventually, the cartel was extended to cover chemical firms in Belgium, Italy, the Netherlands, and England and also a number of other products. Germany was now firmly back in the chemical business and I.G. Farben was soon to become deeply involved in Hitler's program for autarky, the establishment of an independent local supply of gasoline and synthetic rubber, which would allow the Nazi Government to proceed with its military adventures.

CHEMICAL TECHNOLOGY CAN MAKE FUELS

Roughly at the same time that Haber and Bosch were developing their commercial synthesis of ammonia at elevated pressures, another German researcher, Friedrich Bergius at the Technische Hochschule in Hannover, was building equipment to demonstrate the high pressure hydrogenation of heavy oils and powdered coal. Interested in high pressure reactions, including the production of calcium superoxide from lime and oxygen, Bergius saw the need to develop techniques for constructing vessels and valves that would work at high pressures. Recognizing the need for a large source of hydrogen, Bergius turned his attention to the so-called water gas reaction, in which steam reacts with carbon to produce carbon monoxide and hydrogen. In 1914, Bergius succeeded in hydrogenating heavy oils to gasoline at 50 percent yields, working in a 40-liter "bomb" at 430°C and 120 atmospheres, at the same time reducing sulfur in the oils to low levels. During World War I, the emphasis of hydrogenation work switched to coal and lignite to provide design data for large-scale coal hydrogenation plants. Such a unit was finally placed in operation at Rheinau in the early 1920s, using reactors 80 centimeters in diameter and 8 meters long. It was found that the process worked best when powdered coal was fed to the reactor in a slurry made from recycled heavy oil product. Although the process proved workable and even relatively economic, several problems remained to be solved. It was recognized that catalysts should be developed to speed the reaction and that a considerably better yield could probably be achieved.

Now, Bosch at I.G. Farben took another giant step for chemistry and I.G. Farbenindustrie. Well aware that the rest of the world was now also building synthetic ammonia plants, whose output would undoubtedly lead to a glut in the world's supply, Bosch saw a new use for some of the high pressure ammonia plants at Leuna and Oppau. He could convert these to coal hydrogenation plants producing gasoline from coal, if BASF could commercialize the Bergius technology. If successful, this would make Germany independent in the production of motor fuels. And he would try to convince an American oil company, such as Standard Oil of New Jersey, to help finance the project, although this would have to wait until BASF owned the Bergius patents and more development work was done (14, p. 46). Bosch had visited the United States on several occasions in the 1920s, a time when Germany was fraught with post-World War I problems. He noted the general wealth and the exceptional means to carry out expensive pilot plant research work in America and, upon returning from one trip said, "We have neither the money, nor do we have cheap raw materials nor do we have enormous sales. All we have left to us are the people . . . our strength lies only in research or intensive work" (15, p. 1404). It was at that point that Bosch invited the Jersey research executives to Ludwigshafen, leading to the historic agreement between the two companies. BASF acquired rights to the Bergius patents in 1927 and continued the development work, with the goal of developing a process to make both motor fuels and lubricating oils from coal.

The two-step process developed by Matthias Pier's group under the leadership and guidance of Bosch was very sophisticated, even by current standards. Coal dust and highly aromatic recycle oil were injected into the first reactor, operating at 450°C and 200–300 atmospheres under a hydrogen atmosphere. In the second reactor, diesel oil, gasoline, and other liquid hydrocarbons were produced and then distilled in the presence of a catalyst to increase yields. Middle distillates were passed over a tungsten sulfide catalyst, whereby some additional cracking took place, thus increasing the yields of motor fuel.

Though other researchers such as Matthias Pier, Pott, and

Broche,* did much of the development work leading to commercialization, Bergius' contributions were considered as fundamental and he received a Nobel prize in 1931, shared with Carl Bosch. Less well known is the fact that Bergius also developed technology for producing ethylene glycol from ethylene and phenol from chlorobenzene.

Pier and Bosch built on their earlier success by also developing a commercial methanol process at the BASF works in Oppau in 1924. A zinc-copper catalyst was used in a plant built at Leuna which, for the first time, produced methanol and higher alcohols by a technique other than the destructive distillation of wood, which had been used for methanol production since the seventeenth century. Methanol had, in fact, been synthesized from carbon monoxide and hydrogen as early as 1913 by Alwin Mittasch and in 1921 by M. Patard, a French scientist, but lack of experience with high pressure technology delayed commercial application (16, p. 216). In an improved version, the new methanol route became known as the Pier-Mittasch process, which for many years was called the high pressure methanol route. Mittasch, who was in charge of BASF's famous ammonia laboratory,†also contributed to the development of a high pressure urea process, with a 40,000-ton-per-year plant built at Oppau.

The other industrial nations obviously followed these developments with great interest. The I.G. companies were inclined to license some of these technologies, but the cost—in terms of both money and loss of commercial influence by the licensee—was frequently prohibitive and, therefore, often unacceptable. In the case of ammonia, the BASF technology became known to Brunner-Mond engineers inspecting the Oppau plant in 1919. However, it took a great deal of additional research and several years before a commercial plant could be built. The British firm then also de-

---

*The Pott-Broche process was an indirect hydrogenation route, a precursor to what later became known as "donor solvent" technology.

†The ammonia laboratory became a tradition at BASF, the company that is considered the most "process research oriented" among the German Big Three (including Bayer and Hoechst). I had the privilege of working with some of the research and development people in the ammonia laboratory, including its director, Dr. Hans Friz, when Chem Systems and BASF cooperated on the development of a new propylene oxide process in the 1970s. I recognized what many people in the industry already knew. The ammonia laboratory, with its buildings housing multistory pilot plants and with its highly computerized analytical and control equipment, may be the best chemical research laboratory in the world (P.H.S.).

veloped a methanol synthesis. In retrospect, these efforts were extremely important for the company, since they endowed it with the process experience and equipment know-how that later led to ICI's development of high pressure polyethylene technology and steam-methane reforming of liquid hydrocarbons and naphtha. Steam reforming was also developed at BASF, with the first pilot plant placed in operation in 1928.

The success of German chemists in commercializing vapor phase high pressure catalytic processes stimulated worldwide research work on other syntheses. German chemists generally remained in the lead, staying several years ahead of their foreign peers in many research areas. The advanced state of German chemical research work in hydrogenation, synthesis gas conversion, carbonylation and hydroformylation, and high pressure processes in general, was well known and acknowledged and led companies outside Germany—particularly oil companies—to inquire how they could participate in the fruits of this research. Thus, it is not generally known that some of Bergius' work was initially financed, in part, by Royal Dutch Shell, a company that was already one of Jersey's main competitors. However, support was discontinued in the 1920s, when Shell found more petroleum deposits and concluded that coal hydrogenation would be too expensive. This conclusion turned out to be correct, as far as the major oil companies were concerned. Standard Oil (New Jersey) had started its own research program in 1927 in cooperation with BASF, but discontinued the effort in the mid-1930s when "Dad" Joiner's East Texas gusher and subsequent discoveries in Texas and Louisiana, as well as the emerging oil riches of the Middle East, brought crude oil prices down to levels so low as to make synthetic crude oil seem an unlikely prospect for a number of decades to come. However, Germany was in a different situation, with much less access to foreign sources of oil and the possibility of another war on the horizon.

In the early 1930s, a 100,000-ton motor fuel-from-coal plant was built in Leuna, based on improved high pressure hydrogenation technology, followed by similar plants at Gelsenkirchen, Bottrop, and Scholven. By the start of the war, Germany's capacity for motor fuels from coal, using coal hydrogenation, exceeded one million tons per year. A C.I.O.S. team, including Peter Sherwood, later a respected industry consultant, visited most of the coal hydrogenation plants, which had contributed so much to the Nazi war effort. All of the plants used a catalytic process, whereas Bergius had carried out the hydrogenation without a catalyst. At Bottrop, the hydrogenation was carried out on coal-derived pitch in liquid phase (17).

ICI had acquired certain rights to coal hydrogenation technology from the syndicates, which had been financing Bergius' work in the 1930s. For some time, the British company could not decide whether such a plant would ever produce motor fuel economically, but then the British government became concerned about possible future gasoline shortages, particularly if war were to come. A subsidy of eight pence per gallon was therefore offered for gasoline made from coal. Under these circumstances, coal hydrogenation became economical and ICI built several plants in the late 1930s, including two at Billingham and Heysham, with capacities up to 150,000 tons per year. Interestingly, these plants produced LPG* as a by-product and there was no use for this in England in the 1930s. The company thought about possible outlets and eventually worked out technology to reform these liquid hydrocarbons to ammonia and methanol synthesis gas. Coal hydrogenation was thus used in England for a period of time, but it was never as important in that country as in Germany. Also, much of the time, ICI fed creosote oil rather than coal to these plants.†

A route for the production of both fuels and organic chemicals had also come under intensive development in the years before World War II. In 1925, Franz Fischer and Hans Tropsch, working at the Kaiser Wilhelm Institute for Coal Research at Muelheim-Ruhr, succeeded in converting carbon monoxide and hydrogen (synthesis gas) into mixtures of liquid oxygenates and hydrocarbons at pressures considerably more moderate than those employed by Bergius. The approach they took had its roots in the work published by the famous French scientist Paul Sabatier in the early 1900s, which showed that methane could be produced when carbon monoxide and hydrogen were passed under pressure over a nickel catalyst. The catalyst first employed by the German researchers consisted of alkalized iron turnings, although later, cobalt, nickel, and ruthenium were shown to improve yields. Fischer also found that if the pressure was dropped to 1–7 atmospheres, the ratio of hydrocarbons to oxygenates could be reversed, in favor of the former. A great deal of experimental work was done, with the final catalyst used in most of the German plants having a composition of $100Co:5ThO_2:8MgO:200$ Kieselguhr. Rights

*Liquid Petroleum Gases
†Peter Sherwood, personal communication.

to the process were purchased by Ruhrchemie, who built the first commercial Fischer-Tropsch plant in Holten in 1934. During the 1930s, a number of other Fischer-Tropsch plants were built in Germany, six alone in the Ruhr region, with a combined capacity of 400,000 tons per year. These plants did not substantially contribute to liquid fuels production, but were essential for the production of aliphatic chemicals, detergents, synthetic lard, etc.

In addition to the less severe operating conditions needed for this process, it could accommodate a large variety of coals, since gasification and synthesis gas preparation preceded the conversion to more valuable products. This also led to the development of widely different types of gasification reactors, (later referred to as Lurgi, Totzek, and Winkler gasifiers), as needed to handle various types of coal, some of which tended to agglomerate during the heating step. It is significant that German work on coal gasifiers in the 1930s became the basis for essentially all post-World War II work in this area, including much of the U.S. and British research to make synthetic fuels from coal. A number of top German scientists, including Ernst Donath, one of Pier's top assistants and probably Germany's foremost authority on coal hydrogenation technology, helped the U.S. Bureau of Mines to build coal hydrogenation and Fischer-Tropsch demonstration plants in Louisiana in the early 1950s. Figure 1.7 illustrates the process sequence employed in the Fischer-Tropsch (F-T) unit, which employed a Linde-Frank oxygen unit dismantled at Hoechst and re-erected at the Bureau of Mines unit. The F-T synthesis reactor used the so-called ebullated bed technique invented by Hydrocarbon Research Inc. (see also page 305).

Motor and aviation fuel production from coal at the start of World War II exceeded 30,000 barrels per day (BPD), representing probably the most important contribution made by I.G. Farben to Hitler's war machine. This has been disputed by historians, who have pointed out that I.G. Farben's success in inducing the Ethyl Corporation to build a joint venture plant for the production of tetraethyl lead, as requested by the German Ministry of Aviation, was even more significant to the Axis war effort. At the time, Ethyl was owned by Standard of New Jersey and General Motors. The company's decision to go ahead with this project in the mid-1930s, supported by Jersey for commercial reasons, was unsuccessfully opposed by DuPont executives, who rightly claimed that the plant would furnish Germany with technical know-how it did not then possess. As it turned out, a second plant was built by

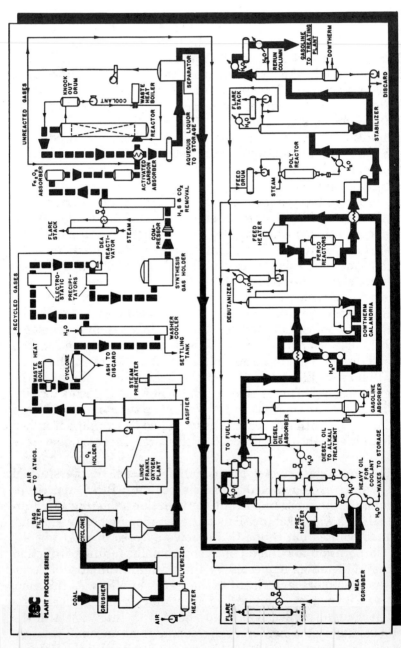

Figure 1.7A Flowsheet of Bureau of Mines modification of gas synthesis process. (*Source:* An American Fischer-Tropsch Plant. In *Modern Chemical Processes*, Vol. III, New York, Reinhold, 1954, pp. 27–45.)

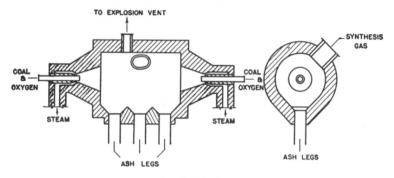

Detail of Horizontal Gasifier

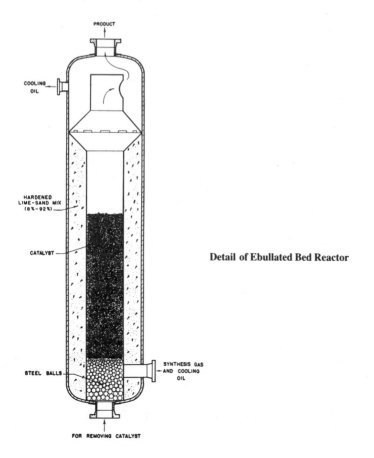

Detail of Ebullated Bed Reactor

Figure 1.7B Equipment details for Bureau of Mines Process.

the German High Command soon after startup of the first unit, but without the knowledge and consent of Ethyl. The refinery operations of the Axis countries could thus be geared to the production of high octane gasoline for Air Force use. While the Wehrmacht was initially able to obtain substantial amounts of crude from the Ploesti fields in Rumania and from Austria, sources of petroleum to German and Italian refineries later dried up, due to intensive bombing of the crude oil fields. I.G. Farben was able to keep its synthetic fuels plants operating fairly well until close to the end of the war. Today, updated versions of F-T technology, to which U.S. firms such as M.W. Kellogg and Badger also contributed, are still in use at the large South African Coal, Gas and Oil Company (SASOL) works in South Africa, which produces large quantities of fuels and petrochemicals. This fact has some significance. The Fischer-Tropsch process can be said to represent the transition from coal tar-based organic chemicals to the current and future organic chemical industry. In this process, synthesis gas is used as the magic "building block."* Versions of the F-T process will, no doubt, be employed at a time when the earth's much more abundant coal may again replace the much more limited oil and natural gas resources of the world, i.e. the current petrochemical feedstocks. At that time, synthesis gas from coal will be converted to the petrochemicals made today from oil and natural gas. But their cost, via F-T processing, will be considerably higher.

ETHYLENE AND BENZENE FROM COKE OVENS

The first two of the three reactive materials—ethylene, benzene, and propylene—that eventually became the foundation of the modern petrochemical industry are present in some quantity in coke-oven gases. Significantly, this represented the only source for these materials for a long time, at least in any appreciable quantities. The large-scale development of Germany's coal tar industry and the advanced state of German chemical research resulted in a more rapid and diverse development in that country of processes for the production of derivatives of both ethylene and benzene. Propylene chemistry came somewhat later, largely due to the fact

---

*This term is used in various parts of this book to denote certain basic chemical molecules that are reacted further to form organic chemicals.

that coke oven gases contain only very small amounts of this material.

In addition to the ammonia washed out of coke-oven gases with sulphuric acid, significant quantities of ethylene are formed under the high temperature reducing conditions that prevail in the coking operation. In the early days of coal coking, ethylene was left in the coke-oven gases, that were generally employed as a fuel for iron and steel production and also for industrial heating and later for residential uses. Because olefins burn with a luminous flame, the presence of ethylene in this gas stream (which also contains hydrogen, carbon monoxide, and light hydrocarbons) gave this combustible mixture the name of "illuminating gas." In most industrial countries, ethylene did not become an important chemical building block until after World War II, although ethylene had been produced "on purpose" even before World War I in Germany by the dehydration of ethanol (18, p. 9). The I.G. Farben companies by the 1930s were recovering coal tar ethylene in substantial amounts and converting it to useful derivatives. This also spurred their research work for producing ethylene by other means, such as via ethane cracking and hydrogenation of acetylene.

Typically, coke-oven gases contain about 1.5 percent ethylene by volume, though the gas supplied from the Saar to the I.G. Farbenindustrie plant at Oppau during World War II contained 2.65 percent ethylene and 0.5 percent propylene. The Linde-Bronn low temperature liquefaction process was used to concentrate the ethylene content to 40 percent, and additional processing further concentrated the stream to 90–99 percent. Figure 1.8 depicts an installation of this type (18, p. 66). In 1943, Germany produced 18,000 tons of ethylene from coke oven gas, representing 17 percent of total German ethylene production in that year. A breakdown of all ethylene sources in that year is shown as follows. (18, p. 36).

Sources of Ethylene Production in Germany in 1943
(Tons per Year)

Source	Production	Percent of Total
Coke-oven gas	18,000	17
Ethane cracking	14,000	13
By-product of arc acetylene process	10,000	9
Hydrogenation of acetylene	33,000	30
Dehydration of ethanol	33,000	30

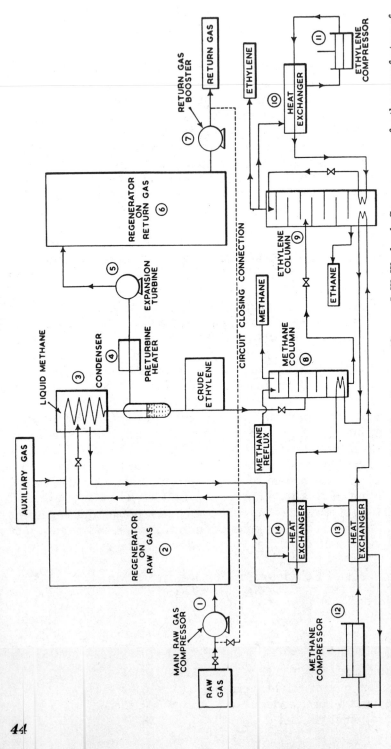

Figure 1.8 Ethylene from coke-oven gas, simplified flow diagram. (*Source:* J. W. Woolcock, Some processes for the manufacture of ethylene. In S. A. Miller, *Ethylene and Its Industrial Derivatives*, London, Ernest Benn Ltd., 1969, p. 66.)

Looking at this table, one might wonder why more ethylene was not produced via hydrocarbon liquids cracking. As early as the turn of the century, so-called "oil gas" was made by cracking petroleum distillates in retorts built for the purpose of enriching low calorific town gas made from coal. Such "carburetting" gases, as they were called, typically contained 20–25 percent ethylene and 13–16 percent propylene, as well as higher olefins and light paraffins. But in Germany, during the war, liquid hydrocarbons were being produced at considerable cost in coal hydrogenation plants and it would not have been logical to convert these critically needed fuels to olefins. Natural gas from the Dutch and German gas fields was very dry and did not contain appreciable amounts of ethane, suitable for making ethylene by direct cracking. And so it was necessary to find a number of other ways to produce wartime ethylene.

It is also noteworthy that German plants did not crack petroleum distillates from the Austrian and Rumanian oil fields, since it would have been easy to develop this technology. In fact, it is surprising that such development work was not done in the mid-1930s, when Germany was importing cheap crude oil from various sources. Most likely, the German High Command felt even then that these supplies would be cut off when the war they expected would finally erupt. As it turned out, Austrian and Rumanian crude oil remained available to Germany throughout the war (except for periodic interruptions resulting from bombing raids).

Dr. Otto Ambros recently confirmed this, stating that the I.G. was insistent on controlling within the German borders the production of all intermediates used to produce Buna rubber.*

Thus, ethanol and acetylene were a much more obvious source of ethylene, particularly in view of the highly developed state of Germany's acetylene industry, which was based on calcium carbide, light hydrocarbon fractions, and methane gas, the latter being feedstocks to the arc process. Acetylene hydrogenation plants were built at Schkopau, Gendorf, Marl (Bunawerke Huels), Ludwigshafen, Leuna, and Auschwitz. Hydrogenation of acetylene to ethylene was carried out with a palladium on silica gel catalyst that had a life of eight months, according to B.I.O.S. reports.

The diversity of ethylene sources attests to the ingenuity of the wartime German chemical industry, whose leaders recognized that

*Dr. Otto Ambros, personal communication.

no one raw material source could satisfy the rapidly rising requirements for this key building block. Ethylene was used for a number of critical wartime needs, including styrene for Buna rubber production, polyethylene, synthetic lubricating oils, and ethylene oxide and glycol. Over 50 percent of the total ethylene was, in fact, used to produce glycol antifreeze for cars and tanks. Synthetic lubricants were made by polymerizing ethylene with anhydrous aluminum chloride, giving an oil with excellent viscosity indices. This technology became obsolete after the war, however.

Whereas ethylene was eventually produced by a number of techniques, benzene was still largely obtained from coke-oven operations. B.I.O.S. Report No. 25, prepared by A.L. Deadman and G.H. Fuidge, of the South Eastern British Gas Board Central Laboratories, gave a comprehensive picture of the German coal tar and "benzole" industries. Although the report concentrated on the period 1939–1945, it also provided a rich historical background. The German coke-oven industry had actually undergone a major change over the half century before World War II. While in 1892, there were 705 by-product coke ovens in Silesia, compared to a total of 500 in the Ruhr and Saar, by 1939 coke production in West Germany was nearly five times greater than in the Eastern part (19). Coal tar was collected and shipped to several very large tar distillers, the most important being Ruetgerswerke A.G., with the largest distillery at Castrop in the Ruhr.

Ruetgerswerke and other companies greatly improved and extended the technology for recovering useful by-products from coal coking. Engineering firms based in the Ruhr became the world experts in designing such plants, exporting the technology to many other countries building a coal and steel industry.

Benzene, later to become the second key petrochemical building block, is traditionally one of the most important chemical by-products of coke-oven operations and the basis of numerous reactions for chemical intermediates and end products. Originally, most of it was recovered from the coke oven gas itself, with the balance obtained from tar distillation. German statistics were actually kept for *benzole*, a term used for benzene and its homologues, toluene and xylene. Annual production of benzole in Germany increased from 220,000 tons in 1932 to 650,000 tons in 1943, or about 62 million gallons, a very large quantity even by today's standards. Of that amount, 52 percent was used in motor fuel and aviation gasoline and the balance for chemical uses and export. Actual benzene available to I.G. Farben plants amounted to approximately 40 million gallons (116,000 tons). One of its most important chemical uses was in the manufacture of styrene for Buna-type rubbers. An indication of the large amounts of benzene that were required for this purpose is given in the following table, which shows the buildup of German Buna capacity relative to natural rubber, which became very scarce (13):

Year	Buna*	Natural Rubber	Total	Percent Buna
1939	14,000	60,000	74,000	19
1940	40,000	26,000	66,000	61
1941	50,000	22,000	72,000	70
1942	69,000	26,000	95,000	73
1943	88,000†	4,000	92,000	95
1944	80,000	3,000	83,000	97

*Approximately 0.21 tons of benzene were required to produce one ton of Buna rubber.
†For short periods of time, German plants produced at a rate exceeding 100,000 tons per year.

Benzene was also employed to make synthetic phenol, maleic anhydride, and lower volume derivatives.

Since less than 100,000 tons of toluene—a critical war material for explosives—were available annually from coke oven operations, the supply was augmented by manufacture of synthetic toluene by the methylation of benzene. This relatively high cost process also yielded some o-xylene by-product. During the course of the war, Ruhrchemie worked on a toluene synthesis from n-heptane, obtained from Fischer-Tropsch processing. The catalyst was chromia-alumina and the reactor was operated on 30-minute reaction-regeneration cycles. German hydrogenation technology, based on earlier work in France and Russia, actually provided the basis for many companies' efforts in the 1940s to convert paraffins or naphthenes in the naphtha boiling range to BTX aromatics, a technology that became known as hydroforming. Process work at Ruhrchemie was completed in 1944 and a 24,000-ton-per-year toluene plant was designed, but it never went on stream. This process and similar ones commercialized in the United States in the early 1940s were precursors for modern catalytic reforming technology, which employs elevated pressures and noble metal catalysts to avoid the severe coking problems encountered in the early work. However, success in this area was to come only in the late 1940s as a result of work at Universal Oil Products Company.

Coke ovens were therefore providing essentially all of Germany's aromatics. The Deadman-Fuidge B.I.O.S. report, which focuses on this subject, contains a great deal of information on the production of various benzene derivatives from coal tar fractions, as practiced in Germany before and during the Second World War. As an example, the following capacities for specific derivatives were listed (19, p. 120):

Location	Tons Per Year
Uerdingen	
Benzaldehyde	500
Benzyl chloride	1,800
Aniline	10,000–12,000
Benzyl alcohol	600
Nitrobenzene	10,000–12,000
Alkyd resin	12,000
Elberfeld and Leverkuesen	
Chlorobenzene	8,400
Nitrochlorobenzene	1,800
Chlorodiphenyl	1,800
Salicylic acid from phenol	1,700

Total German production of phthalic anhydride was estimated at 6600 tons annually, while beta naphthol and other dye intermediates consumed about an equivalent amount of naphthalene raw material. Resorcinol capacity was estimated at 400 tons per year. Phenol production was, of course, very extensive, in the range of 200,000 tons per year. One of the most important uses was in the production of cyclohexanone, an intermediate for Nylon 6 fibers. The Deadman-Fuidge survey is useful also in that it lists a large number of other B.I.O.S. reports on various German plants (19, pp. 166–173).

GERMAN FIBER AND PLASTICS INDUSTRIES WERE VERY ADVANCED

Of particular interest to the Allies was the state of German development in high polymers for the production of synthetic fibers. A C.I.O.S. team headed by LeRoy H Smith of American Viscose surveyed German progress in the fiber sector. Composed of people from DuPont, American Enka, ICI, Courtaulds, and British Nylon Spinners, the team arrived in Leipzig on June 26, 1945 for an extended tour of plants in Germany, Holland, Italy, and Austria. By the time the team visited most of the plants, they were either shut down or operating at extremely low capacities, due to lack of either raw materials or personnel. The final report of this team was published by the Textile Research Institute in 1946 (20). While much of the report dealt with viscose and acetate processes, which were well known, the information obtained on a number of fully synthetic fibers—either in production or in advanced research—was impressive (see Fig. 1.9 representing a page taken from the index of the report). It included Perlon (nylon), polyurethanes, vinyl fibers, polyvinyl alcohol, and polyethylene. Nylon 6/6 had been commercialized by DuPont only just before the outbreak of hostilities, in a plant primarily designed to make fiber for ladies' stockings.

The team members knew that the first true "synthetic" fiber had, in fact, been produced in Germany—based on a vinyl chloride monomer. In 1913, the Griesheim works of Hoechst A.G. had started producing this key chemical on a commercial scale. Dr. Fritz Klatte, who headed this work, regarded vinyl chloride and vinyl acetate monomers as having an excellent potential for the production of man-made fibers, though chemists at that time did not know how to conduct the polymerization of these materials. Hermann Staudinger had not yet charted what others later called "the wonderland of macromolecules of which a single one is often made up of millions of atoms." In the early 1930s, the Wolfen works of I.G. Farben brought a plant on stream to polymerize vinyl chloride, which was treated with chlorine and dissolved in acetone, with the spinning solution passing through a nozzle and PVC fibers recovered in solidified form. The so-called Pe-Ce fiber, the first truly synthetic fiber material, had a number of useful qualities but could not be used for textile production since it softened at 70°C, thus precluding garment washing in hot water. Because of its high chemical resistance, it became a fairly important material for industrial uses. In the mid and late 1930s, the real breakthroughs in synthetic fiber development rapidly rendered this early attempt to imitate natural fibers obsolete.

As the fiber team progressed through several plants and research installations, the history of German nylon development became better known. Evidently, it had been a "catchup" situa-

Figure 1. Page taken from index of report, Synthetic fiber development in Germany. (Source: Synthetic Fiber Development in Germany, Technical Industrial Intelligence Committee, New York, Textile Research Institute, 1946.)

tion, but the German chemists were, as usual, up to the challenge. Aware of DuPont's success in the condensing of adipic acid and hexamethylene diamine (HMDA) to make what is called Nylon 6/6, Paul Schlack, head of I.G. Farben's "Aceta" laboratories in Berlin, was able, in 1938, to self-polymerize caprolactam to produce Nylon 6, which has a very similar polyamide structure to Nylon 6/6. German literature described this as a particularly noteworthy success, since Carothers had apparently claimed that this route was not feasible. DuPont and I.G. Farben then reached a cross-licensing agreement just before the outbreak of hostilities in 1939. Large nylon or Perlon plants, as the fiber was called in Germany, were constructed in Leuna and Ludwigshafen in 1939–1940, with the fiber destined largely for parachutes, tire cord, and other military uses. (See also Chapter 7, which describes the history of synthetic fiber development.)

Actually, German chemical plants had produced both types of nylon during the war. The technical people preferred the caprolactam route, in spite of the undesirable higher water absorption characteristic of Nylon 6, because it was their own development and also because they claimed that it was somewhat cheaper to produce. However, adipic acid and hexamethylene diamine were used as raw materials for the nylon used for film and molding powders made by BASF under the name Igamid. An increasing amount of yarn was actually made from Nylon 6/6 toward the end of the war. Dr. Reppe's butadiene process had been placed in operation in a several thousand ton per month plant in Ludwigshafen, with tetrahydrofuran made as an intermediate. This could be reacted with sodium cyanide to obtain an intermediate to HMDA. The Reppe synthesis could also have been directed to propargyl alcohol, a precursor to hexanediol, from which caprolactam would have been produced. This route was not commercialized before 1945, though Reppe chemistry, based on acetylene later became very important in Germany and in the United States for the production of numerous chemicals made by that route, including some of those listed above. The General Aniline and Film Corporation (GAF), set up after the war in the United States and based on I.G. Farben patents and assets transferred to Switzerland during the war, became the prime manufacturer of these products in the Western Hemisphere.

The fibers team examined a large number of monomer and fiber plants, some completely destroyed by bombings, some burned down by slave labor gangs after cessation of hostilities, and some surprisingly almost intact. In the fibers area, the most interesting development they saw was a continuous viscose process. In the United States and England, the batch technique was still employed in all the plants. Equipment development was also ahead of that in the Allied countries in many cases. The team considered, but then dropped as impractical, the idea of shipping huge xanthane dissolvers or alkali cellulose screws to England or the States. Instead, the team recommended that equipment manufacturers be allowed to inspect the equipment for themselves, rather than using government reports, thus preserving what the team termed as the "free enterprise" spirit, a characterization of mission probably not shared by the conquered German scientists and engineers supplying this information.

From a later perspective, one of the most interesting findings of the fibers team concerned a family of materials called *polyurethanes*, a fiber starting to be produced from hexamethylene di-isocyanate and 1,4 butanediol under the name of Perlon-U. This area of chemistry, where German chemists were then far ahead of the rest of the world as a result of Otto Bayer's research at Leverkuesen, would later lead to DuPont's production of Lycra and Spandex, both specialty fibers with stretch properties. It also led to the Mobay joint venture established by Bayer and Monsanto in the United States for the production of polyurethane plastics, less than ten years after cessation of hostilities. Foamed polyurethanes became the standard material for mattresses made to sell at popular prices.

THE END OF I.G. FARBEN

In 1945, Germany's war machine was shut down and the country divided into four zones. Several years passed before what is now East and West Germany were established as new national entities. Many plants, including the vast Leuna works, were in the Eastern part of prewar Germany and were taken over by the Russians for their own exhaustive studies of German chemical progress. Eventually, these plants were turned over to the East German regime. The largest part of the German chemical industry was, however, located in the Western sector, in the large works at Ludwigshafen, Hoechst, or in the Ruhr and Southern Bavaria.

It is instructive to see just how large a percentage of German chemical production was owned or controlled by I.G. Farben. In 1943, the I.G. had interest in 613 corporations, including 173 in foreign countries, with total assets of 6 billion Reichmarks and it operated with various degrees of influence in 2000 cartels. Figure 1.10 gives an overview of the massive character of I.G. Farben (21). Of course, a number of the companies and plants ended up in the Eastern Zone, under the control of Soviet Russia. Major East German plants that passed to the Russians were Leuna, Schkopau, Wolfen, and Leuna, including Merseburg. As it happened, organic chemical and plastics plants were located to a greater extent in the Leverkuesen, Frankfurt, and Ludwigshafen areas in the Western Zone, while Eastern Germany had more of the fertilizer-, soda ash- and metals-producing capacity.

Although the very name of I.G. Farben is still associated in many people's minds with Hitler's Wehrmacht (tires and gasoline) and with Auschwitz, where a fourth Buna rubber plant was being

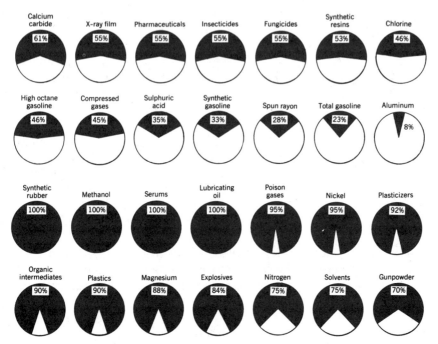

Figure 1.10 Percent of German chemical capacity controlled by the I.G. cartel in 1943. (Excerpted by special permission from *Chemical Engineering*, May 1949, by McGraw-Hill, Inc., New York, NY, 10020.)

built by concentration camp inmates, characterization of the company as an integral part of the Nazi government is too facile. Hitler at first distrusted the firm, since it had several high level Jewish executives when he attained power. Soon, however, he realized that Farben would be indispensable to his plans and from that time on the company became a tool of the Nazi war machine, though few of its top executives became party members. At one point, Dr. Otto Ambros, one of the leading members of the I.G. management board, personally convinced Hitler not to use Tabun nerve gas, a dreaded chemical weapon. The record also seems to show that I.G. Farben's activities under the Hitler regime were not particularly profitable (8, p. 81) and that it was asked to undertake large commercial risks in building plants based on new technologies. Tremendous labor shortages during the latter parts of the war caused the company to use foreign and concentration camp labor, though there was no excuse for the inhuman treatment the workers building the Auschwitz Buna plant received at the hands of inmates with criminal backgrounds, who were used by Farben as "straw bosses" supervising the plant construction. Because thousands of the slave laborers died under these conditions, several of the I.G. executives were convicted at the Nuremberg trial. Their contention that the plant was completely separate from the concentration camp and they they actually may have saved people from the gas chambers by providing employment did not help them escape conviction.

From 1945 to 1950, defeated industrial Germany remained almost at a standstill. In addition to the problems caused by severe shortages of food and fuels, the Allied occupying powers were reluctant to let Germany rebuild its production capacity, which had made the Wehrmacht one of the strongest fighting machines in military history. Production of war materials, such as synthetic rubber, was proscribed for a several-year period, though German industrialists later complained that this was largely an attempt at delaying the resumption of trade competition. In any event, Allied controls clearly slowed the rebirth of German chemical manufacture. Because most able-bodied persons had eventually been conscripted into the army or home defense corps, laboratory and development work had almost stopped by the conclusion of the war and was only slowly resumed thereafter.

The I.G. Farben combine was abolished and the manufacturing plants regrouped largely under the aegis of the three major, original firms: BASF, Hoechst, and Bayer. Several smaller concerns, some partly owned by the three major entities, were again set up as independent operations. For each 1000 marks of I.G. Farbenindustrie, shareholders were given 285 Deutschmark (DM) worth of Bayer shares, 250 DM of BASF, 210 DM of Hoechst, 25 DM of Cassella, 60 DM of Chemieverwaltung (which held 50 percent of Huels), and 50 DM of Rheinstahl. The surviving companies then slowly resumed operations. Thus, in 1951, Hoechst was "reborn" under the careful supervision and guidance of the Allies, although the German executives who would run the firm were able to exert a certain amount of influence on the capitalization and management scheme eventually adopted. The new Hoechst included plants at Hoechst, Griesheim, Gendorf, Bobingen, Gersthofen, Offenbach, and Hersfeld. Hoechst was also reorganized to own 100 percent of Knapsack, Kalle, and two other firms, and lesser percentages of the engineering firm Friedrich Uhde, as well as of Wacker-Chemie, Ruhrchemie, Cassella Farbwerke, and several other firms. Similar arrangements were made for the other two major members of the old I.G. combine.

Two coal hydrogenation plants remained in operation at the end of the war, one operated by Gelsenberg Benzin in Gelsenkirchen and the other by Union Rheinische Braunkohle in Wesseling, near Cologne. In the late 1940s, these plants were converted into refineries and used to upgrade heavy crude oil residues by hydrogenating these cuts over an appropriate catalyst. Together with two other (shut down) hydrogenation plants at Scholven and Bottrop, these plants could process up to 1.4 million tons of oil residues per year, producing moderate quantities of medium octane gasoline, as well as middle distillates and heavy fuel oil. A few years later, all of these plants were shut down, as modern American refining technology started to be used throughout Germany and the rest of Europe, which was importing cheap Middle Eastern crude oil.

The U.S. Government, at the start of the war, seized the assets of I.G. Farben in the United States, including a number of its manufacturing facilities. After the war was over, it took some time to sort out the ownership question, since the I.G. had transferred a substantial amount of control to a Swiss company, Interhandel, before the outbreak of this hostilities. Eventually, a new company, General Aniline and Film Corporation, was set up by the United States Government to take over the I.G.'s confiscated operations in the U.S. In this manner, a substantial amount of I.G. know-how, including chemicals based on Reppe acetylene chemistry as well as the full range of I.G. detergent intermediates came on the U.S. market. Figure 1.11, taken from a paper published in the early 1950s, describes the production of detergent powders at the General Aniline plant in Linden, New Jersey (22).

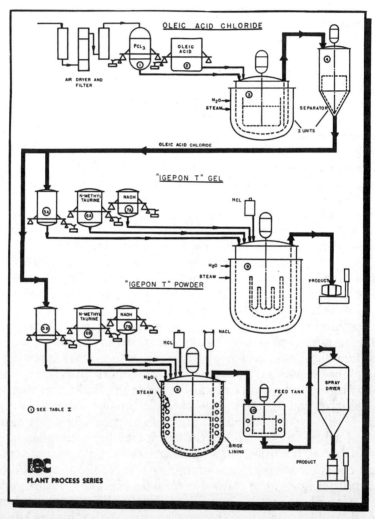

Figure 1.11 Flowsheet for production of Igepon T at Linden, NJ plant of General Aniline & Film Corporation. (*Source:* M. L. Kastens and J. J. Ayo, Jr., Pioneer Surfactant, In *Modern Chemical Processes,* Vol. II, Editors of *Industrial and Chemical Engineering,* eds., New York, Reinhold, 1951, p. 122.)

Developmental research in the United States, England, France, and Russia after the war was facilitated by studies of the prolific German plant and laboratory reports filed by the visiting teams. The availability of this information gave petrochemical researchers useful starting points for process and catalyst improvements and insights into areas where German chemists had tried various approaches and failed. Today, these reports have little significance, although they continue to be available in large stacks—now seldom consulted—in the Military Section of the National Archives in Washington, DC, and in many boxes stored in a facility on the Beltway in Maryland. A number of these reports are also available at the Library of Congress and several companies (e.g., Exxon) have certain reports on microfilm. They were a contribution of defeated Germany to the world's knowledge of state-of-the-art organic chemistry, part of the price that Germany had to pay for starting and losing a war. Interestingly, these reports were later also used in patent infringement cases to demonstrate what know-how had in this manner been placed into the public domain.

Up to the beginning of hostilities, Germany's chemical industry was the most advanced in the world. Though much of the theory of chemistry and physical chemistry had been elucidated by scientists in other countries—notably France, England, and Russia—German chemists had most often taken the lead in reducing theory to practice and in building the first plant. One reason why this occurred in Germany rather than in the other countries certainly relates to that country's extensive coal and steel industry and to the fact that Germany had few colonies outside Europe and therefore had a greater need to develop industrial self-sufficiency and exports. This accounted for Germany's successful effort to develop a synthetic dyestuffs industry in the late 1800s, and a nitrogen fertilizers and explosives industry prior to World War I. The domination of chemists over engineers in German industry was at first a great strength, though it became a drawback when chemical engineering became the key discipline for plant design.

A fundamental reason why Germany had become a leader in industrial chemistry relates to the early development of its educational systems and to the high esteem that technical training commanded in that country. German technical schools served as an ideal training ground for technicians, who would then go into industry, imbued with a desire for technical achievement and recognition. As an institution of higher learning and research, the

Kaiser Wilhelm Institute was unsurpassed for a long period of time. But a number of other universities in Germany were also sending into industry a cadre of highly training chemists and technicians bent on reaping the rewards of high scientific achievement.

An interesting perhaps somewhat controversial perspective on the role of I.G. Farben in fostering industrial innovation was provided by Peter J.T. Morris, who now works at the Center for History of Chemistry (CHOC) at the University of Pennsylvania. Morris spent a great deal of time studying the records of the German combine. He had access to essentially all of the available documents, which are voluminous, to say the least. He claims that I.G. Farben research was often not particularly creative or cost effective and that much of the innovation came from outside the firm. However, "the company succeeded because of its superb development work . . . a result of using highly qualified scientists and engineers for this work and using the same team of technologists for the whole project from laboratory bench to full-scale plant." The I.G. also had a policy of broadening a field of research by taking out a vast number of patents, which tended to inspire awe and to effectively dominate an area. Morris concluded that German chemistry in many fields was, in fact, not very far ahead of that in the United States, but that the I.G. was able to exploit certain areas—such as acetylene chemistry—in a manner that made the German chemical industry unique in its time. He also states that due to the fact that "technical affairs within the I.G. lay with the scientifically trained managers, the technocrats" and that strong personalities such as ter Meer, Ambros, Krauch, and Buetefisch dominated decision making, errors were sometimes made in terms of research management and even process selection (8).

German industrial processes tended to be set up along textbook chemistry lines, a sequence of reactions that would eventually lead to the desired product. Although this is the only way to make dyestuffs and pharmaceuticals, it is often not the simplest route to large-volume chemical intermediates. When Fritz Haber received the Nobel Prize, he stated in his acceptance speech that the days of complex chemistry were over. In this viewpoint, he was certainly wrong. Many more organic chemical reactions were discovered over the next 50 years, and in many other cases new catalysts and novel reaction sequences could produce a new or old chemical product in fewer steps, but with reactions that Haber would certainly consider complex. Emphasis shifted to a considerable extent from chemistry to chemical engineering and this resulted in new approaches in process visualization through the development of novel or improved unit operations techniques. Some of these developments had occurred in the 1920s and 1930s and many more were the successful result of intensive work during the 1939–1945 period, when American industry was forced to build large plants for the production of aviation gasoline, explosives, synthetic rubber, solvents, and other key war materials, with chemical engineers given the task to accomplish the work in record time to meet compressed timetables. America's chemical industry, by the end of the war, had succeeded in building a number of plants that were ahead of the state of the art in Germany.

The origins of the industry that started production of petrochemicals are to a greater extent in Germany than in any one other country and the original feedstock for bulk organic chemicals was, in fact, coal. At a time when polyethylene and styrene production were essentially in their infancy, the bulk of German ethylene came from calcium carbide-based acetylene, from coke-oven gas, and from the cracking of Fischer-Tropsch liquids based on coal. Benzene was almost entirely coal-derived and synthesis gas for ammonia and ethylene was produced by "shifting" a carbon monoxide-rich gas from coking operations to hydrogen. Ingenious use of its own raw materials had brought German industrial chemistry a long way, but the end of this period was in sight. With coal prices only likely to rise due to increasing depletion of the more accessible and larger coal mining seams, the cost of producing the "building blocks" for the manufacture of plastics, synthetic rubber, solvents, and other derivatives was viewed as becoming increasingly unattractive, relative to the cost of natural gas and petroleum. This was of no consequence during the war, but it placed German chemical companies in an increasingly uncompetitive business posture thereafter.

By the early 1950s, the German chemical industry was back in business, having lost six or seven years of momentum in the aftermath of war. But the U.S. petrochemical industry was already well along in its drive toward becoming one of the most dynamic enterprises the world economy had ever seen. Although the technical information obtained from the postwar inspections of German plants and laboratories did contribute in some degree to the petrochemical industry's rapid development, other reasons were more important. The single most important of these was the wartime need to produce high octane gasoline and synthetic rubber from domestic feedstocks. In the course of meeting this challenge, the chemical producers on the U.S. Gulf Coast also found themselves sitting on what must have seemed like a virtually inexhaustible supply of cheap natural gas, the ideal raw material for the production of most organic chemicals. During the period when the German industry was recovering from the war and rebuilding its coal and steel as well as its chemical industries, petrochemical technology was advancing rapidly in North America. By the time the I.G. Farben daughter companies were again a world force, the technical and economic initiative for the production of bulk organic chemicals had passed to the United States.

REFERENCES

1. Report No. 189. *Synthetic Rubber Plant, Chemische Werke Huels*. Washington, D.C.: Office of the Publication Board, Department of Commerce.
2. John M. DeBell, W. C. Goggin, and Waltor E. Gloor (1946). *German Plastics Practice*. DeBell and Richardson, Springfield MA 1946.
3. Frank A. Howard (1947). *Buna Rubber—The Birth of An Industry*, New York, Van Nostrand Company.
4. Combined Intelligence Objectives Subcommittee. *Report SHAEF Gen. Staff G-2, RG331*. Entry 13D, Box 93. Washington, DC: National Archives.
5. Combined Intelligence Objectives Subcommittee. *Technical Report on the Manufacture of Miscellaneous Chemicals in Plants of I.G. Farbenindustrie*. G-2 Division, SHAEF (Rear) APO 413.
6. R. Brightman (1957). Manchester and the origin of the dyestuffs industry, *Chemistry and Industry*, January 26, 86-91.
7. D. W. F. Hardie and J. D. Pratt (1966). *A History of the Modern British Chemical Industry*, London, Pergamon Press.
8. Peter J. T. Morris (1982). "The Development of Acetylene and Buna Rubber at I.G. Farben." Ph.D. thesis, Oxford University.
9. John Graham Smith (1979). *The Origins and Early Development of the Heavy Chemical Industry in France*, Oxford, Clarendon Press.
10. F. A. Lowenhein and M. K. Moran, eds. (1975). *Faith, Keyes, and Clark's Industrial Chemicals* 4th Ed., New York, John Wiley & Sons.
11. I. F. Haber (1971). *The Chemical Industry 1900-1930*, Oxford, Clarendon Press.
12. Alexander Findlay (1937). *A Hundred Years of Chemistry*, London, Duckworth.
13. Fritz ter Meer (1966). *Die I.G.: Ihre Entstehung, Entwicklung, and Bedeutung* (Personal Memoirs), Krefeld, Germany.
14. Joseph Borkin (1978). *The Crime and Punishment of I.G. Farben*, New York, Free Press.

15. Edward Faber, ed. (1961). *Great Chemists,* New York, Interscience.
16. Bruce F. Leach (1983). *Applied Industrial Catalysis,* Vol. 2, New York, Academic Press.
17. Peter W. Sherwood et al. (1946). "Catalysts for Coal Hydrogenation," *F.I.A.T. Final Report No. 741,* March 15.
18. S. A. Miller (1969). *Ethylene and Its Industrial Derivatives,* London, Ernest Benn Ltd.
19. A. L. Deadman and G. H. Fuidge (1950). "The German Coal Tar and Benzole Industries During the Period 1939-1945." *British Intelligence Objectives Subcommittee, Report No. 25.* London.
20. *Synthetic Fiber Development In Germany* (1946). Technical Industrial Intelligence Committee, New York, Textile Research Institute.
21. Karl Falk (1949). What has happened to Germany's divided chemical industry?, *Chemical Engineering,* May, 144-147.
22. M. L. Kastens and J. J. Ayo, Jr. (1952). Pioneer Surfactant, In *Modern Chemical Processes,* Vol. II, Editors of *Industrial and Chemical Engineering,* eds. New York, Reinhold.

ADDITIONAL READING

American Chemical Society (1966). *Advances in Chemistry Series,* Kekulé Centennial, Washington, DC, American Chemical Society.

American Chemical Society (1980). *Advances in Chemistry Series 190,* History of Chemical Engineering, Washington, DC, American Chemical Society.

Appl, Max (1986). Ammonia Synthesis and the Development of Catalytic and High Pressure processes in the Chemical Industry, Dr. H.L. Roy Memorial Lecture, Hyderabad, India, December 19.

Baeumler, Ernst (1968). *A Century of Chemistry,* Duesseldorf, Econ Verlag.

The BASF Digest, Volume II, 1965.

British Intelligence Objectives Subcommittee (1946). *Some Miscellaneous Organic Intermediates and Products Manufactured (mainly) by I.G. Farben,* FR 1154, Item 22, Washington, DC, Office of Technical Services, Department of Commerce.

British Intelligence Objectives Subcommittee (1946). "German practice in the production and utilisation of high boiling coal tar chemicals," *Report No. 1783.*

Lee Niedringhaus Davis (1984). *The Corporate Alchemists,* New York, Davis William Morris.

Festa, Roger, ed. (1983). *Profiles in Chemistry (Fritz Haber),* Vol. 60, No. 6, Storrs, Connecticut: University of Connecticut.

Fuel Age, No. 8, 1946.

Goran, Morris (1967). *The Story of Fritz Haber,* Norman, Oklahoma, University of Oklahoma Press.

Hohenberg, Paul M. (1983). *Chemicals in Western Europe: 1850-1914,* Chicago, Rand McNally.

Kraenzlein, Paul (1980). *Chemie Im Revier: Huels,* Duesseldorf, Econ Verlag.

Report on the Petroleum and Synthetic Oil Industry of Germany (1947), London, Ministry of Fuel and Power.

Rieche, Alfred (1970). *Outline of Industrial Organic Chemistry,* New York, Chemical Publishing.

Steinert, O. and W. Roggersdorf (1965). *In the Realm of Chemistry,* Duesseldorf, Econ Verlag.

Stranges, Anthony N. (1984). *Friedrich Bergius and the Rise of the German Synthetic Fuels Industry.* ISIS, **75**, 643–647.

Vogt, Hans-Heinrich (1975). *Chemiker im Kreutzverhoer,* Koeln, Germany, Aulis Verlag.

Von Nagel, Alfred (1971). *Aethylen,* Badische Anilin & Soda-Fabrik A. G. Ludwigshafen.

Von Nagel, Alfred (1970). *Fuchsin, Alizarin, Judigo,* Badische Anilin & Soda-Fabrik A. G. Ludwigshafen.

Williams, Revor I., ed. (1978). *A History of Technology,* "The Twentieth Century c.1900–1950," Vol. V, Oxford, Clarendon Press.

Winnacker, Karl (1972). *Challenging Years: My Life In Chemistry,* trans. David Goodman, London, Sidgwick & Jackson.

2 / Early Petrochemical Production in the United States

Looking back now, it is difficult to select any single reason that would account for the dramatic growth of the U.S. petrochemical industry from a tiny base in the late 1920s. It was not the discovery of vast new sources of inexpensive hydrocarbons, since there had, for some time, been ample supplies of paraffins and, more recently, olefins from refinery cracking operations, that could be converted to chemicals. Nor was it a surge in the demand for products that could now be produced more economically from petroleum feedstocks, since the petrochemical industry gathered its momentum during the Depression years, when consumer demand was lagging and there was no lack of organic chemicals produced from coke-oven by-products. Favorable economics due to chemical engineering breakthroughs were probably a factor to some extent, in that companies by then were starting to build larger plants that could produce chemicals more cheaply. But in the final analysis, companies started to make petrochemicals because conditions were ripe for a change in the technology and feedstocks for the production of organic chemical intermediates. The management of several enlightened oil and chemical companies led this industrial transformation.

The fact that natural gas or petroleum—derived from hydrocarbons—would be a better chemical feedstock than coal had been obvious for a long time, since hydrocarbons are available in gaseous or liquid form, while coal must be converted from a solid to a liquid or a gas before its contained carbon and hydrogen can be subjected to further chemical processing. The problem with using crude oil-derived feedstocks had been that paraffins—the main constituents of crude oil—are relatively nonreactive. Until the development of various petroleum cracking processes, the more reactive hydrocarbons (e.g., those with double bonds, known as *olefins*) had not been available in refinery streams.

The invention of the Burton thermal cracker in 1912, and various improvements thereafter, changed this situation forever. They gave refiners the means to "crack" heavier crude oil fractions in order to obtain higher yields of gasoline, while at the same time producing offgases that contained some olefins. The Dubbs cracker—also a thermal type—improved this technology further, so that by the middle of the 1920s most refineries were equipped with some type of cracking installation. Eugene Houdry's lifelong work on catalytic cracking led, in the late-1930s, to the construction of a large number of fixed bed "cat crackers," which could truly be considered as key in the transition to modern refining practice. In the 1920s, however, refinery offgases were used only as fuel gas for firing crude stills and cracking furnaces. Refineries were becoming major consumers of fuel, as more sophisticated upgrading facilities were installed to increase the production of gasoline and aviation fuel. The value of cracker offgases as chemical feedstocks was still largely unrealized.

While this seems obvious to us now, it was not always appreciated that it is the availability of chemical feedstocks that leads technology development and subsequent commercial application. Thus, in the 1800s, the companies involved in the production of coal-based gases and coal tar (i.e., the coal companies, the gas companies, and the steel companies with coke ovens) had "missed the boat" as far as the production of chemicals was concerned. In Germany, France, England, and later in the United States, it had been the chemical companies that had seized the opportunity to take feedstocks made as by-products in the coke ovens and convert these into a rich variety of intermediates and end products. Now, a new feedstock—refinery offgases—containing valuable olefins was becoming available in increasing quantities and the question was whether history would repeat itself; that is, whether the refiners operating the crude oil cracking stills would let chemical companies take over the gases emanating from these units and convert their reactive constituents to chemicals. Although refiners knew that they had potentially valuable reactive hydrocarbons in their by-product offgases, and some worked on petrochemical technology, most of the petroleum companies did not initially consider this as an opportunity to expand and diversify their operations. Many of these companies felt that chemicals manufacture could never achieve the scale of their petroleum production, refining, and marketing activities and in this judgment they have been correct to the present time. But a few of the oil companies perceived the opportunity and entered the petrochemical industry. Others indirectly helped the industry, with contributions in petroleum refinery technology and equipment design that were applicable to petrochemicals production.

Not surprisingly, the development of technology for aliphatic chemicals, the type of products for which refinery offgases and natural gas feedstocks were best suited, had lagged aromatic chemicals technology (related to coke over gases) by a considerable degree. Of the major ethylene derivatives in use today, only ethylene glycol, glycol ethers, and ethyl alcohol were produced in any appreciable amount by the mid-1930s. Vinyl monomers were virtually unknown as commercial items and polyethylene had not yet been discovered. Therefore, the presence of ethylene in refinery offgases was not immediately considered as a major opportunity, even by companies that were starting to look into the production of petrochemicals. Union Carbide was the only early exception.

Natural gas (largely containing methane) was available from wells in many parts of the country and at an attractive price. But there had been no need to consider methane as a chemical feedstock, particularly since the locations where it had been discovered were generally far from the market. Thus, natural gas was often left in the ground or else flared, since the large pipelines to the Midwest and to the Eastern seaboard would only start to be constructed during World War II. Ammonia, later the most important methane-based chemical, was at that time mostly produced from coal.

Reviewing history from today's perspective, certain events and accomplishments stand out as key contributions to the foundation of the U.S. petrochemical industry. The following seem, in retrospect, to be among the most important:

1. Union Carbide's pioneering work on the production of ethylene and ethylene derivatives, starting from the company's base as a producer-consumer of acetylene and industrial gases.

2. The formation of Shell Development Company, its construction of a chemical laboratory at Emeryville, California, and Shell's decision to build the first ammonia plant, based on natural gas, near its Martinez refinery on San Francisco Bay.

3. Establishment of Dow Chemical's Texas Division at Freeport, including construction of a large open-architecture manufacturing plant that would serve as a model for many other petrochemical complexes on the Gulf Coast.

4. Standard Oil of New Jersey's (hereafter often called Jersey) development of catalytic approaches—partly based on German know-how—for the production of high octane gasoline blending components and the company's development of a steam cracking process to convert petroleum distillates into olefins and butadiene.

Other key events or milestones also suggest themselves, so that my decision to focus on these four companies is somewhat arbitrary. Still, their activities over this period did provide a solid foundation for the later rapid growth of the U.S. petrochemical industry. There is also a certain amount of "poetic justice" in the choice of these firms: Two oil companies and two chemical companies seeing an opportunity from different perspectives, but certainly understanding that one existed. Shell was already a multinational company, with an appreciation of chemistry and a desire to diversify in the United States, as it had started to do in Europe. Jersey had a strong interest in hydrogenation and other catalytic technology—partly gained from I.G. Farben, as will be further explained—and an early preoccupation with the use of thermal cracking for producing unsaturated hydrocarbons at its Baton Rouge refinery. Union Carbide, whose pioneering interest in the production of reactive hydrocarbons and aliphatic chemicals had made it an early developer of ethylene and ethylene derivatives technology. And Dow Chemical—with origins near the Michigan salt caverns that supplied the raw material for large-scale chlorine and caustic production—which took the lead in the production of bromine and magnesium from sea water, and whose research led to the production of chlorine and chlorinated derivatives, phenol, and styrene. These companies, perhaps more than any others, provided the driving forces that shaped the early course of petrochemical industry development.

What happened was that a new and eventually giant industry was born during that period, which saw the United States finally become a force to be reckoned with in the chemical field. In its 50th Anniversary Review Issue, published in 1973, *Chemical & Engineering News* put it this way:

"... For chemistry, the twenties truly were "roaring," a time of building on all fronts—scientific, technological, business, and industrial . . . eight future Nobelists were all active, the seeds of their later work already bearing fruit . . . eminent men, industrial chemists, chemical engineers . . . were the people who were coming up with new (made-in or modified-in America) process technology, new synthetic routes using new raw materials, new equipment, new products, and were working out the mathematics of equipment design that moved applied industrial chemistry from rough-and-ready pipestill art to sophisticated modern engineering. But the chemical work is more than sophisticated science and elegant engineering. Then, as now, a key part of the chemical team were the industrialists and businessmen who put all the science and engineering together, added required financing and marketing, to get the needed products to the consumer. These were the people who in the twenties moved the U.S. chemical industry through its first round of diversification, mainly through merger, and thus greatly broadened the product base of the industry. An incomplete listing might include these names and connections: Leo H. Baekeland (Bakelite Corp. merged into Union Carbide), Bradley Dewey (cofounder of Dewey & Almy, now part of W. R. Grace), Herbert H. Dow, Lammot DuPont, Otto Haas, Elon Hooker, Eugene Meyer (Allied), A. Cressy Morrison (Union Carbide), William H. Nichols (Allied), John F. Queeny (Monsanto), Henry H. Reichhold, John Stauffer, Orlando Weber (Allied)." (1, pp. 26–27).

As these men and other leaders were building a broad and comprehensive base for the U.S. chemical industry, the raw materials base was starting a dramatic shift. Between 1921 and 1939, the production of organic chemicals *not derived from coal tar* rose from 21 million pounds valued at $9.3 million to 3 billion pounds, with a value of $394 million. Coal tar chemicals production in 1939, according to the U.S. Tariff Commission, still amounted to only 303 million pounds, valued at $260 million. The average 1939 price for petrochemicals was, in fact, 13 cents per pound versus 87 cents for coal tar derived chemicals. The average price of noncoal tar chemicals had, over the period, been reduced by a factor of three, from a 1921 level of 43 cents per pound. Cheaper raw materials and greatly improved manufacturing techniques had made this possible, resulting in the opening up of new markets for plants built on a much larger scale. Glycols, aldehydes, esters, amines, and ketones were the first group of aliphatic chemicals produced in large quantities from natural gas, gas liquids, and refinery off-gases. The Bureau of Standards and the American Petroleum Institute had undertaken extensive investigations into the physical and thermal properties of pure hydrocarbons. By 1931, 192 of these molecules had been isolated and purified for study. This, in turn, led to research in the laboratories of chemical and oil companies interested in the synthesis of higher-octane gasoline components, lubricants, and various organic chemicals previously made exclusively from coal-derived feedstocks.

It was increasingly understood that refineries could become the "front end" of chemical plants capable of producing a variety of synthetic aliphatic and aromatic chemicals. Would the oil companies seize this chance to upgrade some of their by-product streams largely destined for fuel uses, or would they relinquish this opportunity to the chemical companies, as the coal and steel industries had done two or three generations earlier?

The answers to these questions were far from clear in the late 1930s, when most oil companies were still primarily interested in pumping oil out of the ground and trying to improve the profits of their refining and marketing operations. It was also a period when the large international chemical companies had perfected a system of international cartels, patent cross-licensing agreements, and other *ententes cordiales* that made the chemical industry a very restricted club that was very successful in keeping out potential new competitors.

But the seeds of a new industry were already being sown by oil companies like Jersey and Shell, who soon discovered that the cracking and reforming operations they had undertaken to improve product yields and quality in petroleum would produce valuable chemical raw materials. Why not think about expanding this activity to produce intermediates and finished chemicals—a field that seemed to have high profitability? And so these efforts produced a move toward the use (and perhaps domination) of petroleum-based feedstocks that would start to replace the traditional coal tar-derived building blocks. But these seeds were also being sown by chemical companies such as Union Carbide and Dow, whose technology and market leadership in the application of these new feedstocks in some respects played into the hands of their future adversaries—the many oil companies, who would, in the 1950s, bring an end to the clublike system under which the chemical industry had operated up to this time. The approaches the four companies used to usher in the petrochemical era are sketched below.

UNION CARBIDE—ETHYLENE AND ITS DERIVATIVES

In the late 1970s, in a forested area near Danbury, Connecticut, Union Carbide constructed one of the largest corporate headquarters in America. The highly modern and efficient four-story structure housed 3000 people, who were involved in directing the business affairs of the firm. In a restructuring program carried out soon after its move from New York to Danbury, the company reviewed all its major and minor business areas and decided to concentrate on being a leader in a more limited number of activities. Chosen were the areas where the company had traditionally been a major factor, including batteries, antifreeze, polyethylene, alcohols, industrial gases, catalysts, and carbon products, among others.* Over this period, the company divested itself of a large number of chemical manufacturing activities it had developed over the years when Union Carbide was probably the largest and most diverse producer of synthetic organic chemicals in the world. But that era had now passed, supplanted by a new environment characterized by lower chemical growth rates and extreme competition from domestic and foreign companies. These circumstances also forced other chemical producers to review their portfolios and to retain, for the long term, only those products which they could hope to produce with enough strength and leadership to assure an acceptable profit margin.

About 400 miles southeast of its headquarters, Union Carbide still operates one of its most important facilities, the sprawling South Charleston, West Virginia, complex. Over the years, this

*In 1986, Union Carbide, threatened with a takeover by GAF Corporation, went through another major restructuring program. As a result, the company also divested various consumer products operations.

operation contributed much to the success and growth of the giant enterprise. In many respects, it can be said that the roots of the company are still in South Charleston, and in a very small town called Clendenin not far from there. Thus, a corporate information officer in Danbury admitted that information on the earlier years of the firm was not available there. "All that history should be available in Charleston, however," the person who was contacted was able to explain, proudly (and also correctly), as it turned out.

To understand Union Carbide's contributions to the petrochemical industry, the time frame must be shifted back to when petrochemicals were not even known as such. We must look at the first half of the twentieth century, including America's first love affair with the automobile, the growth of the oil and gas industry, and the different manner in which research work was carried out before companies built dedicated R&D laboratories. It was a business environment where decisions to build plants were often made in an opportunistic manner—where companies would try to sell a product that could be synthesized rather than making a chemical needed by an established market.

In Indianapolis in 1904, Carl G. Fisher, a bicycle shop owner, and James A. Allison, his partner and a person of some means, saw an interesting business opportunity. In those days, bicycles had carbon lamps, but Fisher had become aware that acetylene lamps were being used in Europe for portable lighting. These were in the form of steel cylinders filled with a porous mass impregnated with acetone, in which acetylene was dissolved under pressure. The two men formed the Prest-O-Lite Company to commercialize this idea in the United States. Their timing was right, since this was also the start of a major surge in the automobile industry and cars were soon fitted with acetylene headlights of the same type. The Prest-O-Lite Company developed a nationwide automobile service system and soon became the largest single consumer of calcium carbide and, probably, of acetone in the United States. A few years later, in a second development, oxy-acetylene welding became industrially important and so Prest-O-Lite also began selling acetylene in cylinders made for this purpose, again becoming the predominant supplier. Cylinder oxygen, also needed for welding started to be supplied by other firms.

The largest producer of calcium carbide was the Union Carbide Company. Formed in Chicago in the late 1800s by a group consisting of the People's Gas Light and Coke Company and miscellaneous partners, Union Carbide had taken over the American rights to calcium carbide manufacture from the inventors of the process. It had built several plants and was the sole supplier to Prest-O-Lite. With acetylene demand for automobile and other lighting uses and for welding equipment rising rapidly, Prest-O-Lite found itself in a classical situation, facing one of the first "make-or-buy" decisions in the history of the young American aliphatic chemical industry. Union Carbide had close to a monopoly on calcium carbide manufacture, but perhaps there was another way that Prest-O-Lite could make acetylene.

Up to this time, research was generally carried out either in universities or by inventors, who often worked in independent laboratories. Inquiries made by Prest-O-Lite revealed that the Mellon Institute of Industrial Research in Pittsburgh might be a good place to develop another way to produce acetylene. Founded by a group including the Mellon family, the Institute had already gained some prominence by 1913, when it was asked to take on this project. The person the Institute hired was a man of considerable talent and inventiveness. Dr. George O. Curme, Jr. had just returned from studying chemistry in Germany and was looking for a major challenge. His name is now closely linked to the many developments that followed this association.* In less than three years, Curme and his co-workers had placed in operation a high frequency electric arc process that produced acetylene from a gas oil feedstock. Perhaps just as importantly, the gases produced in the arc contained one-half mol of ethylene for every mol of acetylene. Curme, who was primarily an organic chemist, came to realize that almost every chemical that was then being made from acetylene, including acetaldehyde and acetone, as well as many others, could likely be made less expensively from ethylene, since the new process would avoid the costly step involving the manufacture of calcium carbide.† At this time, the Mellon Institute also had a research contract from Union Carbide covering acetylene derivatives technology. However, it was judged that there would be no conflict in working on ethylene derivatives and so Curme also threw himself into this project with vigor. The first target was the production of ethanol.

Ethyl alcohol had first been produced from ethylene in 1828 in

---

*Some of the people associated with Curme in his work were J. N. Compton, C. O. Young, E. W. Reid, H. R. Curme, C. J. Herrly, and H. A. Morton.

†Curme evidently saw in this new technology a means, for the first time, of producing ethylene in potentially large quantities and he further correctly concluded that ethylene would become a lower cost future feedstock than acetylene—*P.H.S.*

the laboratory of Michael Faraday, using the same sulfuric acid technology still in use in some olefin hydration plants today. Nothing came of this until 1855, when Berthelot continued this work and showed that it was also possible to make isopropanol from propylene by this route. Nevertheless, there was little commercial significance in such a synthesis. Whereas ethylene was available in coke-oven gases, ethyl alcohol was cheap to produce from a number of agricultural feedstocks. (On the other hand, very little propylene is found in coke-oven gases.) In 1900, a company was set up in Virginia to make ethyl ether from ethylene, the rationale being to try and get around the heavy tax on fermentation alcohol from which ether was then produced. However, shortly thereafter, Congress dropped the tax on grain alcohol used as a chemical feedstock and ironically alcohol thereafter became the feedstock to make ethylene (instead of vice-versa).

Another possible ethylene derivative that suggested itself to George Curme was dichloroethyl sulfide, made from diethyl sulfate, which became known during World War I as "mustard gas." In 1914, the Mellon Institute was asked by the Chemical Warfare Service to look into the production of mustard gas from ethylene, since alcohol was now a critical material related to the country's needs for food and explosives and it was considered desirable to eliminate its use as a chemical feedstock. But now another issue emerged. Although the arc process was cheaper than the calcium carbide route and produced some ethylene, expensive electric power was required. Perhaps still another way might be found to produce ethylene.

In 1917, the work at Mellon Institute seemed to be on a course that was likely to produce commercial results. Prest-O-Lite was continuing to sponsor Curme's work on acetylene* and ethylene production technology and on ethylene derivatives. The work on mustard gas had led to a synthesis of ethylene chlorohydrin, a possible intermediate to diethyl sulfate, but also a chemical that Curme recognized as having immediate potential for conversion to ethylene glycol. This was an important issue, since earlier attempts to make glycol from ethylene dichloride had been largely unsuccessful. Union Carbide, still sponsoring work at Mellon on

---

*Union Carbide, in 1923, established Niacet (Niagara-Acetylene) Chemical Company in joint venture with Shawinigan Chemical Company to make acetylene derivatives at Niagara Falls, New York. Thus, in retrospect, it did not place all its bets on ethylene.

acetylene derivatives, was following Prest-O-Lite's work with interest and was aware of the government's desire to encourage manufacture of ethylene in a new way. Now Curme was talking about the possible thermal cracking of ethane. Ethane was abundantly available in natural gas in many states other than Texas and Oklahoma, including New York, Pennsylvania, Ohio, and West Virginia. But such a process would need technology not required in separating the products from the electric arc. It would be necessary to use low temperature fractionation to separate ethane from other natural gas constitutents and, if ethane could be successfully cracked, to separate ethylene from uncracked ethane. Another fairly recent development now became significant. In 1911, Union Carbide had bought an interest in the American arm of the German company that was the leader in oxygen manufacture via liquefaction of air: the Linde Air Products Company. The Chemical Warfare Service now asked Linde to cooperate with Curme—with whom Linde executives had become acquainted as a result of some of their own sponsored work at the Institute—on a process using refrigeration technology to make ethylene from natural gas. It became more and more evident that Prest-O-Lite, Linde, the National Carbon Company,* and Union Carbide were linked in a number of ways. It evidently seemed logical to put everything under one roof and so the United Carbide and Carbon Company was founded in 1917. In 1935, Curme wrote "I was distinctly relieved to have the Carbide Company come to my rescue by consolidating with the Prest-O-Lite Company . . . it was a stroke of fortune to have the aid, rather than the opposition, of an experienced manufacturing group in the important project that was beginning to emerge" (2).

Linde's laboratory in Tonawanda, New York,† became the center of subsequent research work on the production of ethylene, with J. A. Rafferty, Assistant Works Manager, in responsible charge. Ethane was separated at low temperatures and cracked in an electrically heated silica tube. Much work was required to develop analytical procedures, but this was seen as an essential element of the program. Eventually, a small plant was constructed to make ethylene for the war effort, but it did not go into operation until shortly after the armistice was signed. It was not a very sophisti-

---

*A company founded in 1886, which had also become a producer of calcium carbide.

†This town, close to Buffalo, was the site of a large steel works operated by Bethlehem Steel Company, including a battery of coke ovens, coal tar distillation units, etc.

cated operation. First, natural gas was fractionated into its components, with ethane recovered and stored in cylinders. The cracking
step then followed, with the ethane-ethylene mixture again stored
in cylinders. Finally, more refrigeration was applied, with product
ethylene transferred to a third group of cylinders. Not surprisingly,
the cost of this operation was never low enough to be useful for a
commercial plant, though it must be considered as a major step
forward in technology (3).

Meanwhile, work continued in Pittsburgh on making various
ethylene derivatives, including a synthetic route to acetone, then
produced commercially via fermentation. A chlorohydrin plant
for the production of ethylene oxide was designed, using a large
amount of stoneware, including cooling coils made with that material, as well as silver-lined pumps and sterling silver check valves,
to cope with corrosive streams. Studies were also proceeding on
making ethyl alcohol, with particular emphasis on the purification steps.

In 1920, a subsidiary called the Carbide and Carbon Chemicals
Corporation was established with the goal of commercializing the
production of a number of aliphatic chemicals. But the company's
corporate management was far from convinced about its future.
The ethylene plant was not considered a great success and, with
the war over, mustard gas was no longer required. There was, however, some promise in developing ethylene glycol as an antifreeze
compound. In 1917, Dr. Harold Hibbert of the Mellon Institute obtained U.S. Patent 1,213,368, which described the use of this material for lowering the freezing point of water in automotive cooling
systems. Ethylene oxide, ethyl alcohol, acetone, and a few other
derivatives were also believed to have a future for a company that
now had some definite thoughts on how ethylene might perhaps
be manufactured in a more economical manner. And so, the company started looking for a production site.

Today, the Kanawha Valley of West Virginia is still an important industrial production center. Its name derived from an Indian
tribe that once lived in the area, the Kanawha River flows north-
west for almost 100 miles before emptying into the Ohio River at
Point Pleasant, West Virginia. Such chemical firms as Diamond
Shamrock, DuPont, NL Industries, FMC Corporation and Monsanto eventually conducted operations in the valley. But the largest
operator by far is Union Carbide Corporation, with plants at South
Charleston and Institute, numerous lesser installations, and a corporate technical center.

The valley is actually quite narrow, with industrial, business, and residential areas in close proximity at some points. So much development took place as time went by, that the surrounding hills also became quite populated. Charleston, the hub of the area, was served by the Chesapeake and Ohio and the Baltimore and Ohio Railroads, as well as by tugboats going up and down the busy river.

Clearly, the region had much to offer to America's industry, as it expanded from the East Coast toward the Midwest, frequently along the Ohio River Valley. Indians were known to have taken salt from nearby springs for many years and the first commercial salt furnace was built by Elisha Brooks in 1797 and operated at 150 pounds per day. Salt production peaked in the mid-1800s and then declined, due to competition from richer brines in Michigan and elsewhere. In 1915, the Warner-Klipstein Company was formed to produce chlorine and caustic soda, the latter for a local glass industry. A number of years later, Klipstein was taken over by Westvaco Corporation, which added carbon disulfide and carbon tetrachloride to the product line. The Belle Alkali Company, eventually a division of Diamond Shamrock, was another early operator of electrolysis cells for chlorine-caustic production in the valley.

Coal has always been an important resource in Appalachia and particularly in West Virginia. The cannel coal mined in the upper Kanawha Valley turned out to be an excellent material for use in the destructive distillation process employed to produce "benzol," alternately known as "coal oil" and used for illumination in lamps in the late 1800s. Kerosene replaced this material, when oil and gas became cheap and plentiful in the region. Thus, one of the first major plants built in the valley was a glass factory that used natural gas for heating and melting the furnace ingredients. A carbon black plant, based on gas, was built in 1915 to supply the new tire industry in Akron. Early carbon black plants were fairly crude, using a technique that produced a "channel black" similar to the "lamp black" material employed in printing ink. Carbon black was probably the first major petrochemical, although plants for its production are now much more sophisticated.

The Union Carbide Chemical team looking for a site for an ethylene derivatives plant, was impressed by the potential offered by the Kanawha Valley. While there were other regions in the United States with larger supplies of natural gas, ample reserves of ethane-rich gas were available in the valley. Gas production in

West Virginia at that time was about 240 billion cubic feet annually, far in excess of foreseeable industrial and residential requirements in the region. Moreover, excellent river and rail transportation were at hand and West Virginia was also close to the large East Coast markets.

In the 1920s, operations in the oil and gas fields were still quite primitive, with minimal processing employed to condition the raw crude oil coming up from the well. Recovered oil was stored in tanks, where the light hydrocarbons were allowed to "weather off" before the oil was loaded into tank cars and shipped to refineries. West Virginia natural gas was fairly rich, containing both light hydrocarbons and condensates. Gasoline, the main desired product, was recovered in a simple heavy oil absorption plant, with the rich gases stripped off and either sold or vented. The gas stream, which contained ethane and propane,* was what the Union Carbide people were interested in and they went looking for an absorption plant that they could buy and operate to recover these hydrocarbons. Such a plant was found at Clendenin, about 20 miles above Charleston. The assets of the Clendenin Gasoline Company were purchased by the Carbide and Carbon Chemicals Company in 1920.

It seems hard to understand today, but it appears to be true that up to the 1920s, very little technological contact had been established between the petroleum and chemical industries. The former were oriented toward fuels and lubricants, the latter toward chemicals and the use of coke-oven by-products as primary feedstocks. This curious situation is now seen to account for the fact that the Linde engineers who examined the operations of the Clendenin Plant were struck by the "crudity and inefficiency of . . . this industry, and of the entire allied petroleum industry." In particular, they were amazed by the "apparent complete ignorance of the principles and practices of rectification," which was employed by chemical firms not only in the separation of air, but also in the fractionation and further separation of coke oven gas constituents and in the manufacture of such chemicals as ethyl alcohol and acetone. (3, p. 32).

Life in the West Virginia gas fields provided other contrasts as well to the engineers and visiting executives who were now planning the future of what would be a new industrial enterprise. In

---

*Propane cracking yields significant amounts of propylene, together with ethylene.

1920, there were few paved roads in this part of West Virginia and it was impossible to drive from Clendenin to Charleston at certain times of the year. One rail line went through the town, and the train serving the intervening communities of Pinch, Blue Creek, Falling Rock, and Reamer was usually filled with a complement of local folk who provided fascinating material for conversation for the corporate visitors going back to New York. The town of Clendenin itself consisted of a station house, a bank, some residences, a restaurant or two, a few small stores, and several stables. The gasoline plant was about a half mile from town. James Rafferty, now head of the new chemical division, had initially scouted this region on horseback.

The first important achievement of the Carbide and Linde engineers, now exposed to the rough and ready operations in the oil industry, was the development of a more efficient method of carrying out the weathering process then in general use. The "stabilizing column," as it was termed at Clendenin, became the standard and universal name for a tower employed for the purpose of removing light ends from gasoline-range naphthas. Carbide obtained patents on this device and started licensing the process, but the patents were later successfully challenged and no royalties were apparently ever collected.

Next, the low temperature technique Linde used for air separation, and modified only slightly for ethylene manufacture at the Buffalo plant, was further changed to allow operation at higher temperatures with less refrigeration, since chilling was only required to separate methane and ethane. At the same time, column pressures were raised, corresponding to the relatively higher temperatures now used for component separation. The system developed at Clendenin is the precursor for thousands of plants built later to separate light hydrocarbon components in natural gasoline, as well as for the manufacture or transformation of ethylene, propylene, and other light olefins.

A research laboratory was set up at Clendenin, and here Curme and his co-workers resumed their development work on ethylene and propylene derivatives, including ethylene chlorohydrin, ethylene oxide, ethylene glycol, ethanol, ethanolamines and other chemicals. Curme also started publishing a number of technical articles on the uses of ethylene and propylene, which provided a great deal of vitally needed information on the products being studied, including ethylene oxide. Meanwhile, a hydrocarbon separations plant and a cracking plant were completed and went on stream in the summer of 1921. What this really meant was that Union Carbide now had a plant that could separate light hydrocarbons and make limited quantities of ethylene that could hopefully be transformed into derivatives. The company now had to find markets for these products.

The timing was not propitious, since startup of the plant took place at the end of the postwar boom. But now the previously established synergy of Union Carbide's several parts again came to the rescue of the group which had pioneered the investment at Clendenin. With Prest-O-Lite's and Linde's bottled acetylene and oxygen business starting to meet competition from bottled hydrocarbon gases marketed by competitors, the chemical division conceived of the idea of bottling mixed light hydrocarbon gases from the Clendenin plant, which were then marketed by the Linde-Prest-O-Lite organization under the Pyrofax trademark. Soon thereafter, an important market was identified—the use of liqufied petroleum gas sold in cylinders for household use in isolated locations, where no town gas was available. Thus, a Union Carbide subsidiary became one of the first distributors of this product, which soon became a major new industry. For a period of time, the company's success in developing this new opportunity, coupled with its slow progress in finding markets for new ethylene derivatives, slowed down the thrust into aliphatic chemicals production. Meanwhile, Pyrofax and Pyrogen, a propane-propylene mixture for oxygen cutting, became money-making products. Pyrofax was also sold as a fuel gas component to the Graf Zeppelin, with Carbide supplying bottled gas both in New Jersey and in Recife, Brazil, providing an additional number of memorable stories for the company's archives. Basically, the only products sold commercially from the Clendenin plant were hydrocarbons. This was not at all what Curme had originally envisioned and when he was later asked what was produced there, he had a tendency to reply "mostly mistakes." However, the accomplishments at Clendenin were vital to the next major step, the decision to establish manufacture on a commercial scale, which was made soon thereafter.

Actually, the laboratory work carried out at Clendenin, as well as in a new research facility in Long Island City, was making good progress. By 1925, technology for producing isopropanol, acetone, ethanol, acetaldehyde, crotonaldehyde, butanol, ethylene oxide, glycol, and glycol ethers was in relatively advanced development. Many economic studies were made over this period, with the object of somehow coming up with a money-making project at relatively low initial production volumes. Finally, a project was passed by the Union Carbide board.

The location selected was South Charleston, West Virginia, where an available site included an abandoned Rollins Chemical Company plant. The first U.S. plant specifically designed to produce ethylene and representing the results of Union Carbide's work at Mellon Institute, Tonawanda, and Clendenin was linked to a chlorohydrin unit, where the entire ethylene output was converted in a single reactor sized at 10,000 pounds per day. Chlorine was available across the fence. The chlorohydrin was largely converted to ethylene glycol, which was sold to explosives manufacturers and for other small uses. At first, no intermediate ethylene oxide was produced, but shortly after startup, a technique was devised to separate the ethylene oxide as an intermediate product.

In 1926, the company started producing an ether based on ethylene oxide and cellulose and sold it under the name of Cellosolve. The product had originally been conceived as a possible solvent for Carnauba wax and, when this didn't work out, as a carrier liquid for essential oils. This attempt met with equally dismal results. However, when tried as a solvent for nitrocellulose lacquers, Cellosolve was an instant success. Carbide had no problems in expanding the product's use as a solvent for other lacquers and varnishes. This glycol ether became the first ethylene derivative produced and sold in significant quantities by Union Carbide.

An unexpected problem encountered by the company in connection with Cellosolve production was recalled by one of Carbide's senior executives, Joseph G. Davidson, in his medalist speech to the Society of Chemical Industry in the mid-1950s (4). In 1925, "Prohibition" (of alcohol consumption) was in effect and the Internal Revenue Service, charged with compliance, became very suspicious of what the company described as its process for making ethylene glycol ethyl ether, which required the use of ethyl alcohol as a feedstock. Davidson told the agent that you took 70 gallons of alcohol and 44 pounds of ethylene oxide and then recovered 63 gallons of alcohol for recycle. "Where did the other seven gallons of alcohol go?" the agent wanted to know. There was no way to convince the agent that the alcohol had been converted to another chemical and so Davidson had to go to Washington, where the IRS had a chemist in its employ. There, the permit was then granted.

In 1927, marketing efforts on a glycol antifreeze, to be known as Prestone, started in earnest. Early applications in automobile engines had failed, because of ethylene glycol's tendency to loosen rust and scale and to seep through joints and cracks in cooling system pipes and hoses. This problem was solved with the help of additives and through better understanding of antifreeze fluid application and use. Prestone then became a huge success, with steady buildup in demand from that point on. Liquid-cooled aircraft engines also became an important market for this product. Carbide gained a 14-year monopoly, before DuPont and Dow also became producers just before World War II.

Outlets had also been found for ethylene gas—as a ripening agent for fruit and as a refrigerant. Ethylene chlorohydrin was sold in limited quantities to produce Novocaine and for carrying out specialized epoxidations. Davidson, who had worked with Curme at Mellon, was at that time manager of chemical sales.

Another advance came in the late 1920s with ethylene dichloride, then the unavoidable by-product of glycol production. Only limited sales opportunities had at first been developed for this chlorinated hydrocarbon, which had found some use in the extraction of vegetable oils and for degreasing wool. Then, almost overnight, it became a prime dry cleaning fluid. Shortly thereafter, it was discovered that it was also an excellent solvent for tetraethyl lead, the gasoline octane booster and, somewhat later, for specialty rubbers, as well.

By 1928, Carbide was also producing and selling diethylene glycol, triethylene glycol, and triethanolamine, all as a result of intensive efforts to find markets for these materials, which had previously been either unavailable or very expensive. During the following year, the company finally started production of acetone, which could now at last be made cheaper synthetically than by the traditional fermentation route.

The year 1929 also saw the first production of vinyl chloride, made by cracking ethylene dichloride. Early attempts to develop a polymer made from the new material were unsuccessful, however, due to the rigidity and poor light stability of polyvinyl chloride (PVC), the new plastic. It was time for George Curme once again to recall his studies in Germany. He knew that vinyl acetate had been successfully polymerized there long ago, giving a material with almost exactly opposite qualities. Thus enlightened, Carbide researchers found that copolymers of vinyl chloride and vinyl acetate gave vastly improved properties, leading to a number of interesting new products. The largest customer was a rapidly-growing record company—RCA (Radio Corporation of America). The product was called Vinylite. Though B.F. Goodrich had, in the meantime, found the secret of making "plasticizers" to soften the rigid qualities of PVC, Union Carbide also had found a suitable solution to the problem, with a number of possible markets. (See Chapter 6.) A decade later, the Bakelite Company, a pioneering firm in thermoset plastics, was acquired to pursue more vigorously the plastics area of the company's business.

In 1930, Union Carbide entered the production of synthetic ethyl alcohol. Successful commercialization of this process was partly the result of the application of special construction materials for handling sulphuric acid in various concentrations; here, Carbide's Alloy Division played an important contributory role. Sale of ethyl alcohol—a controversial business during Prohibition—was placed in the hands of an established fermentation-based firm: the U.S. Industrial Alcohol Company.* Some ethanol was also used captively for making ethyl ether, ethyl acetate, ethanolamine, and other such derivatives. Ethylene oxide sales began to pick up. It was now also being used as a fumigant and for the manufacture of a variety of adducts (e.g., for the production of detergents).

The history of synthetic organic chemical development at Union Carbide is a synopsis of all the elements that allowed the creation of a petrochemical industry: feedstocks, technology, development of markets. Before ethylene and propylene were available in refinery streams in any quantity, Curme and co-workers recognized the possibility of using abundantly available, cheap natural gas components as a feedstock and they set about devising technology to crack these to the desired reactive olefins. The small-scale research work at Mellon Institute led logically to the demonstration of cracking at Tonawanda, followed by the "skunk works" at Clendenin in the gas fields of West Virginia. Then it was up to the drive and creativity of salesmen like Joe Davidson to create the markets that allow Union Carbide to make South Charleston, the first grass roots petrochemical complex, a success.

In 1926, Union Carbide made six compounds derived from ethylene and two from propylene. By 1934, this had dramatically increased to 35 from ethylene and 15 from propylene (5).

*Later to be called National Distillers and Chemical Corporation.

And finally, 15 years after the first synthesis of the product, a tank car of diethyl sulfate was produced and sold. History does not record whether the product was used for a less ignoble purpose than the production of mustard gas. The record shows, however, that George Curme, by that time Vice President of Research for Union Carbide and Chemicals, and several of his friends and long-time co-workers rode the tank car out of the plant gate and to the freight yard on the edge of town, waving flags in the air!

SHELL CHEMICAL—AMMONIA, PROPYLENE, AND SOLVENTS

In 1927, the management of the Shell Group of companies took stock of the world situation in hydrocarbon fuels and aliphatic chemicals production. In the United States, Shell's chief competitor, Standard of New Jersey, had taken its first step toward the production of chemicals from petroleum feedstocks—the manufacture of isopropyl alcohol from propylene at Bayway, New Jersey—and had initially encountered a lot of problems in product separations, due to the impure nature of its feedstock. Nevertheless, it appeared that Jersey would soon be a successful "petrochemicals" producer. In Europe, I.G. Farbenindustrie was achieving success in hydrogenating coal to fuel oil and gasoline, which could soon develop into competition for Shell's worldwide fuels business. If chemical companies were now developing technology for the production of hydrocarbon fuels, perhaps it was time for oil companies to move into chemicals. At a time when "strategic" thinking was not yet common, Shell decided that it should start to look at taking a major step into the chemical field, to make sure it would not be left behind.* The company decided upon the following approach:

- Develop and commercialize technology to utilize either refinery "waste" streams or natural gas and gas liquids, or both.
- Emphasize these activities in the United States, which had ample proven reserves of hydrocarbon feedstocks and where

*Some of the key executives who made substantial contributions to Shell Chemicals' early entry into petrochemicals were C. B. DeBruijn, President Shell Chemical 1931-1941; Daniel Pyzel, Vice President Shell Chemical, 1929-1943; J. B. A. Kessler, Chairman Shell Chemical 1929-1943; and S. S. Lawrence, Sales Manager.

Shell also had substantial-sized refineries with thermal cracking units.

• Bring in the necessary academic talent to help ensure the success of Shell's new "chemical strategy."

The products that Shell decided to focus on were logical: ammonia and aliphatic chemicals. Ammonia could conceivably be produced as readily from natural gas as from coal gas, although this had not been done before. Ethylene, propylene, and butylenes were available in substantial quantities in refinery cracker offgases—15–20 percent by volume—and these could, via known chemistry, be readily converted to alcohols and thence to other oxygenates. Recognizing that much larger supplies of olefins would eventually be required, Shell started research work in its Amsterdam laboratories on steam cracking butane to ethylene and higher olefins. However, the supply of gas liquids in Europe was limited, leading to the conclusion that the United States was a more fruitful place for continuing this development program.

Two important choices had to be made: where to set up the laboratory and who should be placed in charge of research. With large Shell refineries at Wood River, Illinois, and Martinez, California, the choice of location soon narrowed to the areas around St. Louis, Missouri, and San Francisco. Both had good universities nearby and therefore offered the contact with academia that was felt to be important. The final selection of Emeryville, California, was based not only on proximity to Berkeley, but also on the fact that it was completely zoned for industry and in many ways ideally suited for what Shell had in mind for its research center.

Identification of an appropriate chief research administrator was next. The ideal candidate should preferably be a brilliant chemist with a proven track record as an administrator, a person who well understood the difference between basic and applied research, and preferably someone with industrial experience. Shell's board of directors chose Dr. E. Clifford Williams, who was at the time dean of the science faculty at London University and who had spent several years with the British Dyestuffs Corporation. One of his achievements at London University had been to establish a chemical engineering curriculum, which was an uncommon discipline in those days. Williams' qualifications were considered to be excellent and Shell therefore proceeded with an offer. He accepted the position and immediately started planning the laboratory in California. It was built within a space of only four months and the staff started work in late 1928.

Shell's first excursion into petrochemicals actually did not involve the Emeryville group to any great extent, since plans were well along by the time the laboratory went into operation. The Royal Dutch Group decided in 1927 to license the Mont Cenis ammonia process, which used a pressure of only 100 atmospheres and was therefore outside the scope of the Haber-Bosch patents controlled by I.G. Farben. A 20-ton-per-day ammonia plant based on coke-oven gases produced at Ymuiden, Holland, was placed in operation in 1929 and a second plant, based on using natural gas as a raw material, was soon in the planning stage. It was decided that this plant should be built in California. There, natural gas was plentiful and, in addition, there was a vast agricultural system and, as yet, no ammonia fertilizer plants, such as had been built on the East Coast in the early and mid-1920s.* The production of ammonia from natural gas rather than coke oven gas or coal gasification required a different method of preparing the hydrogen and here Shell ran into some luck in the form of available experience in California. The local gas utilities had faced a problem some years earlier when natural gas had become available by pipeline and they had found that the gas had too high a heating value (above 1000 Btu per 1000 cubic feet) to be compatible with the typical 500 Btu gas the company was then manufacturing and distributing. Research had then been done to "reform" the high Btu gas with steam to bring its Btu content down to the lower level.† Shell arranged to buy natural gas from these companies and they, in turn, agreed to share their experience in gas reforming with Shell. The Southern California Gas Company, which had recently switched its system to high Btu natural gas, made a reforming unit of the type described above available to Shell for its studies (6).

The ammonia plant was a strange amalgamation of European

---

*Allied Chemical had been the first company to build a synthetic ammonia plant in the United States at Hopewell, Virginia. The plant went into operation in 1928, based on research work carried out by Allied at Syracuse, New York, starting in 1921. It used coal as a feedstock (7).

†Effectively, this converts some of the methane to carbon monoxide, carbon dioxide, and water vapor. It results in a larger amount of gas with a lower average heating value, more like the gas made in the traditional town gas systems, where steam was passed over hot coal to make a heating gas.

and U.S. technology. Shell had purchased two ammonia plants in Europe—completely equipped and instrumented—including gauges that were calibrated to give pressure readings in kilograms per square centimeter and temperature in degrees Centigrade. These plants were modified to include the equipment required to reform high Btu natural gas. The units went on stream in August 1931. The timing, however, was exquisitely poor, with the Great Depression just beginning. Ammonia prices started falling sharply and the operation of the Shell plant became highly uneconomical. Nevertheless, operations continued and valuable early experience was gained on a process that has, in modified form, become one of the mainstays of the petrochemical industry.

The first product that actually emerged from the laboratory research efforts at Emeryville was secondary butyl alcohol. Increasing amounts of normal and isobutylene were becoming available from thermal cracking operations based on the Dubbs or Tube-and-Tank crackers that were becoming a standard feature of refineries designed to increase the yield of gasoline from crude oil. No obvious use had been found for any of the olefins—except for Jersey's isopropyl alcohol plant based on propylene. C_4 olefins, being higher-boiling, could be condensed with cooling water and were thus even more readily captured for possible upgrading. A pilot plant was built to study the absorption of butylenes in sulfuric acid of different concentrations, using the refinery mixed butylene cut as a feedstock. The Shell chemists' extensive knowledge of absorption and extraction technology allowed them to efficiently separate the isobutylene and n-butylene adducts successively, utilizing first a 65 percent and then a 90 percent concentration of acid and leaving behind the saturated C_4 cut. These adducts were then hydrolyzed to the alcohols. A small sec-butyl alcohol plant was built in 1931, but this was no great success, since little market could be developed for this material.

The Emeryville chemists next worked on the dehydrogenation of secondary butyl alcohol to methyl ethyl ketone (MEK), which they had, in any case, been contemplating. This turned out to be considerably more successful. A small MEK plant was put on stream in late 1931, followed by a full-scale unit in 1933. This chemical had only been available in small quantities before, based on by-product recovery from wood distillation, but it had the immediate potential of a large market as a solvent for almost all organic materials, including nitrocellulose lacquers, cellulose acetate, and for the perfume industry. Soon, it was also used in printing inks, in solvent dewaxing of petroleum cuts, and in insecticides.

Availability of isobutylene from the C_4 extraction also led to the manufacture of tertiary butyl alcohol. As it turned out, this remained a specialty chemical for many years and, in fact, only very recently became an important gasoline octane enhancer coproduced by Arco Chemical in conjunction with propylene oxide manufacture. Shell's sales of this product never became very large. All of these plants were built on a small site adjacent to the Martinez refinery.

Emeryville soon saw another outlet for isobutylene, with possibly enormous consequences for Shell's refinery operations. In the early 1930s, research work on high compression engines had led the U.S. Army Air Corps to adopt the "octane" system for rating gasoline performance (n-heptane has a zero rating and iso-octane a rating of 100). At that time, aviation gasoline had a rating of around 70 octane and iso-octane was basically a "laboratory curiosity," available for testing purposes but not in volume as a "high octane" fuel. In the separation of isobutylene from the other C_4 components, the acid-hydrocarbon mixture was kept at a low temperature. However, it was found that when a mixture of isobutylene and sulfuric acid was heated, two moles of iso-butylene would combine to form di-isobutylene, a material very close in composition to iso-octane. Known hydrogenation technology could then be used to convert the so-called dimer to the desired iso-octane product. The hydrogenation was carried out in the ammonia plant, where ample hydrogen was available. Starting in 1934, Shell Chemical began to sell carload quantities of iso-octane to the U.S. Air Force at approximately $2.00 per gallon. It was blended with lower octane fuel and then leaded with 3cc of tetraethyl lead fluid (TEL). to give an aviation fuel with an octane rating of 100.

Production of isopropyl alcohol and acetone followed in 1934, a few years after the startup of a similar plant by Union Carbide. Acetone had long been produced via fermentation by such companies as Commercial Solvents Corporation, but this process formed by-products that were difficult to remove completely. The ability to produce 99 percent purity acetone in a normal manner that gave essentially no by-products was a major selling point and this product soon became the most important item in Shell Chemical's now growing line of petrochemicals. A large market for acetone had already been established as a solvent for greases, dyes, and synthetic resins; as a component of automobile finishes; and as a spinning solvent for rayon. Shell quickly became one of the largest suppliers and also shortly entered the production of such acetone derivatives as diacetone alcohol, mesityl oxide, methyl isobutyl ketone, and other chemicals in the acetone chain.

Although development of processes for the manufacture of alcohols and ketones had propelled Shell into the petrochemical arena, this was not as the result of any major research breakthrough. However, by the late 1930s, the company was working on another process that would become a far more important contribution to petrochemical process technology; the manufacture of synthetic glycerin. Williams, still active in research at Emeryville, had gained considerable prior background in chlorination technology and was aware, from work carried out in Russia in the late 1880s, that propylene and chlorine could combine in quite a different manner, depending on reaction conditions. At low temperatures, chlorine added across the double bond to form dichloropropane. At 500°C, however, the chlorine atoms left the double bond intact to form allyl chloride. And allyl chloride could be readily converted to allyl alcohol and glycerin. The latter product, available as a by-product from tallow splitting, already had a large market in soaps, explosives, and alkyd resins—170 million pounds in 1936. Shell perfected a glycerin synthesis and built a pilot plant in 1937. The process was announced in an important address to the American Petroleum Institute by Williams in November 1938.

The technology was later described in detail in a paper Williams presented at the December 1940 American Institute of Chemical Engineers meeting in New Orleans. In it, he traced the history of various proposed attempts to make glycerin synthetically, by conventional techniques or via fermentation. Then, he listed different techniques studied by Shell to arrive at a high yield, economical synthesis of allyl chloride, which eventually led to the 85 percent yields obtained in the high temperature chlorination of propylene. He then turned to the hydrolysis reaction to allyl alcohol, describing how Shell had investigated both alkali and acid conditions, finally selecting the latter route, using cuprous chloride catalyst. Chlorohydration of the anhydrous alcohol was not difficult as a laboratory procedure, but here the main contribution was the development of a continuous process in a packed tower filled with gaseous chlorine. Finally, a continuous hydrolysis step to glycerin was devised, using a stirred autoclave. Williams then described an alternative route to glycerin, also developed by Shell, which allowed the elimination of one step by direct chlorohydration of allyl chloride, followed again by hydrolysis. Epichlorohydrin and glycidol could be produced as a coproduct, depending on how the hydrolysis was carried out (see Fig. 2.1). Thus, as Williams pointed out, Shell had developed a comprehensive approach to convert propylene to glycerin in several parallel steps, with the possibility of ending up not only with glycerin, but also with several important intermediates and coproducts, as desired. He published a number of details on vapor-liquid equilibrium data obtained for various mixtures, on reaction conditions, and on the construction of different sections of the pilot plant. Shell Chemical's achievement must, even now, be considered a *tour de force* in chemical engineering practice and a great contribution to petrochemical process development (e.g., free radical reaction systems, combination of various unit operations).

Ironically, the company hesitated to proceed to commercialization. Natural glycerin was relatively inexpensive and a large glyc-

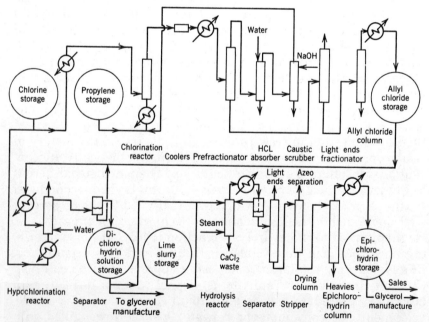

Figure 2.1 Flowsheet for epichlorohydrin process. (*Source:* From Dr. E. Clifford Williams, AIChE Meeting, New Orleans, December, 1940.)

erin plant would have to be built to achieve favorable economics. For some time, Shell negotiated with DuPont—which had chlorine and was a major buyer of glycerin—but no deal could be made. Soon, the war intervened and it was another ten years before Shell's first glycerin plant was built in Houston, Texas. Thus, Shell's biggest technology achievement at Emeryville did not emerge from the pilot plant until after the war years, when so much other petrochemical development was taking place in other laboratories and plants.

In October 1948, Shell Development Company received the Kirkpatrick Award for Chemical Engineering Achievement, which recognizes important contributions to advances in the chemical industry. The award specifically cited the development of the synthetic glycerin process, but also referred to "a long-term program of pioneering in petrochemicals and other outstanding applications of chemical engineering in the petroleum industry." In a long list of Shell Development Company achievements, the following were highlighted in the award citation:

Process or Products	Year of First Commercial Operation	Plants Built for Each Process
Sec. butyl alcohol	1930	4
Isooctane, cold acid process	1934	13
Isopropyl alcohol and acetone	1935	4
Petroleum alkyl phenols	1937	2
Alkylation of paraffins with olefins (with other companies)	1939	28
Toluene recovery by extraction distillation	1940	11
Butadiene via dichlorobutane	1941	1

DOW CHEMICAL—CHLORINE AND BROMINE CHEMISTRY LEAD TO THE GULF COAST

Late in 1938, Willard H. Dow and A. P. "Dutch" Beutel, a top operating manager at Midland, Michigan, were driving on a road between Houston and Freeport, Texas. They had been in that area several times before and were fascinated by the sight of large flares shooting up from 6-inch and 8-inch pipes used to vent the associated gas from operating oil wells. "It was so bright there at night," Beutel later recounted, "that you could read a newspaper by the light of a flare, while driving along at night in a car." What Dow and Beutel were doing, while ostensibly checking on operations of their oil well acidizing crews, was making the final selection of a site for a new chemical plant the company was planning to construct on the Gulf Coast, the first to be built in that area by a major U.S. chemical company.

Willard Dow's father, Herbert Henry Dow, a college chemistry teacher from Cleveland, had come to Midland in 1890 after concluding that a possible fortune was buried underground in the form of a rich rock salt deposit containing bromine, as well as ordinary salt. He had devised a method of separating the two chemicals and, using borrowed money, had built a cell plant and evaporation unit over the deposit, which was mined by leaching with water. While the company was hardly an overnight success, sale of bromides and bleach powder (the latter to textile and cotton mills) eventually formed the basis of a solid undertaking. Soon, the company extracted not only chlorine, bromine, and sodium from the brine, but magnesium and calcium as well. The business branched out into synthetic dyes, fertilizers, food preservatives, solvents, such as carbon tetrachloride, and chemical intermediates, including caustic soda. Dow Chemical became a bulk supplier to other chemical companies, which were being established at a rapid pace across the country.

During World War I, Dow, like Union Carbide, had become involved in the production of mustard gas, using small amounts of ethylene produced from the dehydration of alcohol. Under the leadership of Herbert Dow and later Willard Dow, who had received a chemical engineering degree at the University of Michigan, the company had by the mid-1920s become a large producer of chlorine, caustic, calcium chloride, phenol, and, somewhat later, vinylidene chloride (Saran), ethyl cellulose (Ethocel), and other consumer-oriented products. Phenol, at first primarily a disinfectant, soon became an important intermediate for formaldehyde resins and insecticides, with Dow a major supplier. The company also became the first U.S. firm to develop a strong interest in styrene and polystyrene, but a number of problems and lack of management interest delayed real progress in this area until just before the war.

The Midland site had many advantages, including large salt deposits nearby, which could first be mined to produce feedstock for the electrolytic cells and later also used to dispose the vast quantities of spent brines generated in the processes employed at that site. The supply of bromine was always fairly limited, but that was no problem, at first, since demand was also low. The situation changed dramatically, however, when it was discovered that the addition of tetraethyl lead in ethylene dibromide fluid would greatly improve the efficiency of the automobile engine by eliminating its tendency to "knock" during the compression stroke. General Motors and Standard Oil (N.J.) subsequently founded the Ethyl Corporation and a new industry was born.

The monumentally successful, classical research work on anti-knock agents by Thomas Midgley, Jr. can only be described in outline form here. Employed by "Boss" Kettering, who had set up the Dayton Research Laboratory (later the Delco Division of General Motors), Midgley had been given the task of finding the cause of knocking and to see how it could be eliminated. The remarkable thing is that Midgley was not even trained in chemistry, having received a degree in mechanical engineering from Cornell. Over a period of several years Midgley, with a group of later also very distinguished people assisting him, systematically learned how certain substances inhibit knocking.* It was found that these materials could retard the rupture in the molecular chains of straight-chain (unbranched) hydrocarbons, the gasoline components most likely to break and then ignite spontaneously under the high pressures and temperatures at the end of the compression stroke. The first materials showing promise as antiknock agents were organic compounds, including aniline. Later, at Kettering's suggestion, alkyl compounds of selenium and tellurium were found to be more effective, but still not good enough. At Wilson's suggestion, it was then decided to try other metals, using Langmuir's theory of atomic structure and the Period Table of Elements as a guide. This finally led, in 1921, to the identification by Midgley and Hochwalt of tetraethyl lead, a product far better for inhibiting engine knock than any other discovered before or since that time. The search for

---

*Persons contributing to Midgley's work on antiknock fluids were Alan R. Albright, Carrol A. Hochwalt, and Charles A. Thomas (all from Delco at that time); Robert E. Wilson and Charles S. Venable, then both professors at M.I.T.; and Charles M. A. Stine, Willis Harrington, and Elmer K. Bolton of DuPont.

a satisfactory antiknock agent was now over. Ethylene dibromide was added to tetraethyl lead to eliminate deposits of lead on engine valves (8). Figure 2.2 shows how the octane rating of gasoline and engine compression ratios rose steadily after the discovery of the effect of "ethyl" as the new additive was called.

The rapid rise in tetraethyl lead consumption in the 1920s pointed to a need for sources beyond the natural brines available in inland areas. By 1931, bromine demand had risen to 9 million pounds per year—roughly four times the consumption rate in the early 1920s—and both Dow and Ethyl started to look at sea water as a more logical long-term source. Dow had already done a great deal of work on a sea-water extraction process, which involved treatment with chlorine, sulfuric acid, and soda ash. It required a location where the spent sea water would not dilute the incoming feed stream and where no industrial wastes would be present. In 1931, after a careful survey of logical sites, Dow built a pilot plant at Cape Fear, North Carolina, that was sized to extract and purify 550 pounds per day of bromine. Successful operation of this unit resulted in the design of the 15,000-pound-per-day plant at Kure Beach, North Carolina, which started up in early 1934. The basic process involved (1) oxidizing the bromine-containing brine with chlorine to liberate the bromine, followed by air blowing to free the bromine and absorbing it in an alkali carbonate solution, and (2) treating the bromine in the form of a solution of sodium bromide and bromate with sulfuric acid to liberate the bromine. Ethylene was produced via dehydration of ethyl alcohol vapor passed over kaolin catalyst. The ethylene was then reacted with bromine to make 16,000 pounds per day of ethylene dibromide.

Although the Ethyl-Dow joint venture alleviated one of the problems of the Midland site, two others caused Dow Chemical to take steps to establish still another site, which also had to be on sea water. Disposal of brines was becoming a major problem again at Midland. The company had also become a producer of magnesium and was developing another process to tap sea water as a major raw materials source.

The Dow people were not unfamiliar with the Gulf Coast and its extensive oil and gas operations. For some time, the company's Dowell subsidiary had sold muriatic (dilute hydrochloric) acid to acidize oil wells. But around this time, the company found it could perform another, eventually far more important oil field service. In one of those fascinating "accidents" when industry history is

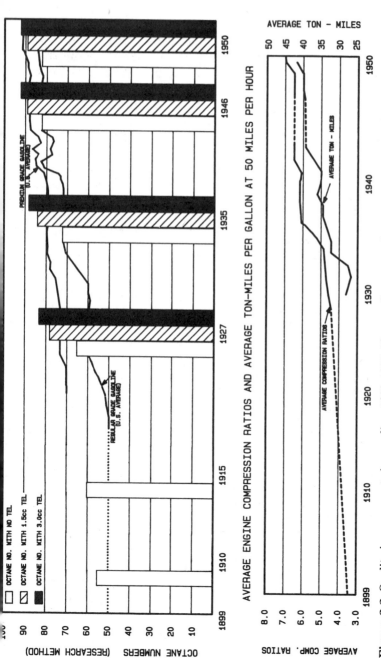

Figure 2.2 Quality improvements in gasoline: 1899–1950. (*Source:* Octane numbers 1940–1942 and average ton-miles per gallon, from C. L. McCoen, 1951, Economic relationship of engine-fuel research, American Petroleum Institute, Midyear meeting Tulsa, OK, May 3.) Octane numbers prior to 1910 assumed to have remained constant. Octane numbers 1946–1950 from Ethyl Corporation surveys. Average compression ratios from *Automotive Industries* and Ethyl Corporation data.

made, Beutel had been in charge of an operation which involved trying for the first time to pump spent brine into a particularly tight sand formation near Midland. Using a large pump that developed 600 psig discharge pressure, the crew was at first unsuccessful in pumping waste brine into the Parma sand, some 900 feet down. Suddenly, the pressure dropped sharply and the brine poured down into the formation. The well had, in fact, been "fractured," thus allowing brine to flow into newly formed cracks in the formation. Beutel was never granted a patent on this technique, but it became the basis for one of Dowell's most important oil field services—oil-well fracturing—where pressures up to 10,000 psig were used to break tight oil-sand formations to produce more oil. Dow Chemical's steadily increasing involvement in oil well services therefore brought its executives to the Gulf Coast with increasing frequency.

Dow Chemical's magnesium operations were not without problems, in that the company first had to convince the U.S. government and the airframe industry that the metal had special virtues. The company had started producing magnesium on a small scale in the early 1930s, in association with the Cleveland Cliffs Company. Domestic interest in this lightest of metals was almost nonexistent, but orders from England, France, Germany, and Japan kept production rising. Dow was convinced that a war was coming and that United States manufacturers would soon recognize the advantage of magnesium. Therefore, it was time to look for a larger supply of raw materials and Dow knew that every 1000 gallons of sea water contained the equivalent of ten pounds of magnesium and a half pound of bromine.

Pressure to build on another site was also mounting from other directions. Underground storage of brine near Midland was beginning to create pollution problems, due to leakage into the aquifers that fed the nearby Tittabawassee River. At Kure Beach, electric power was becoming costly and transportation costs for shipping soda ash and sulfuric acid to that location were rising to a point where something had to be done. In Midland, Dow had started small-scale production of ethylene oxide from chlorohydrin and was trying to decide where a large supply of ethylene might be developed. Union Carbide had shown, more than ten years before, that natural gas-based ethane was an ideal feedstock for this purpose.

A plant on the Texas Gulf Coast would meet all the requirements. Electricity was cheap, natural gas and oil were plentiful, and sea water provided most of the balance of raw materials for a plant that would produce chlorine-caustic, ethylene glycol, ethylene dibromide, and magnesium. A source of lime needed for the chlorhydrin process and for magnesia was also available—in large mounds of oyster shells! This was the ideal location. Nevertheless, the directors of Dow hesitated for some time. They felt that the proposed project involved the most important decision ever made by the management of the firm. The directors finally decided to meet in Corpus Christi, Texas, to make a final selection between that location and Freeport on the Brazos River. Corpus Christi offered better schools and housing, good shopping facilities, and many other advantages. But Willard Dow and Beutel favored Freeport, an ideal location in all other respects, including vast salt domes for spent brine disposal. When the directors assembled in Corpus Christi, the weather was terrible—cold and blustery. The group then went to Freeport. Over a few hours' time, the weather had become balmy and the site looked inviting. The decision was made then and there. Over the next several weeks, the company bought several thousand acres of land along the coast and on the Brazos River. Then, in a major departure from previous practice, it was decided to bring in an outside firm, the Austin Corporation, to help design and build the plant. It started up just before the outbreak of hostilities in Europe.

Initial design for the Freeport plant involved an integrated production line that would convert sea water and natural gas annually into 12 million pounds of magnesium, 60,000 tons of chorine, 66,000 tons of caustic, 25 million pounds of ethylene, 15 million pounds (each) of ethylene glycol, ethylene dichloride and vinylidene chloride, and 28.5 million pounds of ethylene dibromide. Shortly thereafter, a styrene plant, the first major U.S. facility to make this material, was constructed at nearby Velasco, Texas. Freeport would become the model for a series of other petrochemical complexes to be built on a line between the Mexican border and Lake Charles. There were good reasons why Dow, able to extract its most important raw materials from sea water, and to buy inexpensive natural gas for its other important needs, was the first to locate on the Gulf Coast. So it was Dow that naturally led the way.

Beutel became an honorary Texan and a champion of the "open construction" plants, so different from the plants traditionally located inside large buildings and built in Europe and in the United States for many years. The warm climate on the Gulf Coast precluded the need for burying pipes below the frostline or locating facilities inside heated areas. But all U.S. companies did not immediately adopt the new construction techniques, even when locating in the Deep South. During World War II, Marion Boyer, superintendent of Jersey's Baton Rouge refinery was talking to William Haynes, an industry historian who published a number of books on the development of the domestic chemical industry. Boyer pointed to an adjacent plant where DuPont was producing tetraethyl lead. "See that fine building by the river?" he said, "that is their original unit. We told them they did not have to build a fine University Hall like that. But no, they knew how to build a chemical plant, and they did. They learned quickly enough! Just look at the rest of the property" (9).

The savings involved in building and maintaining a chemical plant in the warm southern climate were considered to amount to one-third to one-half of the cost of building comparable facilities inside an enclosed structure in a cold, northern location. At a testimonial dinner at the Warwick Hotel in Houston in 1966, honoring Beutel's 50 years with Dow, it was said, "He is a man with boundless energy and drive, a man of ideas and imagination. Most of all, Dutch Beutel is the pioneering personality of the chemical industry in the Southwest."

Many companies followed Dow to the Gulf Coast to establish petrochemical plants in an area where cheap feedstocks and a friendly climate were at hand. The basis for the economic superiority of U.S. petrochemical production was being established for a long time to come.

STANDARD OIL COMPANY (N.J.)—HYDROGENATION, OLEFINS, AND AROMATICS

Standard Oil of New Jersey's interest in chemical production technology stemmed from the company's decision to study the application of chemical engineering techniques to the upgrading of crude oil fractions. In the late 1920s, the directors of the company concurred that it was timely to upgrade the state of technology in its refineries, which were processing a variety of crude oils domestically, as well as abroad. In a wide ranging reorganization in 1927, all corporate research and engineering functions were transferred to Standard Oil Development (S.O.D.) Company, a new subsidiary that had been set up under Edgar M. Clark, a director of the parent company with substantial background in refining technology, including participation in the development of the Burton-Clark cracking still. Frank A. Howard, an engineer and patent attorney, was placed in charge of operations. Of some interest is the fact that Humble Oil, a subsidiary located in Texas and at that time not wholly owned by Jersey, maintained a separate research organization, as did Imperial Oil, Jersey's Canadian subsidiary. Extensive exchange of information eventually became an important factor among the groups, though Humble people tended to be rather independent until the company was fully absorbed by Jersey.

One of the first key steps taken by Clark and Howard was to establish close liaison with the chemical engineering department at the Massachusetts Institute of Technology, and specifically with Professor Warren K. Lewis who headed the department at that time. In addition, Jersey persuaded Robert T. Haslam, another professor of chemical engineering at M.I.T., to take a leave of absence and organize the company's effort to set up research work at Jersey's Baton Rouge refinery, which would soon serve as the key proving ground for many of the company's chemical processes and projects. Haslam, in turn, hired Robert P. Russell, who brought with him a dozen or so M.I.T. graduates to help staff the new Louisiana R&D group.

Jersey had entered into a relationship with I.G. Farbenindustrie in the late 1920s, after that firm had succeeded in demonstrating the high pressure hydrogenation of powdered coal. But Jersey saw the technology's potential quite differently from the researchers at I.G. Farben, being primarily interested in heavy oil upgrading through hydrogenation. In 1927, the two companies signed an agreement whereby Jersey would erect and operate a heavy oil hydrogenation plant at Baton Rouge under a broad patent and licensing arrangement, involving extensive know-how sharing and cross-licensing features. Test facilities were eventually built at Baton Rouge and at Bayway, both key refineries in the Jersey system. The startup and early operations of these plants became part of the S.O.D. folklore, since it took a great deal of time and a series of minor mishaps to gain operating experience with high pressure hydrogenation technology. One survivor of this period recalls that a number of barrels, initially provided for collecting the product, were diverted to a more immediate use—for engineers to dive into when they thought some part of the system "was about to blow."

In 1930 the original agreement was extended to cover other areas of technical cooperation between the companies, the common thread being the development of fuels and chemicals from coal or by hydrogenation of oils. The I.G. was already working on Buna rubbers and included this technology in the broad-scaled agreement (10).

Pilot plant work on the I.G. Farben acetylene arc process was also carried out at Baton Rouge (see Chapter 1). The development of the new acetylene process had been closely associated with the German synthetic rubber program, since the I.G. chemists had worked out a route to butadiene from acetylene with acetaldehyde as an intermediate product. In the test work at Baton Rouge, the emphasis was placed primarily on the production of acetylene and acetaldehyde, given the fact that Buna-S rubber was, at that time, considered an inferior product by the domestic rubber companies and since there was no shortage of natural rubber. Acetaldehyde would be made by the hydration of acetylene over a pumice catalyst. The Jersey engineers now saw an opportunity to make a useful product—acetic acid—from acetaldehyde. Process work on acetaldehyde proceeded slowly and, at one time, the Jersey group visited I.G. plants in Ludwigshafen, Oppau, Hoechst, and Knapsack to study the Germany plants. As a result, it was decided to switch to a mercury catalyst in sulfuric acid to effect this conversion. Eventually, a process of this kind was developed in Baton Rouge; however, it was decided not to proceed with such a plant in the United States. As a result of agreements entered into by Jersey several years later, the arc process know-how was transferred back to I.G. and later used in the wartime plants to make Buna rubber for the Axis powers.

Economical production of hydrogen was also a key part of a wide-ranging research program mapped out for Baton Rouge, since it turned out that I.G. Farben had developed a series of suitable steam reforming catalysts. As the work developed, Jersey's management became more and more convinced that hydrogenation (or "hydrocracking," as it later was called) would become the key refining step of the future, based on the predominance of very heavy crudes known to exist all over the world. Jersey's interest in the joint R&D program with I.G. Farben was, therefore, based primarily on its focus on *fuel* products and the contractual arrangements very much spoke to that point. Thus, Jersey would control the worldwide application (outside Germany) of the jointly developed technology for the production of fuels, while I.G. Farben would be in control of the application of technology for *chemicals* emanating from the program (11). The companies would, however, share in the rewards for both types of products in a predetermined manner. In 1930, a third patent-pooling and licensing entity was set up to handle borderline cases. Farben assigned to that company (known as the Joint American Study Company or JASCO) its rights outside of Germany to such technology areas as paraffin oxidation, acetylene manufacture, naphtha reforming, and Buna rubbers, all of which were apparently considered "borderline" situations at the time. Standard Oil Development obtained the right to license or use this technology.

Soon after these agreements had been signed, vast new oil deposits were discovered in the United States in the Middle East with the result that hydrogenation technology for the production of synthetic crude oil was put on the shelf—for many years, as it turned out. To Jersey—and eventually to the U.S. war effort—the most useful results of the German/U.S. cooperation were the product areas assigned to JASCO, as well as the process experience gained in hydrogenation (and dehydrogenation) technology, even though this technology would not be applied to the production of synthetic crude from coal. It did lead to hydrotreating processes for sulfur removal and lube oil treatment and also to such transformations as hydrogenation of di-isobutylene to iso-octane, and to hydroforming (i.e., catalytic reforming of naphtha), which could be used to make nitration-grade toluene. Perhaps just as importantly, it provided a major stimulus for the study of catalytic processes of various kinds, which led Jersey's researchers into a number of chemical as well as refining applications.

Petrochemical raw materials had, of course, been available for a long time in most refineries, although they were basically unappreciated by-products of operations conducted for the production of gasoline and other fuels. In the 1920s and early 1930s, most refineries had installed thermal cracking units, usually of the Dubbs or Tube-and-Tank types (Figures 4.2 and 4.3). Both of these operated at elevated pressures—on the order of 500–1000 psig—and at temperatures close to 1000°F. Cracking took place under thermal "soaking" conditions in large reaction drums containing no catalyst. The feedstocks to these thermal crackers ranged from crude and reduced crude oil to gas oil and naphtha fractions. The main purpose of these operations was to increase the yield of gasoline on crude oil or, in the case of naphtha feedstocks, to raise the octane rating of the gasoline by increasing its aromatics content. As engine octane requirements rose, the percent of cracked gasoline blended into the total gasoline mixture also rose substantially, from 16 percent in 1919 to over 30 percent in 1929. (see Table 2.1). This also more than doubled the amount of reactive olefins present in the cracked gases coming off the thermal conversion units and increasingly brought the presence of these materials—still largely burned as fuel—to the attention of refiners and technologists (see Table 2.2).

In thermal cracking operations on a range of feedstocks, the ethylene content of cracked gases varied from 2.5 percent to over 6 percent, while propylene could run as high as 20 percent, and the combined butylene-butadiene content as high as 17 percent. The Gyro Process, another development in thermal cracking to increase gasoline yields, produced offgases containing over 20 percent ethylene. Considering the large crude runs in many refineries, the amounts of olefins and butadiene available for potential transformation into high octane gasoline fractions or chemicals were becoming appreciable.

An early development program leading to the production of a

Table 2.1   U.S. Production of Gasoline by Methods: 1919-1929 (Millions of Barrels)

Year	Total	Straight Distillation	Cracking	Natural Gasoline
1919	99.7	75.8 (76%)	15.5 (16%)	8.4 (8%)
1920	122.3	96.9 (79%)	16.2 (13%)	9.2 (18%)
1921	130.9	98.9 (76%)	21.3 (16%)	10.7 (8%)
1922	156.1	118.6 (76%)	25.4 (16%)	12.1 (8%)
1923	193.8	146.1 (75%)	28.3 (15%)	19.4 (10%)
1924	222.9	166.3 (75%)	34.4 (15%)	22.2 (10%)
1925	266.8	171.4 (64%)	68.6 (26%)	26.8 (10%)
1926	304.5	178.3 (59%)	93.7 (30%)	32.5 (11%)
1927	337.3	197.0 (58%)	101.2 (30%)	39.1 (12%)
1928	385.0	219.2 (57%)	122.6 (31%)	43.2 (12%)
1929	441.8	244.9 (55%)	143.7 (33%)	53.2 (12%)

Source: API, (1950), *Petroleum Facts and Figures,* 225.

Table 2.2 Thermal Cracking of East Texas Gas Oil

Cracking Conditions

Pressure—350 psig
Temperature—950°F

Yield

60 percent gasoline with research octane
rating of 74

Gas Analysis (percent by volume)*

Methane and uncondensables	39.2
Ethylene	3.9
Ethane	21.0
Propylene	7.4
Propane	16.2
Butylenes	2.6
Butadiene	2.3
Others	7.7

*Cracked gas yield was approximately 13 percent by weight of gas oil charged to unit.
(*Source:* Carleton Ellis (1937). *The Chemistry of Petroleum Derivatives,* New York, Reinhold.)

useful chemical was commercialized at Jersey's Bayway refinery in 1922—the production of tetraethyl lead (TEL) by the reaction of ethyl chloride and lead/sodium alloy. A similar plant was built by DuPont at Deepwater, New Jersey, in 1923. Jersey and DuPont at first used ethyl alcohol to produce the ethyl chloride, since the amount of ethylene required was small and the cost of recovering pure ethylene from a refinery stream far exceeded the raw material cost advantage relative to using fermentation alcohol as a feedstock. Only Union Carbide had, by that time, worked on any commercial uses for the C_2 olefin and, in fact, it was some time before low temperature separation processes were perfected to the degree necessary to achieve the really large-scale use of ethylene for the manufacture of derivatives.

As time went by, Ethyl Corporation and DuPont needed much larger quantities of ethylene for the production of TEL. Jersey and Ethyl considered several alternate processes, with the Jersey scientists concentrating on the production of ethylene via propane cracking. At one point, Alco Products Company was brought in to design the first propane cracker and associated ethylene recovery units. Such a plant was built and then turned over to Ethyl. It served as a model for Jersey's future steam crackers. In the 1930s, Jersey started using naphtha and even heavier feedstocks, which required solving many problems associated with furnace operation, as well as the recovery and purification of by-products. Whereas Union Carbide had been first in deliberately cracking a light hydrocarbon to ethylene, Jersey pioneered the technology later termed "heavy-liquids cracking."

Thermal reforming of naphtha was also practiced extensively in the 1930s. This was carried out at temperatures of 1000°F or higher and at somewhat lower pressure and produced a gasoline stream high in olefins and aromatics. One of the major drawbacks of this type of operation was high coke and gas formation, requiring very frequent decoking and cleaning. Another problem was the tendency of olefinic components in the gasoline to form undesirable gums and polymers. As an example, a naphtha fraction containing 96 percent naphthenes and paraffins cracking at 1100°F and 60 seconds contact time produced a 32 percent yield of a gasoline-range product containing 36 percent aromatics and 35 percent unsaturates, as well as 0.38 pounds of coke and 1800 cubic feet of gas per barrel of naphtha feedstock. At a charge rate of 5000 barrels per day, almost a ton of coke was laid down daily in the reaction vessel. The cracked gases contained a large quantity of lower olefins, as well as substantial amounts of butadiene.

Earlier, Jersey and Humble researchers had gone to work on ways and means to upgrade the copious quantities of olefins emanating from their thermal cracking operations. At Bayway, New Jersey, site of a large Esso refinery, a plant was built to convert propylene to isopropyl alcohol, based on patents by Carleton Ellis, one of the most eminent organic chemists of his time and the author of the definitive book on organic chemical technology at a later stage of his career (12). Ellis had studied Berthelot's work involving the reaction of propylene with sulphuric acid, followed by hydrolysis of the isopropyl hydrogen sulphate and Ellis' patents disclosed a process to carry out this reaction commercially. As mentioned earlier, this plant at first ran into production difficulties, due to Jersey's inexperience in producing a pure feedstock through careful fractional distillation. The problem was eventually solved and other alcohols were then produced in due course. Meanwhile, research work at Standard Oil Development Company involving other reactions of olefinic compounds was achieving some success.

One of the first results was the extension of the same type of technology. It was found that hot sulfuric acid could be used to combine iso- and normal butylenes to make a high octane dimer, substantially increasing the gasoline yield from a given amount of isobutylene. Both Shell and S.O.D. were studying this approach and placed small plants in operation in 1936. Shortly thereafter, a far more important process was conceived. Butylene and isobutane could also be reacted with sulfuric acid to make a product that did not need to be hydrogenated. This "alkylation" process had first been described in an article published by the research depeartment of the Anglo-Iranian Oil Company. Humble researchers quickly confirmed the thesis, following which the company arranged to obtain rights to the patents and started isobutane alkylation in an existing dimer plant in the summer of 1938. Alkylation became the basis for much of the aviation fuel made from refinery C_4 streams during World War II.

An important process from a later petrochemical perspective was also at first oriented toward military needs. This was the development of technology to make toluene from petroleum naphtha fractions instead of from the traditional coke-oven light oils. Jersey's interest in the production of synthetic toluene from petroleum dated from 1933, when Haslam wrote to the Army Ordnance Department informing them that benzene, toluene, and xylene had been found in product streams from certain naphtha feedstocks that had been subjected to thermal treatment under hydrogen-rich conditions. Samples were submitted to the government shortly thereafter. Although these proved as yet unsatisfactory for nitration to TNT, Army sources encouraged the S.O.D. scientists to continue the experimental work. By 1936, much better results were being obtained, although toluene purity was still well below that of the coal-derived material and yields were disappointingly low. Executives of S.O.D. now decided to try a different approach, again turning to German technology, which had been made available to Jersey under the I.G. agreements. This information included data on the use of alumina-molybdenum oxide catalysts operated at 900–1000°F and 200–300 psig to process low octane naphthas into high octane aromatic gasolines. The reaction system operated for about 12 hours, when regeneration was required, due to carbon deposits and conversion of molybdenum oxide to sulfide.

Oxygen content of the regeneration gas was 1-1.5 percent at the beginning, increasing to 10-15 percent at the end of the reactivation, following which the reactor was put back into reforming service. The German process had been under development for aviation gasoline manufacture, but not for the production of high purity aromatics. Jersey experimenters realized that this technology, which soon became known as the "hydroforming" process, could be used to produce a cut rich in benzene-toluene-xylene (BTX) aromatics, which could then be extracted and fractionated to produce the desired toluene, with benzene and xylene as other desired coproducts.

The hydroforming process was carried out in a series of fixed beds that could be periodically regenerated, similar to the Houdry fixed-bed catalytic cracking reactors. When operated for gasoline production, the yield of "hydroformate" was about 72 percent, and this was blended with light naphtha to give a final mixture containing 50-55 percent aromatics, having an unleaded motor octane rating around 80. Regeneration temperature was 1020-1030°F and catalyst life—with 12-hour reaction-regeneration cycles—was about six months. This process was obviously better suited for aromatics, and specifically toluene production, than the thermal cracked streams previously available for extracting aromatics cuts. However, further modifications were required to improve and optimize yields.

A pilot plant was built in 1938 to demonstrate the technology and the results were good, with a large yield of toluene. The naphtha feed was selected from crudes containing high amounts of naphthenes (easy to convert to aromatics) and fractionated to obtain a 180-230°F cut, containing extensive amounts of methylcyclohexane and dimethyl cyclopentane. This was fed to the hydroformer. Later, a two-stage process was developed, where the product from the first reforming reactor was fractionated to obtain a narrow cut for further processing in a second reforming step, resulting in a toluene content of 90-95 percent in the stream going to extraction. Attention also turned to the extraction step, where Jersey had already obtained substantial experience in extracting undesirable aromatics from paraffins, such as kerosene, through the use of the Edeleanu* sulfur dioxide extraction system.

---

*Edeleanu was a Rumanian chemist who invented a number of petroleum extraction processes, including some for producing lubricating oil stocks.

This technique was now applied to separate toluene and other aromatics from reformate. The process involved chilling the stream to 60° below zero, contacting it with liquid SO_2, and treating the mixture with light paraffinic lubricating oil. Two phases were formed, one of which contained the aromatics cut mixed with the SO_2 and some of the oil, while paraffins from the reformate separated in the other phase. However, the lubricating oil gave undesirable impurities in the aromatics cut, since some of its constituents were close to toluene in boiling range. In further work, a higher-boiling, narrow range kerosene fraction was substituted for the lube oil, making it easy to separate the aromatics wash oil, as well as the solvent. A final chemical treatment was also added. The resulting 99+ percent toluene was now found suitable for nitration by the Army Arsenal at Picatinny, Maryland.

It was 1940, and the Army's interest in obtaining a high purity source of toluene was becoming acute. An order for 20,000 gallons was obtained by Jersey, but now it was found that no single refinery had all the equipment to produce the material, which had been offered to the Army at $1.70 per gallon. The feedstocks were assembled by Humble at Baytown, Texas, and distilled to produce a narrow cut suitable for reforming. This was then shipped by tanker to Bayway, New Jersey, where it was hydroformed in a converted hydrogenation pilot plant and redistilled. Following that, it was loaded into 22 tank cars and returned by rail to Baytown, where the toluene was extracted in the Edeleanu unit. This material was then shipped to Baton Rouge, Louisiana, for distillation and acid treatment and finally delivered to the Army. The company's cost was $135,000, with Jersey sustaining a loss of over $90,000 on this first large order for synthetic toluene from petroleum feedstocks. Business improved considerably after that (13). Humble built the Baytown Ordnance Works for the government and this plant produced more than half of the total amount of petroleum toluene for the U.S. war effort.

Probably, the most important contribution made by Standard Oil Development Company was the fluid-bed catalytic cracking process. This technology, which was a logical successor to Houdry fixed-bed cat cracking, eventually revolutionized the petroleum refining industry and provided hitherto unimaginably large supplies of olefins for conversion to fuel and petrochemical products. This technology was developed during the Second World War and is described in Chapter 3.

FEEDSTOCK SELECTION: JUDGMENTS AND ACTIONS

The four companies identified as being ahead of many of their peers in the utilization of petroleum-based feedstocks must have pondered the reluctance of some of the other large chemicals producers to consider a switch to hydrocarbons from coal. After all, coal-based organic chemistry was not an old, established industry in the United States at that time. The first coke ovens had only been installed in 1893 by the Semet-Solvay Company and recovery of coal tar chemicals had only been commenced in 1910 by Semet-Solvay, jointly with Barrett Chemical Company (both later divisions of Allied Chemical). World War I had, of course, greatly spurred this industry, due to the need for such products as ammonia, toluene, and phenol. Yet, it is interesting to reflect that by the early 1930s, when the promise of petrochemicals was starting to become a reality, U.S. production of coal-derived organics had only been carried out for 20 years or so.

Nevertheless, DuPont in 1938 told ICI that it could produce any chemical from coal and that it did not want to place its future in the hands of the oil companies. "In the field of carbon monoxide chemistry," a DuPont man told J.W. Armit of ICI, it "has an answer to anything the oil companies can do from hydrocarbon gases" (14, p. 321). ICI, by that time, had used German technology to construct coal hydrogenation plants to make both naphthas and light hydrocarbons, which could serve as feedstocks in a similar manner to crude oil. ICI also considered molasses as a very viable British raw material, in that Distillers Company Ltd. was producing large quantities of ethyl alcohol and acetone at very low prices from it and ICI could produce ethylene from the alcohol. In the 1930s, ICI used ethylene from this source to make ethylene oxide, glycol and later, polyethylene. Acetaldehyde obtained from dehydration of ethyl alcohol, could be transformed to yield butanol, acetic acid, acetic anhydride, and acetone. Thus, as late as 1944, ICI apparently gave relatively equal weight to coal, oil, and molasses as feedstocks for the production of heavy organic chemicals (Fig. 2.3) (14, p. 320).

In the United States, the transition from coal and agricultural feedstocks to petroleum and natural-gas-based feedstocks is very evident from a consideration of oxygenated solvents production in the 1930s and 1940s (See Figure 2.4). Dupont was the main producer of coal-based solvents, with production varying

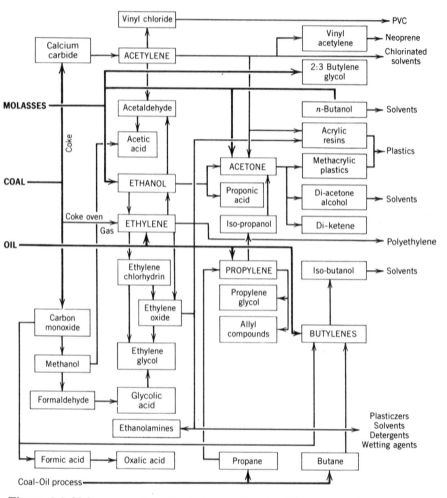

Figure 2.3 Molasses, coal, or oil: choices confronting ICI in 1944. (*Source:* W. J. Reader, *Imperial Chemical Industries, A History,* Vol. II, 1970, 1975, Oxford University Press, Oxford, p. 320.)

between 100 and 200 million pounds per year over this period. Fermentation alcohol was by far the largest volume oxygenate until almost the end of World War II, with production greatly spurred by the need for butadiene, used for making synthetic rubber. But by the 1940s, the combined synthetic solvent production of Carbide, Shell, Enjay (Standard Oil Company, N.J.) and others started to exceed the production of grain-based ethanol.

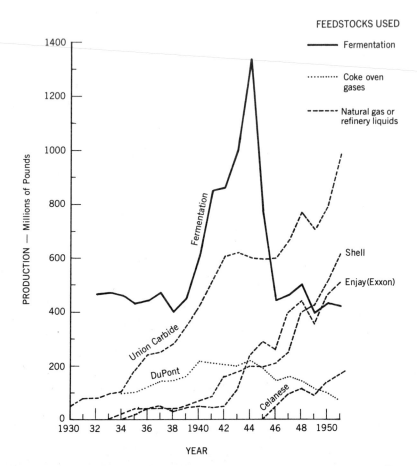

Figure 2.4 Oxygenated solvents production in the 1930s and 1940s. (*Source: A. Jonnard, personal communication.*)

Coal-based solvent production declined to negligible amounts by 1950, and synthetic (ethylene-based) alcohol almost totally replaced fermentation-based alcohol, due to its higher purity.

The activities of the four American companies who pioneered many of the advances in the use of hydrocarbon feedstocks don't tell the whole story, of course. Certainly, there is no intention to slight the relevant activities of many other firms during this period, when the petrochemical industry was still in its infancy. Some contributions made by other firms to the development of the U.S. petrochemicals industry in the period before World War II are detailed below. DuPont is not included, first since a great deal of information on the Wilmington firm is covered in Chapter 7 on synthetic fibers and elsewhere in this book, and also because DuPont refrained from committing itself to petrochemicals until the answer became very clear. The same can be said for a number of the other traditional U.S. chemical firms, who were slow to embrace the prospective feedstock change from coal, molasses or calcium carbide-based acetylene.

Some other noteworthy achievements include the following:

Carbon Black (several firms). As mentioned earlier, this material, so vital for tire production, is, in a certain sense, the earliest petrochemical, although some would argue with the definition. The Channel Black process used in the earliest plants was replaced by the cyclical Thermal Black process, first used by the Thermatomic Carbon Company in Louisiana in 1922. The modern Furnace Black process, using either gas or oil, was introduced in 1928. Godfrey L. Cabot Inc., and United Carbon Company were early leaders. An oil-based carbon black plant is depicted in Figure 2.5 (15).

Ethyl Corporation. The production of tetraethyl lead, ethyl chloride, and ethylene dibromide represented an outstanding example of early process development and commercialization of petrochemical products. Ethyl Corporation later severed its ties to Jersey and General Motors (which had established the company), and became a producer of a number of other petrochemicals, partly based on internal research.

Monsanto. Drs. Charles A. Thomas and Carroll A. Hochwalt, both ex-General Motors Corporation and outstanding research chemists, led Monsanto into the plastics era after Edgar Queeny, Monsanto's president, established a new subsidiary, Monsanto Petroleum Chemicals Inc., in 1936 (16, p. 221). The company started producing polyvinyl butyral and vinyl acetate resins in the mid-1930s, acquired Fiberloid, a major plastics producer, in 1938 and closely followed Dow's entry into styrene and polystyrene.

Sharples Chemicals. A very innovative company for its time, Sharples in 1926 built a plant at Belle, West Virginia that converted pentanes fractionated out of field gasolines to amyl alcohol and amyl acetates. The process was based on chlorination, fol-

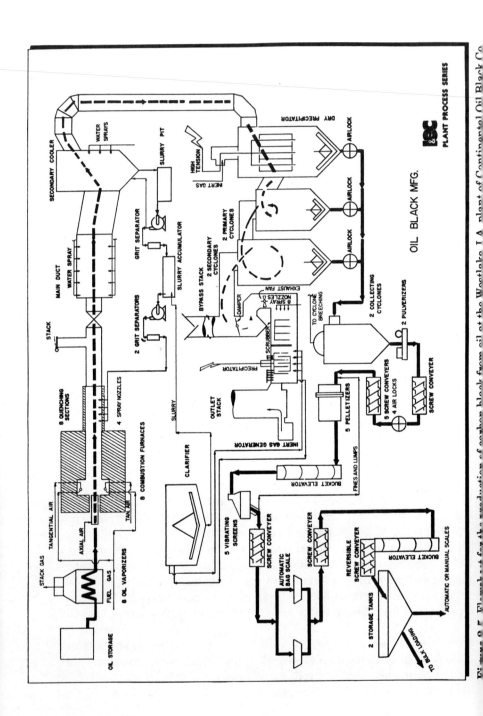

Figure 9.5 Flow sheet for the production of carbon black from oil at the Westlake, LA, plant of Continental Oil Black Co.

lowed by hydrolysis with caustic. Sharples later became part of the company known today as Pennwalt (17).

Rohm and Haas. Began commercial production in 1934 of methylamines via high-pressure catalytic dehydration of ammonia and methanol (16, p. 223). Commenced production of methyl methacrylate resins in the mid-1930s, with product marketed under the Plexiglas trade name.

Commercial Solvents and Cities Service. Commenced production of methanol from natural gas in 1927 and 1929, respectively. The Commercial Solvents plant had a capacity of 3 million gallons per year and the Cities Service plant 6 million gallons. (DuPont had built a 32 million gallon plant at Belle, West Virginia in 1927, but it was based on coke.)

It is also interesting to record here that M. W. Kellogg, the founder of the engineering construction firm that still bears his name, bought natural gas deposits in Texas in the 1930s, because his company's early work in gas reforming technology convinced him that methane would be a key feedstock of the future.

Although this chapter has focused entirely on American companies' pioneering activities in developing technology for the conversion of hydrocarbons to chemicals, it would be quite wrong to leave readers with the impression that there were no important contributions in this area by companies in Europe. This should be apparent from a consideration of some of the developments described in Chapter 1, which, of course, concentrates primarily on the German chemical industry. Rather than attempting to give a quick and sketchy summary of non-U.S. petrochemical developments, it seems more appropriate to give one important example—namely, ICI's work on the production of ammonia and methanol from liquid hydrocarbons in the mid-1930s, when these materials were available as by-products from "synthetic petrol" plants.

The ICI site in Billingham on the River Tee near the North England coal fields was acquired in 1918 by Brunner Mond (later merged into ICI) to get into the synthetic ammonia business. The required technical information was to have come from details observed in captured plants at Oppau in Germany. Thus, instead of entering into a cooperative agreement with BASF/I.G. Farben after the war and building ammonia plants under a German license (as the French company O.N.I.A. had done) the British firm decided to develop its own version of the Haber-Bosch process. This turned out to be much harder than expected, in spite of the fact that Francis Freeth, a leading Brunner Mond chemist, was able to inspect the BASF plant at Oppau in 1919 over the objections of the German company (18). At the British company's Winnington laboratory, a number of chemists and engineers over a period of several years developed know-how for the design of high pressure reactors, piping, valves, compressors, and other such specialized equipment. A small plant, sized at 500 tons per year of ammonia, was then built at Billingham in 1922.

Although this plant and subsequent expansions were not a great financial success, given the world surplus of nitrogen fertilizers in the 1920s and 1930s, the ICI development program resulted in building up a broad knowledge of high pressure technology, which thereafter benefited the company in a number of ways. Thus, soon after completing work on synthetic ammonia, a methanol process was also developed by the same team. At that time, both ammonia and methanol production were based on synthesis gas derived from the coal water gas reaction, which produces mixtures of carbon monoxide and hydrogen by passing superheated steam over a bed of coal.

ICI acquired certain rights to the Bergius coal hydrogenation patents in the late 1920s and eventually convinced the British government to provide tax incentives for the production of "synthetic petrol" by this technology. The first such plant was constructed at Billingham in the early 1930s. In addition to gasoline-range naphtha, this plant and a second one at Heysham produced substantial quantities of propane and butane as by-products. ICI's interest in utilizing these low-boiling hydrocarbons—quite new to England with its coal- and alcohol-based chemistry and long before the discovery of North Sea crude oil—resulted in a development of great significance to the later petrochemical industry.

Neither the Germans nor the Americans had any particular reason for using propane or butane as feedstocks to produce ammonia or methanol. German industry was then entirely based on coal, while in the United States natural gas was the obvious alternate, that would be used increasingly as an ammonia and methanol feedstock. ICI felt, however, that propane and butane from Billingham and Heysham would be ideal feedstocks for a steam reforming reaction, if appropriate technology could be developed. Among other problems, however, these materials contained sulphur compounds, which were known to be catalyst poisons.

ICI's engineers went back to work to develop a light hydrocarbon reforming process that could serve as a front end to the ammonia synthesis technology the company had successfully developed a decade and a half earlier. The program was an early success and included a number of innovations. One of these involved fabricating the reforming catalyst in the shape of rings and loading these inside the reactor tubes, where the reforming reaction could take place under more controlled conditions. Also, to avoid catalyst poisoning due to sulphur compounds, two guard chambers containing zinc oxide absorbent were placed in parallel ahead of the reformer. These removed the sulphur during operation and could be periodically opened and recharged with fresh absorbent while the alternate unit was left on stream (19).

The ICI reforming process became so successful that ICI later licensed it to many other firms and also made it available to U.S. and Canadian plants during World War II. In the 1950s, ICI further improved the process by developing reforming technology at elevated pressures (see Chapter 11).

By 1940, storm clouds were assembling and the oil and chemical companies would soon be devoting most of their research and development efforts to the production of motor and aviation fuels, synthetic rubber, and other materials critical to America's war effort. The early 1940s would become a fruitful period for the development of a number of new processes to make petrochemical feedstocks, intermediates, and their derivatives. Oil and chemical companies played a major role in helping the United States win many of the important battles, fought not only in the field, but also in the laboratories racing to develop technologies to produce the key war materials. These included not only the fuels, tires, and explosives so vital to the direct effort to win the war, but also synthetic fibers and special plastic materials, ranging from polyethylene and polystyrene to new copolymers and other previously unknown materials. Scientists fleeing to America from the occupied countries contributed greatly to the understanding of complex molecules and to the knowledge of the principles of catalysis, which were starting to be successfully employed in an increasing number of petrochemical syntheses. The know-how exchange with segments of the German chemical industry was, of course, cut off at the start of the war. Thus, the large flow of information collected several years later during the postwar visits and recorded in the British Intelligence Objectives Subcommittee and Combined Intelligence Objectives Subcommittee reports reached an American chemical industry that had for some time achieved technological independence and maturity and was far along in transforming petroleum-based feedstocks into the chemical building blocks of the future.

REFERENCES

1. *Chemical & Engineering News* (1973). 50th Anniversary Issue, January 15.
2. G. O. Curme, Jr. (1935). Industry's toolmaker, *Industrial and Engineering Chemistry*, **27**, February, 223-230.
3. J. N. Compton (1937). *Informal Personal Observations on the History of the Carbide and Carbon Chemical Corporation*, Union Carbide, October 4.
4. Joseph G. Davidson (1955). *Petrochemical Survey—An Anecdotal Reminiscence*, Chemical Industry Medal 1955 Address delivered before the American Section of the Society of Chemical Industry, New York, October 28.
5. R. F. Goldstein and A. L. Waddams (1967). *The Petroleum Chemicals Industry* (Third Edition), London, E. & F.N. Spon Ltd., 10.
6. Kendall Beaton (1957). *Enterprise in Oil: A History of Shell in the United States*, New York, Appleton-Century-Crofts, 523.
7. Allied Chemical Corporation (1968). *A Brief History and Description of Allied Chemical Corporation (1920-1968)*, New York, Allied Chemical Corporation.
8. Thomas Midgley, Jr. (1937). From the periodic table to production, *Industrial and Engineering Chemistry*. **29**, No. 2, February, 241-244. Edward Faber, ed. (1961). *Great Chemists*, New York, Interscience, 1588-1597.
9. Williams Haynes (1946). *Southern Horizons*, New York, Van Nostrand, 254.
10. Joseph Borkin (1978). *The Crime and Punishment of I.G. Farben*, New York, Free Press, 51.
11. Frank A. Howard (1947). *Buna Rubber, The Birth of an Industry*, New York, Van Nostrand, 249-251.
12. Carleton Ellis (1937). *The Chemistry of Petroleum Derivatives*, New York, Reinhold.
13. Charles S. Popple (1952). *Standard Oil Company (New Jersey) in World War II*, New York, Standard Oil.

14. W. J. Reader (1970 and 1975). *Imperial Chemical Industries, A History,* London, Oxford University Press, Vol. II.

15. R. A. Reinke and T. A. Ruble (1950). Oil black, *Modern Chemical Processes,* Volume III, New York, Industrial and Engineering Chemistry, 44ff.

16. Williams Haynes (1954). *American Chemical Industry, A History,* Vol. 5., *Decade of New Products, 1930–39,* New York, Van Nostrand.

17. R. L. Kenyon et al. (1950). Amyl compounds from pentane, *Modern Chemical Processes,* Volume II, New York, Industrial and Engineering Chemistry, 19ff.

18. Carol Kennedy (1986). *ICI; The Company that Changed Our Lives,* London, Century Hutchinson, 16.

19. B. G. Achilladelis (1973). Process innovation in the chemical industry, Ph.D. thesis, England, University of Sussex, England (made available through the courtesy of the Center of History of Chemistry, University of Pennsylvania, Philadelphia, PA).

ADDITIONAL READING

American Chemical Society (1977). *A Brief History of Chemistry In the Kanawha Valley,* Washington, DC, American Chemical Society.

Campbell, Murray, and Halton, Harrison (1951). *Herbert H. Dow, Pioneer in Creative Chemistry,* New York, Appleton-Century-Crofts.

Forrestal, D. J. (1977). *Faith, Hope and $5,000, The Story of Monsanto,* New York, Simon & Schuster.

Green, A. Donald (1977). *An Engineer Putting Chemistry to Work,* Personal Memoirs, Standard Oil of New Jersey.

Larson, Henrietta M. et al. (1971). *History of Standard Oil Company (N.J.) New Horizons 1927–1950,* New York, Harper & Row.

Robert, Joseph C. (1983). *Ethyl: A History of the Corporation and the People Who Made It,* Charlottesville, University Press of Virginia.

Whitehead, Don (1968). *The Dow Story: The History of Dow Chemical Company,* New York, McGraw-Hill.

Union Carbide Corporation (1937). *A Marketing Revolution, Early Sales Efforts of Union Carbide Chemicals Company.*

3 / Cat Crackers: Wartime Fuels and Petrochemical Raw Materials

It seems remarkable to many people now in the industry that, for such a long time, there was so little interest in ethylene, propylene, and the other lower olefins. Then, over a period of only a few years, these unsaturated hydrocarbons became the most important class of chemical raw materials, with ethylene the primary petrochemical building block. Wartime needs turned out to be a major factor in that ethylene, propylene, and all the butylenes played an indispensable role in the production of fuel and chemical products needed for the war effort. Then, when the war was over, these building blocks were in place—ready to be converted to the various derivatives that would be used to produce an array of newly developed consumer products.

The main reason for the rapid ascendancy of olefins as raw materials was actually a combination of two factors. First, the rapidly growing amounts of olefins present in the offgases from refinery processes made it feasible to think in a more sanguine fashion about the utilization of these materials. Second, advances in plastics and synthetic rubber production technology created a large demand for various lower olefins (and diolefins) and these feedstocks were now no longer needed for producing war materials. For ethylene, the key turning points were the development of thermoplastics (polyvinyl chloride, polyethylene), synthetic rubber (styrene), and the greatly expanded demand for antifreeze (ethylene glycol) and, soon thereafter, polyester fibers. For propylene, it was not only the need for motor and aviation gasoline blending stocks for wartime and civilian demands (polymer, cumene, propylene alkylate), but also the growing interest in such propylene-based chemicals as isopropyl alcohol, phenol, acetone, and tetramer for the manufacture of detergents.

Butylenes quickly became indispensable for making high octane blending stocks and for the production of synthetic rubber. The first spurt in butylenes demand thus took place over a period of roughly eight years (i.e., from 1936 to 1944), by which time the Allies no longer worried about supplies of gasoline and synthetic rubber, now amply available for the final stages of the conflict. The second phase started when the war was over and these materials went into the peacetime economy.

The abundant presence of lower olefins in refinery streams in the late 1930s and particularly by the early 1940s was directly tied to the increasing complexity of refinery operations. In the early days of the petroleum industry, primitive stills and dephlegmators basically separated the crude oil into fractions that were roughly proportional to the composition of the oil. Thus, light crudes were used primarily to make gasoline and very heavy crudes to make asphalt and, later, fuel oil. The demand for petroleum products, including kerosene, solvents, and lube oils, was, of course, not necessarily proportional to the amounts readily recovered via simple distillation from the various crude oils. However, techniques were not yet available to modify the yields of the different fractions that made up the crude oil. The only alternative available to refiners, therefore, was to purchase and run crudes that had the proper characteristics for the products they wanted to make.

In the 1920s, "cracking" processes were invented to increase the proportion of lighter materials (primarily gasoline) that could be produced from a given crude oil. These thermal cracking stills were operated at high temperatures and frequently also at elevated pressures. Under these conditions, cracking (i.e., molecular weight reduction) occurred to a varying degree, depending on the specific processing conditions employed. Substantial amounts of additional naphtha in the gasoline boiling range were formed, but the "thermal" gasoline was highly olefinic and required heavy treatment to reduce its tendency to form gums (polymers) in the car engine. Olefinic hydrocarbons were formed in various molecular weight ranges, from partly unsaturated naphthas down to the lower olefins, which formed when smaller hydrocarbon fragments broke off from the larger molecules. A typical offgas stream from a thermal cracker operating at 500 psig and 860°F in the mid-1920s would contain 15-25 percent ethylene, 10-20 percent propylene, and 4-8 percent butylenes. The total gas stream constituted about 6 percent of the feed charged to the cracker.

During the time when thermal cracking was essentially the only means to modify the product distribution obtained from crudes, a period that lasted from 1920 to just before the beginning of World War II, the demand for the lower olefins was very limited, so that little recovery of these materials took place. Also, commercial recovery techniques for olefins were simplistic, consisting of relatively inefficient absorption systems. The use of refrigeration for this purpose started in the 1930s, allowing recovery of larger quantities of these olefins.

A new approach to processing crude oil fractions—called catalytic cracking—then began to take over, with "cat crackers" going into operation in a number of refineries just as the war began. The advent of catalytic cracking was most fortuitous for the United States, since it coincided with a time when Hitler had already marched into the Rhineland (1936) and Japan was starting to plan its aggressive expansion into the Pacific Basin. Commercialization of catalytic cracking, a far more sophisticated process than thermal cracking, provided much larger amounts of olefins, which would soon be desperately required for the war effort, although this fact was not yet appreciated. Catalytic cracking has to this day remained the most important source of butylenes and a very major source of propylene. Ethylene, also available in cat cracker offgases, as well as the propylene and butylenes, were recovered from this source during the war but, in the case of ethylene, for only a short time thereafter. This is because thermal cracking in the presence of steam and at very low furnace residence times, a technology called "steam cracking" that, in effect, evolved from the work carried out by Union Carbide and Linde at Tonawanda, New York, in the early 1920s, became the dominant source of ethylene. In the meantime, major improvements in the recovery and purification sections through the use of more sophisticated, lower temperature refrigerated absorption systems made ethylene production a more elegant and efficient process.

It is interesting now to look back on how the olefin supply situation evolved over the years:

Source	Olefins Produced	Time Period
Coke-oven operations	Ethylene	18th century to World War II
Thermal cracking (petroleum fractions)	Ethylene, propylene, butylenes	1920s to World War II
Ethanol dehydration	Ethylene	1910s to World War II
Catalytic cracking (petroleum fractions)	Ethylene, propylene, butylenes	1939 to present (propylene, butylenes)
Steam cracking (natural gas and petroleum fractions)	Ethylene, propylene, butylenes	1930s to present

The history of ethylene production and recovery from various carbon-bearing raw materials thus spans the full range of fossil energy sources, from coal to petroleum and natural gas. Significantly, it also largely coincides with the development of chemical engineering as a major discipline. This branch of engineering became an important industrial technology considerably later than such other engineering sciences as civil, mechanical, and electrical engineering and was, in fact, largely pioneered in the United States at a time when other industrial countries still divided chemical engineering functions between chemists and mechanical or civil engineers. Chemical engineers developed many of the so-called unit operations* skills and equipment in the years before World War II, with much of the emphasis on the processing and conversion of hydrocarbon fractions—that is, as part of refinery operations. Partly for that reason, the development of fixed- and fluid-bed catalytic cracking technology is covered in some detail in this chapter. Unit operations that were developed during

---

*This term is employed to cover various physical transformations carried out in refineries and chemical plants, (e.g., distillation, absorption, centrifugation, drying, heat exchange, etc.)

the war included, among others, superfractionation, complex heat transfer systems, design of large fixed and fluid bed reaction systems, dense phase solids transport, and continuous (versus previous batch) systems for many types of reactions. These techniques comprise much of what would be considered the essence of chemical engineering practice. They were developed or sharpened to a great extent in the laboratories of several major universities and in company research laboratories and pilot plants. Taken as a whole, they became a new form of applied science that gave American companies, for a period of time, a major advantage in the design and operation of large-scale plants for the production of a number of important hydrocarbons and chemicals. Schools such as the Massachusetts Institute of Technology (M.I.T.), California Institute of Technology and a number of other major universities (e.g., Wisconsin, Minnesota, Delaware, Purdue, Texas, and Cornell) became known for the excellence of their chemical engineering departments and contributed large numbers of graduates to the oil and chemical companies and to the engineering contractors involved in petrochemical projects during and after the war.

GETTING READY FOR WAR

Initially, the production of olefins was not at the top of any priority list prepared by government and industry leaders readying the nation for conflict. The first critical need was to increase the production of 100-octane aviation gasoline, and this resulted in a variety of estimates and surveys made by the Council of National Defense and the Petroleum Industry War Council. Dr. Robert E. Wilson of Standard Oil of Indiana, who headed up the petroleum products section of the former, first estimated high octane aviation gasoline requirements at 71,300 barrels per day, versus a projection less than half as large made by the Armed Services Joint Aeronautical Board. When President Franklin Roosevelt in 1940 announced a goal of 50,000 war planes, Wilson upped his estimate to 190,000 barrels per day. After the nation entered the war, Harold Ickes, former Interior Secretary and more recently appointed petroleum coordinator, then increased the government estimate still further. Even this projection eventually proved to amount to less than half of the 600,000 barrels per day of high octane gasoline the nation would need before the end of hostilities (1).

The really critical period occurred in early 1942, when aviation gasoline supplies were seen to be woefully inadequate. As a first step, small operating changes were effected in most refineries, resulting in raising the 40,000 barrels per day of 100-octane gasoline then being produced by a paltry but still important 6,000 barrels per day. A further step was an increase in tetraethyl lead (TEL) addition from 3 to a new figure of 4 cc per liter, which allowed a production increase of another 10,000 barrels per day. Even greater amounts of lead additive were proposed, but the Air Force decided that this would lead to excessive spark plug fouling on long missions and so this stratagem was wisely dropped. It was around this time that the concept of "octane-barrels" started being used. This relates to the fact that TEL and octane blending components such as toluene are evaluated in terms of how many barrels of gasoline can be raised to what octane number with a given amount of blending component or additive.

A review conducted at that time indicated that the new catalytically cracked gasoline base stocks then starting to be produced in some quantities by Sun Oil Company and Socony Vacuum Company in the so-called Houdry units were excellent for the production of 100-octane aviation fuels. Using these "cat-cracked" naphthas, it was possible to make specification fuel while substantially reducing the amount of high octane alkylate blended into the mixture. Release of these alkylate streams to blend more lower octane naphthas up to gasoline quality added another 15 percent to the nation's supplies in early 1942.

Recognition of the potential of refinery cat crackers to supply both high octane cat naphthas and lower olefins for additional alkylate and polymer gasoline production then led the War Production Board to call for the construction of a number of additional units of this kind. Here was a new refinery process that could transform middle distillates and gas oils, which were of considerably less importance to the war effort, into large amounts of high octane gasoline. The age of catalytic cracking was now at hand.

At this writing, when fluid bed catalytic cracking is essentially the only cat-cracking process used by refineries around the world, it is easy to forget that the fixed bed catalytic process invented by Eugene Houdry (and not the fluid bed process) was the real breakthrough in petroleum refining, although developers of the fluid bed process might disagree. Although fluid bed technology eventually became the dominant process, the Houdry crackers not only demonstrated the principle of catalytic cracking and catalyst regeneration but resulted in the construction of a large number of units by 1941—two years or so before fluid bed crackers were placed in service. Houdry crackers were necessarily physically limited in size because of valve switching and heat transfer problems at high temperatures, but these units contributed very substantially throughout the war and for many years thereafter to the production of fuels and petrochemicals. By 1939, 15 Houdry units were already in operation, with a combined capacity of 212,000 barrels per day. This increased to 24 units by 1944, aggregating 330,000 barrels per day. The first fluid bed cracker came on stream only in May 1942 in Baton Rouge, Louisiana. A third cracking process, the Thermofor moving bed cracker was commercialized in 1943, but it never became important. By the end of the war, total installed U.S. cat cracking capacity was over 900,000 barrels per day.

The fixed-bed Houdry process gave once-through weight yields of 25–40 percent of 400°F end-point gasoline, depending on the quality of the gas oil feedstock. Not only were these yields higher than those obtained from thermal cracking, but the gasoline had an unleaded motor octane in the range of 78–80 and only required mild sulfuric acid treating before blending into aviation gasoline. The high octane number was attributed largely to extensive lower paraffin branching, since the percentage of aromatics in the gasoline was low.* In addition to gasoline, gas oil, and some coke, the process also made 4–6 percent by weight of cracked gases typically containing 16 percent hydrogen, 18 percent methane, 5 percent ethylene, 5 percent ethane, 22 percent propylene, 5 percent propane, 21 percent normal-and isobutylenes, and 8 percent other compounds. The total quantity of lower olefins amounted to about three percent of the feedstock charged to the cat cracker, or of the order of 40 million pounds per year for a cat unit with a fresh feed rate of 15,000 barrels per day. This was a far from insignificant amount of olefins from the perspective of a chemicals manufacturer looking for feedstocks.

---

*Branched paraffins (i.e., paraffin with side chains) and aromatics are more stable than unbranched paraffins under the high temperature and pressure conditions in the engine cylinder during the compression stroke. They therefore have less tendency to spontaneously ignite, which causes the engine to knock or "ping."

The Houdry reactor was designed with feed/product heat exchangers and a preheat furnace, to bring the charge up to 800°F. Catalyst was contained in three parallel reaction vessels operating at 30 psig, with a diameter of 10 feet 7 inches and a height of 38 feet. A mixture of molten salts was used inside the reactor tubes to control the temperature during reaction and regeneration. The automatically controlled cycle was 10 minutes for reaction, 10 minutes for regeneration, and 5 minutes (each) turnaround time between the two types of operation. The regenerator offgases, containing carbon monoxide formed from regeneration air and from the carbon burned off the catalyst, were passed through a combustion chamber, again containing tubes with molten salt circulation. Steam was then produced by circulating the salt mixture through an external boiler (2).

The installed cost of a 15,000 barrel per day plant in 1938 was slightly under $3 million. This plant represented the culmination of the work of one of the most remarkable inventors in the annals of petroleum refining—Eugene Houdry, a man who was neither a chemist nor a chemical engineer by training.

DEVELOPMENT OF FIXED-BED CATALYTIC CRACKING

Eugene J. Houdry was born near Paris in 1892, the son of a family engaged in the metals fabrication business. He graduated with a mechanical engineering degree in 1911, receiving high honors and a gold medal as well as being first in his class. Following graduation, he joined his father's company, but soon enrolled in the Army, where he became a lieutenant in the Tank Corps. He was seriously wounded in 1917, receiving the *Croix de Guerre* and membership in the *Legion d'Honneur* for extraordinary heroism in battle. At the end of the war, he returned to the family business.

Houdry soon developed an extraordinary interest in the automobile and particularly in car engines. Through an interest in car racing, he became aware of the limitations of engine performance, due to the knocking tendency of most available fuels. Visiting the Ford Motor Company in Detroit, as well as attending the Memorial Day Indianapolis 500 race, he recognized the need for more efficient high performance motor fuels. His wartime experiences had also left a deep impression on him regarding the need to produce efficient liquid fuels in countries like France, which did not have adequate amounts of indigenous petroleum resources. Recognizing that France had large lignite* deposits, Houdry decided to make a change in his career and to concentrate on the production of synthetic liquid fuels from lignite. It is not known whether Houdry was aware of Bergius' and other scientists' work in Germany on coal hydrogenation to produce liquid fuels. In any case, he decided to work on pyrolysis† rather than on hydrogenation.

Joining with a group of friends, Houdry in 1922 formed a company to develop technology to convert lignite to synthetic fuels. At that time, a biologist in Nice had disclosed some laboratory results on a process that we would now call a mild pyrolysis, followed by hydrotreating, to form a stable gasoline. Neither the chemist nor Houdry and his group really understood the principles involved in that operation, but the results looked promising. They decided to finance, and later to take over the research work and to build a larger unit near Paris. This installation came on stream in 1923 (3).

Over the next seven years, a great deal was accomplished. One of the most important things Houdry learned was that catalysts containing silica-alumina, with relatively little metal content, were useful in cracking to gasoline the residual tars formed in the pyrolysis. In a real sense, this was the origin of catalytic cracking of heavier oil fractions to make lighter products. He also began to understand catalyst activity and the need and procedure for catalyst regeneration. Accordingly, he became knowledgeable in the preparation of certain types of catalysts and also learned much about the principles of heat transfer.

Nevertheless, Houdry's results on lignite remained unsatisfactory from a commercial standpoint. In the late 1920s, Houdry therefore decided to discontinue work on lignite, since he recognized that his work on the catalytic cracking of heavy liquid tars showed far more promise, at least as far as production of a quality motor fuel was concerned. He now turned his attention to heavy petroleum feedstocks, to be fed to a "catalytic cracking" process, using Venezuelan gas oil as a model hydrocarbon. After a number of experiments with different catalysts, he settled on an acid-activated clay supplied by Pechelbronn Oil Refining Company in San Diego.

*Low grade coal.
†High temperature decomposition (cracking).

By 1930, Houdry had visualized the use of a fixed-bed heat exchanger type reactor for a commercial process, with a bed containing a clay catalyst consisting of 80 percent silica and 20 percent alumina. The regeneration cycle would need temperature control, but water could be circulated through tubes in the reactor during that cycle. The results of the catalytic cracking step were now also becoming much better. Perhaps most importantly, road tests showed the gasoline produced in the cracking step to have good properties as a motor fuel. Houdry was ready to go to the next step, a pilot plant program.

By this time, the large oil companies had become aware of Houdry's experiments. Among the refining companies who reviewed his results and the 50 or more patents that had been filed to cover the development work, the most interested was Vacuum Oil Company (later, Socony Vacuum and still later Mobil Oil Company). Company officials and Houdry agreed to conduct a test at Mobil's Paulsboro, New Jersey, refinery, which proved to be very successful. The Houdry Process Company was founded in 1931, with share participation by Eugene Houdry and by the sponsoring oil company. Between 1931 and 1933, a 200-barrel per day pilot unit was operated in Paulsboro.

The Great Depression caused Socony Vacuum to discontinue its support in 1933. However, Sun Oil Company officials in Philadelphia, who had been following the work due to their proximity to the Paulsboro refinery, decided to sponsor continued development. Sun then also took share participation in the Houdry Process Company. From 1933 to 1937, an improved pilot plant was operated at Sun Oil's Marcus Hook, Delaware, refinery. Much of this work centered on mechanical aspects of the process, including construction materials, vessel internals, and so on. Houdry and Sun also turned to other clay manufacturers, such as the Filtrol Company, to provide samples for further catalyst evaluation.

A review of the state of hydrocarbon cracking technology with and without catalysts, published by Carleton Ellis* in 1937, gives a good picture of what petroleum technologists knew at that time. Due to the large crude oil deposits near the Caspian Sea, Russian scientists had probably done more work than investigators

---

*Ellis, one of the foremost petroleum chemists of his time, published numerous patents and wrote the definitive book on the chemistry of petroleum derivatives. For many years, he was a distinguished professor at Penn State University.

in other countries on petroleum conversion processes using catalysts. Many of their results were available in the published literature. Thus, Russian petroleum chemists had investigated such catalysts as zinc and nickel oxide, alumina, uranyl oxide, titanium dioxide, activated carbon, glass chips, and fused borax to crack gas oils, kerosenes, and various hydrocarbons at temperatures in the range of 300–750°C. Researchers in the United States had investigated ammonium vanadate, silica gels, aluminum and iron chlorides, spent clays, and various other catalytic agents. Most of the difficulties encountered by all of these researchers involved extensive coke laydown on the catalyst during the reaction (4).

Researchers in other companies in the United States were also conducting work on catalytic cracking. While they obtained less tangible results and were therefore not as close to a commercial design as Houdry, the research work done by these investigators greatly augmented the understanding of the mechanisms taking place in cracking hydrocarbons over acid catalysts. Thus, at Universal Oil Products Company (UOP), a considerable amount of prior knowledge had been accumulated regarding the use of natural clays to stabilize gasoline-range naphthas produced in thermal cracking operations. UOP scientists decided to study the use of such clays for the catalytic cracking of gas oils. Experimenting with clays, again supplied by Filtrol Corporation as well as other vendors, the group surmised that for best performance as catalysts, these materials should be "opened up," namely that pores could be created by heating such clays with lime and calcium chloride, followed by acid leaching. Synthetic zeolites, which have such pores or "cages," were already known for their use in trapping impurities in water treatment systems. Now, using pure hydrocarbons as feedstocks, the UOP researchers also concluded that silica-alumina must be a high temperature acid, which promotes the cracking reaction. With this background on pore structure and by further experimentation, the UOP researchers learned to make active cracking catalysts by exchanging the sodium ions of amorphous sodium alumina-silicates with other cations. [A couple of decades later, this work led to the development of cation-exchanged Y-zeolites] (5).

What puzzled researchers at the time was this: How can silica-alumina be an acid? Eventually, it was surmised, using Pauling's rules, that the electron deficiency in the four oxygen atoms attached to the aluminum could be associated with a hydrogen ion to form a so-called protonic or Bronsted acid. Under high temperature conditions, this could then also lead to a so-called Lewis acid. The sodium ions had to be removed and replaced with hydrogen, in order to create acidity. A cracking process taking place over such a catalyst became known as a "carbonium ion" reaction.

A carbonium ion can only be made with an acid catalyst, which can donate protons or accept electron pairs. Such materials include various mineral acids, Friedel Crafts catalysts, porous solids impregnated with acids (such as Kieselguhr), and treated clays of certain structures, all of which have Bronsted acidity. Acid-catalyzed hydrocarbon reactions could be used to explain not only catalytic cracking, but also polymerization, alkylation, and isomerization, as the scientists at UOP and other researchers determined in the mid-1930s. In catalytic cracking, olefins are formed by thermal cracking and these are partly converted to carbonium ions, which remove hydride ions from paraffins, causing further cracking. A chain reaction proceeds as the paraffins are split. The formation of olefins also occurs with dehydrogenation by traces of oxygen and by reaction with carbon on the catalyst.

While great progress was, in fact, being made in understanding the theory of catalytic cracking, Houdry, who probably never understood (or necessarily needed to understand) the theory of catalytic cracking, concentrated on equipment development and on scale-up design, having identified a catalyst that would give the desired results and having finally settled on a commercial process scheme (6). In 1936, Socony Vacuum, which by then was again funding development work, decided to build a 2000 barrel per day semicommercial Houdry unit at Paulsboro, which went on stream that year. Based on the results obtained in this plant, Socony and Sun Oil both decided on full-scale commercialization. The first plant came on stream at Sun Oil's Marcus Hook refinery in 1937, with a fresh feed rate of 15,000 barrels per day. Shortly thereafter, Sun Oil introduced "Nu-Blue" Sunoco gasoline as "the new miracle of gasoline chemistry," made by the Houdry process.

The new process was announced with much fanfare at an American Petroleum Institute meeting in Chicago in November 1938. The presentation was made by Arthur Pew, a founding father of Sun Oil Company, in a paper coauthored by Eugene Houdry and representatives of Sun Oil, Socony and Badger (an engineering firm), the companies that had contributed so much to the success of the process.

Alex Oblad, not long ago retired from the Houdry Process Company, listed among the major accomplishments of Eugene Houdry the following:

- First successful catalytic cracking process.
- First large-scale catalytic process to use air regeneration.
- First commercial production of cracking catalyst from naturally occurring clays.
- First commercial production and use of synthetic silica-alumina catalyst (3).

THE NEXT TECHNOLOGY: CAT CRACKING

Not all the companies watching the successful development of the Houdry cracking process in the late 1930s joined the parade of firms lining up for licenses. Standard of New Jersey, in particular, was one of the companies whose senior management and scientists were not convinced that Houdry's approach, involving short repetitive cycles of reaction and regeneration, was the way to carry out a cracking reaction (i.e., a process which deactivated the catalyst over such a short period of time). Moreover, the licensing fees for a Houdry cracker, the most important process breakthrough the petroleum industry had seen since the advent of thermal cracking stills, were quite high. Jersey and some of the other Standard Oil Companies did engage in negotiations for a worldwide license for the Houdry process (at reduced fees), but were unsuccessful. Most likely, the Jersey management was not surprised or particularly dismayed by this development. The high license fee they would have to pay for each Houdry unit, multiplied by the large number of refineries in the worldwide Jersey system, provided a tremendous incentive to step up the company's research work on an entirely different approach.

The problem could be stated as follows: What is the best way to conduct a process that results in laying down carbon on a catalyst, causing it to deactivate rapidly and to need regeneration and where the heat generated by burning the coke off the catalyst could be used to preheat and vaporize the feed to the reactor? In the Houdry process, this was done with multiple vessels filled with catalyst, which were switched back and forth to serve successively as reactor or regenerator, with much opening and closing of valves—basically an inelegant way to carry out such a reaction, the Jersey engineers thought. Why not have just two large vessels, one a reactor and the other a regenerator, and circulate the catalyst between them? But how do you do that, when calculations showed that the amount of catalyst that had to move back and forth between the vessels would be measured in terms of many thousands of tons per day. Conveyor-type approaches were considered (and were actually later commercialized by Mobil and others in so-called moving bed systems called Thermofor units). However, Jersey's researchers felt the best system would use a technique that was more like the airlift systems used to unload grain elevators, that is through the use of a motive gas to transport the small solids particles. But it quickly became apparent that this approach could not work in this manner. First, the amount of gases that would be needed to make such a system work was far greater than the quantity of reactor vapors or regeneration air calculated to be available. Moreover, there would be grave dangers inherent in such a process. Any flow reversals causing regeneration air to backflow into the reactor would certainly lead to explosions, involving massive amounts of flammable hydrocarbons. What was needed was a system where catalyst could be circulated rapidly between the vessels in a "dense phase," requiring relatively small amounts of motive gas, and forming a seal that would prevent such flow reversals.

A study of known commercial techniques for solids movement showed only that Fritz Winkler had, in 1921, developed a system of keeping fine coal particles in suspension in a new type of gasifier, which some called a "fluidized bed" (see Fig. 3.1). However, Winkler's approach was wholly inapplicable to the requirements of a system that would have to move many tons of catalyst a minute between two vessels (7).*

The next problem: How do you get fine catalyst particles and a small amount of gas to "flow as a liquid"? It seemed like an impossible task. The 100 barrels per day (BPD) pilot plant that had been built at the Esso Laboratories in Baton Rouge, Louisiana, to study the fixed-bed approach had already been modified several times. Then, a further switch was made to a powdered catalyst

---

*Imperial Oil R & D suggested consideration of a tubular cracking process they called "Suspensoid Cracking" but this was also considered impractical (Dr. J. F. Mathis, Personal Communication).

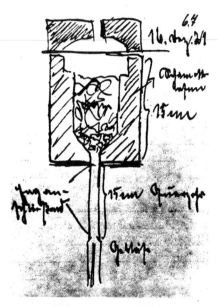

Figure 3.1 Winkler fluidized-bed process. (*Source:* K. Schoenemann, Chemical engineering in Germany, In *History of Chemical Engineering,* William F. Furter, ed., Advances in Chemistry Series 190, American Chemical Society, Washington, DC, 1980, p. 257, with permission.)

and when it was recognized that a conventional airlift system would not work, a Fuller-Kenyon screw pump was provided to transfer the catalyst between the vessels. This approach was also soon dismissed (due to problems with catalyst deactivation and rapid erosion of the pump) leaving the developers groping for other means to circulate the catalyst. Stymied in its quest, Jersey turned the problem over to the man who had become the company's most important academic consultant, Dr. Warren K. Lewis at the Massachusetts Institute of Technology (M.I.T.).

The relationship of this outstanding engineering school with oil companies (notably Jersey and Indiana Standard) had been firmly established in the 1920s, when the development of thermal cracking technology called for new approaches in chemical engineering calculations and design, causing companies to turn to universities with departments able to provide the required technical assistance. As the first school to recognize chemical engineering as a separate discipline, M.I.T. had appointed William H. Walker in 1908 to head up this new teaching area. Walker and Arthur D. Little, who had graduated from M.I.T. in 1885, had also formed a consulting firm, which later became the firm still operating under the name of Arthur D. Little, Inc. Little and Walker, in the early days of chemical engineering at M.I.T., had developed four concepts that formed the foundation for a soon-to-be-established department: (*1*) the grouping together of a number of individual steps common to many industrial processes (e.g., crushing, grinding, extraction, distillation, heat transfer, drying, etc.), and terming them "unit operations," which could be studied as such, regardless of the industry where they were employed, (*2*) formation of a research laboratory of applied chemistry, (*3*) establishment of a school of chemical engineering practice, where students could, under the guidance of M.I.T. professors, study actual plant operating conditions and problems, and (*4*) use of a case study method for solving chemical engineering problems. Chemical engineering became a part of the M.I.T. Chemistry Department in 1912, and a separate department in 1920. More than anything else, the Chemical Engineering Department at M.I.T. provided some of the most important contributions in the transition from batch processing, used largely at that time, to continuous, automated processing. It was also a center for the development of calculation techniques and design parameters for distillation and absorption towers (8).

Lewis entered M.I.T. in 1901 and received an undergraduate degree, after which he studied in Breslau, Germany, returning to M.I.T. to obtain his doctorate degree in 1908. He then joined the faculty and became the first head of the Chemical Engineering Department, when it was finally established as a separate entity. The first edition of a seminal textbook entitled *Principles of Chemical Engineering,* by Walker, Lewis, and McAdams, the latter a leading expert in heat transfer technology, was published in 1923. In 1929, Lewis resigned as department head to devote full time to teaching, thesis supervision and consulting work. By that time, he had become a legendary figure, due to his explosive, overbearing personality and his unusual teaching methods, which had similarities to the alleged Harvard Law School instruction methods immortalized in the film "The Paper Chase".

When in undergraduate school at M.I.T. in the late 1940s, I had "Doc" Lewis as a professor in industrial chemistry and in his class I found out firsthand how he could reduce students to make illogical, irrational statements once an incorrect premise had been identified.

At the end of a series of progressively more absurd or, in any case, incorrect assertions on my part, he proved to the rest of class that if my contentions were correct, you could get cellulose fibers to coalesce into a single homogeneous mass just by squeezing them together. This was obviously ridiculous, as I admitted, with great embarrassment. In spite of such incidents, Lewis was beloved by his students (including myself) and eventually was always able to get the best out of them. He also had the unusual ability "to wring information from a few facts and a relatively simple model. Repeatedly, by using only material and energy balances, he was able to develop unexpected relationships" (9). He taught his students to be clear and concise in their communications as engineers, particularly when addressing non-technical people. I specifically remember him advising his students to "throw the fodder where the calves can get at it."

Lewis had developed close contacts with Standard Oil of New Jersey. One of his assistant professors, Robert P. Russell, had originally been selected to head up Jersey's Baton Rouge laboratories. Later, Robert T. Haslam, an early director of the M.I.T. Practice School, had become manager of Standard Oil Development Company. A number of M.I.T. graduates had gone to work for Jersey and there was a steady flow of professors and executives back and forth between Jersey and Indiana Standard, on the industry side, and M.I.T. During the 1920s and 1930s, M.I.T. professors had made substantial contributions to the development of design techniques for hydrocarbon cracking, recovery, and separations, including (1) Professor Weber's and Professor Meissner's work on establishing the so-called MU charts, which defined the behavior of gases near their critical temperatures and pressures, (2) Professor Hottel's work on furnace cracking coil design principles, and (3) studies by Lewis and others on particle transfer and settling characteristics.

Confronted with the problem of developing a fluidized bed process, Lewis and another eminent M.I.T. professor, Dr. Edwin R. Gilliland, consulted with the Jersey engineers to develop an understanding of the needs for a circulating catalyst system. Basically, the issue was this: regardless of the configuration of the commercial plant, that is, the relative positions of the reactor and regenerator vessels in the structure, the catalyst had to travel in both an "upflow" and "downflow" mode in at least one of the transfers between the two vessels. But whatever knowledge existed on particle settling velocities in this kind of system, the inevitable conclusion seemed to be that the catalyst concentration in the upflow section would be much higher than in the downflow section. Also, how could a "dense bed" in the reactor and regenerator contain enough catalyst—relative to the amount of reaction vapors and regeneration air, respectively—to assure adequate contact time for the required reaction?

Lewis and Gilliland put the problem on their list of thesis topics and soon had several of their brightest graduate students at work. This included one of my fraternity brothers, Warren Fuchs, and I was fortunate to hear about some of the details of this work from him. Largely under Lewis' direction, the students delved into the applicability of Stokes' law* on the settling of catalyst particles moving in a "dense bed." This was new territory, but fortunately the work progressed rapidly once the problem had been properly defined. Within a few months, experiments showed that a stable dense bed could be maintained at velocities substantially higher than the so-called Stokes free fall velocities of individual particles: gas velocities of 1–3 ft/sec could be used, versus a calculated Stokes free fall velocity of 0.1 ft/sec or less for the smallest particle in the powder mixture (10).

In parallel work at M.I.T. and Esso Laboratories in Baton Rouge, the concept of a fluid bed "standpipe" was also studied. A dense column of aerated solids could be made to act just like a liquid at very low gas velocities. The column would then build up a hydrostatic head proportional to the length of the standpipe. This is how one would be able to pressure balance the system, as well as provide the necessary seal to prevent backflow between the vessels.

The work started to look so promising that the 100 BPD pilot plant was rebuilt to incorporate a fluid bed circulating system, as well as reactor and regenerator vessels that could operate in the dense phase. The work at M.I.T. had started in late 1939, and a year later the pilot plant was already in operation. Spurred not only by commercial considerations, but by the near certainty of an impending war that would require major increases in gasoline production by the petroleum industry, Jersey's engineers immediately started on the design of three 12,000 BPD fluid cat crackers, using the data now finally starting to be developed with petroleum feed-

---

*Stokes' law covers the behavior of liquid or solid particles in motion relative to a surrounding fluid (11).

stocks in the revamped Baton Rouge pilot plant. Still, there was a considerable amount of management skepticism whether the system would work—not only to transport 50–100 tons per minute of catalyst—an incredible achievement in itself—but that it would also be safe. To confirm this, a standpipe 100 feet high was built at Baton Rouge by filling a spare fractionating column with catalyst and aerating it. Pressure gauges at the bottom confirmed the buildup in static head* and, when a valve was opened at the bottom, catalyst ran out, as if it were a liquid! The company now knew that the concept would work and went into a crash program to design and construct the first fluid bed cat cracking units.

Fluid cracking, perhaps the most important process refineries would ever use, therefore represented a major achievement for Esso Laboratories, which had succeeded in transforming the theoretical work and laboratory-scale experiments performed at M.I.T. into a commercial process. The two fundamental contributions made by Esso laboratories were (1) the demonstration of a stable fluid dense bed at relatively low velocities, which provided the basis for the successful reactor and regenerator designs, and (2) the standpipe-riser and slide valve concepts that provided the means to circulate large quantities of solids safely between two vessels.

The Jersey executive who had been in charge of overall development of fluid cat cracking technology was a man who would eventually become the president of Standard Oil Development Company, Eger V. Murphree. Murphree had, at one time, been a development engineer at Allied Chemical's synthetic soda ash plant in Syracuse, New York, where he had supervised a number of improvements in the solids handling aspects of this Solvay process plant. He had also collected a strong group of chemical engineers, including Bob Carrier, Osgood Tracy, and Don Green. When Jersey signed the JASCO agreements with I.G. Farben, the company recruited Murphree, who brought his group of outstanding engineers along to Standard Oil's new laboratories in Baton Rouge. Carrier, Tracy, and Green became involved in most of the important chemical projects of Jersey over the next 20 years, including the development of technology for the production of ethylene, ethyl chloride, the arc process for acetylene, hydrogenation, butyl rubber, and butadiene extraction. Murphree, who had studied the possible use of a fluidized approach to convert sodium bicar-

---

*A measure of pressure buildup as a function of liquid depth.

bonate to soda ash, had the right background to think about applying this principle to the catalytic cracking of hydrocarbon fractions (12). Working with Homer Z. Martin, Donald L. Campbell, and C. Wesley Tyson, Murphree led the development of the new process through its various stages. This group eventually became known as the "Four Horsemen" of S.O.D. An outstanding scientist, engineer and administrator, Murphree also became involved in the design of uranium isotope separation plants for the Manhattan Project, shortly after the United States entered the war.

The first fluid cat cracker started up at the Baton Rouge refinery in May 1942. Many other equipment problems had been successfully addressed, including the design of large slide valves to provide shutoff between the vessels, the development of appropriate huge cyclones to prevent excessive catalyst loss from both vessels, and other necessary innovations. After starting up the first "downflow" units, with the reactor placed well below the regenerator (Fig. 3.2), successive design modifications by Jersey and other companies (e.g., Indiana, Kellogg, UOP) progressively improved the configuration of fluid cat crackers, leading to modern designs (see Fig. 3.3). Many catalyst improvements were also made over time, going from the original natural clays to synthetic silica-alumina materials.

Most cat crackers built during the war had feed rates of 10,000–15,000 barrels per day. They produced about 2500 barrels per day of components for alkylate, 2500 barrels of aviation base stock, and 6500 barrels of residual gasoline and heavier products. Together with downstream processing plants (e.g., alkylation, isomerization, vapor recovery, and auxiliary equipment), these units cost about $18 million.

The fluid cat cracking process, which owed a great debt to Eugene Houdry, soon became the dominant technique to crack heavy petroleum fractions to gasoline and light olefins. It was successively modified and improved, leading eventually to the Model IV cat plant design, on which I worked at Bayway, New Jersey, in the early 1950s. Since then, fluid bed technology has also been applied to a number of other processes, with varying degrees of success.

In the petroleum industry, fluid coking, developed in the 1950s by Jersey, and a process on which I hold several patents, was the only other important successful application. Chemical industry uses of fluid bed technology include the production of phthalic

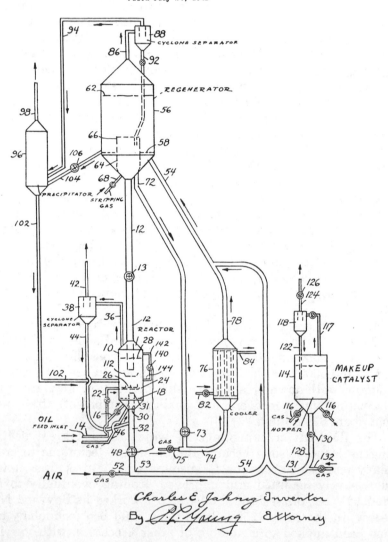

Charles E Jahnig Inventor
By P.L. Young   Attorney

Figure 3.2 Early downflow design. (*Source:* C. E. Jahnig, et al., The development of fluid catalytic cracking, *Heterogeneous Catalysis,* Washington, DC, American Chemical Society, 1983, with permission.)

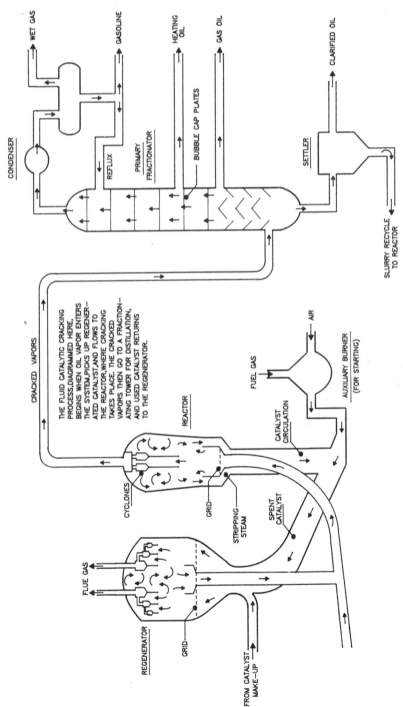

THE FLUID CATALYTIC CRACKING PROCESS, DIAGRAMMED HERE, BEGINS WHEN OIL VAPOR ENTERS THE SYSTEM, PICKS UP REGENERATED CATALYST, AND FLOWS TO THE REACTOR, WHERE CRACKING TAKES PLACE. THE CRACKED VAPORS THEN GO TO A FRACTIONATING TOWER FOR DISTILLATION, AND USED CATALYST RETURNS TO THE REGENERATOR.

WET GAS

GASOLINE

HEATING OIL

GAS OIL

CLARIFIED OIL

CONDENSER

REFLUX

PRIMARY FRACTIONATOR

BUBBLE CAP PLATES

SETTLER

SLURRY RECYCLE TO REACTOR

CRACKED VAPORS

AIR

FUEL GAS

AUXILIARY BURNER (FOR STARTING)

CATALYST CIRCULATION

REACTOR

CYCLONES

GRID

STRIPPING STEAM

SPENT CATALYST

FLUE GAS

REGENERATOR

GRID

FROM CATALYST MAKE-UP

Figure 3.3 Fluid catalytic cracking unit. (*Source:* Standard Oil Co., NJ.)

anhydride from naphthalene, oxychlorination of ethylene to ethylene dichloride, and the synthesis of acrylonitrile from propylene. In all three of these, the Badger company played a major role, working respectively with the Sherwin Williams Company, B.F. Goodrich, and Standard Oil of Ohio in scaling pilot plant results up to commercial designs.

PETROLEUM TECHNOLOGY KEEPS ADVANCING

While cat crackers provided the bulk of wartime gasoline needs, catalytic polymerization and alkylation, which were developed earlier, made a very significant contribution and were indispensable for producing high octane blending stocks throughout the war.

The development of the octane scale itself represented a major cooperative effort between engine manufacturers and the petroleum industry. As noted in Chapter 2, significant advances were made in the 1920s and 1930s in tieing the cause of engine knock to premature ignition of the fuel mixture and in relating hydrocarbon structure (i.e., straight chain versus branched or aromatic) to fuel behavior in the combustion cylinder. Thomas Midgley at General Motors (see Chapter 2) and Professor Charles A. Kraus at Clark University were associated with the original work, leading to the formation of the Ethyl Gasoline Company, a Jersey-General Motors joint venture, in 1924. In September 1926, Dr. Graham Edgar, who headed research at Ethyl, described to a meeting of the American Chemical Society his discovery of a means to rate the octane numbers of a gasoline mixture by comparing its performance in an actual test engine to that of a mixture made up by using adjusted amounts of n-heptane (zero octane) and iso-octane (rated at 100-octane) to obtain similar performance. Among other things, this identified iso-octane as a valuable high octane material that could be used in aviation gasoline suitable for higher compression ratio engines. Shell and Jersey in 1929 had started dimerizing isobutylene in mixed butylene streams to obtain di-isobutylene, an olefin that was subsequently hydrogenated by Ethyl to make iso-octane. Sulfuric acid was used to make the dimer. Later, Jersey used an I.G. Farben catalyst to perform the hydrogenation and took over this step from Ethyl Corporation. However, isobutylene availability was very limited at that time, severely restricting the amount of iso-octane that could be made in this manner.

In the mid 1930s, Shell and Jersey both discovered that at somewhat higher temperatures than those used in cold dimerization, normal and isobutylene combined to form a copolymer (codimer) that could then also be hydrogenated to make iso-octane. This technique expanded to some extent the supply of high octane gasoline raw materials.

In the meantime, work at Universal Oil Products in Des Plaines, Illinois, demonstrated that gaseous olefins could be combined over an acid catalyst to make liquid C_6 and C_9 dimers and trimers with a considerable amount of chain branching, producing relatively high octane value blending stocks in the naphtha boiling range. A number of refiners in the late 1930s built these catalytic polymerization or "cat poly" units to increase gasoline production by recovering and using propylene and butylene previously flared or used as fuel gas.

In 1935, Humble Oil and Refining Company, a Jersey affiliate, which had been supplying the Army Air Force with high octane fuels, decided to expand its production of aviation gasoline by augmenting the supply of lower olefins available for dimerization or other processing. It decided to license a Phillips Petroleum Company process that could be used to crack a mixture of field propane and butanes into more valuable olefins at high temperature (1025°F) and pressure (1700 psig). This plant was built in conjunction with a hot acid plant to make codimer. By 1938, both plants were placed in operation.

Humble's interest in further increasing its production of high octane gasoline fraction also caused its researchers to note a paper published by Anglo-Iranian Oil Company scientists in June 1938.* This described the alkylation of isobutane—obtained by superfractionation from field butanes—with butylene or amylene at low temperature and pressure, again in a bath of sulfuric acid. An important advantage of this process versus cat poly plants

---

*AIOC, the company now known as British Petroleum (BP), appears to have been first to discover the reaction of isoparaffins with olefins in a strong sulfuric acid solution to give high octane blending components. At its research station in Sunbury-on-Thames, AIOC scientists in 1936 worked on reacting n-butene with isobutene, using isopentane as a solvent. As it turned out, the isopentane reacted with the butylenes to give a paraffinic C_9 material with a very high octane rating.

was that no hydrogenation step was required in this method for producing iso-octane. Herb Meyer, the Technical Manager at Baytown, saw immediately that this process would be the best technique to obtain large amounts of high octane blending stock and so Humble quickly started its own work on this process.* However, the relatively close boiling points of isobutane and n-butane (10.9°F vs. 31.1°F) required intensive studies on the design of fractionating columns, the aim being to reduce tray height so that for a large number of trays, as required to effect the separation, the tower size could be limited to an acceptable height. This was, at that time, pioneering work in fractionating tray design, involving new standards for tray spacing, bubble cap design, and tray downcomer sizing. Plant-scale alkylation of C_4 and C_5 olefins with isobutane was commenced by Humble in 1939 and made that company the largest producer of aviation gasoline for the war effort. Geoffrey Lloyd of the United Kingdom Oil Control Board was soon to say that "without 100-octane, we should not have won the Battle of Britain" and it is a fact that this high performance fuel, "spiked" with aromatics such as cumene (also produced by alkylation), gave British Spitfires and Hurricanes a distinct advantage over the much larger planes of the Luftwaffe. Thus it was that I.G. Farben technology, which had been used to hydrogenate dimer and to produce aromatics via hydroforming, helped to turn the tide of the war against Germany.

These developments also proved significant from a chemical standpoint. Olefin supplies had been expanded through the construction of a plant that had been specifically designed by Humble to produce propylene, butylene and amylenes—a major step forward from the recovery of these materials as by-products from thermal cracking. Second, liquid and vapor phase alkylation and polymerization were *chemical* processes, although they were employed to make a fuel product.

Alkylation also produced another effective high octane blending component for "rich mixtures" of aviation gasoline. In the United States, the Air Force had determined that the addition of substituted aromatics to aviation gasoline would give a mixture with a 100/130 octane rating, which was desirable for high power take-offs on short landing strips and aircraft carriers. The Petroleum Administration for War (PAW) asked the industry in late 1941 to

---

*Dr. J. F. Mathis, personal communication.

determine whether the supply of suitable aromatics could be augmented by a synthetic route. By early 1942, Shell had succeeded in adapting the UOP alkylation process to make cumene (isopropyl benzene) from coal tar benzene and propylene. By mid-1942, Shell was operating synthetic cumene plants at Wood River, Illinois, and at Norco, Louisiana. Shell offered its technology free to all competitors and by 1943, 19 plants were using this process in the United States and in Canada.

In another development, Standard of Indiana developed and built a paraffin isomerization unit to produce large amounts of high octane isopentane and isohexane from the normal paraffin isomers. A number of other such plants were also constructed by Indiana and its licensees.

The results of the various programs for producing high octane gasoline were impressive. By the end of 1943, 100-octane gasoline blending stock production had increased to 260,000 barrels daily, up from 80,000 barrels per day in early 1942. Finally, by 1944, the refining industry was able to keep up with the armed services' demands for high octane fuel for aviation and other motor uses. And the production and use of propylene, butylenes, and amylenes from cat crackers and thermal crackers had become so substantial that it became almost inevitable that these materials would find other uses when wartime priorities would no longer apply.

THE OTHER PROBLEM: SYNTHETIC RUBBER

While the aviation gasoline program was the driving force in spurring the U.S. refining industry to build what could be called a number of chemical feedstock factories, the synthetic rubber program, in many respects, was just as important to the development of the U.S. petrochemical industry. Although thermoplastics and synthetic fibers later became much larger consumers of petrochemical building blocks, the manufacture of synthetic elastomers (rubber) represented the first instance where synthetic polymers were produced in very large quantities from petroleum-based feedstocks. By the middle of the war, the Rubber Reserve Program had sponsored the construction of a number of styrene and butadiene plants, which required a large supply of olefin feedstocks—ethylene and butylenes. But this course of events was far from apparent at the start of the war. The history of the rubber program has been amply recorded elsewhere (13), but a brief overview will provide a petrochemical perspective.

German chemists had made a reasonable rubber substitute from butadiene as early as World War I, when Fritz Hofman, a pharmacist working for Bayer, made synthetic rubber tires for the Kaiser's car from methyl-isoprene (14). However, when world natural rubber prices dropped as low as 3 cents per pound in 1933, work on synthetic tire rubber was discontinued. In the United States, Thiokol Corporation and DuPont developed oil-resistant rubbers in the late 1920s and early 1930s, respectively, but these materials found only small specialized uses.

When Hitler came to power, he quickly grasped the need for an autarkic program for German raw materials self-sufficiency. He therefore asked I.G. Farben to resume work on synthetic rubber, recognizing the likelihood of a natural rubber cutoff in case of war. By 1934, BASF and Bayer had developed Buna-S rubber, which was a polymer with 25 percent styrene, contained in a butadiene chain. An agreement made between I.G. Farben and General Tire and Rubber at that time led the U.S. firm to conclude that Buna rubber was not yet suitable for tire manufacture. Another version, Buna-N, made with acrylonitrile, was also produced as a specialty material in small quantities in an I.G. plant. Both types of Buna rubber were of interest to Standard Oil of Jersey, which obtained rights to use the technology through its broad exchange agreement with I.G. Farben, detailed elsewhere. The U.S. rubber companies continued to study these materials and, by 1940, Goodyear had a one-ton-per-day pilot plant in operation to make a synthetic rubber for tire treads. Production of Buna-type rubbers in Germany had reached 20,000 tons by that time and the product was starting to be used in tires and tank treads.

The United States now entered the war and by early 1942, it was clear that Japan would control the natural rubber plantations in Southeast Asia. At that time, the U.S. Government reserve stockpile of rubber stood at 500,000 tons, equal to only two-thirds of U.S. consumption for a single year. A program was initiated for collecting and reclaiming rubber from discarded tires, but this would be far from adequate for future rubber supplies. The problem of developing a synthetic rubber industry suitable for making tires for America's rapidly growing war needs was now becoming critical. Some time before, it had been turned over to Jesse Jones, then Chairman of the Reconstruction Finance Corporation (RFC), the agency that supervised the nation's rubber stockpile, in conjunction with its broader charter of surveying and safeguarding the nation's stockpile of critical materials. Soon, several other government agencies also became involved in what was to become, for a period of time, a program fraught with technology arguments and politics.

It was obvious from the beginning that styrene-butadiene rubber, based on the Buna-S patents, would be the backbone of the nation's synthetic rubber program. To make this possible, Jersey made I.G. Farben's and its own patent information available on a royalty-free basis to the government and to the companies that would produce the rubber and rubber intermediates for the government program. However, Jersey had been unable to convince the Germans to turn over the "know-how" necessary to use their patents. The Rubber Reserve Company, created by the RFC, had, in 1941, requested the four largest rubber companies, Goodyear, Goodrich, Firestone, and U.S. Rubber (later Uniroyal) to each build a 10,000-ton Buna-S plant. Shortly after the war broke out, this was raised to 30,000 ton plants for each company, but now, in addition to the need for developing Buna manufacturing know-how, a major stumbling block appeared: where would the styrene and butadiene come from? Styrene was barely known as a chemical intermediate. Butadiene was present in small amounts in streams from thermal crackers but was not being recovered. The problem of providing large amounts of the two monomers for a rubber program that would eventually produce over 700,000 tons per year of what would later be called GR-S or SBR rubber appeared staggering to government and industry planners.

The technological and logistics questions confronting government and industry planners were overwhelming and the need to solve these problems and to start construction of plants—but what kind of plants?—made the situation critical and seemingly beyond a rapid solution. Issues included sources of raw materials, technology for the intermediates and for making suitable quality Buna-S rubber, provision of construction materials and size and location of plants.

It was immediately recognized that the rapid expansion of a fledgling industry to a large, essentially multicompany enterprise would require the full and effective exchange of all technical information at a time when secrecy was still the normal *modus operandi* of the chemical industry. The Rubber Reserve Program addressed the latter issue as a first step by establishing a Technical Committee comprised of representatives of the government and the companies participating in the program. Eventually, 36 companies joined in this agreement.

The Technical Committee then directed the companies to study the German work on Buna-S elastomer polymerization and, if possible, to improve the process so as to allow large-scale production to commence as soon as possible. Information available from the Jersey–I.G. Farben agreements indicated that the rate of polymerization was quite low, but the reasons were not apparent. Work carried out under great time pressure soon resulted in a determination that the emulsifiers used by the Germans—principally linoleic acid and conjugated stearates—in fact acted as inhibitors to the reaction. Also, some of the impurities present in the then commercially available butadiene were also acting as inhibitors. It was discovered, however, that certain initiators could be added to speed the reaction. In particular, potassium persulfate-dodecyl mercaptan was seen to be effective as an initiator and to control polymer chain length. This allowed the production of polymers of sufficient plasticity to permit handling on conventional rubber processing equipment (15). Unit operations were studied and optimized to allow scaling up production line size. Chemical engineers again made major contributions here, developing systems for continuous polymerization, improved agitators, monomer stripping facilities, rapid coagulation, and new drying equipment.

DEVELOPMENT OF STYRENE PRODUCTION

Now, the Technical Committee faced the question of how to produce the immense amounts of styrene and butadiene that would be required to produce GR-S rubber in the quantities necessary to replace the natural rubber no longer available from the Malay Peninsula.

The styrene problem turned out to be somewhat easier to solve, though this again required a great deal of government-industry cooperation. Styrene was far from well known as a chemical at that time, although Dow Chemical and Monsanto were starting to produce small amounts of polystyrene plastic resin from monomer made by Dow. That company had started to work on styrene technology in the early 1930s, about the same time as the German chemists. In fact, there had been a long hiatus between the mid-1800s, when Berthelot had first identified styrene and indene as pyrolysis products and had carried out the first thermal dehydrogenation of ethylbenzene, and 1925, when Ostromislenski and Shepard definitively studied the dehydrogenation of ethylbenzene and cumene at 450–700°C (16). Dow's major contributions were the development of a heterogeneous catalyst and of an inhibitor injected to prevent styrene polymerization during the final monomer purification step.

Other companies, including Union Carbide, Koppers, Monsanto, UOP and others had done research work on either ethylbenzene or styrene technology. But Dow had built a monomer plant in 1937 and had by far the most experience. Carbide had worked on another approach, involving an oxidation step, with a semiworks plant constructed at Institute, West Virginia.

After studying the various technologies available, the Technical Committee decided to put Dow Chemical in charge of the program. The company was asked to build large styrene plants at Torrance, California; Velasco, Texas; and Sarnia, Ontario, using Dow technology, and to supervise construction of several other plants. Union Carbide was authorized to build a large plant based on its process adjacent to its pilot plant. Monsanto built an ethylbenzene-styrene plant in Texas City, Texas, using a combination of Dow and Monsanto technology, in design partnership with the Lummus Company, an engineering firm. And Koppers was authorized to build a plant at Kobuta, Pennsylvania, using a vapor phase alkylation process, which was based on contributions by UOP, Phillips Petroleum, and Koppers.

U.S. production of styrene, which was less than 2 million pounds per month in 1941, rose to 20 million pounds monthly by the end of 1943 and to 40 million pounds monthly—close to half a billion pounds per year—by the end of 1944. Styrene became the largest user of benzene, a situation that has continued to the present, although styrene monomer outlets have broadly diversified since that time. During the war, the benzene was primarily sourced from coal tar distillers, reacted with ethylene recovered from cat crackers or thermal crackers or produced via dehydration of ethanol. Some benzene also came from petroleum sources (i.e., hydroformers and steam crackers).

A list of the styrene plants eventually placed in operation follows. For each plant, the rated capacity, as well as the maximum production rate achieved is indicated:

Wartime Styrene Plant Output (Metric Tons per Year)

Plant	Rated Capacity	Maximum Production
Union Carbide and Carbide Institute, West Virginia	25,000	17,000
Dow Chemical		
Torrance, California	25,000	19,000
Velasco, Texas	50,000	61,000
Koppers		
Kobuta, Pennsylvania	37,500	29,000
Monsanto		
Texas City, Texas	50,000	53,000

Source: Ref. 13, Herbert and Bisio, p. 131.

BUTADIENE FROM VARIOUS SOURCES

The butadiene program ran into political as well as raw materials and process problems. Butadiene would have to be made "on purpose" and in large quantities; this precluded primary reliance on by-product recovery from thermal cracking. A number of possible routes were identified, but they soon boiled down to the following approaches:

1. Dehydrogenation of butylenes (or conceivably butane). In the case of butylene, this material was becoming available in increasing amounts from cat crackers.
2. High temperature cracking of naphtha, a technology under investigation by Jersey, which had already placed a propane cracker in operation and was studying the steam cracking of heavier petroleum fractions, which would produce substantial amounts of butylenes and butadiene.
3. Chlorination-dehydrochlorination of butylenes, an approach known to Shell as a result of its work on glycerin intermediates.

4. Reduction of ethyl alcohol to acetaldehyde, aldol condensation, followed by dehydration and dehydrogenation to butadiene.

Interestingly, the use of acetylene for the production of acetaldehyde—the main production used in Germany—was never seriously considered in the United States.

As soon as the agricultural lobby became aware of the possibility of using grain-based alcohols to make a critical war material, it mobilized its friends in the Senate and House of Representatives. As a result, the Senate's Gillette Subcommittee on Agriculture and Forestry strongly supported this route, which would also use large government surpluses of grain. The committee's position was bolstered by the fact that the supply of butylenes (see first butadiene option above) was still limited, while the need for 100-octane gasoline, which depended on butylenes, was very high. This led government members of the Technical Committee to listen to the Gillette Subcommittee's case for the alcohol-based route, which was somewhat more complicated and expensive. For a while, it even appeared that all butadiene would be made from alcohol. It was "politics as usual" and months of delay were encountered before a decision on a butadiene supply program was eventually made. The breakthrough came after President Roosevelt appointed Bernard M. Baruch, an elder statesman and presidential adviser, to head up the Rubber Program with two eminent scientists, James B Conant, president of Harvard, and Karl T. Compton, president of M.I.T., to investigate the situation, and to advise Baruch. One of the first decisions made was to produce butadiene from both types of feedstock. Alcohol would nevertheless provide the bulk of the butadiene during the earlier parts of the war.

The eventual butadiene program adopted had important consequences, not only for the rubber program, but for a petrochemical industry now starting to make major contributions to the war effort.

In early 1941, Shell decided to build a small butadiene plant, based on a chlorination route that had also been developed in Germany. Starting up in 1942, this little plant produced 4,000 tons of butadiene, enough for over a million average-size automobile tires. In that year, this plant was "the towering giant of the American synthetic rubber industry," according to a book covering the history of Shell Oil Company. (17) Eventually, the plant's capacity was doubled. However, wartime shortages of chlorine kept this route from becoming a major butadiene source in the later parts of the conflict.

Grain alcohol did become an important source of butadiene, largely because Union Carbide had developed a suitable American process of this kind. The company built plants at Institute, West Virginia, and Louisville, Kentucky, and Koppers built a third. Together, these units had a capacity of 242,000 tons per year or roughly one half of total U.S. butadiene production. Although this butadiene was somewhat more expensive than that produced from petroleum, the influence of the agricultural lobby remained strong and, in addition, the government had decided not to put all its eggs in one basket, recognizing the alternate need for butylenes in aviation gasoline.

Jersey and its subsidiary, Humble Oil, took the lead in building plants to make butadiene from hydrocarbon fractions. In this, they divided the company's efforts, so that the two possible routes could be used as soon as possible. The company had amassed considerable experience in steam cracking various heavy naphtha fractions to achieve relatively high butadiene yields. Three such units were placed in operation between January 1942 and March 1943, each with a larger capacity than the previous plant. The last unit, known as QBLA ("Quickie Butadiene" in Louisiana), with a capacity of 10,500 tons of butadiene was erected so rapidly that no time was taken to individually size the fractionating columns. The vendor was advised to make them all the same size to gain time!*

Jersey had already studied the extraction of butadiene from mixed C_4 streams, as a consequence of its cooperative work with I.G. Farben. It was then discovered that ammoniacal copper solutions were an excellent solvent for butadiene contained in mixed butylenes. Jersey's patents in this area eventually produced substantial licensing income for the company.

Butylene dehydrogenation plants were built by Jersey at Baton Rouge, Louisiana, and by Humble at Baytown, Texas. Thus, a 30,000-ton butadiene plant was built at Baytown at a cost of $19 million and was placed in operation in September 1943. When all of the dehydrogenation and cracking plants were on stream, Jersey's production of butadiene was 98,000 tons annually, amount-

---

*Dr. Bert W. Struth, personal communication.

ing to one-third of the nation's butadiene supplies from petroleum sources. Phillips Petroleum and the Houdry company contributed with technology to dehydrogenate butylene to butadiene, thus substantially expanding the raw material supply for making the conjugated diolefin. Some work was also done on butane dehydrogenation and a small plant of this kind was built on the West Coast by the Standard Oil Company of California.

Production of synthetic rubber rose rapidly in the United States once the government and industry planners were able to agree on technology and raw material issues (Fig. 3.4). During the latter stages of the war, Bradley Dewey, a founder of Dewey and Almy Chemical Company, which later formed the nucleus of W. R. Grace's chemical group, headed the rubber program. As indicated in Figure 3.5, GR-S rubber production*, which was 3,700 tons in 1942, reached 181,000 tons in 1943, and 668,000 tons in 1944. Butadiene production from alcohol exceeded that from petroleum in 1943 and 1944, but petroleum-based production was substantially higher by 1945 (Fig. 3.6) and this has remained the dominant process since that time.

Butyl rubber also came into its own during World War II, though in a smaller way. German chemists had, in 1929, succeeded in polymerizing isobutylene, but had found it impossible to vulcanize this material. In 1937, Sparks and Thomas at Standard Oil Development Company incorporated small amounts of butadiene in isobutylene and produced an elastomer that would not only vulcanize but had good initial "tack" and aged satisfactorily. Later, isoprene was also found to be useful as a comonomer with isobutylene. An important chemical engineering achievement in connection with the development of butyl rubber was the fact that polymerization had to be carried out at −140°F, even though the reaction was highly exothermic. Also, extremely high purity requirements called for further advances in fractionation techniques at low temperatures. When the design was judged ready for commercial realization, the government requested the immediate construction of a plant to make butyl rubber, since this product was uniquely effective for making tire inner tubes. The plant, which was authorized a few days before Pearl Harbor, did make a valu-

*Still called Buna-S by many people, due to its German origin, the main synthetic rubber production in the United States for tire manufacture was known as GR-S rubber.

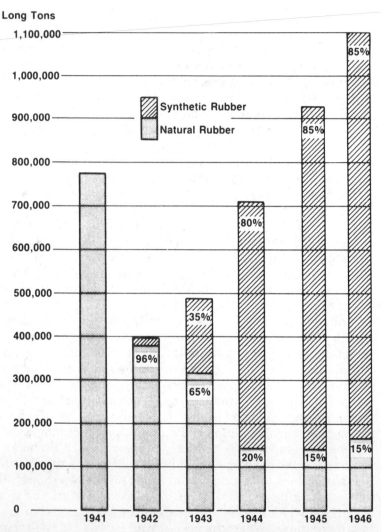

Figure 3.4 U.S. rubber consumption, natural and synthetic, 1941-1946. (*Source:* Herbert and Bisio, *Synthetic Rubber: A Project That Had to Succeed,* (Contributions in Economics & Economic History, No. 63, Greenwood Press, Inc., Westport, CT, 1985), p. 126. Copyright © 1985 by Vernon Herbert and Attilio Bisio. Reprinted with permission.)

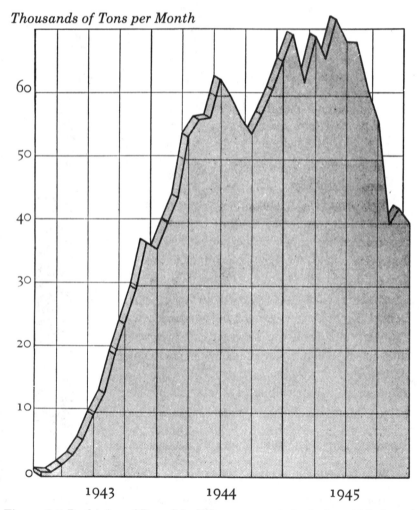

Figure 3.5 Production of Buna-S in U.S. government plants from 1943 through 1945. (*Source:* Charles S. Popple, *Standard Oil Company (N.J.) in World War II,* Standard Oil Co. (NJ), New York, 1952, p. 72. Reprinted with permission from Exxon Corporation.)

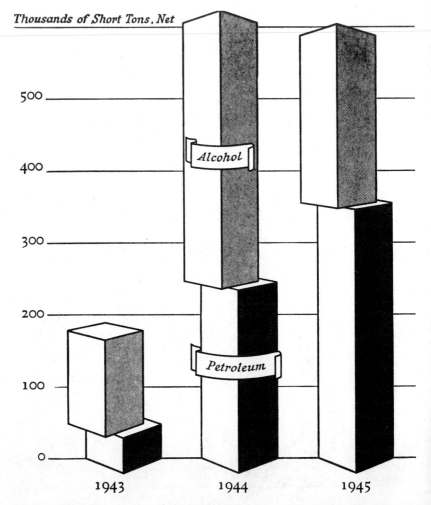

Figure 3.6 Production of butadiene from petroleum and from alcohol, 1943-1945. (*Source:* Charles S. Popple, *Standard Oil Company (N.J.) in World War II.* Standard Oil Company (NJ), New York, 1952, p. 74. Reprinted with permission from Exxon Corporation.)

able contribution to the nation's war effort, but its importance was limited, compared to the GR-S rubber program. At maximum capacity, about 2,450 barrels per day of isobutylene were converted to butyl rubber.

Ethylene for styrene. Propylene for poly gasoline, alkylate and cumene. Butylenes for codimer, butadiene, and butyl rubber. Amylene for alkylate. These were the new feedstocks that produced the essential wartime fuels and chemical products. By the end of the war, the many cat crackers and a number of dedicated naphtha and gas oil steam crackers were churning out these olefins at an enormous rate. And soon after the cessation of hostilities, government requirements for high octane fuels, tires, plastics, and other products made from these olefins dropped to low levels, making huge quantities of chemicals available for civilian uses. GR-S rubber production dropped back to 408,000 tons in 1947 and below 300,000 tons by 1949. Aviation gasoline demand experienced a similar drop, though civilian consumption soon started to take up the slack.

Government investment in chemical plants and facilities during the hostilities amounted to about $3.4 billion, of which $2.9 billion went for ammunition and explosives plants. A total of $470 million was spent on plants for synthetic ammonia, toluene, chlorine, and other chemical facilities, and these were, at the end of the war, assigned to the Surplus Property Administration. Chemical and oil companies were logical purchasers of many of these plants, which were often built on or adjacent to their own plant sites. Many of the refining and chemical production plants built during the war were, however, financed by the companies rather than by the U.S. government, although in most cases, construction was the result of government supply contracts.

When companies purchased government-built plants after the war, they were able to buy these facilities on a very favorable basis, as shown by the following selected examples:

Plant	Original Cost	Price Paid to Government
Esso-Baton Rouge, Louisiana Butadiene from naphtha (6,800 MT/year)	$1,985,000	$325,000

Plant	Original Cost	Price Paid to Government
Monsanto-Texas City, Texas Styrene (50,000 MT/year)	$19,200,000	$9,900,000
DuPont-Louisville, Kentucky Neoprene (60,000 MT/year)	$37,600,000	$13,300,000
Davison-Baltimore, Maryland Cracking catalyst	$2,056,000	$176,000

Source: Ref. 13 (Herbert and Bisio, p. 164).

Refiners and chemical intermediates manufacturers, who had participated in such a substantial manner in the war effort, were now ready to supply copious amounts of petrochemicals to meet pent-up consumer demand for products that could be made from these materials. The stage was set for the next phase of development.

REFERENCES

1. Kendall Beaton (1957). *Enterprise in Oil: A History of Shell in the United States,* New York, Appleton-Century-Crofts, 574–577.
2. A. N. Sachanan (1940). *Conversion of Petroleum,* New York, Reinhold, 143ff.
3. Alex G. Oblad (1983). The contributions of Eugene J. Houdry to the development of catalytic cracking, *Heterogeneous Catalysis: Selected American Histories* Washington, DC, American Chemical Society, pp. 61–75.
4. Carleton Ellis (1937). *The Chemistry of Petroleum Derivatives,* New York, Reinhold.
5. Charles L. Thomas (1983). A history of early catalytic cracking research at Universal Oil Products Company, *Heterogeneous Catalysis: Selected American Histories,* Washington, DC, American Chemical Society, pp. 241–245.
6. U.S. Patent 2,078,247 assigned to E. J. Houdry and issued in 1937 was filed in 1932. It describes the principles of the process entitled "Catalytic Conversion of Higher Boiling Hydrocarbons into Lower Boiling Hydrocarbons."
7. Karl Schoenemann (1980). Chemical engineering in Germany, *Advances in Chemistry,* Series 190. Washington, DC: American Chemical Society, p. 249.
8. J. R. Fair. (1983) Historical Development of distillation equipment, A.I.Ch.E. Symposium Series.
9. *A Dollar To A Doughnut, The Lewis Story,* privately printed, (M.I.T.) 1955.

10. C. E. Jahnig, H. Z. Martin, and D. L. Campbell (1983). The development of fluid catalytic cracking, *Heterogenous Catalysis: Selected American Histories,* Washington, D.C. American Chemical Society, pp. 273–291.

11. Robert H. Perry, Cecil H. Chilton, Sidney D. Kirkpatrick (1963). *Perry's Chemical Engineer's Handbook,* Fourth Edition, Chapter V, Particle dynamics, New York, McGraw-Hill, 5–59.

12. A. Donald Green (1977). *An Engineer Putting Chemistry to Work,* personal memoirs, Standard Oil of New Jersey.

13. For example: Vernon Herbert and Attilio Bisio (1985). *Synthetic Rubber: A Project That Had to Succeed,* Westport, Connecticut, Greenwood Press; Frank Howard (1947). *Buna Rubber, The Birth-of an Industry,* New York, Van Nostrand Company; Charles S. Popple (1952). *Standard Oil Company (New Jersey) in World War II,* New York, Standard Oil; Kendall Beaton (1957). *Enterprise In Oil: A History of Shell in the United States,* New York, Appleton-Century-Crofts.

14. Peter J. T. Morris (1986). *Polymer Pioneers, A Popular History of the Science and Technology of Large Molecules,* Philadelphia, Center of History and Chemistry, 12.

15. R. L. Babb et al. (1952). Synthetic rubber polymerization practices, *Industrial and Engineering Chemistry,* **44**, May, 724–730.

16. R. H. Boundy et al. (1952). Styrene, its polymers, copolymers and derivatives, American Chemical Society Monograph 115, New York, Reinhold.

17. Kendall Beaton (1957). *Enterprise in Oil: A History of Shell in the United States,* New York, Appleton-Century-Crofts, p. 593.

ADDITIONAL READING

Babcock, Glenn D. *History of the U.S. Rubber Company,* Indiana Business Report No. 3, University of Indiana Graduate School of Business.

Enos, J. L. (1962). *Petroleum, Progress of Profits: A History of Process Innovation,* Cambridge, Mass., MIT Press.

Furter, William F. ed. (1980). *History of Chemical Engineering,* Washington, DC, American Chemical Society.

Hooper, John H. D. (1986). The alkylation process—A golden anniversary, *Chemistry & Industry,* October 20, 685–686.

Larson, Henrietta and Kenneth Porter (1959). *History of Humble Oil & Refining Company: A Study in Industrial Growth,* New York, Harper & Bros.

Larson, Henrietta M. et al. (1971). *History of Standard Oil Company (N.J.) New Horizons 1927-1950,* New York, Harper & Row.

Miller, S. A. ed. (1969). *Ethylene and Its Industrial Derivatives,* London, Ernest Benn.

M.I.T. (1980). *The Improbable Achievement: Chemical Engineering at M.I.T.,* Cambridge, Mass., M.I.T. Department of Chemical Engineering.

Synthetic Rubber, The Story of an Industry, New York, International Institute of Synthetic Rubber Producers.

Thomas, Charles L. (1983). *A History of Early Catalytic Cracking Research and Universal Oil Products Company,* American Chemical Society.

Williamson, Harold F., et al. (1963). *The American Petroleum Industry,* Evanston, Ill., Northwestern University Press.

4 / Aromatic Feedstocks from Petroleum: Universal Oil Products Company (UOP)

The employment of petroleum fractions for the specific production of BTX aromatics (benzene, toluene, xylenes) proceeded at a slower pace than the use of crude-derived hydrocarbons for conversion to olefins. Coal tar distillation could provide all the benzene, toluene, and xylenes the United States required for any conceivable chemical purposes up to the start of World War II. The iron and steel industry, at that time, generated as a by-product close to 200 million gallons per year of benzene, far more than was required for manufacture of chemical derivatives produced from this aromatic building block up to that time. Styrene, which later became the largest benzene derivative, was almost unknown as a commercial product. Thus, in the 1930s, benzene was used primarily for the manufacture of chlorobenzenes, phenol, maleic anhydride, and aniline. Toluene di-isocyanate (TDI) and polyurethanes, later two of the main toluene derivatives, were unknown, while polyester fiber, eventually the main outlet for xylenes, had not been considered as a feasible product by Wallace Carothers and other synthetic fiber chemists active in the 1930s.

Toluene, however, did have one important chemical outlet—the production of explosives, including trinitrotoluene (TNT). As the likelihood of war increased, the U.S. Army Ordnance Department studied potentially scarce domestic resources and recognized that

157

toluene supplies could become short at a time when the need for explosives and ammunition was mounting. Moreover, toluene distilled from coal tar did not always have the high degree of purity required to meet nitration-grade specifications. Catalytic hydroforming of petroleum naphtha fractions represented an alternate route to toluene and other aromatics, but was not yet commercially practiced. In 1939, Ordnance Department officers therefore approached several oil companies and asked them to step up their development work on the naphtha hydroforming process, which had been identified as a result of the Jersey-I.G. Farben exchange agreements. Moreover, industry and government recognized that hydroforming technology was closely tied to an important new use for aromatics: the production of high octane gasoline.

At the start of the war, aviation gasoline was largely a blend of iso-octane and other high octane aliphatic refinery streams. The possibility of making aviation fuels with aromatic blending stocks had been recognized, but catalytic reforming was barely known by the industry. A 1939 article in the Annual Refinery Issue of *World Petroleum* said, "Scientists are now trying to establish the . . . secrets of these reactions . . . the system is much more complicated than the synthesis of iso-octane or the production of alkylate from butylene and isobutane" (1).

As the war progressed, the synthetic rubber program presented a second, very critical demand for aromatics: styrene. Although supplies of coal tar benzene were theoretically sufficient to meet this need, petroleum-derived benzene, often produced in refineries adjacent to the synthetic rubber plants, was used to make a substantial part of the styrene for GR-S rubber, the name used by the military for the butadiene-styrene elastomer the Germans referred to as Buna-S rubber. Nevertheless, up to the late 1940s, the total amount of petroleum-based benzene used for chemicals was under 10 percent of total U.S. consumption.

A small amount of aromatics had always been produced in refineries practicing thermal cracking. But thermal reformers, as they were called, raised naphtha octane primarily through the formation of branched and olefinic molecules rather than via the aromatization of naphthenes. First used in 1931, thermal reforming was carried out at severe conditions: pressures of 500–1000 psig and temperatures of 1000–1075°F. Typical yields varied from 70–90 percent on naphtha feedstocks, with the reformed gasoline having a research octane rating of around 70 (clear) at the higher yield levels, with yields dropping to 70 percent or lower when a 90 (clear)-octane gasoline was produced. The process therefore had a limited potential for the production of high octane gasoline, with yield losses becoming prohibitive if the octane level was pushed too far. Coke formation was not a major problem, the yield loss being primarily to lower olefins and paraffins. The large amounts of C_3 and C_4 olefins produced in this process led to the development of *catalytic polymerization* as a means to supplement gasoline production with a blendstock having a relatively high octane value. This process—which effectively produces a high octane product in the gasoline boiling range by combining two molecules of a C_3 or C_4 olefin—was developed by a company destined to play a significant role in the development of petroleum refining technology, Universal Oil Products Company (UOP).

A number of small refineries were provided with thermal reforming plus so-called "cat poly" units and this precluded the need (for some time) to install catalytic cracking units, which together with catalytic reforming, later became the main technology to make high octane gasolines. (By 1957, there still were 34 operable *thermal* reformers with a combined capacity of 220,000 barrels per day.)

In 1939, Standard Oil of New Jersey, Standard Oil of Indiana, and M. W. Kellogg introduced the fixed-bed catalytic "hydroforming" process, largely based on German technology and catalyst know-how. The first unit went on stream at an Indiana affiliate, Pan American Refining Company, in Texas City, Texas, in November 1940 (2). The catalytic process differed radically from thermal reforming. Whereas the latter produced relatively limited amounts of aromatics, relying mainly on cracking paraffins and naphthenes to produce shorter branched and straight chain paraffins and olefins, catalytic hydroforming increased gasoline octane primarily through catalytic dehydrogenation and dehydroisomerization of naphthenes to form aromatics. Hydrogen split off from saturated paraffins and naphthenes is made as a by-product in this type of process. The catalyst was molybdenum oxide-alumina. Recycle hydrogen was employed to mitigate catalyst coking. Typical conditions were pressures in the range of 150–300 psig and temperatures from 850-1000°F. On-stream time for the reactors was 4-8 hours. There were usually four reactors, with two on stream and two under regeneration. In the latter step, air was admitted to the bed containing spent catalyst, whereby partially reduced molybdenum oxide was reoxidized, the sulfur that had reacted with the molybdenum was burned off as sulfur dioxide, and coke on the catalyst was converted to carbon oxides and discharged to the atmosphere.

The economic advantage of *catalytic hydroforming* versus *thermal reforming plus catalytic polymerization* was considerable. On a typical East Texas naphtha, the catalytic process could achieve a yield (expressed as volume percent on feed) of around 85 percent while also providing some increase in research octane number. Thermal reforming of the same feedstock involved a considerably lower yield of gasoline at any given higher octane rating. More importantly, hydroformed naphtha had a much higher aromatics content, thus making this stream a new source for BTX aromatics. A typical comparison of the two processes is shown in Table 4.1 (3). Over the course of the war, a number of fixed-bed hydroformers were built and placed in operation. In addition to producing large amounts of high octane aviation gasoline, these units also made about 170 million gallons per year of high purity toluene in the peak war year (1944).

When producing toluene, catalytic hydroformers were charged with a narrow-boiling (180–230°F) feedstock, giving a toluene cut containing 85–90 percent aromatics. When aviation gasoline blendstock was desired, it could be produced without shutting down by charging a wider-boiling feedstock. Typically, for every 100 barrels of feedstock, 77 barrels of aviation blendstock were produced. To this were added 21 barrels of isopentane fractionated from natural gasoline, resulting in 98 barrels of aviation fuel. This was then "leaded up" to obtain a so-called F-3 octane rating of 100.

Standard Oil Company of California also developed a hydroforming process, which was first installed at its Richmond, California, refinery in February 1943. It had a shorter reaction-regeneration cycle and employed only three (eventually four) reactors—with only one in the regeneration mode at any time. The catalyst was an improved version of the molybdenum-alumina type and, by the end of the war, was installed in a majority of all operating hydroformers (see also Fig. 4.1). An interesting fact is that at Richmond mixed xylenes were separated and fractionated to produce an o-xylene cut. This was used to make phthalic anhydride via catalytic oxidation by a proprietary Chevron* process,

---

*This name, which was used for the company's gasoline brands, eventually was adopted as the name of Standard Oil Company (California) to differentiate the firm from the other Standard Oil successor companies.

Table 4.1   Thermal Reforming Versus Fixed-Bed Hydroforming of East Texas Virgin Heavy Naphtha

	Thermal Reforming	Fixed-Bed Hydroforming
Temperature, °F	1045	930
Pressure, psig	1000	200
Space velocity, v/hr/v	—	0.5
Recycle gas rate, SCF/bbl	—	2890
Hydrogen in recycle, vol. %	—	70
Yields, Wt. %		
H$_2$ + CH$_4$	5.5	4.0
C$_2$H$_4$	0.6	—
C$_2$H$_6$	5.6	2.0
C$_3$H$_6$	3.2	—
C$_3$H$_8$	6.7	4.6
Total light hydrocarbons	**21.6**	**10.6**
Gasoline (400°F endpoint)	**70.6**	**86.9**
Tar	**7.8**	—
Carbon	—	0.2
	Reforming Plus Catalytic Polymerization of Propylene and Butylene	
C$_4$ + Gasoline		
Vol.% on feed	74.1	85.2
Gravity, °API	51.8	46.4
Reid vapor pressure, psi	7.9	6.5
Research octane (clear)	80.3	81.3

(*Source:* See ref 3.)

the first to employ xylene instead of naphthalene as a feedstock (4). Phthalic anhydride production in the United States, previously wholly based on naphthalene, had risen from 3,350 tons in 1930 to 29,000 tons in 1940 and to 62,000 tons in 1944, largely due to wartime uses of phthalate esters for PVC (polyvinyl chloride) plasticizers. These found a particular use in coated fabrics that could withstand repeated flexing at subzero temperatures.

Shortly after the war, Jersey, Kellogg, and Indiana combined efforts to try and develop a process that would avoid the cyclical operation required for fixed-bed hydroformers. Jersey had solved

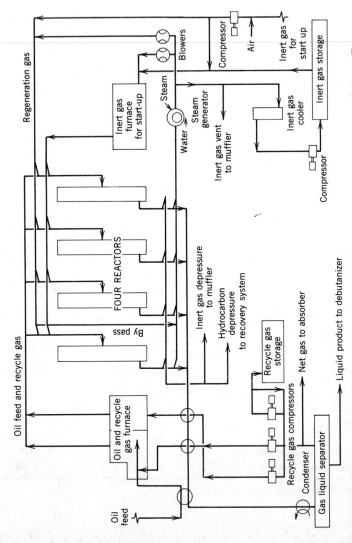

Figure 4.1 Standard Oil of California catalytic reformer—catalyst section. (*Source:* Energy Publications, *The Petroleum Engineer*, May 1946.)

a similar problem by using a fluid bed system and continuous catalyst circulation for dealing with the coke laydown that occurs in the cat cracking of gas oils. The company now took the lead in the development of a *fluid bed reforming* process (called fluid hydroforming), which would allow continuous regeneration of a relatively conventional hydroforming catalyst in a separate vessel. The first commercial fluid hydroformer went on stream at the Destrahan, Louisiana, refinery of Pan-American Southern Company in the early 1950s. Four other units were eventually built. The process was not particularly successful, however, because backmixing in the large diameter fluid bed reactor vessels placed an effective upper limit on gasoline octane. After much pilot work at Jersey's Bayway refinery, it was determined that this was due to overcracking of the desired products as a result of their being recycled back down from the top of the fluid bed. The Standard Oil Development engineers therefore had to settle for a lower-octane product than they might have hoped for. Nevertheless, a plant was built, using internal reactor baffles to mitigate the backmixing problem. Then, several other plants were built. However, a serious explosion in one of the larger units (a Standard of Indiana plant in Whiting, Indiana) made refinery people skeptical about the safety of this process, which operated around 200 psig, a high pressure for a process that used small differential pressures to control catalyst circulation between the two vessels (fluid catalytic cracking is operated close to atmospheric pressure). The explosion was, however, due to an operating error on startup not necessarily associated with system pressure differentials. Eventually, all of the fluid hydroforming units were shut down and both Jersey and Indiana turned their attention to fixed bed regenerative processes, using noble metals catalysts. By that time, however, another company had established a considerable lead over the traditional innovators in refining technology.

In 1949, Universal Oil Products Company stunned the industry by announcing a continuous, high pressure reforming process *that did not need catalyst regeneration,* since there was no laydown of coke during the reaction. It was based on the use of an entirely different catalyst, containing a noble metal: *platinum.* The yield of high octane gasoline obtained with this process was 95 volume percent, 10 percent higher than fixed-bed hydroforming and some 30 percent higher than that obtained in thermal reformers, some of which were still in operation. As might be expected, the process was an almost immediate success and, by the end of 1951, 25 units were either in operation, under construction or under contract. UOP's development of the process—known as *platforming*—was the company's most notable achievement since its development of the Dubbs cracking process in the early 1920s.

To understand UOP's role as the leading research and engineering firm active in the development of technology for refining processes and petrochemical feedstocks, we must go back to the early days of petroleum refining. The story of UOP is closely tied to the history of refining and catalysis and involves several eminent pioneers in the field.

ASPHALT PROCESSING WAS AN EARLY START

In 1913, the Standard Asphalt Company, whose main business was the production of asphalt and synthetic rubber from petroleum residues, purchased a number of asphalt production patents issued to Jesse Dubbs. A corporation called National Hydrocarbon Company was then set up to exploit the patents. Dubbs was the manager of a small California refinery, who had been working on improvements in asphalt manufacture. To Frank Belnap, patent counsel of Standard Asphalt, it appeared that some of the patents had a broader potential than the production of improved asphalt, since they contained similarities to the work that Belnap knew Dr. W. M. Burton had been conducting at Standard Oil (Indiana). There, the company had started to process crude oil fractions at elevated temperatures and pressures to produce additional amounts of lighter products in the gasoline and kerosene boiling range. Large quantities of coke formed in the process did, however, require frequent shutdowns for cleaning out the equipment.

Standard Asphalt accordingly bought out all of Dubbs' rights, including a key patent application of Jesse Dubbs covering thermal cracking, which later was issued as U.S. 1,123,503 (January 5, 1915) and changed its name to the Universal Oil Products Company (5). Dubbs' son, who had the picturesque name of Carbon Petroleum (C.P.) Dubbs, was placed in charge of further research. Dr. Gustav Egloff—later well known in the refining industry as "Gasoline Gus"—had already been hired by the firm as a senior chemist. Other capable chemists and chemical engineers soon joined the staff.

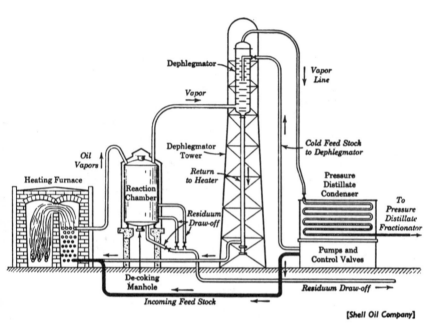

Figure 4.2 Flowsheet of early Dubbs unit. (*Source:* John L. Enos, *Petroleum Progress and Profits*, M.I.T. Press, Cambridge, MA, 1961, pp. 78, 83.)

In 1919, C. P. Dubbs filed a patent (U.S. 1,392,629) on a "clean recirculating" process, which covered a system where oil passed through thermal cracking tubes and the heavy residue was separated and discharged from the system as tar, while heavier distillates were "recirculated" to the cracking step. In distinction from the Burton units and even to the more advanced Burton-Clark tube cracking stills first installed at Indiana's Wood River (Illinois) refinery, the Dubbs crackers were able to operate continuously, with reflux for dilution, and they could crack crudes as well as gas oils. The Dubbs patent was issued in 1921 and the process was soon placed in commercial operation, with UOP guaranteeing a 23 percent yield of gasoline and a 24-hour cleanout period for the typical 250 BPD* Dubbs units then being installed. Royalty was set at 15 cents per barrel. By 1923, the process had been widely accepted by the refining industry. A flowsheet of an early Dubbs unit is shown in Figure 4.2 and the apparatus described in the "clean recirculation" patent shown in Figure 4.3 (6).

*BPD (barrels per day) is the most common unit refiners use as a measure of flow rate.

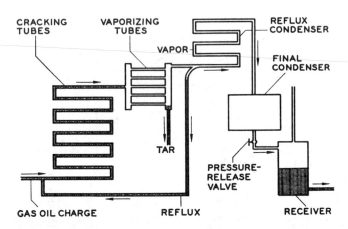

Figure 4.3 (*a*) Dubbs apparatus for "clean recirculation." (*Source:* H. F. Williamson et al. *The American Petroleum Industry, The Age of Energy (1899–1959)*, Evanston, IL, Northwestern University Press, 1963, p. 158.)

Figure 4.4 illustrates the Cross process, another cracker of that period, while Figure 4.5 depicts a bubble-cap type fractionating tower, which became standard for the industry for many years. The Dubbs process was licensed to Shell Oil, Standard of California, and a number of independent refiners not associated with the Standard Oil group of companies. The Standard Oil associated firms had continued the development of the Burton process, as well as combining it with the Cross process, which took the reaction up to 600 psig in an insulated reaction chamber.

Litigation now ensued among Standard of Indiana, which had led the development of the Burton and Burton-Clark processes, the Texas Company, with the Holms-Manley process and UOP, the engineering company claiming that the Burton process was infringing the Dubbs patents. A lengthy and costly legal battle followed, which showed no sign of abatement throughout the 1920s. UOP's royalty income kept increasing over this period, but the company's success was overshadowed by the patent issue. Eventually, Shell Oil, which was then paying substantial royalties to UOP, approached California Standard, and together the companies came up with a solution. They decided to join forces to buy UOP! In addition to debentures used for the purchase, funds also

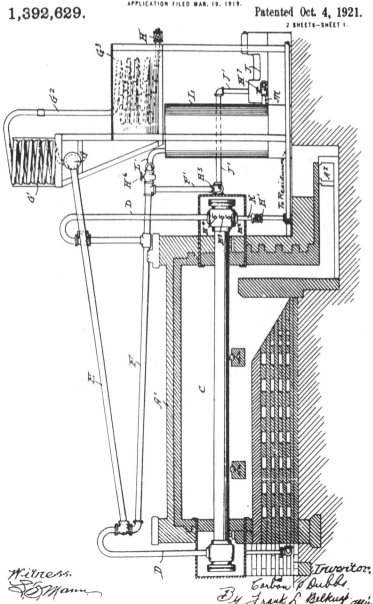

Figure 4.3 (*b*) Equipment details for Dubbs apparatus for clean recirculation. (*Source:* As for Fig. 4.3*a*, p. 158.)

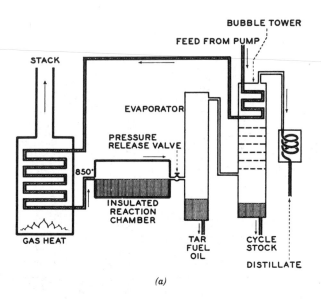

(a)

	Cross system	Pressure distillate system
Barrels of oil treated per unit per average operating day including cleaning	500	150
Barrels of gasoline produced per day per unit	125	50
Installation cost of one unit	$40,000.00	$50,000.00
Installation cost per barrel of oil treated per day	$80.00	$333.00
Installation cost per barrel of gasoline per day	$320.00	$1,000.00
Barrels of fuel oil required per barrel of gasoline produced	0.20	0.50
Total cost per barrel of gasoline	$3.73	$4.79

(b)

Figure 4.4 (*a*) The Cross process with bubble tower. (*Source:* H. F. Williamson et al., *The American Petroleum Industry, The Age of Energy (1899–1959)*, Evanston, IL, Northwestern University Press, 1963, p. 382.) (*b*) Comparison of cross system and conventional bulk pressure system, 1921. (*Source:* Leslie, *Motor Fuels*, 378.)

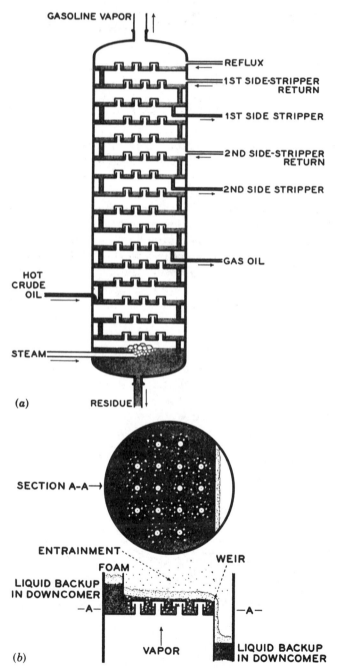

GASOLINE VAPOR

REFLUX

1ST SIDE-STRIPPER RETURN

1ST SIDE STRIPPER

2ND SIDE-STRIPPER RETURN

2ND SIDE STRIPPER

GAS OIL

HOT CRUDE OIL

STEAM

(a)

RESIDUE

SECTION A-A→

ENTRAINMENT

WEIR

FOAM

LIQUID BACKUP IN DOWNCOMER

—A—

—A—

VAPOR

LIQUID BACKUP IN DOWNCOMER

(b)

Figure 4.5 (*a*) Diagram of a bubble-cap type fractionating tower. (*b*) Details of tray design. (*Source:* H. F. Williamson et al., *The American Petroleum Industry, The Age of Energy (1899–1959),* Evanston, IL, Northwestern University Press, 1963, pp. 400, 401.)

came from the sale of paid-up licenses for the Dubbs process, which they were able to negotiate with a number of the large oil companies that had been opposing UOP. In addition, the companies buying UOP also received licenses for any developments made by UOP for the following twelve years. Thus, the two oil companies were able to solve the dispute, but in the process UOP lost its independence and also a substantial source of future revenues for some time to come.

Settlement of the litigation with Indiana in the 1930s did provided UOP with an atmosphere much more conducive to carrying out advanced research. The level of understanding of various types of chemical reactions had risen appreciably in the years between 1915 and 1930. Similar to researchers working for the large chemical companies in Germany and other industrial countries, the scientists at UOP recognized the great strides being made in catalysis and they turned their attention to the development of more advanced technology that would use more elegant* techniques to reshape the molecules of petroleum feedstocks.

Concern in the United States was also mounting at that time regarding potential future shortages of crude oil supplies (This was just before the discovery of vast new reservoirs of oil in East Texas.) These perceptions of possible supply shortages led to renewed interest in the German work on coal hydrogenation and in catalytic processes for hydrocarbon conversion, in general. Egloff, who in any case felt that new approaches to shaping petroleum molecules were needed, was sent to Europe on several occasions to recruit research talent there.

The company first attracted an important German researcher in Hans Tropsch (see Chapter 1), but his tenure at UOP was relatively limited, as he soon returned to Germany with a serious illness. But an even bigger "catch" was made in the person of Vladimir Ipatieff. Egloff met Ipatieff in Germany and asked him to come to the United States to head up a laboratory to study catalytic hydrocarbon conversions. The Russian chemist was then at the peak of his career and, with Paul Sabatier, was recognized as one

---

*Thermal cracking, in some ways, could be likened to "hitting a large molecule with a sledgehammer."

of the fathers of modern catalysis. The collaboration between UOP and Ipatieff was another important milestone in the history of the company and tied many of its later successes to chemical research work that had originated in Europe.

CATALYSIS: IPATIEFF, SABATIER, AND OTHER GIANTS

The fact that such a thing as a catalytic effect might exist was probably first noted by Sir Humphrey Davy in England around 1820, who observed that a hot platinum wire could "catalyze" the conversion of ethyl alcohol to acetic acid. In 1831, Peregrine Phillips used platinum to oxidize SO_2 to SO_3, (7) although he never lived to see the development of the so-called Contact* process for the production of sulfuric acid. Somewhat earlier, Thenard observed the decomposition of hydrogen peroxide over an active material, obviously also acting as a "catalyst." Jons Jakob Berzelius and Michael Faraday in the late 1830s developed theories covering these interesting effects, but their conclusions were later found to be only partially correct. Ludwig Mond† used a catalyst to develop steam reforming technology, but did not attempt to elucidate the underlying theory involved, which would explain the effects that were providing the desired results—in this case, the production of carbon monoxide and hydrogen from gaseous or liquid hydrocarbons in the presence of steam. Ostwald in Germany is considered by some to be the first researcher to understand the specific action of a catalyst, working around the turn of the century on the oxidation of ammonia to nitric acid (see Chapter 1) and on the acid-catalyzed hydrolysis of methyl acetate. He correctly defined a catalyst as "a substance which changes the velocity of a reaction without appearing in its end-product." He did not explain, however, how the catalyst did its work.

Two French chemists, Marcelin Berthelot and Paul Sabatier, made valuable contributions in studying catalytic effects in organic synthesis. Shortly after Woehler, in Germany, had synthe-

---

*From "Kontact," the German word for catalyst.

†Founder of a predecessor company to ICI in England called Brunner Mond.

sized urea from ammonium cyanate, Berthelot had been able to produce acetylene and ethylene from alcohol by passing it over a red-hot metallic surface. Then, around the turn of the century, Sabatier, together with the Abbé Jean-Baptiste Senderens, found that finely divided nickel could be used to great advantage in effecting the hydrogenation of acetylene to ethylene and of ethylene to ethane. Benzene could be hydrogenated to cyclohexane, while fatty acids, such as oleic acid, could be converted into solid acids such as stearic acid.* He also found that platinum was an excellent hydrogenation and dehydrogenation catalyst (8).

It wasn't only British, French, and German chemists who were eludicating the structure of hydrocarbons and organic chemicals and attempting to synthesize them in the mid-1800s. In Russia, Alexander Butlerov and Vladimir Markovnikov were among the most eminent chemists of their day. Butlerov, who was engaged in major disputes with Kekulé, first proposed correct formulas for ethylene and higher olefins, recognizing the significance of the double and triple bond in reactive hydrocarbons. Markovnikov demonstrated the mutual interactions of the atoms in a molecule, using as an example the addition of chlorine or bromine atoms to a hydrocarbon molecule, the reaction that eventually was given his name. It is now thought that the decade from 1860 to 1870 was the turning point from the old to the new view of organic chemistry.

Vladimir Nikolaevitch Ipatieff was born in 1867 into the czarist nobility and he received a classical Russian education, attending military school, but concentrating on scientific subjects. He joined the Russian Physical-Chemical Society in 1890 and soon came into personal contact with such eminent personalities as Mendeleev and Beilstein. Concentrating his work on chemical reactions involving double bonds, he was one of the first to determine the structure of isoprene by studying the decomposition of natural rubber and then to synthesize the isoprene molecule. In 1900, Ipatieff became interested in the pyrolysis of alcohols and soon discovered the role and specific action of catalysts, such as aluminum oxide, zinc, and copper in dehydration and dehydrogenation reactions. A retrospective view of his work indicates that he was the first to understand the function of metal oxides as catalysts. At about the same time that Sabatier was doing his historic hydrogenation

---

*Today, it is common knowledge that some shortening and cooking oils are hydrogenated (solid) or unsaturated (olefinic).

experiments on the ethylene/hydrogen/ethane system (9), Ipatieff demonstrated that a catalyst can perform a reaction a great number of times before undergoing change and he was able to explain the effects occurring at the catalyst surface. He described reaction equilibria and the reversibility of reactions (as Sabatier was also able to do) and, perhaps most importantly, he identified the need for large surface areas to provide the required catalytic effect, as required by a heterogeneous catalyst. He also showed that reactions can proceed at high temperatures without decomposition of the reactants. Sabatier and Ipatieff, working on different systems in laboratories far apart from each other, thus drew a number of parallel conclusions, but Ipatieff was able to come up with explanations that were much closer to what we now know occurs in a catalytic reaction.

Over the next several years, Ipatieff also turned his attention to the action of silica, alumina, and clays on the production of olefins from alcohols. He learned how to prepare catalysts with high activity and, as a result, sometimes received what would now be called consulting assignments. As an example, the German firm of Schering, which had been working on the production of ethylene from ethanol, asked Ipatieff to help in the preparation of high yield catalysts, which they were themselves unable to accomplish. Ipatieff may therefore have been the first "consultant" for the development of catalytic processes.

Shortly before World War I, Ipatieff received an assignment to work in the Nobel Brothers Laboratory in Baku on the Caspian Sea where, as early as 1880, benzene and naphthalene had been extracted from crude oil fractions (10). There, research was starting to be carried out on methods to produce gasoline from crude oil. This work was discontinued, however, when Russia was drawn into the conflict. Much later, Ipatieff recognized the similarity of these studies to the development of cracking stills in the United States in the late 1920s.

Following the Russian Revolution, Ipatieff attempted to accommodate himself to the Bolsheviks, who had ousted the czar and had eliminated, or chased out of the country, most of the titled families. His work was recognized by Lenin, who appointed him to a high research post. Thereafter, the Russian scientist achieved considerable prominence under the new Communist regime, devoting his government-sponsored research work primarily to high pressure reactions. Over this period, he received a number of scientific awards. He also frequently attended international chemical society meetings, where he exchanged ideas with BASF's Drs. Caro and Wilstatter, and such other famous German chemists as Bergius, Haber, and Nernst. He also met Sabatier. In 1928, Ipatieff was awarded the coveted Berthelot Medal by the French Society of Industrial Chemistry.

As time went on, the increasingly totalitarian nature of the Russian regime became a factor in Ipatieff's life and work. As recounted in his memoirs (11), Ipatieff recognized that he could not continue his career under the conditions prevalent in the Soviet Union after Stalin came to power. Several of his friends and co-workers disappeared or were executed by a government that no longer respected the individual and created an atmosphere of fear and repression. Thus, when Egloff provided the opportunity to leave, the Russian scientist and his wife finally decided to emigrate to the United States. Arriving in Chicago at the age of 62, he immediately joined UOP and was also appointed to a professorship of chemistry at Northwestern University.

Ipatieff's work and contributions at UOP have been fondly recollected by his friend and co-worker, Herman Pines (12,13). When the famous Russian chemist joined the firm, the two scientists initially collaborated to demonstrate the principle of alkylation of olefins. In 1932, they produced the first alkylate, using an aluminum chloride catalyst promoted by hydrochloric acid. The next important discovery of Ipatieff and another co-worker R. E. Schaad was the development of a solid phosphoric acid catalyst (H_3PO_4 + Kieselguhr) to effect this type of hydrocarbon conversion, which was termed catalytic polymerization. The product, in the form of a trimer, was used as a gasoline blending component, called cat poly gasoline, in a plant built by Shell Oil at its East Chicago, Indiana, refinery. In a later adaptation of this process, involving dimerization and hydrogenation of butenes, an even higher octane blending component was made for the production of aviation gasoline. During World War II, the same catalyst was widely used to alkylate benzene with propylene to make cumene for blending into aviation gasoline. (Later, cumene became the major intermediate for the production of phenol, although a liquid phase alkylation process was eventually also widely used.) Ipatieff's olefin polymerization process was also employed to make tetramer, a propylene-based "oligomer" found useful by the detergent industry.

These research accomplishments, which led to processes we consider commonplace today, must be seen as having commenced at a time when catalytic cracking was just starting to be developed. Until this time, only thermal processes were available to modify (i.e., largely reduce) the size of petroleum molecules. Moreover, the ability of processes to transform gaseous components like propylene and butylene into liquids boiling in the gasoline range must have seemed almost miraculous to the relatively unsophisticated refining industry. It is, therefore, not surprising that Ipatieff was considered, at that time, as the foremost expert in catalytic reactions in connection with petroleum refining. Many other UOP developments were aided by suggestions from Ipatieff, who was, for over 15 years, the company's resident expert on catalysis.

Of course, Ipatieff came into a fertile field, since the refining industry was at that time well behind the chemical industry in understanding the actions and use of catalysts. This seems evident from a paper published as late as 1940 by an author writing about the refining industry, who characterized "Dubbs phosphoric acid plants" (i.e., catalytic polymerization units licensed by UOP) as using "a catalyst that appears to play the part of a true catalyst or at least a semicatalyst" (whatever that meant). Thus, UOP had to do a considerable amount of missionary work to get refiners to understand the application of catalysts in an industry used to doing things largely by the application of heat and sometimes also elevated pressure.

Between 1935 and 1939, Ipatieff authored or coauthored over 50 papers and applied for dozens of patents. He became a member of the National Academy of Sciences and received the Gibbs Medal for his many achievements. At Northwestern, where he was an inspiration to his students, his problems with the English language led to many anecdotes. He is probably best remembered by his students and coworkers for his frequent statement "ve did zis in St. Petersburg (now Leningrad-P.H.S.) thirty years ago."

Ipatieff died in 1952. Though many honors were conferred on him during his lifetime, he never received the Nobel Prize, which had been awarded to his rival Sabatier. In his autobiography, *My Life as a Chemist,* his disappointment and professional jealousy often came to the surface. History does tend to vindicate Ipatieff's feelings in that the breadth and scope of his discoveries and the validity of his theories must now be considered as equal in many ways to the accomplishments of Sabatier.

PLATFORMING—UOP'S BIGGEST BREAKTHROUGH

Vladimir Haensel, whose father was a friend of Ipatieff's, started at UOP with a summer job in 1935, working as a technician in the catalytic reforming laboratory. At that time, the main catalyst under study for this reaction was chromia-alumina, reactions being carried out at atmospheric pressure and with no hydrogen applied to the system. This summer job evidently pointed Haensel in the direction that would later lead to his major discovery. Haensel went back for a master's degree at M.I.T. and then joined UOP on a full-time basis in 1937. While working there, he studied for his doctorate in Ipatieff's high pressure laboratory at Northwestern. In 1941, he was again employed full-time at UOP, but under the direction of Ipatieff. Haensel recalled that, around that time, one of the major problems identified by Egloff was coke formation in the naphtha reforming reaction, much of the research work being directed toward a solution of this problem, which required plants to shut down frequently for catalyst regeneration (14).

Shortly after the war, Haensel joined one of the military teams that inspected German refinery and chemical plants. No doubt this exposure to German technology improved his insight into catalytic processes for hydrocarbon conversions (see also Chapter 1).

During the mid-1940s, UOP concentrated on hydrocracking reactions using various types of catalysts, including nickel and platinum on silica-alumina supports. By this time, a great deal more was understood about the types of reactions that occur in systems involving the transformation of paraffins and naphthenes into aromatics. Catalytic reforming of naphthas actually comprises a large number of reactions, the most important of which are summarized in Table 4.2. Paraffins are dehydrogenated to olefins, which can then cyclize to form aromatic rings, naphthenes (saturated rings) are dehydrogenated to aromatics, etc. Catalyst research work on the reforming reaction became much more focused when the nature of these reactions—and their interactions—became increasingly clear. The extent to which each of these reactions takes place is primarily dependent on the catalyst or catalysts used, the composition of the naphtha, and the reaction conditions. It eventually became apparent that the isomerization and hydrocracking reactions require the catalyst to have two entirely different functions, namely, hydrogenation/dehydrogenation and acidity. The

Table 4.2 Important Reactions in Catalytic Reforming

Dehydrogenation Reactions (examples)

(1) Dehydrogenation of cyclohexanes to aromatics

methylcyclohexane $\longrightarrow$ toluene $+ 3H_2$

(2) Dehydrocyclization of paraffins and olefins to aromatics

(a) $n\text{-}C_7H_{16}$ $\longrightarrow$ toluene $+ 4H_2$

(b) $n\text{-}C_7H_{14}$ $\longrightarrow$ toluene $+ 3H_2$

Isomerization Reactions (examples)

(1) Isomerization of n-paraffins to isoparaffins

n-heptane $\rightarrow$ 2-methylhexane

(2) Hydroisomerization of olefins to isoparaffins

heptene-1 $+ H_2 \rightarrow$ 2-methylhexane

(3) Isomerization of alkylcyclopentanes to cyclohexanes

methylcyclopentane $\longrightarrow$ cyclohexane

Hydrocracking Reactions (examples)

(1) Hydrocracking of paraffins
   (a) $C_9H_{20} + H_2 \rightarrow C_5H_{12} + C_4H_{10}$
   (b) $C_9H_{20} + H_2 \rightarrow CH_4 + C_8H_{18}$
(2) Hydrodesulfurization*

methylthiophene $+ 4H_2 \rightarrow C_5H_{12} + H_2S$

Source: Paul W. Emmett, ed. (1958), *Catalysis,* Vol. VI, New York, Reinhold Publishing Company.

*Carried out ahead of the platforming reactor.

two functions may reside in the same catalyst component or in two different components. Transition metal oxide catalysts, such as chromia-alumina and molybdena-alumina are examples of the former, while silica-alumina catalysts doped with an active metal ion, are examples of the latter and are known as "dual-function" catalysts.

Ipatieff's counsel and help influenced much of this work. In Haensel's own words, Ipatieff "was always available for discussion and consultations and anyone would have been foolish not to take advantage of the opportunity." Moreover, the two scientists coauthored a number technical papers during this period, including one in 1947 describing the demethylation of branched chain paraffins with nickel or cobalt catalysts at pressures up to 500 psig, which gave unusual insights into the complex nature of the multiple reactions occurring in such a system.

In view of his later contributions to the development of platforming, it is significant that much of Ipatieff's early work in Russia involved high pressure reactions under hydrogen atmosphere, as well as acid-catalyzed reactions. The use of platinum and nickel in aromatization reactions had been known from other Russian work and from studies by Komarewsky and Riesz at the Illinois Institute of Technology (15). What was about to happen was a major advance in the technology of catalytic reforming.

Haensel and his co-workers had been studying hydrocracking reactions of kerosene fractions, using nickel-silica-alumina catalysts. At that time, one of the tests for six-member ring naphthene content was to pass the desulfurized product over a 5 percent platinum on carbon catalyst at low space velocities; only these particular naphthenes were converted into aromatics. The gasoline fractions produced by hydrocracking were analyzed in this manner and much of the work concentrated on feeds with high naphthene content. The objective was to obtain gasoline fractions with high octane numbers, if possible.

One time, no desulfurized naphtha fraction was available and the virgin naphtha was passed over the platinum catalyst at the usual conditions. The catalyst promptly died, as did a number of other catalyst preparations. However, the nagging thought persisted: there must be a temperature and hydrogen partial pressure high enough to cause the platinum sulfide obviously formed to be reduced back to active platinum. Accordingly, a platinum-aluminum catalyst was selected and a further set of experiments commenced.

Operating at 500 psig, with high hydrogen partial pressures, it was decided to start raising the reaction temperature well above the level then recommended for platinum catalysts, that is, close to 450°C, which was 200°C or so higher than what was thought the catalyst could stand. The results looked very good, being equal to or better than the yields then being achieved in conventional hydroformers using conventional metal oxide catalysts, and they also gave higher octane values. *Moreover, there was no coking!* As the reaction studies at UOP proceeded, it became obvious that a "breakthrough" was at hand. What was happening was that at the high temperatures and high partial pressures of hydrogen employed, the coke laid down during the aromatization reaction was continually removed by the hydrogen in the recycle gas (14). And the fact that sulfur was present in the feedstock actually enhanced the reaction.*

Now, a commercial problem had to be solved. At a concentration of 3 percent platinum on alumina, the catalyst was far too expensive. By this time, under the guidance and leadership of C. G. Gerhold, manager of UOP laboratories and an outstanding chemical engineer in his own right, the group turned its attention to decreasing the platinum content. Soon thereafter, to their great satisfaction, the researchers were able to achieve excellent results at platinum contents an order of magnitude lower, in the range of 0.3 to 0.7 percent (16,17). During this period, a further major discovery was made. When the catalyst support was prepared from aluminum chloride instead of aluminum nitrate, the finished catalyst activity was even higher than before and, much more importantly, remained high, instead of declining. The proper control and maintenance of catalyst acidity was soon understood to be a very key requirement. Eventually, this led to the low platinum-content fluorided, or chlorided, catalysts that became the standard for UOP's Platforming process.

An understanding of the various reactions taking place also allowed the creation of a commercial design that would take maximum advantage of the dual functional nature of the catalyst. Platforming units were designed with three reactors in series. In the first reactor, dehydrogenation and dehydroisomerization of naphthenes and paraffins were the main reactions, with high endother-

---

*In the eventual commercial version, lower pressures were used to obtain higher octanes and this again required feed desulphurization. However, some "sulphiding" of the catalyst became standard procedure.

micity (heat absorption) giving a large (120°F) temperature drop. By the time the charge went through the third reactor, the temperature only dropped 10°F from the entrance to the exit of the bed, since hydrocracking and dehydrocyclization were now the primary reactions. External reheat was used to bring stream temperature back to about 930°F at each reactor inlet.

Reaction pressure was also an important variable. Pressures below 700 pounds per square inch favored the aromatics-forming reaction, while high pressure levels increased hydrocracking, thus producing more branched paraffins (also high octane materials) and less hydrogen. This feature of the process allowed UOP to tailor the design of platforming units to the specific requirements of the operator: gasoline blending components, aromatics for chemicals, or both in some cases.

A technical paper on the new process was presented by a UOP executive at the Western Petroleum Refiners' Association in San Antonio in April 1949. There, Elmer Sondregger, the superintendent of a small plant of the Old Dutch Refinery at Muskegon, Michigan, heard the presentation, and on his way home stopped in at UOP's office in Des Plaines. He allowed that he had a small thermal reforming unit that he felt could probably be converted to use that new process. A contract was signed then and there and six months later the conversion was completed and the revamped unit placed onstream. But after three hours, the unit had to be shut down due to excessive heating of the outer shell. A new reactor inner liner was designed and installed and the unit was then placed back onstream without further problems. A flowsheet depicting the installation of the new platforming process at Old Dutch Refining Company is shown on Figure 4.6 and typical operating results in Table 4.3 (18).

The plant became an instant success. One of the most important processes in the history of petroleum refining—and petrochemicals feedstock production—had now been launched—the accomplishment of Ipatieff's disciple and friend, Val Haensel, strongly supported by C. G. Gerhold and R. E. Sutherland, who were able to convince UOP management to allocate half of UOP's technical manpower to this development effort.

It came just in time for UOP. In 1944, as a result of its owners' concern about possible antitrust problems, UOP had become an independent firm and the stock owned by the oil companies had been placed into a trust, with net royalty income going to the

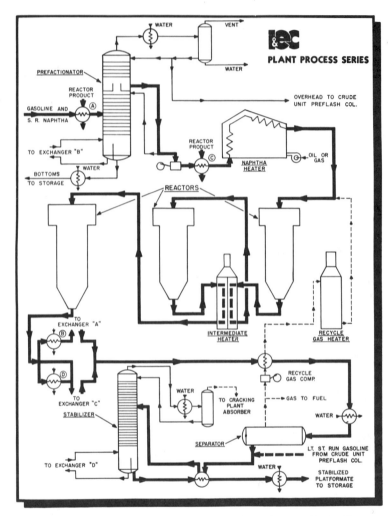

Figure 4.6 Flowsheet for Platforming of gasoline. (*Source:* M. L. Kastens and R. E. Sutherland, Platinum Reforming of Gasoline, *Modern Chemical Process,* Vol. 2, Editors of *Industrial and Chemical Engineering,* eds., New York, Reinhold, 1952, pp. 193–204.)

American Chemical Society. The company's royalty income had been dropping and the firm was again involved in some litigation. Success with the platforming process completely changed the picture. By January 1958, or less than 10 years after startup of the

Old Dutch reformer, UOP had installed 106 platforming units with a total capacity of 755,000 barrels per day (BPD) (3). By this time, several other developers had placed onstream their own versions of noble metal catalytic reforming processes.

Some statistics are useful in illustrating the impact of the new reforming technologies on the U.S. refining industry. Total U.S. catalytic reforming capacity with noble metal catalysts had by then reached 1.5 million BPD, equal to 15 percent of the total crude distillation capacity. In 1950, about 2 percent of the U.S.

Table 4.3   Performance Data—Old Dutch Platforming Unit February 6-9, 1950

Operating Conditions	
Av. reactor pressure, psi gauge	720
Av. reactor temp., °F	890
Observed rates and yields, vol.% of charge	
Reactor charge	100
Stabilized Platformate	92.6
Calcd. 10-lb. vapor pressure Platformate	
Yield	97.1
Outside butane required	4.5

Result of Platforming Reaction	Reactor Charge	Stabilized Platformate
Inspection		
Paraffins, %	62	61
Olefins, %	0	1
Naphthenes, %	33	1
Aromatics, %	5	37
Sp.gr., °API	58.1	57.4
Octane No.		
Research		
Clear	52.5	81.3
Plus 3 cc. TEL	70.2	93.9
Motor		
Clear	48.9	75.5
Plus 3 cc. TEL	68.5	87.4

(*Source:* See reference 18, reprinted with permission from *Industrial and Engineering Chemistry,* **42,** 528, April 1950. Copyright American Chemical Society.

motor gasoline pool was catalytic reformate. This figure rose to 30 percent by the late 1950s. Availability of higher octane blending components allowed automobile manufacturers to increase engine compression ratios, with the result that the unleaded research octane number of regular gasoline rose from 73.5 to 84.0, and that of premium grade gasoline from 80.0 to 91.2 over this period. Whereas catalytic cracking capacity also increased greatly over this time, reforming made it possible to upgrade very low octane virgin naphtha fractions to valuable gasoline components in a manner never possible before that time in such an efficient and economical manner.

Successful commercialization of the Platforming process started a veritable boom in catalytic reforming technology development. Two years after the successful startup of the Old Dutch Refining Company's platforming unit, three new reforming processes were announced and by 1956 seven more processes were available from other developers. Several of these were of the cyclical regenerative type,* which used a noble metal catalyst, but operated at a lower pressure and gave a slightly higher product octane rating (versus Platforming) at the expense of somewhat higher operating costs. Indiana's Ultraforming and Jersey's Powerforming processes, both of the latter type, as well as Atlantic Refining's Catforming (later combined with Sinclair-Baker technology and adapted to use the Engelhard catalyst) came closest to matching the achievement of UOP. Chevron, about ten years later, made a further contribution by developing an improved catalyst, using both platinum and rhenium. It was UOP, however, that had been first with noble metal reforming.

Among the many honors bestowed on Val Haensel were the A.I.Ch.E. Chemical Pioneer Award (1967), the Perkin Medal (1967), the Eugene Houdry Award in Applied Catalysis (1977) and membership in the National Academy of Sciences (1971) and the National Academy of Engineering (1974). In 1973, President Nixon presented him the National Medal of Science "for his outstanding research in the catalytic reforming of hydrocarbons, which has greatly enhanced the economic value of our petroleum natural resources."

---

*Versus UOP's process, which did not require regeneration.

GETTING THE AROMATICS OUT OF REFORMATE

The rapid increase in the availability of BTX aromatics from petroleum processing operations did not go unnoticed by the chemical community. It came just in time, because it was becoming apparent that benzene production by the steel industry had peaked and would henceforth decline. Thus, in 1950, benzene from coal tar distillation amounted to 184 million gallons, but by 1960 it had dropped to 147 million (by 1970 it was below 100 million gallons). Benzene demand for various chemical derivatives would rise more than threefold between 1950 and 1960, requiring large amounts of petroleum-based products to supplement the material from coal tar distillers.

U.S. Benzene Consumption (Million Gallons)

Year	For Ethylbenzene	For Cyclohexane	For Maleic Anhydride
1950	63	15	3
1960	201	40	17

Starting shortly after the end of the war, the United States had become a net importer of benzene, which was brought in from European countries and other parts of the world. Imports varied from year to year, but averaged 40 to 50 million gallons in the early and mid-1950s. These imports helped to support the rapid growth of benzene derivatives, which saw total benzene demand rise above 300 million gallons in 1955, a figure that also included the large amount used in the production of synthetic rubber. A considerable incentive was, therefore, available for refiners to distill benzene out of reformed petroleum fractions and sell it to chemical producers. This made sense, because benzene, being a lower octane material, is not as valuable as toluene or xylene in the gasoline pool. As late as 1950, only 10 million gallons of petroleum-derived benzene had found their way into chemical applications. By 1955, this had risen to 99 million gallons and by 1960 petrochemical benzene reached 309 million gallons, more than double the amount produced from coal tar. To achieve such levels of benzene production, another technology development had occurred—the separation of aromatics fractions from mixed hydrocarbon streams by a process considerably simpler and more economical than was known before that time and also developed by UOP.

The extraction and separation of benzene from mixed refinery streams is not a simple proposition and it is further complicated by the fact that benzene forms azeotropes with a number of non-aromatic hydrocarbons. Three methods are available to effect this separation: (*1*) liquid-liquid extraction, (*2*) extraction distillation, and (*3*) azeotropic distillation. In all of these techniques, another material is introduced to effect the separation. Extraction was used during World War II, but the sulfur dioxide solvent, which had been developed for other refinery extraction applications (e.g., lube oils, kerosene) was not especially selective. Somewhat improved extractive and azeotropic distillation processes for aromatics were commercialized by Shell Oil and Union Oil, respectively, the latter using methyl ethyl ketone and water as the azeotroping agent (19). However, neither of these relatively complex processes was a major improvement, nor was a Sun Oil charcoal adsorption route, Arosorb, announced in the early 1950s. Then, in 1952, Dow Chemical and UOP combined efforts in the development of the Udex process, which almost immediately became the standard of the industry.

The Udex process was unique in that it combined liquid-liquid extraction and extractive distillation of the rich solvent, followed by two-stage stripping of this solvent. In contrast to all previous processes, this technology, which was basically made feasible by the commercialization of platforming, made it possible to charge a wide-boiling feedstock to an extraction section, followed by simple fractionation to produce high purity benzene, toluene, and xylenes. The solvent consisted of a mixture of glycols and water and was noncorrosive, inexpensive, and highly stable. The process was far less complicated than sulfur dioxide extraction, as shown on Figure 4.7 (20). Udex investment requirements were correspondingly modest and operating costs were low—another major success for UOP.

The combination of the Platforming and Udex technologies placed UOP in a position to serve as the prime licensor of aromatics technology to the petroleum and chemical industries. For refiners, the Udex process could produce high octane blending stocks, or it could separate undesired aromatics from paraffinic naphtha or kerosene cuts destined for solvent or other uses. Refiners wishing to sell BTX aromatics or individual aromatics (e.g., mixed xylenes)

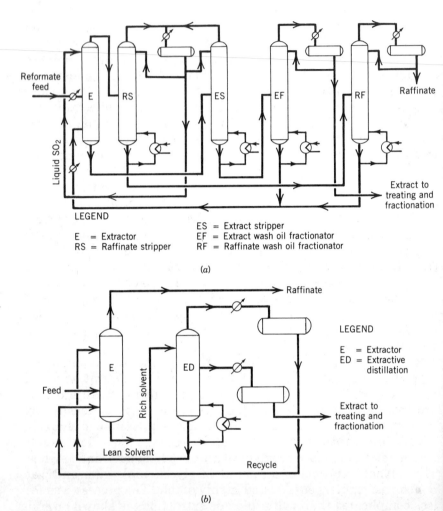

LEGEND

E = Extractor
RS = Raffinate stripper

ES = Extract stripper
EF = Extract wash oil fractionator
RF = Raffinate wash oil fractionator

(a)

LEGEND

E = Extractor
ED = Extractive distillation

(b)

Figure 4.7 Modified sulfur dioxide extraction process (*a*) and Udex process (*b*). (*Source:* G. F. Asselin and R. A. Persak, BTX Aromatics Extraction: Past, Present and Future, UOP Process Division Technology Conference, Des Plaines, Illinois, 1975. Courtesy UOP Inc.)

to petrochemical producers could use the Udex process on a portion of their reformed naphtha stream, while blending the balance into gasoline. And those petrochemical companies who wanted to be independent of refinery suppliers could install reforming, extraction, and fractionation facilities to make their own benzene, toluene, and xylene feedstocks by purchasing low-octane naphthas as their primary feedstock.

A block diagram of a typical aromatics "complex" in the early 1950s is shown in Figure 4.8. In this scheme, 10,000 barrels per day of East Texas naphtha are sent to fractionation to prepare appropriate feedstocks for platforming. The fractionation system and the reformer were designed for "blocked (sequential) operation" to produce either aromatics for chemicals production or a high octane motor fuel blendstock. In operating for aromatics, the *reformate* was sent to Udex extraction, followed by distillation, to produce benzene, toluene, and a mixed xylene-ethylbenzene cut. Costs for the platforming operation are shown in Table 4.4 and the cost of operating the entire complex to make gasoline and aromatics is summarized in Table 4.5. The gasoline price of 12 cents per gallon and the natural gas price of 10 cents per million BTU have a nostalgic quality. A very short payout time of two years was projected for the process (21).

More than 75 Udex units were constructed, ranging from 180 to 28,000 barrels per day of charge capacity. Then, in 1959, UOP joined Shell to commercialize an even better, relatively similar process, using a solvent termed "Sulfolane." Higher aromatics recoveries and lower utility costs due to greater solvent selectivity gave this process an important advantage over Udex at a time when competition among aromatics producers was intense. Only a few more Udex plants were built after that time. Although some of the original Udex plants are still in operation at this writing, most others were converted to the use of Sulfolane solvent. No better technology than Sulfolane has been developed since that time, although various chemicals, such as n-methylpyrollidone (NMP), dimethylsulphoxide (DMS), dimethylformamide (DMF), and other such "supersolvents" were proposed and, to a limited extent, employed in a few units in countries outside the United States.

The development of Platforming and, soon thereafter, of the Udex process, not only solved UOP's financial problems, but cemented the company's position as the prime source of petroleum refining process techniques. While many of the larger oil companies, such as Jersey, Mobil, Indiana, Chevron, and other majors (e.g., Sinclair), developed and licensed their own refining technologies, UOP has remained the largest source of refining know-how, particularly for the many large and small independent oil companies.

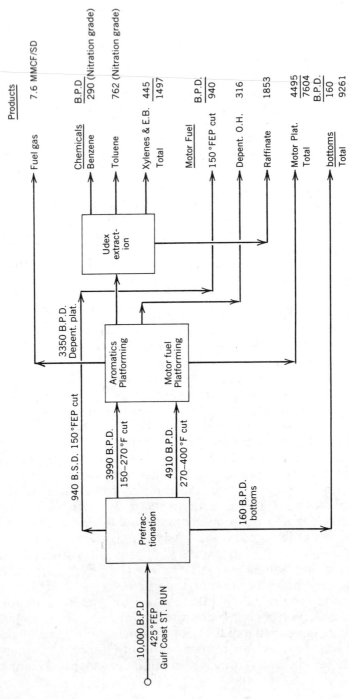

Figure 4.8 Production of aromatics. Blocked-out aromatics-motor fuel operation, (*Source:* David Read, Production of high purity atomatics for chemicals, paper presented at API's Division of Refining, May 14, 1952. Reprinted with permission by UOP Inc.)

Table 4.4   Estimated Platforming Operating Costs*

	Cents per Barrel of Reactor Feed
1. Operating supervision	
1/3 man per shift at $3.00/hour	0.3
2. Operating labor	
1 operator per shift at $2.75/hour	0.7
1 helper per shift at $2.40/hour	0.7
3. Catalyst	7.0
4. Utilities	
Fuel gas at 10 cents/MM Btu's	
Cooling water at 1 cent/1,000 gal	
Electric power at 1 cent/kwh	
Steam at 25 cents/1,000 lb	
Total utilities	**5.5**
5. Royalty	7.5
6. Taxes and insurance	
Estimated at 2.5%/year of $3.2 MM	2.6
7. Maintenance:	
Estimated at 3%/year of $3.2 MM	3.1
Total	**27.4**

Source: D. Read (see reference 21, reprinted with permission by UOP Inc.).

Basis: Charging 3,990 bbl per Stream Day of 150–270°F or 4,910 bbl per Stream Day of 270–400°F Naphtha in Blocked-out Operation

Later, UOP, alone or in partnership with operating companies, developed a number of other processes for the production and conversion of aromatics. As an example, the company was approached by Ashland Oil in the early 1950s to jointly develop and license a toluene dealkylation process based on Ashland's successful research work in the dealkylation of naphthalene. It became known as the Hydeal process. In the early 1970s, UOP undertook to further develop and license a process developed by Toray (formerly Toyo Rayon) for the disproportionation (transalkylation) of toluene and C_9 aromatics to benzene and xylenes. Known commercially as the Tatoray process, more than 15 units have been licensed after the first UOP-designed unit came onstream in 1978. More recently, British Petroleum (BP) and UOP have joined forces to commercialize a process known as Cyclar for the production of aromatics from LPG (liquid propane gas) fractions (propane and butanes) over a zeolite catalyst. Generally, UOP has been able to

Table 4.5 Economics of Operations

Basis: Charging 10,000 Bbl per Stream Day of 425°F Endpoint Gulf Coast
Straight-run Gasoline

Investment: $6,745,000 (Incl. Utility Generation and Tankage)

Value of products	Cents Per Gallon	Aromatics/Motor Fuel	
		Barrels Per Stream Day	Dollars Per Stream Day
Benzene	50.0	290	6,090
Toluene	20.0	762	6,401
Xylenes and ethylbenzene	20.0	445	3,738
Motor fuel: 92 octane no., premium	12.0	7,604	38,324
400°F plus bottoms	8.5	160	570
Total liquids	—	**9,261**	**55,123**
Fuel gas at 10 cents/MM Btu	—	—	511
Total value of products		—	**55,634**
Cost of charge stock (425°F endpoint Gulf Coast straight run)	9.25	**10,000**	**38,800**
Operating costs			
Prefractionation			493
Platforming			2,431
Udex extraction			1,380
Tetraethyl lead at 0.26 cent/ milliliter			1,510
Maintenance at 2%/year on auxiliary equipment			72
Taxes and insurance at 2.5%/ year on auxiliary equipment			90
Administration and overhead, estimated at			500
Interest at 4% on investment			780
Amortization at 20%/year of investment			3,900
Total operating costs			**11,156**
Net earnings before income tax, and amortization, $/stream day			**9,578**
Net earnings before income tax but after deduction for amortization, $/year			**$1,970,000**
Payout time before income-tax and amortization charges			**2.03 years**

Source: D. Read (see reference 21, reprinted with permission by UOP Inc.)

assemble a combination of processing "blocks" that would allow a producer to make any desired combination and relative quantity of benzene, toluene, and xylene isomers from every conceivable feedstock.

A UNIQUE SEPARATIONS TECHNOLOGY

A major success story for UOP over the past two decades was the development of the Parex process for the recovery of high purity paraxylene by separating it from its isomers in the liquid phase, using a simulated countercurrent solid bed adsorption technology. As in the case of Platforming with Ipatieff and Haensel, the successful development of the Parex process resulted from the leadership of Donald B. Broughton.

Born in Rugby, England, in 1917, Broughton came to the United States with his family when he was seven years old and settled first in Philadelphia, where his father worked for the railroad. After graduating from Pennsylvania State College in 1938, and receiving a master's degree in chemical engineering from M.I.T. in 1939, he worked briefly in the pilot plant division of Rohm and Haas Company and returned to M.I.T., where he obtained a doctor of science degree in 1943. Appointed an instructor in chemical engineering at M.I.T. in 1942, he was promoted to assistant professor in 1946 and remained at M.I.T. until he joined UOP in 1949.

At UOP, Broughton was first instrumental in the development of the Udex and Sulfolane processes described earlier. However, Don Broughton's most significant contribution at UOP was in the development of the Sorbex separations technology.

Sorbex accomplishes the selective adsorptive separation of a component or a group of components by maintaining a continuous countercurrent flow of liquid and solid adsorbent (22,23). In a Sorbex unit, the feed and product streams enter and leave the adsorbent bed continuously, without interruptions and at essentially constant composition. As in all true countercurrent processes, the adsorbent progressively undergoes adsorption and desorption, based solely on axial concentration gradients of the various components within the bed. Feed injection, adsorption, elution, desorption, and product withdrawal all take place simultaneously, but at different points within a single bed of adsorbent. No adsorbent cycling, flushing, or washing is required, since the countercurrent flow of the solid and the liquid acts as an internal enriching flush, similar to the role of the internal reflux in a fractionation column.

The countercurrent flow of liquid and solid is achieved without actual movement of the solid. Such movement is not practical because of absorbent attrition and the impossibility of assuring uniform plug flow of the solid. Instead, a stationary bed of adsorbent is used. The countercurrent motion of liquid and solid is achieved by periodically displacing the positions at which the process streams enter and leave the bed of adsorbent. Don Broughton realized that if the positions of the liquid feed and withdrawal points are shifted in the same direction as the fluid flow down the bed, the countercurrent motion of the solid in the opposite direction could be simulated.

Because it is not practical to physically move the feed and product lines, a manifold of fixed lines is attached to a number of fixed, evenly spaced nozzles and distributors within the bed. Rather than moving the lines, the displacement of the feed and withdrawal points is accomplished by, at fixed time intervals, shifting each of the process streams to the next line immediately below. For this purpose, Broughton and other UOP engineers developed a highly specialized rotary valve which, on the one side, is connected to the continuous process streams—feed, desorbent, extract, and raffinate—while the other is connected to the bed manifold. At any given moment, only the process lines are active. After a suitable time interval, the valve shifts to its next position and each process flow is switched to the adjacent line immediately below. A liquid pump maintains the connection between the bottom and the top of the bed so that, functionally, the bed has no top or bottom; it is equivalent to an annular bed.

Figure 4.9 illustrates the basic configuration of a Sorbex unit and the typical concentration profiles encountered within the bed of adsorbent. In an actual countercurrent operation, the concentration profiles would be stationary, but in a Sorbex unit the concentration profiles move downward and follow the process streams as they move, thus establishing a relative counterflow between the solid adsorbent and the circulating liquid. The figure illustrates a typical case in which the desorbent is heavier than either the extract or the raffinate; other Sorbex applications may use a desorbent that is lighter than either product stream.

The first application of the Sorbex principle was in the Molex

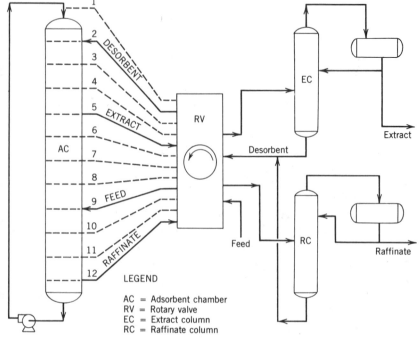

Figure 4.9 Sorbex-simulated moving bed for adsorptive separation. (*Source:* Adsorptive Separations by Simulated Moving Bed Technology: The Sorbex Process, International Conference on Fundamentals of Adsorption, Schloss Elmau, Upper Bavaria, West Germany, May 6–11, 1983. Courtesy UOP Inc.)

process for the separation of linear paraffins from branched paraffins. First commercialized in 1964, more than 20 Molex units were licensed to this time. Most Molex units recover linear paraffins in the C_{10} to C_{14} carbon range, or heavier, for the production of biodegradable synthetic detergents, but the Molex process has also been used to raise the octane value of gasoline by enriching the concentration of branched paraffins.

In 1971, the Sorbex technology was commercialized for the recovery of high purity paraxylene in the Parex process. The Parex process quickly replaced fractional crystallization as the preferred process for the recovery of paraxylene and, over the past decade, has been used in about 90 percent of all new paraxylene capacity built or licensed worldwide. More than 35 Parex units have been licensed to date. In later years, the Sorbex technology has also been commercialized to separate olefins from paraffins, to recover individual cresol isomers, to separate fructose from glucose, to separate cumene (isopropyltoluene) isomers and, in general, in applications in which conventional separation techniques, like fractionation or crystallization, would be too costly or virtually impossible.

Broughton remained with UOP all his life and further contributed to improving, modifying, and expanding the Sorbex technology. He died in 1984 while still active at UOP.*

As noted in this and the previous chapter, many other firms made outstanding contributions to the development of refining, aromatics, and petrochemical technology. One important example is afforded by the Sinclair Research Laboratories at Harvey, Illinois, under the direction of John W. Teter and including such personalities as Carl D. Keith (later a director of Engelhard and Chem Systems), William P. Hettinger, and Joseph Verdol (later licensing manager for Arco Chemical). This outstanding research organization came up with numerous processes for hydrocarbon conversions, developing superior catalysts and always staying close to the leader, UOP. One Sinclair process, developed originally for separating isobutylene, is now, 30 years later, the leading technology for making the high octane gasoline additive MTBE (methyl tertiary butyl ether).

UOP's net income from royalties, process engineering, and catalyst sales was impressively large for many years, with a substantial portion of its profits resulting from licensing its Platforming, Udex, Sulfolane, and Parex processes and supplying Platforming catalysts and Parex absorbents. This steady income allowed the company to expand its research and diversification efforts substantially. Over the years, UOP has contributed substantially to the development of fluid catalytic cracking (FCC), hydrocracking, dehydrogenation, and alkylation technology and has licensed processes in these areas extensively. Also, over the past 20 years, UOP undertook a number of ventures outside the petroleum field, some more successful than others. Although UOP enjoyed additional success in its later process developments, it made its biggest and most unique contribution to the refining and chemical industry by providing routes to low cost, plentiful aromatics.

*Don Broughton was also an excellent teacher—as I found out during my junior year at M.I.T.—(*P.H.S.*).

REFERENCES

1. *World Petroleum* (1939). Annual Refinery Issue.
2. D. S. Smith and L. W. Moore (1941). Hydroforming is new dehydrogenation process, *The Petroleum Engineer*, April.
3. Paul W. Emmett, ed. (1958). *Catalysis, Volume VI, Alkylation, Isomerization, Polymerization, Cracking, and Hydroforming*, New York, Reinhold, p. 631.
4. Phthalic anhydride breaks a coal tar tradition, *Chemical Engineering*, August 1946.
5. John L. Enos (1962). *Petroleum, Progress and Profits: A History of Process Innovation*, Cambridge, Mass., M.I.T. Press, p. 67.
6. Williamson, Harold F., et al. (1963). *The American Petroleum Industry*, Evanston, Ill., Northwestern University Press.
7. Don F. Hardie and J. Davidson Pratt, (1966) *A History of the Modern British Chemical Industry*, p. 16.
8. Edward Farber (1953). *Nobel Prize Winners in Chemistry (1901-1951)*, New York, Abelard-Schuman, pp. 51-55.
9. Les hydrogenations directés sur le nickel, *Bulletin de la Société Chimique de France*, S.5 V.6 MEM., (1939.)
10. R. Holroyd (1958). The development of the petroleum chemical industry in Britain, *Chemistry and Industry*, July 19, 900-909.
11. V. N. Ipatieff (1946). *The Life of a Chemist. Memoirs of V. N. Ipatieff*, Stanford, Cal., Stanford University Press.
12. Herman Pines (1981). My mentor, Ipatieff, *Chemtech*, February (1981). 78-82.
13. Herman Pines (1983). V. N. Ipatieff: As I Knew Him, American Chemical Society Monograph, *Heterogeneous Catalysis*.
14. V. Haensel (1983). The development of the platforming process—Some personal and catalytic recollections, American Chemical Society Monograph, *Heterogeneous Catalysis*.
15. V. I. Komarewsky and C. H. Riess (1948). Catalytic reforming of straight run gasoline increases aromatics content, *Oil and Gas Journal*, June 24, 90ff.
16. V. Haensel, U. S. Patent 2,479,100, assigned to UOP.
17. V. Haensel, U. S. Patent 2,479,109, assigned to UOP.
18. M. L. Kastens and R. E. Sutherland (1952). Platinum reforming of gasoline, *Modern Chemical Processes*, **II**, 193-204. Also *Industrial and Engineering Chemistry*, **42**, 528, April 1950.
19. Fred L. Hartley (1945). Commercial synthesis of toluene by hydroforming and recovery by azeotropic distillation, *Petroleum Refiner*, **24** (12), December, 519-524.
20. G. F. Asselin and R. A. Persak (1975). BTX Aromatics extraction: Past, present and future, UOP Process Division Technology Conference. Des Plaines, Illinois.
21. David Read (1952). Production of high-purity aromatics for chemicals, presented at API's Division of Refining, May 14.

22. D. B. Broughton (1978). Adsorptive separation (liquids), *Kirk-Othmer: Encyclopedia of Chemical Technology,* Vol. 1, Third Edition, New York, John Wiley and Co.

23. D. B. Broughton and S. A. Gembicki (1983). Adsorptive separations by simulated moving bed technology: The Sorbex process, International Conference on Fundamentals of Adsorption, Schloss Elmau, Upper Bavaria, West Germany, May 6-11.

ADDITIONAL READING

Broughton, D. B. and G. F. Asselin (1967). Production of high purity aromatics by the Sulfolane Process, Paper presented to the Seventh World Petroleum Congress.

Catalytic Reforming: The Search for Higher Octanes, American Institute for Chemical Engineering paper, Houston, Texas, March 4, 1971.

Egloff, Gustav (1940). Improved processes in the manufacture of motor fuels from petroleum, *Petroleum Engineer,* **11** (10), 21-26.

Grote, H. W. (1958). The Udex process, *Chemical Engineering Progress,* **54** (8), 43-48, August.

Grote, H. W. and D. B. Broughton (1959). Use of the Udex process for refinery octane balancing. Presented to the API's Division of Refining, May 28.

Haensel, V. (1950). Platforming, *Petroleum Refiner,* **29** (4), April, 131-136.

Haensel V. and V. N. Ipatieff (1947). Selective demethylation of paraffin hydrocarbons, *Industrial & Engineering Chemistry,* **23,** July, 853-855.

Hill, L. R. et al. (1946). Hydroforming: A catalytic method for naphtha upgrading, *National Petroleum News,* **38** (23), June 5.

Ipatieff, V. N., D. B. Carson, and G. Egloff (1935). Polymerization, a new source of gasoline, *Industrial and Engineering Chemistry,* **27** (9), September, 1077-1081.

Sterba, M. J. and V. Haensel (1971). Catalytic reforming: Its role in the manufacture of petroleum and petrochemical products. Yesterday, today, and tomorrow, *World Petroleum,* June.

5 / The Old Order: Cooperation and Cartels

Executives and lawyers at Exxon Corporation are more sensitive on the subject of antitrust issues than their peers at most other oil and chemical companies. Thus, business dealings between Exxon—formerly Standard Oil Company (N.J.)—and outside firms are scrutinized more carefully, from an antitrust standpoint, than those at many other companies. Exxon's preoccupation with avoiding any conceivable antitrust violations could easily be rooted in the 1911 Supreme Court decision that dissolved the Standard Oil Trust, thereby dividing the Rockefeller-controlled petroleum empire into a number of independent companies, including Standard of New Jersey. To some extent, this is undoubtedly the case. More likely, however, the company's attitude on antitrust violations is related to a later event, when Jersey unexpectedly became the company that received the full brunt of the Roosevelt Administration's antitrust campaign. The attention of both the executive and legislative branches of the U.S. government was turned on Jersey, not because the company had behaved in a more reprehensible fashion than many other U.S. firms that had formed production and sales alliances with domestic or foreign companies, but because it had entered into a broad technology exchange and market definition agreement in 1929 with I.G. Farbenindustrie, which lasted until the start of World War II and gave each party control over technology for the production of specified chemicals and synthetic fuels in each other's sphere of influence (chemicals for the I.G. and fuels for Jersey). As a result of this agreement, Jersey was subjected to the most unfavorable possible publicity. Just before war broke out, the company agreed to sign a consent decree that effectively terminated the Jersey-I.G. relationship.*

Jersey officials testifying before Congressional committees during this period claimed that the company, as a result of its agreements with the German combine, had obtained valuable information covering the production of high octane fuels and synthetic rubber. They also stated that the company's decision to accept the consent decree was made to allow the country to get on with the war effort and did not imply any "guilt" on the part of Jersey. The records of such hearings were published and, in this case, contain a very large amount of both written and oral information. It has, therefore, been possible for historians to evaluate the circumstances at the time, particularly when these records are combined with information obtained from German documents seized at the conclusion of the war. In several books dealing with this subject (1-4), different aspects of the case are highlighted, depending on the authors' viewpoint, and this makes it difficult to form a judgment on all the issues involved. Certain points do, however, emerge with considerable clarity.

First, it becomes evident that the I.G., which had, whether it wanted to or not, become an agent of the Nazi government, had been successful in obtaining a considerable amount of information useful for the German war effort through its association with its American partner. For example, the I.G. had requested and received full information on the production of butyl rubber (a Jersey invention)† and tetraethyl lead (from Ethyl Corporation, 50 percent owned by Jersey), while Standard had been almost totally unsuccessful in obtaining know-how on Buna rubber production from its German partner, who only released the Buna *patent information* to Jersey (1, pp. 82–84; 2, p. 502). The I.G. had also been

---

*Details of this and two other consent judgments entered into by Jersey are described in a booklet entitled "Antitrust Guide 1979" distributed to all Exxon employees. In 1985, the consent decree referred to in this chapter was finally set aside by the federal government.

†However, Jersey's research on butyl rubber was, in fact, based on earlier information received from I.G. Farben, which had not been able to make a satisfactory synthetic rubber from isobutylene.

successful in getting Jersey to build a demonstration plant for the arc acetylene process. This know-how was then taken back to Germany and was later indispensable for the production of Buna rubber during the war. Jersey did, however, obtain information and know-how in such areas as (1) *hydroforming,* which proved to be very important in producing toluene and other aviation gasoline components from petroleum fractions, and (2) *steam-methane reforming* technology to produce hydrogen. In the case of tetraethyl lead, the hearings did not emphasize that the U.S. government had, in fact, given its official sanction to this transfer of know-how to the Nazi government. Although Jersey did gain the right to use the Buna patents to build synthetic rubber plants in the United States, the Germans never provided the technical know-how necessary to use these patents. Nevertheless, the antitrust action unfairly accused Jersey of having established a monopoly with the I.G. to keep other U.S. companies from building synthetic rubber plants. Actually, Jersey had approached the Army and Navy munitions boards as soon as it received the Buna patents to advise that the United States should immediately proceed with a synthetic rubber program. It was the government that dragged its feet at that point.* In retrospect, it appears that Jersey was primarily guilty of having signed an agreement that was difficult to enforce as it related to the exchange of know-how on synthetic rubber technology, for there was nothing in the agreement that would allow Jersey to force I.G. Farben to yield the Buna information it was entitled to receive, while the Germans had obtained valuable U.S. know-how in other areas, in time to use in their planning for war.

Second, a review of the Jersey-I.G. agreements shows that these were primarily technology-exchange agreements of the type that were—and still are—frequently entered into by manufacturing firms who convey exclusive licenses covering patented inventions. These agreements were, in fact, not the type of far-reaching cartel arrangements typical of the period between the wars, when technology-exchange agreements were used as a springboard for market sharing, price fixing, and other actions characteristic of cartels. Jersey had entered into its agreements with the I.G. mainly because of its concern that the Germans might become major com-

---

*James W. Carr, Jr., ex-Jersey official and author of *50 Year History of Exxon Research Laboratories,* personal communication.

petitors in the world fuel market, with gasoline produced via coal hydrogenation. To induce the Germans to let Jersey effectively control this technology outside of Germany, Jersey agreed to finance pilot-plant research and to exchange chemical know-how with the Germans, thus giving the I.G. effective control in much of the world over the production of chemicals covered in the agreement.

Third, it is a fact that the antitrust action taken against Jersey was only one of many other such actions conducted by Thurman Arnold's "trustbusting" team in the late 1930s, when the Roosevelt administration turned its attention to correcting what it perceived to be the excesses of "Big Business", condoned by previous Republican administrations. The Standard Oil case received a great deal more publicity than the others, because it occurred just before the war and because Jersey was judged by many as being guilty of having been too friendly with the Nazi industrialists.* It was not really brought out to any great extent that many other American firms had also built extensive relationships with I.G. Farben over the previous 20 years and that the chemical industry of the world was, in effect, a series of "clubs," with I.G. Farben a "charter member."

Many firms outside of Germany were, in the 1920s and 1930s, eager to obtain the benefits of advanced German chemical technology and, as a result, entered into complex bilateral or multilateral agreements that gave the I.G. an inordinate amount of influence in the chemical industries of other countries. Although a few firms tended to resist some of the I.G.'s attempts to gain even more influence and were inclined to treat the German companies' actions with suspicion and countermoves when these were considered as unfair or unreasonable, they often cooperated in other areas, using technology-exchange agreements as the basis for such cooperation. In fact, during the period from roughly 1910 to the start of World War II—with only a short interruption during World War I—this practice was the rule rather than the exception. It was a period when international cartels blossomed into an effective and pervasive business practice, covering products rang-

---

*Jersey officials felt that they were largely vindicated when Rubber Director William Jeffers, in June 1943, stated "had it not been for the research and engineering development carried out by Standard Oil of New Jersey prior to Pearl Harbor, the synthetic rubber program would be one and one-half years behind what it is now" (3).

ing from commodities, such as sugar and natural rubber, to manufactured products such as chemical fertilizers, aluminum, and electric light bulbs. American firms were not in the forefront of these schemes to reduce or essentially eliminate competition, since U.S. antimonopoly and antitrust laws, such as the Clayton and Sherman Acts, were much stricter than those in foreign countries. Also, unlike many foreign governments, the United States government did not participate in or abet the establishment of these cartels. Nevertheless, many of the large domestic chemical companies participated in international cooperation agreements, establishing complex relationships with foreign firms through various types of patent and process-exchange agreements that went considerably beyond the intent of the patent system.

The manufacture of heavy organic chemicals, fertilizers, dyestuffs, and a number of other chemicals during the period between the wars was a closely held business, with each segment controlled by a limited number of companies that wanted to keep things the way they were. Cooperation between internationally oriented companies producing similar lines of chemicals was extensive and the business was conducted in an atmosphere of "noblesse oblige" between the large companies that controlled specific chemical product areas. Market sharing on a local and international level was normal practice in these cases, so that competition in the true sense of the word was often nonexistent in most of the countries involved in cartel arrangements.

When World War II broke out, many companies on both sides of the conflict anticipated that, when hostilities were over, the old order would resume. In fact, this did occur in Europe, to some extent, before the European Economic Community imposed anticartel legislation. In the United States, however, a different set of conditions prevailed, with a number of new firms poised to enter the rapidly expanding chemical business. Government agencies and Congress were determined to prevent, through vigorous enforcement of the antitrust laws, a recurrence of the old, anticompetitive alliances. The chemical industry now became highly competitive, although traditional producers still showed no particular desire to share their technology with the newcomers. By the mid- to late 1950s, the number of companies producing some of the key chemicals had expanded considerably and it became evident that the old days might be gone forever. Soon thereafter, the same thing started to occur in Europe, although at a slower pace, with traditional chemicals producers remaining in a strong position. A smaller number of "outside" firms did, however, enter the industry.

Development and control of technology was the basis for the original establishment of cartels among chemical manufacturers. Technology development was also the cause of their demise. After World War II, the companies that had dominated various areas of chemical production found to their chagrin that they could no longer use technology control in the same manner as before. In addition to government suits aimed specifically at lessening the degree of domination stemming from technology control, companies were confronted with an increasing number of innovations from new sources, such as engineering firms and research establishments. Inventors could now also hope for receptivity among potential new entrants to the industry, who still found it difficult to obtain technology from the old-line firms in the industry. This much more open environment has continued since that time, but to understand the transition it is necessary to look at the system under which much of the chemical industry operated before the war.

THE BIRTH AND GROWTH OF CARTELS

In an era when "cartel" is considered to be a dirty word, it is easy to forget that cartels were a way of life for a long period of time. In the United States, cartels were, in fact, illegal and in their relations with foreign firms, domestic producers had to be careful to avoid stretching collaborative activities beyond the point where it was felt there could be prosecution under the antitrust laws. But a considerable amount of such "stretching" did take place.

In Europe, the situation was much easier and the atmosphere more conducive. Here, there were explicit market-sharing schemes, both within a country and between firms in a number of different countries. There was considerable exchange of information on prices and frequent consultations on how to deal with business problems threatening the cartel. This method of conducting business had become well established and, as far as the producers were concerned, was the only rational means to deal with a problem that is common to a number of industries, including the chemical industry and which, in the absence of government action, provides a perfectly good reason for "competitors" to form a cartel: For products that have a relatively inelastic demand and whose total supply exceeds the demand, severe competition among the producers will injure all of them. For example, only so much sulfuric acid is needed to make ammonium sulfate fertilizers at any given time, or only so many tons of soda ash to make the total amount of glass produced and sold in any one year. If companies producing sulfuric acid or soda ash, utilizing relatively similar technologies and producing materials of similar quality, decided to compete on the basis of price, chaos would generally follow. Theoretically, if one producer cuts the price, he would tend to get most of the business, or at least sell as much as he can produce. With two or three producers sharing a market, the first producer's major gain in market share would seriously hurt the others and there would then be no choice on their part but to match the price cut or to face the possibility of going out of business. Little additional soda ash would have been sold as a result of a price cut in this material, since the world would not install more glass windows as a result of a small reduction in glass price, conceivably resulting from cheaper soda ash. Actually, the glass producer would probably not even drop his price, but would try to keep the additional profit made from buying cheaper soda ash. With a lower soda ash price now established, the winner is therefore the glass manufacturer, who has increased his profit margins. The loser is the entire soda ash industry—the several producers who all cut their price to match the first price cutter and then ended up with more or less the same market share as before, a lower sales revenue, and therefore lower profits or even losses.

Cartels were established to avoid such problems. In such an arrangement, the soda ash manufacturers simply did not take unilateral steps, such as price cuts, to gain market share.

Although it was often easy to establish the original cartel, these associations did, at times, run into difficulties, as the number of participants grew and the members became more difficult to monitor and control. When only two or three firms cooperated in a cartel, it was relatively easier to deal with issues such as expansion of demand (i.e., which firm would build the next plant) or exports (how would a particular market be shared). With more firms in the cartel, the situation became more complex and frequently tenuous. Most of the time, however, cartel arrangements were manageable, even if specific arrangements fell apart for short periods from time to time. Mutual interest in reestablishing order generally made the participants decide soon enough to "bury the hatchet."

In studying the operation of cartels originally based on manufacturing technology, one is struck by the fact that the participating companies would have stayed within the bounds of allowable conduct, if they had decided to limit their cooperation to exclusive or nonexclusive licenses and to the exchange of technical know-how under such licensing arrangements. Ownership of a patent does give a person or a company monopolistic control over the invention in all the countries in which the patent is filed. This includes also the right to grant licenses under the patent to other companies (i.e., for other companies to practice the invention and to pay royalties to the patent holder). Patent ownership also allows the companies granting licenses to specify the capacity of plants built under such licenses and to limit the licensees' freedom to sell the product in other countries, at least to some extent. These types of arrangements do not, however, allow companies to fix prices nor to engage in market-sharing arrangements. The monopoly powers granted under the patent laws are, of course, not applicable to companies that do not even have patent-licensing agreements with each other, but which, through other forms of association or through the exchange of share ownership, act to limit competition among the members of the cartel and act in concert against potential newcomers.

Regardless of patent arrangements, manufacturing cartels were, in fact, most often established by companies that found it convenient to cooperate closely on technology and manufacturing issues. They then used these contacts to establish what were considered as "orderly" marketing arrangements on a global basis. The fact that technology developments are of such great importance to chemicals producers gave companies the incentive to maintain good channels of communications with their licensed "competitors." One of these companies might make an important improvement in a process or might become aware of a serious threat to the cartel, posed by process technology being developed outside the group. If successful, such an "outside" development could conceivably render the existing industry obsolete. This would be a far more serious threat than new technology developed by one of the members of the cartel, since in the latter case the fortunate producer would normally just use the invention to bargain for a larger market share and for (higher) licensing fees from fellow members of the cartel. But in a well-organized cartel, private inventors were generally forced to deal with the cartel rather than with individual producers. This made their position much weaker and helped to maintain the dominant position of the cartel, which could, if desired, agree to buy off the inventor and shelve the new technology to avoid making new capital investments.

Cartels were particularly important to the weaker producers, who found membership in the cartel essential to keeping their less efficient production facilities in operation under the price umbrella set by the cartel. It goes without saying that this price was set at a higher level than would have been the case in a truly competitive environment.

The fact that many chemical products are of strategic national importance—for example, nitric acid for fertilizers and explosives, caustic soda for refineries, soda ash for glass manufacture—actually provided a rationale for governments to support the existence of certain cartels. These tended to keep in operation some of the less efficient plants in the countries involved or kept the ownership and control of such plants from falling into the hands of foreign producers, who would not have the country's best interests in mind, in case of war. Governments could therefore rationalize certain cartels on the basis of national security.

Cartels varied in form, breadth, and degree of control. In their looser manifestation, they affected market prices only to some extent or for certain intervals, because at least some of the participants did not consider themselves strongly bound by cartel rules. In their more highly perfected form, cartels eliminated all competition through jointly owned selling agencies and by means of financial and organizational ties between cartel members.

An interesting distinction can be made between "defensive" and "aggressive" cartels. The former usually involved commodities such as sugar, natural rubber or Chilean natural fertilizer (in the early 1900s), which were generally in oversupply and whose price was therefore in constant danger of falling so low as to become ruinous to the producers. Government sponsorship of cartel arrangements allowed companies engaged in the production of such commodities to annually review supply restriction and market-sharing arrangements. That this did not always work as intended did not alter the fact that cartels were an accepted business practice. Some of the original "defensive" cartels, such as the one set up by the natural rubber producing countries, were kept intact even when demand had risen to the point where supply restrictions were probably no longer required. The OPEC (Organization of Petroleum Exporting Countries) crude oil cartel, which flourished between 1973 and 1982 and will probably regain strength in the 1990s, is, in a sense, a defensive cartel, even though its members acted very aggressively during its heyday.

"Aggressive" cartels went considerably beyond restricting the supply of an overabundant commodity—for example, to keep coffee bean farmers or tin producers from being ruined by overproduction or to keep governments from being overthrown when a bumper farm crop caused a plunge in commodity prices. They were, in fact, private business arrangements set up by manufacturers to maximize profits by limiting competition and arranging sales prices among the producers participating in the cartel. In the case of government-sponsored cartels involving commodities, where such factors as output quotas and selling prices were open knowledge, the cartels formed by manufacturing firms involved private agreements between businessmen, which often violated the law and, in the United States, usually ended up in antitrust actions.

The Nobel explosives cartel and the alkali cartel were among the first associations involving a number of international manufacturing firms. Alfred Nobel had patented his formula for dynamite in the mid-1860s and had then built a highly profitable empire of manufacturing branches all over the world. But in 1881, the basic patent ran out and a number of new firms began to produce dynamite or related types of explosives. Nobel's profits rapidly eroded, as the price of dynamite dropped sharply, due to heavy competition. In the Nobel boardroom, it was time to take positive action and the term "cartel" began to be heard. Over the next seven years, price-fixing accords were signed with a number of German firms; similar agreements were signed with competitors by Nobel subsidiaries in France and Latin America. A British-German firm, The Nobel-Dynamite Trust Company, Ltd., was set up to combine the interests of firms in both of these countries and the trust then proceeded to set up spheres of influence throughout the world, including a profit-sharing arrangement known as the General Pooling Agreement (5).

In his long and extremely informative book on the history of ICI, W. J. Reader, makes some interesting comments on the formation of cartels, which, in his judgment, acted to inhibit the development of new technology (6, pp. 468–469):

"Once their affairs were running prosperously, the exponents of the new technologies in explosives and in alkali showed little inclination to search for radical innovation on the patterns of the 1870s. Between the mid-seventies and 1914, there was a development of capital importance—smokeless powder, which enormously accelerated the development of weapons—but apart from that, the explosives makers were well content with the group of blasting explosives invented by Alfred Nobel, and beyond the explosives field they saw no point in going. In alkali, Ernest Solvay initiated the development of Semet-Solvay coke ovens and he saw the importance of electrochemistry. Except in Germany, however, his zeal for technical progress, particularly in electrolysis, found little support among his associates. Brunner Mond concentrated wholeheartedly (and very successfully) on soda ash and its near relations, paying very little attention to anything else, in spite of occasional unease about dependence on one group of products—until the Great War decisively broadened their outlook. For a matter of more than forty years before 1914 . . . the two branches of the chemical industry—explosives and alkali—were technically unadventurous in the matter of technical innovations. . . .

. . . "[What is seen here is] a record of industrial diplomacy directed to one end: the regulation, throughout the world, of competition between makers in the same industry, with a view to the protection of profits in normal times and, at moments of crisis, survival. This was the objective in the explosives industry of the formation of the Nobel-Dynamite Trust Company (1886), of the General Pooling Agreement (1889) between the Trust Company and German powder companies, and of the long negotiations between the European companies and DuPont between 1897 and the outbreak of the Great War. In the alkali industry, the Solvay group single-mindedly pursued the aim of keeping its members out of each other's way and of presenting a united front to such outside competition as presented itself.

"As soon as competition begins to bite, particularly in periods of bad trade or in a market no longer expanding, businessmen usually try to moderate its force (using) mergers, takeover, price agreement, market sharing, restriction of output . . . what was exceptional about companies in explosives and in alkali was not that they did these things, but that they did them so successfully".

It appears that DuPont was, at first, unwilling to join the Nobel group. However, when in 1897, a German member of the trust made plans to build a plant to make detonators, propellants, and blasting agents in New Jersey, DuPont executives traveled to London and reluctantly decided to have their company become a member of the club. For 10 years thereafter, world trade was divided into three parts; European, American, and "syndicated" territories. The result of this arrangement was satisfactory to all parties; there would be no invasion of Europe or America by firms in the opposite territory and, in the "syndicated" third area, mostly Latin America, prices were fixed and profits shared by all members (5).

In 1907, under the Sherman Act, the U.S. government filed an antitrust action against DuPont, which effectively ended the arrangement. Antitrust action also resulted in splitting off from DuPont two parts of the business that became the Hercules and Atlas Powder Companies. However, shortly thereafter, the DuPont lawyers conducted a careful review of the details of the Sherman Act, resulting in a finding that seemed to indicate an approach that would not be in violation. Although market sharing and price fixing were clearly illegal, the Sherman Act recognized the fact that patent laws allowed inventors effective monopoly privileges, including the right to license inventions on an exclusive basis. Thus, it was possible to exchange patents and confidential know-how as a more sophisticated means of communication. It would not be as effective or as blatant as the previous type of arrangement, but it could be extremely useful as a new form of cooperation. The DuPont and ICI lawyers rewrote the agreements, using patent and know-how exchange as the basis to form a new association, which became a powerful force in the period between the two world wars (5). In 1929, DuPont and ICI, the successor company to the British Nobel interests, formed a far-reaching alliance that comprised synthetic fertilizers, dyestuffs, coal hydrogenation, alkali (Brunner Mond) and other products. From the standpoint of ICI, at least, it was a "cartel-maker's world" (6).

A broad study of cartels conducted in the late 1940s by the Twentieth Century Fund offered this viewpoint on the role of patent cross-licensing agreements (2, p. 10):

"Not all patents and processes agreements are illegal, of course, nor do they necessarily constitute cartels or reinforced cartels. Only when they go beyond the recognized and legitimate scope of patent privileges duly conferred and impose mutual restrictions or create contractual rights which impair freedom of opportunity in trade and impede competitive adjustments in open markets do they take on the character of a cartel arrangement. The patent cross-licensing agreement has been an important device used by American and foreign firms to establish a degree of control over international markets much greater than would have been possible under a separate and independent exercise of their respective monopoly privileges based on patent grants. Through these arrangements, the parties have divided world markets, allocated output, and fixed prices . . . they have frequently extended the scope of these arrangements to products and processes not at the moment subject to patents . . . and they have made these arrangements . . . on a permanent basis."

While the referenced study is based on a great deal of research, containing thousands of citations, the objective reader is struck by a certain amount of antibusiness bias in portions of the text. It also seems that at the Senate hearings,* the mode of questioning that was used elicited answers from company spokesmen that could easily lead to later innocent or deliberate misinterpretations of the record covering these hearings. Nevertheless, the Twentieth Century Fund study may be one of the best references available on chemical cartels in the nineteenth and twentieth centuries.

Some of the important international chemical cartels were in nitrogen and in dyestuffs. Export cartels were set up to cover a large number of other products. In the United States, these were not necessarily illegal and even today, certain types of export cartels are allowed to operate (e.g., the Nitrex cartel for fertilizer exports). However, what were purported to be export cartels, in some cases were, in fact, worldwide market-sharing arrangements involving a large number of companies in the same business, which also included restrictions on sale of related foreign products in the United States. This was true in the case of the alkali cartel, which included Solvay, ICI, I.G. Farben, and the U.S. export association known as Alkasso.

ALKALI CARTEL ILLUSTRATES ROLE OF TECHNOLOGY

The alkali cartel is symbolic, since it was the oldest such association, covering the manufacture and sale of the first chemical deliberately produced by synthetic means on an industrial scale—soda ash. The technology on which the alkali cartel of the late 1800s was based was the Solvay process, a successor to the original soda ash process, invented by Leblanc.

The chemical name for soda ash is sodium carbonate, but it received its common name from the fact that in the earliest days

---

*Several congressional committees, including a committee headed by Senator Bone, conducted lengthy investigations of business practices before World War II—often with a highly adversary attitude toward business leaders.

soda ash was made in Spain by burning seaweed. This resulted in combining the ocean's salt (sodium) with the organic carbon found in the seaweed, forming the "soda ash," which could then be leached out, recovered, and sold.* The French glass industry became heavily dependent on this material in the 1700s. Thus, when the British navy cut off Spanish exports during the war in which the British Armada decisively defeated the Spanish fleet, the French Academy offered a prize of 12,000 Francs to the person inventing a process to replace natural soda ash. Leblanc worked on this for three years and succeeded magnificently when he roasted a "salt cake" made with salt, sulfuric acid (sodium sulfate), charcoal, and chalk. Sodium carbonate formed when this black ash was leached with water and the soda ash could then be crystallized and recovered.

A number of countries built soda ash plants based on Leblanc's process. About 80 years after its discovery, however, this process also became the first chemical technology to be totally obsolesced by another route, the Solvay process, which was substantially cheaper. In 1863, Ernest Solvay, a Belgian chemist found that when a salt solution was saturated with coke-oven ammonia and allowed to contact carbon dioxide gas made by heating limestone, sodium bicarbonate was formed. This material could be decomposed to sodium carbonate (soda ash) by simple heating. By the time the Solvay process swept through the industrial world, soda ash was used not only for glass manufacture, but for making soap and a number of other important products.

Solvay, together with his family, now proceeded to set up a series of manufacturing entities in different countries using patent ownership as a basis for exerting worldwide control over the use of his invention. Solvay and Ludwig Mond set up Brunner Mond in Great Britain in 1872 with an exclusive license on the Solvay process. That company and Solvay then established the Solvay Process Company in New York. Meanwhile, Solvay had licensed a number of other subsidiaries in Germany, Holland, France, Italy, Russia, and other countries to practice the manufacture of soda ash by the new route. The companies were linked not only by common technology, but also by marketing agreements involving

---

*Soda ash is a strong alkali or base (the opposite of an acid) because the sodium part of the molecule, which is also a constituent of caustic soda, is stronger as an alkali or base than the carbonate part is an acid.

price fixing and division of sales territories. Solvay and I.G. Farben jointly owned Aussiger Verein, a company that exploited the process in Czechoslovakia, Poland, Yugoslavia, Hungary, and Rumania and were also members of the German Soda Syndicate. The Belgian company owned about 25 percent of the stock of ICI (the successor company to Brunner Mond), and roughly the same percentage of Allied Chemical & Dye, the successor to the Solvay Process Company in the United States.

Although Allied Chemical & Dye Company was closely linked to Brunner Mond and Solvay, it is quite clear that it did not always "play the game" as the Europeans might have wanted it played. Headed by Orlando F. Weber, a strong individualist who resented the stake that the European companies had gained in Allied, the company refused to cooperate in the sharing of world markets in alkalis, much to the distress of the part owners of his company. In fact, Weber in 1920 told Solvay and Brunner Mond that "his new combine would be as complete if not more complete and more wealthy than I.G." Allied, which had a public stock offering that year, was, in fact, bigger than the I.G. and the combination of British companies that would later become ICI. Allied's reluctance to play ball with its European counterparts is said to have contributed to Brunner Mond's decision to join Nobel Industries and form ICI. This merger included the United Alkali Company (successor to the British Leblanc process companies but now producing electrolytic chlorine and caustic) and also British Dyestuffs Corporation, which had been formed through previous mergers of Levinstein, Ltd. and British Alizarine, both old-line British dye producers. The merger of the four companies into ICI was strongly supported by the Baldwin government—as a counter to the rising force known as I.G. Farben.

The soda ash produced by the Solvay process had, by then, been challenged by caustic soda produced via electrolysis. This technology was first commercially practiced in 1890 by Chemische Fabrik Elektron-Griesheim in Germany, using a diaphragm cell patented four years earlier (7). Still later, both soda ash and electrolytic caustic were challenged by natural soda ash produced from the rich Trona deposits discovered in this century. These developments spelled the end of the alkali cartel. But, during its time, the alkali association based on the Solvay process was the original, archtypical cartel that set the pattern for the world chemical industry.

NITROGEN CARTEL SHOWS TECHNIQUES EMPLOYED

In the 1920s, there was intense activity among several of the leading European chemical firms in extending the technology of ammonia production. Several different versions of the original Haber-Bosch process were put into commercial operation in different countries and numerous patents were issued, covering reactor and tube design, catalyst manufacture, refrigeration systems, and other parts of the basic ammonia process. Several patented designs assigned to some of the more important companies in the field are depicted in Figure 5.1. Yet, while these firms competed vigorously with each other in coming up with incremental, patentable improvements in the manufacture of ammonia, which they could license to other firms at a profit, they were also concerned that their activities in the market place should not result in unstable pricing and unexpected invasion of the home market by overeager competitors.

The nitrogen cartel is a good example of how cartels functioned to limit supply in an oversupplied environment. Organized in 1929, when world capacity in ammonia and in nitrate fertilizers exceeded world consumption by over 100 percent, nitrogen producers turned to cartel control as the only possible salvation. By dividing markets, allocating exports, and cooperating on sales, producers attempted to raise prices, which had recently dropped over 20 percent. The German Nitrogen Syndicate stated the following objectives for the cartel: "The Syndicate (cartel) just concluded aims at bringing the production of nitrogen fertilizers, which has lately risen out of proportion to requirements, back to the level of consumption. By eliminating unsound competition on the nitrogen market, it is intended to prevent losses both in production and distribution of nitrogeneous fertilizers and thus enable the industry to supply agriculture with cheaper fertilizers in the future." (2)

By 1930, the cartel had effected a reduction of 10 percent in French fertilizer output and a 50 percent reduction in British production. Members were paid to reduce output. For example, 4.5 million Deutschmarks were paid by the German syndicate to the major Dutch nitrogen company to induce closure of a portion of one plant, thus limiting its total output. A later agreement paid the Belgian nitrogen group 12 pence for every 100 kilograms of nitrogen sold by cartel members in their home and foreign markets to compensate the Belgians for restricting their output. Earlier,

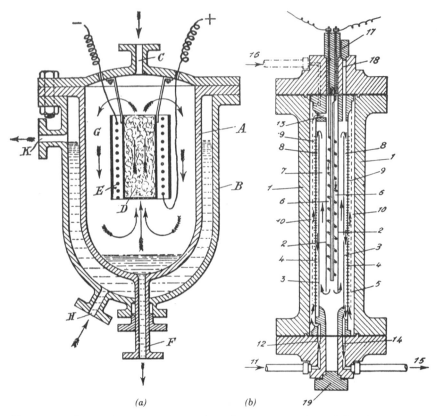

Figure 5.1 Ammonia process patents issued to some members of the nitrogen cartel. (*a*) Apparatus for the synthesis of ammonia (B.A.S.F., 1910). (*b*) Catalyst tube (L. Casale, 1925). (*Source:* Harold Tongue, *The Design and Construction of High Pressure Chemical Plant*, Van Nostrand, New York, 1934.) (For three other patented designs, see pg. 214.)

the German nitrogen producers association had paid 75 million Belgian Francs to the same group to stop construction of an incomplete plant at Ressaix-Laval (2, p. 161).

In 1933, I.G. Farben, which led the German nitrogen cartel, blocked a potential capacity expansion in the United States by refusing to license Hercules Powder Company for ammonia production. In its letter to Hercules, it advised that "because of our

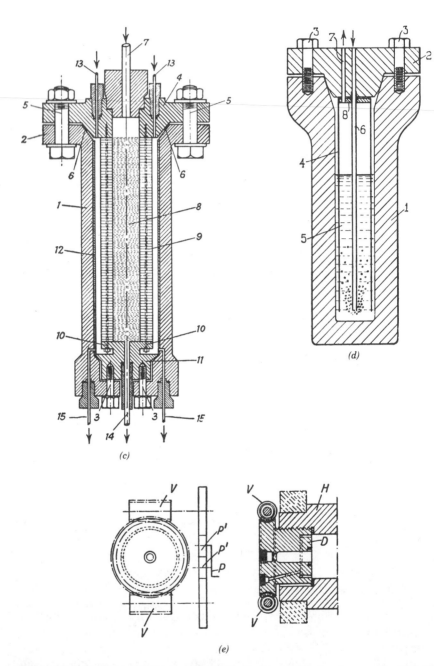

Figure 5.1 *(Continued)* (c) Catalyst tube for the synthesis of ammonia (Norsk Hydro Elec. kvall., September, 1924). (d) High pressure reaction vessel (Imperial Chemical Industries, 1928). (e) Catalyst tube for ammonia synthesis (L'Air Liquide, January, 1921). (*Source:* As for Fig. 5.1a, b.)

214

other nitrogen interests, we are not in a position to permit your firm to use our process and experience. . . ." These other interests included a previous license to DuPont (2, p. 161).

The nitrogen cartel found it had a difficult task on its hands, since world nitrogen capacity increased from 3,278,000 tons in 1929 to 5,082,300 tons by 1934. This huge amount of new capacity further depressed prices, a trend that was aggravated by the world recession, which acted to cut demand in spite of price reductions. In the early years of the Great Depression, the cartel had found it possible to resist price drops, for example in ammonium sulphate. By 1932, however, the price for this commodity had dropped from approximately 9£ per ton to around 6£ and the cartel regrouped to try and defend the price at this level. Eventually, a 20–30 percent price rise was achieved.

An interesting tactic used by the cartel to protect weaker producers was to establish "economic capacity." This was defined as "the minimum requirement for economic operation." Two units with a similar maximum capacity of 50,000 tons per year might have been operated by a strong producer with lower costs and a weaker producer. The former's "economic capacity", (i.e., the capacity at which he could still operate with some profit margin) might have been 25,000 tons, while the weaker producer's was 35,000 tons. The cartel allowed the weaker producer to operate at the higher capacity, so that both producers could have a viable operation, with the stronger producer enjoying higher profits, due to lower costs.

These tactics were symptomatic of European cartels in the first third of the twentieth century. As noted, such cartels used various tactics to restrict supply and to coordinate world prices. Nevertheless, they often met with only limited success or their influence was limited to certain periods of time, after which more powerful economic or political forces took over.

CARTELS AND POWER POLITICS

It is not surprising that chemicals producers found it easy or perhaps even necessary, in their view, to adopt the cartel approach. In the chemical industry, new products and processes constantly threaten to disturb the established order, involving the stability of markets and the economic viability of manufacturing plants. By engaging in what was sometimes called "business diplomacy," companies involved in cartel arrangements were able to deal with these threats and to devise strategies to maintain control or to redress balances as a result of different firms gaining specific advantages, usually through technology breakthroughs. Industry progress through a system of negotiations rather than free competition was therefore a distinctive characteristic of the chemical industry before World War II.

Stocking and Watkins, describing the condition of the chemical industry in the period before World War I, put the situation this way (2, p. 364):

"The threat of industrial chemistry to vested business interests—its corrosive action on long-established economic boundaries—has given powerful impetus to unified control in the chemical industries. To protect customary markets from the capricious onslaughts of chemical technology and insure development of new techniques and new products in an orderly manner—from the standpoint of their business interests—chemical companies have resorted to various expedients. These range from comprehensive written agreements, perpetual patent pools, and intercompany exchange of stocks, to casual gentlemen's understandings, nebulous codes of business ethics and friendly favoritism in commercial relations".

Taylor and Sudnik, in a book covering the history of DuPont, said it somewhat differently (8):

"Each of the major integrated chemical enterprises—I.G. Farben, ICI, DuPont—developed a 'foreign policy' that encompassed a range of mutual problems, including not only market restraints, but also technological exchanges, joint ventures, intercompany investments and related matters".

I.G. Farben, more than any other firm, promoted and shaped the cartelization of the international chemical industry and controlled or influenced many of its most important sectors during the period between the wars. Although Germany had been thoroughly defeated in World War I and then punished severely by the Treaty of Versailles, the I.G. made a rapid comeback to reassume a dominant position vis-a-vis the chemical firms in the Allied countries. Fundamentally, the reason for this was the wide lead in technology held in many chemical processes by different companies in the I.G. group. These technological advances were successfully withheld, in large part, from the Allied scientists visiting the German plants and laboratories after World War I. Severely pressed by the need to make reparation payments to the victorious Allies and eager to reestablish their industries and to rebuild factories using the new and more efficient processes under development during the war years, firms such as BASF, Bayer, Kalle, and others rapidly regained a leading position in their traditional activities. As soon as the new or rebuilt plants were in operation, the I.G. systematically built or rebuilt alliances with most of the large international chemical firms in England, France, Italy, Belgium, the United States, and many other countries.

These alliances were not always true cartel arrangements, particularly in the United States. However, there were no such restrictions in many European countries and even in the United States a number of contracts and arrangements were negotiated, that either had some of the characteristics of cartels or were cross-licensing agreement that, in effect, gave I.G. Farben a great deal of influence and control over the development of the U.S. chemical industry. The U.S. firms entering into these agreements did so, in part, to gain access to I.G. technology—for which they often paid a high price, not only in terms of money and know-how feedback, but also with respect to restricting their activities in areas where the I.G. had agreements with other firms. There was, however, another reason why U.S. companies decided to enter into such agreements. By doing so, they effectively kept the I.G. from entering into direct manufacture in the United States, which it often threatened to do, whether this was its real intention or not. The various agreements, in total, gave the I.G. a surprising degree of influence and control over the activities of U.S. chemical companies, while at the same time providing its U.S. licensees a strong position in various industry sectors, including protection from potential domestic competitors, which the I.G. would decline to license.

It has been claimed, for example, that the Senate Committee investigation on antitrust issues, headed by Senator Bone, brought out that Farben kept Jersey from using the jointly developed acetylene know-how for building plants for the production of acetaldehyde and acetic anhydride. This was allegedly done to protect the interests of other I.G. Farben clients in the United States, who had licensed technology to make these products from Farben (2, p. 502). Jersey people recently contacted claim that Jersey never had good technology for making these acetylene derivatives and did not seriously contemplate the construction of such plants. A more likely case of Farben influence in the United States revolves around the claim that the I.G. allegedly turned down the Hercules Powder Company request for an ammonia technology license in deference to Farben's then existing license agreement on ammonia with DuPont. Nevertheless, the record shows that DuPont was always wary, attempting to be careful not to break the antitrust laws and was often in an adversary position to the large German combine.

Some American firms entered into worldwide market sharing agreements with Farben, although the significance and extent of these agreements is difficult to pin down in retrospect. An understanding between BASF and DuPont on division of tetraethyl lead markets was apparently followed by a direct agreement in this area in 1926 between Farben and Ethyl Corporation. This was noted in an examination of company documents by Joseph C. Robert, who wrote a historical biography of Ethyl Corporation. He concluded that "(it) was never of commercial importance" (9). DuPont, however, was on record opposing the transfer of tetraethyl lead technology to a potential future enemy. Among the major international chemicals companies, it appears that DuPont, ICI, and Allied were companies that often tended to balk at the unfavorable, one-sided arrangements frequently offered by I.G., although these firms did have extensive technical and commercial relationships with the German combine.

The relationship between the I.G. and ICI is quite useful in illustrating some of the aspects of cartel operation in the years between the world wars. In the mid-1920s, three of the most important product areas involving these two companies were nitrogen, dyestuffs, and the German hydrogenation technology (i.e., oil from coal). Both groups had important interests in the first two chemicals, ICI having made substantial advances in ammonia production technology, while the I.G. was stronger in dyestuffs technology and had a dominant lead in coal hydrogenation. The two companies had already cooperated in alkali and other matters, but also had a series of relationships with other firms (notably ICI with DuPont), which limited to some extent, their ability to bargain with each other. In a series of meetings in 1926 and 1927, ICI and Farben attempted to come to terms that would define, for a long period of time, their respective positions in the three chemical areas under negotiation (6, Vol. II, pp. 38–47).

- ICI claimed it was willing to let I.G. purchase a limited number of ICI shares in return for German know-how in coal hydrogenation and advanced technology in dyestuffs. World markets would be shared, with the British Empire for ICI, Europe for the Germans, and sales quotas or other sharing arrangements for both America and the Far East. ICI would build a coal hydrogenation plant to commercialize this technology and profits would be divided.
- I.G. Farben took a different approach. It proposed a massive exchange of ICI and I.G. shares—perhaps up to 30 percent and a profit pool for all products, with the I.G. receiving two-thirds of the profits. I.G. did not really expect ICI to accept this proposition, but was apparently still waiting to see whether it could conclude a global arrangement with Standard Oil or Shell on coal hydrogenation.

With no progress in sight, the companies adjourned their negotiations. However, several months later, delegations for the two firms met again and the Germans advanced the follow proposition.

- In view of ICI's "inferior" position in dyestuffs, the I.G. was willing not to sell some of its products in the United Kingdom, provided that ICI would yield most, if not all, of the export market in dyestuffs to the I.G. The Germans would "leave" ICI with the manufacture of about 70 percent of U.K. dyestuffs requirements, with the balances imported into Britain from Germany.

In a follow-up meeting, the I.G. also requested that ICI hold up its ammonia expansion in Billingham until the nitrogen production by the I.G. and its associate in Norway, Norsk Hydro, was "fully absorbed."

ICI flatly rejected these proposals and the companies never did come to terms on these issues. Nevertheless, Chairman Bosch of BASF, who had headed up the German negotiations, for some time thereafter, admonished Sir Alfred Mond that the latter had previously agreed to certain restrictions on dyestuffs in return for the I.G.'s cooperation on oil-from-coal technology. With respect to ammonia, he said that "ICI's production ought to conform to the fundamental principles laid down at the commencement of our various discussions and which, owing to a too extensive interpretation of 'National Requirements' are naturally in danger of being broken down." Mond rejected this approach on several counts, citing the likely stultification of Britain's technical skills in organic chemistry and the endangering of national security (6, Vol. II, p. 46).

Although ICI did obtain rights to the hydrogenation technology, the company never entered into the astonishingly unfavorable commercial arrangements proposed by I.G. Farben during these negotiations. This episode does, however, illustrate how large firms approached issues of worldwide technology exchange, market sharing, and interlocking of commercial interests through share ownership. A number of other dealings between the two firms before and after this period did achieve positive conclusions, including those in dyestuffs and alkali.

FEWER PRODUCERS ALLOWED BETTER CONTROL

Considering the large number of competitors making most commodity chemicals today, it is illuminating to note the relatively small number of manufacturers for chemicals that were produced in the 1930s. For example, there were only three or four U.S. firms producing acetic acid, antifreeze mixtures, and synthetic ammonia as compared to 6, 12, and over 30 producers, respectively of these same chemicals in that late 1970s. Often, a single firm truly dominated the production or marketing of a given chemical. Examples are Union Carbide in certain industrial gases, Allied Chemical in ammonium sulfate and nitrate fertilizers, and Dow in chlorine and bromine derivatives. In other cases, two companies held almost the entire market—for example, Union Carbide and Air Reduction in acetylene production from calcium carbide. When three or even four producers existed, one or two often used their output captively, letting the other one or two companies control the merchant and export markets.

While U.S. companies competed to a greater extent than many of their European counterparts, they also tended to recognize "spheres of interest" in which given companies held a preeminent position that would not be challenged. A *Business Week* article stated "chemical companies traditionally don't go out of their way to compete directly with each other in the same markets" (10).

Fortune magazine in a 1937 featured article on the U.S. chemical industry offered some interesting characterizations (11):

> ". . . the chemical industry, despite its slowly lowering curve of real prices, is an "orderly" industry. It was practicing "cooperation" long before General Johnson invented it in 1933. It has seldom been bedeviled by overproduction, has had no private depressions of its own, and has not often involved itself in long or bloody price wars. The alcohol sector of the industry has frequently been guilty of disorderly conduct, and alkali made by the Solvay process has gone into some nasty brawls with electrolytic alkali. But, by and large, the chemical industry has regulated itself in a manner that would please even a Soviet Commissar. . . . Its gentlemanly instincts are all against pushing and crowding. . . . The industry . . . is . . . the practitioner of one definite sort of planned economy. . . .

> "Today, the whole chemical picture has an air of financial stability that is unusual in so new an industry. There is no evidence of fighting among its companies for position: price structures are steady. . . . This is the unique industry that knows its costs and refuses to sacrifice profits for the sake of volume. Competition is chemical . . . but the surface, the financial surface, is serene. And it will probably continue to be: new developments seek outlets through established chemical industrial channels, for there lie the talent and the money for development, one as vital as the other for any new process."

Managers in companies competing in commodity chemicals today can be excused if they become wistful when they read a description of their industry as it existed in prewar days. But it was a situation that was coming to an end.

Wartime conditions, in any case, changed the rules under which the industry was to operate, in that the government specifically asked companies to cooperate (rather than compete) in building and operating plants making strategic materials, including most chemicals. Pricing was frequently set by large government purchase contracts and inventions were pooled for the common good of the United States and its allies. A number of plants built under government sponsorship (e.g., ammonia and nitric acid units) involved chemicals whose production and marketing, before the war, was controlled under the type of conditions described by *Fortune* magazine. At the conclusion of hostilities, many of these plants were bought by companies not previously involved in the manufacture of these chemicals, thus broadening the extent of participation in such segments of the industry outside the domain of the traditional producers. It is evident that the old-line manufacturers then realized that, in many respects, the industry was undergoing a major change and that the more comfortable conditions typical of earlier times could not be recaptured. Moreover, the attitude of the American government, with respect to antitrust issues, had undergone a dramatic change—from a permissive stance in the 1920s and 1930s to a relatively punitive role in the later stages of the Roosevelt administration.

What actually occurred was a vigorous rebirth of a policy to enforce existing antitrust laws, such as the Sherman Act, which had once been strongly enforced (e.g., in the Theodore Roosevelt era), but had essentially been allowed to lapse under the pro-business Republican administrations of the 1920s and early 1930s. Such an enforcement policy was still low on the priority list of Franklin Roosevelt's early terms in office, but when Thurman Arnold took charge of the Antitrust Division of the Justice Department in the late 1930s, things began to change. A number of suits were then brought against DuPont, ICI, I.G. Farben (through their U.S. subsidiary, General Aniline and Film Corporation), and a number of other firms. Products involved included explosives, titanium metal, dyestuffs, nitrogen, and methyl methacrylate. Not surprisingly, the companies involved in these actions felt that these attacks on a well-established system were largely based on the political motives of the New Deal administration. The antitrust action against Standard Oil of New Jersey, as described earlier, was also in that category, and in view of the nature of Jersey's partner, represented an untenable situation for the U.S. firm.

In a number of respects, government claims in antitrust actions went well beyond reasonable interpretation of monopolistic or oligopolistic practice and, for that reason, the government did not always win these suits. For example, government lawyers suggested that it was improper for one company to decide to make one group of dyestuffs and for a second company to make another group, claiming that this was a deliberate attempt to stifle competition and to reduce the potential number of producers. They also suggested that it was illegal for a company to cut price to induce another firm not to enter into the manufacture of a chemical. In general, these are accepted, legal business practices. It is now widely conceded that the Roosevelt Administration went overboard in its sweeping interpretations of antitrust legislation. Later administrations were more moderate, but still enforced such legislation with some vigor.

The U.S. government's position in the interpretation and enforcement of the antitrust laws is a subject too broad to be dealt with in detail here. Certainly, Section I of the Sherman Act, which prohibits arrangements between competitors to control price and to divide markets, has been enforced vigorously much of the time and the mere existence of such arrangements has been judged as being anticompetitive, even if full proof was not available. The Clayton Act, adopted in 1913, further defined business arrangements judged as being anticompetitive, including "vertical" as well as "horizontal" integrations. ("Vertical" integrations involve the acquisition of customers or raw materials suppliers, while "horizontal" integrations cover competitors making the same product.) In the 1930s, during the worst years of the Depression, it appears that the U.S. government may have shared the views of corporations that "implicit" stabilization of markets via cooperative arrangements among producers were possibly desirable at that time to stem economic decline and to protect shrinking markets (8). But in the late 1940s and during the 1950s, it was largely the provisions of the Clayton Act that caused the Justice Department to break up such combinations as the acquisition of Visking (a large polyethylene fabricator) by Union Carbide and the large DuPont shareholding in General Motors Corporation. In the latter case, the Federal Trade Commission ruled that DuPont's ownership in GM allowed the chemical firm undue control over GM's purchases of automobile finishes and interior fabrics (12).

The use of the patent laws for anticompetitive purposes has frequently been a source of controversy, since a patent gives the owner *per se* monopolistic powers. Companies have rightly come under attack, however, where cross-licensing (exchange of patents rights between two companies) provisions were seen as being part of an illegal plan to dominate an industry. Compulsory licensing of patents* has then, at times, often been decreed as a remedy, as was the case for nylon.

The American government seemed determined, after the war,

---

*In such a case, the court rules that a patent holder must grant one or more licenses to another company, who will then be a competitor.

to use its position as the strongest member of the wartime alliance to impose on the rest of the world its views on how business should be conducted. Thus, in 1944, Francis Biddle, Attorney General of the United States, said to a meeting of the Harvard Law School Alumni Association that at the end of the war there would be a striking contrast between the free enterprise system and a cartelized Europe. He said that the American system was set up to give everybody an equal business opportunity, which is inconsistent with a scheme that involved output quotas, market divisions, and decisions regarding who may enter a business area. He then strongly attacked the division of world markets and the agreements that kept foreign products out of the United States, while restricting certain U.S. exports, likening such agreements to treaties among foreign powers (13).

Although the force of U.S. government actions had, at the start of the war, been aimed to a considerable extent at I.G. Farben and its worldwide agreements, which came to the fore as a result of the rubber shortage, later actions were directed against any other cartel arrangements of which the government became aware. A particular target were the DuPont-ICI Patents and Processes Agreements that the two companies had signed in 1929, shortly after ICI's negotiations with I.G. Farben had broken down. These agreements covered a broad cross-licensing and know-how exchange program involving many products, as well as future inventions that would be made by both firms. The accords were largely the result of a judgment by the two companies that, together, they would be better able to counter the technical and commercial initiatives of I.G. Farben, while also recognizing exclusive trading territories for ICI and DuPont. The 1929 agreements were typical of an era and by 1944, they were judged, by the Antitrust Division, to be an illegal means of conducting business. ICI and DuPont therefore recognized that the usefulness of their agreements was coming to an end. In fact, the companies had already started their separation process by a new agreement, several years earlier, that ended their cooperation in nylon. The government action against DuPont and ICI continued for three years after the cessation of hostilities, but even while depositions were being taken, the companies were negotiating an end to their historical omnibus agreement and a document to this effect was signed on June 30, 1948. Soon thereafter, the companies also agreed to end their joint ownership of foreign companies such as Canadian Industries Limited in Canada and Duperial in Argentina and they began to compete on a worldwide basis (6).

The prewar cartel system is effectively obsolete in the chemical industry today as a result of vigorous enforcement of the price fixing and market sharing provisions of the Sherman and Clayton Acts in the United States and corresponding enforcement of Article 85 of the Treaty of Rome in the European Common market. In Japan, a form of market sharing is still practiced under the watchful eye of the Ministry of Trade and Industry. The Webb Act (sometimes called the Webb-Pomerene Act), passed in 1919, does allow certain types of cooperation by U.S. firms in the export market, but only up to a point. Thus, in 1944, the Justice Department sued the U.S. Alkali Export Association (Alkasso) and a number of large U.S. and foreign chlor-alkali producers under the Sherman Act, when it determined that the Webb Act had apparently been used as a means of intercompany cooperation in the allocation of alkali markets, including agreements not to invade each other's markets (14). In another example, the Anti-Cartel Commission of the EEC (European Economic Community) undertook a sweeping investigation of the European polypropylene business in 1985 and subsequently imposed large fines on a number of producers who had allegedly colluded over the period 1977–1983 in market allocations and in setting product prices (15).

While the cartel system ceased to have an effect on the development of the chemical industry after World War II, it represents a very important historical milestone. For a considerable period of time, when many important inventions were being made, the industry was shaped by a system involving either cartels or other, more gentle forms of cooperation, comprising carefully negotiated company positions, spheres of influence, and expressions of foreign and domestic commercial policy. Basically, the cartel system suited an industry that frowned on unseemly competitive behavior, with a small number of major firms controlling the manufacture and marketing of many of the important industrial chemicals. It was an industry based on closely held technology that was more often licensed to friendly firms in other countries than to potentially troublesome new competitors in the home country. In this manner, the large chemical companies could retain their dominant domestic positions while fashioning far-reaching foreign alliances that would largely remain intact until World War II brought an end to this comfortable but legally untenable epoch.

REFERENCES

1. Joseph Borkin (1978). *The Crime and Punishment of I.G. Farben,* New York, Free Press.
2. George W. Stocking and Myron W. Watkins (1950). *Cartels in Action,* New York, Twentieth Century Fund.
3. Frank A. Howard (1947). *Buna Rubber, The Birth of an Industry,* New York, Van Nostrand.
4. Peter J. T. Morris (1982). "The Development of Acetylene and Buna Rubber at I.G. Farben," Ph.D. thesis, Oxford University, England.
5. Lee Niedringhaus Davis (1984). *The Corporate Alchemists,* New York, William Morris, p. 77.
6. W. J. Reader (1970, 1975). *Imperial Chemical Industries, a History,* 2 vols., London, Oxford University Press.
7. Aaron J. Ihde (1964). *The Development of Modern Chemistry,* New York, Harper & Row, p. 448.
8. Graham D. Taylor and Patricia E. Sudnik (1984). *DuPont and the International Chemical Industry,* G.K. Hall & Co., p. 92.
9. Joseph C. Robert (1983). *Ethyl: A History of the Corporation and the People Who Made It,* Charlottesville, University Press of Virginia.
10. *Business Week,* November 25, 1944.
11. Chemical industry I, *Fortune,* December 1937, pp. 157-162.
12. Law enforcer's anti-trust legacy, *Chemical Week,* November 23, 1957, pp. 79-85.
13. Francis Biddle (1944). Cartels: An approach to the problem, address given at the Annual Dinner of the Harvard Law School Alumni Association, February 23, 1944.
14. Wendell Berge (1944). The Webb Act, In *Cartels—Challenge to a Free World,* Washington, DC, Public Affairs Press.
15. The polypropylene cartel—a remarkable tale of collusion, *European Chemical News,* September 8, 1986, Vol. 47, 12.

ADDITIONAL READING

Dutton, William S. (1942). *DuPont: One Hundred and Forty Years,* New York, Charles Scribner's & Sons.
Kennedy, Carol (1986). *ICI: The Company That Changed Our Lives,* London, Century Hutchinson.
Popple, Charles S. (1952). *Standard Oil Company (New Jersey) in World War II,* New York, Standard Oil.
ter Meer, Fritz (1966). *Die I.G.; Ihre Entstehung, Entwicklung und Bedeutung* (personal memoirs), Krefeld, Germany.
Tongue, Harold (1934). *The Design and Construction of High Pressure Chemical Plant,* New York, Van Nostrand.

6 / Plastics: The Engine for Growth

The war was over, it was time to get back to normal life, but many things would never be the same again. Much of Europe and Japan lay in ruins. The Russian armies had claimed Eastern Europe, including a significant part of prewar Germany, which would now become a Russian satellite. In America, which had gone through the war with no damage to its industries and cities, servicemen were returning to an economy that had worked overtime to supply the war effort and now had to make the transition to peacetime. American industry had broadly expanded and diversified, with many new plants built to manufacture war equipment and to supply high octane fuels, synthetic rubber, explosives, and other products to support the war effort. It was still in high gear after V-E Day, and when the bombs were dropped on Hiroshima and Nagasaki. Japan surrendered only a few days later. The war was suddenly over. After the victorious Allies celebrated the defeat of Hitler's and Tojo's war machines, they turned their attention to rebuilding a different kind of world.

Among the industry sectors that would never be the same again was the American chemical industry. Previously dependent almost exclusively on raw materials derived from coal tar, chemicals manufacturers were now using a large array of petrochemical feedstocks coming out of refinery process units built to supply the aviation fuel and synthetic rubber production efforts. The large factories that such companies as Dow, Monsanto, Union Carbide, and Goodyear had built in record time with government contracts were now going to be available to manufacture consumer goods. And, from new refinery units, copious quantities of ethylene, propylene, BTX aromatics, and other attractive raw materials were available in streams not yet diverted to chemical uses.

The Great Depression of the 1930s had lasted until just before the start of the war, with American industry deeply in the doldrums. Unprecedented unemployment over much of the period had sharply decreased consumer demand. International trade had seriously suffered from world protectionism and the deficit financing of the Roosevelt administration had only barely kept the economy moving along. Then the war came and the United States now had a mission. "Saving the world for democracy" not only meant sending destroyers and planes to Europe. It also required the massive buildup of America's industrial might to match the German and Japanese war machines and to supply not only American armed forces requirements, but also a wide variety of critical supplies to Great Britain, Russia, and other countries fighting the common enemy. It was easy to forget the breadlines of the 1930s while working double shifts in an aircraft plant to meet President Roosevelt's target of 50,000 war planes. Women, up to recently worried about their husbands on relief or on WPA (Works Progress Administration) projects, were soon in demand as welders, machinists, or factory workers. By the time the U.S. entered the war, the economy was in full swing.

Now, the servicemen were returning to an economy flush with wartime savings and with an unprecedented, unfilled demand for consumer goods. Wartime priorities had made it necessary, even patriotic, to defer many normal family expenditures. New automobiles had not been available for several years and little priority had been given to the construction of new housing. Monies earned during the war had often gone into war bonds and other savings, but now the war was over and it was time to address personal needs that went back, in many cases, to the early years of the Depression. New families by the millions, including many that had resulted from hasty wartime marriages, were bursting out of small apartments or houses shared with parents, relatives, or friends. With wartime savings and discharge pay in their hands, servicemen and their families now started to buy houses, cars, appliances, and civilian clothes.

Plastics consumption grew at an astounding rate between 1947 and 1950. In a review article published in January 1951, *Modern Plastics* gave the following figures to illustrate this phenomenon, including not only thermoplastic but also thermoset resins:

Production of Plastic Molding and Extrusion Materials (1940 Through 1950)

	Thermoplastic Totals (lbs)	Thermoset Totals (lbs)
1940	20,300,000	98,000,000
1946	239,000,000	175,000,000
1950	508,000,000	286,000,000

This was 20 percent compounded annual growth during the last four years—and polyethylene had barely been introduced. However, producers of refrigerator containers and bags, liners for shipping bags, paper coatings, plastic bottles, and food wrappers were now starting to clamor for this new plastic, which was in extremely short supply (1).

Wartime experiences had also exposed people to many new types of products and materials. Nylon parachutes, butyl rubber life rafts, Plexiglas airplane windows, and plastic raincoats made both servicemen and women factory workers aware of the many new materials developed for wartime needs. Because many of these were superior to comparable prewar goods, the factories that had churned out these articles during the war would have no difficulty in keeping their plants in operation when the war was over. It was not difficult to recognize that these products would now become a permanent part of the peacetime economy.

Surveys conducted in 1945 and 1946 showed that consumers in the United States would buy more goods in 1946 than at any time in the nation's history. The consensus was that if labor and management could work together, the unsatisfied demand for consumer goods would keep the economy humming for at least five years. A report turned out by the Committee for Economic Development (CED) under the chairmanship of Paul G. Hoffman correlated the opinions of more than 1,500 manufacturers and trade associations with respect to likely short-term demand of various goods. The conclusion was that the overall value of products manufactured in 1947 would be $80.5 million versus $56.8 million in 1939, an increase of 42 percent. In specific categories, the expected increases were even much larger. For example, the report projected a 76 percent increase in automobiles; 68 percent in electric appliances; 97 percent in aircraft and aircraft parts; and 81 percent in radios, tubes, and phonographs (2).

Manufacturers warned that these demand increases could hardly be met, due to the lag time required to build new manufacturing facilities, such as those for automobile assembly lines. For example, General Motors claimed that its production in 1946 would be no higher than in 1941, since new facilities could not become effective until 1947 or even 1948. A great deal of retooling was going to be required but here, as well, a lot of changes were going on and many of the changes related to plastics. The CED survey showed that the plastic industry's principal customers' demands ran far ahead of the general consumption total in many cases and that plastics would capture a market equivalent to two and one-half times their 1939 dollar volume, an increase far greater than for any other industry.

Some examples illustrate how plastics were beginning to make significant inroads as a material for consumer goods. A 1942 automobile had only minor plastics parts, with phenolic resins and laminates used for knobs, door trim, and brake bands; cellulose acetate butyrate for steering wheel horn buttons; polyvinyl butyral in safety glass; plus small amounts of thermoset resins in electrical applications. Now, automobile manufacturers were contemplating "artificial leather" (i.e., vinyl) seat upholstery, glass fiber reinforced polyester fenders, plastic tops for convertibles, and various decorative parts made from an assortment of thermoplastic and thermoset materials. The pounds of plastic going into each car would thus increase significantly. In other consumer applications, polystyrene would be used in refrigerators; phenolics, instead of aluminum agitators in washing machines; plastic handles in electric irons; and high impact polystyrene in radio cabinets and flashlights. And dolls could now be made even more realistically than before from PVC paste resins.

Much of the impetus for greater use of plastics in many applications came from women who had been involved in the defense and war effort. In a paper delivered during the war in Britain, a new consumer society was visualized in the following terms. "For the first time," the author stated, "thousands of women, uprooted from their homes, served . . . on a national scale and came in contact with modern machinery used in the war effort, machinery designed to perform with the utmost economy of effort and materials" (3). He suggested that after the war, women would be design aware and critical and would not put up with badly designed, cheaply made products. In a "Britain Can Make It" exposition held in London in 1946, the main theme was the application of war technology to civilian products.

By January 1947, it was clear that consumer demand projections made only 12-18 months earlier had actually been far too low. Thus, durable goods production in October 1946 had run at a level 214 percent over the 1935-1939 average and 25 percent over the first half of 1946. All-time peaks were reached in the production of gas ranges, radios, washing machines, and vacuum cleaners. A distinct shortage of both fabricating capacity and resins was being experienced by an economy insatiable in its demand for a variety of consumer goods. And this situation was projected to continue and to become, if anything, even more hectic. A survey of molders, conducted around this time, indicated that more than half expected a 50-300 percent increase in their production volume in 1948 versus 1946.

Plastics had been around before the war, of course, but for a number of reasons, plastics growth had been relatively moderate. Thermoset resins, such as phenolics and melamine, had made inroads in certain markets, but had never experienced really dramatic growth. Typical uses were in decorative light fittings, candlesticks, fluted boxes, jewelry, and small radio cabinets. While one of the main problems with phenolics was poor coloring ability, urea and melamine resins allowed molders to produce brightly colored dinnerware and other attractive objects for domestic use. Cellulose nitrate and acetate had been known for some time, but these materials had few established markets and this limited their growth potential. Typical consumer uses were in combs, toothbrush handles, toys, refrigerator parts, and in packaging. Cellulose acetate butyrate was used for screw driver handles and in a few other applications.

In 1935, injection molding machines started to be imported from Germany and their automatic action and short molding cycles drew attention to the fact that thermoplastics, such as cellulose acetate, conferred a substantial processing advantage. By 1940, more than 700 injection molding machines, produced by seven domestic makers, were in use in the United States. Foster Grant Corporation, an early molder of thermoset, as well as cellulose nitrate and acetate resins into such articles as combs and barrettes and later, eyeglass frames was an early importer of German injection molding equipment.* Figures 6.1 and 6.2 illustrate a variety of modern plastics processing techniques.

The advent of cheap thermoplastics such as polystyrene and polyvinyl chloride (PVC) was the trigger for explosive expansion. Here were resins that could be melted and then molded, extruded, thermoformed, or cast into sheets without the use of high pressures or chemical "cross-linkers," as was the case for thermosets. Transparent or translucent resins could be easily colored, could readily be blown or cast into thick films and sheets, and could be melted and resolidified several times, thus allowing recycling of excess materials from the molding machines. Most importantly, molding cycles for thermoplastic resins were 5 to 10 times faster than for thermosets—8 or 10 seconds instead of a minute or more. In the 1930s, of course, the resins that would soon become the "commodity thermoplastics" were barely known. Those thermoplastics available (cellulose acetate, methyl methacrylate, and others) were either expensive or had certain important drawbacks. Thus, injection molding of thermoplastics was not yet a large business. It took off as soon as the war was over.

Plastics also had to overcome an image problem. Although the world was becoming conscious of the potential of plastics and other polymers, these materials, which were transforming so many aspects of consumer applications, were often considered less desirable than the products—glass, wood, and metals—they were replacing. In these early days of the mass production plastics industry, poor quality was often a problem, particularly as inexperienced and poorly financed fabricators entered the business. Plastics, for a period of time, therefore acquired an image of cheapness and low quality, frequently well deserved. Yet, in spite of this, plastics were starting to penetrate more and more markets, with toys, packaging goods, shower curtains, phonograph records, and picnicware now increasingly made from these new materials. Also, by the late 1940s, consumer resistance to plastics was largely overcome, as the industry learned to improve quality control and the cost of plastic goods steadily dropped, making these products even more attractive as substitutes or in new market applications.

Statistics for the plastics industry show that between 1939 and

*Dr. Robert Purvin, personal communication.

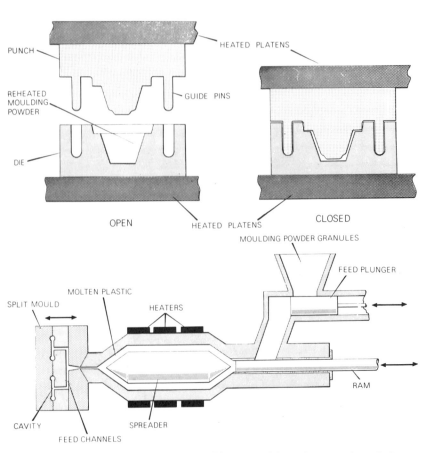

Figure 6.1 Diagram of injection molding machine. (*Source: Our Industry: Petroleum,* London, The British Petroleum Co., Ltd., 1977, p. 395.)

1946, the production of all synthetic resins and cellulosic plastics materials rose from 247 million to 1.2 billion pounds. This fivefold increase signaled the beginning of a new phase for plastics. While over this period the production of phenolic molding powders doubled from 65 to 140 million pounds, polystyrene consumption went from less than 1 million pounds in 1939 to 150 million pounds in 1947, and vinyl resins from one million to 235 million pounds over the same period (4).

Industry groups visiting German plants shortly after the end of the war recognized that a similar pattern in the use of plastics

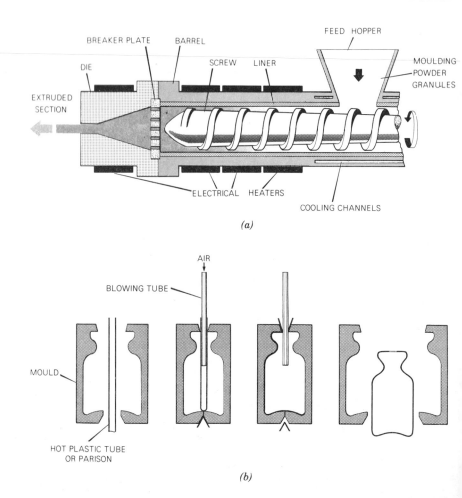

Figure 6.2 (*a*) Extruder. (*b*) Principle of blow molding. (*Source: Our Industry: Petroleum,* London, The British Petroleum Co., Ltd., 1977, p. 395.)

had taken place in that country in the 1930s and during the war years, with the rise in production of various types of thermoplastics and thermosets about at the same rapid rate as in the United States. German technology in polystyrene and certain grades of PVC was somewhat ahead of that in the United States, though U.S. technology was better in other plastics areas.

How is it that plastics suddenly became a household word, that a family of new materials was starting to replace so many conventional materials, including glass, wood, steel, aluminum, and paper? It is easier now, 40 years or so later, to obtain a perspective on the origins, development, and growth of the polymer industries, of which plastics became the most important sector. And to do that we must return to the middle of the eighteenth century, when the only material we would today classify as a "plastic" was shellac—a natural product that could be melted and then molded into objects. Up to that time, no chemist had succeeded in making a material of this type *on purpose.*

EARLY HISTORY OF PLASTICS

It is probably useful to start with definitions. According to one source, "plastics are man-made materials that can be shaped in almost any form. They may be any color of the rainbow, or as clear and colorless as crystal. Plastics may have the hardness of steel or the softness of silk. Manufacturers can shape them into long-wearing machine parts or into women's stockings. The word 'plastics' comes from the Greek word 'plastikos,' which means 'able to be molded' "(5). Another source defines plastics as "nonmetallic basic engineering materials that can be formed and shaped by many methods"(6).

Some people have said that the modern plastics industry was born in 1839. That year, Charles Goodyear discovered that when rubber was reacted with a small amount of sulfur, a stronger, yet still elastic, material was obtained, with more resistance to heat or cold. Twelve years later, his brother Nelson Goodyear incorporated a much higher amount of sulfur in the rubber and obtained a hard material he called "Ebonite," due to its resemblance to ebony. He fabricated and exhibited furniture made from Ebonite and the material was soon also used for the telegraph machine, buttons, and other items. Shortly before this time, Charles Mackintosh had developed a rubberized fabric used in raincoats.

An even more important step occurred when, in 1846, Alexander Parkes, a Birmingham chemist, found that he could produce shaped objects by dissolving nitrocellulose—an explosive—in a solvent and then evaporating the solvent from a mold. He mixed the material, which became known as "Parkesine," with castor oil and coloring matter and was able to mold the mixture into decorative and other useful articles (7, p. 11). Nitrocellulose was shortly thereafter used for the preparation of photographic film and for other applications. Later, British Xylonite, Ltd. became a successful producer of nitrocellulose plastics by improved methods, including greatly reduced costs for the solvent.

Rubber and cellulose are both long and complex molecules, whose structure can be modified through the action of chemicals and solvents. When inventors and scientists learned that these materials would be transformed into a state where they could be shaped, molded or spun into useful objects, a new industry was born. Both rubber and cellulose are, of course, not man-made. Only much later was it possible for chemists to synthesize molecules that would have even better properties than these natural materials.

In 1868, John and Isaiah Hyatt, engaged in the printing business in Albany, New York, responded to the challenge of a $10,000 prize offered by the firm of Phelan and Colender to anyone who would develop a manufacturing technique for billiard balls without having to kill elephants to obtain tusks for the ivory traditionally used for this purpose. Eventually, the Hyatt brothers found that camphor could be used as a solvent for nitrocellulose, then employing heat and pressure to mold solid billiard balls from the paste. Hyatt's plastics were given the name of "Celluloid" and could be used to mold many types of brightly colored objects. Denture plates could even be made from this material.

Cellulose acetate was first produced in a laboratory at the Sorbonne University in Paris in 1865, but the discovery remained dormant for many years. The product was soluble only in then relatively expensive solvents, such as chloroform, and it required the use of costly acetic anhydride for its preparation. An American, G. W. Miles, in 1905 patented a simple process to modify the chemical nature of cellulose to allow acetone to be used as a solvent. Several firms, including Bayer in Germany and Lustron in the United States, manufactured small amounts of "acetate silk" in this manner around 1898.

A few years earlier, in 1892, three Englishmen, Charles Cross, Edward Bevan, and Clayton Beadle had spun cellulose dissolved in an ammoniacal solution of a copper salt (termed "viscose") into a precipitating bath, giving a shiny fiber they named *rayon*. It was the realization of a prophesy made over 200 years earlier by

Robert Hooks in England when he wrote, "I have often thought that probably there might be a way found out to make an artificial glutinous composition much resembling that excrement out of which the silkworm wiredraws his clew." The process regenerated cellulose in the form of fine threads, which had many of the properties of silk at a fraction of its cost. The British firm of Courtaulds, a silk weaver, was the first to make rayon fiber commercially, with production starting in 1895.

"Plastics" and "man-made fibers" were by now a reality, related by the fact that both of these materials consisted of long-chain molecules (e.g., cellulose), though this fact was not yet well understood. Two Swiss brothers, Camille and Henri Dreyfus, started manufacturing cellulose acetate lacquers and plastic film on a reasonable commercial scale in Basel just before World War I. After thousands of experiments, the brothers were able to produce excellent samples of acetate continuous filament yarn (8). To aid the Allied cause in World War I, the brothers emigrated to England and set up a plant to make nonflammable airplane dope from the same material. After the war, "artificial silk" production began. The product was given the name of "Celanese" (for "cellulose" and "ease of care,") and the company's name itself was later changed to British Celanese. Manufacture of acetate in sheet, rod and tube form was commenced in the United States in 1927 by the Celluloid Company under license from the Celanese Corporation. From a production rate of 200,000 pounds per year in 1931, total acetate molding powder, sheet and yarn sales rose to almost 4.7 million pounds in 1934 and to 12 million pounds in 1939. Price reductions in the acetic anhydride used as a raw material, from $1.25 per pound in 1930 to 35 cents in 1939, greatly spurred the use of acetate plastics. Acetate yarn and film production exceeded 50,000,000 pounds by the start of the war.

Cellophane sheets, produced from viscose, were first made in Vosges, France, just before the start of World War I. They were based on patents by a Swiss textile chemist, who used cellulose solutions to make table cloths impervious to dirt and stains. Later, transparent sheets and films were also made. Shortly thereafter, DuPont purchased the patent rights and trademark for Cellophane. Manufacturing facilities were established in the United States several years later. DuPont improved the process by developing, in 1927, a means to make Cellophane moisture proof. Since the manufacture of cellophane, a clear plastic film, was a fore-

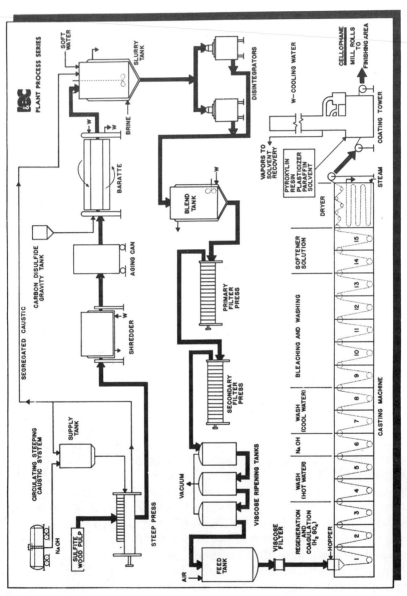

Figure 6.3 Flowsheet for the manufacture of cellophane at the Clinton, Iowa plant of E.I. duPont de Nemours & Co., Inc. (*Source:* Cellophane, A Series of Articles Describing Chemical Manufacturing *Industrial and Engineer-*

238

runner to later petrochemical technology, a flowsheet depicting a cellophane plant is shown on Figure 6.3 (9).

All of these "plastics" had at least in part, been produced from natural materials, such as wool- or cotton-based cellulose and natural rubber. Another natural material, casein, which is derived from milk, achieved some success in Europe for the manufacture of buttons and jewelry. Plastics derived from these sources are termed "man-made", since they are derived from natural materials that have been modified by man through the application of chemicals. The term "synthetics" is used for materials totally synthesized in the laboratory. A major breakthrough, therefore, came with the development of a totally synthetic plastic material, phenol-formaldehyde resins, the result of studies by Dr. Leo Baekeland in Yonkers, New York in 1905.

THE DISCOVERY OF THERMOSET RESINS

Chemists had produced resinlike materials from phenol and formaldehyde several decades before the turn of the century, but were unable to develop commercial applications for a product that could not be crystallized or distilled. It had been recognized that phenol reacts with various aldehydes to give a wide array of products, but these were usually in the form of a resinous mass that was unsuitable for shaping into useful objects. Both alkali and acid had been used as catalysts, but neither proved satisfactory. The product was either a gelled material that was only a poor substitute for shellac or a hard mass with an unstable structure, due to the bubbles that formed during the curing process.

Baekeland, whose original objective was to develop synthetic varnishes as substitutes for shellac, gained a broad perspective on the relative effect of acids and alkalis on the reaction, as well as an understanding of the effect of the ratio of aldehyde and phenol on the final product. He defined two reactions, one where a thermoplastic material he termed "Novolak" could be formed in an acid-catalyzed system, using an excess of formaldehyde, and another, where an alkali catalyst could be used to cross-link the polymer into a resin suitable for molding, later called "Bakelite." He also showed that the use of pressure in the curing step could eliminate the formation of bubbles in the final resin. The key result of Baekeland's work was the ability to produce a very hard, totally synthetic material that faithfully reproduced the contour of a mold, did not absorb water, did not melt, and was a poor conductor of electricity. Baekeland also learned to incorporate wood flour in the molding powder to produce, under heat and pressure, strong, heat-resistant parts that would not crack or split apart on aging.

Bakeland's work therefore resulted in two important new totally synthetic products: phenol-formaldehyde resins for molding hard objects and Novolak resins for coatings and varnishes. The first sale of eight barrels of Novolak resins was made to Western Electric in 1909.

Baekeland did not propose a correct formula for the compounds he was able to produce, since little was known about molecular structures in the early 1900s. Only some 20 years later, when Professor Hermann Staudinger, in Germany, performed his outstanding research work, was an understanding gained of the structure of both thermoplastic and thermosetting plastics. It is now known that in the Bakelite molding powder, phenol molecules are linked by the $-CH_2-$ groups of formaldehyde molecules into long chains. After the molding process, these chains are then cross-linked into complicated three-dimensional networks, as illustrated in Figure 6.4 (10).

The General Bakelite Company was formed in 1910 to make molded parts, laminated sheets, and insulating varnishes, with most of the products going into electrical applications. One of General Bakelite's first molded products was an improved Bakelite billiard ball (11). Many other uses developed over the following two decades in paneling, switchboards, tabletops, counters, gear wheels, washing machine agitators, pump housings, and electrical applications. Phenol-formaldehyde resins are good insulators for domestic uses, though they have limitations for high voltage or high frequency applications.

An interesting sidelight in connection with Baekeland's discovery of phenol-formaldehyde resins involves Thomas Edison, America's most famous inventor. Around 1900, Edison started to carry out chemicals and plastics research, in part because of his interest in the production of phonograph records (at the time, 50 million pounds of shellac were being imported annually for this purpose). A collaborator, Jonas Aylsworth, patented in 1910 the use of cross-linking compounds to transform Novolak-type varnishes into a hard surface that could be used for taking sound track imprints, as used in phonograph records. Together, they formed the

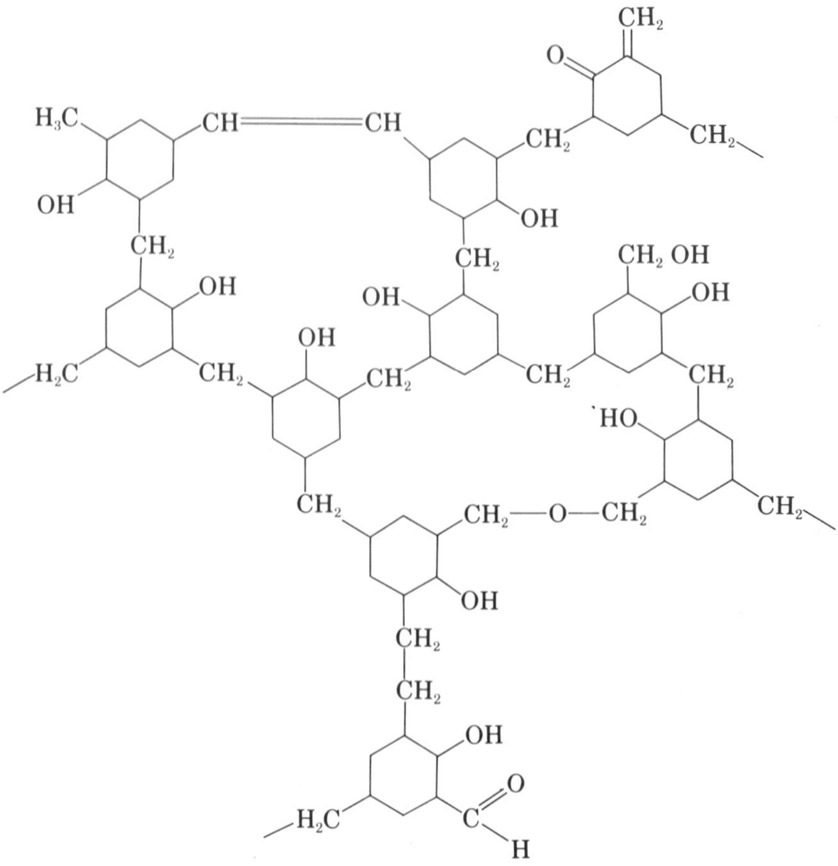

Figure 6.4 Molecular linkages and phenol-formaldehyde resins. Redrawn from Frank Sherwood Taylor, *A History of Industrial Chemistry,* New York, Abelard-Schumann, 1957, p. 259).

Condensite Company to manufacture phenolic resins and, for a period of time, they were involved in bitter patent litigation with Baekeland.* Condensite had quickly become a larger user of phenol, still mostly imported from Europe. When World War I broke out, stocks were quickly exhausted and phenol became a critical war material, for example for the manufacture of trinitrophenol (picric acid). At that time, no synthetic phenol was produced in the

*Later, the companies decided to merge and form the Bakelite Corporation.

United States and coal tar supplies were still very limited. Unable to convince any chemical companies to make this material, Edison, now well established with laboratories and fabrication shops, decided to go into phenol production. A synthetic process, using benzene sulfonation followed by caustic fusion, was known from the literature, but actual production techniques were covered by foreign trade secrets. Edison assigned 40 people on his staff to a crash program to develop a commercial process. Within a week, plant construction was commenced and about two months later the plant was producing six tons of phenol per day. Barrett (later a division of Allied Chemical) started producing synthetic phenol in 1915 and Dow Chemical built a large plant in 1917, so by then there was ample supply. Phenol prices had reached $1.50 per pound in 1914, but dropped to 65 cents per pound before the war was over. Edison had ceased manufacture by that time (12,13).

Formaldehyde, the other part of the phenolic resin molecule, had only very minor markets at the time that Baekeland was developing a commercial use for this chemical. Heyden Chemical Works (later part of Heyden-Newport, acquired in the 1950s by Tenneco) had started limited production in 1901, first using a copper and later a silver catalyst and German know-how. Formaldehyde's usefulness for making plastics and resin varnishes spurred its consumption after 1910 and these applications have remained the largest outlet for this reactive material. By 1920, production reached 10 million pounds. Production technology has not changed appreciably over the years. A flowsheet for a plant built around 1950 is shown on Figure 6.5 (14).

The feedstock on which production of formaldehyde is based—methanol—was long available, but from an unusual source: the destructive distillation of wood, practiced in many countries. In 1900, U.S. production of methanol was 5 million gallons a year, and it stayed below 10 million gallons until synthetic methanol production (from coke or natural gas via reforming) was commenced in the late 1920s. However, methanol production in the 1910–1930 period was adequate for satisfying the requirements for formaldehyde as used in the new phenol-formaldehyde and, later, other thermoset resins.

An important drawback for phenolic resins was the fact that phenolic plastics (phenoplasts) are highly colored and are not odorless. In 1928, the British Cyanides Company commercialized, under the name of "Beetle," amino-formaldehyde resins, which could

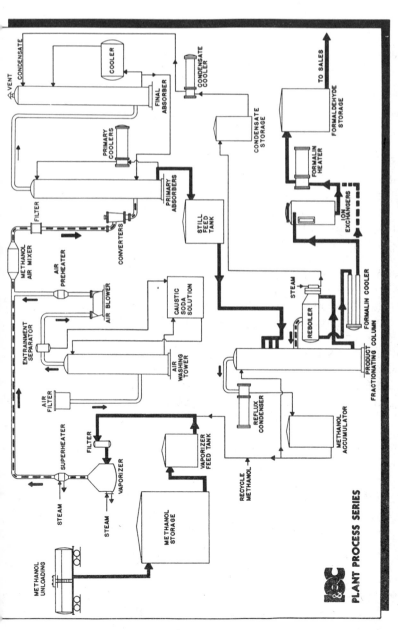

Figure 6.5 Flowsheet for production of formaldehyde from methanol at Calumet City, IL, plant of Spencer Chemical Co. (*Source*: R. N. Hader, R. D. Wallace, and R. W. McKinney, Formaldehyde from Methanol. *Industrial and Engineering Chemistry*, eds, Modern Chemical Processes, Vol. 3, New York, Reinhold 1954, p. 83.)

be used to produce colorless, odorless, and light-fast molded articles by a reaction mechanism similar to Baekeland's. Both urea and melamine were suitable amino-type raw materials for the production of these resins, which were molded into decorative articles and tableware of any desired color and shade, including translucent finishes. American Cyanamid, through an agreement with British Cyanamid Company, was early among U.S. companies active in the production of amino-formaldehyde thermosetting resins and molded articles. Later, the company started producing its famous Formica brand of thermoset laminates, using this technology.

The Bakelite Company was acquired by Union Carbide in 1939. Leo Baekeland had served as head of the company until that time, collecting many honors along the way. Charles Kettering of General Motors presented a biographical memoir about his friend to the National Academy of Sciences shortly after Baekeland's death in 1944. In his eulogy, Kettering recalled Baekeland's early discoveries in photographic papers as a young chemist in Belgium, his native country. He had then sold the rights for his invention to George Eastman, for $1 million, a huge amount of money in those days. Baekeland had subsequently emigrated to the United States, where he first worked in electrochemistry, contributing to Elon Hooker's work on the diaphragm cell. This was followed by his studies on phenol-formaldehyde resins and the formation of General Bakelite and, later, the Bakelite Company. By the time he died, Baekeland had filed over 400 patents. In Bakelite phenolic resin, Kettering had found an ideal material with suitable dielectric strength and resistance to temperature, oil and chemicals to produce the "Delco" Ignition and Starting System that became one of General Motors' main contributions to the modern automobile. Kettering and Baekeland had remained friends from that time on.

Some 30 American firms were engaged in the manufacture of the so-called phenoplasts for sale or for their own consumption by the late 1930s, since Baekeland's patents on phenol-formaldehyde resins had expired some years earlier. In 1940, production of phenolic resins for casting, molding and other uses was 58 million pounds, while production of urea-formaldehyde resins reached 21 million pounds.

Thermoplastics before World War II comprised primarily cellulosics, as described earlier, although DuPont was in production with methyl methacrylate (MMA) at Belle, West Virginia. Rohm and Haas was also producing MMA molding powder and Monsanto was making polyvinyl butyral for automobile safety glass. Also, polyamide molding resin (DuPont's nylon 6,6 powder) was starting to be produced. However, cellulose acetate was still by far the most important polymeric material, with 175 million pounds produced in 1940 for conversion into fibers, film, sheeting, and molded plastics. In 1941, 38 million pounds of cellulosic plastics were used in molding and other typical "plastics" applications (15).

Celanese and Tennessee Eastman (Kodak) were important producers of cellulose acetate resins. Eastman had established a chemical operation in Kingsport, Tennessee, in the 1920s to make materials for the production of photographic film, including acetic anhydride and cellulose acetate. Perley Wilcox, later president of Tennessee Eastman, saw plastics production as a suitable diversification and so the company started selling acetate molding in the mid-1930s under the Tenite label.*

While thermoset resins and thermoplastics based on cellulose were experiencing accelerated growth in the decade before the outbreak of World War II, even more exciting developments were taking place in the thermoplastic field. It was during the 1930s that the outstanding polymer chemists of the day were finally unraveling the structure of various types of long-chain molecules. This made it possible to approach with more confidence the synthesis of a number of polymers that had far greater versatility than the thermosets—leading to polystyrene and polyvinyl chloride, and to an understanding of the structure of polyethylene, which was discovered quite accidentally. The sequence of events that led up to these discoveries and some of the contributions of specific researchers are covered in the next section.

THERMOPLASTICS—MODERN POLYMER SCIENCE

In 1861, Thomas Graham in England proposed the name "colloids" for viscous material that could not pass through a semipermeable membrane, although it could be dissolved. Table jelly and natural rubber solutions in benzene were examples, and some thought that such materials must have high molecular weights. In fact, rough measurements made at the time—not very accurate

*J. S. Sorrels, Tennessee Eastman Co., personal communication.

by today's standards—showed that molecular weights could be as high as 10,000 for cellulose nitrate, 12,000 for rubber, and 40,000 for starch. Nevertheless, many chemists were reluctant to believe in the fact of such high molecular weights and developed the theory that these materials consisted of small molecules held together by "secondary" chemical forces to form clusters they called "micelles." These would behave as if they were large molecules (7, p. 17).

In 1920, The Svedberg, a Swedish scientist, used an ultracentrifuge to show that polymers were true molecules of hitherto unimagined size. He claimed that molecular weights could be as high as one million and that a single molecule could contain hundreds of thousands of atoms. Svedberg, who received the Nobel prize for his work, was not able to explain, however, how these atoms were, in fact, combined to form these "high polymers." The scientific community, which had been used to thinking of polymers being formed through interactions between colloidal micelles, therefore found it hard to accept Svedberg's explanations. It was even more skeptical when Professor Staudinger—later known as the "grandfather of modern polymer science"—proposed that in these materials the atoms were linked not in blocks or networks but in extremely long chains. It took close to 30 years for Staudinger to receive his Nobel prize, so much opposition did he encounter to this revolutionary vision.

Staudinger concentrated on the structure of macromolecules—that is, of long chains in which individual units (monomers) are connected to each other by covalent double bonds. Although he also studied cellulosic chains,* his model (study) compounds mostly involved carbon and hydrogen atoms, which he polymerized to form both rubberlike and solid (plastic) materials. Rubber molecules evidently contained double bonds, while plastic materials did not. In this manner, Staudinger obtained direct, experimental evidence for the validity of a rubber formula he had postulated in 1920. In 1932, Staudinger published a paper covering the possibility of stereoregular structure in polymers—a terminology that relates to the means by which the d- or l-form†of certain isomers arranged themselves along the chain. An orderly arrange-

---

*Containing carbon, hydrogen, and oxygen atoms.
†The right- or left-handed form.

ment would produce crystallinity, due to a regular structure, while a random arrangement would produce a more flexible polymer.

Around the same time, Professor Herman Mark used the new x-ray crystallography technique to develop a theory of the structure of large molecules, somewhat analogous to that of Staudinger. He became director of polymer research for I.G. Farbenindustrie in the 1930s and there directed the development of a number of synthetic thermoplastic polymers, including polystyrene. Among other things, he concluded that differences in reaction conditions could produce widely different polymers, due to different degrees of chain branching (7, p. 52).

Acceptance of the "long-chain" theory covering large molecules (instead of explaining polymers in terms of colloidal micelles) opened up a much better understanding of the structure of both rubber and plastic materials. The elasticity and softness in elastomers could be attributed to a "wriggling" of flexible chains, while the fact that vulcanization of natural rubber with sulfur hardened the rubber could be explained by assuming that this process resulted in "cross-linking" a number of sites in the chains, giving much less flexibility. The new theory also explained the fact that rubber regains its shape after the forces stretching or compressing it are released.

The elucidation of the large molecule theory by Staudinger, Mark, and others during this period therefore allowed researchers to understand better the subject of crystallinity or noncrystallinity in rubberlike and plastic materials. Natural rubber is noncrystalline at room temperature, which is why it is elastic, whereas gutta-percha, the isomer of natural rubber, is crystalline. The difference was evidently due to the method in which the sidechains on the two materials are arranged, the former being the so-called "cis" form and the other the "trans" form. Buna rubber is less crystalline than natural rubber, which makes vulcanized Buna a less satisfactory tire material, although it was found that incorporating large amounts of carbon black would make Buna almost as good as natural rubber in this application. Polystyrene is also noncrystalline, in spite of its glasslike appearance, due to the stiffness of the polystyrene molecule, containing primarily benzene rings (16).

This was the start of an exciting period, with new discoveries and a greater understanding developing swiftly on both sides of the Atlantic. Mark, who left Germany in time to become a distinguished Professor of Polymer Science of Brooklyn Polytechnic Institute, wrote in 1976 (17):

> ". . . progressive leaders in many industries—including plastics, textiles, rubber, coatings, films, and adhesives—immediately recognized the importance of fundamental and applied polymer research and wasted no time in advancing it through grants to universities and through the establishment of large research laboratories in their own organizations. . .
>
> ". . . Once the basic concepts of this new branch of chemistry were firmly established, polymer chemists settled down to useful and practical work: synthesis of new monomers, quantitative study of the mechanism of polymerization processes in bulk, solution, suspension, and emulsion; characterization of macromolecules in solution on the basis of statistical thermodynamics; study of the fundamentals of the behavior in the solid state. The result was a better understanding of the properties of rubbers, plastics, and fibers."

An extremely important discovery during this critical period was that polymers with linear or branched structures (later called thermoplastics) soften without chemical change when heated and cooled, whereas thermosetting polymers form polymer networks when heated. Once formed, they do not soften on heating.

It was understood that polymerization could be induced by different mechanisms and could occur under widely different conditions, depending on the monomers involved. It was now also known that there are two main types of polymerization: (1) chain-growth or addition polymerization, which usually involves monomers with a carbon-carbon double bond, and (2) condensation or step growth polymerization, which is simply a chemical reaction carried out repeatedly, which might throw off a by-product, such as water. In chain-growth polymerization, an initiator, usually a free-radical, but sometimes an ion or a catalyst, could be used. The free-radical or ion reacts with the monomer and is incorporated into the end of the chain, turning the monomer itself into a radical. This monomer then reacts with another molecule of monomer and so forth. The polymerization eventually stops for one of several reasons.

Another important development involved the different procedures for effecting polymerization—now known as bulk, solution, suspension, and emulsion methods. In bulk or mass polymerization, the monomer and initiator are combined in a vessel and heated to a certain temperature, where polymerization starts to occur. Because polymer formation is exothermic (gives off heat), one of the major problems in such a system is heat transfer. The other forms of polymerization are therefore all designed, at least in part, to deal with this problem. In solution polymerization, the reactants are soluble in a liquid that acts as a heat sink and reduces the viscosity of the reaction mixture. In suspension polymerization, the monomer and catalyst are suspended in a continuous phase, such as water, which again acts as a heat sink. Emulsion polymerization is similar to suspension, except that an emulsifying agent is used to form micelles (stable droplets in the nonreactive suspending medium) and the reaction occurs inside these micelles, where the polymer grows. This form of polymerization takes the longest time—as much as 10 minutes—and can be used to produce extremely high molecular weight polymers. It was developed during the war to produce synthetic rubber latex and is also used to make vinyl paste resins. After the war, Frank Mayo at U.S. Rubber Company and others made key contributions to the theory of the kinetics of copolymerization (7, p. 21).

It was recognized that polymer structures are held together by chemical bonds of various types. An understanding of the energy content of these bonds could be used to predict the effect of heat and light on polymer structure and, therefore, stability. Thus, if the polymer bond resulting from the polymerization is the weakest bond, the material will depolymerize upon heating (thermoplastics). If the side group bonds are the weaker link, the material will carbonize rather than depolymerize (thermosets). In some cases, both effects may be present. Other modes of polymer degradation occur, but the relative amount of bond energy provides a reliable guide to the breakdown mechanism. As most polymers are shaped under the application of heat, an understanding of this phenomenon provided the breakthrough necessary to allow the modern plastics industry to develop as it did.

An appreciation of the structure of linear and branched polymers also led to the development of synthetic fibers and to Carothers' work (see Chapter 7). In fact, it is not generally realized that the successful development of thermoplastic polymers preceded Carothers' discoveries by only a few years. The most important thermoplastic polymers are polyvinyl chloride (PVC), polystyrene, and polyethylene—products that were essentially unknown as commercial products until the 1930s. Significantly, all three of these are based on the double (vinyl) bond in ethylene, a chemical only present to a limited extent in coke-oven gases, but, as we now know, capable of being made in almost unlimited quantities by cracking petroleum and natural gas-based feedstocks. As it turned out, the elucidation of the structure of thermoplastic resins produced from ethylene coincided with a time when ethylene and other olefins became broadly available in wartime cracking plants, a situation perhaps best characterized as petrochemical serendipity. The origins and early development of the three major thermoplastic polymers is described below.

POLYVINYL CHLORIDE

Although it was known as early as the middle of the nineteenth century that vinyl chloride could be transformed into a solid (polymer) by exposure to sunlight, there was no interest in so-called vinyl chemistry until the early 1900s. Production of acetylene had by then become important, since this product found widespread use as an illuminating gas. But between 1905 and 1909, the advent of the electric light bulb started to spell the end of the gaslight era. As a result, there was soon an oversupply of acetylene or, more accurately, of calcium carbide, the raw material for acetylene production, whose price dropped very sharply. No doubt as a consequence of the unexpected availability of potentially large quantities of inexpensive acetylene,* research commenced on using this reactive hydrocarbon as a chemical feedstock. In 1912, Fritz Klatte assigned a patent to Griesheim-Elektron in Germany that claimed the manufacture of vinyl chloride monomer from acetylene and hydrogen chloride, using mercuric chloride catalyst. This work also comprised studies on the polymerization of the monomer, using peroxide initiators. Nevertheless, neither this research, nor work carried out in Russia, led to commercial application. The Russian work was at that time directed toward the development of a rubber substitute.

By the late 1920s, several companies were again working on developing polymers from vinyl compounds (i.e., monomers that

---

*This chemical has a triple bond, versus a double bond for ethylene and the other olefins.

had a double bond in their structure). In the United States, where B.F. Goodrich had started to show great interest in this type of chemistry, Union Carbide had also decided that this would be a good area for research. One reason was that the company had become interested in developing a synthetic product for tung oil, used in varnishes. The price of tung oil traditionally went through wild swings and it would therefore be desirable to find a substitute. And the company's analysis of tung oil showed a double bond structure similar to that of vinyl chloride (18). Another reason for Carbide's interest related to the fact that its ethylene oxide plant, which used the chlorohydrin process, was producing large amounts of ethylene dichloride (EDC) by-product, for which there was no good outlet. Looking at possible derivatives of this material, attention settled on vinyl chloride, which could be produced in reasonable yields by cracking the by-product EDC, a procedure that produced the vinyl bond in the vinyl chloride, formed by splitting off hydrogen chloride. Although this process would be somewhat more complicated than synthesizing vinyl chloride directly from acetylene and hydrogen chloride, ethylene dichloride was available to Union Carbide at essentially no cost from the ethylene oxide plant.

A major problem developers had to overcome, however, was the rigidity of the polyvinyl chloride (PVC) polymer. This rigidity made processing the resin into useful products extremely difficult. Union Carbide decided to turn again to the Mellon Institute in Pittsburgh, where so much of its previous successful work on ethylene derivatives had been carried out. Under the leadership of E. W. Reid, various approaches were tried, until an interesting observation pointed the way toward a solution. It was known that vinyl acetate resins, at that time being produced by the Shawinigan Company in Canada, had a characteristic that was essentially the opposite of PVC polymers—they were too soft and had too low a melting point. Perhaps a combination of the two resins would work! Studies on the copolymerization of vinyl chloride and vinyl acetate at Mellon Institute showed that plastic resins could be produced with properties intermediate between those of PVC and polyvinyl acetate. The result was a material the company called Vinylite (19). Floor tiles and phonograph records made of Vinylite were exhibited at the Chicago World's Fair in 1933. Encouraged, Union Carbide built a five-million-pound-per-year Vinylite plant in 1936. Other uses were soon found for the material in can coating and fabric coating, although it took several more years for sales to reach a meaningful level.

Another approach to deal with the stiffness problem of PVC was discovered in the mid-1930s by Waldo Semon at B.F. Goodrich. He found that "plasticizers," such as tritolyl phosphate, could be used to transform PVC into a rubberlike material. Named Koroseal, this material was used for wire and cable insulation and in other applications where flexibility was desired (20). Union Carbide and Goodrich scientists also developed a number of additives, such as heat stabilizers and lubricants, to facilitate processing and improve the characteristics of the plastic end products (tubing, molded shapes, wall coverings, draperies, dentures, and insulation). As knowledge about PVC polymer disseminated, the Navy's and Air Force's interest was piqued by the fact that PVC performed far better than rubber in coating wires and cables submerged in seawater or subjected to extreme temperatures. This application was developed jointly by Goodrich and General Electric Company. Flameproofing of garments through the use of PVC-coated fabrics was also of great interest for war applications. The rigidity of PVC had some advantages, of course. It could, for example, be used to fabricate pressure and drainage piping and this eventually became its biggest market.

Development of PVC technology in Germany roughly paralleled that in the United States. The ample availability of acetylene and hydrogen chloride facilitated the large-scale production of vinyl chloride monomer and made PVC a relatively low cost product, once the technology was elucidated. Actually, it was the I.G. Farben companies active in Buna rubber development and production who had extra acetylene capacity available and who could now use some of this material for the manufacture of PVC. The company called the product "Igelit," a name taken from I.G. and "Vinylite." Unplasticized PVC was used for piping, while plasticized material went into shoe soles, insulation, upholstery, and phonograph records. In Germany during World War II, vinyl chloride was copolymerized with dimethyl maleate or methyl acrylate to obtain a softer material that could be processed without the use of other plasticizers.

In England, production of PVC compounds started just before the beginning of the war, using polymer imported from Union Carbide in the United States. A 1,500-ton plant for the manufacture of monomer from acetylene and hydrogen chloride was built by ICI at Runcorn during the war and was expanded to 5,000 tons when it was realized, shortly thereafter, that natural rubber supply would likely be cut off for the remainder of the conflict. Distillers Chemicals Ltd. (DCL) also worked on vinyl chloride monomer process technology. It based its process on ethylene produced via dehydration of alcohol. Like Union Carbide, the company made vinyl chloride by cracking ethylene dichloride, which DCL made "on purpose" (rather than as a by-product) via chlorination of ethylene.

Production of vinyl resins in the United States remained at a relatively modest level until just before the start of the war, with statistics for 1939 showing a total of only slightly over one million pounds produced in that year. However, a number of potential new uses had been developed over the previous several years, such as rigid sheets in 1938, flexible sheeting in 1939, and Vinyon textile fibers in 1939, the latter being PVC copolymers with polyvinyl alcohol. Further developments during the war included "Plastisol" and "Organisol" paste and solution resins for a variety of specialized molding applications.

PVC became the "workhorse" plastic for hundreds of military uses. In view of the loss of natural rubber supply and the fact that synthetic rubber production did not become effective until the middle of the war, plasticized PVC was a welcome substitute for many applications where rubber might otherwise have been employed. In many of these, it was superior to rubber. The production of vinyl chloride monomer and PVC therefore rose very rapidly in the early 1940s. By the end of the war, enough plants had been built to allow U.S. PVC production to reach 120 million pounds per year.

POLYSTYRENE

Many investigators had a role in the identification of styrene as a reactive monomer; in the synthesis of styrene from hydrocarbon feedstocks; and in the development of processes for the production of polystyrene, one of the most versatile of the plastics. However, the key factor in the growth of polystyrene was the fact that styrene was produced in very large quantities as an intermediate for the production of Buna S (known in the United States as GRS) synthetic rubber. For this reason, a number of styrene monomer plants were erected both in Germany, and later in the United

States and Canada. When the production of synthetic rubber was no longer a critical war priority item, styrene became, for a time, the most important monomer for the production of plastics.

Styrene was first isolated as a compound in 1831 as a distillation product from aromatic materials such as cassia oils* and camphor. In 1845, two British scientists showed that styrene could be transformed into a solid material upon heating. Shortly thereafter, Berthelot, in France, synthesized styrene by pyrolyzing hydrocarbons in a hot tube—a type of "brute force" dehydrogenation later carried out with the aid of a catalyst.

The first recognition of the commercial potential of polystyrene came in England in 1911, when Matthews filed a British patent covering thermal and catalytic processes for polymerizing styrene to a hard material that, according to the patent claims, could be used to make articles then produced from wood, glass, celluloid and hard rubber. A major problem, however, made it difficult to use this invention—styrene monomer was so reactive that it was difficult to purify it and, particularly, to store it. Another invention, by two French researchers, provided the answer when they found that aromatic amines and phenols acted as inhibitors to the premature polymerization of styrene, which had a tendency to occur in the final distillation column or in storage.

Naugatuck Chemical Company in 1925, was the first firm to build a polystyrene plant, aided by an eminent Russian scientist, I. I. Ostromislenski, who had worked in the area of vinyl chemistry for many years. One of his key patents, filed in 1927, was entitled "Process for Manufacturing Plastic Compositions and Products Obtained Thereby." He described several polymerization processes, showing the different properties that could be obtained under various reaction conditions. Naugatuck and Ostromislenski had not, however, followed Berthelot's lead in preparing styrene by the dehydration of ethylbenzene. Instead, they conceived an expensive process involving dehydrohalogenation of chlorinated ethylbenzene. This not only gave a high cost product but also resulted in a polymer that had a tendency to yellow. The main outlet was in a denture material called "Victron." Predictably, the product was not a big success (19).

Scientists at Dow Chemical and I.G. Farben started development work on a commercial dehydrogenation process for styrene

*Obtained from the bark of trees that was also ground up to make cinnamon.

around 1930. The German work proceeded much faster, driven by the need for monomer to make Buna-S rubber. In 1929, Dr. Wulff at Ludwigshafen and Professor Mark were responsible for developing the I.G. technology for styrene monomer. Trolitol polystyrene plastics were developed shortly thereafter. A number of polystyrene plants were built in the late 1930s at Ludwigshafen and at Schkopau, near Leuna, in Eastern Germany.

The work at Dow proceeded much more slowly, with no encouragement from top management for several years. In fact, Willard Dow apparently told his research manager at one time to drop work on styrene and to concentrate on cellulosic plastics, since Dow was already involved in Ethocel and other cellulosic products. Nevertheless, "bootlegged" work continued at Dow, leading to the development of a practical dehydrogenation catalyst. The work was done under a different code name than "styrene" and was supported by company treasurer Earl Bennett, who had apparently been convinced by several key Dow researchers who were sure that they had a potentially successful product on their hands. Dow polystyrene was put on the market in 1937 under the trade name Styron and had a crystalline clarity far superior to Naugatuck's material 10 years earlier. Shortly after Dow started producing and selling the resin, Monsanto and the Bakelite Company also began marketing the Dow material. The most important aspect of Dow's development was, of course, the fact that when the synthetic rubber program finally got underway, Dow was in a technical position to supervise the construction of a number of large styrene plants. In 1947, Drs. R. R. Dreisbach and J. Grebe received the Hyatt award for the development of a process for the production of pure styrene and its polymerization to polystyrene. (Much later, I met Ken Bowen, who had been the manager of Dow Chemical's first styrene plant just before the war. Now, in the early 1970s, retired from Dow, he approached Conoco with the idea that ethylene could be produced more economically by filling steam cracker tubes with a catalyst. Chem Systems organized some experiments to try and prove this out, but unfortunately the results were unconvincing.)

The fact that German manufacturers had a lead of several years in the production of styrene polymers is evident. When DeBell's C.I.O.S. team surveyed German plastics practice just after cessation of hostilities (see Chapter 1), they found a surprisingly large variation of styrenic resin products and production processes.

From a chemical standpoint, these included styrene-acrylonitrile and styrene acrylate copolymers, and from a process standpoint, various techniques of polymerization, including mass, emulsion, and two-stage systems. Technology for the production of impact as well as crystal polymers was extensive. German polystyrene uses ranged from fuse and igniter-cap parts and gas-mask breathing parts in military applications to combs, egg cups, printing plates, and drinking glasses (21). DeBell also found that styrene was starting to be used in conjunction with polyesters "as a potting compound and in laminates." This foreshadowed today's extensive use of styrene in fiberglass-reinforced polyesters.

In the United States, polystyrene production rose from 190,000 pounds in 1938 to 15 million pounds in 1945. Polystyrene had become an important new plastic in the U.S. economy, going not only into various injection molding applications, but also into adhesives, emulsions, and foams. With a huge amount of wartime styrene capacity waiting to be exploited for the civilian market, the only issue was how fast new polymerization and fabrication plants could be built to convert the monomer into a myriad of consumer products.

Monsanto bought the styrene plant it had built and operated for the government in Texas City, Texas. Behind this move was the guiding spirit of Joe Mares– like "Dutch" Beutel, with whom he had founded the Texas Chemical Council, another "larger than life" figure in early U.S. petrochemicals. Mares had been in charge of Monsanto's patent department before the war and had subsequently headed up the company's development group, which he had pointed toward petrochemicals. At the end of the war, he had tried to engineer a joint venture, based on hydrocarbons, with Mobil Oil, but this plan was dropped when the price of molasses collapsed and alcohol was thought to be a cheaper feedstock for making ethylene derivatives. But now Mares was put in charge of the Texas City styrene plant and he immediately proceeded to add a large polystyrene unit. The 1947 ammonium nitrate explosion in the harbor at Texas City destroyed much of this plant, but it was soon rebuilt and expanded. Mares had hoped that his contributions in petrochemicals would propel him to the top at Monsanto. When this didn't happen, he left to form a consulting firm with Henry Groppe. There he helped to establish and run Petrotex Chemical (a joint venture between FMC Corporation and Tenneco to make butadiene) and El Paso Natural Gas Products Company (a joint venture to make styrene, ethylene and polyethylene in the West Texas gas fields near Odessa).*

And this brings us to the third major thermoplastic, the product obtained by the polymerization of the simplest possible monomer—ethylene.

POLYETHYLENE

In May 1945, *Modern Plastics* magazine reviewed an article entitled "Polyethylene—Its Packaging Possibilities," which had appeared in *Modern Packaging* in December 1944. Among other things, the article stated that polyethylene film "had an extremely low vapor-transmission rate, low moisture absorption, could be heat-sealed, remained flexible at low temperatures and is colorless and non-toxic." The author also said that "the plastic can be molded, extruded, welded, cemented, embossed, blow-molded, swagged and drawn." In what was surely one of the most prophetic statements made for a new chemical material, he then concluded that "in film form, this (product) should be suitable for packaging . . ." (22).

In 1944, polyethylene was barely known to the plastics industry. Production in the United States had only started one year earlier and use of the new material was limited to military applications, primarily including the shielding of high frequency coaxial cables and wire insulation. Only a few years later, polyethylene, in many ways the most versatile of plastics, had become the fastest growing synthetic material in the world. More than any other chemical product, it became the "engine" for the growth of the U.S. petrochemical industry.

Polyethylene is the simplest of all possible polymers, consisting as it does of simple units containing one carbon and two hydrogen atoms ($-CH_2-$), linked together in some form. The fact that a compound of this structure could exist was first visualized by a German chemist, Hans von Pechmann, in 1898, when he decomposed an ethereal solution of diazomethane to obtain a compound he called "polymethylene." The product he examined was of relatively low molecular weight, although later work with the same raw material produced "polymethylene" polymers with molecular

*Henry Groppe, personal communication.

weights above three million. These were unbranched, linear polymers. Branching procedures for these materials were later discovered by other researchers, still using diazoalkanes as starting materials. Although this work was of theoretical interest, the high cost of the raw material convinced researchers that production of polymethylene would be impractical from any commercial point of view. Up to that time, no one had attempted or perhaps even thought about trying to polymerize ethylene directly.

Research work on polyethylene, which turned out to be one of the most important inventions of the twentieth century, commenced in England in what might be called a classical manner, since at the time the work was initiated only very general objectives had been set. In every company there occur times when the processes it employs commercially seem to have reached a degree of improvement that is considered close to maximum efficiency—although this may not, in fact, be the case. The company then looks for new fields to conquer. At such times, the research team may, for example, try an entirely new process route to one of its chemical products, often using a different raw material. But this is not always feasible or obvious. In these earlier times, when research departments usually had greater license for independent action, research managers might alternately decide that it would be useful just to extend the frontiers of knowledge in a given area in the hope of making a fundamental discovery that might potentially lead to a new product or line of products. As described in Chapter 7, this is how Carothers of DuPont discovered the structure of nylon, and this is also how ICI, in the 1930s, discovered polyethylene.

Under the leadership of Francis A. Freeth, who was research director from 1921 to 1927, ICI's Alkali Group had built a research laboratory at Winnington, having decided that new products would be necessary for the group to maintain its traditional leadership position in the company. The good financial performance of the group had greatly helped the company's fortunes during the early years of the Depression, but also had aroused considerable jealousy in ICI's Dyestuffs Group, whose acknowledged technical excellence in organic chemistry had not recently provided the expected profits for the company. Winnington, which had traditionally been less technically oriented than Dyestuffs, identified high pressure reactions as an interesting field for exploratory research work, since there was little experience with reactions at pressures above those used in hydrogenation processes, such as coal liquefaction or ammonia synthesis. This kind of "blue sky" research particularly appealed to Freeth, who liked the "open-ended pursuit of answers to which the questions had not yet been asked"—in terms of industrial applications. "What are they doing?" he inquired of Brunner Mond at one time "examining last month's cost with a microscope when they should be surveying the horizon with a telescope?" (23).

ICI had, for some time, supported research studies at the University of Leyden, in Holland, which specialized in high pressure equipment design and experimentation. Also, physicists P. W. Bridgman and J. B. Conant at Harvard had published extensively on their work at high pressures. Now, Winnington asked Dr. A. Michels, who headed up the research work at Leyden, to assist the Alkali Group in setting up bench scale apparatus in its laboratory, where it would try and develop practical applications for high pressure reactions (24). Since Billingham, another ICI production site, had the relatively high pressure ammonia plants and Dyestuffs employed the most experienced organic chemists, these groups were asked to assist the Alkali Group by supplying research people to a combined effort aimed at exploring the effect of high pressure technologies on chemical synthesis.

Thus, in January 1932, J. C. Swallow and Michael Perrin from the Alkali Group were joined at Winnington by E. W. Fawcett from Dyestuffs and R. O. Gibson from Billingham. Gibson had already studied under Michels at Leyden and was familiar with apparatus that could take pressures up to 20,000 atmospheres. Research management had set a general objective: See what would happen when a variety of chemicals were brought together for the first time at pressure levels far above those ever used by other researchers (25).

A number of experiments were carried out, but without particularly notable results. Then, on Friday, March 24, 1932, 20 cubic centimeters of ethylene and benzaldehyde, intended to react with each other, were measured into the autoclave and the pressure was raised to 2000 atmospheres. The tube was then placed into a bath at 170°C and left overnight (see Figure 6.6). When Fawcett and Gibson returned in the morning, it was evident that a leak had developed and that the chamber had been emptied of gases. But when the researchers examined the inside of the reaction tube, it was clear that something had happened. The inside tube wall

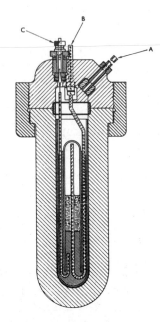

Figure 6.6 Gas-reaction vessel in which polythene was first observed. (*Source:* R. O. Gibson, *The Discovery of Polythene,* Royal Institute of Chemistry Lecture Series, No. 1, 1964, Royal Institute of Chemistry, London, England, p. 16.)

looked like it had been dipped in paraffin wax and this was duly noted by Gibson. The white material was polyethylene!

A few days later, the experiment was repeated but the results were disappointing. No deposit was found in the tube, but there also had been no leak. Additional experiments also gave no positive results, with some resulting in fairly serious explosions. It was frustrating to be unable to recreate the conditions under which the first experiment had been performed and the danger of further explosions signaled caution. Work on the reaction was discontinued and the Dyestuffs Group withdrew its support. At Winnington, the research management proscribed further work on this reaction, which was considered dangerous and whose potential had not yet been acknowledged by management.

In December 1935, Perrin and two others decided to resume work on reacting ethylene, but unofficially, during off hours. The team had already surmised that benzaldehyde had played no particular role in the reaction. In this new attempt, they used somewhat lower purity ethylene. Employing the original type of experimental bomb and again a 170°C bath, they attempted to raise pressure to 200 atmospheres. To their considerable surprise, they found it impossible to hold pressure at that level, even when adding more ethylene, and Perrin now recognized that a polymer was probably being formed inside the bomb. Soon, they dropped pressure and opened up the apparatus and, according to Perrin's recollections, "masses of snowy white powder spilled out . . . we had made at least ten grams . . . something like a hundred times more than all the previous yields put together."

Shortly thereafter, the team concluded that a small amount of oxygen impurity in the ethylene feedstock had acted as a catalyst for the polymerization. A little less oxygen and nothing would have happened. A little more, and there would have been an explosion. Perrin and his group had reliably rediscovered polyethylene and soon found that the conditions of polymer formation were reproducible. In February 1936, the first British patent specification had been filed and a brand name "Alkthene" (for Alkali Division Polyethylene) had been chosen. Early that year, the first film had been cast from a hot solution on to a glass plate, molded articles had been produced, and the excellent dielectric properties of the material had been recognized.

It was time to make a commercial process out of a laboratory production technique that still required digging polymer by hand out of a reaction vessel. Professor Michels again contributed, by designing a compressor that used mercury pistons as a liquid. And the ICI engineers came up with an *autoclave* reactor, containing a motor-driven stirrer, to keep the polymer from adhering to the walls, as it was being formed.

The first plant was constructed, coming onstream on September 1, 1939 with a nominal capacity of 100 tons per year. It was built by the Alkali Division, based on its successful sponsorship of the research work, even though ICI, through its earlier acquisition of Mouldrite Plastics, had finally established a Plastics Division. Ten tons of polyethylene were sold in 1939, all for electrical purposes. This application, primarily for airborne radar installations, accounted for essentially all of the polyethylene made and sold during the war. By 1945, the company was able to produce and sell 1,500 tons per year.

Fortunately for ICI, it had filed a composition-of-matter patent for polyethylene in the United States soon after filing in England.

This broadest type of a patent protects an invention no matter what process is employed to make it. ICI's decision turned out to be critical, since Union Carbide had been independently developing a polyethylene process around the same time. ICI had beaten Union Carbide to the U.S. Patent Office by only a few months.

This time, ICI had also scored a clean sweep against its old rival I.G. Farben. Just before the outbreak of the war, the I.G. heard about the development and asked ICI for information about the new material. The British company, in line with previous such requests and information exchanges, pondered the question. At first, it considered asking the Germans to provide, in return for polyethylene know-how, combined information on Buna Rubber, "Oppanol" (polyisobutylene rubber and lube oil additives), polystyrene, and polyvinyl chloride. However, even this was not considered enough, in view of the outstanding nature of the polyethylene invention and so ICI finally decided that it would not supply the information to the German company under any circumstances. The result was that during the early part of the war, aircraft operated by the Axis countries had much bulkier radar sets than Allied planes. Shortly thereafter, BASF developed a polyethylene process, based on a tubular (not autoclave) reactor, and the material then found its way into similar dielectric uses in German war equipment. It was called "Lupolen," taken from Ludwigshafen and polyethylene (21, pp. 131–140). Much later, Dr. H. Hopf, a high level research executive, confirmed that his group's visit to Winnington just before the war helped I.G. Farben's rapid development of a German polyethylene process.* Dr. Otto Ambros, a leading polymer chemist at BASF, later also in charge of Buna Rubber development, apparently said during the course of the group's visit to Winnington, "I don't know how we missed it" (23).

The Allies also used polyethylene-insulated radar in ships and ground installations. Developmental applications in high voltage power cables, shortwave sets, and in television were also being studied and soon became a commercial reality. A polyethylene-insulated telephone trunk line was installed in 1941 between New York and Washington, with polymer supplied by ICI.

In 1941, a DuPont group visited the ICI plant, and was provided with information to build polyethylene facilities in the United States under license. Two plants were erected in the United States

---

*Dr. Robert Purvin, personal communication.

during the war. One was a DuPont plant using ICI technology obtained under the companies' 1929 Patents and Processes Agreement and the other a Union Carbide plant that used a tubular reactor design developed by the company, which had received a polyethylene license from ICI.

By 1946, several different commercial polyethylene processes were in operation. All of these involved the free-radical polymerization of ethylene to produce a high molecular weight polymer under highly exothermic conditions. Reaction pressures were in the range of 15,000–40,000 pounds per square inch (1,000 to almost 3,000 atmospheres). The reaction initiation temperature was 100–200°C and either oxygen or an organic peroxide were used as initiators.

Although the autoclave and tubular reactor processes differed somewhat in terms of polymerization conditions, the polyethylenes obtained from either type of reactor all had a relatively low density (0.915 to 0.935 grams/cubic centimeter) and therefore low crystallinity and a high molecular weight. Product characteristics, in terms of molecular weight range, branching, and degree of crystallinity, could be varied through independent control of pressure, temperature (varied through the use of cooling jackets), and the amount of initiator employed. The polymerization was carried out with ethylene in the form of a dense gas above its critical temperature and the material was characterized by extensive chain branching. These polymers became known as low density polyethylene (LDPE) and were all based on the original work of ICI.

High density polyethylene (HDPE), which appeared as a commercial product some 12 years later, was, in a minor way, based on a discovery made in Germany during World War II, although its importance was not appreciated at the time. An I.G. Farben chemist was attempting to synthesize a lubricating oil from ethylene, using titanium tetrachloride and aluminum powder as a catalyst. He obtained an oily product and also a white powder he was not able to identify. About 10 years later, Dr. Karl Ziegler, working at the Max Planck Institute in Muehlheim-Ruhr, carried out related experiments with somewhat altered catalysts and realized that he had discovered a form of polyethylene quite different from that obtained in the high pressure process. Using alkyl aluminum compounds and titanium tetrachloride as a catalyst, he was able to polymerize ethylene at atmospheric pressure and close to ambient temperature to produce polyethylene that had a higher density and considerably greater crystallinity than that obtained in the high pressure process. This polymer had essentially no chain branching and produced a highly oriented and therefore crystalline arrangement. Work by Standard Oil (Indiana) and Phillips Petroleum, using a transition metal oxide catalyst at somewhat elevated pressure, also resulted in linear polyethylenes with little branching and high crystallinity.

By the late 1950s, some 10 years after the end of the war, both high and low pressure polyethylene had been firmly established in their respective markets. High density polyethylene produced by the low pressure process was considered particularly good for applications where hardness, rigidity, and high strength were important. Low density, high pressure polyethylene was used for its flexibility, toughness, and the clarity of its films. The discovery and development of so-called stereo regular polymers, such as high density polyethylene is covered in detail in Chapter 8.

Although polyethylene was well known for specialized uses during the war, it took several years for this product to make a breakthrough in consumer applications. In the January 1947 issue of *Modern Plastics,* which reviewed expected plant construction projects for the coming year, polyethylene was not even covered among the categories of plastics resins surveyed in the article, although mention was made of DuPont's plans for building a polyethylene plant at Orange, Texas.

In an antitrust settlement in 1952, the U.S. government and ICI agreed that the British firm would license its polyethylene technology in the United States on a nonexclusive basis and licenses were then granted to a number of firms. Union Carbide also expanded capacity and two other firms obtained licenses from BASF on its tubular process. These plants were built because consumers had discovered the many uses for polyethylene, with the largest demand in packaging applications. In 1955, *Chemical Week* characterized the rise in polyethylene production as "phenomenal." Production had increased by 50 percent in the previous year (26). Polyethylene demand rose from 200 million pounds in 1954 to 600 million pounds in 1958. In 1960, polyethylene consumption exceeded 1.2 billion pounds. Shortly before, it had become the largest volume plastic resin in the United States.

Plastics have become the universal material that can perform almost, although not quite all of the functions of a host of other materials, from paper to wood, metals, and glass. Essentially all of the plastics, which have replaced these traditional materials in many applications, are now made wholly, or in part, from petrochemicals (Fig. 6.7). Articles produced from styrenic resins and methacrylates are not quite as clear or as strong as those made from glass, but they are lighter, safer and usually less expensive. Polyethylene film has not only replaced cellophane but also paper in many packaging applications. High density polyethylene and PVC are now used for drums, bins, and bottles that were previously made from steel, wood, or glass. PVC siding and window frames partly replace wood or aluminum, while PVC pipe substitutes for steel or cast iron in above- or below-ground applications. Thermoset plastics are still employed for many molding applications, where rigidity and heat stability are required. Polyurethane plastics provide a compromise between elastomers and plastics.

Plastics passed through three distinct stages: cellulosics, thermosets, and finally thermoplastics, the latter being integrally tied to the major petrochemical "building blocks." Cellulosics first showed the potential for plastics and gave the man-made fiber industry a good start, but these polymers had too many limitations to allow broad-scale substitution for other materials. The thermosets, including the phenolics and the amino resins, created an injection-molding industry and provided consumers with a further indication of things to come. These resins, however, had drawbacks due to limitations in processing techniques, such as long cycle times in the mold, poor performance characteristics in many applications, and the fact that they could not be blown into films or cast into thin sheets.

The thermoplastic resins were far more versatile and also less expensive to produce, an "unbeatable combination" relative to thermosets. Rapid growth of thermoplastics was spurred by the fact that some of the large plants built during the war for producing synthetic elastomers could be converted to make thermoplastic polymers and were thus able to make products for consumer markets. These plants also allowed economies of scale never experienced before in the production of organic chemical products. With ethylene prices dropping to levels as low as two to three cents per pound, with rapidly increasing quantities of inexpensive benzene available from refineries, and with chlorine or hydrogen chloride available at low prices (the latter being the by-product of chlor-alkali plants usually built for producing caustic soda rather than chlorine), it was no wonder that the production of polyeth-

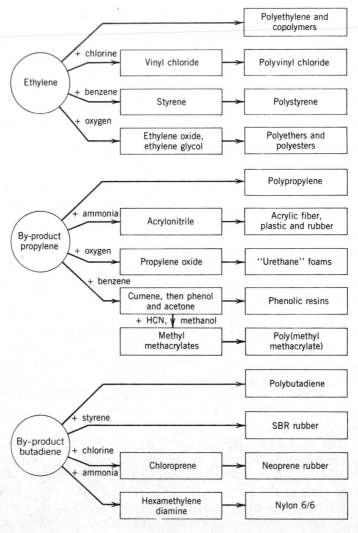

Figure 6.7 Important monomers and polymers derived from ethylene, propylene, and butadiene.

ylene, polystyrene, and PVC became highly economical and therefore attracted many new producers.

And while the price of these "building blocks" has now escalated by a factor of five or more since the 1940s, the substitution of plastics for competitive materials is still far from complete. Although

The Ubiquitous Products of the Petrochemical Industry

Packaging

Washing-up liquid
bottles
Mineral and carbonated
drink bottles
Caps for bottles and
aerosols
Carboys for industrial
chemicals
Coatings for tinplate
cans
Bottle crates
Tote boxes
Flexible packaging for
frozen food
Yoghurt and cream
containers
Stretch and shrink
wrap for pallets
Industrial strapping
Refuse sacks
Sterile packs for
medical use

Building

Shuttering and
molds for concrete
Damp course film
Thermal insulation
Window frames,
guttering, drainage
pipes
Gas, sewage and
water pipes
Electrical conduit
Foaming agents for
plasterboard
Binders for
particleboard and
plywood
Solvents for paints
Insulation and
sheathing for
power, telephone
and TV wire and
cables
Electrical plugs,
sockets and
switches
Vandal-proof and
security glazing
Building film for
site cover during
construction

Other uses

in the home . . .
Molded chairs
Mattresses
Decorative laminates
Vinyl wall coverings
Washing-up bowls
Canisters for food
Buckets
Bristles for brushes
Floor tiles
Soles, heels and
shoes
Washing machine
drums and
agitators
Microchip toy casings

. . . in the office . . .
Telephone handsets
Pocket calculator
casings
VDU housings

**. . . and all over
the place**
Printed circuit
laminates
Audio and video
tapes
Cassette housings
and drives
Adhesives
Telephone poles
Road markers and
paints
Fishing nets, ropes,
string
Fish and vegetable
boxes
Horticultural film
Powder and liquid
detergents
Dry cleaning fluids
Disposable syringes
Contact lenses
Artificial hips and
other replacement
surgical items
Anti-skid road
surfacing

Textiles

Fibers for:

Coats	Skirts	Carpet pile	Tarpau-lins
Suits	Socks	fibers	Soil
Underwear	Stockings	Carpet backing	stabili-
Shirts	Curtains	fabrics	sation fabrics
	Uphol-stery fabrics	Pillow fillings	Industrial cloth-ing
		Quilt fillings	Fireproof cloth-ing

Transport

Dashboards	Knobs	Antifreeze
Bumpers	Seat foam	Truck cabs
Radiator grilles	Seat covers	Train bodies
Gasoline tanks	Interior linings	Bus and coach parts
Tyres and inner tubes	Anti-corro-sion treatment	Aircraft parts
Laminate film for safety glass	Paints	Yacht parts
Battery cases	Brake fluids	Space shuttle elements
Wire insulation	Degreasing solvents	

Figure 6.8 Petrochemicals in Use—A few examples (*Source:* Shell Oil Company, *The Petroleum Handbook,* 6th ed., New York, Elsevier, 1983.)

plastics became the most important petrochemical consumer product, "petrochemicals" now comprise an incredibly broad part of our everyday life. Figure 6.8 gives a representative illustration of this fact, as shown in a recent Shell publication.

Together with synthetic fibers, elastomers, solvents, coatings, and other synthetic materials, plastics provided petrochemicals producers the basis for double-digit annual growth rates for many of the important organic chemicals made from oil and natural gas. During the 1950s and 1960s, there was little letup in this phenomenal spurt in production. By the 1970s, plastics had, in fact, replaced a large percentage of traditional materials in many uses. By 1979, the volume of all plastics materials produced exceeded the production of iron and steel.

REFERENCES

1. *Modern Plastics,* **28,** January 1951, pp. 55–64, 140–146.
2. What's ahead for 1946, *Modern Plastics,* **23,** January 1946, pp. 91–106.
3. Paper presented before Royal Society of Arts, London, England, 1943.
4. Stanford Research Institute. *Chemical Economics Handbook,* Menlo Park, California, Stanford Research Institute, and Government Statistics.
5. *World Book,* Volume P, 1954, p. 494.
6. J. Henry Dubois and F. W. John (1981). *Plastics, Sixth Edition,* New York, Van Nostrand Reinhold.
7. Morris Kaufman (1968). *Giant Molecules, The Technology of Plastics, Fibers and Rubber,* New York, Doubleday.
8. Harold Blancke (President, Celanese Corporation) (1952). "Celanese Corporation of America, The Founders and the Early Years," speech to the Newcomen Society, New York.
9. G. C. Inskeep and R. Van Horn (1950). Cellophane, a series of articles describing chemical manufacturing plants, by the editors of *Industrial and Engineering Chemistry,* New York, Reinhold, Vol. III, pp. 118ff.
10. F. Sherwood Taylor (1957). *A History of Industrial Chemistry,* New York, Abelard-Schumann, p. 259.
11. Peter J. T. Morris (1986). *Polymer Pioneers—A Popular History of the Science and Technology of Large Molecules,* Philadelphia, The Center of History of Chemistry, p. 40.
12. Byron M. Vanderbilt (1971). *Thomas Edison, Chemist,* Chapter 8, Organic chemicals; Chapter 8, Organic chemicals and naval research, Washington, DC, American Chemical Society.
13. R. L. Kenyon and N. Boehmer (1950). Phenol Sulfonation, Modern Chemical Processes, a series of articles describing chemical manufacturing plants, by

the editors of *Industrial and Engineering Chemistry,* New York, Reinhold, Vol. II, pp. 33ff.

14. R. N. Hader, R. D. Wallace, and R. W. McKinney, Formaldehyde from Methanol, a series of articles describing chemical manufacturing plants, by the editors of *Industrial and Engineering Chemistry,* New York, Reinhold, Vol. III, pp. 79ff.

15. John DeBell (1941). Thermoplastics, *Modern Plastics,* January.

16. C. W. Bunn (1957). Achievements of industrial chemicals—Hydrocarbon macromolecules, *Chemistry & Industry,* April 6, 404–410.

17. Hermann Mark (1976). Polymer chemistry: The last 100 years, *Chemical & Engineering News,* April 6, p. 183.

18. Joseph G. Davidson (1956). Petrochemical survey, An anecdoctal reminiscence, chemistry industry medal, 1955 address, *Chemistry & Industry,* May 19, 392–398.

19. Reginald L. Wakeman (1947). *The Chemistry of Commercial Plastics,* New York, Reinhold, p. 304.

20. Vinyl chloride polymers, *Kirk-Othmer Encyclopedia,* Vol. 14, New York, Wiley, p. 306.

21. John M. DeBell et al. (1946). *German Plastics Practice,* from the Quartermaster Reports, Washington, DC, Department of Commerce.

22. C. S. Myers (1944). Polyethylene—Its packaging possibilities, *Modern Packaging,* December, 18, 122–123, 158, 160.

23. Carol Kennedy (1986). *ICI: The Company That Changed Our Lives,* London, Century Hutchinson, pp. 60–61.

24. Martin Sherwood (1983). Polyethylene and its origins, *Chemistry & Industry,* March 21, 237–242.

25. W. J. Reader (1970, 1975). Mid-century materials, Plastics, *Imperial Chemical Industries: A History, Vol. II,* London, Oxford University Press, p. 349ff.

26. Report on plastics, *Chemical Week,* November 19, 1955.

ADDITIONAL READING

Bishop, R. B. (1971). *Practical Polymerization for Polystyrene,* Boston, Mass., Cahners Book.

Dubois, J. Harry (1972). *Plastics History U.S.A.,* Boston, Mass., Cahners Books.

Forrestal, D. J. (1977). *Faith, Hope & $5000, The Story of Monsanto,* New York, Simon & Schuster.

Gibson, R. O. (1964). The discovery of polythene, Royal Institute of Chemistry Lecture Series, No. 1, p. 16.

Goggin, W. C. (1946). Advances in plastics in the United States and Germany, *Industrial & Engineering Chemistry,* **24,** No. 3, February 10.

Haynes, William. *American Chemical Industry, A History,* six volumes, New York, D. Von Nostrand 1945–1954.

Raff, R. A. V. and J. B. Allison (1956). *Polyethylene,* New York, Interscience Publisher Inc.

Rodriguez, Ferdinand (1982). *Principles of Polymer Systems,* New York, McGraw-Hill.

Union Carbide Corporation. *A Biography of Leon Henrik Baekeland (1863–1944),* Union Carbide Corporation.

Wittcoff, Harold A. and Bryan G. Reuben (1980). *Industrial Organic Chemicals In Perspective, Parts I & II,* New York, Wiley.

7 / From Cellulosic to Synthetic Fibers

Although "plastics" were the petrochemical product that captured everybody's imagination,* the development of synthetic fibers was the crowning achievement of the organic chemists and chemical engineers whose careers spanned the transition from coal-based to petroleum-based raw materials. Closely following the advances in polymer chemistry made in the early 1930s, the new synthetic fibers were all made from monomers that could initially be produced from coal-based feedstocks. But it was the ample availability of low cost petrochemical feedstocks that allowed synthetics to become inexpensive enough to capture roughly half of the total fiber market. Within a span of only a little over 10 years, the chemical industry developed three fibers—polyamide, acrylic, and polyester—able to supplant or replace, in various applications, the natural and cellulosic (man-made) fibers that had been used up to that time. The new fibers were either superior in quality or less expensive than those they were replacing, or both. As a result, all consumption growth in fibers from then on was in the synthetics, rather than in the traditional fibers (wool, rayon, cotton, and silk). Considering the explosive growth in postwar consumer demand for

*Many will remember the film *"The Graduate"*, in which Dustin Hoffman, Mrs. Robinson's improbable young lover, is advised to choose a career in "plastics."

all kinds of personal and commercial goods produced from fibers, the development of synthetics had arrived just in time.

The birth and early years of the synthetic fiber industry are fascinating, not only from a scientific standpoint, but also because of the roles that some of the key companies played—or did not play—as the technology for the production of these new materials became known. In retrospect, DuPont was in a class by itself in first pioneering the development of the polyamide they called "nylon"— and a little later in diligently pursuing the development and commercialization of acrylic and polyester fibers. The I.G. Farben companies, principally Agfa and, later, Bayer and others, were not far behind, although, in the case of nylon, the Germans were fortunate in identifying a route to polyamide fibers not considered feasible and therefore not patented by Carothers of DuPont. Similarly, the fact that Carothers had little success in making fibers from aliphatic polyesters left a second loophole for later researchers to exploit, so that a team operating in a small industrial laboratory operated by the Calico Printers Association in England was able to make the key invention that led to polyester fibers.

Acrylic fiber development was largely the result of goal-oriented research* by several companies, including DuPont, Bayer, Monsanto, and Union Carbide. In some respects, this development work was less dramatic, although certainly no less important than the work on the other two fibers. Acrylic fibers became a reality when companies found out how to modify and spin polyacrylonitrile and how to dye the fibers so obtained to produce a material that was acceptable to the customer (more about this later).

Some of the other firms that participated in the transition from man-made to synthetic fibers included ICI, Courtaulds, American Viscose, Rhône-Poulenc, and Toyo Rayon. Surprisingly, Courtaulds, a firm originally larger and more powerful than ICI and endowed with an immense amount of fiber spinning and application know-how, managed to come out rather worse than might have been expected in the transition from natural and man-made to synthetic fibers. In the 1930s, ICI stayed out of fibers to avoid upsetting its dealings with Courtaulds, which involved the supply of

*This term (also called mission-oriented research) is used to describe a process where a research group has a fairly specific idea of what it hopes to invent and attempts to achieve success as quickly as possible, rather than developing a broad patent position and a number of subsidiary inventions as a new area is explored.

heavy organic and inorganic chemicals to that firm. As recounted in W. J. Readers' voluminous, yet extremely readable book on the history of ICI, that company's management at first had considerable misgivings about entering the fibers field (1).

> "Plastics and fibres shared similar technology, but in ICI they were seen as presenting vastly different commercial problems. With plastics, people in ICI felt fairly happy. They represented business of a kind they understood and which, they considered, fell fairly within their field: business, that is to say, in supplying other manufacturers with materials for their own activities. Fibres were different altogether. The field was dominated by Courtaulds—rich, successful, supposedly technically very expert, and a valued customer of ICI. Little was known in ICI about the technique of spinning and there were alleged to be arcane mysteries in the marketing of fibres to the textile industry. Moreover, the consumer market—the fashion trade, even—lay not far away, and that was no place for a self-respecting chemical firm".

Some 10 years later, ICI used its Patents and Processes Agreement with DuPont to enter the nylon business. At that early stage, however, it was careful to offer a joint interest in this venture—called British Nylon Spinners (B.N.S.)—to Courtaulds. When ICI was later able to gain control of the Calico Printers Association's (C.P.A.) polyester fiber technology, it decided that it would henceforth pursue an independent course from Courtaulds and it was eventually able to take over Courtaulds' interest in B.N.S.

Many technological developments were needed to produce synthetic fibers of suitable quality at prices that consumers would be able to afford. At the laboratory bench level, it took an enormous number of experiments to eventually identify the organic chemical building blocks that would combine to produce polymers of the requisite molecular chain length and configuration to emulate the natural and man-made fibers. At the spinning and processing end, it was necessary to develop new equipment and processes to extrude (spin), dry, collect, stretch, and further process the fibers to obtain suitable tensile strength, appearance, dyeability, and other features. New synthesis routes had to be conceived to make large quantities of previously fairly esoteric organic chemicals—such as adipic acid, hexamethylene diamine, caprolactam, and terephthalic acid (all intermediates for making synthetic fibers)—at acceptable cost. This required a great deal of original chemistry and chemical engineering, with some of the key work carried out under wartime conditions. Innovation in production schemes for all of the monomers continued well into the late 1950s. Behind most of the earlier developments was the genius of DuPont's Dr. Wallace Carothers, whose pioneering research created the synthetic fiber industry as we know it today.

INSPIRED RESEARCH BY CAROTHERS

It is useful to consider the state of the textile fiber industry at the time when synthetic fibers had just come on the market and the natural and cellulosic (man-made) fibers still dominated the industry. In 1949–1950, textile fiber consumption in the United States was approximately six billion pounds per year (Table 7.1 and Figure 7.1). Cotton was still, by far, the largest-selling fiber, followed by the man-made cellulosics (rayon, acetate, etc.) and then wool. In 1949, the total amount of synthetic fibers produced—

Table 7.1   Textile, Fiber Consumption During Immediate Postwar Years (Million Pounds Per Year)

	1949	1950	1951
Cotton	3,838	4,720	4,500
Wool			
Apparel	350	441	425
Carpet	161	196	115
Total	511	637	540
Silk	4	8	5
Cellulosic man-made			
Viscose rayon	648	804	823
Cupra rayon	12	14	18
Acetate rayon	318	436	419
Rayon imports	16	38	107
Total	994	1,352	1,367
Synthetic fibers	92	145	170
Total fibers	5,439	6,862	6,582

Source: Address by J. B. Quig, E. I. DuPont de Nemours & Company, to the Chemical Marketing Research Association, October 1951.

largely nylon—was 92 million pounds, or only 1½ percent of total fiber consumption.

If we consider that the world first heard about nylon in 1938, this is hardly surprising. Much more amazing is the fact that, as a result of the abundance and low cost of petrochemical feedstocks and the superior properties of these new materials, synthetic fiber demand surpassed the combined consumption of natural and cellulosic fibers by the mid-1960s. DuPont and the other companies had spearheaded one of the major industrial developments of this century.

DuPont's interest in fibers was actually an outgrowth of its familiarity with nitrocellulose explosives, which were used for the production of smokeless powder. Shortly after the end of World War I, DuPont evaluated fiber production from nitrocellulose, but soon concluded that the vicose process offered better opportunities

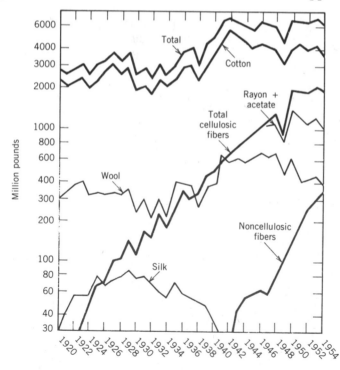

Figure 7.1 U.S. fiber consumption. (*Source:* C. W. Bendigo, Acrylic fibers, copyright by Chemical Marketing Research Association, Staten Island, New York, November 14–15, 1955).

to produce the "artificial silk" it was looking for. After obtaining a license from the Comptoir des Textiles Artificiels in 1920, the DuPont Fibersilk Company was established. A 3 million pound per year plant was built in Buffalo, New York, a year later. In 1925, a second plant was constructed at Old Hickory, Tennessee. The product was made in only one form—continuous filament—first collected on a glass bobbin and later produced by bucket spinning. This fiber had high luster and could be brightly colored, but it was also harsh, fairly weak, and lacked uniformity.

In 1925, the DuPont sales organization decided to stop trying to imitate silk with this material and the product's name was changed to "rayon." In 1927, an important discovery was made. By chopping the filament into short lengths and spinning yarn from these fiber segments by conventional means, a new and more widely useful product was made available to the textile industry— it was known as "staple" and used in clothing. A high-tenacity continuous filament rayon fiber, named "Cordura," was developed in the early 1930s and used in tire cord.

In the late 1920s, DuPont also obtained rights to manufacture another fiber—cellulose acetate yarn—through negotiations with Usines du Rhône and Rhodiaceta (later combined to form Rhône-Poulenc). Production of yarn at the Waynesboro, Virginia, plant began in 1929, followed by acetate staple in 1937. By the late 1930s, DuPont was producing rayon, acetate staple, and yarn, as well as rayon filament. In the course of developing and selling its products, the company also gained an immense amount of fiber spinning and processing know-how (2).

In the early 1930s, when Carothers started his work, this much was known about fibers: Both natural and artificial fibers were based on molecules containing long chains. Cellulose provided these chains for cotton and flax, which were raw materials for the most important natural vegetable fibers. Proteins from animals, such as sheep or the silkworm, gave the long chains found in wool and silk. Later, it was found that the properties of cellulose could be modified to produce fibers not found in nature, such as viscose (rayon) and acetate. But at this time, little success had been obtained in producing, through chemical synthesis, the long-chain molecules that would give fibers derived from these polymers acceptable commercial quality. German chemists produced fibers from polyvinyl chloride (known as Pe-C fiber) and from polyvinyl alcohol in the early 1930s (the latter by Wacker Chemie), but these experiments did not result in commercial products at that time.

When DuPont, in 1929, set a goal of developing a new, superior fiber that would overcome the drawbacks of rayon and acetate, the company first considered a further modification of cellulose, for example using amino- instead of nitro- groups. This area of investigation eventually failed, but then another approach was conceived, and although this line of research was not directed specifically at fiber development, it did eventually lead to the discovery of nylon.

Similar to ICI's discovery of polyethylene (see Chapter 6) in one important respect, this research work by DuPont was undertaken not to develop a specific process or product, but rather to stretch the frontiers of scientific knowledge. In 1927, the company decided that it would soon need new products to assure the continued, successful growth of the corporation. Accordingly, it set up a separate new laboratory dedicated to "filling in the gaps of knowledge affecting important chemical processes, which might be of value for future applied research." A search was made for a qualified person to head the staff of this new research center and the choice fell on Carothers, at that time an instructor at Harvard University.

Carothers, then 32 years old, was already well known in the scientific community. Recipient of a doctor of philosophy degree at the University of Illinois, Carothers had published extensively on the application of the electron theory to the double bond, a body of work that was considered fundamentally important for decades thereafter. He also worked on catalytic reactions of various kinds, concentrating on the action of promoters and catalyst poisons. Lured to Harvard by Professor James Conant, then head of Harvard's prestigious chemistry department, Carothers turned his attention to the structure of long molecules via polymerization.

It appears that Carothers was always more interested in research than in teaching. Although popular with his students, he recognized research as his primary goal in life. When the offer from DuPont came along, he accepted immediately, since it gave him the opportunity to explore new frontiers under conditions of almost unlimited financial backing. Soon after joining DuPont, he chose to concentrate on polymerization by condensation, including work on the structure of substances of high molecular weight. In 1928, he commenced work on polycondensation to make linear polymers with long-chain lengths.

One of Carothers' first successes was the work done on a process for neoprene rubber in the late 1920s. Father Nieuwland at Notre Dame University had published some exciting results on dimers and trimers of acetylene. Carothers and Arnold Collins extended his work to higher polymers and found that the incorporation of chlorine—apparently derived from the cuprous chloride catalyst employed—gave a stable, rubbery material with a structure similar to isoprene. It was soon found that a suitable monomer could be produced by reacting acetylene dimer with HCl, which could then be polymerized to "chloroprene" rubber, a material with high resistance to chemical and ozone. Marketed as Neoprene, it is still used today as an important specialty rubber (3).

The story of Carothers' discovery of nylon will only be briefly summarized here. Basically, the development of the nylon process went through three stages, (1) fundamental research on various monomers, (2) specific studies on various polyamides, and (3) process development on the manufacture of the intermediates and on the polymerization and spinning of the new fiber.

Carothers' early work on the condensation of dibasic acids and glycols was disappointing, since it produced relatively low molecular weight units (in the 2000–5000 range) with unsuitable chains. He then turned his attention to amides and found that he was able to produce hard, waxlike polymers, good in that respect but not suitable for spinning, since they were insoluble in organic solvents.* Around this time, the molecular still was discovered and this allowed Carothers to form polymers at higher temperatures and longer contact times under vacuum, without breaking down the molecules. With the new equipment, he was able to produce "superpolymers," with molecular weights of 10,000 or higher. He also started to make polymers that could be spun into fibers. Further, by cold drawing these fibers, he could obtain properties quite superior to those of unstretched fibers. X-ray studies showed these drawn fibers to have a degree of crystallinity and orientation similar to those of silk and of rayon filaments after they had been stretched under tension. On the other hand, these "superpolyesters" still had too low a melting point, making them unsuitable for use as textile fibers (4).

At DuPont, there was much skepticism at this time as to whether the research carried out would eventually produce a com-

---

*Many fibers are produced by dissolving polymer in an appropriate organic solvent and then extruding the liquid through small holes in "spinnerets" into a bath of cold liquid or into a heated empty vessel. Here, the solvent separates from the polymer, now in strands of continuous fiber, which are then taken up on a spool for further processing.

mercial fiber. The group working on this project felt encouraged by the results, however, and continued its investigations. The breakthrough came soon thereafter, when, after many tries and failures, Carothers decided to attempt to make "superpolyamides" from dibasic acids and diamines. Carothers selected 9-aminononanoic acid as a model compound and now, for the first time, he obtained rather good polymers, with a relatively high melting point of 195°C. In February 1935, a superpolymer was produced from another dibasic acid-amine pair of compounds: hexamethylene diamine and adipic acid. This polymer, termed nylon 6/6 for the number of carbon atoms in each of the two reacting monomers, could be converted to a fiber by melt spinning or by dry spinning. The cold-drawn fibers had high tensile strength and elasticity. They were insoluble in solvents that attacked many other fiber polymers and melted at 263°C. A completely new, practical synthetic fiber had now been developed—at least in the laboratory.

DuPont wasted no time in putting this discovery into commercial practice. Adipic acid could be produced from phenol and a program to make adipic in substantial quantities was now placed in the hands of Roger Williams, at that time chemical director of the ammonia department. Hexamethylene diamine (HMDA) production technology also developed rapidly. One of the early routes was based on furfural derived from oat hulls or corn cobs, which was converted to adiponitrile through a series of steps involving intermediate production of 1,4-dichlorobutane. This was then reacted with sodium cyanide to obtain the nitrile. But DuPont was already contemplating other, less complicated routes to HMDA.

In 1938, DuPont decided to go ahead with its first commercial nylon plant at Seaford, Delaware. Other plants and an expansion at Seaford followed soon thereafter. C. H. Greenewalt, who headed up the Chemical Department at DuPont in those years and later became DuPont's chief executive officer, was thoroughly identified with one of the company's most important inventions.

GERMAN DEVELOPMENT WORK WAS ALONG A DIFFERENT PATH

Paul Schlack (see Chapter 1), then head of Aceta's Berlin laboratories, a part of the I.G. Farben combine, started to work on polycondensation in 1928, several years before Carothers. Not surprisingly, he had also based his early work on the condensation of acids (adipic, sebacic) and glycols and also determined that polyamides were probably a more likely type of monomer. He eventually settled on e-aminocaproic acid, but found great difficulty in purifying this material and obtaining a reasonable polymer. Schlack apparently recognized at this point that diamines might be useful as the other part of the fiber molecule. In 1932, I.G. Farben chemists were developing new technology for synthesizing amines, but when Schlack asked them if they would prepare diamines, he could not obtain their cooperation. Several years went by without further progress. It appears, in fact, that Schlack was actually working in other areas for the next few years. Publication of Carothers' first patent in 1937 stunned the German chemist, who now recognized how close he had come several years earlier to the discovery of nylon.

Work was immediately resumed on synthetic fiber development, but there was now the issue of dealing with Carothers' patent claims. Although the world was moving closer to war, international chemical companies were still respecting each other's patent rights, an important issue for the I.G., which was receiving royalty income from its inventions in various foreign countries. Schlack turned back to aminocaproic acid and looked at different methods of purification and copolymerization. Although this did not produce notable results, he eventually made an important observation: It appeared that some of the acid was transformed into the lactam. And now Schlack started looking carefully at this rather unusual material that could be "opened up" to have an amino group at one end and an acid group at the other—a material called caprolactam. It looked very much like an intermediate that might polymerize into a long-chain, high molecular weight polyamide. Schlack wondered: Had Carothers realized that polyamide chains could possibly be made from a single monomer? He went back to study the patent and was puzzled and pleased to find that Carothers stated categorically that caprolactam could not be converted into a suitable polymer—*a conclusion that shortly proved to be wrong and allowed I.G. Farben to develop its own nylon, independent of DuPont's patents.* Recognizing that hydrochloric acid would probably be a suitable catalyst, Schlack heated caprolactam to 240°C and watched what happened. His very first experiment proved successful. Literally within days, the group at Aceta's laboratory in Wolfen (near Berlin) had spun nylon filament from caprolactam polymer and had also cast 2–3 centimeter rods of the polyamide. These were the precursors of today's nylon engineering resins (5).

Visiting DuPont executives had been unaware of these developments when they arrived at Wolfen in 1938, and they were, of course, astounded at what they found. Accordingly, in mid-1939, DuPont and I.G. Farben signed a cross-licensing agreement on nylon. Not long thereafter, the United States and Germany went to war. In Germany, a nylon 6 plant was built at Wolfen, located in what later became the Russian sector. At the end of the war, some of the engineers from Wolfen and from Leuna, also in East Germany, escaped to the Allied sector and joined the staff of Farbenfabriken Bayer. The first West German nylon (Perlon) plant was built near Leverkuesen, with monomer production at Uerdingen and a fiber-spinning plant at Dormagen, across the Rhine.

No company in any other country matched the prewar achievements of DuPont and I.G. Farben in the development of synthetic fiber technology. This statement might be disputed by Toyo Rayon Company, now called Toray Industries, which came up with a nylon 6 process just before the war, apparently getting around the Schlack patent with a different catalyst.* The fact is that DuPont and I.G.'s Aceta Laboratories had independently developed different versions of a polyamide constructed of six-member monomers. Carothers had made the breakthrough, but had not patented a wide enough area. Schlack had his chance to succeed before Carothers, but had not been able to prevail before learning that Carothers had linked an acid and an amine to make a long-chain polyamide that could be spun into an excellent artificial fiber. It is fair to say that DuPont and the German chemists and engineers had independently achieved success by combining their backgrounds and skill in rayon manufacture and in organic chemical synthesis to come up with what was one of the most important chemical inventions of the century.

Knowing DuPont's philosophy on feedstocks at the time the first nylon plants came onstream, it is doubtful that anyone thought that synthetic fibers would soon be produced exclusively from "petrochemicals." DuPont was proud to tell the world that it had made a synthetic fiber "from coal, air, and water," which was true

---

*Dr. N. Yoda, Director of the Board, Toray Industries, Inc., personal communication.

at that time. Phenol, recovered from coke-oven gases or synthesized from coal-derived benzene, became the first raw material for both types of nylon. But, within a short period of time, both benzene and phenol would be made from petroleum feedstocks. And petroleum-derived benzene would be converted to cyclohexane, which soon became the primary intermediate for adipic acid.

POLYESTER—THE SECOND "MIRACLE FIBER"

The genius of Wallace Carothers was in no way diminished by the fact that he had not only "missed" nylon 6, but also another type of fiber, in some ways superior to nylon, that could be produced from *aromatic* polyesters. He had, in fact, developed what he called "superpolymers" from polyesters in his early work and two of his patents, issued in 1937, covered such high molecular weight compounds. However, these polymers were somewhat unstable, with melting points too low for making textile fibers. Carothers did not succeed, because his research was largely limited to *aliphatic* polyesters and because his success in polyamides caused him to concentrate his subsequent work on these materials. In some respects, Carothers preoccupation with his major discovery—polyamide fibers—had much in common with Karl Ziegler's decision to concentrate on low density polyethylene, effectively allowing Guilio Natto to surge ahead of Ziegler and develop polypropylene and other commercial stereospecific polymers (see Chapter 8).

In England in 1939, J. R. Whinfield and J. T. Dickson, working in a laboratory operated by the Calico Printers Association Ltd., studied Carothers disclosures and patent claims carefully. This industrial research laboratory, set up by an association that dated almost back to the Industrial Revolution, was rather unique since, at that time, chemical research work was still the domain of corporate laboratories or universities. The two organic chemists noted that Carothers had given up on polyester molecules as a suitable composition for synthetic fibers because the aliphatic polyesters he had synthesized (*1*) lacked the chemical stability of polyamides and (*2*) had too low a melting point (Carothers had, nevertheless, patented aliphatic polyesters). Whinfield and Dickson quickly recognized, however, that Carothers either had not studied aromatic polyesters or else had also obtained disappointing results with molecules of this configuration. In any case, he had not included these materials in his patents. They therefore decided to concentrate on synthesizing superpolymers from these materials.

Ethylene glycol was the obvious alcohol part of such a molecule and so they set out to find a suitable aromatic acid. According to records, they did not have to try many aromatic compounds before arriving at terephthalic acid. This material, which has two carboxyl groups in the para position on the benzene ring, was a fairly rare chemical, used, however, in textile dying, and for that reason it was available in their laboratory. Reacting the two chemicals with a suitable catalyst and distilling off the water in a vacuum still, they were soon able to produce a high polymeric polyester with excellent properties and a high melting point of 240°C. And, as they surmised, their invention proved eminently patentable (6).

Polyester fibers have many of the qualities of nylon and some unusual ones of their own. After cold drawing, the fibers are extremely insensitive to water and resistant to most solvents. But, most importantly, they are able to duplicate the resilience properties of wool, particularly when "crimped," which is more difficult to achieve with nylon fibers. Moreover, when compared to natural fibers, which lose their shape under the influence of heat and moisture, polyesters can be "heat set" by exposing the fibers in fabric form to elevated temperatures. Short of thermal degradation, which occurs at extreme conditions of time-temperature exposures, polyester fibers can take a permanent "set," a characteristic that would later allow manufacturers to make "permanent press" garments.

The Calico Printers Association (C.P.A.) could not have anticipated all of these benefits at the time Whinfield and Dickson filed their historic patent application, but it recognized that it had an important invention on its hands. One wonders what course polyester fiber development would have taken if the discovery had not occurred during wartime conditions, and C.P.A. had simply published its results and waited for the world to react. However, Rex Whinfield was by that time working for the U.K. Ministry of Supply. By agreement with C.P.A., his former employer, who felt that production of polyester fibers might aid the British war effort, Whinfield now asked ICI to evaluate the new product and to assess the possibility of going into production as soon as possible. It appears that ICI was selected because the company produced one of the two monomers—ethylene glycol—and because it was already involved in fiber production through its British Nylon Spinners (B.N.S.) venture with Courtaulds. The latter, although it was the major British textile firm at the time, was apparently not asked about its possible interest in the invention. ICI subsequently negotiated a preliminary agreement with C.P.A. and started to work on this new fiber, to which Whinfield had already given the name Terylene (Fig. 7.2a).

Since polyester fibers were not produced before the end of the war, the main beneficiary of these developments was not the Allied war effort but ICI, which soon used its license from C.P.A. to make an independent entry into the fiber business. Still involved in B.N.S. with Courtaulds, ICI was determined to keep this new invention from its partner, since ICI by this time had decided that it would face the consequences of a falling-out with the then dominant U.K. fiber producer, even if that meant the loss of Courtaulds' chemical business. One important roadblock had to be cleared, however. B.N.S. had earlier been licensed by DuPont with that company's fiber melt-spinning technology and, seeing ICI about to develop an independent fiber activity, Courtaulds now took the posi-

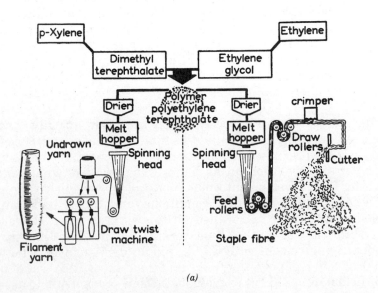

(a)

Figure 7.2(a) Manufacture of Terylene polyester fiber by ICI, (*Source:* R. W. Moncrieff, *Man-made Fibres,* 4th ed., New York, Wiley, 1971.)

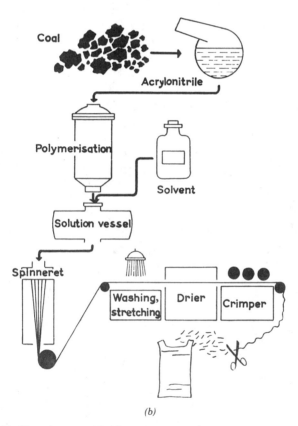

(b)

Figure 7.2(*b*) Manufacture of Dralon acrylic fiber by Farbenfabriken Bayer, A.G. (*Source:* Same as for Fig. 7.2*a*).

tion that ICI could not use this technology outside of B.N.S. for producing polyester fibers. But Courtaulds must have recognized that it would not win this battle, in view of the longstanding relationship between DuPont and ICI (i.e., the famous Patents and Processes Agreement that had, in the 1920s and 1930s, resulted in such a close relationship between the British and American firms). As it turned out, DuPont was very interested in ICI's polyester fiber technology and was therefore willing to deal. In a Solomon-like decision, designed to keep within the letter of its nylon spinning technology license agreement with B.N.S., DuPont now decided to issue independent melt spinning licenses to ICI and Courtaulds.

And, consequently ICI could proceed independently with Terylene
(1). The first plant, with a capacity of 5,000 tons per year, was
approved by the ICI board in late 1950.

Actually, DuPont had not been idle with respect to extending its
fiber development work. In early 1944, Dr. E. F. Izard, in DuPont's
Pioneering Research Section, unaware of Whinfield and Dickson's
work, had also come across polyethylene terephthalate and had
developed an excellent polyester fiber. It was only after the end of
the war, when the British government had relaxed the wartime
secrecy restrictions covering patent applications of military value,
that DuPont became aware of the Whinfield-Dickson patent. But,
while ICI and DuPont were very close—too close, as U.S. antitrust
lawyers later successfully claimed—the Patent and Processes
Agreement, which called for technology exchanges in many areas,
allowed each of the companies to treat "major inventions" in a
different manner from normal technology improvements. DuPont
had taken such a position on nylon and ICI, which had also done so
on high pressure polyethylene, now also took this position on
polyester fibers. Basically, what this meant was that ICI was under
no obligation to routinely provide DuPont with its Terylene
know-how under the principles of the broad intercompany technology exchange agreement. DuPont engineers visited ICI's laboratories and found that both companies had been working on the
same type of fiber, but it was clear that ICI held the dominant
patent position. There was no choice but for DuPont to purchase the
U.S. rights to the Whinfield and Dickson patent application from
ICI. This was done in 1946. (The patent actually did not issue until
1949.) DuPont had filed other patents, including one on the use of
litharge as a catalyst for the ester interchange, which it claimed
was better than ICI's catalyst and which it claimed gave them a
better fiber. But, no matter! ICI had the basic patent.

With this issue settled, DuPont set out to produce its second
synthetic fiber. At Seaford, a nylon pilot was converted in 1948 to
melt spin polyester fiber. The fiber was called Dacron, and it was
essentially a duplicate of ICI's Terylene. The first DuPont polyester
fibers sold for commercial use were produced in the Seaford,
Delaware, semiworks plant in 1950, which produced both staple
and yarn, with a capacity of about 1.5 million pounds per year.

A major problem in developing a commercial process for
polyester fiber intermediates was the fact that it was extremely difficult to purify terephthalic acid, which was produced by nitric acid

oxidation of p-xylene. The approach used by both ICI and DuPont was to separate the aromatic acid from its impurities—largely p-carboxybenzaldehyde—by esterifying the acid with methanol and separating the relatively pure dimethyl terephthalate (DMT) from the balance of the oxidation products. The ester could then be reacted with ethylene glycol to give the polymer, with methanol recovered and recycled. This was the only technology employed, until Scientific Design Company and Amoco Chemicals cooperated to devise an air oxidation process for p-xylene. Amoco later developed a catalytic hydrogenation process to purify terephthalic acid, which could then be directly esterified without prior conversion to DMT.

THE THIRD SYNTHETIC FIBER—ACRYLICS

Before describing the development of acrylic fibers, it is useful to review some general chemical background. In the late 1920s and early 1930s, it became known that "giant molecules" could be formed by two different approaches: condensation polymerization and addition polymerization.

Polyamide and polyester fibers are produced from polymers made by condensation polymerization, while acrylic fibers are made from polymers obtained by addition polymerization, a process that involves joining unsaturated (e.g., vinyl) compounds to form a long chain with a high molecular weight. Using a suitable catalyst, this process can be readily carried out at low temperatures. The carbon chains formed can be laterally substituted in a number of ways, depending on what monomers or comonomers are employed. Acrylic fibers are based on polymers that contain a high percentage of acrylonitrile, generally in combination with other monomers, although DuPont's Orlon and Bayer's Dralon were originally made of 100 percent acrylonitrile. In this polymer, the molecules are flexible chains of carbon atoms with CN (cyanide) groups bound to CH groups and attached to every second carbon in the chain. Considering the fact that in forming this type of polymer it is possible to use several types of vinyl comonomers together with acrylonitrile, it is easy to see why various firms used different approaches to make acrylic fiber monomers, once this type of synthetic fiber structure became known.

Thorough familiarity with the state of knowledge on vinyl plas-

tic polymers led DuPont's Rayon Department, in 1941, to study
the possible development of an acrylic fiber. Actually, I.G. Farben
chemists had, as early as 1929, obtained a patent on an acrylonitrile polymer, but there was apparently no immediate appreciation
of the significance of this patent for the production of fibers. The
Agfa laboratory at Wolfen in the 1930s carried out some work on
spinning acrylic fibers by producing a polymer and extruding the
fibers into a bath, but the researchers there had not succeeded in
obtaining a suitable textile fiber. In 1939, Otto Bayer and P. Kurtz
at Bayer-Leverkuesen patented a practical acrylonitrile production
process, using acetylene feedstock. Then, in 1941, both DuPont and
Bayer discovered a solvent for acrylic polymers that made it possible to dissolve and then extrude the polymer solution—dimethylformamide (DMF). German work was, however, discontinued in
favor of nylon development, and was not resumed until well after
the end of the war. DuPont apparently also did not do much more
development work in this area until 1946.

Shortly after the end of the war, several American firms started
to work on an acrylic fiber. By this time, it was appreciated that
acrylonitrile could be copolymerized with a number of vinyl compounds, including vinyl chloride, vinyl pyridine and acrylic esters.
Depending on which comonomer was used, a variety of properties
could be obtained. DuPont had earlier found that acrylic fiber was
extremely difficult to dye. However, acrylic fibers had such outstanding resistance to deterioration by sunlight and to attack by
moths and mildew and had such high "bulking" power that it was
apparent that these fibers would find a large market, even though
they might never be used as conventional textile fibers that could
be properly dyed to any color. Thus, DuPont decided to build a
6-million-pound-per-year Orlon plant in Camden, South Carolina,
that started production in 1950, making yarns that were marketed
for use in awnings and window curtains (7). Early shirts made
of Orlon acrylic fiber were rather unsatisfactory, as some readers
may remember, being available only in white and having a rather
clammy feel in their original version.

DuPont followed by building a staple fiber plant, bringing its
polyacrylonitrile fiber capacity up to 37 million pounds by 1952.
By this time, several other U.S. firms had developed acrylic copolymer technology that resulted in fibers with considerably better
properties. One of these firms was Union Carbide, which built an
8-million-pound-per-year plant in 1952 for making its Dynel fiber,

which contained 40 percent acrylonitrile and 60 percent vinyl chloride. The polymer could be dissolved in acetone, extruded into a water bath, dried, stretched, cut, and crimped. The fiber was then chopped into staple length and stabilized. It was sold for $1.25 per pound—versus wool at $2.49 per pound at that time (8). It was washable, almost shrink proof, and had the texture and warmth of wool. It could be dyed a full range of colors and would take a permanent crease. Dynel and other acrylic fibers containing 35–85 percent acrylonitrile became known as "modacrylic fibers." Eastman Kodak was one of the companies that later produced a fiber of this type. (The sensitivity of the modacrylics to heat closed many potential applications for these fibers. Production of modacrylics today in the United States is only about 10 percent of that for acrylics.)

Monsanto started work on an acrylic fiber in 1942 and published a number of patents on various copolymers in the 1940s. By 1949, the company felt that it was ready to go commercial. However, for a firm not previously engaged in fiber production, the risk to proceed alone was considered too great. The Monsanto executives decided to approach a textile fiber company to form a joint venture and the company selected was American Viscose, a major rayon producer. The joint company, named Chemstrand, was then provided a license to use Monsanto's technology and it proceeded to build a plant for Acrilan, as the acrylic copolymer was later named. When this plant came onstream in the early 1950s, however, the fibers produced turned out to have such serious flaws that the venture came close to cratering. Although the fibers could be dyed, they ruptured under stress (e.g., when bending a sweater at the elbow) and the undyed substrate showed through, a problem that became known as "fibrillating." For a period of time, Acrilan production was curtailed, so that more laboratory work could be done to try and solve the problem.

But now occurred one of the more interesting developments in the history of the postwar chemical industry, a major stroke of good fortune for Monsanto and its partner, American Viscose. What transpired effectively allowed Monsanto and its partner to firmly establish Chemstrand as a synthetic fiber producer and gave the two companies both time and a rationale to solve the problem with Acrilan. The U.S. government had, for some time, advised DuPont that the Justice Department would most likely proceed with antitrust litigation against it and ICI, focusing par-

ticularly on their technology exchanges covering the production
of nylon. The actual suit was filed in 1950. DuPont soon recognized that if it wanted to get the government off its back, it would
probably have to license nylon know-how to companies other than
ICI. It therefore started casting about for a likely licensee, at first
just to find out what a suitable fee for licensing its patents and
know-how might be. The company initially approached Eastman
Kodak, which was a suitable candidate due to its production of
acetate fibers, but Eastman was unwilling to pay the type of money
DuPont wanted for its proposed license. DuPont next turned to
Monsanto and, in contrast to Eastman, found the company's management very excited about being offered this licensing opportunity. Intense negotiations were carried out over a period of more
than a year and it appears that they came close to breaking down
several times. However, in June 1951, an historic agreement was
signed. For a payment of about $120 million—a tremendous figure
for those days and large even by modern standards—Chemstrand
obtained a license to produce nylon and its intermediates, with
DuPont supplying engineers to help design, build, and start up the
plant. Chemstrand's 50 million-pound-per-year nylon plant went
into operation in Pensacola, Florida, in 1953, a year after the
startup of the Acrilan plant in Decatur, Alabama. The DuPont
license covered more than 300 patents, plus an option on improvement patents and know-how for the following five years, with some
additional payments required for exercising that option.

Chemstrand's nylon plant was a tremendous success, almost
from the start, and this experience gave its two partners confidence
in the synthetic fibers business. By 1955, the fibrillation problem
with Acrilan had been solved and production was soon resumed.
Six years later, Monsanto acquired American Viscose's interest
in Chemstrand and absorbed the company as a wholly-owned
subsidiary (9). Acrilan fibers gained a substantial share of the U.S.
market for acrylic fibers.

Other U.S. companies, including American Cyanamid, also
commercialized acrylic fibers. Cyanamid was a producer of acrylonitrile, based on low cost acetylene available at its Niagara Falls
site, and it later built a more modern "acrylo" plant at Fortier,
Louisiana.

Acrylic fibers were also produced in Germany in the early 1950s.
Bayer again took the lead, building the first plant in Dormagen
in 1953. Most of the company's production was in the form of sta-

ple fiber. It also acquired know-how on continuous acrylic filament fiber development from Cassella and soon started producing a more silklike acrylic fiber. Bayer's acrylic fibers were sold under the trade name of Dralon (see Figure 7.2*b*), which became an important export product. Acrylonitrile production was assigned to the Bayer-BP Chemicals joint petrochemical venture at Dormagen, known as Erdoelchemie. Bayer went on to become one of the world's leading acrylic fiber producers. Courtaulds, which had to share nylon with ICI and had lost out on polyester fiber completely, also became a major acrylic fiber producer. But the British firm missed out on the other two big synthetics, having later decided to relinquish nylon to ICI.

Celanese, the other British producer of man-made fibers, had earlier transferred its man-made fiber business from the U.K. to America. In the early 1960s, the company bought a nylon license from ICI and together the two companies established Fiber Industries, Inc., a joint venture that later also produced polyester fibers. Celanese remained an important producer of man-made and synthetic fibers. American Viscose, on the other hand, was ultimately acquired by FMC Corporation.

AND NOW—PHENOMENAL GROWTH

Over a 20-year period from the advent of synthetic fibers around 1950, total fiber demand in the United States increased from six and one half billion to over ten billion pounds. And the growth was almost entirely in synthetics. In 1969, total natural fiber consumption (cotton, wool, silk) was 4.3 billion pounds, almost exactly equal to the consumption of these fibers in 1949. Rayon and acetate fiber consumption in 1969 was 1.7 billion pounds, up from slightly under 1 billion pounds 20 years earlier. But total synthetic fiber production in 1969 had increased to 3.5 billion pounds. Table 7.2 shows what happened over this period, while Table 7.3 gives an overview of end-use markets in 1954 and 1966. Table 7.3 shows that man-made and synthetic fibers made the greatest inroads in home furnishings markets.

Both nylon 6 and nylon 6/6 were eventually produced in the United States. Most nylon fiber was in filament form, although about 15 percent was made as staple. The main markets were in carpets, women's apparel, and knit goods, as well as in the replace-

Table 7.2   Synthetics Take Most of the Growth in Textile Fiber
Consumption (Million Pounds Per Year)

	1949	1969
Natural fibers		
(cotton, wool, silk)	4,353	4,285
Total cellulosics (rayon, acetate)	994	1,735
Textile glass	—	500
Synthetics		
Polyester		1,280
Polyamides		1,370
Acrylics		535
Polyolefins		265
Total	92	3,480
Grand total	5,439	9,970

Source: R. W. Moncrieff (1971), *Man-Made Fibres*, New York, Wiley.

ment tire market, where nylon tire cord's tendency toward "flat spotting" was less of a problem. Later, polyester tire cord took over from nylon. By 1978, there were six U.S. producers of nylon 6/6, with total production capacity of 1.15 billion pounds and seven nylon 6 producers, with a combined capacity of 465 million pounds. DuPont and Monsanto dominated the former, while Allied and American Enka were the largest producers of nylon 6, Allied hav-

Table 7.3   End Use Markets for Fibers in All Applications (U.S.)

	Percent of All Fibers Used		Percent of Man-Made and Synthetics Used	
	1954	1966	1954	1966
Women's and children's wear	19	20	28	21
Men's and boys' wear	21	20	11	11
Home furnishings	21	28	12	29
Other consumer uses	10	11	10	12
Industrial uses	23	18	33	23
Exports	6	3	7	4

Source: R. W. Moncrieff (1971), *Man-Made Fibres*, New York, Wiley.

ing established caprolactam and nylon 6 production at Hopewell, Virginia, in 1955.

The technology of nylon production was greatly advanced by a development made by the Scientific Design Company (SD) in the late 1950s. Up to that time, adipic acid had been produced via nitric acid oxidation of cyclohexane, with adipic yields reduced through the formation of a substantial amount of other organic acids as by-products of this somewhat non-selective oxidation. When cyclohexane is oxidized, it forms mixtures of cyclohexanol and cyclohexanone as intermediates. These are then further oxidized as the ring structure is attacked, with adipic acid the main product. It had, for some time, been recognized that a more desirable approach would be to first make only cyclohexanol and then use nitric acid under somewhat milder and more controlled conditions to make adipic acid in higher yields. Scientific Design became aware of Russian work that showed how alcohols could be "tied up" as borate esters to keep from being further oxidized—and this was considered a promising lead to a new adipic acid process. Research work in SD's laboratory soon resulted in a process that could make cyclohexanol in high yields by a technique that tied the -ol up as the borate ester and then "sprung" the alcohol through another reaction in a separate vessel—a fundamental, new way of obtaining high yields of adipic acid. Chemstrand took an exclusive U.S. license on this process, which was later also licensed by SD to such foreign firms as ICI, Rhône-Poulenc, Bayer, and Mitsubishi Chemical (10).

This process was not licensed to DuPont, however. Observers speculated whether it was pride or the basic economics of its own nylon monomer plant that kept DuPont from licensing the SD route. Probably the latter, because a few years later DuPont licensed SD's borate ester technology to make the C_{12} diacid (dodecane-dioic acid) for its "miracle fiber" Qiana. Unfortunately, that product never lived up to DuPont's anticipations and, like Corfam (the company's synthetic leather), Qiana was eventually dropped from the product line.

DuPont remained the largest polyester fiber producer. These fibers are sold to a greater extent in staple form. However, filament is produced for the tire cord market and textured filament for knitted apparel. An important use for polyester fibers has always been in blends with cotton and wool for the production of "permanent press" garments. Similar to nylon, polyester staple found large markets in carpet production.* At one time, 13 U.S. firms were producing polyester fibers, with Eastman Kodak and Fiber Industries the largest, next to DuPont. Hoechst became a worldwide supplier with its Trevira fiber, and established a strong position in the United States.

Acrylic fiber markets were primarily in carpets and in bulky knits, such as sweaters—in other words, as a replacement for wool. By 1970, the growth of acrylic and modacrylic fibers had started to slow, as wool replacement markets became somewhat saturated. Six producers were making these fibers, with Monsanto and DuPont the largest manufacturers.

VARIOUS PETROCHEMICAL INTERMEDIATES USED TO MAKE SYNTHETIC FIBERS

The rapid growth of the synthetic fiber industry resulted in a correspondingly dramatic growth in the demand for the important fiber raw materials, including cyclohexane, phenol, p-xylene, acrylonitrile, and others. Table 7.4 indicates the approximate amounts of these intermediates required to produce a pound of each of the fibers.

As discussed hereunder and elsewhere in this book, a number of different production routes were developed to make the intermediates for these fibers. By the end of the 1950s, all of the adipic acid was produced from cyclohexane. However, several different ways had been found to make the hexamethylene diamine, including routes from adipic acid, butadiene, and acrylonitrile (via adiponitrile). Table 7.5 indicates the different processes, together with the companies practicing these routes in the 1960s.

Cyclohexane, which was a specialty hydrocarbon before the development of nylon, now became a key petrochemical intermediate. In 1955, there were three cyclohexane producers, with a total production capacity of 37 million pounds per year. By 1965, 10 producers were making 280 million pounds per year (11). A relatively modest amount of this total was extracted from petroleum

---

*Polyester fibers later lost most of the carpet market to nylon, which currently holds 89 percent of the carpet synthetic fiber market, versus 7 percent for polyester and 3 percent for wool.

Table 7.4   Petrochemical Demand for Fiber Production Conversion Factors (in pounds of raw material per pound of fiber produced)

Nylon 6/6	0.62 adipic acid, 0.55 hexamethylene diamine requiring alternately: (a) 0.42 cyclohexane, 0.39 butadiene (b) 0.42 cyclohexane, 0.70 acrylonitrile (c) 1.35 cyclohexane
Polyester	1.01 dimethyl terephthalate 0.32 ethylene glycol (Requiring 0.89 p-xylene)
Nylon 6	1.18 phenol or 1.35 cyclohexane
Acrylic	0.90 acrylonitrile
Modacrylic	0.50 acrylonitrile
Olefin	1.0 polypropylene

Source: Chem Systems Inc.

streams, the balance being produced via hydrogenation of benzene. Almost half of U.S. cyclohexane production was exported, much of it to Europe, where the price of benzene and hydrogen was usually much higher than in the United States. Exports also went to Japan. UOP and IFP (The French Petroleum Institute) supplied the technology for most of the cyclohexane plants built in the United States, IFP having developed an unusual, very effective slurry catalyst process. Phillips, Conoco, Union Oil, and Gulf became the largest merchant sellers of cyclohexane. Monsanto and DuPont were the largest buyers. Back integration into hydrocarbon feedstocks was not considered important by most of the fiber producers, although Monsanto later decided to build a petrochemical complex at Chocolate Bayou, Texas.

P-xylene production for polyester fibers experienced a similar surge. In 1954, the first year for which production data are available, p-xylene consumption reached 59 million pounds. By 1965, production exceeded 400 million pounds and it rose above 1 billion pounds at the turn of the decade. To produce these huge quantities of the para isomer, which only constitutes 15–20 percent of the usual mixed xylene streams coming from catalytic reformers, technology had to be developed (*1*) to increase the amount of p-xylene via isomerization of meta-xylene, which is the most abundant isomer (o-xylene is also a desired product in that it is used for making phthalic anhydride), and (*2*) to separate and purify the p-xylene ef-

Table 7.5 Routes to Nylon 6/6

DuPont

Cyclohexane ⟶ adipic acid ⟶ Nylon 6/6

Butadiene ⟶ adiponitrile ⟶ HMDA ⟶ (to Nylon 6/6)

Monsanto (old process)

Cyclohexane ⟶ adipic acid ⟶ Nylon 6/6

adipic acid ↓ adiponitrile ⟶ HMDA ⟶ (to Nylon 6/6)

Monsanto (new process)

Cyclohexane ⟶ adipic acid ⟶ Nylon 6/6

Acrylonitrile ⟶* adiponitrile ⟶ HMDA ⟶ (to Nylon 6/6)

Celanese and Fiber Industries

Cyclohexane
↓
cyclohexanol-cyclohexanone oil ⟶ adipic acid ⟶ Nylon 6/6
↓
other oxidation products

1,6-hexanediol ⟶ HMDA ⟶ (to Nylon 6/6)

Beaunit-El Paso (Russian know-how)

Cyclohexane ⟶ adipic acid ⟶ Nylon 6/6

adipic acid ↓ adiponitrile ⟶ HMDA ⟶ (to Nylon 6/6)

*Electrochemical process. (*Source:* Chem Systems Inc.)

ficiently. For a number of years, this was done by crystallization technology developed by ICI and others. Isomerization processes were developed by UOP, Sinclair, Engelhard, and Mobil Research.

Chevron, Sinclair (later absorbed by Atlantic Richfield), and Enjay (later Exxon Chemical) were the largest producers of p-xylene. DuPont was, by far, the largest buyer. Amoco Chemicals, which built the first direct oxidation terephthalic acid plant, developed its own captive supply of p-xylene. Again, a very substantial amount of this key fiber intermediate went into export markets, helping to keep the U.S. petrochemical industry in an expansive mode.

For acrylic fibers, the key monomer was, of course, acrylonitrile. This reactive monomer had, before the introduction of acrylic and modacrylic fibers, been used in Buna-N rubber and as a modifier for plastics and resins. Originally produced from ethylene oxide and hydrogen cyanide gas (a German development), later production techniques included the reaction of acetylene and hydrogen cyanide (Germany and American Cyanamid) and the oxidation of propylene with nitric oxide (DuPont). In the late 1950s, several companies, including Sohio, Distillers Ltd. (England), Montecatini-Edison (Italy), and O.S.W. (Austria) developed routes for the ammoxidation of propylene with air and ammonia. Sohio and Montecatini used the fluid-bed approach, which was effective due to the high exotherm (heat release) of this reaction. Working with the Badger Company, the most experienced U.S. contractor in the application of fluid-bed technology to chemical reactions, Sohio ended up with the best process, which it commercialized in 1960. In many ways, this process was considered one of the most important achievements of its time. It substantially lowered the production cost of acrylonitrile and allowed Sohio to become the dominant U.S. producer and world licensor. Over the following decade, Sohio introduced several new generations of catalyst. The company always remained a merchant producer, with DuPont, Monsanto, Union Carbide, and American Cyanamid, the main acrylic fiber manufacturers, as customers.

In this and Chapter 6, we have looked at the development of the plastics and synthetic fiber industries, which owe so much to the availability of reasonably priced, abundant petrochemicals. Synthetic rubbers or elastomers, as they are often called, were covered somewhat more briefly in Chapter 3. All three of these materials are very largely based on ethylene, propylene, butadiene, benzene, and the xylenes, the key petrochemical "building blocks" produced, respectively, in steam cracking plants and in catalytic reformers (see Chapter 4). Figure 7.3 provides an overview of important intermediates and end products made from these petroleum-based raw materials.

With refineries and steam crackers turning out ever-increasing amounts of these raw materials, so ideally suited for the production of such a large variety of chemicals and derivatives, there was never any question of turning back to coal or to other feedstocks—not until the 1970s, in any case, when the OPEC nations started to control the world supply of crude oil and called into question

Feedstock	Important Derivatives		End Products
Ethylene	Polyethylene (high and low density)		Plastics
	Styrene →	Polystyrene	Plastics
	Ethylene oxide →	Glycol	Antifreeze, fibers
	Vinyl chloride →	PVC	Plastics
	Ethanol		Solvent
	E.P. rubber		Elastomer
	Vinyl acetate		Adhesives, plastics
Propylene	Cumene →	Phenol	Plastics, nylon 6 (fibers)
	Polypropylene		Plastics, fibers
	Propylene oxide →	Glycol	Plastics
	Acrylonitrile		Fibers, plastics
	Isopropyl alcohol		Solvents
	Acetone		Solvents, plastics
	Acrylates		Coatings, adhesives

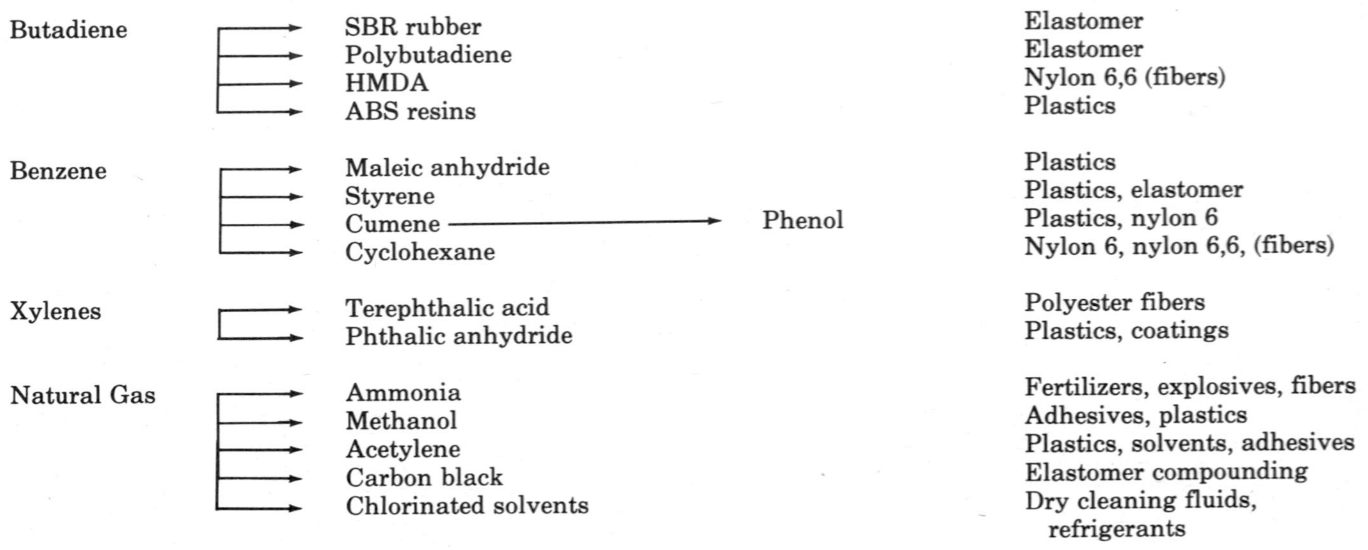

Butadiene
- SBR rubber → Elastomer
- Polybutadiene → Elastomer
- HMDA → Nylon 6,6 (fibers)
- ABS resins → Plastics

Benzene
- Maleic anhydride → Plastics
- Styrene → Plastics, elastomer
- Cumene → Phenol → Plastics, nylon 6
- Cyclohexane → Nylon 6, nylon 6,6, (fibers)

Xylenes
- Terephthalic acid → Polyester fibers
- Phthalic anhydride → Plastics, coatings

Natural Gas
- Ammonia → Fertilizers, explosives, fibers
- Methanol → Adhesives, plastics
- Acetylene → Plastics, solvents, adhesives
- Carbon black → Elastomer compounding
- Chlorinated solvents → Dry cleaning fluids, refrigerants

Figure 7.3 Petrochemical overview (*Source:* Chem Systems Inc.)

the issue of future petrochemical feedstocks. Between 1946 and the late 1960s, petrochemicals enjoyed a golden era, with the United States becoming supplier to the world and every company with any ambition to make the new petroleum-based chemicals interested in joining the parade.

Unfortunately, there was not enough room for everybody and domestic feedstock pricing also became a major issue. But we are getting ahead of the story. The next chapters bring the industry through its exciting growth period and also deal with some of the economic and business problems that arose during this time.

REFERENCES

1. W. J. Reader (1970, 1975). *Imperial Chemical Industries, a History,* 2 vols., London, Oxford University Press, Vol. 2, p. 365.
2. DuPont & Company. *The Early Days of DuPont Fibers (1919–1949),* Wilmington, DE, DuPont & Co.
3. C. S. Marvel and C. E. Carraher, Jr. (1984). Carothers, chemist, *Chemtech,* December, 716–719.
4. C. K. Bolton (1942). Development of nylon, *Industrial and Engineering Chemistry,* **34,** January, 53ff.
5. B. Achilladelis (1970). A study in technological history, part I—The manufacture of "Perlon" (nylon 6) and caprolactam by I.G. Farbenindustrie, *Chemistry & Industry,* December 5.
6. R. W. Moncrieff (1971). *Man-Made Fibres,* New York, Wiley, p. 405.
7. Polyacrylonitrile, *Chemical Engineering,* August 1951, p. 129.
8. Acrylic copolymers, *Chemical Engineering,* August 1951. p. 130.
9. D. J. Forrestal (1977). *Faith, Hope, and $5,000: The Story of Monsanto,* New York, Simon & Schuster, Chapter 8 pp. 131–134.
10. Ralph Landau (1981). Process innovation, *Chemistry and Industry,* May 2, 321ff.
11. Robert Stobaugh (1966). *Petrochemical Manufacturing and Marketing Guide,* Houston, Gulf Publishing, 1966. Volume 1, pp. 42–43.

ADDITIONAL READING

Bendigo, C. W. (1955). The acrylic fibers, Chemical Marketing Research Association Paper, November 14–15.
Dupont, E.I. Biographical memoir of Wallace Hume Carothers, Wilmington, Del., E.I. DuPont de Nemours & Co., Public Relations Department.

Kennedy, Carol (1986). *ICI: The Company That Changed Our Lives,* London, Century Hutchinson.

Kent, James A., ed. Man-made textile fibers, *Riegel's Industrial Chemistry,* New York, Reinhold.

Quig, J. B. (1951). Synthesis of Orlon acrylic fiber and Dacron polyester fiber, Chemical Market Research Association Paper, October 16.

Reader W. J. (1975). *Imperial Chemical Industries: A History,* Volume 2, Chapter 20, Mid Century Materials II: Fibres.

Stobaugh, Robert B. (1971). Acrylonitrile: How, where, who—future, *Hydrocarbon Processing,* January, 109ff.

Winnacker, Karl (1972). *Challenging Years: My Life in Chemistry,* trans. David Goodman, London, Sidgwick & Jackson.

8 / The Rush into Petrochemicals

By the late 1940s, with the war safely over and the peacetime economy booming, it had become evident that an entirely different U.S. chemical industry was starting to emerge. Previously, an integral part of a well-ordered system of international producers, largely operating under a benign atmosphere of *noblesse oblige,* this industry would now set the standard for the chemical world of the future. Most significantly, there would henceforth be a much larger number of "players," who would engage in an arena far more competitive than anything seen up to that time. Here, companies would vie to gain for themselves the benefits expected from the rapid development of the new markets provided by the plastics, fibers, and other synthetics, which were now being made at low cost from natural gas and petroleum feedstocks. The Europeans would try for a period of time to turn back the clock and resurrect the cozy prewar arrangements, involving market sharing, pricing agreements, and other aspects of the old cartels. It was the only industrial world they ever knew ("plus ça change, plus c'est la même chose," was surely their first approach), but this ultimately proved to be a futile effort. In fact, the European Economic Community soon enacted antitrust laws not dissimilar from those in the United States.

Not surprisingly, U.S. companies had a running start in the race to become the dominant chemical producers of the future.

302

Whereas in Europe and Japan much of the manufacturing industry had been destroyed in Allied bombing raids, the United States entered the peacetime era with an imposing array of refineries and petrochemical plants. These were far larger and more diverse than any such European or Japanese installations before the war, and they frequently utilized technologies not known or perfected before 1939. Although England had never actually been invaded, and such countries as France, Belgium, and the Netherlands had ended up on the winning side, these countries' industries would not be rebuilt for several years. American help was provided through the Marshall Plan and other means, but time was needed to bring the European allies' manufacturing infrastructure back to normal. Even more time was required in Germany and Japan, in spite of the relatively benevolent attitude of the Allies, who recognized the fallacies of the harsh covenants of the Treaty of Versailles, which had been concluded after the 1918 Armistice. A number of years later, it was ruefully recognized that the vanquished Axis countries had gained a considerable advantage, in that they had received an opportunity to completely rebuild and modernize their aging prewar industries. There is no evidence, however, that this issue was on anyone's mind in the immediate postwar years, when Germany, Japan, and Italy were struggling to get back on their feet and the new enemy was the Soviet Union.

In most respects, American industry saw the postwar period as an era of maximum opportunity. Newly built manufacturing plants and cheap hydrocarbon feedstocks were in place, the U.S. consumer economy was booming, and the destruction of foreign manufacturing capacity had provided a unique opportunity for exports. Not only export of products, such as chemical derivatives and fabricated goods, but also export of industrial plants and engineering services. It did not take the American engineering contracting industry very long to determine that technology and recently developed specialized construction skills were now needed to build refineries and fertilizer and petrochemical plants in Europe, and so such companies as Kellogg, Stone and Webster, Foster Wheeler, and others soon established European offices, sending U.S. supervisors to train low cost local designers and draftsmen in modern American construction techniques.

Military teams consisting of engineers and chemists were sent from the United States and England to survey the German chemical plants and laboratories to extract what useful information they could obtain from the supervisors and chemists still left at many of the bombed-out installations (see Chapter 1). In the production of such chemicals as ethylene, propylene, butadiene, and synthetic rubber, not much useful information turned up, as the chemical engineering breakthroughs made in the production of these chemicals in the United States during the war had outstripped many of the achievements of the I.G. Farben companies. In other areas, the information obtained was much more useful. These visits also confirmed the fact that it would take the vaunted German companies a number of years to try and recoup their prewar positions, particularly since the Allied Occupation Powers, for a period of time, prohibited the resumption of chemical manufacturing operations that were considered as having been a key part of the Nazi war effort. As might be expected, a considerable amount of latitude was allowed in the interpretation of this mandate, which slowed down the reconstruction of the German chemical industry. In any case, half of that industry was now in East Germany, with the production sites remaining in the Western sector representing the remnant of an industry truncated by the victorious Allies.

In Europe, one of the first priorities was the construction of new oil refineries, since so much of the continent's refining capacity had been destroyed by bombing or artillery shelling during the war. While Europe's requirements for gasoline were very low, due to a much smaller car population—a trend that continued for many years thereafter—there was a great need for kerosene, diesel fuel, and heating oils. American, British, and French oil companies soon started on major refinery reconstruction and expansion programs, leading to large new installations such as an Esso refinery in Fawley on the English Channel, and a British Petroleum refinery in Fos, near Marseilles. The first wave of European construction involved principally refining units, tankage, oil tankers, docks, and unloading stations. In the next phase, these and other European firms, such as British Petroleum and Companie Francaise des Petroles (CFP), would add steam crackers and aromatics extraction plants, based on U.S. technology developed during the war, and would also start to think about "going downstream" (i.e., into the production of petrochemical derivatives). But that came five to eight years later.

Another priority was for the construction of fertilizer plants, to allow European farmers to rebuild their agriculture. European technology for ammonia, nitric acid, urea,* and other nitrogen fertilizers was still dominant and so a number of these plants were built by European as well as U.S. contractors, who obtained the technology from firms such as ICI, Kuhlmann, and Montecatini. Before the war, these companies had been far more chary in granting licenses, with the I.G. companies exerting considerable influence, but this was now a different world, with the German cartel no longer a factor and fertilizer technology becoming more freely available on payment of an appropriate licensing fee.

In West Germany, with its industries at a standstill and its economy faced with the major problem of rebuilding what had been destroyed under Hitler, it was a time to find salable commodities. Chemical technology was in that category, since the patent laws, suspended during the war, were again being respected by the international community, although, as noted elsewhere, much German technology know-how could be abstracted from the postwar military inspection reports. Soon, a number of American firms started to approach German firms for licenses to manufacture chemicals such as polyethylene, dimethyl terephthalate—an intermediate for the new polyester fibers—urea, and others. Fischer-Tropsch chemistry seemed an ideal technology for transforming inexpensive natural gas to a variety of liquid hydrocarbons, alcohols, and other chemical intermediates. A group headed by "Dobie" Keith of Hydrocarbon Research Inc., a company engaged in refining process development work, obtained a license to use German technology in such a plant, to be constructed in Brownsville, Texas, by a company called Carthage Hydrocol (2). This plant was never a commercial success because it soon turned out that the products could be made more cheaply by conventional petrochemical technology. Perhaps the main reason for its demise was the fact that during the time the project was conceived and built, the price of natural gas had quintupled, although by today's standards the gas price was still an excellent deal. It had risen from 3 cents to 15 cents per thousand cubic feet.† (By the late 1970s, the price was $3.00 per thousand cubic feet or higher.)

---

*Urea, a product made by reacting ammonia and carbon dioxide, may have been the first synthetic organic produced in the laboratory. It was accidentally synthesized by Freidrich Woehler in 1828 (1).

†Dr. Robert Purvin, personal communication.

Companies that had built various types of chemical plants for the war effort now negotiated with the government to acquire these facilities to make products for the peacetime economy. B.F. Goodrich purchased the 60,000-ton GRS rubber plant and then converted a portion of this unit to make additional polyvinyl chloride (PVC) resins. Koppers bought the 37,500-ton styrene monomer plant at Kobuta, Pennsylvania, and started construction of a polystyrene plant, having successfully piloted such a process in a 1-ton-per-day pilot plant. Monsanto bought the 50,000-ton government-owned styrene plant it had constructed at Texas City, Texas, and announced that, by 1947, it would have 80 million pounds of polystyrene production capacity in place, much of it in Springfield, Massachusetts. Dow bought the styrene plant it had built at Velasco, Texas, adding this capacity to its smaller supply from Midland, and also expanded polystyrene capacity, as resin supplies were becoming very tight. With Monsanto, Koppers, Dow, and Union Carbide all producing large amounts of styrene monomer, and with the technology well known to many other companies through wartime exposure, it was clear that the production of this chemical would henceforth involve a large number of suppliers. An Exxon styrene catalyst (1707) and soon thereafter a Shell catalyst (A-105), were produced under license by several catalyst companies and could therefore be purchased by other would-be producers. The stage was thus set for strong future competition, which would soon also involve the styrene plant at Sarnia, Ontario. Dow had built that unit for the Canadian government and it was now to be operated by the government-owned Polymer Corporation (later privatized under the name Polysar).

Before the war, the large international chemical companies on both sides of the conflict had been linked in a variety of cartels, export associations, and patent and process exchange agreements. No doubt, some executives had expected a resumption of old relationships, as had occurred after World War I. But history was not going to repeat itself. In the United States, the government had seized the properties of I.G. Farben and, for some time after the end of the war, had kept control of these facilities, which were principally owned by the General Aniline and Film Corporation (GAF), a subsidiary of the old I.G. Moreover, the administration had given a clear warning to U.S. producers that the government would no longer tolerate the types of cooperative arrangements that had often inhibited prospective new entrants to the industry. A number of antitrust suits were filed by the Justice Department for several years after the war (see also Chapter 5). American producers were now considered to have been put on notice that the government expected the chemical industry to be truly competitive. If, in the 1920s and 1930s, U.S. chemical producers were at some disadvantage to the Germans, and if this caused the more friendly Harding, Coolidge, and Hoover administrations to wink at somewhat questionable "technical-exchange arrangements," government officials in the Truman and Eisenhower era saw things very differently. Victory at war and a healthy manufacturing industry, enjoying the benefits of economies of large scale operation, were considered to be providing American firms a large enough advantage in the international arena.

Chemical companies now started to branch out into areas that, in many cases, had been the domain of a very limited number of established producers. For example, Celanese Corporation, up to then only involved in acetate fibers and plastics, constructed a multiproduct propane oxidation plant at Bishop, Texas, the first of its kind in the world. This remarkable, uncatalyzed vapor-phase process yielded, as major coproducts, acetaldehyde, formaldehyde, and methanol, along with a spectrum of higher oxygenates. A series of distillations recovered and purified the various aldehydes, alcohols, and ketones produced. The chief reason for the plant was to make acetic acid, the major raw material for cellulose acetate. This was accomplished by liquid phase oxidation of acetaldehyde.

Celanese's pioneer effort began when it hired Joe Bludworth, who had done experimental work on the conversion of propane to "foul-smelling chemicals." Bludworth joined Celanese at Cumberland, Maryland, and began to direct research and development on hydrocarbon oxidation. When Celanese was confident it could scale up, the company looked toward Texas as a source of inexpensive natural gas and LPG. It completed the Bishop plant near the end of World War II. Bludworth relocated to the area. He would have been the natural choice to head Celanese's budding Chemical Division, but he was hardly a diplomatic administrator. Instead, he was a tough, combative, controversial, domineering figure. Consequently, Celanese went outside the company to find a Chemical Division general manager. It hired John Fennebresque, an able young chemical engineer from Monsanto, described by some old Celanese hands as "the only man they could find who could outtalk Joe Bludworth.*

While Fennebresque was general manager of the Chemical Division, Nat Robertson discovered that liquid-phase oxidation of butane was much more selective than the vapor-phase oxidation Celanese was practicing. It yielded copious quantities of acetic acid directly. There were some coproducts, notably methyl ethyl ketone, formic acid, propionic acid, and ethyl acetate, but the array was small compared with that from vapor-phase oxidation. In 1952, Celanese built a plant at Pampa, Texas, to commercialize the new liquid-phase technology.

Ethylene production had risen rapidly during the war, since all of the important ethylene derivatives were involved in applications tied to the war effort (see Table 8.1). Production of SBR rubber (including butadiene from ethanol), antifreeze solution (glycols), PVC resins, tetraethyl lead (TEL), and solvent alcohol consumed essentially all of the ethylene produced during the war. In most cases, the ethylene was sent "across the fence" to adjacent derivatives units in locations like Baton Rouge, Louisiana; Freeport, Texas; Institute, West Virginia; and others. At a time well before the so-called "spaghetti bowl" of pipelines had been built along much of the Gulf Coast, companies planning ethylene derivatives plants had to locate next to refineries recovering ethylene from cat cracker offgases or adjacent to steam crackers. Thus, Ethyl Corporation's ethyl chloride plant and a government-owned SBR plant were in enclaves inside Jersey's Baton Rouge refinery, where the nation's first steam cracker dedicated to the merchant market had been built, just before the war, to supply Ethyl—a joint venture company owned 50-50 by Jersey and General Motors Corporation.

Union Carbide became the largest ethylene producer, serving its own needs as well as the merchant market, with several plants built along the Gulf Coast. In an imaginative manner, Carbide people went around Texas to make deals to buy deethanizer overhead streams from natural gasoline plants. At a time when natural gas was sold on a cubic foot basis, ethane—which has a higher heating value than methane—did not command a premium from gas pipelines purchasing the gas. So, when Union Carbide offered to buy ethane—the best ethylene feedstock—for its heating value

*Celanese Corporation, personal communication.

**Table 8.1   Ethylene Consumption in Derivatives
Manufacture (1940-1946)**

Tons/Year of Ethylene Converted to:

Year	Ethanol	Ethyl Benzene	Ethylene Oxide	Ethylene Dichloride	Ethyl Chloride
1940	63,000	500	41,500	9,000	3,000
1942	97,000	1,500	73,500	13,000	9,000
1944	117,000	50,000	85,000	22,000	25,000
1946	135,000	58,000	78,000	27,000	28,500

Source: *Chemical Economics Handbook*, SRI International.

(higher than that of methane) rather than on a volume basis (as was then customary), the gasoline plant operators were happy to sell the ethane-rich deethanizer overhead stream to Carbide. It then built an ethane gathering pipeline system to collect these streams and bring them to its plants.*

In the early 1950s, National Distillers Products Corporation, a company that up to then had largely been involved in products related to fermentation alcohol, decided to build a grass-roots petrochemical installation in Tuscola, Illinois. Part of the reason for this important step was that its new chief executive officer, Jack Bierwirth, Sr., was a teetotaler and wanted the company to diversify out of the whiskey business. In a sense, this decision by a company previously 100 percent dedicated to fermentation chemistry also provided a convincing U.S. answer to the prewar ICI feedstock question of "molasses, coal, or oil?" (see Chapter 2). In a joint venture with its feedstock supplier, Panhandle Eastern Pipeline Company, National Distillers constructed a "straddle plant" to extract ethane from Panhandle's natural gas pipeline coming to Illinois from the Kansas and Oklahoma gas fields. This supplied a 200 million pound per year ethylene plant feeding a synthetic alcohol unit (justified by a contract from DuPont, which had found Shell too expensive) and, soon thereafter, a polyethylene plant.† The ethylene unit, large for its time, required an investment of under $10 million and could make ethylene for 2.3 cents per pound! Polyethy-

*Robert Purvin, personal communication.

†Dr. Aimison Jonnard, personal communication.

lene technology (patents and know-how) were licensed from ICI and National Distillers was also able to lure Ralph Knight away from DuPont to head up its new polymer business.

Other straddle plants were built, as gas transmission companies recognized that they could profitably extract and sell ethane and higher components out of the natural gas they were sending to the Middle West and to the East Coast, while still meeting the minimum heating value specifications on the remaining pipeline gas. Such a plant was, for example, built by Tenneco Gas Transmission Company at Brandenburg, Kentucky, supplying ethane and gas liquids to Olin Mathieson (later Olin Corporation), which built a cracker and downstream petrochemical units at adjacent Doe Run, Kentucky. Based on this plant, Olin became an important producer of ethylene oxide, propylene oxide, glycols, and polyols, the latter used, in part, for the manufacture of flexible urethane foams.

A number of joint ventures were established between companies basic in hydrocarbon raw materials and chemical firms interested in converting these hydrocarbons into plastics, solvents, and various other petrochemical end products. Examples of such joint ventures were Jefferson Chemical (Texaco and American Cyanamid), Petrotex Chemical (Tenneco and FMC Corporation), Sunolin (Sun Oil and Olin), Chemplex (Skelly Oil and American Can Company) and a partnership formed by El Paso Natural Gas and Rexall Drug Company. All of these were established in the 1950s, a time when "vertical integration" was considered extremely important. The gas-rich companies wanted to get into petrochemicals, while their chemical partners were "back-integrating" to assure a long-term feedstock supply.

KOREAN WAR PROVIDES EXTRA BOOST

The first few postwar years had served to largely satisfy the pent-up consumer demand and now the economy would get another boost. In 1950, the United States again found itself at war. Although this conflict was far less traumatic than the battle with the Axis powers, the Korean war provided a second major stimulus to the U.S. economy. In early 1952, defense mobilizer Charles E. Wilson pointed out:

"Never before on so vast a scale has any nation attempted to build military strength and at the same time expand its basic economy, maintain high levels of production of consumer goods and assist in the arming of allies throughout the world."

Thus, in 1951-1952, the U.S. refining and chemical industry embarked on its largest expansion program yet. Refiners upped capital spending by 118 percent, while planning an expansion of refining capacity from 7 million to 8 million barrels per day. Chlorine capacity would rise from 2.1 million tons in 1951 to 3.4 million in 1954. The same was true for many other industries. Just before the outbreak of the Korean conflict in 1950, steel production was well under 100 million tons. By 1954, it was approaching 120 million, a figure never again to be exceeded by U.S. producers.

Fertilizer production was also increasing rapidly. The government set a goal of 2.9 million tons of nitrogen a year for 1954, 80 percent higher than the amount turned out in 1951. Several World War II ammonia plants were reactivated and a number of new units were under construction, aided by the favorable tax legislation enacted by the business-minded Eisenhower administration.

With production facilities coming on stream at a rapid pace in most sectors of heavy industry, concern was starting to be expressed regarding the future. Certainly, demand was still growing rapidly, but what would happen when this war was over and government requirements would suddenly drop, leaving only the civilian economy to absorb the huge supply of chemicals emanating from the nation's factories? And what would occur when government wage and price controls were removed? Chemical industry pretax profits were at record levels in 1950 and 1951, but in 1951 so were taxes, so that industry net profits were actually down from the year before. Inflation had raised prices by 225 percent over the 1939 level, but government controls had stabilized costs over the past couple of years. Now, there was concern about a resumption of inflation when controls came off again.

Another problem identified around that time was an apparent shortage of chemical engineers. In spite of the fact that these engineers were known to have made some of the greatest contributions in providing the high octane fuels, synthetic rubber and other goods needed to "make the world safe for democracy," the profession was not attracting anywhere near the number of students required to keep the industry growing and continuing to innovate. A shortage of up to 60,000 chemical engineers was widely forecast.

The early 1950s were thus a period of continued growth, but also of a rising number of worries. Perhaps the most pervasive concern involved the recognition that too many companies were investing in chemicals manufacture, now that this industry had become a wide-open arena in which almost anybody with enough money had a chance to play. And, as noted above, profits were also starting to decline. In an address delivered to an industry group in early 1954, Robert E. Hulse, a vice-president of National Distillers and Chemical Corporation, made some poignant observations (3):

> "In the past few years there has been a certain amount of glamour and romance attached by the general public to the word 'petrochemicals.' ... In fact, one president of a petroleum company recently stated off the record that the chief factor in influencing its entry into the petrochemical field via ammonia was the number of letters from stockholders asking why his company had not entered the field of petrochemicals ... (yet) the petroleum industry, with its special tax treatment for depletion (etc.) currently averages a higher return on investment than the petrochemical field ... the year 1954 has been and will be characterized by abnormally low return on investment for many petrochemical projects ... it is a year in which supply has caught up with demand on most petrochemicals ... the volume of sales of major petrochemicals is at least as high, if not higher than in preceding years, but new and expanded productive capacity has made excess material available for sale.... Currently, it would be difficult to find any major petrochemical in short supply, except where new demands have developed, due to changes in technology or new products."

Listening to a speech of this kind at an important industry forum, the audience must have wondered whether the bloom was now off the rose, at least for a while. However, Hulse ended his address on an optimistic note saying,

> "I still feel that petrochemicals are on the steep slope of the growth curve and that any change in the growth pattern will be of a temporary nature ... increased markets and new uses will take care of the present overproduction on many of the products. ..."

History doesn't record how many people asked themselves around this time why things had changed so much from the conditions that prevailed in the 1930s, or why so many new producers had been able to enter the industry and had built up the supply of many of the new petrochemicals to the point where it had started to outpace demand. Perhaps a lot of this was obvious—the drive to build more and more capacity in view of burgeoning demand growth; the opportunity for large-scale exports, due to lagging foreign capacity buildups; the low cost of feedstocks just waiting to be converted to higher-value petrochemicals. Surely the fact that the government strongly encouraged competition and was ready to attack the old cartels or related arrangements among the traditional producers also played a key part in the proliferation of producers that was now taking place. But another factor was probably even more important: the growing availability of technology to new entrants, a totally new situation for the chemical industry. Over the years 1948–1955, it became possible, for the first time, for any new producer to obtain a license to make most of the major petrochemicals.

PETROCHEMICAL TECHNOLOGY BECOMES BROADLY AVAILABLE

There are between 40 and 60 important petrochemicals, depending on definitions and viewpoints, although in the early 1950s, the number was still somewhat smaller, since such chemicals as vinyl chloride and vinyl acetate were, in the 1950s still made from coal-based acetylene. They became "petrochemicals" a bit later, when acetylene started being made from natural gas, and they unquestionably were considered "petrochemicals" still later when their manufacture was switched to ethylene. Similarly, all benzene derivatives were originally coal-based, except that by the mid-1950s much of the benzene was already obtained from catalytic reforming of petroleum naphthas. All of these products were experiencing high growth rates and were therefore not only of great interest to existing chemical producers, but were also attracting attention from potential new entrants. Soon, most of these chemicals were being produced by at least 5 and sometimes as many as 15 U.S. companies, a far cry from the 1930s, when it was unusual to find more than three companies making a given chemical. Often, this had been due to the fact that manufacturing technology was closely controlled by a small number of international producers. How did this change come about?

Looking back, it now seems evident that a number of circumstances combined to allow this very important development to occur, a situation where new producers could gain access to technology that existing producers used to guard so jealously that it was next to impossible for outsiders to enter the industry. Below, we will discuss the major reasons, not necessarily in the order of their importance.

1. A substantial amount of technology transfer had taken place during the war years, providing petrochemical manufacturing processes to a number of companies that then continued to make these chemicals after the war. Examples of products in this category include styrene, ammonia and butadiene. In most cases, some ingenuity was required for new producers to benefit from information in the "public domain," since this was usually not enough to build a plant with confidence. Two interesting cases illustrate this point.

Butadiene. By the time the Korean war came, the alcohol-based butadiene plants were shut down and would not be restarted. Yet, there was a sudden great need for butadiene, due to insufficient capacity. As Bob Purvin recently recollected, it seemed obvious to him (ex-Humble and then a principal of the consulting firm of Purvin & Gertz) that it should be possible to build a large plant to dehydrogenate butane to butadiene, using a standard dehydrogenation catalyst. He interested Fluor, the engineering firm, and Houdry in such a project, but there was little commercial information available. But it was known that Chevron had operated a process of this kind during the war. Purvin contacted Otto Miller,* the refinery manager at one of the Chevron plants in California (whom he knew) and arranged to take Carl Mueller, an executive from Bankers Trust with him to show him that the technology had been made to work. Chevron was obliged to disclose the data, since this had been a government plant. Soon thereafter, Cabot Corporation and the investment firm of Loeb Rhodes & Company became financial backers of Texas Butadiene and Chemical Corporation, a new firm set up to make butadiene and butylenes (for avi-

---

*Later president of Standard Oil Company of California (Chevron).

ation gasoline) from amply available Gulf Coast butane. The plant was a huge success. Other such plants were later built.*

Styrene. Foster-Grant Corporation had been one of the largest plastics molders before the war, instrumental in importing from Germany injection molding machinery, as well as "polystyrol" resin. After the war was over, Joe Foster became interested in manufacturing polystyrene resins, as well as styrene monomer. By this time, some people involved in this product area had left Dow for other companies and it was possible for Foster-Grant to attract them to help build these plants. However, there were two problems. While these people were able to bring much required know-how (now partly in the public domain, due to publication of details in the C.I.O.S. and F.I.A.T. reports), there were important Dow and Koppers patents that would apparently preclude Foster-Grant from building and operating styrene and polystyrene plants. Careful study by Foster-Grant's consultants, Purvin & Gertz, convinced the company that it would be possible to operate the styrene reactor in a temperature range such as to get around the Dow patent. This concept proved successful and the company built a 12 million pound per year styrene plant, using a Shell catalyst. Subsequently, another consultant allegedly helped Foster-Grant to get around his own patent (assigned to Koppers) on suspension polymerization of styrene to polystyrene, thus putting Foster-Grant into the polystyrene business.

Foster-Grant (later acquired by Hoechst) was for many years one of the largest U.S. producers of styrene and polystyrene.*

2. Partly as a result of wartime sharing of information—formal or informal, as the case may have been—a considerable amount of manufacturing know-how proliferated through the industry. Often, this was combined with catalyst or other know-how contained in the great multitude of reports filed by the teams that had inspected the German installations after the war. In some cases, useful catalysts could now also be purchased from vendors in the United States. A combination of information and catalyst know-how, together with reasonable chemical engineering skills, could therefore be used by new producers to design their plants. Examples of products in this category include propylene oxide,

*Dr. Robert Purvin, personal communication.

vinyl chloride, phthalic anhydride, and the production of acrylates from acetylene. Thus, anybody wishing to design an ethylene oxide plant was greatly helped by studying B.I.O.S. Report FR 1154, which described the unit at Gendorf (4). As another example, Rohm and Haas used I.G. Farben technology described in postwar inspection reports to build a hydrogen cyanide plant after the war. This made it possible for the company to stop relying on its competitor, DuPont, for this raw material for methyl methacrylate (Plexiglas acrylic) (5).

While there were a few false starts, including some fiascos where plants had to be entirely written off, the risk-reward ratio was quite favorable. Perhaps most importantly, it was still possible to build rather small plants at modest cost, which made it easier to decide to build a plant even when the technology had not been fully demonstrated. Building a 10 million pound-per-year plant costing only about $2 million seemed a reasonable way to enter a market growing by 20–50 million pounds per year, even if the design was not totally proven out and some modifications might have to be made after startup.

The availability of German technical know-how, which had been placed into the public domain through the publication of the many C.I.O.S. and other military inspection reports after the war, may have had another important consequence. It may also have effectively resulted in the dissemination of some non-German "know-how" covering technical information on plants in the United States and in other Allied countries. Employees of chemical firms generally sign secrecy agreements with their employer that protect the firm's know-how, the term used for proprietary information that cannot be patented for various reasons (i.e., the trade secrets, as they are often called). These secrecy agreements can let employees who join competitors "off the hook" if similar information is available from sources outside the company. One can surmise that in some cases, employees who left a chemical firm and joined a competitor or another engineering company may have used the availability of German know-how as justification for applying some of what they had learned in their previous work to the design and operation of similar plants built by other companies after the war.

3. Before World War II, the managers and technical employees of chemical firms tended to join companies for their entire career.

If they changed jobs, they would not likely have gone to work for a competitor. This situation changed after the war, with more job switching and greater opportunities for know-how dissemination.

My recent discussion with a design engineer who worked for Union Carbide in the 1930s was quite illuminating in this respect. During these Depression years, people were happy enough to be at work and South Charleston, West Virginia, was almost a "boom town" in those days. Joe Davidson, then sales manager and later a Union Carbide chief executive officer, told the employees at company affairs, "You are employed here for your career, it's that kind of a company." There was no thought of leaving to go work for a competitor. And while there was much social contact with the DuPont engineers working at nearby Belle, West Virginia, including at engineering society meetings, great care was exercised not to reveal any trade secrets. This kind of informal acceptance of the rules of the game apparently precluded the need for employee secrecy agreements, later a common practice.* A high level executive in one of the large traditional U.S. chemical companies indicated that his firm had only instituted in the early 1950s the practice of having technical employees sign restrictive secrecy agreements covering company know-how. Thus, people leaving such a firm before that time would have been more difficult to bring to account, should they have revealed company trade secrets to a firm they had decided to join.

Dr. Ralph Landau of Scientific Design Company wrote in the 1960s, "the partial breaking down of secrecy barriers in the chemical industry is increasing the exchange of information and ideas among companies. This, in turn, increases the trend toward more licensing of processes" (6).

4. Engineering contractors became know-how sources for the first time, having built a number of plants during the war years, with suitable licensing arrangements made, where appropriate, with patent holders. Chemicals in this category include ethylene, ammonia, carbon black, methanol, BTX aromatics, and cumene.

5. Licensing became much more frequent as a source of technology for new producers. In some cases, such as polyethylene, there was more than one producer-licensor, so that a certain amount of competition soon developed among licensors, although none of the operating companies offering polyethylene know-how went out of

*Donald Thompson, formerly of Union Carbide, personal communication.

its way to sell licenses at that time. As mentioned earlier, relative to such chemicals as urea and dimethyl terephthalate,* there was also a definite interest on the part of European firms to obtain income by licensing their technology to American companies. In one of the more unusual situations, DuPont licensed Chemstrand, a Monsanto-American Viscose joint venture, with its nylon technology to avoid antitrust penalties stemming from its domination of this field and its cooperation with ICI (see Chapter 7).

6. In a departure from prewar practice, some brand new technologies, developed by operating companies, were made available for license to any and all comers. A good example is the Hercules-Distillers phenol/acetone process, which was commercialized in 1953 and forever changed the way that phenol would be produced.

Also, what turned out to be another important event had taken place in the industry. A new firm—Scientific Design Company, Inc.—had been formed for the sole purpose of developing and licensing petrochemical technology. SD, as the company was called, probably succeeded beyond its founders' wildest dreams in achieving its original objectives. And, in many cases, the technologies offered by SD had roots in Europe.

ENTER SCIENTIFIC DESIGN COMPANY

Some of the early achievements of Scientific Design Company illustrate the results of successful research, often based on or combined with the technology transfers that characterized the decade following the end of World War II. The company was founded in 1946 by Ralph Landau and Harry Rehnberg, who had become acquainted when both worked on the Manhattan Project during the war. Landau, who had received a doctorate in chemical engineering at M.I.T., had worked for the Kellex Division of M. W. Kellogg, involved in the uranium separation plant. At M.I.T., Landau had met Bob Egbert, also studying for a doctorate, who had then worked for Union Carbide for several years. Egbert joined Scientific Design shortly after its formation, to become a third

*This technology had been developed by Dynamit-Nobel, the German member of the original Nobel group.

founder. The three talented engineers recognized a major opportunity and they immediately adopted an international outlook.

As Landau noted in his 1978 speech to the Newcomen Society (7):

> "we perceived a need for organic and 'petrochemical' technology as a result of World War II . . . the greatest areas of devastation (Europe and Japan) offered us broader market opportunities than a more prosperous U.S. . . . and because we knew that innovation and proprietary 'high technology' had been the keys to the successful development of roughly comparable companies like UOP and M. W. Kellogg in the petroleum field, we started our own original research early in our career."

Thus, many of SD's successes were closely linked to the fact that its founders viewed Europe and later Japan as areas of great opportunity for technology acquisition and development and for technology licensing. This theme appeared again and again in SD's advertisements and articles written during and after this period. Several examples of Scientific Design's early successes are chronicled below.

Ethylene Oxide and Glycol

By the late 1940s, ethylene glycol was already one of the largest volume ethylene derivatives and growing rapidly. Between 1940 and 1950, ethylene oxide consumption rose from 49,000 to 206,000 tons, with almost 70 percent converted to the monoglycol and the balance used as follows: heavier glycols (7.9 percent), glycol ethers (5.7 percent), ethanolamines (5.5 percent), acrylonitrile (5.7 percent), and nonionic surfactants (6.2 percent). At this time, there were three producers: Union Carbide, Dow, and Jefferson Chemical (a joint venture of Texaco and American Cyanamid). The latter two companies employed the chlorohydrin route, while Union Carbide uniquely used a direct oxidation process it had commercialized in 1937. Typical of this era, Union Carbide did not grant licenses on its technology and enjoyed the benefits of its more economical process, relative to the chlorhydrin route.

Potential new producers could proceed to build chlorhydrin plants, since this was already old technology and know-how was available at reasonable costs, or from German plant inspection reports. However, this route was not particularly attractive for a new producer. It entailed either manufacture or purchase of chlorine, which in the process was converted to a relatively low value by-product, ethylene dichloride, as well as to calcium chloride, also an undesirable by-product. The economic advantage of a direct oxidation process was then in the range of two to three cents per pound of ethylene oxide, which was a 20–30 percent saving over the chlorohydrin route.

Landau and his co-workers saw this situation as one fraught with great opportunity. The group studied the Union Carbide process, and particularly the Carbide patents, and felt that it would be possible to develop a better direct route without danger of infringement. This, in fact, led to the first research work by SD, carried out in an office building in the middle of Manhattan. The team working on this development was probably one of the most capable group of chemists and chemical engineers ever assembled in a small, entrepreneurial company. They had considerable achievements already to their credit from earlier work with other companies. As occurred so often in the mission-oriented research atmosphere prevalent at SD in those days, the group defined the objective and started to work.

Some of the studies carried out by SD at that time went back to the earliest work on this reaction by Lefort in France and Twigg in England. This was then used as a basis for new kinetic studies on the mechanisms defining conversion and selectivity obtained with the improved silver catalyst to be used in this reaction. Other studies involved the comparison of different catalyst shapes for a fixed-bed reactor, as well as studies on a fluid-bed system. Eventually, a fixed bed was selected, because fluid-bed operation gave lower yields, primarily due to back mixing, and the reaction did not need a regeneration system, for which the fluid-bed process is particularly suitable. Eventually, a specific process design was conceived, which resulted in a higher yield than that thought to be achieved at that time by Union Carbide. Some patents were later granted to SD on its process design and its catalyst system.

The time had come to build a pilot reactor at a commercial site. Now, an arrangement was made with Petrochemicals Ltd. in England, whereby the British firm built a pilot plant in return for an exclusive British license on SD's new direct oxidation process. The results were convincing and SD was on its way with the new technology. It had also proved that technology rights and license agreements can be traded for the feedback of know-how that could then be sold or licensed to many other firms.

SD now attempted to find a U.S. company to build the first plant based on its process. But the breakthrough came in Europe, when

Naphtachimie, a joint venture of Pechiney and Kuhlmann, decided to use the SD process in a new ethylene oxide and ethylene glycol plant in Lavera, France. Naphtachimie designed the glycol plant, apparently without much difficulty, since generalized know-how for this reaction was in the public domain. The Naphtachimie plant started up successfully in 1953 and was subsequently expanded. A license was granted to Allied Chemical and then a second European plant based on the SD process was built by Société Chimique des Derives du Petrole in Antwerp, Belgium. A "grass roots" oxide-glycol plant, designed and built by SD for the GAF Corporation (the I.G. Farben successor company in the United States, but now completely divorced from its former owners), then came onstream in 1958.

Other plants were also on the drawing boards. By 1960, U.S. ethylene glycol production had risen to well over 500 million pounds. Union Carbide remained the largest producer, increasing its capacity throughout the years, while other companies were competing by licensing outside technology. By now, there was a choice of two licensors, since a direct oxidation process had also been developed by Shell Chemical, using oxygen instead of air as the oxidant.* The Shell process had lower *capital* cost but higher *operating* costs, since it required expensive pure oxygen from an air separation plant. Shell supplied the technology and the catalyst and signed up several contractors to design and build plants for licensees of its process.

For many years thereafter Shell and SD vied with each other to grant licenses for new ethylene oxide projects all over the world, with SD maintaining an edge over its competitor for a long time. Competition between licensors to sign up a new licensee can be just as vigorous as between manufacturers of the product itself and the battles between Scientific Design and Shell/Lummus (Lummus was frequently selected as the contractor designing the Shell process EO plant) were a good example. For a while, I headed up the group at SD that engaged in these contests and it was actually a lot of fun (as well as hard work), particularly if you won. The battlefield comprised three elements: royalties, engineering fees, and catalyst sales conditions. There was often some flexibility in all of these and the challenge was to offer the new licensee a deal that he evaluated as being superior to the Shell/Lummus offering. Ralph Landau's skill in negotiating license deals was unsurpassed.

*The growing market for oxygen instead of air for chemical process oxidations created major business opportunities for companies such as Air Products and Chemicals, the Linde Division of Union Carbide, and Big Three Industries.

By the early 1980's, SD had granted close to 100 licenses. The company's income from royalties, catalyst sales, and engineering fees remained very substantial for over 30 years. But the most significant aspect of this story is that fact that SD had successfully identified a major petrochemical process development opportunity, opening up ethylene oxide-glycol manufacture for a multitude of firms worldwide. This was repeated for a number of other chemicals over the next 15 years.

Chlorinated Solvents

Chlorinated derivatives of C_1 and C_2 hydrocarbons, including methyl chloride, trichloroethylene, carbon tetrachloride, and perchloroethylene, had long been manufactured from acetylene by successive chlorinations. However, acetylene was relatively expensive, particularly in areas where power costs (for making calcium carbide) were high. In the United States, where natural gas became the preferred feedstock for almost any chemical, it was of some interest to determine whether chlorinated solvents could be produced directly from natural gas. This would involve a type of technology never practiced commercially on this scale: thermal chlorination. This process is based on a free-radical reaction that takes place under highly corrosive conditions. In the early 1950s, SD found out that Allied Chemical was looking for such a process to install at its Moundsville, West Virginia, plant, but had had difficulty in locating suitable technology. By this time, SD already had a very active European office set up to look for technologies saleable in the U.S. market—particularly processes that could be further improved by SD's chemical engineers. Allied's quest became the next challenge for the young firm.

A suitable process was, in fact, soon found at a Montecatini pilot plant in Novarra, Italy, where natural gas, recently discovered in the Po Valley, had stimulated research on the direct chlorination of methane. Far from optimized, the process was taken back by SD to its Port Washington laboratory and there it was refined and improved. A plant was then designed for Allied Chemical, which went into operation in 1954. In addition to cutting hydrocarbon costs by 75 percent, this process also provided hydrogen chloride by-product. A year later, Pechiney in France approached SD to ask whether the company could use the same technology to make perchloroethylene (a dry cleaning fluid) from light liquid hydrocarbons and chlorine at its St. Auban plant in the Maritime Alps. Although a more difficult application, with even greater corrosion problems, which involved the use of glass, graphite, nickel, and other relatively exotic materials, this process was successfully commercialized by SD and Pechiney in 1956, after major startup problems had almost doomed the plant. The plant also made very high purity hydrogen chloride by-product gas suitable for reaction with acetylene to make vinyl chloride monomer.

SD's ability to take technology back and forth across the Atlantic gave the firm a tremendous advantage over companies thinking along less global lines. Within a decade, most chlorinated solvents were produced via hot chlorination technology. Dow and PPG Industries developed comparable processes. Although SD did not achieve nearly as much success in licensing its chlorinated solvents technology as it did with ethylene oxide and some of its other developments, SD's experience with a process it found in an Italian pilot plant provided the chemical community with additional evidence that foreign technology should not be neglected in planning new petrochemical projects.

Maleic Anhydride

One of the oldest derivatives of coal-tar based benzene, maleic anhydride had, over the years, found a surprisingly large number of applications in such diverse areas as pharmaceuticals, agricultural chemicals, and coating resins. In the late 1940s, maleic anhydride also became a major intermediate for polyester resins, thermoset materials, usually reinforced with fiberglass, that were used in the construction of boats, storage tanks, and other large molded objects. Much of the maleic anhydride was recovered as a by-product from phthalic anhydride plants, but it was also made on purpose in rather small plants, using antiquated technology.

Since maleic acid and anhydride were both products of coke-oven derived feedstocks (naphthalene or benzene), the major maleic producers before the war were tar distillers, such as Koppers and the National Aniline Division of Allied Chemical.* Maleic anhydride was still a minor chemical at that time, with total U.S. production in 1941 below five million pounds.

---

*Actually, the Barrett Division of Allied Chemical recovered the chemicals from coke-oven gases, including the benzene transferred to National Aniline.

In the early 1950s, Reichhold Chemicals built a maleic anhydride plant, but then ran into operating difficulties. SD engineers were called in to improve plant operations, including assistance in developing a better catalyst. SD's engineers recognized that it would be possible to improve this process substantially by making a number of important modifications to the flowsheet. This was accomplished over the next 12–18 months. SD now had another process it would be able to license broadly to the world.

Again, the first application of the new process was made in Europe, this time for Compagnie Française des Matières Colorantes, a Kuhlmann subsidiary. Shortly after joining SD, I saw the complete calculations for this plant—including heat and material balances, equipment process design, critical mechanical design items (e.g., certain heat exchangers), and flowsheets—as prepared by Bob Egbert, Vice-President of Engineering for SD and one of the original partners in the firm. I have the distinct recollection that the calculations and mechanical sketches defining the entire plant and developed with great chemical engineering skill, occupied the space of barely 30 pages of cross-hatched paper. I am still impressed by this engineering *tour-de-force*, when I think about it.

Within a short number of years, SD licensed several U.S. manufacturers with its maleic anhydride technology, including such companies as Koppers, American Cyanamid, Tenneco (Heyden-Newport), and Monsanto. Not many years later, a large percentage of the world's maleic anhydride capacity was based on the SD process. By 1950, U.S. maleic production had risen to 16 million pounds and by 1960 it had further increased fivefold to 90 million pounds, much of it made in plants designed by SD.

Scientific Design opened up maleic anhydride technology by developing superior know-how in cooperation with an operating company and then offering it to any firm willing to pay royalties and to buy a process design package from the engineering firm. Figure 8.1, a reproduction of an SD advertisement in the late 1950s, illustrates how the company positioned itself as a purveyor of petrochemical processes.

In connection with its assignment at Reichhold, SD also acquired the services of Tom Brown, who later became Vice-President of Sales at SD and, together with Ralph Landau, contributed greatly to the firm's worldwide licensing program, particularly during the late 1950s in Japan.

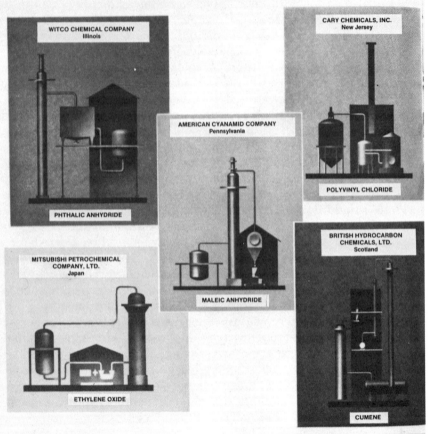

The pay-off is in production

SD announces successful start-ups of 5 more plants

Exclusive emphasis on chemical process skill enables SD to undertake complete and integrated responsibility for all phases of a project, from earliest planning to plant start-up.

For further information on SD's process skill and international services, write for SD's Process Skill Brochure.

SCIENTIFIC DESIGN COMPANY, INC.

EXECUTIVE OFFICES: TWO PARK AVENUE, NEW YORK 16, NEW YORK
THE SD GROUP:
SD Plants Inc., New York • SD Plants, Canada Ltd., Toronto
SD Plants Ltd., London, England • Catalyst Development Corporation, New Jersey
Société Française des Services Techniques S.a.r.l., Paris, France

Figure 8.1 SD advertisement–late 1950s. (*Source: Chemical Week.*)

325

Terephthalic Acid

The development of process technology for the manufacture of synthetic fiber monomers must have been particularly appealing to the technical management of SD: (*1*) fiber production was growing rapidly while (*2*) the technology for the monomers, as well as the fibers, remained very close held. Polyester fibers had been invented by the Calico Printers Association, which had signed an exclusive arrangement with ICI during the war. DuPont had paid ICI for a license for the United States and had become the sole U.S. producer at that time. Now, Landau and his group again pondered a major challenge.

As noted in Chapter 7, it is very difficult to purify terephthalic acid made via nitric acid oxidation of p-xylene. Accordingly, the acid had to be esterified with methanol to obtain the more easily purified methyl ester (DMT), which was then reacted with ethylene glycol. In addition to the purification problems caused by its use, nitric acid has other drawbacks as an oxidant in that the lower oxides of nitrogen produced must be recovered and reoxidized back to the acid, a fairly expensive procedure that can also involve major pollution problems. Landau and his co-workers recognized the potential simplicity of using air as the oxidant, but such a process would require a catalyst system not then known.

The search for such a catalyst occupied a relatively long period at the Port Washington, New York, laboratory, where the firm had converted a garage to a research facility when it could no longer continue working in the office building on Park Avenue. At that time, the company's fortunes were not yet shining very brightly, and, in fact, some of the design engineers were working in the laboratory . One interesting early by-product of this research work was a process to alkylate benzene with propylene to make cumene (isopropyl benzene) and p-di-isopropyl benzene (p-dipb), the latter a product that SD felt might be a reasonable terephthalic acid precursor. Before the terephthalic acid breakthrough came, SD had an opportunity to design a cumene plant for Allied Chemical, which had just licensed the new cumene-based Hercules-Distillers phenol process, and this kept some money coming in. The French firm, Kuhlmann, supported some of the earlier work on the p-dipb route, although it never used the process then being developed.

The search for a suitable catalyst for a new reaction can quickly be successful or it may never succeed. A combination of skill and luck are involved in most cases and sometimes researchers are close to quitting when the break finally comes. When Al Saffer, then research director, and his team finally reached for the right bottle on the laboratory shelf, they knew within hours that the problem was solved. An excellent catalyst for the oxidation had been identified—basically metallic bromine in an acetate solution. With this catalyst system, it was possible to convert either p-dipb or p-xylene to terephthalic acid in very high yields. P-xylene would be a better feedstock—it was available in large quantities from aromatic gasoline blending stocks. It was clear that a major breakthrough was at hand.

In 1956, SD sold worldwide rights to its oxidation technology (now termed the Mid-Century Process) to Amoco Chemicals Corporation, which had been funding the later part of this work, but SD had already granted several lucrative licenses outside the United States, including one to ICI, which gave particular pleasure to Landau. It turned out that SD had beaten ICI to the patent office with the bromine technology by only two weeks. ICI, the company that had commercialized the original process for Terylene polyester using nitric acid oxidation, had recently developed technology along the same lines as Scientific Design.

While SD understandably takes great credit for its "breakthrough" in the development of a new catalyst for p-xylene oxidation, much credit also goes to Amoco Chemicals for developing and commercializing the technology at its first plant in Joliet, Illinois. This was done at great expense and over a considerable period of time, aided by some of the SD engineers that had worked on catalyst development and had submitted the process design for the actual plant in cooperation with Amoco's engineers. Later, Amoco developed a purification process that made it possible for fiber producers to use terephthalic acid directly, rather than dimethyl terephthalate. Convincing the conservative fiber industry to change its mode of operation was a major accomplishment for Amoco.

Other licensees of the Mid-Century technology, including ICI, Maruzen, and Mitsui Petrochemicals, also made major contributions in perfecting a sound, commercial process. Amoco later also used the technology to develop routes to isophtalic acid, trimellitic anhydride, and other specialty aromatic acids.

Sale of its technology to Amoco gave Scientific Design Company the financial wherewithal to proceed with a broad range of other research and development projects, which will not be further detailed here. Much later, SD changed its name to Halcon International and used a new propylene oxide process to become a major manufacturer of this chemical in a joint venture with Arco Chemical.

SD's invention of improved technology to produce aromatic acids and the sale of this technology to Amoco, highlighted two important points:

- It indicated that the laboratory and development staff of a small engineering firm could perform research work every bit as good as that coming out of the laboratories of a DuPont or Union Carbide. Not only that, but the costs of SD's research work were an order of magnitude lower than typical R&D costs in operating companies, partly because SD usually did not build an expensive pilot plant to prove out the process at a larger scale.
- By completing the development and commercialization of the process, a major oil company was able to become an important "player" in the petrochemical field, a situation symptomatic of what was happening in many other parts of the petrochemical industry. The Mid-Century process has since been responsible for a large part of Amoco Chemical's profits.

Hercules had earlier licensed dimethyl terephthalate (DMT) technology from Germany and, together with Amoco, became a worthy competitor to DuPont. As it turned out, polyester fibers were then just at their threshold of sustained growth and there was ample room for all of these companies to participate in that dynamic business for some time into the future. Amoco and Hercules became the main suppliers to the merchant market and a number of companies, in addition to DuPont, then entered the manufacture of these "miracle" fibers.

Scientific Design's history was not an unbroken string of successes. An early project to build a monochloroacetic acid plant for Stauffer Chemical turned out badly, due to serious corrosion problems. These could have been avoided with different construction materials and SD's recommendations in this area may not have been accepted by Stauffer. As another example, the first use of the (later widely practiced) cyclohexane oxidation process in an Australian plant built for Monsanto was unsuccessful, with the plant

never achieving close to design operations. I was the project manager on that venture, which, unfortunately, turned into an expensive pilot plant. Later, Monsanto's Chemstrand joint venture
became an important licensee of this process.

Some SD projects eventually succeeded due to sheer persever-
ance rather than brilliance. In one of these, I found out the hard
way the meaning of the word "know-how," the term used to cover
confidential information that is not patentable but is nevertheless very important in the design and operation of a plant. In the
1950s, the only contractor from whom companies could get a license for building a phthalic anhydride plant was the German
firm Chemiebau von Zieren, which had obtained this technology
under license from an I.G. Farben successor company. SD was usually undaunted when asked to supply technology, so when Witco
Chemical was interested in becoming a phthalic anhydride producer, SD offered to design and build a 20 million pound-per-year
plant and I was asked to head up the project.

We found a considerable amount of design information in
C.I.O.S. and F.I.A.T. reports (8), although our reactor design differed from that shown in Figure 8.2. A consultant was engaged
to learn more. We then developed a catalyst and subsequently designed and built the plant. My family and I now took an apart-
ment on the outskirts of Chicago, where the plant had been constructed and I turned my attention to starting up the plant. This
experience soon became a nightmare! First, the molten salt solution, used to cool the reactor tubes, leaked through pinholes in
almost every seam where tubes had been welded into the reactor
shell. Over 4,000 tubes had to be rewelded several times in place
by welders in the middle of one of the coldest winters in Chicago,
before an effective welding rod and flux were found to make the
reactors tight (special know-how). Then, we experienced a series of
fires and explosions in the piping downstream of the reactors and
in the so-called "switch condensers" that collected the phthalic
anhydride product by subliming it on chilled tube walls. (These
were then periodically "switched" to steam to melt the product
off the walls into a tank below.) The explosions and fires continued for weeks. We were at wit's end. Frantically, we looked for a
consultant, who had worked in a phthalic plant. When we eventually found one, he told us that for the plant to operate without
these mishaps, it would be necessary to *passivate* the piping downstream of the reactors by circulating a special solution through

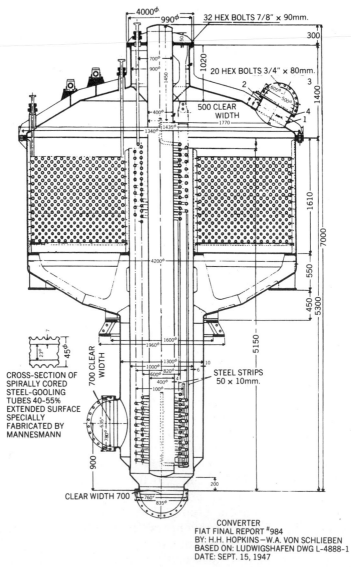

Figure 8.2 Phthalic reactor design. (*Source:* F.I.A.T. Final Report 984.)

them before restarting the plant. This would prevent iron oxide from reacting with phthalic and by-product maleic acid, forming iron phthalates and maleates, which promoted spontaneous ignition in the stream leaving the reactors (such materials are called "pyrophoric compounds"). Armed with this priceless know-how, for which we paid a few hundred dollars, as I recall, we successfully started up the plant.

It is this kind of knowledge, separate from patent rights, that often allows companies to charge royalties of from 1 to 3 percent on the sales price of the product to be made. Another way of saying it is this: If a licensor cannot provide all the required know-how under the license agreement, "caveat emptor."

Scientific Design, of course, was not the only independent source of new petrochemical technology. Although SD was essentially unique as an organization, boasting a research laboratory, advanced chemical engineering design techniques and great licensing skills, there were other success stories. Now, there was considerably greater opportunity for researchers not affiliated with any commercial firm to develop technology and to license or sell the corresponding patent rights to a number of companies. The best example of this was the success of Karl Ziegler, who discovered high density polyethylene.

ZIEGLER AND LINEAR POLYOLEFINS

Many outstanding chemists had advanced the field of organic and polymer chemistry in the early to mid-1900s, but they had often worked directly for a producing company or else had published their results without obtaining much financial benefit from their labors. To a large extent, this was a consequence of the fact that a few large companies controlled the manufacture of most chemicals and derivatives, so that inventors were generally forced to make a deal with an existing producer. The dramatic changes taking place in the postwar chemical industry made it easier for an inventor to find a potential new producer willing to sponsor research work on the basis that success in such research would then allow the sponsoring firm to have suitable technology to enter the field in question. That being the case, it followed that the inventor was now also in a much better position to strike a more favorable bargain with an existing producer, should he decide to approach such a company with his research concept.

Karl Ziegler had worked at the Kaiser Wilhelm Institute during the war, after a number of years of teaching chemistry at several universities. When the Institute's facilities came under Russian control shortly before the end of the war, Ziegler helped to reestablish the research center at Muelheim in the Ruhr, where it was renamed the Max Planck Institute. Here, Ziegler was able to resume his work in the area that interested him more than any others: the reactions of organic compounds of metals. And because the Institute had been used as the wartime repository of lithium, a metal that reacts with hydrocarbons, Ziegler found himself with what was certainly the largest amount of this material that had ever been collected in one place. Here then were ideal conditions to study new approaches to the polymerization of olefins.

Certainly, Ziegler was aware of the work previously carried out in this area by a number of previous researchers, including the wartime work at BASF (see Chapter 6). But Ziegler now took the art much further and eventually developed the technology for low pressure, high density polyethylene. Using lithium hydride, he was able to get ethylene molecules to form lithium ethyl, which could then be reacted with additional ethylene to form lithium butyl and so on. Ziegler termed this the *Aufbau* (literally "growth" but later termed "chain growth") reaction and this work led to his momentous discovery of a means to produce linear polymers from a lower olefin. His significant finding was that in this reaction the next unit always added on to one of the ends of the chain, thus giving unbranched and therefore "linear" polymers. This resulted in quite a different form of polyethylene than that made in the ICI high pressure process, which gave a great deal of chain branching. As a result of further research by Ziegler and his co-workers, working at ambient pressure with no external application of heat to start the reaction, an optimum catalyst system based on titanium and aluminum alkyl was eventually selected. This, of course, was a major improvement over the high pressure process, although the products made by the two routes were different enough to create important end uses for both types of polymer.

Strangely, Ziegler's outstanding accomplishments were not immediately appreciated (or perhaps understood) by some of his German peers. As recounted in *The Chain Straighteners* (9), the announcement of the Aufbau reaction and the low pressure polymerization of olefins was allegedly greeted with some derision by Bayer's research director, Dr. Otto Bayer, who made a bad pun on the word *Muehlheimer*, a man from Muehlheim-Ruhr. *Muelleimer*, spelled slightly differently, is the German word for garbage pail. Hopefully, some sort of apology was offered at a later time.

Ziegler's strong-willed personality and supreme confidence worked to his advantage, but also to his detriment. He decided at an early stage that he would personally decide on a licensing policy and he negotiated licensing agreements without the help of an experienced lawyer. Having previously made a favorable deal between himself and the Institute, he was in a position to negotiate all contracts and he did so because he stood to personally benefit very substantially from the licensing income derived from his inventions. Ziegler signed early agreements with Shell and Montecatini and later with many others. Basically, he gave licenses on his patents and the companies then had to develop their own processes, based on these patents, with some assistance from Ziegler and the Institute. Most likely, Ziegler could have made even more lucrative arrangements if he had relied on experienced counsel to assist in his negotiations and in the drafting of licensing agreements. But that was not his style.

Ziegler also was not careful in protecting his know-how. After granting a polyethylene license to Montecatini, he had invited some of its chemists to work at the Institute and they were evidently free to transmit much of the know-how they absorbed to Professor Guilio Natta, then a consultant for Montecatini in Milan. This turned out to be a serious error by Ziegler, since it appears that he was sure that the chain growth reaction would not work on propylene and he therefore did not apply for patents in that area. Even if he thought the reaction might work, he was apparently more interested, as a thorough German scientist, in first perfecting the work on the new type of polyethylene he had discovered.

Several polymer scientists, including Hermann Staudinger, Herman Mark, Paul Flory, and Calvin Schildknecht had visualized the possibility that linear polymers could be formed with regularly or irregularly alternating side chains. Such so-called stereospecific polymers might not only be made from olefins but also from vinyl alcohols or other compounds and would have a very high degree of crystallinity. However, none of these chemists knew how such chains could be synthesized and there remained considerable differences of opinion on the general subject.

Natta was familiar with the area as a result of his work in synthetic rubber, which resulted in a butadiene-based synthetic elastomer plant in Ferrara just before the war. He had also worked on olefin dimers and trimers, but with quite different catalyst systems. When he became aware of Ziegler's work on polyethylene, however, he immediately concluded that the catalyst system being used could be the answer to the synthesis of crystalline polymers with side chains. In any case, Montecatini and Natta decided that polypropylene represented an extremely interesting area, not yet covered by any of Ziegler's patents. Natta's research work, which was based on a catalyst system very similar to that of Ziegler, was almost immediately successful. He and his group then went on to polymerize a number of other monomers to produce stereoregular polyolefins. Significant, they learned how the methyl alkyl-titanium chloride catalyst system could be modified to control the location of the methyl groups on the chain (i.e., how to increase or decrease the amount of stereoregularity to produce polymers with more or less stiffness or elasticity) (10). High degrees of crystallinity could be achieved when all the methyl groups were on one side, a condition Natta called "isotactic" polypropylene. "Atactic" polypropylene, on the other hand, had random locations for methyl sidechains and therefore no stereo regularity. It acted like a rubber. Figure 8.3 shows three steric configurations of the polypropylene molecule.

Another important application of Ziegler's growth reaction was in the production of so-called alpha olefins and linear alcohols, used in detergents and plasticizers. Ethyl Corporation and Continental Oil both negotiated for licenses to use the aluminum alkyl technology, developing and commercializing processes in the 1960s. Ethyl Corporation was interested in producing both linear (alpha) olefins and linear alcohols, while Conoco Chemicals* developed a process to make exclusively linear alcohols, which the company called Alfols. The Ethyl process was more versatile, since it could use recycles to vary the relative amounts of different molecular weight olefins and alcohols. Conoco, on the other hand, produced as a valuable by-product a very pure alumina that was used as a catalyst carrier. An important issue in the development of these technologies was the fact that up to that point (with the exception of some Fischer-Tropsch products) detergent-range alcohols came largely from such natural products as coconut and tallow oils, whose supply and price tended to vary over a wide

---

*Now a separate company–"spun off" from Continental Oil–called Vista Chemical.

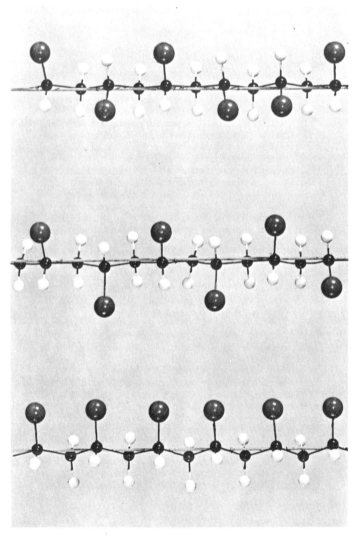

Figure 8.3 Three possible forms of polypropylene. *Top:* actactic; *middle:* syndiotactic; *bottom:* isotactic. (*Source:* Morris Kaufman, *Giant Molecules, The Technology of Plastics, Fibers and Rubber,* New York, Doubleday, 1968, p. 60.)

range. Here then was another area where petrochemistry was able to supplant and to a considerable extent displace natural materials (11,12)

Ten years later, Ziegler and Natta jointly received the Nobel Prize for Chemistry. Unfortunately, the two men had had a falling out when Ziegler had accused Natta of improperly using the information obtained by the Montecatini researchers at Muehlheim-Ruhr. In fact, Natta had later agreed that 30 percent of the royalties collected by Montecatini on polypropylene would go to Ziegler. Nevertheless, the rift between the two men was never healed. Ziegler catalyst systems were later also used to make stereospecific synthetic rubbers, including 1,4 polybutadiene and polyisoprene.

The first low pressure polyethylene plant was built by Hoechst in 1955 (13). Hercules Chemical had an opportunity to strike a deal with Ziegler on polyethylene at an early point, but couldn't quite make up its mind. It moved much more rapidly on polypropylene, however, taking licenses from Ziegler as well as Montecatini. Later, Hercules became the world leader in polypropylene production.* A typical Hercules slurry process flowsheet for a polypropylene plant is shown in Figure 8.4.

By 1957, six plants using Ziegler technology came onstream (see Table 8.2).

A large number of European, United States, and Japanese companies were able to obtain licenses to make linear polyethylene or polypropylene or both types of resin. In addition, researchers at Standard of Indiana and at Phillips Petroleum had developed their own quite different catalyst systems to make a linear type of polyethylene. Phillips brought a high density polyethylene plant on stream in 1957, with a capacity of 75 million pounds per year. Several other firms had also worked on polypropylene. In the case of both polymers, it took many years to sort out all of the conflicting patent priority dates and claims.† Fifteen U.S. companies eventually became producers of linear polyethylene and 17 became producers of polypropylene. Some of these firms did not build plants until the 1960s or 1970s, but the numbers indicate the range of

---

*In the 1980s, Hercules and Montecatini (now Montedison) merged their worldwide polypropylene plants and technology to form a company called Himont.

†Phillips Petroleum eventually emerged as having priority on the discovery of linear polymers of olefins.

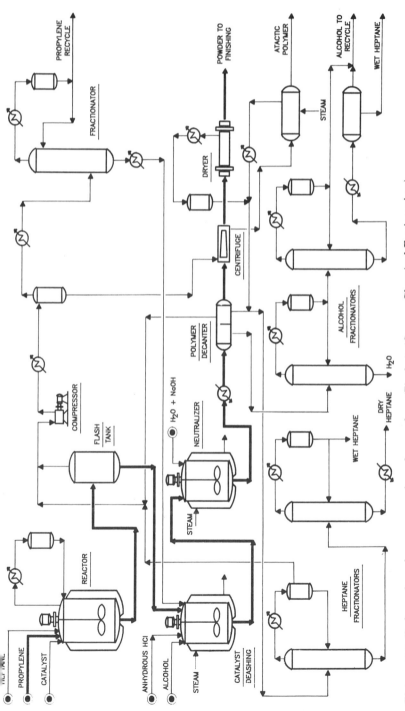

Figure 8.4 Hydrocarbon slurry process for polypropylene (Ziegler). (*Source: Chemical Engineering.*)

337

Table 8.2   Plants Using Ziegler Technology by 1957

Company	Product	Plant Location	Annual Capacity (Million Lbs)
Celanese	Polyolefins	Houston, TX	40
Hercules	High-density polyethylene	Parlin, NJ	30
W. R. Grace	High-density polyethylene	Baton Rouge, LA	50
Montecatini	Polypropylene	Ferrara, Italy	15
Farbwerke Hoechst	Polypropylene	Frankfurt, Germany	16.8
Hercules Powder	Polypropylene	Parlin, NJ	20

Source: Ref. 14.

competitors that were eventually able to enter these sectors of the industry.

NUMEROUS PRODUCERS—A NEW COMPETITIVE ENVIRONMENT

It was, by now, becoming difficult to find many similarities between the chemical industry of the 1930s versus that of the 1950s. Whereas the prewar industry was steeped in tradition and based on a "live-and-let live" mentality, the postwar petrochemical industry was as competitive as the most liberal economists might have wished. And while technology in the old days was closely held and only available under very restrictive circumstances to companies willing to play the game, now there were usually a number of options for obtaining the know-how to build specific plants. The excess capacity that often developed due to overenthusiasm regarding the prospects of the industry would correct itself as product demand kept growing. Nevertheless, there was often a problem of oversupply.

This situation was actually already surfacing in the mid-1950s. Thus, in 1954, six producers had acetaldehyde capacity totalling 860 million pounds per year (Union Carbide had almost half of that), but consumption was barely 700 million pounds per year and dropping, since both acetic anhydride and cellulose acetate had been on a major downtrend since 1950 (15). Four acrylonitrile producers in 1955 had capacity totaling 204 million pounds per year, but consumption was only 130 million pounds per year, with fibers taking the largest percent. Acrylonitrile prices had dropped from 53 cents per pound to 27 cents per pound over the previous two years in the face of such oversupply (16). An interesting point here is that in the case of both products, new technology was about to be introduced, leading to the construction of considerably more capacity in the near future (Wacker process for acetaldehyde; Sohio process for acrylonitrile).

In spite of the industry's frequent bouts with overcapacity, leading sometimes to major price reductions, as shown in the example on acrylonitrile, pricing was still relatively good in most cases. An industry that had been used to very high margins might, in other words, have to content itself with more moderate margins. This would be all right if volume was high, which it was, of course. Thus, an optimistic mood prevailed much of the time and the industry was definitely considered as "the place to be." The traditional chemical companies, which still produced most of the petrochemicals, were thus joined by groups of other entrants including oil companies, gas companies and diversified firms (later called "conglomerates"), which saw the petrochemicals business as an excellent area for diversification. Although feedstock control had never been an important issue in chemicals production, firms with large hydrocarbon reserves somehow felt—incorrectly, as it later turned out—that they would have a substantial advantage over their competitors by being "back integrated." And so, many oil and gas companies proceeded to build ammonia and ethylene plants to go "downstream" into olefins and aromatics derivatives. In one instance, a chemical company, Allied Chemical, went "upstream" by acquiring the Union Texas Natural Gas Corporation (actually, a successor to Union Sulphur Company, founded by Herman Frasch). A number of joint ventures were also established between "feedstock companies" and downstream firms: for example, Jefferson Chemical (Texaco and American Cyanamid), Chemplex (Getty and American Can), and El Paso Products Company (El Paso Natural Gas and Rexall Drug Company). All of these joint ventures built steam crackers and none of these firms is in existence as a joint venture at this writing.

Oil companies that built steam crackers were just as interested in the merchant market as in their downstream operations. Gulf

Oil and others therefore promoted the construction of a vast ethylene pipeline network all over the Gulf Coast, which made it possible for many other firms to build ethylene derivatives plants at locations of their own choice (see Fig. 8.5).

The oil companies also entered the production of petrochemical intermediates in a major way. Fuel products were growing at only the rate of the Gross National Product or less. But petrochemicals, made from the raw materials in the gas fields and refineries, were growing at 10 to 15 percent annually, or several times faster. Surely, this would be a great area for business diversification. The only question was—how far to go "downstream"? That would have to be decided but, in the meantime, there was plenty to do. In addition to building ethylene capacity, Gulf Oil started to produce cyclohexane, styrene, and ammonia. Amoco Chemicals went into terephthalic acid, high density polyethylene, and into a joint venture in polypropylene. Phillips Petroleum added to its elastomer business by including high density polyethylene. Shell added ethylene oxide and glycol, and so on. Jersey also decided to enter the plastics business, first signing a license with Ziegler. As mentioned earlier, these licenses only entitled licensees to use the patents, but did not give them a process. That had to be developed by the licensee. According to Irv Leibson, who headed up this development program for Humble, Standard Oil Development Company,

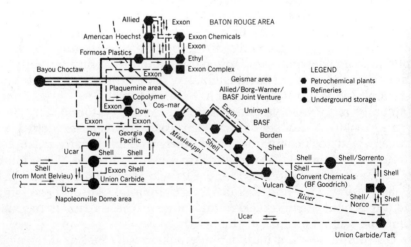

Figure 8.5 Ethylene pipeline network in Louisiana. (*Source:* Allied Chemical.)

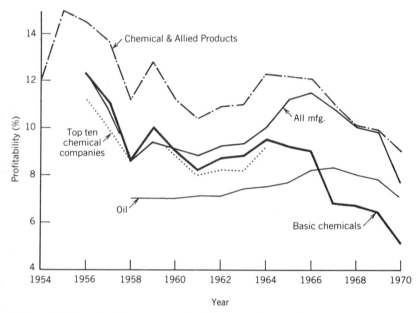

Figure 8.6 Profitability on gross fixed assets. (*Source:* Government Statistics).

the Jersey research arm, had problems developing a high density polyethylene product with low ash content. Accordingly, work was switched to polypropylene.* In the mid-1950s, Jersey president Jack Rathbone approved construction of the company's first polymer plant—a polypropylene unit at Humble's Baytown refinery. Soon thereafter, Humble was absorbed into the parent company, a fact that might have been associated with Baytown's new foray into petrochemicals.

It is probably true that for many oil companies petrochemicals manufacture appeared attractive not only due to the requirements for hydrocarbon raw materials, but also because "Chemicals and Allied Products" (A Commerce Department classification) had relatively high profitability on fixed assets, certainly much higher than the refining industry. Moreover, the world was awash with oil and the huge cash flow the oil companies enjoyed was far larger than what was needed to drill holes in the ground. Petrochemicals and then fertilizers were an attractive area for investment. The oil

*Irv Leibson, personal communication.

companies built petrochemical plants, bought fertilizer companies, then built more fertilizer capacity. At one point, Jersey was building ammonia plants in nine countries, including Spain, Lebanon, Cyprus, Pakistan, and the Philippines.*

By the mid-1950s, the U.S. petrochemical industry had become a vast enterprise, still growing rapidly, with as many as 10 or 15 companies frequently producing a given chemical. An industry with so many producers—including others still in the wings—was bound to run into profitability problems as time went by (see Fig. 8.6). But in the 1950s, profits were still good. U.S. companies, in fact, were starting to expand their petrochemical activities abroad.

REFERENCES

1. George W. Stocking and Myron W. Watkins (1950). *Cartels in Action,* New York, Twentieth Century Fund, p. 366.

2. P. C. Keith (1946). *Oil and Gas Journal,* **45,** No. 6, 102.

3. R. E. Hulse (1954). Petrochemicals, Chemical Marketing Research Association Paper, New York, May 20.

4. British Intelligence Objectives Subcommittee, Report FR 1154, Item No. 22, p. 40ff.

5. Sheldon Hochheiser (1986). *Rohm and Haas—History of a Chemical Company,* Philadelphia, University of Pennsylvania Press, p. 87.

6. Ralph Landau, ed. (1966). *The Chemical Plant—From Process Selection to Commercial Operation,* New York. Reichhold.

7. Ralph Landau (1978). An entrepreneurial chemical company, speech to the Newcomen Society, October.

8. British Intelligence Objectives Subcommittee, Report No. 984 Supplement No. 1, Manufacture of Phthalic Anhydride by I.G. Farbenindustrie.

9. R. McMillan (1979). *The Chain Straighteners,* London, Macmillan, p. 40.

10. Peter J. T. Morris (1986). *Polymer Pioneers—A Popular History of the Science and Technology of Large Molecules,* Philadelphia, The Center of History of Chemistry, p. 83.

11. P. H. Washecheck (1980). Aliphatic alcohols via Ziegler chemistry, ACS Meeting, Houston, Texas, March.

12. P. A. Lobo et al. (1962). The alfol alcohol process, *Chemical Engineering Progress,* **58,** No. 5, May.

13. Karl Winnacker (1972). *Challenging Years: My Life in Chemistry* (trans. David Goodman) London, Sidgwick & Jackson, p. 207.

14. Polypropylene makes a 3-nation debut, *Chemical Week,* December 7, 1957, p. 31.

*Aimison Jonnard, personal communication.

15. Acetaldehyde poser: How much and where? *Chemical Week,* October 9, 1954.
16. Enough—For how long? *Chemical Week,* October 1, 1955.

ADDITIONAL READING

The battle for production, *Chemical Engineering,* February 1952, p. 143ff.

Drawing on Europe's Ideas, *Business Week,* June 4, 1955.

Internationaler Erfahrungsaustausch Aus Amerikanischer Sicht, *Chemische Industrie* **X,** September 1958, 468ff.

Landau, Ralph, ed. (1966). *The Chemical Plant—From Process Selection to Commercial Operation,* New York, Reichhold.

Landau, Ralph (1953). Ethylene oxide by direct oxidation, *Petroleum Refiner,* September.

Landau, Ralph and T. P. Brown (1959). Expansion by acquiring foreign know-how, *Chemical Industry International,* March.

Landau, Ralph, Process Innovation, *Chemistry & Industry,* May 2, 1981.

McMillan, R. (1979). *The Chain Straighteners,* London, Macmillan.

Stobaugh, Robert B. (1966). *Petrochemical Manufacturing and Marketing Guide,* Houston, Gulf Publishing.

Winnacker, Karl (1972). *Challenging Years: My Life in Chemistry,* trans. David Goodman, London, Sidgwick & Jackson.

9 / International Development and Growth

Chapters 3, 4, and 6 describe how the petrochemical industry came of age in the United States when the rising demand for various consumer and military products called for a feedstock base far larger than that available from the coke ovens of the iron and steel industry. In the course of this transition, a considerable amount of new technology had to be developed and many known processes were modified or transformed to meet new requirements. Much of the underlying basic chemistry had origins in various European countries, notably Germany, England, the U.S.S.R., and France. But wartime needs and continued development work thereafter resulted in a number of technological advances that created a large new American industry, different in many ways from the chemical industry that existed in the United States and Europe before the war. What soon became known as the "petrochemical industry" presented a formidable challenge to Europe and the rest of the world. A large number of modern plants, using continuous processing techniques in the conversion of inexpensive Gulf Coast feedstocks, were now supplying various organic intermediates to the plastics, synthetic fiber, and other new industries. Over a short period of time, American industry had made chemistry synonymous with "big business"—alongside steel, glass, cement, and other so-called heavy industries. Before the war, the chemical in-

344

dustry could be considered as an assemblage of diverse smaller business segments, such as explosives, dyestuffs, textiles, fertilizers, and fine chemicals. With the creation of the petrochemical industry, there was now a very large and relatively coherent new industry that would soon be one of the biggest contributors to the U.S. Gross National Product (GNP).

It was clear that companies in Western Europe and Japan would have to evaluate the significance of this change and to assess its consequences on their domestic industries. Certainly, steps would have to be taken to emulate, in a manner appropriate to local circumstances, many of the industrial developments that had taken place in the United States and, to some extent, in Canada. And there was considerable urgency to get started. For a number of countries in these regions, it was simply inadmissible to concede an important part of the world's chemical market to a greatly transformed North American chemical industry, which had now become the low cost producer of many, if not most, bulk commodity organic chemicals.

Over the period from 1946 to 1960, Western Europe and Japan carried out a major transition to produce aliphatic and aromatic chemicals from petroleum rather than coal-based feedstocks. Neither region was a producer of either oil or gas (in any substantial quantities) and this made it far more difficult for chemical producers in these areas to abandon the use of locally available coal or ethyl alcohol and other agriculturally-derived feedstocks. Nevertheless, both Europe and Japan found the need for this transition compelling. In Europe, it occurred earlier, but at a moderate rate. Japan waited somewhat longer, but was then in a hurry to accomplish it as quickly as possible. This chapter describes what happened in both of these geographic regions.

POSTWAR EUROPE CONSIDERS THE TRANSITION FROM COAL

Dealing with the ravages of a devastating war was the first priority in most of the Western European countries. As the next step, the large firms in continental Europe had to reestablish and reorganize themselves for carrying out business in the latter part of the twentieth century. Here, too, there were things to be learned from the large American companies, now called "multinationals," which were not only operating plants using new technologies, but were also setting up large global business systems to move products around the world. Significantly, these companies were also more adept at seeing Europe as a total trading area rather than as a series of individual countries.

Some chemical industry leaders in postwar Europe were unwilling to concede that the American petrochemical industry was based on real technology breakthroughs. After all, had not such "petrochemicals" as styrene, ethylene glycol, ammonia, methanol, phenol, and many others been produced in Europe before the war with European technology, often before their manufacture had been commenced on the other side of the ocean? True, the American firms making these products from natural gas and oil had a raw materials cost advantage, but presumably this would soon be overcome, since Europe's refineries would certainly be rebuilt and modernized, and cheap crude oil from the Middle East was now amply available at low prices. Presumably, this would soon provide Europe's chemical industry with the reactive hydrocarbon streams now being converted to a number of conventional chemical intermediates in the United States.

Such chauvinistic views as were sometimes expressed regarding technology issues were, in many cases, inappropriate, as process technology does not stand still. It was true, for example, that in the early 1940s, German technology in polystyrene and polyvinyl chloride resins was about at the same state of development as in the United States. That could be surmised when going through the copious information contained in the B.I.O.S. and F.I.A.T. reports covering the visits of the Allied military inspection teams sent into German plastics plants right after V-E Day. But, in the case of many of the chemicals involved, including these thermoplastic polymers, which were in their infancy in the 1940s, U.S. producers were continuing to move along a steep "learning curve" at a time when the German factories largely lay in ruins. Advances continued to be made over the period when the I.G. cartel was being dismembered and its successor companies had not yet been reestablished. Thus, by the early 1950s, U.S. polymer technology was well ahead of German research, a point recently made by Frank Reese, then a Monsanto research executive involved in that company's PVC and polystyrene business.* Superior resin technology helped

---

*Francis Reese, personal communication.

Monsanto and Dow gain early footholds as suppliers to the European plastics market.

The same was true for a number of other process technologies. Not surprisingly, chemical research and development work in Europe had been severely curtailed during the German occupation. In Italy and Germany, this type of work was assigned low priority after it became clear that the war would be lost. Chemical researchers then also became more concerned with family safety than with advances in technology. It would now take some time to get the research work cranked up again. Meanwhile, development work was steadily progressing in U.S. companies' research laboratories and in U.S. universities, as well as in private research and engineering companies.

While some European industrialists tended to deprecate the advances made in America during the war and thereafter, others quickly recognized that U.S. technology in many areas would be very beneficial for revamping and modernizing certain parts of Europe's chemical industry—particularly the production of olefins, olefin derivatives, and aromatics from petroleum. But some years would pass before a program to switch from oil to coal was in full swing.

The British chemical industry was in reasonably good shape. Its plants had largely remained in operation, often with the benefit of some American technology transfers during the war. But England's industry was still largely based on local coal—not on petroleum, which had to be imported.

In Japan, there was much concern. The Japanese chemical industry had traditionally been less innovative and now a particularly serious "technology gap" was foreseen. Moreover, major changes in industry structure had been promulgated by the Allied Occupation Government and it was evident that it would take a longer time for the chemical industry to reestablish itself under a new format that deemphasized the role of the old Zaibatsu industrial and banking combines. As described later in this chapter, the Japanese petrochemical industry only came into being in the late 1950s, but it made remarkable progress thereafter.

In retrospect, it is clear that European producers found it much more difficult than originally expected to build a competitive petrochemical industry that could compete in most respects with its American counterpart. There were many reasons for this, not the least being the fact that it took time for European companies to adjust their raw materials thinking from coal to petroleum-based feedstocks. Perhaps a more basic reason, however, was related to nationalism—specifically, the problems Europeans faced in adjusting their thinking to the concept of building large plants to supply a total European market. Although Western Europe has a population roughly equal to that of the United States, it actually consists of a number of countries that traditionally maintained separate identities, as well as quite separate industries. This was based not only on a strong tradition of independence, but because many countries had periodically engaged in bloody wars. Industrial independence necessarily meant that each country tended to build small plants for the home market. Even in countries with a relatively large population, such as France and Great Britain, chemical firms planning new projects in the postwar period found it difficult to build a large enough plant that would have reasonably attractive economics. Substantial exports were needed to build such plants, but the products in question would not necessarily be saleable in adjacent European countries, since potential purchasers were still averse to being dependent on supply from across the border. On the other hand, building a large plant partly sized for exports to other parts of the world entailed substantial risks, since American firms were now often in a better position to supply such Third World markets. In fact, U.S. firms were now increasing their exports to the European market itself since, as mentioned earlier, they were able to see Europe as an integral market area. Historical European attitudes, traditions, and prejudices were not an issue for American companies.

Shortly after the cessation of hostilities, a few far-seeing statesmen felt that the time had come for European countries to join in a federation that would, among other things, coordinate and combine many of their industrial activities. Such an amalgamation would presumably also help to wipe out the mistrust and animosity that had characterized the relationships between many of these countries for such a long time. But the Treaty of Rome, which established the European Economic Community (EEC) in 1957, was a greatly watered-down version of the concepts advanced by these visionary leaders.

The creation of the so-called European Common Market and the European Free Trade Association (EFTA) in the late 1950s was a consequence of recognizing a need to broaden the local market potential for European firms, while erecting a tariff wall against

American and other non-European imports. However, these trade groupings were less than effective in achieving the objective of creating European (rather than countrywide) markets that could be served from large plants in individual countries, whereby one country would produce one particular chemical and a second country would manufacture another, both to be freely traded within the associations. This concept took a long time to take hold. By excluding some European countries, notably Great Britain, the EEC did not become a strong enough trading area to deal effectively with international trade issues. And the animosities and suspicions between the countries making up the EEC would take a number of years to abate. England did later join the European Common Market and the EFTA group was dissolved soon thereafter. But Europe remained a far less coherent industrial and trading area than the United States, with continuing disadvantages due to local practices and traditions.

Not only were local markets too small, but there were also too many companies making the same products. In France, Germany, Belgium, and elsewhere, it took a long time to consolidate the industry into a smaller number of stronger companies that could compete more effectively with their foreign counterparts. Significantly, mergers between companies in different European countries were almost impossible under EEC statutes. In many cases, such mergers would have greatly improved competitiveness by creating larger entities. As a matter of fact, there was relatively little interest in such mergers. Nationalism thus remained an important factor in the development of the postwar European chemical industry.

Significantly, it was the international oil companies that took the lead in establishing a European petrochemical industry. Unburdened by traditions associated with coal-based chemistry, these firms saw the European opportunity in terms of diversification of their historical roles as suppliers of fuels and lubricants. They also had another driving force, related to the European pattern of fuel products demand. The market for gasoline was relatively small, based on the limited number of automobiles then on the roads. Thus, other outlets were needed for the naphtha associated with the crudes being run through the refineries, which were primarily operated to produce fuel oils, diesel fuel, lubricants, and asphalt. Naphtha, of course, is a prime feedstock for the production of olefins and aromatics. It was therefore natural to think about converting naphtha to petrochemical building blocks, such as ethylene, propylene, butadiene, and benzene.

At a relatively early stage, Standard Oil (N.J.) built petrochemical production centers next to Jersey-owned refineries in England, France, and Germany and elsewhere, including France's first steam cracker, a 30,000-ton-per-year unit at Port Jerôme in Normandy. British Petroleum (formerly the Anglo-Iranian Oil Company) took a somewhat different tack, but with the same objective. Instead of building wholly owned crackers and selling olefins and aromatics to other firms brought to the site to build derivatives plants, BP sought joint ventures with traditional European chemical companies. These partnerships comprised a cracker, as well as downstream users. Within a short time, BP set up Naphtachimie in France (with Kuhlman and Pechiney), Erdoelchemie in Germany (with Bayer), and British Hydrocarbon Chemicals in England (with Distillers Corporation). Shell took an intermediate course, partly establishing joint ventures (e.g., Rheinische Olefinwerke with BASF) and partly building petrochemical facilities next to its refineries (e.g., at Pernis, in Holland).

Standard Oil (N.J.), Mobil, Gulf, and other international oil companies eventually also built a number of aromatics plants at various European refineries, thus creating a large local supply of benzene, toluene and xylenes from petroleum. Jersey's so-called Powerforming technology for reforming naphtha to BTX aromatics (see Chapter 4) was not only used in the company's own refineries, but was also widely licensed to other refiners, large and small. Bert Struth, whom I already knew at Esso Engineering and who joined Chem Systems during its early days, earned his spurs by going around Europe in the late 1950s, starting up Esso-licensed reformers in various picturesque and not-so-picturesque locations. He told me that dealing with labor unions and Communist agitators in Italy probably took up more of his time than solving some of the operating problems at the plants he helped to start up.

The oil companies thus progressed with greater vigor into petrochemicals than many of the traditional European chemical firms, which remained wedded for some time to feedstocks derived from the coal and steel industry. Government actions were, in some cases, also instrumental in fostering the establishment of European petrochemical installations. In Italy, in the late 1950s, the government decided to aid the impoverished Mezzogiorno region (consisting of Sardinia, Southern Italy, and Sicily) by providing large grants and low interest loans for the construction of chemical, plastics and synthetic fiber plants. History records that this turned out to be a poor way to establish a new local industry, which was built far too large for the geographical market it could economically serve. The Italian program did create one of the largest postwar refinery-petrochemical companies, Società Italiana di Resine (SIR), which, for a time, was a major factor in the European Common Market, but later went bankrupt.

The superior economics of producing chemical end-products from petroleum-based feedstocks—with the use of newly developed American technology—eventually became an irresistible driving force in the conversion of a number of European installations from coal to hydrocarbons. A poignant example was butadiene production at Huels. Before and during the war, butadiene was largely produced from acetylene made by the arc process, using low molecular weight hydrocarbons recovered from coal hydrogenation (although small quantities of natural gas liquids from the German gas fields were also used to supplement coal). This production mode for butadiene became a problem after the war, when coal hydrogenation was largely discontinued and coal became increasingly expensive. In 1953, a French firm with interests in synthetic rubber production offered Huels a long time supply contract for alcohol produced from red wine—available in large surplus quantities in that country—which could be used to produce butadiene, using one of the earlier process technologies. The offer elicited much humor in Germany at a time when this was a rare commodity. Journalists suggested that instead of importing ethanol, a red wine pipeline should be installed, running directly from Bordeaux to the Ruhr, so that other, more broadly shared benefits could be derived from the proposed transaction. It was also suggested that if the deal went through, it would be appropriate to say "Salut!" or "Prost" after changing an automobile tire. In the event, Huels turned down the French alcohol as too expensive a material for its future production of Buna rubber (1, pp. 120–121). Huels was still adding electric arc facilities over this period, as not only acetylene but also the associated ethylene were needed in increasing quantities for the production of vinyl chloride and detergent intermediates. Meanwhile, production costs kept rising and raw materials supply was a continuing problem. Moreover, rubber exports were not competitive, relative to U.S. producers. The company finally decided that it should, as soon as possible, adopt the process technique used for the production of GR-S rubber in the United States, which was based on the dehydrogenation of butylene or of natural gas-based liquids or refinery butane. Studies showed that dehydrogenation of normal butane would represent the best approach for use at Marl. It was some time, however, before enough butane would be available from German refineries to make this a practical alternative. During the time that the supply of butane was being studied, Huels took a license from the Houdry Corporation,* covering a process for the dehydrogenation of butane to butadiene. A catalyst plant was built, jointly owned by Huels and Houdry. Finally, in 1956, the decision was made to proceed with the new butadiene plant, which commenced operations in 1958—13 years after the end of the war (1, pp. 122-123).

The 1950s, then, were the years when European and Japanese chemical producers had to decide how to adapt to a new international industry and to select the product slates they saw as being most appropriate to their circumstances and to their visions of the future. The timing of their actions and the choices they ultimately made represent a wide variety of reactions and views of the future. These were, to some extent, also related to the circumstances specific to the country involved.

The French industry took a fairly long time to consolidate its organic chemicals business, because smaller firms in that country were more resistant to giving up their individuality. Also, the low cost of hydroelectric power in the French Alpine region, which had provided some of its companies an important competitive advantage, slowed the transition from electrochemistry to petrochemistry. German firms tended to be more skeptical of the benefits of oil versus coal feedstocks and generally did not embrace petrochemistry with great enthusiasm. They were also more interested in rebuilding and then expanding their specialty chemicals and pharmaceutical operations than in plunging into the production of bulk organic chemicals made from oil. Except for BASF, which acquired an oil company (Wintershall), the I.G. Farben successor companies depended on refiners to provide reactive hydrocarbon streams, rather than using their own capital to build expensive crackers. England, Belgium, and the Netherlands made somewhat more rapid progress into petrochemicals, because of the more extensive programs undertaken by the oil companies in those countries, as well as due to stronger government support.

*This company later became a division of Air Products and Chemicals Corporation.

An important factor acting as a spur to drive the European and Japanese industries into the production of petrochemicals was the need to build synthetic fiber and plastics plants to make up for a lack of indigenous raw materials. Since Europe and Japan import much of their wool and all of their cotton, the advent of nylon, polyester, and acrylic fibers was an even greater boon for these regions than for the United States. Also, due to their more limited timber resources, Europe and Japan saw plastics as an important locally produced substitute for wood and paper in many building and packaging applications. Largely for that reason, German per capita consumption of plastics, in due course, rose above that in the United States and it has remained there ever since.

While the European chemical industry was rebuilding some of its prewar plants and deciding what technologies and feedstocks to use in the future, U.S. firms found Europe an excellent outlet for chemical exports. Companies such as DuPont, Union Carbide, and Monsanto established sales offices at an early point and many others followed. Some of these companies also set up or acquired limited European manufacturing operations before the war. The new sales offices were often set up quite independently, acting primarily as order takers, with product shipped to European customers from U.S. plants in 55 gallon drums. It was not an ideal way to supply bulk chemicals, which are freight sensitive, but for a time it was the best, or only source, of the chemical involved.

Some of the most important products exported to Europe and Japan in the early and mid-1950s were petroleum-derived aromatics. The commercialization of modern catalytic reforming and extraction technology made large quantities of benzene and mixed xylenes available to the U.S. petrochemical industry. In some cases, the markets available to use these materials grew more slowly than the supply, leading producers to look at the export market. This seemed reasonable, since Europe and Japan were still deriving aromatics from coal tar, a more expensive source. The career of one of the early aromatics traders, Dewey Mark, was launched after Cosden Petroleum Company built a Udex extraction unit in Big Spring, Texas, in the early 1950s. The company had signed a five-year contract in 1952 to deliver xylene to a large domestic chemical firm. Soon after the plant went into operation, the customer advised Cosden that it could not take the material, since its plans had changed. However, Cosden did not let the company off the hook and so another buyer had to be found. As it turned out, Japanese chemical companies around this time started to require very pure xylenes to make fiber monomers and recognized that such material was becoming available in the States. Fallek Chemical, an international trading firm, accordingly sold the Cosden xylene to Japan. This was the start of a long relationship between Fallek and Dewey Mark. After the Cosden contract with the original buyer ran out, Fallek started exporting large amounts of Cosden xylene directly to Japan and Europe. Udex-derived benzene also had a purity that could not be matched by coal tar-derived material and therefore became a preferred product in many applications. Fallek and Cosden therefore cooperated to market Cosden's benzene in Europe and Japan, as well.

Eastern States Petroleum Company in Houston was another firm that built one of the early Udex units. Ed Von Doersten, later president of Ashland Chemical Company, and Tom Moran, now president of the Petrochemical Founders' Club,* were active in selling part of the company's production of benzene, toluene and solvent xylenes abroad. At first, this material moved in drums and sometimes in tramp steamers. A terminal was eventually established in Dortrecht, Holland, and then a second one at Leghorn, Italy. Between 1956 and 1959, Eastern States' annual sales of aromatic solvents to Europe increased from 40,000 to 250,000 barrels (5,000 to 33,000 metric tons).†

In the late 1950s, firms in Italy and Japan developed technology to make phthalic anhydride from ortho-xylene (instead of the traditional naphthalene feedstock). Fallek was again able to act as an intermediary by convincing Cosden and other U.S. firms to install superfractionators that could separate the ortho fraction from the other close-boiling xylene isomers. By the early 1960s, export of o-xylene had become a huge business. By that time, Dewey Mark had joined Tenneco, which had built a large aromatics complex at Chalmette, Louisiana. This plant shipped as much as 50,000 tons per year of o-xylene to Europe and Japan and counted a number of the major German firms, including BASF, as customers for benzene and ethylbenzene, the feedstock for styrene monomer.

In the early 1950s, Charley Steuber, then involved in selling drum quantities of Union Carbide's oxygenated chemicals to

---

*This organization of roughly 300 members meets once a year for a "black tie" dinner at the annual convention of the Chemical Division of the National Petroleum Refiners Association, usually held in San Antonio, Texas.

†Ed Von Doersten, personal communication.

Europe, approached the company with an idea. Why not convert a war surplus 10,000 ton T-2 tanker into a compartmented bulk cargo vessel that would ship organic chemicals to a proposed European terminal, from which deliveries could be made to customers on the Continent? When Carbide turned down this idea, he left and founded his own company to carry out this plan. The first converted tanker, named *Freddie,* was placed in operation, delivering to a terminal in the Netherlands. A second vessel, *Alchemist,* was commissioned in 1961 with a capacity around 20,000 tons. Soon thereafter, other companies followed this example. To avoid corrosion during shipment, Dimethcote, a zinc-cladding material, was used for the construction of the compartments. Stainless steel valves, pipes, and fittings were also employed.*

American export of chemicals of various kinds thus increased rapidly during the 1950s. The value of total exports of all chemicals rose from $163 million in 1939 to $1.3 billion in 1955 (2). Among the more important exported petrochemicals in the mid-1950s were carbon black, synthetic phenol, ethylene glycol, butanol, vinyl resins, and polystyrene resins. Whereas, in 1929, chemical imports and exports had been essentially in balance, imports stayed at a low level throughout the 1950s and much of the 1960s (e.g., around $300 million in 1955), while exports boomed.

As European economic conditions normalized and then started to improve rapidly, consumption levels for various consumer items rose correspondingly, resulting in accelerated demand growth for chemicals and synthetics. This provided increasing rationale for the construction of local plants, partly to stem the rising wave of imports. European production of organic chemical intermediates and particularly of plastics were now increasing at a rapid rate (Fig. 9.1). Firms in the United States thus had to decide on policies to continue to serve this expanding market. Options in most cases included (1) a step-up in exports, if possible, (2) construction of wholly owned plants in one or more countries, (3) joint ventures with local firms, or (4) licensing U.S. technology to foreign firms, with payment either in the form of royalty income or part ownership of a foreign entity using the technology. All of these techniques were employed, the choice depending on the company and on circumstances.

Monsanto generally took a conservative approach. The company had developed outstanding polystyrene technology, for

*Dewey Mark, personal communication.

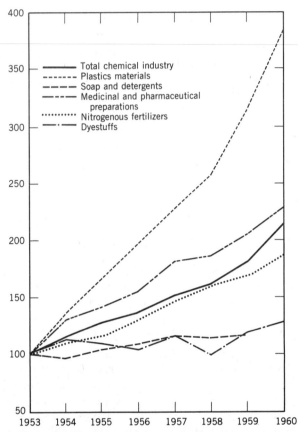

Figure 9.1 Development of the European chemical industry and certain branches (1953 = 100). (*Source: The Chemical Industry in Europe, 1960–1961,* O.E.C.D.)

which there was great demand in Europe. To capitalize on its position, Monsanto entered into a number of joint ventures with European firms (e.g., in France, England, and Spain) to build styrene and polystyrene plants.

Dow was considerably bolder in its European strategy. Midland management decided, soon after the end of the war, that it should establish a strong presence in Europe, but it had little international experience. Partly for this reason, the company engaged the services of Zoltan Merszei, a Hungarian with a strong entrepreneurial bent, who persuasively urged Dow's management to let him guide Dow's penetration of the European market. Merszei built up a large export business to Europe and other parts of the world, selling many of Dow's traditional products, including polystyrene and chlorinated solvents. By the mid-1950s, Merszei was able to show that wholly owned European manufacturing facilities should now be erected by the Midland firm.* Several small projects were approved by Dow's management. Not many years later, a large grass roots petrochemical complex was built in Terneuzen, Holland, the first by a U.S. chemical firm. Dow could now continue to be competitive with the European companies, which by the end of the 1950s were again starting to produce commodity chemicals on a fairly large scale. Later, Dow built a second complex at Stade, Germany. Both complexes were centered on a large chlor-alkali facility that could transfer chlorine at low cost to downstream users. Derivatives plants made traditional Dow products, such as ethylene oxide, vinyl chloride, chlorinated solvents, and propylene oxide. Dow's selection of Holland (for logistical reasons involving intra-European trade) and later of Germany (due to availability of low cost nuclear power) were symptomatic of the way U.S. firms were not constrained in any manner regarding optimum plant location in the Common Market. Later, some of the European firms, notably ICI, BASF, and Montedison, followed this example.

Union Carbide was among the first chemical companies to establish European petrochemical operations, with ethylene glycol and polyethylene plants built in the late 1950s in Antwerp, Belgium. Recent discussions with ex-Carbide executives indicated that there was a considerable amount of study work in the early 1960s involving the construction of a grass roots petrochemical complex similar in concept to the plants that Dow built at Terneuzen. However, Union Carbide management eventually turned down this project. Later, there was considerable regret that this decision allowed Dow to become what many felt was the world's preeminent petrochemicals producer. Up to that point, Union Carbide had been the leader in that field.

Most of the major U.S. chemical companies sooner or later established wholly owned manufacturing plants or joint ventures in Europe. DuPont built fiber plants in Northern Ireland, but also entered into a joint venture for urethane intermediates in France. Wyandotte Chemical and Kuhlmann built a jointly owned polyols

*Zoltan Merszei, personal communication.

plant, also in France. Union Carbide entered into joint ventures with Montedison (Celene, producing glycols, amines, surfactants, LDPE), with Distillers Corporation (BXL, Ltd. producing LDPE, PVC film) and with Fostfatbolaget in Sweden (Unifos, LDPE). PPG Industries entered into a joint venture with Rumianca in Italy to make PPG's line of chlorinated solvents. Celanese and K.Z.K. in Holland negotiated a joint venture to make methanol derivatives, acetic acid and other products. And Tennessee Eastman and Huels established Faserwerke Huels, using Eastman's technology to make polyester fiber for the European market.

In addition to Shell, other U.S. oil companies also established a number of European joint ventures. Thus, Phillips Petroleum hooked up with Petrofina in Belgium (Petrochim—olefins, cumene, aromatics, ethylene glycol), with Rhône Poulenc (polyolefins), with Calvo Sotelo, Foret, and Cros in Spain (Calatrava—butadiene, SBR rubber, carbon black, HDPE), and with ICI (refinery products). Gulf entered joint ventures with Banco Bilbao and several other companies in Spain (Fertiberia—ammonia, urea, fertilizers and Rio Tinto—(aromatics, cyclohexane). Chevron established joint ventures with Progil and Antar (California Atlantique—paraxylene) with CFR and Progil (Petrosynthèse—detergent intermediates) with BP (Grange Chemical—phthalic anhydride and alkylates), and with CEPSA and INI in Spain (Repesa—fertilizers).

U.S. chemical investment abroad increased rapidly, rising from $572 million in 1950 to over $3 billion by 1964. Between 1964 and 1967, it rose by an additional 1.7 billion. About 40 percent of this investment was directed to Europe, primarily the Common Market, Britain, and Scandinavia. During this period, investment in foreign chemical projects averaged 17 percent of all U.S. foreign investments, a figure roughly double the prewar level. It is reasonable to surmise that this substantial increase was largely due to superior American technology and high worldwide growth rates for the products involved.

Funds for foreign investments came from (*1*) transfer of capital abroad, (*2*) reinvestment of earnings from foreign operations, (*3*) reinvestment of depreciation cash flow, and (*4*) foreign borrowing. The latter method became very popular when the Eurobond market was established in the early 1960s. Merszei recently claimed that essentially all of Dow's capital requirements in Europe were met from locally generated cash and from local borrowings.* To fa-

*Zoltan Merszei, personal communication.

cilitate its financial transactions, Dow purchased a small bank in Zurich. Dow's European headquarters were also located in Switzerland and remain there to this time, at Horgen near Zurich.

Brussels, which had been selected as the seat of the European Economic Commission, became one of the favorite cities for locating corporate offices designed to serve the Common Market. Thus, Monsanto established its headquarters there, as did Esso Chemical and ICI.* The British firm, which had established manufacturing operations in Holland, Spain, France and elsewhere by that time, created ICI-Europa to look after its activities on the Continent. Meanwhile, the chemical firms on the Continent had started major programs to launch their operations into the petrochemical arena.

THE EUROPEAN RESPONSE

Although it took some time for Europe's chemical manufacturers to build up momentum, the switch to petrochemicals was in full swing by the end of the 1950s. Perhaps for this reason, the Chemical Marketing Research Association (CMRA) featured a review of the status of the European chemical industry at its October 1960 annual meeting, held in Portsmouth, New Hampshire. Papers presented on the condition of the chemical industries in Germany, France, England, and Italy at that time gave a good deal of information regarding the progress of petrochemicals manufacture in these key European countries. Some of the following is taken from these papers (3).

Germany

While slow to get started, production of synthetics in the German Federal Republic started to boom in the late 1950s (see Fig. 9.2). Plastics production, already fairly significant in 1955, almost doubled over the next four years, increasing at almost twice the rate as in the United States. This is noted on Table 9.1 from the paper by H. Sinkel of Huels, which also provides information for several other countries and for the world as a whole. In 1959, German production of PVC and copolymers was about 140,000 tons, polyethylene and polypropylene 60,000 tons, and acrylic and methacrylic polymers 25,000 tons. Production of noncellulosic

---

* Brussels was also later selected as the headquarters of the European Petrochemical Association. Eric Yates, originally with Monsanto Europe, remains active as secretary of EPCA.

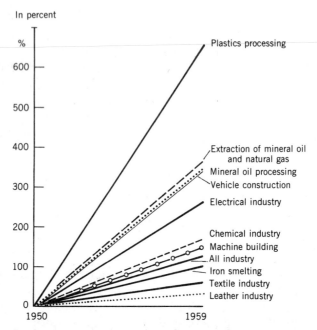

Figure 9.2 Production increases in various German industries, 1950–1959. (*Source:* H. Sinkel, The Chemical Industry in Germany, paper presented at the Chemical Marketing Research Association, Portsmouth, New Hampshire, October 3, 1960.)

fibers also accelerated strongly toward the end of the 1950s. In a 12-month period in 1958–1959, total production of non-cellulosic staple and yarn (largely nylon, polyester, and acrylics) increased from 24,000 to 38,000 tons.

Nevertheless, coal-based chemicals at that time still constituted a larger percentage of total production than those based on petroleum feedstocks. Such key chemicals as ammonia and methanol were still made via coal gasification, while acetylene remained the main feedstock for vinyl chloride, acrylonitrile, vinyl acetate, and other important organics. Benzene and other aromatics were still largely derived from coal tar processing, although imports were starting to become important. It was estimated that only 40 percent of the total volume of organic chemicals produced in Germany in 1960 were based on petroleum or natural gas, versus 80 percent in the United States at that time. Acetylene was projected to remain the preferred feedstock versus ethylene, due to the favorable cost of coal and electricity in the Ruhr basin. This feedstock choice had already been proved wrong for butadiene at Huels, but, as noted earlier, German companies were reluctant to abandon their traditional coal-based chemistry. Still, the C.M.R.A. paper projected substantial future increases in the production of "petrochemicals," acknowledging the fact that German coal tar supplies would not increase at anywhere near the rate required to supply feedstocks for the production of organic intermediates. With German refineries at that time likewise unable to meet the demand for reactive hydrocarbon streams, substantially increased imports of propylene, butylenes, benzene, and xylenes were foreseen.

The large I.G. Farben successor companies were well reestablished and in vigorous competition. Bayer, BASF, and Hoechst each had turnovers over $ 500 million, and all had some involvement with petrochemicals. Huels, Wacker, Kali-Chemie, Dynamit-Nobel, Henkel, and Degussa were smaller, though increasingly important companies in the German chemical industry.

At the time Sinkel's paper was published, Germany was experiencing an unprecedented economic boom, often referred to as "the German Miracle." Unemployment was almost nonexistent and laborers (called "guest workers") were being imported from Turkey, Yugoslavia, and other countries still in poor economic straits. In Germany, strong economic growth was sustained for a number of years thereafter, with continued beneficial effect on various industries, including the new petrochemical industry.

France

The prewar bulk chemical industry in France basically comprised three types of companies: Collieries (coke oven operators process-

Table 9.1 Plastics Production in Metric Tons

Country	1955	1958	1959
United States	1,700,000	2,115,000	2,510,000
Germany	425,000	621,000	795,000
Great Britain	330,000	425,000	510,000
France	95,000	210,000	290,000
Italy	98,000	165,000	250,000
Japan	95,000	300,000	415,000
World Total (Approx.)	**3,200,000**	**4,800,000**	**6,000,000**

Source: See ref. 3.

ing coal tars), electrochemical producers, and fertilizer companies. Important companies in the first group included Houillères du Bassin du Nord (H.B.N.) near Calais, Houillères du Bassin du Lorraine (H.B.L.), near the German border, and Houilleres du Bassin du Midi (H.B.M.) in the South of France. Electrochemical producers generally were also involved in aluminum and other industries that were heavy users of electric power. Pechiney, Progil, and Ugine, all with operations south of Lyon in the Haute Savoie or in the Maritime Alps, were the most important in this group. These companies were the primary chlorine producers and used cheap hydropower to produce calcium carbide for the manufacture of acetylene. Kuhlmann was primarily a fertilizer producer, but with some joint ventures with collieries. In a subsidiary role were companies with a background in fermentation chemistry (alcohol, acetone, etc.) notably Usine de Melle. And, of course, there was Rhône-Poulenc, a firm preeminent in the production of man-made fibers, as well as organic intermediates, fertilizers, and pharmaceuticals.

The event that launched the petrochemical industry in France was the discovery of large deposits of very sour (sulfur-containing) natural gas near Lacq in the Southwest, close to the Pyrenees. Processing of hydrogen sulfide for the production of elemental sulfur for the fertilizer industry and other uses started shortly after the end of the war. A steam cracker was later constructed by Société Nationale des Pétroles D'Aquitaine (S.N.P.A.) and, a number of other joint venture companies were established to make a variety of derivatives on this site. These included Acetalacq (acetaldehyde), Aquitaine Chimie (ammonia, methanol from natural gas), Azolacq (ammonia), Methanolacq (methanol), and Vinylacq (vinyl chloride).

Marcel Bohy, who was an executive with CdF Chimie for many years and later on the board of Rhône Poulenc, recently mentioned that the management of French chemical companies was really alerted to the promise of petrochemicals when Dr. Carl Wurster of BASF spoke on this subject in Paris in the early 1950s. Wurster particularly emphasized the role of chemical research and process development, which, according to Bohy, was not as close to the consciousness of these executives as it became soon thereafter. For example, the Gillet family, the major shareholders in Rhône Poulenc, was more familiar with textile activities than with producing the monomers that were used to make the synthetic fibers.

This changed rather quickly after that. Rhône Poulenc was the first French firm to launch a major petrochemical project not based on Lacq gas—a synthetic phenol plant in 1954.*

In the 1950s, some of the collieries, which had already been producing some ethylene recovered from coke oven gases (e.g., H.B.L. at Mazingarbe), entered into joint ventures with chemical companies to make synthetics. A typical case was Ethylène-Plastique, established by H.B.N., Pechiney, and Air Liquide to make high pressure polyethylene. Oil companies also formed joint ventures with chemical firms, including Naphtachimie (see earlier in this chapter), Shell-St. Gobain (the latter a glass company with chemical operations), Standard-Kuhlmann, and Progil-Antar (the latter a smaller independent French oil refiner). Another example was Manolène, a joint venture company established to produce high density polyethylene, which was formed by Rhône-Poulenc, Kuhlmann, and Compagnie Française de Raffinage (C.F.R.), France's large international oil company. Acetylene was produced in Lorraine via methane cracking and used for the manufacture of acrylonitrile.

Similar to the situation in Germany, French petrochemical production was expanding rapidly by the end of the 1950s. For example, in 1959, ethylene production rose by 112 percent, methanol production by 74 percent, and PVC production by 48 percent. Carbon black production rose from 20,000 tons in 1956 to 66,000 tons in 1960, an increase of 230 percent. And plastics production increased from 35,000 tons in 1952 to 250,000 tons in 1960.

Technology for the production of petrochemicals in France came largely from outside the country, except in the fertilizer area, where such firms as Kuhlmann, Air Liquide-Grande Paroisse, and O.N.I.A. were technically advanced and very active. As was the case in most other European countries around that time, steam cracking technology came from firms such as Lummus and Stone and Webster, ethylene oxide know-how from Scientific Design (e.g., for Naphthachimie and Marles-Kuhlmann), and polyethylene technology from German, United States, or British firms.

France's chemical industry not only started with a relatively large number of companies, but also formed innumerable joint ventures, some containing a large number of partners. When big steam crackers started to be built in France, they were often shared by

*Marcel Bohy, personal communication.

four or five companies, a good example being the Feyzin cracker near the Belgian border, which was also shared by Solvay, a Belgian firm with large capacity in vinyl chloride and PVC. By the late 1960s, there were 160 chemical joint ventures in France, of which Ugine-Kuhlmann had 44, Progil 34, Pechiney-St. Gobain 28, Rhone Poulenc 24, and Charbonnages de France 19.* It would take a great deal of time and a number of restructuring efforts by a series of governments to transform the French chemical industry into a reasonable number of companies with large enough plants to compete effectively within the Common Market and outside Europe. By 1972, however, Mike Hyde's *Chemical Insight*, a new and well-received newsletter on the world chemical industry, reported that ATO-Chimie, by then France's largest petrochemical group, was building the world's biggest polyethylene plant.

Great Britain

England's petrochemical industry came into being earlier than that in the other European countries, partly as a result of an infusion of American technology, but also due to important British technology developed in the early 1940s. Of particular importance was the work carried out at the ICI hydrogenation plant at Billingham, which had been constructed with German know-how. Here, hydrogenation work was directed at modifying the properties of various hydrocarbon fractions, one of the goals being to develop higher octane motor fuels. ICI, Shell, and Trinidad Leaseholds in 1941 built a gas oil hydrogenation plant at Heysham which, together with Billingham, produced about a half million tons per year of aviation fuels in this manner. Billingham also studied the dehydrogenation of cyclohexane, using a platinum catalyst, and came close to making the type of discoveries that UOP announced in the late 1940s, when it commercialzed its Platforming process (see Chapter 4).

Other noteworthy British accomplishments were (*1*) the start of production of a detergent based on olefins from wax cracking, as carried out by Shell in 1942 at Stanlow and (*2*) the Catarole process, an early oil-cracking technology practiced by Petrochemicals Ltd., at Partington, which produced both olefins and aromatics, using a copper-iron catalyst. This process was later abandoned as uneconomical, versus modern thermal steam cracking. (5)

*Dr. Aimison Jonnard, personal communication.

Like Germany, England remained wedded to coal as a chemical feedstock for longer than might seem reasonable, though petrochemical technology was implemented rapidly for the production of various derivatives. And when England's petrochemical industry started to grow, it developed its own characteristics. For example, polyethylene consumption grew much more rapidly in England than on the Continent, as did the consumption of solvents and synthetic detergents produced from petroleum feedstocks. Conversely, demand for ethylene oxide and ethylbenzene rose much more slowly than in some other European countries, such as Germany.

An indication of the progress of petrochemicals production in Great Britain is afforded by the fact that between 1948 and 1958, nearly $280 million was spent in this sector, which was then receiving a higher proportion of total industrial investment than any other British industry. This figure was also far larger than the corresponding investment figures for any other European country during this period. The major firms investing in organic chemicals manufacture were ICI, British Hydrocarbon Chemicals (a BP-Distillers joint venture), Courtaulds, Monsanto, Shell, and The Distillers Company itself.

Production of what was called "petroleum chemicals" in England tripled between 1953 and 1959, as indicated by the following table, taken from the C.M.R.A. paper (5).

Table 9.2   U.K. Production of Petroleum Chemicals, 1953-1959

Year	Output (Carbon Content) Thousands of Short Tons
1953	140
1954	180
1955	220
1956	240
1957	300
1958	330
1959	420

The rapid growth of low density polyethylene production in England also illustrates the remarkable growth of British petrochemicals in the 1950s and particularly between 1958 and the late 1960s. Of course, prices dropped sharply over the same period (Fig. 9.3) (6).

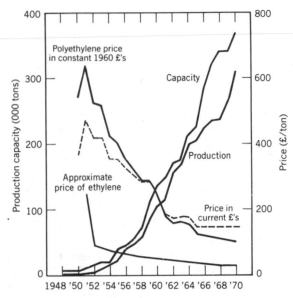

Figure 9.3 Production and price for low density polyethylene in Britain, 1948–1968. (*Source:* B. G. Reuben and M. L. Burstall, *The Chemical Economy,* London, Longman Group, 1973.)

In 1954, two-thirds of all chemicals were still based on coal and fermentation conversion technology. By 1959, this proportion was down to half. Thus, British Hydrocarbon Chemicals started the manufacture of synthetic ethanol from ethylene in the mid-1950s, constituting a significant switch for one of its partners, the Distillers Company. England also started production of p-xylene at an early stage, since ICI, the discoverer of Terylene, needed this feedstock for its growing polyester fiber business. ICI and Phillips Petroleum joined in constructing a new petrochemical refinery, which supplied aromatics and other hydrocarbons to ICI.

Not surprisingly, synthetic fiber production in the U.K. also grew faster than in other European countries. The growth rate for synthetic fibers in Great Britain was strikingly similar to that in the United States, after adjusting for a five-year time lag (see Fig. 9.4). By the end of the 1950s, British capacity for nylon was 70 million pounds, for polyester 50 million pounds and for acrylic fibers 30 million pounds per year. At this time, total German production of noncellulosic man-made fibers was well under 100 million pounds per year.

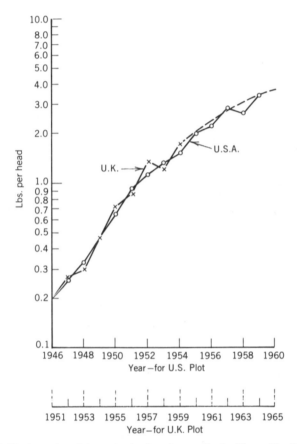

Figure 9.4 Postwar trend in output of main synthetic fibers (lbs/head) in the United States and the United Kingdom. (*Source:* J. H. Townsend, paper presented at the Chemical Marketing Research Association, Portsmouth, New Hampshire, October 3, 1960.)

In contrast to France, Germany and several of the other European countries, a single firm, ICI, dominated the British chemical industry, with activities across most of its sectors. In the petrochemical area, however Shell, British Hydrocarbon Chemicals and, later, Esso Chemical were a match for ICI in some areas—notably steam cracking and the production of organic solvents. In 1959, ICI's worldwide turnover was $1.4 billion, slightly under Union Carbide's ($1.5 billion) but considerably larger than that of Dow ($720 million) and Allied Chemical ($705 million).

Italy

Similar to the case of ICI in Great Britain, Montecatini was the early, dominant factor in the Italian chemical industry. This traditional old firm, with its rich background in research as well as in the production of a variety of chemicals before the war, led Italy's thrust into the petrochemical industry. Within a short time, however, Ente Nazionale Idrocarburi (ENI), the government oil monopoly, created a petrochemical subsidiary, ANIC, which quickly became a second important producer of petroleum-based chemicals. Then, Società Italiana Resine (SIR) became the third major company making important investments in this sector, which started to be heavily subsidized by the Italian government, as noted earlier.

Discovery of natural gas deposits in the Po Valley in the early 1950s was an important raw materials "breakthrough" for Italy, which had little or no crude oil and only poor quality coals. Thus, ammonia production was switched to natural gas at an early stage. Significantly, the first Italian steam cracker was already under construction in Ferrara in 1950, also based on Po Valley hydrocarbon feedstocks. Between 1954 and 1959, Italian steam cracking capacity, based on carbon content, rose from 16,000 to 180,000 tons.

Italy's plastics industry grew at a rapid pace. The country's industrial leaders took pride in the fact that Italy had constructed the first European PVC plant outside Germany in 1936 (a 1200-ton-per-year unit). PVC started as, and has always remained Italy's most important plastic material. Moreover, Montecatini and Prof. Guilio Natta were first to develop polypropylene, which was commercialized in Ferrara in 1957.

In the early 1960s, Montecatini merged with the Edison Group, a state-owned electricity monopoly that already had substantial chemical operations at Porto Maghera and Mantova, and at Priolo in Sicily. Edison was a substantial producer of such plastic resins as polyethylene, polystyrene, polyvinyl chloride, and polyvinyl acetate. Shortly after the merger, the combined firm, now called Montedison, put on stream a giant petrochemical complex at Brindisi in the Mezzogiorno region.

ANIC, the ENI affiliate, became particularly active in the production of synthetic elastomers and carbon black. This firm, as well as Montedison, SIR, and others, vied with each other to receive government grants and low interest loans to build petrochemical plants in the Mezzogiorno region, as noted earlier. As a result, there was much unneeded duplication of plants [e.g., six producers of polyamide (nylon) fibers in Italy by 1959]. It took a number of years and a great deal of later government intervention to reduce the glut of excess Italian petrochemical capacity.

While European firms were building up their petrochemical activities, U.S. firms did not slow their drive to become important factors in this arena. And they continued to benefit from advantages that went well beyond their strong position in petrochemical technology. American companies were much larger (except for ICI), more profitable, and they were considered to be better managed in a more modern manner than their European counterparts. Financial strength helped U.S. multinational companies to obtain larger amounts of credit from European banks and in plowing back more cash flow from operations into new investments. It also made it easier for U.S. firms to make acquisitions, although U.S. chemical firms were less inclined to do this than firms in the automobile, communications, and other industries. As noted earlier, the antitrust covenants of the Treaty of Rome actually made it easier for U.S. companies to buy European companies than for European firms to contemplate such mergers and acquisitions, a point not particularly appreciated by industrial circles on the Continent.

While some American companies saw the demise of the old cartels as an opportunity to establish European operations, others were not sure that the system was really dead. In the late 1960s, Chem Systems was asked by an oil company to make a study that would assess opportunities for the production of chlorinated solvents in the European Common Market. Dow had recently started production of these materials at Terneuzen, Holland, and had quickly captured 20 percent of the market. Our consultants visited many members of the prewar chlor-alkali "club," as well as a number of customers and distributors. What we found was that while the old producers had not been thrilled to welcome Dow to Europe, they admitted that they really could not keep out this strong and aggressive company, which had gone around and talked to all of the producers to tell them of its plans. (This was much later also confirmed to me by Zoltan Merszei.*) Accordingly, they had given up market share to Dow. Hearing this story, our client became con-

---

*Zoltan Merszei, personal communication.

Table 9.3   Chemicals and Allied Products: Sales by American-owned Plants Abroad and Exports from the U.S.: Selected Years, 1957-1967 (millions of dollars)

Year	Sales by U.S. Plants Abroad	Exports from the United States	Total
1957	$2,411	$1,376	$3,787
1959	2,950	1,558	4,508
1961	3,890	1,789	5,679
1963	5,130	2,009	7,139
1965	6,851	2,402	9,253
1967	9,000	2,803	11,803

Source: House Ways and Means Committee (ref. 7).

vinced that "Dow had joined the cartel," which was actually not at all the case. In any event, our client decided that this game was not for him and cancelled the project.

As U.S. companies started to invest more heavily abroad, the ratio of sales from their foreign plants to exports from the U.S. increased rapidly. This is shown in Table 9.3, taken from information compiled in 1968 by the House Ways and Means Committee as it studied foreign trade issues.

The higher profits enjoyed by U.S. companies also allowed them to invest more funds in research, which helped them to maintain their technological lead. In the early 1960s, profit margins of large corporations in the United States, running at the level of 6 to 7 percent of turnover, were over double those of large firms in the Common Market.

It seemed to Europeans that American firms had all the advantages: larger turnover, much higher profits, more money to spend on research, higher productivity, lower raw materials cost, and greater freedom to do business in Europe than the European firms themselves. In a widely read book, *The American Challenge,* written in the late 1960s by J. J. Servan-Schreiber (8), European industrial and government leaders were castigated for allowing American firms to achieve such a dominating presence in France and in the rest of Europe. An American businessman in Frankfurt was quoted by Servan-Schreiber as saying (8, pp. 3-9),

"The Treaty of Rome is the sweetest deal ever to come out of Europe. It's what brought us here . . . we're making money. And we're going to make a lot more. Whether the political negotiations in Brussels move ahead or not, prospects in commerce and industry are better for us here than they are in the United States."

And with respect to management practices, Servan-Schreiber gave the following illuminating quotation by another U.S. executive (8, p. 8),

"If a German manager wants to increase his production, he studies all the factors that go into the manufacture of his product. But, if I want to increase my production, I add to these same calculations our research and market predictions, so that I will know not only how to produce, but how to produce the desired quantity at the lowest cost. What interests me is my profit margin. What interests my European competitor is a factory that produces. 'It isn't the same thing.' "

The science of marketing was actually quite new to Europe. Servan-Schreiber quoted a McGraw-Hill report that stated (8, p. 9):

"The founders of the Common Market, men like Robert Schuman, Jean Monnet, and Walter Hallstein, can be proud of helping break down the barriers dividing Europe. But it is American business that has understood their idea and is helping Europe understand its own potential by applying, with some variations, the same methods America used to build its own enormous market."

During the 1960s and early 1970s, American firms continued to penetrate the European market, adding substantially to their investments on the Continent and in Great Britain. But Servan-Schreiber's Cassandra-like warnings had overstated the situation. U.S. chemical companies did not achieve anywhere close to a dominant position in any sectors of the European petrochemical industry. While additional U.S. firms, such as Ethyl Corporation, Amoco Chemical, and Oxirane* built plants based on proprietary U.S. technology, other ventures, such as the steam cracker, styrene, and cumene plants built by Gulf Oil in Holland were based largely on

*A joint venture of Arco Chemical and Halcon International, the successor company to Scientific Design Company—see Chapter 8.

corporate desire to establish a presence in the European market. Such moves were often not solidly based and led to early withdrawals when economic conditions turned down.

An indication of the relatively low total market shares of American firms in Europe's petrochemical industry is provided in Tables 9.4, 9.5, and 9.6, which list European producers of ethylene oxide, styrene, and cumene in 1972, a year when U.S. firms had not yet started their broad withdrawal from the European chemical arena (9). Other petrochemicals generally followed a similar pattern, except where American technology was not made available for license to European firms (e.g., terephthalic acid, propylene oxide). It is, however, significant to note that U.S. technology was

Table 9.4   European Ethylene Oxide Capacity (1972)

Country	Company	Thousands of Metric Tons/Year
Belgium	Basant	120
	Petrochim*	20
	Union Carbide†	120
France	Ethylox	90
	Naphthachimie	170
Germany	BASF	45
	Erdoelchemie	60
	Hoechst	160
	Huels	130
Italy	ANIC	25
	Montedison	70
Netherlands	Dow†	90
	Shell	215
Spain	Alcudia	11
	IQA	11
Sweden	MODO	40
United Kingdom	ICI	125
	Shell	45
	Union Carbide†	25

Source: Chem Systems. Multiclient Subscriber Report (1972)
*Joint venture including a U.S. firm (Petrofina/Phillips Petroleum)
†U.S. firm.

Table 9.5   European Styrene Capacity (1972)

Country	Company	Thousands of Metric Tons/Year
France	A.T.O.	80
	CdF Chimie	100
	S.N.P.A.	45
Germany	BASF	270
	Huels	170
	ROW (Shell/BASF)	240
Italy	ANIC	20
	Montedison	130
	SIR	50
Netherlands	Dow*	240
	Gulf*	220
	Shell	30
United Kingdom	Forth (BP/Monsanto)†	65
	I.S.R.	60
	Shell	75

Source: Chem Systems, Multiclient Subscriber Report (1972)
*U.S. firm.
†Joint venture including a U.S. firm.

Table 9.6   European Cumene Capacity (1972)

Country	Company	Thousands of Metric Tons/Year
Benelux	Gulf*	150
	Petrochim†	30
France	Rhone Progil	215
	Shell	100
Germany	Huls	100
	Veba	200
Italy	Montedison	70
	Saras	200
	SIR	150
United Kingdom	BP Chemicals	90

Source: Chem Systems, Multiclient Subscriber Report (1972).
*U.S. firm.
†Joint venture including a U.S. firm (Petrofina/Phillips Petroleum).

employed in many, if not most, of the plants listed in the three tables.

In a paper published around the same time as Servan-Schreiber's book, J. A. Stewart of ICI gave quite a different view of the relative influence and positions of U.S. versus European firms (10). He conceded that U.S. firms had a number of advantages stemming from their size, the large home market in which they operated, the fact that typical order sizes in the U.S. were several times larger than those in Europe and that U.S. firms were better capitalized, thus providing their workers the potential of achieving higher productivity. On the other hand, he was quite unwilling to endow U.S. companies with any magic advantages over their European counterparts, particularly in the area of technology and innovation. He claimed that Europeans were traditionally just as inventive as Americans, although the latter had perhaps done a better job of transforming inventions to commercial practice. Now, however, technology could be licensed by anyone willing to pay the license fees and this was allowing European firms to attack their market in the same way as American firms were doing. He went on to strongly criticize America for the "unfair" American Selling Price (ASP) system governing its import duties and suggested that it was now time for Europe to do something about this particular U.S. advantage. Projecting the near-term entry of Great Britain into the EEC, Stewart foresaw greater future cooperation between European firms and a time, not far in the future, when Europe's chemical companies would start major investments in the United States.

Rereading, some 20 years later, the views of Servan-Schreiber and Stewart, it is easy to conclude that Stewart's were the more prophetic. American companies had the greatest impact on Europe's petrochemical industry, in terms of product exports and technology transfers, but not in terms of investment and local industry domination. Trade in chemicals was heavily positive for American firms through the 1950s, 1960s, and 1970s, helping to establish and maintain a favorable U.S. balance of trade throughout this period. Thus, in an 11-year period from 1958 to 1968, chemicals and allied products earned an export surplus of more than $16 billion (2, p. 297). A substantial part of U.S. chemical exports were in petrochemicals and their derivatives. Technology transfers were very extensive, as U.S. firms were even more willing to license foreign companies than domestic competitors. A Booz Allen and

Hamilton study published in the late 1960s indicated that between January 1961 and December 1967, American companies producing chemicals and allied products concluded 150 licensing agreements with foreign groups and an additional 45 such agreements were made by rubber and plastics companies. While a number of petrochemical technologies were, in fact, developed in Europe (high and low pressure polyethylene, polypropylene, polyester fibers, urea, and others) a much greater number of processes were developed in the United States and licensed to European firms. Perhaps most importantly, the international oil companies, and U.S. engineering firms were largely responsible for building the steam crackers, reformers, and aromatics plants that provided the European petrochemical industry its basic foundation.

PETROCHEMICAL DEVELOPMENT IN JAPAN

The Japanese chemical industry differs from that of most other industrial countries in that it only dates back to the Meiji Restoration in the late 1860s, when Japan finally threw off its feudal origins to become a modern state. Government production of portland cement was commenced in 1871, sulfuric acid in 1872, caustic soda in 1880, and calcium carbide in 1904. Compared to European countries and the United States, Japan was therefore considerably behind in its chemical development. The same was, of course, true for many of its other industries.

Involved in three major wars with China, Russia, and the Western Allies between 1890 and 1918, Japan rapidly built up its explosives and fertilizer industries to meet the requirements of its new military machine, as well as its growing population. Over this time period, the major Zaibatsu groups, including Mitsui and Mitsubishi, also developed Japan's coal mining industry and started the production of coal chemicals, based on coke-oven operations. Viscose rayon production was established between 1907 and 1916 by two individuals and eventually led to the founding of Teikoku Rayon Company (now known as Teijin).

The country's chemical industry grew rapidly in the 1920s and 1930s, with the creation of a large number of firms. Synthetic ammonia production commenced in 1923, not long after such plants started being built in other parts of the world. This period also saw the start of a considerable amount of original chemical research, frequently patterned after development work in other countries. Nihon Synthetic Chemical Industry Company developed an acetic acid process in 1929 and Gosei Kogyo Company came up with independent methanol technology in 1932. High pressure coal hydrogenation was commenced in 1938 jointly by the Japanese Navy and South Manchuria Railroad Company, based on Manchurian coal deposits. During the same year, Professor Sakurada and Dr. Tomonari invented a process to make Vinyon fiber from polyvinyl alcohol.

Although in many respects Japan's chemical industry developed along fairly traditional lines, there were also special circumstances unique to Japan. Perhaps the most important of these was the fact that the country has very limited domestic raw materials resources. Japan imports 98 percent of its petroleum; 100 percent of its industrial salt, cotton, and wool; 85 percent of its iron ore; and 50 percent of its metallurgical coal. Consequently, most manufactured products carry a relatively high cost and there is a great need to develop exports to pay for the country's substantial import requirements. But the chemical industry, based increasingly on imported raw materials and, as it developed, on a great deal of imported technology, could not be counted on to redress the trade balance for some time.

Bombing raids toward the end of World War II eventually destroyed a large part of the country's chemical manufacturing base. In 1945, sulphuric acid production was 380,000 tons per year, corresponding to only 25 percent of prewar capacity. Other examples were rayon production, which was at 39 percent and calcium carbide at 40 percent of prewar capacity. For the first several years after the armistice, chemical firms struggled to reestablish prewar operations, with some Japanese and some U.S. government help. Then, the Korean war resulted in a boom for the Japanese economy, among other things allowing Japanese chemical firms to complete the rebuilding of their factories and to expand into many other areas.

By world standards, Japanese chemical companies in the mid-1950s were quite small. Sumitomo Chemical, Mitsubishi Chemical, and Showa Denko had sales volumes only one-fifth as large as those of Hoechst, Bayer, and BASF and one-third as large as Montecatini's. The small size of the Japanese firms exacerbated their problems, in terms of available capital for research and development and in their ability to compete in foreign trade. Shortage of investment capital was acute, with the result that companies operated with a high ratio of debt to equity capital, giving the banks a great deal of influence and control. In addition, the Ministry of International Trade and Industry (M.I.T.I.) closely monitored and controlled the acquisition of foreign technology and the investment programs of the Japanese firms.

Japan's petrochemical industry came into being in the late 1950s as a result of a fundamental study carried out by a Petrochemical Technology Committee set up by M.I.T.I. The committee had 20 executives from Japanese chemical firms, including Mr. T. Ishida and Dr. N. Nakajima from the Mitsui Group, Mr. K. Ikeda from Mitsubishi Petrochemical, and Mr. M. Masai from Sumitomo Chemical. Recognizing that other industrial countries had or were establishing a petrochemical industry, the committee assessed Japan's ability to emulate such a development and concluded that this would be next to impossible, unless imported technology were employed. This was particularly so, because the country's state of knowledge in certain industrial areas was considered extremely backward. While ammonia technology was quite advanced, there was little experience in the design and operation of plants that contained streams of highly flammable liquids at high pressures. Also, Japanese knowledge of instrumentation and process control was quite limited and the discipline of chemical engineering was not well developed. For these and other reasons, including the need to get started quickly, the Committee decided that all petrochemical technology should be imported rather than developed locally. In retrospect, this continues to appear as having been a very wise decision. Japanese companies, in this manner, would not only receive process technology to build various types of modern plants, but would also gain a great deal of general knowledge of modern design techniques, equipment and instrumentation.

The Committee started deliberations in November 1954 and finished its work three months later. Soon thereafter, three petrochemical complexes were authorized to be built, managed by Mitsui Petrochemical at Iwakuni (not far from Hiroshima), Mitsubishi Chemical at Yokkaichi (near Nagoya), and Sumitomo Chemical at Niihama (on Shikoku Island). A fourth complex was authorized shortly thereafter for Nippon Petrochemical, to be built at Kawasaki (near Tokyo). All of these complexes were based on central steam crackers. The first such cracker, a 20,000-ton-per-year Stone and Webster unit, started up in Iwakuni in 1958. Dr. A.

Mazume of Teijin recently noted that Japan did not have the option of using refinery offgases as a basis for a petrochemical industry since the American Occupation Government after World War II had a policy of not allowing Japan to build large refineries. Thus, cat crackers big enough to justify recovery of ethylene and other olefins were not available. As a result, Japan's petrochemical industry was largely based on cracking imported naphtha.* Moreover, as was pointed out to me by Dr. Y. Torii of Mitsui Petrochemical Industries Ltd., Japan really had no need to build cat crackers at that stage, due to the low consumption of gasoline in Japan in those years.†

Another engineering firm that furnished some of the earliest technology to Japan was Scientific Design, which licensed ethylene oxide and glycol know-how to Mitsui Petrochemical and Mitsubishi Petrochemical, and cumene technology to Mitsui. The technology transfers were usually arranged by the trading companies of the Zaibatsu groups involved (e.g., Mitsui & Company [Mitsui Bussan Kaisha] for Mitsui Petrochemical).

It should come as no great surprise that even in those early days of the country's petrochemical industry, the Japanese showed that they were good bargainers with the Westerners who were furnishing the badly needed process technology. M.I.T.I. directed the three process companies seeking ethylene process technology to bargain jointly with the U.S. contractors vying for this business. As a result, Stone and Webster agreed to a rather substantial discount to the three firms in order to be selected. They were rewarded by the fact that for some time thereafter, all Japanese steam crackers were designed by Stone and Webster. Mitsui Petrochemical's Noburo Nakajima, who had come from Miike Gosei (one of the three founding firms of Mitsui Petrochemical, together with Mitsui Chemical and Mitsui Mining) also turned out to be a tough negotiator. In his lengthy bargaining sessions with SD for several licenses, he and Akira Kume of Mitsui & Company were masters of the "bad guy, good guy" routine, well known in negotiating circles.‡ In the end, both Mitsui and SD were happy with the outcome.

Mitsui also became interested in terephthalic acid (TPA) technology since a possible by-product of cumene production was

---

*Dr. A. Mazume, personal communications.
†Dr. Y. Torii, personal communication.
‡Shigeru Ishihara, personal communication.

di-isopropyl benzene, a conceivable precursor to TPA. However, SD convinced Mitsui that its just-discovered Mid-Century route based on para-xylene was superior, leading to another license agreement. Maruzen Petrochemical also took a TPA license from SD around the same time.

Another firm that sold a great deal of process technology to Japan was Universal Oil Products Company (UOP). This was accomplished through the close relationship it established with Japan Gasoline Company, a large Japanese engineering firm and contractor. UOP may have been the first U.S. firm to license petrochemical technology to a Japanese firm when a small Udex extraction unit was built by Mitsubishi Oil, a joint venture partner of Getty Oil Company, in the early 1950s. Chuck Campbell, later a Vice President of Chem Systems, lived in Japan for Getty Oil at that time and participated in this transaction. The plant was erected by Chiyoda Engineering, which later became one of the largest Japanese contractors, headed by Tamaki-san, who had come to Chiyoda from Mitsubishi Oil. Another example of close Japanese-U.S. engineering company cooperation was the relationship of the Lummus Company of Bloomfield, New Jersey, with Toyo Engineering Company, whereby the latter gained access to Lummus' steam cracking technology and other processes for the construction of plants in Japan and, later, for export to companies in other parts of Asia and to the U.S.S.R.

Establishment of steam-cracking installations utilizing naphtha feedstock was as logical in Japan as it was in Europe, again due to the fact that the country's refining industry was more oriented toward the production of fuel oil than gasoline. In fact, when allocating imported crude oil to refineries, the government would authorize first 1.0 and later 2.3 barrels of crude oil for every barrel of naphtha cracked to petrochemicals, thus creating an important incentive to build crackers and adjoining derivatives plants to use the ethylene, propylene, and the other reactive streams coming from the crackers. Between 1960 and 1970, the use of naphtha as a chemical feedstock rose from 17 to 46 percent of all naphtha produced in Japanese refineries, even though gasoline production tripled over this period.

The advent of steam cracking brought about major changes in the production techniques for various other chemicals. Ammonia, which had been produced partly via electrolysis of water and partly from coke-oven offgases was now increasingly produced

from the by-product gases coming from cracking plants. Aromatics
started being recovered in large quantities from steam cracker pyrolysis gasoline and from catalytic reformers, although the Japanese iron and steel industry remained an important source of benzene (in contrast to what happened in the United States). By 1970,
70 percent of Japan's domestic toluene and 84 percent of its xylene
came from petroleum feedstocks, although 55 percent of its benzene
was still recovered from coal tar processing. (In fact, it took some
time for Japanese chemical companies to accept the purer benzene
produced from petroleum sources. When Udex-derived benzene was
first shipped from the United States to Japan, it was rejected since
"it didn't smell like coal-based benzene."*)

Petrochemical technology obsolesced Japan's fermentation
units when it was decided to start producing ethanol, acetone, and
butanol from petroleum feedstocks rather than from agricultural
wastes. The switch from acetylene to ethylene also proceeded fairly
rapidly in Japan, due to the high cost of coal and electric power
and government incentives to increase steam-cracking capacity.

While a great deal of Japanese petrochemical technology was
bought from engineering firms, such as Stone and Webster, Scientific Design and UOP, early licenses were also negotiated with
U.S. and European operating companies. Examples are high
pressure polyethylene (DuPont), polypropylene (Montecatini), phe-
nol/acetone (Hercules/Distillers), and acrylonitrile (Sohio). Mitsu
Petrochemical almost signed up for a high pressure polyethylene
license from ICI, but at the last moment switched to Ziegler linear polyethylene.† In some cases, joint ventures were formed with
such U.S. firms as DuPont, Dow, Union Carbide, Celanese, and
a number of others. Several of the Japanese oil companies were
partly owned by foreign firms, and some of these, such as Shell
and Esso also entered the petrochemical field, e.g., Shell and Mitsubishi Chemical, who founded *Mitsubishi Yuka* (Japanese for
"Mitsubishi Petrochemical").

The purchase of know-how through licensing arrangements required the outlay of what the Japanese considered as very substantial fees. Between 1957 and 1960, the start of Japan's entry
into petrochemicals, the annual cost of import licenses rose from
$4 million to $12 million per year. Over this period, total petro

*Kurt Duldner, Fallek Chemical, personal communication.

†Shigeru Ishihara, personal communication.

hemical investment increased from $62 million to $225 million, a ubstantial part of this being the cost of imported equipment and machinery.

Over the 1960s, Japan's chemical industry continued to import a great deal of foreign petrochemical technology. Some examples are dimethyl terephthalate from Dynamit Nobel and Hercules, actaldehyde from Wacker, polybutene from Amoco, as well as chlorinated solvents, maleic anhydride, and Nylon 6/6 intermediates technology from Scientific Design. Over this period, a number of other petrochemical complexes were constructed, including those of Tonen Sekiyu Kagaku at Kawasaki, Maruzen at Chiba, Daikywa at Yokkaichi, Idemitsu at Tokuyama, and Mitsubishi Chemical at Mizushima.

While it is a fact that a substantial part of Japan's chemical technology was imported, Japanese research also contributed in various sectors. Toyo Rayon developed a process for Nylon 6 during World War II. At Kyoto University, Professor S. Kodama analyzed polyethylene taken from the radar wires of a downed B-29 bomber and subsequently took the lead in developing technology for a high pressure process (later, however, an ICI license was taken by Sumitomo Chemical for Japan's first polyethylene plant) (11). Japan Catalytic Chemical Industry Company (Nippon Shokubai) commercialized its own phthalic anhydride process in 951 as well as an ethylene oxide and glycol process in 1959. In the early 1960s, Dr. Gomi, who headed research at Kureha Chemical Industry Company, developed unique technology to produce vinyl chloride by first cracking a liquid hydrocarbon at extremely high temperatures to obtain a stream containing dilute mixtures of ethylene and acetylene, followed by reaction with chlorine and hydrogen chloride, respectively. Later, Dr. Gomi also pioneered crude oil cracking to ethylene, at one point in cooperation with Union Carbide. Gomi became a senior adviser and representative of Chem Systems in the late 1970s, based on our personal friendship going back over some 20 years.

In a paper published in 1960, Dr. Ryogi Negishi of Nippon Petrochemical provided a large amount of statistical information on Japan's petrochemical industry at the time (12). One of the interesting conclusions drawn by Dr. Negishi was the fact that for a number of products Japan's industry was about 10 years behind the United States. Thus, in nylon, polyethylene and in synthetic detergents, Japan's production in 1960 was about equal to 1950 statistics in the United States. Still, considering Japan's smaller population, it was evident that the country was catching up fairly rapidly.

Japanese companies proved adept at modifying and improving petrochemical technologies and then exporting them to other countries, including to the West in many cases. In another good paper Dr. Alfred Saffer of Halcon International (formerly Scientific Design) and J. Yoshida of Nihon Oxirane track the timing for (1) the commercialization of certain process technologies in the West, (2) introduction of these technologies in Japan, and (3) export of technology for the product from Japan (11). In some cases, only a few years elapsed between (2) and (3). Many Japanese companies eventually became successful licensors, as indicated in Table 9.7 taken from that paper. Japanese companies continued to develop novel technology suited to the specific characteristics of Japan's chemical and refining industries. Thus, Mitsubishi Rayon and Japan Catalytic both developed technology to make methyl methacrylate from butylenes, since this steam cracker by-product finds relatively less use in Japanese refineries (versus the United States). In the United States, methyl methacrylate is still produced from acetone and hydrogen cyanide. Mitsubishi Chemical also found butylenes useful as a feedstock for making maleic anhydride, which is produced from benzene or butane in the United States and Western Europe.

In summary, over a relatively short period from 1955 to 1970, Japan built a huge petrochemical industry, with participation by a very large number of companies. Initially very much behind in chemical technology development, Japan was able to purchase modern processes from the West in order to be able to build plants employing the most modern technology available at the time. While the amount of indigenous technology development was initially modest, Japanese firms were often able to improve the technology licensed from the outside, thus making it suitable for reexport. As time went by, an increasing amount of technology was also developed in Japan.

One of the most successful Japanese developments was the work carried out by Mitsui Petrochemical in high activity polyethylene and polypropylene catalysts. Mitsui took a Ziegler license and then developed its own HDPE process. The company's management did not, however, take a foreign license in polypropylene technology, choosing instead to try and develop a process that would out-

Table 9.7A Chemical Technology Trade by Japanese Companies (in billions of yen)

	1972	1973	1974	1975	1976
Imports	41	25	27	27	29
Exports	16	17	23	22	26
Gap	25	8	4	5	3

Source: A. Saffer and J. A. Yoshida, (1980) Sources of technology *Chemtech,* November, 670–673.

rank the Natta-Montecatini patents. In this, it was partly successful. But unknown to Dr. Yasuji Torii, Mitsui's research executive, Montedison (successor company to Montecatini) was developing a similar high yield, high productivity catalyst that would avoid the problems of catalyst removal (deashing) from the polypropylene product. The story of the independent development work carried out by these firms in the 1970s, which ended in a cross-licensing

Table 9.7B Typical Processes Exported by Japanese Companies (1960-1978)

Technology	No. of Plants	Licensors
Acrylonitrile	2	Asahi Chemical
HDPE	9	Mitsui Petrochemical, Asahi Chemical, Mitsubishi Petrochemical
LDPE	8	Sumitomo Chemical, Toyo Soda, Mitsubishi Petrochemical
PVC	33	Sumitomo Chemical, Kanegafuchi, Japanese Zeon, Shinetsu Chemical
Polyols	3	Sanyo Chemical, Mitsui Toatsu
Polypropylene	12	Mitsui Petrochemical, Mitsubishi Petrochemical
Propylene oxide (chlorohydrin)	2	Nippon Soda, Mitsui Toatsu
ABS & SBR	8	Japan Synthetic Rubber
Ethylene	1	Mitsubishi Petrochemical

Source: A. Saffer and J. A. Yoshida, (1980) Sources of technology *Chemtech,* November, 670–673.

and joint venture agreement initialed by Dr. Torii and Dr. Italo Trapasso of Montedison, has been recounted in a fascinating chapter of a recent book (13). By the early 1970s, when the world would learn to try and cope with the effects of the "oil shock" and its various consequences, Japan had, in all respects, become a key producer of the full range of petrochemicals.

THE REST OF THE WORLD

This chapter has focused on industry developments in Western Europe and Japan, because these two regions followed the United States fairly closely in the establishment of their petrochemical activities. As a consequence, the production levels of most petrochemicals in the three regions were, for a long time, higher than those in the Comecon countries and in China. Several of the Communist countries did eventually become fairly large producers. And certain industrialized oil-rich countries, such as Canada, as well as some of the Third World countries, such as Iran, Saudi Arabia and Libya, plunged headlong into petrochemical projects when the world oil crisis appeared to give them a springboard (see Chapter 12).

Russia's and the rest of Eastern Europe's problem in establishing an oil- and gas-based chemical industry had more to do with finance and national priorities than with technology. Eastern Germany contained at least half of prewar Germany's chemical plant and many German chemists and engineers had stayed behind after the country was divided. As for Russia, it had long been a large oil producer and, as a consequence, a great deal of organic chemistry based on hydrocarbon feedstocks had been published over the years. (See Chapter 4 on Ipatieff's early work, for example.) But in spite of more than adequate knowledge of the required process technology, the pace of converting chemical plants from coal tar to hydrocarbon feedstocks and of building new chemicals plants in both of these technologically advanced countries was slow. There were simply not enough funds available for that, given the other items in these countries' five-year plans, as well as the military priorities arising as a consequence of the cold war.

Then by the early 1970s, Russia, Germany, and several of the other Comecon countries became very good customers of European and Japanese engineering firms anxious to secure the business to supply equipment and technology to the Eastern Bloc. Often unable or unwilling to pay for these plants in hard cash, the Comecon countries generally insisted on so-called "compensation deals," which called for the payment of services in the form of exports of a large percentage of the chemicals that would be produced in these plants. In most cases, plant purchases also involved long term loans from Western banks, guaranteed by the export credit agencies of the countries involved. The technology came from Western contractors or operating companies and, in many cases, approval was required—but almost always granted—by the governments involved. In this manner, Eastern Europe built a sizeable petrochemical industry over time, though still far smaller, in the case of most products, than that in Western Europe.

A comprehensive review of compensation deals with Eastern Europe was published in the late 1970s by *European Chemicals News* (14). The magazine lists over 100 such deals concluded in the years 1972 to 1978. The following are examples of only a few agreements concluded in the first year (1972):

- A 250,000-ton-per-year ethylene plant for Bulgaria, furnished by the French contractor Technip.
- An 80,000-ton-per-year polypropylene plant for Czechoslovakia, based on an Amoco process and furnished by Chisso and C. Itoh, a trading company in Japan.
- A 120,000-ton-per-year low density polyethylene plant for the U.S.S.R., with technology and equipment furnished by Salzgitter in Germany.

The sale of petrochemical process plants to Eastern Europe had two unfavorable effects on the Western countries, namely (1) loss of exports to Eastern Europe, and (2) the emergence of a rising tide of chemicals coming back from Eastern European plants and representing payments under compensation deals. These now had to be absorbed in Western markets. Since this problem became particularly acute just at the time when the European petrochemical industry was facing the recession caused by the first "oil shock," many operating companies that had licensed process technology to the East had second thoughts about the deals they had made.

An indication of the relative size of Eastern's Europe's petrochemical industry is afforded by figures published in two industry journals and shown in Tables 9.8 and 9.9 (15,16).

Table 9.8   Eastern European Petrochemical Production Capacities (1979) (thousands of metric tons)

	Ethylene	LDPE	HDPE
Russia	1,500,000	600,000	300,000
Czechoslovakia	700,000	150,000	80,000
Bulgaria	600,000	100,000	10,000
GDR (East Germany)	600,000	50,000	20,000
Romania	550,000	100,000	40,000
Poland	400,000	160,000	—
Hungary	250,000	60,000	60,000
Yugoslavia	250,000	130,000	50,000

Source: European Chemical News, March 17, 1980.

In synthetic ammonia, Russian capacity by the mid-1980s was higher than installed ammonia capacity in the United States. Synthetic rubber capacity was about 90 percent of U.S. capacity. However, Russia's ethylene capacity was far lower than that in either the United States or Western Europe and has stayed lower to the present time.

To cite another example of Eastern's Europe's petrochemical development, Chem Systems included such information in a study on the world styrene and styrenic resins business it published

Table 9.9   Eastern Europe's Chemical Industry (selected statistics, figures in thousand of metric tons)

	1981	1984
Russia		
Synthetic ammonia	14,718	17,445
Plastics	4,089	4,819
Synthetic rubber	1,860	1,850
East Germany		
Synthetic ammonia	1,203	Not available
Plastics	998	1,085
Synthetic rubber	155	152
Bulgaria		
Synthetic ammonia	1,023	1,138
Plastics	290	418
Synthetic rubber	30	26

Source: Chemical and Engineering News, June 9, 1986, p. 85, American Chemical Society, with permission.

in 1986. It shows a Eastern European styrene monomer capacity of 1.35 million metric tons in 1984, versus a Western European capacity of 3.4 million tons for the same year. For polystyrene resins, the corresponding figures were 791,000 tons for Eastern Europe versus 1.9 million tons for Western Europe (17). These figures show that Eastern Europe had been catching up over the six years when petrochemical construction was abating in the West.

Although Eastern Europe's petrochemical development program was relatively slow for the reasons indicated, East German and Russian research work in the areas was extensive over much of the period of the industry's growth and development. Researchers in most U.S. and other Western and Japanese companies were thoroughly aware of this work, particularly in the area of catalysis. In fact, publication of Russian work often led researchers in the West to consider new approaches. A good example of this was Halcon's development work covering the use of borate esters for the production of nylon intermediates from cyclohexane, as described elsewhere. This breakthrough was acknowledged to have been inspired by Russian work in a related area.

Russia pioneered certain process technologies, among which the synthesis of isoprene from formaldehyde stands out in my recollection. In some cases, Russian know-how was used by U.S. companies as a basis for getting into the production of certain chemicals, where a license from a Western company was either unavailable or too expensive. In the late 1960s, El Paso Products Company and Beaunit decided to build a nylon business based on El Paso's petrochemical production know-how and aromatic feedstocks and on Beaunit's position as a fiber producer. The companies decided to use Russian know-how for the cyclohexane oxidation step in a plant built at Odessa, Texas. At some point, Chem Systems was asked to assist in improving the operations of this unit. Based on our exposure to this project, it can be said that whatever the problems were at the time, Russian know-how was not the main cause.

The "internationalization" of the petrochemical industry proceeded in several stages. After the United States and Canada established this new industry in time to help win a major war, the more advanced European nations were forced to respond. England was in the best position, having suffered the least wartime damage. And the German companies, which had actually started to use a small amount of natural gas and oil feedstocks during the war, started to think hard about how to switch a much larger percentage of their production from the traditional base of coal to a more elegant source of carbon, i.e. petroleum feedstocks.

By the late 1950s, Germany, France, and some of the other European countries were well on the way to becoming petrochemical producers of some size, with a strong "assist" from the international oil companies operating refineries in these countries. And about that time, Japan decided that it would have to catch up as quickly as possible, with maximum reliance on imported technology. It was very successful in this endeavor.

Government priorities for military expenditures and for other industries kept Eastern Europe from establishing significant petrochemical operations until the late 1960s and early 1970s. Then, favorable financing arrangements from Western contractors anxious to obtain this business, made it possible for Russia and the other Comecon nations to build up a significant petrochemical capability in just a few years.

Finally, in the mid 1970s, the oil-rich countries decided that they had an advantage (some of them felt even a *right*) to build petrochemical plants, based on the fact that they had some of the most inexpensive and abundant raw materials of the required quality at a time when the rest of the world was short and was wondering what the future cost and availability of these feedstocks would be.

By this time, it was possible for any potential new producer in any part of the world to obtain modern production know-how, via licensing agreements, for manufacturing all but a few petrochemical products. Technology easily jumps over national borders. Dissemination of chemical manufacturing know-how was now essentially wide open, with obvious consequences for capacity additions in all parts of the world.

REFERENCES

1. P. Kranzlein (1980). *Chemie im Revier—Huels,* Duesseldorf, Econ. Verlag.
2. Jules Backman (1970). *The Economics of the Chemical Industry,* published by Manufacturing Chemists Association, February.
3. Chemical Marketing Research Association annual meeting, Portsmouth, NH, October 3, 1960, Papers by H. Sinkel, Jacques Roche, J. H. Townsend, G. Ballabio (CMRA Papers 315, 316, 317, 318).

4. R. Holroyd (1958). The development of the petroleum industry in Britain, *Chemistry and Industry,* July 19, 900–909.

5. J. H. Townsend (1960). The U.K. chemical industry, CMRA Paper 317, Chemical Market Research annual meeting, Portsmouth, NH, October 3.

6. B. G. Reuben and M. L. Burstall (1973). *The Chemical Economy,* London, Longman Group.

7. House Ways and Means Committee, Foreign Trade and Tariff Proposals, Part 2, June 5 and 10, 1968, Washington, DC, 1968, p. 548.

8. J. J. Servan-Schreiber (1968). *Le Defi American (The American Challenge),* New York, Atheneum.

9. Chem Systems, Information taken from the company's process evaluation/research planning (PERP) reports, a multiclient subscription program.

10. J. A. Stewart, Imperial Chemical Industries, West European chemical industry, CMRA Paper 665.

11. A. Saffer and J. A. Yoshida (1980). Sources of technology, *Chemtech,* November, pp. 670–673.

12. Dr. Ryogi Negishi (1961). Petrochemical industry features and its relation to industry in Japan, Presented before the Chemical Marketing Research Association, San Francisco, CA Nov. 28–Dec. 1, 1961.

13. P. R. Nayak and J. M. Ketteringham (1986). *Breakthroughs,* New York, Rawson Associates, pp. 286–1313.

14. *European Chemical News,* Chemscope, July 21, 1978, pp. 32–61.

15. *European Chemical News,* March 17, 1980, p. 22.

16. *Chemical and Engineering News,* June 9, 1986, p. 85.

17. Chem Systems Inc., World Styrene/Styrenics Industry, published in May 1985, New York, (A multiclient subscriber study.)

ADDITIONAL READING

The Chemical Industry in Europe (1954–1955), (1958–1959), and (1960–1961). Annual Review published by the Organization of Economic Cooperation and Development (O.E.C.D.).

Japan gets into petrochemicals, *Chemical & Engineering News,* May 2, 1956.

Morikawa, K. (1961). Basic problems of chemical market research in Japan, Presented before the Chemical Marketing Research Association, San Francisco, CA Nov. 28–Dec. 1, 1961.

Shohara, W. (1961). Chemical industry highlights in Japan, Presented before the Chemical Marketing Association, San Francisco, CA Nov. 28–Dec. 1, 1961.

Williams, Roger (1961). Chemical trends in the European Community, CMRA Paper 553.

10 / Winners and Losers: The Case of Vinyl Chloride

The dynamic growth of the U.S. petrochemical industry over the 25-year period following World War II will be studied for a long time. Seldom has such a multifaceted industry grown so rapidly, with such a large number of participants and with so many improvements in technology. But there was also a darker side, for in spite of rapidly growing markets and major breakthroughs in the technology and economics of manufacture, many of the companies participating in this industry did not even come close to achieving acceptable investment returns much of the time. Profitless growth was not a completely new phenomenon, since episodes of this kind in earlier times had led to the establishment of manufacturing cartels to prevent disruptive pricing and to avoid major battles over market share. But the era of cartels had come to a close in the 1940s and now the large number of competitors producing most of the important petrochemicals, and the much more stringent enforcement of antitrust laws, made cartels a relic of the past. Competition was particularly severe in ethylene and in many of the ethylene derivatives, such as ethylene glycol, polyethylene, styrene, and vinyl chloride. And for many of the other petrochemicals, the situation was not much better.

The often self-destructive behavior of petrochemical companies, competing with ever more efficient technologies in a rapidly

390

expanding market, has recently been echoed in other industries—for example, in the manufacture of integrated circuits for electronic applications. In such situations, the palpable dilemma that industry participants acknowledge, join to condemn, but cannot seem to do anything about is this: When technology breakthroughs become available to any company financially able to build a new plant and when more than one of these companies believes that it can thereby establish or protect a dominant position, the stage has generally been set for a period of very competitive pricing and minimal or nonexisting profits. This situation became the rule, rather than the exception for many products, much of the time, in the petro-chemical industry, starting in the mid-1960s. The earlier years of this period were a time of *de novo* entry for many new participants wanting to become involved in this dynamic industry. The latter period was characterized by efforts designed to force a shakeout of weaker producers—the companies that did not want to play the next chip in an increasingly expensive poker game.

When the Boston Consulting Group (BCG) started expounding the application of its famous Experience Curve and found a few converts in the chemical industry, these companies thought they now had a rationale for their profitless quest for increasing market share. However, BCG's own experience had, in considerable measure, been gained in industries where one company had acquired, and could also maintain, a large market share relative to a number of smaller competitors. Through the experience gained in manufacturing and selling much larger quantities of a given product, the industry leader conceptually made higher profits, which allowed that company to spend more funds for research, for production improvements, and for marketing the product. This always kept it well ahead of its competitors, proving the wisdom of the Experience Curve.

In the petrochemical industry, the Experience Curve (more often called the "learning curve") also applied, but to the entire industry more than to one specific producer. Thus, in products such as ethylene, ammonia, styrene, and also vinyl chloride, there are usually a number of producers using the same general technology. As time goes by, their manufacturing costs decrease, as they learn to improve catalyst activity, add energy saving schemes, and obtain capcity increases through minor debottlenecking investments. The company with the largest market share may move down the Experience Curve a little faster than the others, but not much faster.

Obtaining a larger market share (e.g., going from 10 to 15 percent market share) does not usually confer noticeably large cost advantages to the company involved, which might by that time be the largest U.S. producer.

Manufacturing costs in the chemical industry are strongly affected by technology breakthroughs, and these can be the result of inventions by any company (not necessarily the currently strongest producer) with a combination of research dedication, skill, and some luck. Moreover, technology dissemination, experience gained by contractors, and the construction of ever larger plants with improved economics of scale can also play a decisive role. This is what often happened in the petrochemical industry over this period.

If the breakthrough was made by an engineering firm, it would then mount an effort to license as many operating companies as possible with the new technology, since this produced an attractive combination of royalties and engineering-construction fees. As a result, a new player could often become the low cost producer for a period of time.

If the invention was made by an operating company, it would then attempt to commercialize the invention as soon as possible. Even though it might have no previous experience in manufacturing the chemical in question, this company could now become the low cost producer. To summarize: the tenets of the Experience Curve did not hold in the chemical industry, because in most petrochemical product areas, the industry leader could not maintain a dominant low cost position versus competitors for an extended period of time.

In the 1950s and 1960s, when the plants were not yet prohibitively large and costly, and when markets were still growing rapidly much of the time, the temptation to build new plants to serve these expanding markets was truly irresistible. If the industry added a bit too much capacity at certain times, due to excessive optimism regarding immediate demand growth, it was recognized that the market would soon catch up. Thus, a new wave of expansions would be planned and executed, hopefully with even better technology. And when a company built new plants with improved technology that would yield several million dollars per year of additional annual profits on paper, it anticipated that it would be in production a year or two before the competition caught up technologically and that some of the smaller players would now perhaps fold their tents and leave the business. And if this did not happen and even more new companies entered the business by building large new plants using the latest technologies, the existing producers could only hope that the industry would, at some point, come to its senses. But this happened much later, when the seductive music of double-digit growth had finally stopped. And, at this point, the players looked back and wondered why they had effectively given away the results of so much of their astoundingly successful research to the American consumer in the form of lower and lower prices, without keeping the financial benefits for themselves.

There were, of course, instances, such as in acrylonitrile, terephthalic acid, and propylene oxide, where Sohio, Amoco, and Oxirane Corporation, respectively, developed new production routes so much better than existing processes that they were able to become economically dominant producers, in spite of selective licensing (only foreign in the case of Amoco and Oxirane). But these were exceptions. In most other chemicals, the results of successful research were usually much less rewarding. If the new route represented a substantial economic improvement, but was not judged to be able to provide a dominant position, the company making the invention usually embarked on a licensing program, settling for the income provided by royalties and catalyst sales, as well as the presumed benefits of becoming a reasonably low cost producer. In other cases, the company could not establish a controlling position, because it could not obtain broad patent protection to keep competitors from developing relatively similar process routes. In still other cases, such as Badger-Sherwin Williams' fluid-bed phthalic anhydride process, the new technology was not so much better that it forced a wave of shutdowns. Here, the new technology just added one or two new competitors and upgraded the economics of some of the existing producers, who switched to the new process.

In the petrochemical industry, advances in technology involve either a less expensive raw material, fewer process steps, a more selective catalyst, or a combination thereof. Although many such advances were made, involving most of the important petrochemicals manufactured over this period, history shows that most of these did not provide a large enough economic advantage to shut down the more efficient existing producers. The technology improvements primarily increased competition in the industry and lowered the sales price of the product in question. They did usually contribute to a shakeout of the smaller companies using the older technologies.

Over the roughly 25-year period of rapid expansion of the industry, the manufacturing technology for most of the 40 or so "primary" and "secondary" petrochemicals underwent progressive change. For some of these (e.g., acrylonitrile, acrylic acid, acetic acid, chlorinated solvents, vinyl acetate), research resulted in the identification of a less expensive petrochemical raw material. In others (e.g., phenol, propylene oxide, adipic acid, hexamethylene diamine), a more efficient process was developed, that did not involve the use of a secondary reactant, such as chlorine, sulfuric acid, or nitric acid. In some cases (terephthalic acid, phthalic anhydride), new processes involving alternate feedstocks, although dramatic in their impact on the industry, did not confer a large enough advantage to shut down the most efficient producer or all plants using the older technologies. Thus, in terephthalic acid, the Mid-Century Process developed by Scientific Design and Amoco Chemicals, which eventually made Amoco the world's largest terephthalic acid producer, never was able to shut down the DMT (dimethyl terephthalate) plants operated by DuPont, Hercules, and Hoechst. In phthalic anhydride, the breakthrough by BASF involving the use of o-xylene instead of naphthalene feedstock was not dramatic enough to shut down every naphthalene-based plant. In fact, it was subsequently countered by the fluid-bed naphthalene process developed by Badger and Sherwin Williams, which gave that raw material a new life for a period of time. Throughout this period of competition among phthalic anhydride process developers and users, the price of phthalic anhydride fell, as companies attempted to use the pricing advantage conferred by better technology to force other competitors to leave the business.

Often, the fact that new process routes allowed the use of alternate raw materials made the selection of technology for a new plant somewhat of a gamble, since it was difficult to predict the likely future prices of the two possible feedstocks. A good example is maleic anhydride, where Chem Systems, Monsanto, and others eventually developed processes based on n-butane, instead of the traditional benzene feedstock. Here, there was a tradeoff among plant investment, reactor yields, and feedstock price, with a substantial advantage for butane-based plants, unless the price of benzene fell to the low end of its cyclical range and butane near the high end. Eventually, most U.S. plants used butane-based reaction systems. Other process developments gave a simpler choice for companies evaluating new plants, particularly those involving a switch from acetylene to ethylene or propylene feedstock—olefins took over essentially all of these applications.

In most cases, the changes brought about by technological innovation occurred over a substantial period of time. There were a number of milestones, starting with patent filing dates. Then, at a later time, came the announcement of the new process, authorization by a company's management to build the first plant based on the new process, eventual startup, and the subsequent actions taken by the process developer. In most cases, these actions involved the granting of foreign and often also domestic licenses. Then, there were the countermoves by the other producers and process developers. These involved various decisions regarding either conversions to the new technology (if licensable), development and/or adoption of an alternate technology (where available), or eventual shutdown. This sequence of events was the rule for many, if not most, of the important petrochemicals. Each chemical in a way, contributed its own "case history."

In this chapter, we trace the changes that took place in the manufacture of vinyl chloride monomer over a period lasting from the late 1950s to the early 1970s. This chemical was selected because, in many respects, its history is a microcosm of the entire industry. To follow the development of vinyl chloride production over this period of time is to understand most of the salient issues that make up the history of growth and technological change during the "go-go" years of the petrochemical industry.

Some of the key developments that chronicle the market growth, technology changes, and profitability problems of vinyl chloride production are summarized below:

- From 1952 to 1970, the demand for vinyl chloride, primarily used for the production of polyvinyl chloride (PVC) resins and copolymers, rose from 321 million pounds per year to four billion pounds per year (see Fig. 10.1).
- Over the same period, the size of typical new vinyl chloride monomer plants increased from 30 million pounds per year to one billion pounds per year.

- At the start of this period, acetylene was the preferred raw material for vinyl chloride production. By the early 1970s, almost every producer was using ethylene.
- A dramatic process breakthrough, known as *ethylene oxychlorination,* was developed during this period and was eventually adopted by every new or remaining producer. However, more than one company developed versions of this type of process, so that oxychlorination technology did not give any one producer a dominant position.
- Several large companies became new entrants to the industry during the time interval under study. All of them presumably expected to become profitable producers with a substantial market share, but all of them found this objective unattainable. Their entry, in combination, did result in a number of other companies exiting the industry. It also greatly aggravated the already intense competition among the various existing and new producers.
- The price of PVC resins, which was in the range of 38 cents per pound in 1952, dropped to 16 cents per pound in 1961. Monomer

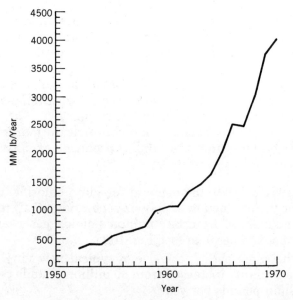

Figure 10.1 U.S. production of vinyl chloride monomer. (*Source:* Chem Systems.)

prices correspondingly fell from 13 cents to 6 cents per pound (1). This is remarkable when you consider that the consumer price index for all commodities rose from 87.0 to 92.0 over the same period and the index for fuel oil and coal from 78.0 to 91.0 (1967 = 100). Thus, vinyl chloride and PVC prices were dropping by over 50 percent while the consumer price index was rising.

The history of the vinyl chloride industry over the period in question is discussed in the balance of this chapter, enlivened to some extent by some of the more interesting events and sidelights.

BECOMING A VINYL CHLORIDE PRODUCER

The following were traditional reasons why companies might decide to manufacture vinyl chloride.

Back Integration from PVC. A company would conclude that it should be able to make vinyl chloride more profitably than it could buy it on the merchant market. In the early years, when there was no merchant market, a company that wanted to produce PVC resins would have had to make vinyl chloride as well. Of course, the company would have needed access to suitable technology, which was not always the case in the early days.

Chlor-Alkali Producer. A company with substantial chlorine-caustic capacity might view forward integration into vinyl chloride monomer as a logical step, particularly if the company felt more secure in marketing the caustic soda (than the chlorine) part of its production. Vinyl chloride is by far the largest outlet for chlorine, and this provides a good rationale for moving forward into production of monomer.

Forward Integration from Hydrocarbon Feedstock. This became the primary reasons why oil companies that built steam crackers decided to get into the vinyl chloride business. Vinyl chloride eventually became one of the largest ethylene users, not as big as polyethylene, but bigger than styrene, vinyl acetate, and several other ethylene derivatives.

Synergy with Other Operations. This might relate to one or more of the above rationales, but could also involve other reasons. Thus, Dow Chemicals and Union Carbide made ethylene dichloride by-product from their ethylene oxide plants, which they could use as part of the feedstock for making vinyl monomer. Dow produced chlorinated solvents by a hot chlorination step that allowed the utilization of heavy by-products obtained in vinyl chloride manufacture. Ethyl Corporation made ethyl chloride, which required hydrogen chloride (HCl) gas as a feedstock. It could obtain this from an adjacent vinyl chloride plant, since HCl comes off as a by-product from cracking ethylene dichloride to vinyl chloride (see Fig. 10.2). Thus, Ethyl, Dow, and Union Carbide are examples of companies with special reasons that made vinyl chloride monomer manufacture more attractive to them than to producers without these synergies.

Development of Improved Technology. To the extent that companies made research breakthroughs or improvement in vinyl

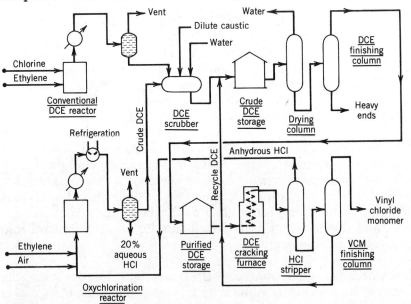

Figure 10.2 Vinyl chloride from ethylene with oxychlorination. (*Source:* E.F. Edwards and T. Weaver, New route to vinyl chloride, *Chem. Eng. Progress* **61**(1) 22(1965). Reproduced by permission of the American Institute of Chemical Engineers.)

chloride manufacturing technology, such firms might decide to enter in or to broaden their participation in the vinyl chloride monomer (VCM) business.

BACKGROUND TO CHANGE

In the United States, the original producers of vinyl chloride were Union Carbide and Goodrich (see Chapters 2 and 6), followed by Dow Chemical and Ethyl Corporation soon after the end of World War II. Production of the monomer rose from roughly 300 million pounds in the early 1950s to slightly over 1 billion pounds in 1960. Essentially, no merchant market existed for monomer until 1955, when Dow started a program of selling vinyl chloride as a commodity. This resulted in the construction of a number of small PVC plants by a new group of producers including Cary Chemical (later bought by Tenneco), Borden Chemical, Pantasote Chemical, Escambia, and others (2). PVC production technology had recently become available from firms such as Scientific Design and Blaw-Knox, both of which had engineered a simple, off-the-shelf design, suitable for new, unsophisticated producers. Vinyl chloride was now being shipped by barge, tanker, or tank truck and delivered into these companies' feed tanks rather than being pumped "across the fence" to the VCM manufacturers own PVC plant, as had previously been the case. Merchant sales of monomer reached 30 percent of total VCM production by 1958 and stayed in that range for many years thereafter. Ethyl Corporation also became a large supplier to the merchant market in the late 1950s. Merchant sales established the price of monomer, at 10–11 cents per pound in 1955–1960.

There was little change in vinyl chloride manufacturing technology between the late 1930s and the end of the 1950s. Basically, manufacturers had two choices. The simpler route was to react acetylene with hydrogen chloride gas over a heterogenous mercuric chloride catalyst, which produced vinyl chloride in high yields. The HCl gas was generally obtained by burning chlorine with hydrogen, although it was sometimes available as a by-product from other operations. The other process route to make vinyl chloride was to thermally crack ethylene dichloride (EDC), which could be obtained via chlorination of ethylene or as a by-product from ethylene oxide manufacture. This cracking step gave HCl gas as a by-product. If acetylene was available at the same location, the company could produce additional VCM by reacting the HCl offgases with the acetylene. This type of installation became known as a "balanced" plant.

Acetylene was, in the earlier time, produced by the traditional calcium carbide process, as practiced by companies such as Union Carbide, Air Reduction, and others. Ethylene was available via recovery from cat cracker offgases or from steam cracking of natural gas liquids or petroleum fractions.

In 1960, the following companies were engaged in the production of vinyl chloride and all of them (except Ethyl) produced PVC resin as well: Allied Chemical, Cumberland Chemicals (later Airco), Diamond Alkali, Dow Chemical, Ethyl Corporation, General Tire and Rubber, Goodrich, Goodyear, American Chemical,* Union Carbide, and Monsanto.

NEW ACETYLENE PROCESSES

In the 1950s, BASF, which had pioneered the development of the so-called Reppe chemicals, based on acetylene, announced the successful commercialization of a high yield, economically attractive *flame-cracking* process to convert methane to acetylene.† This new acetylene route involved feeding a mixture of methane and oxygen to a burner, reaching a temperature of about 1500°C for about a tenth of a second and then quenching the stream to 80°C. The resulting product gases contained about 30 percent acetylene. Soon thereafter, Société Belge de l'Azôte (S.B.A.) announced a similar process. At the time, acetylene was still produced almost exclusively from calcium carbide in the United States, as well as in Europe and elsewhere. The so-called flame-cracking technologies would now make acetylene a "petrochemical," since it was now based on natural gas feedstock. Acetylene was, at that time, being used as raw material not only for vinyl chloride, but also for vinyl acetate, acrylonitrile, and other intermediates. An attractive additional feature of these new technologies was that the product

---

*Joint venture between Stauffer and Atlantic Richfield.

†This development was also known as the Sachsse process. (See Chapter 1 for a vignette on the inventor.)

gases contained substantial quantities of carbon monoxide, which could be further processed to make ammonia, methanol, and other useful products.

American Cyanamid, a major acrylonitrile producer, first decided to build an acetylene plant, using the new flame cracking process, at Fortier, Louisiana, where it would also produce ammonia from the carbon oxides and hydrogen by-product obtained in the manufacture of acetylene. Vinyl chloride producers also became very interested in flame-cracking technology, which would lower the cost of the hydrocarbon portion of the VCM molecule. Soon thereafter, Union Carbide and Monsanto decided to use hydrocarbon-based acetylene in their Gulf Coast plants. More significantly, as a result of their studies of the new process, additional producers of vinyl chloride made their appearance. Borden Chemical and United States Rubber Company decided to build a joint venture monomer plant at Geismar, Louisiana, where Borden erected a BASF process acetylene plant, with offgases used to produce ammonia and methanol. The joint venture was known as Monochem. Tenneco Chemical, now owner of Cary Chemical, decided to back integrate by building a "balanced" VCM plant on the Gulf Coast. It licensed the S.B.A. acetylene technology, which had been further developed by M. W. Kellogg. This would now bring the number of VCM manufacturers to 13, none of the earlier producers having as yet dropped out.

THE PRICE OF MONOMER AND PVC HEADS DOWN

Dow Chemical had been watching the proliferation of vinyl chloride and PVC producers since the mid-1950s. The company had, of course, promoted the entry of a number of new PVC producers when it became a supplier of merchant monomer in the 1950s. And the advent of the new producers was, no doubt, a factor in the drop in price for general purpose resin from 38 cents per pound in 1950–1954 to 31 cents in 1955, 27 cents in 1956, 23.5 cents in 1958, and 18 cents in 1961, where the price stayed for a long time thereafter. In 1952, the VCM price was 13 cents per pound, giving a gross margin of 25 cents for the integrated producers in that year. At that time, Dow Chemical also produced a small amount of PVC resin, but it was far more interested in the monomer. Dow found that the combination of ethylene, propylene, and chlorine-based intermediates, which included ethylene and propylene oxide and their derivatives, vinyl chloride, and several chlorinated solvents, provided a great deal of manufacturing synergy that should allow the company to be the dominant, low cost producer of all of these commodities. The company's dedication to PVC had never been great and so its strategy to become the dominant merchant monomer supplier was reasonable. Among other things, it would let Dow expand and continue to balance its integrated operations at Freeport, Texas, and at its new Plaquemine, Lousiana, site. While the price of PVC resins was bound to drop, as the domination of the integrated producers started to wane, Dow expected to come out on top, with greater sales and profits from all the intermediates, including vinyl chloride. Vinyl chloride prices did drop somewhat from 13 cents per pound in 1952 (before merchant monomer was available) to 10–11 cents per pound in 1955–1960, but this was a far smaller decline than for PVC resins. Accordingly, Dow Chemical exited the PVC resin business a few years later (3).

In 1961, Dow evidently became impatient, since its market share had not increased to the extent it had anticipated. No one was quitting the vinyl chloride monomer business and new producers were starting to appear on the horizon. The company now made a decision that some people in the industry still remember today. It announced that it was dropping the price of monomer by about 4 cents (a 33 percent price drop) to a new price of 8 cents per pound. This was a bombshell! What the company seemed to be saying was: Let's see who can afford to stay in this business! Dow knew that some producers, such as Ethyl, also had good production economics and would not decide to quit. Some others might decide to shut down and, if they were producers of PVC resins, become buyers in the merchant market served by Dow. New producers were, at the same time, warned: This will not now be a profitable business to build and to start depreciating a new plant.

It is hard to say whether Dow made a gross miscalculation, since the strategy seems sound in retrospect and a number of shutdowns did later take place. However, in the period following Dow's pricing move, a technological factor intervened that made it possible for several other vinyl chloride producers to achieve lower production costs and which lured several other new producers into the field: the development of ethylene oxychlorination.

THE ETHYLENE OXYCHLORINATION PROCESS

The fact that ethylene dichloride cracking required suitable disposition of by-product HCl gas had always been regarded as a problem, although "balanced" plants, which reacted the HCl with acetylene to make more VCM, provided a solution in some cases. This use of acetylene to react the by-product HCl only worked, of course, if the acetylene was available nearby (it cannot be piped over long distances, since it is a hazardous material, prone to explosions). Also, the manufacturer always had to produce twice as much monomer as would be made from ethylene alone to achieve the proper stoichiometric balance. If acetylene was not available, VCM manufacturers cracking EDC would either need another outlet for the HCl by-product, such as manufacture of ethyl chloride, or face a disposal problem. Often, HCl was therefore absorbed in water and sold at low prices in the form of muriatic acid, used to clean metal surfaces. The problem of identifying a reasonable "sink" for the hydrogen chloride had traditionally led VCM manufacturers to use acetylene rather than ethylene feedstock, thus avoiding the HCl disposal problem altogether.

There was, however, another option for the HCl gas—it could theroretically be oxidized back to chlorine. This technology, known as the Deacon process, had been invented many years earlier and involved the use of a cupric chloride catalyst. The trouble was that the chlorine produced in this manner was more expensive than the price at which it could be purchased, even when hydrogen chloride was charged to the Deacon plant at disposal value. On that basis, the Deacon process was a nonstarter. In the early 1960s, however, several companies decided on another tack. Why not try to use a Deacon-type catalyst in the presence of ethylene as well as HCl and oxygen to produce ethylene dichloride, thus compressing two steps into one? A number of problems would have to be solved, most importantly the high exothermicity (heat release) that would result from this reaction. The problem of catalyst "hot spots," which occur in reactions of this type, would have to be addressed in particular.

Three U.S. companies—Dow, Goodrich, and Stauffer—worked on ethylene oxychlorination around the same time, later to be joined by Toyo Soda and Vulcan. Dow's process may have been the earliest developed, but the company was silent on the subject and never offered it for license, as far as I know. Stauffer Chemical, which operated its joint venture plant in Watson, California, started work on oxychlorination in 1960, most likely because the plant's capacity was limited by the amount of HCl the joint venture could convert to ethyl chloride in an adjacent plant. In 1961, Stauffer successfully developed a fixed-bed ethylene oxychlorination process, which used several reactor beds in series to deal with the problem of exotherm and catalyst hotspotting. Goodrich Chemical received the most publicity when it announced, in 1964, that, in combination with the Badger Company, it had successfully commercialized its own oxychlorination process, using a fluidized-bed reactor. Goodrich decided to use the new process to build a giant VCM plant at Calvert City, Kentucky, with a capacity of 400 million pounds per year. This was far larger than any of Dow's or Ethyl's plants at that time.

The oxychlorination process (Fig. 10.2) provided even better economics than those achievable with Sachsse acetylene (4). More importantly, it made it possible to construct a balanced vinyl chloride plant without the need for acetylene, since HCl from the EDC cracking step could now produce additional EDC by reaction with more ethylene, thus completing the cycle. In this respect, the oxychlorination was particularly attractive to oil companies that wanted to use only ethylene—which they produced in abundance— to make the monomer. A comparison of the different routes to vinyl monomer is shown in Table 10.1, with relative economics in Table 10.2 (4, pp. 21–26). A list of vinyl chloride producers in 1964 is shown in Table 10.3, which also includes plant sizes and locations (5).

VCM DEMAND CONTINUES TO GROW

One reason why even some of the weaker vinyl chloride producers were not ready to shut down their plants—in spite of relatively poor economics—was the fact that vinyl chloride consumption continued to rise rapidly. Between 1960 and 1964, annual PVC production had increased from 1.0 to 1.64 billion pounds. Monomer nameplate capacity was not much more than two billion pounds and in 1965 VCM consumption actually reached the two billion pound level, an increase of almost 400 million pounds over the previous year. Meanwhile, with demand outpacing supply, the

Table 10.1 Major Process Routes to Vinyl Chloride

1. Addition of HCl to Acetylene

$$HC \equiv CH + HCl \xrightarrow[\text{+ HgCl2}]{\text{activated carbon}} CH_2 = CHCl$$
$$\text{(acetylene)} \qquad\qquad\qquad\qquad \text{(vinyl chloride)}$$

2. Balanced Ethylene/Acetylene VCM Production

$$CH_2 = CH_2 + Cl_2 \longrightarrow CH_2Cl - CH_2Cl$$
$$\text{(ethylene)} \qquad\qquad \text{(ethylene dichloride—EDC)}$$

$$CH_2Cl - CH_2Cl \xrightarrow[\text{cracking}]{900\text{-}950°F} CH_2 = CHCl + HCl$$
$$\qquad\qquad\qquad\qquad\qquad \text{(vinyl chloride)}$$

$$HC \equiv CH + HCl \longrightarrow CH_2 = CHCl$$
$$\qquad\qquad\qquad\qquad \text{(vinyl chloride)}$$

3. Balanced Oxychlorination Process

$$CH_2 = CH_2 + Cl_2 \longrightarrow CH_2Cl - CH_2Cl$$

$$CH_2 = CH_2 + HCl + ½ O_2 \xrightarrow[\text{CuCl}_2]{\text{Oxychlorination}} CH_2Cl - CH_2Cl + H_2O$$

$$CH_2Cl - CH_2Cl \xrightarrow[\text{cracking}]{900\text{-}950°F} CH_2 = CHCl + HCl$$

Source: Chem Systems.

contract price of VCM, which had dropped to as low as 6.2 cents per pound on the spot market, again stabilized around 8 cents. A headline in the December 12th, 1964 issue of *Chemical Week* announced "Vinyl: Not Enough To Go Around." (5)

Predictably, there now came another period of incremental capacity additions by a number of the producers. Almost every one of them saw this as a time to debottleneck, if at all possible. Dow, Ethyl, and Monochem were among the companies adding substantial capacity, as well as Union Carbide at Texas City. Allied Chemical, which had built an ethylene plant in Louisiana, was now planning a Gulf Coast monomer plant, as were other companies, such as Wyandotte, PPG, Chemplex, and a proposed joint venture company formed by Conoco and Stauffer. In 1966, vinyl chloride production reached 2.5 billion pounds. It was widely projected that PVC resin consumption could reach 5 billion pounds by 1975.

Table 10.2 Production Economics for Vinyl Chloride (1964)

	Ethylene Route		Acetylene Route
	Conventional	Oxychlorination	
		(dollars per short ton)	
Raw materials			
Ethylene @ 4.5 cents/lb	42.84	43.56	—
Chlorine @ $50/ton	60.25	33.70	—
By-product HCl @ $25/ton	(14.75)	—	—
Acetylene @ 8 cents/lb	—	—	67.84
HCl @ $50/ton	—	—	29.84
Total Raw Materials	88.34	77.26	97.64
Other conversion costs	10.42	12.21	6.98
S.G.&A. costs	1.50	1.50	1.50
Capital charges, royalty, profit	22.00	26.00	18.00
Minimum profitable selling price			
$/Short ton	122	117	124
Cents/lb	6.1	5.8	6.2
Capital Investment:	$5,460,000	$6,400,000	$4,590,000

Source: Chemical Engineering Progress, 61(1), January 1965, pp. 21–26. Reproduced by permission of the American Institute of Chemical Engineers.

Table 10.3 U.S. Vinyl Chloride Producers—1964

Company	Location	Plant Size (MM lb/yr)	Feedstock
Allied	Moundsville, WV	150	Carbide acetylene
American Chemical (Stauffer, JV)	Watson, CA	70	Ethylene
Cumberland Chemical (Airco)	Calvert City, KY	60	Carbide acetylene
Diamond Alkali	Deer Park, TX	100	Balanced acetylene/ethylene
Dow Chemical	Freeport, TX	100	Ethylene
	Plaquemine, LA	100	Ethylene
Ethyl	Baton Rouge, LA	160	Ethylene
	Houston, TX	80	Ethylene
General Tire	Ashtabula, OH	30	Carbide acetylene
Goodrich	Calvert City, KY	400	Ethylene
	Louisville, KY	120	Carbide acetylene
Goodyear	Niagara Falls, NY	40	Carbide acetylene
	Niagara Falls, NY	70	Carbide acetylene
Monochem (Borden-U.S. Rubber)	Geismar, LA	150	BASF acetylene
Monsanto	Texas City, TX	150	Balanced ethylene/acetylene
Tenneco Chemicals	Houston, TX	200	SBA (Societé Belge de l'Azôte)-acetylene
Union Carbide	South Charleston, WV	120	Carbide acetylene
	Texas City, TX	150	Balanced acetylene/ethylene
Total		**2250**	

Source: Chemical Marketing Reporter and other publications.

It was a strange situation and one that must have been particularly disturbing to the executives of companies involved in the production of chemicals before World War II, when there were rarely more than two or three producers of a given chemical. Here were 15 or so producers of vinyl chloride, none with a market share greater than 10-15 percent, competing fiercely in a still rapidly growing market. And while none were able to achieve a decent return on new capacity at the price that monomer was sold, several continued to invest. And so the pattern continued.

In late 1966, PPG announced its decision to enter VCM production with a 300 million pound per year plant, based on its own oxychlorination technology. No doubt the company felt it belonged in this business as much as anybody. PPG was one of the largest chlorine producers. It was involved in the production of chlorinated solvents and, like Dow, it would achieve some production synergies by integrating vinyl chloride production with other manufacturing steps at Lake Charles, Louisiana. And the company was also able to line up some customers in the PVC business.

In the same year, Stauffer and Conoco made a decision to build a large joint venture plant. For Stauffer, this would be a major expansion of its monomer capacity, this time on the Gulf Coast; for Conoco, this would be an opportunity to build an ethylene plant to supply not only this monomer unit, but also its synthetic detergent alcohols plant. But now a rather amazing thing happened, given the large number of vinyl chloride and PVC producers and the ferocious competition taking place in both business areas. The Federal Trade Commission summoned executives of the two companies to Washington and told them to break up the newly formed joint venture, since it would violate the antitrust laws. The Sherman and Clayton Acts had previously been used to prevent joint ventures in the chemical industry (e.g., a proposed combination between Pennwalt and Olin in chlorates), based on the principle that either of the two partners could have gone into the business alone and that the partnership would act to reduce potential competition.* But now, antitrust action was being taken in a product area

---

*The Federal Trade Commission complaint stated that in 1965 there were 13 vinyl chloride producers, with the top 4 and top 9 firms, respectively, accounting for 62.9 and 91.2 percent of total industry production. For the record, it was also noted that the top 4 PVC producers accounted for 47.3 percent of the market and the top 8 for 70.7 percent, with an overall total of 28 producers.

where competition was probably more vigorous than the fathers of the historic antitrust acts might ever have imagined. Nevertheless, the companies had no choice but to comply. Conoco agreed to build the monomer plant by itself (with licensed Stauffer technology) and to divest a PVC production company, Thompson-Apex, that Conoco had recently acquired (6). Stauffer and Conoco later proceeded to build PVC plants individually.

By this time, not only vinyl chloride but also PVC polymerization plants had expanded greatly in size. This was particularly true for plants producing resin for the fabrication of PVC pipe, now increasingly used for various industrial, commercial, and domestic applications. Very large reactors were used in suspension and mass polymerization processes. Figure 10.3 depicts a Pechiney-St. Gobain mass polymerization reactor and plant design furnished around this time by the French firm of Peciney-St. Gobain (7).

In 1968, forecasters decided that the year when PVC production would reach five billion pounds would now be as early as 1972, versus 1975, as predicted earlier. Goodrich had decided to expand its Calvert City plant to one billion pounds of capacity and Allied approved the new plant in Baton Rouge, Louisiana. But all was not well at the moment. In *Oil, Paint and Drug Reporter,* October 14, 1968, the headline read "Vinyl Chloride Monomer's Market: Brisk Growth but Problems Loom." Monomer capacity was now over 3.7 billion pounds, but consumption was not rising rapidly just now, with industry output not expected to top 2.7 billion pounds in 1968. At this juncture, some of the fringe producers finally decided to throw in the towel. It was also time for some of the stronger producers to think about shutting down some older plants that still used acetylene. General Tire, Goodyear, Air Reduction (Cumberland), and Diamond Shamrock decided to quit. Allied would shut down its Moundsville plant when Baton Rouge came on line. Meanwhile, Dow announced a big new 700 million pound plant in Oyster Creek, Texas, close to Freeport (8).

A combination of temporarily sagging demand growth and oversupply also brought about a disastrous drop in vinyl monomer price—it sank to 4.5 cents per pound. In early 1969, Monsanto, which had developed its own oxychlorination process, shut down its sole plant at Texas City, Texas. Soon thereafter, Union Carbide decided to close down its acetylene-based plant in Charleston, West Virginia. These shutdowns brought industry capacity down to 3.6 million pounds, providing a better supply/demand balance.

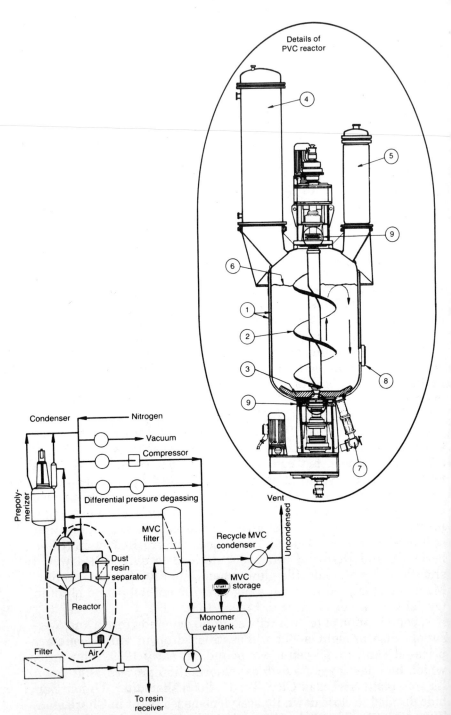

Figure 10.3 Flowsheet of PVC polymerization plant and details of a polymerization reactor. (*Source:* Gulf Publishing Co., PVC mass polymerization, *Hydrocarbon Processing,* May 1981, p. 143.)

There was now renewed hope in the industry that things would get better.

In October 1969, this hope was rudely shattered. Shell Chemical announced its decision to enter the vinyl chloride business by building a 700 million pound per year plant at Deer Park, Texas. Citing a projected 10 percent compounded annual growth for monomer as soon as demand perked up again, Shell said it decided to become a major player in this market. From Shell Chemical, the following rationale was heard: The company was a major ethylene producer, it had had a long experience in the production of chlorinated hydrocarbons (see Chapters 2 and 3), it could use oxychlorination to soak up by-product HCl from other operations, and it was already a producer of such plastics as polystyrene, polypropylene, and epoxy resins. From the industry's standpoint, however, it was clear that this was at least one competitor too many. PPG had also just announced a new monomer plant in Puerto Rico, where it had already decided to build a joint venture ethylene plant with Commonwealth Oil Refining Company (CORCO). In the October 20, 1969 issue, the *Oil, Paint and Drug Reporter* headlined "VCM Facility for Shell Confirmed; It Will Be Bigger Than We Thought." The article pointed to the fact that PPG had just started up in Puerto Rico, but that perhaps some older domestic capacity might now shut down (9).

Table 10.4 details vinyl chloride producers and plants in 1972, by which time it had become only too clear that vinyl monomer production would remain a difficult arena in which to make a profit (10). Vinyl chloride production in the United States, and in Europe and Japan as well, had become too competitive. But perhaps plants built away from the major petrochemical centers would offer a better opportunity with less intense competition. Around that time, Chem Systems had been working jointly with Diamond Alkali and Oronzio de Nora, a private Italian company that was perhaps the world's most important source of technology for chlorine cells at that time. Would it be possible, the companies asked, to design an inexpensive, small cracker that would make a stream of relatively low concentration ethylene, which could then be reacted with chlorine to make ethylene dichloride and vinyl chloride? Such a plant could be built in developing nations, which wanted to build PVC plants to supply local needs, but could not afford to build giant ethylene plants. Soon, we came up with such a design, which would be available from the two

Table 10.4   U.S. Vinyl Chloride Producers (1972 versus 1964)
(MM lb/yr)

Company	Location	1964	1972
Allied	Moundsville, WV	150	Shut down
	Baton Rouge, LA	—	300
American Chemical	Watson, CA	70	170
Conoco		—	600
Cumberland Chemical	Calvert City, KY	60	Shut down
Diamond Alkali	Deer Park, TX	100	Shut down
Dow Chemical	Freeport, TX	100	180
	Oyster Creek, TX	—	700
	Plaquemine, LA	100	340
Ethyl	Baton Rouge, LA	160	270
	Houston, TX	80	150
General Tire	Ashtabula, OH	30	Shut down
Goodrich	Calvert City, KY	400	1000
	Louisville, KY	120	Shut down
	Niagara Falls, NY	40	Shut down
Goodyear	Niagara Falls, NY	70	Shut down
Monochem	Geismar, LA	150	300
Monsanto	Texas City, TX	150	Shut down
PPG	Lake Charles, LA	—	300
	Puerto Rico	—	500
Shell	Houston, TX	—	800
	Norco, LA	—	800 (1974)
Tenneco Chemicals	Houston, TX	200	255
Union Carbide	Texas City, TX	120	Shut down
	South Charleston, WV	150	Shut down
Total		**2250**	**5865**

Source: *Chemical Marketing Reporter* and other publications.

sponsoring companies under the name of the "Dianor" Process. Unfortunately, such a plant was never built, largely because by that time the world was starting to be obsessed with the "large plant" syndrome (see Chapter 11). But there were some compensations to having worked with the venerable Milanese firm. When I visited Vittorio de Nora at his summer home in St. Jean-Cap Ferrat on the French Riviera, where a salt-water swimming pool overlooked an outside elevator going down to the yacht mooring below, and I heard about Vittorio's and his wife's "his and hers" jets, it became plain that at least a part of Europe had long recovered from the ravages of war and that the patrician life-style of European industrial aristocrats was alive and well.

AND THE GAME CONTINUED

In the 1970s, there were no more surprises nor any important technological developments in the vinyl chloride industry. There was no improvement in the profitability of producers, except for very brief periods. One more new producer, Georgia Pacific, decided to build a large monomer plant as a result of this pulp and paper company's decision to go into the plastics business, which was encroaching on its wood and paper markets. One of the earlier producers—Diamond Shamrock (previously Diamond Alkali)—reentered monomer production with a new one-billion-pound-per-year plant, after arranging a favorable ethylene deal with Phillips, but then exited the business again several years later. Several of the larger producers, including Goodrich, built more capacity, mostly to their sorrow, as it later turned out. Shell started up its second large plant at Norco, Louisiana, in 1974, then shut it down a few years later, announcing that vinyl chloride was no longer viewed as a key product for Shell. PPG admitted that it had made a mistake to build in Puerto Rico, now that the island's favorable tax treatment no longer applied and its partner, CORCO, had gone into bankruptcy. Goodrich, at one point, announced that it would henceforth consider PVC (including VCM) its most important strategic business area (ahead of tires). Then, a few years later, it again changed its strategy—it would stay in VCM and PVC, but it would not stake the future of the company on this business. Dow Chemical, which had plans to invest in several other typical "Dow Complexes," as it had done in Freeport, Plaquemine, Terneuzen, and Stade (the latter two in Europe), and generally included VCM production, dropped the concept of further growth in commodity chemicals in the early 1980s. At least for now! And so it went.

THE SCOREBOARD

There were many losers in the production of vinyl chloride monomer. Who were the winners? Here it is only possible to make surmises. On that basis, one can tentatively conclude that, for at least some of the earlier players, vinyl chloride production probably brought more satisfaction than for most of the later entrants.

Goodrich Chemical. It was always the leader in PVC resin production, including many specialty grades. In the 1960s, the company also profited by being a producer rather than a buyer of monomer. It also earned substantial royalties from licensing its oxychlorination technology. Goodrich has remained the largest U.S. producer of PVC resins, strongly committed to this business.

Ethyl Corporation. It did fairly well in monomer production, due to the specific nature of its manufacturing complex, including the production of ethyl chloride. Ethyl refrained from a policy of reinvestment to maintain or gain market share and left the business when it made no sense to stay.

Dow Chemical. For Dow, the vinyl monomer business has probably been more profitable over the years than for any of its competitors because of (1) good technology, (2) large capacity, usually installed ahead of its competitors, (3) integration of VCM manufacture with other products, and (4) a substantial export business. However, Dow has not done nearly as well as it once surely hoped, and it has experienced many periods when profits must have been very low or nonexistent in vinyl chloride.

Stauffer Chemical. The company's small West Coast plant was undoubtedly profitable for some time, due to a location advantage. More importantly, Stauffer earned substantial royalties from licensing its fixed-bed oxychlorination technology to companies all over the world. The Federal Trade Commission's directive preventing Stauffer from building a monomer plant must have eventually been considered a real blessing in disguise.

Although these companies probably did better than most of the others, it is unlikely that any of them considered vinyl chloride production a good business much of the time. It also seems safe to say that none of the other vinyl chloride manufacturers considered themselves as "winners" in the production of this chemical. One of the "losers" in this business was Shell Chemical, which entered late and never did establish itself very well, in spite of building two efficient, world-scale plants with excellent technology. Shell, which claims its VCM operations were profitable between 1970 and

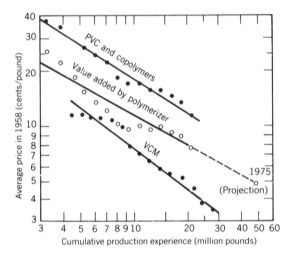

Figure 10.4 Experience curves for VCM price, PVC price, and value added by polymerizer. U.S. Tariff Commission, Boston Consulting Group, and Manufacturing Chemists Association figures are combined with the GNP deflator (1958 base year) and authors' estimates of future production. A 3 percent inflation projection through 1975 is incorporated. (*Source:* Reproduced with permission from *Hydrocarbon Processing,* February 1973.)

1978,* eventually discovered that there was a major handicap to being a vinyl chloride producer if you did not produce the chlorine and also were not captive in PVC production. If you did both of these (e.g., like Goodrich), you had a chance. If neither one, it was difficult. Shell also came in rather late, when PVC demand was flattening and when environmental issues relating to the release of VCM monomer caused producers to have to spend large sums of capital to revise VCM plant design and operation.

Some of the other firms made money in the early days, but never became big players. And as for the winners, these companies would, no doubt, concede that they once thought the game would produce a much greater return than they ultimately enjoyed. A pictorial representation of the Experience Curves for VCM and PVC production, from a 1973 article, gives a grim picture of an industry that consistently became less profitable with time (Fig. 10.4). Similar curves could be developed for a number of other key petrochemicals.

*Shell Chemical, personal communications.

THE CONCLUSIONS

What can we make of this history of a multibillion-pound product that lured so many companies into the chemical industry and then provided them with so little return for their efforts? Why did the development of ever more efficient production techniques not allow the inventors to make meaningful profits as their inventions became commercially successful? Why didn't backward or forward integration strategies provide the benefits that companies had hoped to enjoy through the employment of these techniques?

Some of the answers to these questions are contained in the early parts of this chapter. They are perhaps best restated as three fundamental conditions that were (and still are) required to become a financially successful producer of a petrochemical commodity:

1. *A new process technique not only has to provide substantially better economics than the existing technology it replaces, but it also has to be unique, patented, and not easily duplicated by others. That is, the process must be a real "breakthrough," that cannot readily be emulated by competitors.*

2. *When a commodity chemical is produced by a large number of competitors, none of whom has a commanding market share, the ensuing competition will provide a pattern where no company can be a really profitable producer.*

3. *Unless high entry barriers exist for a new producer, due to specialized technology, high capital cost, or other reasons, a product with attractive market growth prospects will attract too many producers.*

Some further thoughts on these matters are expressed in Chapter 13.

REFERENCES

1. Vinyl makers vie for position, *Chemical Week,* September 11, 1965, 39–40.
2. P. E. Newman and A. R. Smith (1958). Small polyvinyl chloride plants. Technological developments and economic considerations. Paper presented at XXXI Congrès Internationale de Chimie Industrielle, Liège Belgium, September.
3. Vinyl chloride monomers market: Brisk growth, but problems loom, *Oil, Paint & Drug Reporter,* October 14, 1968, p. 33.

4. E. F. Edwards and Theodore Weaver (1965). New route to vinyl chloride, *Chemical Engineering Progress,* **61** (1), January.

5. Vinyl: Not enough to go around, *Chemical Week,* December 12, 1964, 91-94.

6. Vinyl chloride bust-up order forcing Stauffer-Conoco split and sales of two other firms, *Oil, Paint & Drug Reporter,* October 16, 1967.

7. *Hydrocarbon Processing,* Mass Polymerization of Vinyl Chloride, May 1981, p. 143.

8. Vinyl chloride mart upheaval: Small plants fleeing the scene as big units reach completion, *Oil, Paint & Drug Reporter,* April 29, 1968. p. 3.

9. VCM facility for Shell confirmed; It will be bigger than we thought, *Oil Paint & Drug Reporter,* October 20, 1969, p. 3.

10. D. P. Keane, Robert B. Stobaugh, and Phillip L. Townsend (1973). Vinyl chloride, how, where, who———future! *Hydrocarbon Processing,* February, 99-106.

ADDITIONAL READING

Acetylene, Vol. 1, pp. 192-243; Vinyl chloride polymers, Vol. 23, pp. 865-885, *Kirk-Othmer Encyclopedia,* New York, Wiley Interscience.

Brous, S. J. (1945). Future chemical needs of the plastics industry, Chemical Marketing Research Association Paper, Cleveland, Ohio, December 13.

Chemical profile, vinyl chloride, *Oil, Paint & Drug Reporter,* March 17, 1969.

Richards, J. C. Jr. (1952). Vinyl resins, presented at Chemical Marketing Research Conference, September. Chicago, Ill.

The vinyls today, *Chemical Week,* November 16, 1957, 71-73, 75-76, 78, 80.

11 / Large Plants: The New Economics

Those of us active in the industry in the mid-1960s were becoming aware of the fact that the size of new plants was increasing at a remarkable rate. The annual production of chemicals and plastics was growing rapidly and, as a result, each company contemplating a new unit could build a bigger plant for a given slice of the market. Thus, maleic plants increased from a typical capacity of 10 million pounds per year in the late 1950s to 20–30 million pounds 10 years later; phenol plants grew from 20 to the level of 50 million pounds per year; and vinyl chloride plants increased from 50 to 100–200 million pounds per year by the early 1960s. At first, these capacity increases did not require any particular breakthroughs in equipment design. In fact, many times it involved the duplication of reaction systems (i.e., building two reaction "trains" instead of one), although the "back end" or purification section of the plant was often designed with a single set of larger distillation columns, which were easier and less risky to scale up. This approach was in the tradition of a conservative industry that was not used to putting all of its eggs in one basket, as far as the more complicated reaction section of the plant was concerned. The result was that the economics of operating a plant with twice the capacity of its predecessor were not nearly as good as if an entire "single-train" unit had been constructed for the new capacity. This more risky

418

approach lowers the investment-related cost per pound of product made.

By the early 1960s, however, a number of firms involved in the design of petrochemical plants were working on this concept—large, single-train plants. These would provide substantially lower production costs, if all the equipment could be successfully scaled up to the required dimensions and the plants could be made to operate in a reliable manner, without the use of duplicate equipment in key parts of the installation.

The conservative approach to chemical plant design was, in fact, a vestige of traditional practice found among European chemical producers. Anybody who, in the 1950s, visited the sprawling chemical works built in such countries as England, France and Germany, found that production facilities for many of the chemical intermediates were made up of a large number of reaction and distillation systems of various histories and sizes. Moreover, plant additions were almost invariably made in incremental fashion, rather than by constructing a single large new plant to replace several of the older units. This was also true in the United States, at that time, but to a lesser extent. Here, a new plant more often replaced several smaller existing units, although the new plant would still have substantial sparing (duplicating) of critical equipment items. An important point is that the experience gained as a result of constructing large oil refinery process plants during World War II gave U.S. contractors and operating companies a considerable degree of confidence in keeping key equipment items operating over a longer period of time. This eventually also prompted petrochemical manufacturers to think about building larger plants. At first, this resulted only in larger diameter distillation columns and heat exchangers; later, in larger dimensioned reaction systems. Eventually, it led to the modern single-train plant.

Of course, a number of limitations had to be overcome in order for designers to avoid the necessity of duplicating specific equipment items rather than just building a single larger unit. In the case of distillation towers and other large vessels, there was a practical limitation if the vessel had to be shipped to its final destination by rail. The size of the flatbed car and the required clearances for tracks and tunnels generally limits the diameter of vessels being transported in this manner to about 12 feet and the overall length of towers to a size that can be accommodated by the specific shipment route. Larger diameter vessels and particularly tall vessels either have to be shipped by barge, if water transportation is feasible, or by truck. These limitations often made it necessary to fabricate large vessels in several pieces and to weld these together in the field, a practice that required the development of techniques to stress relieve (anneal) field welds in a satisfactory manner.

Rotating equipment also presented special scale up problems. Pumps were relatively easier to fabricate in larger sizes, though in the case of high-pressure pumps problems could arise. In the 1950s, I participated in the startup of part of Esso Chemical's Fawley refinery in England, where we had designed a catalytic polymerization unit that required a 20-stage vertical pump. The pump was used to pressure a propylene stream up to several thousand pounds per square inch, which was the pressure level required for the polymerization reaction. The pump, an Ingersoll-Rand unit, was the largest ever built for this purpose and was driven by a motor connected to the pump by a right-angle gear drive. When the big moment came and the button was pushed to start up the pump, it operated for about 20 seconds and then ground to a screeching halt. It turned out that the thrust exerted by the motor on the gear drive displaced the pump rotor enough—actually only a few thousands of an inch—to close the minute gap between a number of the shaft-mounted rotors and the pump casing, causing the pump to seize and stop functioning. It took eight weeks to redesign and refabricate the pump and driver system. After that, we successfully started up the plant. We now knew how to design a pump assembly and driver for a large cat poly plant, but the delay was costly.

Compressors represented a different kind of problem. Until the mid-1950s, essentially all of the compressors that brought a gas stream up to any reasonable pressure level were of the reciprocating* type, since manufacturers were not yet able to design centrifugal compressors to do this job. Reciprocating compressors had a size limitation related to piston and cylinder design and, in addition, required a considerable amount of maintenance. As many chemical process streams contain solids or can form polymers and gums and as plant upsets can result in liquids being carried over to the next process step—often a compressor—the reciprocating units were frequently in danger of being seriously damaged. Thus,

---

*Such compressors use pistons to compress the gases inside cylinders, similar to the principle used in automobile engines.

even if it was possible to use larger "recips," as they were called, prudent design practice called for installing two or even three or four such units in parallel, so that one unit could be out of action for maintenance while the plant was kept running with the other compressors. Single train units were designed to use a large centrifugal compressor that could be reliably kept on stream for a year or more. A number of design problems had to be solved to produce such a compressor and incorporate it in the plant design.

Equipment fouling was also an important issue for many heat exchanger applications, including distillation column reboilers, quench exchangers downstream of cracking reactors and other such difficult services. Much had to be learned with respect to the design and operation of such units. For example, it became obvious that a dirty or "fouling" stream should flow through the tube side rather than through the shell side, where solids can more easily accumulate in dead spots and that the exchanger heads must be designed in a manner to avoid buildup of solids in "pockets".

Other types of unit operations were also often difficult to scale up, as plant throughput increased. This included the centrifuges used for separating crystallized solids from liquid streams, an operation that is employed, for example, to recover terephthalic or adipic acid in fiber monomer plants. The design of large crystallizers themselves presented challenging problems for the chemical engineers scaling plants up to higher and higher capacities. As vessel height and diameter increased, the behavior of the mixture from which crystals were to be recovered through chilling and subsequent separation became more difficult to predict. Large liquid-phase reaction systems could also be difficult to scale up if the reaction was diffusion controlled (i.e., if the reaction depended on the creation of sufficient bubble surface area for the reactants to achieve adequate contact and for the products to diffuse away from the reaction sites). Major theoretical and practical studies of mixing energy requirements and stirred tank configuration and baffling were needed to design reaction systems that would match in the plant the yields achieved in test reactors or in pilot plants, where the new process technology had been developed.

At Scientific Design Company, where we were developing new processes for the production of terephthalic acid, cyclohexanol (for adipic acid), glycerine, and other petrochemicals, this was an exciting time for chemical engineers. And it was the same situation in the engineering departments of most of the large chemical and oil companies and in the offices of the engineering contractors involved in chemical plant design.

Plant sizes were increasing, equipment of various types was becoming larger, and the engineers contemplating the design of the next plant were gaining increasing confidence in their ability to come up with a process and mechanical design that would avoid the necessity of installing duplicate equipment items in parallel. And this was just in time, because an important driving force was now at work: improving the economics of scale to the greatest possible degree to gain at least a small edge over competitors.

In an industry that had become more and more competitive, it was essential in the 1960s to achieve the lowest possible unit cost of operation. To understand the principles involved, a short review of the various elements of production cost may be helpful (see Table 11.1). In an operating plant, costs can be divided into "variable" costs, that relate to the rate at which the plant is operated and "fixed costs" that stay more or less constant, regardless of production level. Variable costs include raw materials, utilities,

Table 11.1   Typical Economics of Manufacture for a Bulk Organic Chemical Product (in cents/lb)

Costs	Small Plant*	Large Plant* ("Single Train")
Variable Costs		
Raw materials	5.2	5.2
Utilities	1.0	0.7
Other (e.g., catalyst)	0.5	0.5
Total *Variable* costs (¢/lb)	**6.7**	**6.4**
Fixed Costs		
Labor	0.6	0.2
Maintenance	1.6	0.8
Depreciation	4.0	2.0
Overheads	2.0	1.0
Total *Fixed* costs (¢/lb)	**8.2**	**4.0**
Total *Production* costs (¢/lb) (before return on investment)	**14.9**	**10.4**

* For this fictitious example, the "small" plant has been assumed to have a capacity of 100,000,000 lb/yr and an investment cost of $40,000,000 while the "large" plant has a capacity of 600,000,000 lb/yr and an investment cost of $110,000,000.

and the cost of chemicals used as catalysts, treating agents, and so on. Fixed costs comprise labor and maintenance charges, insurance, and other plant overheads. Depreciation is also a fixed cost, but it is a bookkeeping charge, rather than an actual cash outlay. From the above, it follows that a substantial percentage of the fixed costs are seen to be related to the capital investment for the plant.

Companies engaged in an effort to lower unit production costs must look at both the variable and fixed costs to see where economies can be made. Variable costs can be reduced by utilizing a less expensive feedstock, by increasing yields from a given feedstock, or by achieving utilities savings through more efficient plant design. All of these items are under periodic study and contribute to a gradual lowering of operating costs (although inflation will, of course, work in the opposite direction and can more than offset the savings made through more efficient processing).

In the 1950s and particularly in the 1960s, when inflation rates were low, the development of improved techniques in plant design was instrumental in the achievement of substantially higher yields and lower utilities costs (i.e., considerably reduced variable costs) in a number of different types of plants (e.g., ethylene oxide, acrylonitrile, methanol, etc.). Operating companies traditionally tend to be more preoccupied with the "variable" rather than with the "fixed" portion of their production costs. This is true for two reasons. First, fixed costs are frequently a smaller part of the total cost, relative to variable cost, particularly when depreciation charges are excluded. Second, once a plant is built, only variable costs change to any appreciable extent. Engineering contractors on the other hand, focus primarily on selling plants and therefore tend to be more interested in providing designs leading to lower plant investment. When contractors bid against each other on new projects, the firm that comes up with the lowest bid on a lump sum contract will, all other things being equal, get the job. Since capital cost is associated with the "fixed" costs of unit production, it follows that the engineering contractors were effectively working on developing designs that resulted in lowering the fixed cost portion of the total production costs.

In the early 1960s, it seemed to become obvious that if it were possible to just scale up every piece of equipment to double or triple its previous size, the fixed cost of making each pound of product could be substantially decreased. Experience with estimates for various plant capacities indicated that it was often reasonable to use a six-tenths factor to factor up the investment for a smaller plant to that of a larger plant, provided the latter also had only one "train" (i.e., no equipment duplication). Thus, if a 100-million-pound-per-year plant cost $10 million, a 200-million-pound-per-year plant of substantially the same design (i.e., with every piece of equipment designed with twice the capacity) might cost [$(200/100)^{0.6} \times$ $10 million] or a little over $15 million. In this example, the effect would be to achieve a 0.25 cents per pound decrease in the depreciation charge per pound of product. There would be a further 0.75 cents per pound decrease in the price required to achieve a 30 percent pretax return in investment.* These numbers were significant at a time when ethylene price was in the range of 3 cents per pound.

And so, by the early 1960s, there was an increasing awareness of the need to achieve improvements in production economics and this fortunately coincided with a time when manufacturers were gaining success in scaling up equipment sizes. This now created an atmosphere where it became possible to build really large single-train plants for many petrochemical products. As mentioned earlier, many of these large conceptual designs had been developed by contractors rather than by operating companies. Contractors were promoting these large plant designs in an agressive manner, publishing articles that illustrated the advantages of building large plants (Fig. 11.1) (1). A big selling point was the fact that new entrants could now build plants that promised to produce the chemical involved at a lower production cost than could be achieved by most of the existing manufacturers. As it happened, the first of the "new breed" of giant plants was usually (but not always) built by a company with experience in manufacturing the chemical under consideration. This was because the contractor who had designed the new plant usually wanted or needed the experience of the operating company to make it work. But after that, any other company would be able to hire that engineering firm to build a copy of the plant and to use the contractor's startup crew to place it in successful operation. In this manner, the latest technology was, in effect, made available to the entire industry!

---

*Companies use this method to calculate what is often called a "transfer price"—meaning a calculated price that includes manufacturing cost plus a desired pretax return. Much of the time, the actual market price achieved is lower than that.

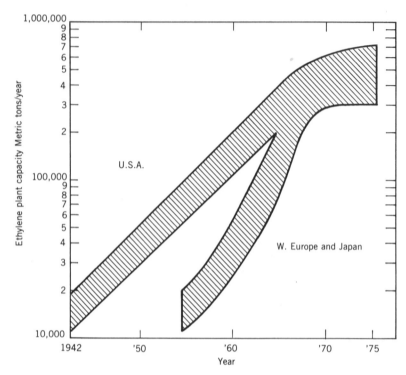

Figure 11.1 Ethylene plant size: increasing capacity with time. (*Source:* W. Tucker and M. A. Abrahams, Heavier feedstock trends: the changing economics of petrochemical production, presented at the World Congress of the Société de la Chimie Industrielle, Valley Forge, PA, October 1976.)

Since ammonia and ethylene are the two most important petro-chemicals, it is not surprising that the large, single-train concept was first applied to these two products. In the case of both of these chemicals, the successful design approach involved every section of the plant, from the furnace area through compression and pu-rification sections, and included a thorough optimization of energy requirements and utilization. Many people in various companies had a hand in the design of the new ammonia and ethylene plants and it is therefore difficult to be totally fair in assigning credits for these innovations. It is generally acknowledged that ICI and M. W. Kellogg were the two companies most responsible for the de-velopments that culminated in the design of the new, single-train ammonia plants, though several other contractors would dispute the point. In the case of ethylene, the credits must be spread more widely, to such companies as Esso Chemical, Stone and Webster, Lummus, M. W. Kellogg, Foster-Wheeler, and Selas (a furnace designer).

The rest of this chapter covers the development of large plant designs and the effect of applying economics of scale to the production of ammonia and ethylene in the early 1960s.

LARGE SINGLE-TRAIN AMMONIA PLANTS

To understand the technological improvements that allowed designers to come up with the modern single-train flowsheet for ammonia, it is necessary to briefly describe the basic process.

Ammonia forms when three mols of hydrogen combine with one mol of nitrogen, according to the following equation:

$$N_2 + 3 H_2 \rightarrow 2 NH_3$$

Use of high pressure favors the reaction, since there is a contraction in gas volume when four mols of feed gas are reduced to two mols of product. This is why Haber decided to use a pressure of 3000 pounds per square inch in his original work (Fig. 11.2) and why ammonia plants since that time have always used elevated pressure for this reaction. The reaction is carried out in a reactor filled with an appropriate catalyst, which speeds up the conversion to a practical rate. The synthesis is carried out at a temperature of between 850°and 1,000°F.

A number of alternatives are available to prepare the two reactants, hydrogen and nitrogen. In the simplest, but usually the most expensive case, these two gases are recovered from other operations in relatively pure form and are then compressed and fed to the ammonia converter. Much more typically, ammonia plants are built on a "grass roots" or "greenfield" basis (both terms that seem to apply well to ammonia plants) and in such cases the synthesis gas mixture of hydrogen and nitrogen must be prepared from a hydrocarbon (or coal), steam, and air. Many options exist here, but in most cases a hydrocarbon gas or distillate is sent through externally fired furnace tubes filled with nickel catalyst, where it is "reformed" in the presence of steam into a mixture of hydrogen, hydrocarbons, carbon monoxide (CO), carbon dioxide

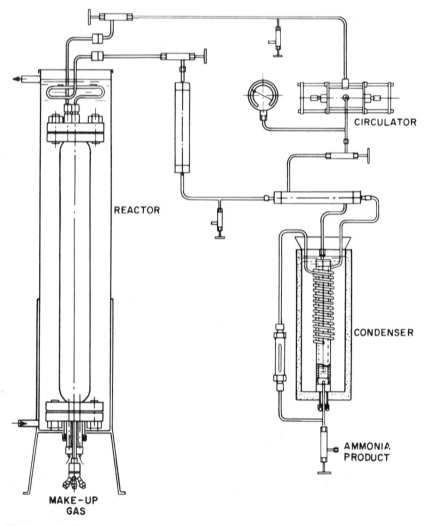

REACTOR

CIRCULATOR

CONDENSER

AMMONIA PRODUCT

MAKE-UP GAS

Figure 11.2 Experimental apparatus used by Haber and LeRossignol. Ammonia is condensed from the converter exit gas and gas recycled. (*Source:* A. V. Slack and G. Russell James, eds., *Ammonia,* Part I, New York, Marcel Dekker, 1973, p. 14)

(CO_2), and water vapor (steam). In a subsequent step, air is added and the mixture is sent to a secondary reformer, where the balance of the hydrocarbons is converted to hydrogen, carbon oxides, and water vapor. Following that, the carbon monoxide is further reacted with steam over a catalyst to produce additional hydrogen and more carbon dioxide by the so-called water gas shift reaction.

The remaining mixture now contains essentially only hydrogen, nitrogen, and carbon dioxide, as well as some residual water vapor. It is now easy to scrub out all but a small amount of the carbon dioxide with one of a number of appropriate solvents, and to condense out the water. A so-called methanation step is used to remove the minor residual amounts of carbon oxides by converting them to methane and water. What remains is a mixture of nitrogen and hydrogen in the desired ratio, plus a minor amount of methane, which is harmless to the ammonia catalyst and represents only a minor yield loss.

To develop the modern, single-train plant design, two key issues had to be addressed:

1. Until the late 1950s, all reformers were designed to operate at atmospheric pressure, since no technology had been developed to carry out this reaction at relatively high pressures and correspondingly higher temperatures. A single-train plant would have to carry out the reforming step under pressure to balance out more closely the pressure levels of the reforming and ammonia synthesis reactions.

2. To bring this nitrogen and hydrogen up to the pressure required in the conversion to ammonia, multistage reciprocating compressors were traditionally used. These cost more than centrifugal compressors and also have size limitations, so that several such units were needed, even in relatively small ammonia plants. Centrifugal compressors are only reasonably efficient above a certain minimum gas volume, which even as early as 1927 engineers with ICI had calculated as corresponding to around 1,000 tons/day of ammonia, synthesized at 3,700 psig.* Single stream output of this magnitude was only required from the late 1960s.

*ICI, personal communication.

Designers most likely visualized, well before the development of the modern ammonia plant flowsheet, that it might eventually be possible to carry out the reforming step under pressure, so that the gases leaving the reformer would be at a high enough pressure level to allow the use of a centrifugal compressor. This much simpler and less maintenance-prone machine could then raise the properly prepared "synthesis gas" mixture of hydrogen and nitrogen to a suitable pressure for the ammonia convertor. But when ICI started working on the pressure reforming of hydrocarbon distillates, the company's objective seems to have been broader than the design of an optimized single-train ammonia plant. The ICI engineers knew that reforming under pressure would reduce compression costs, since it would be cheaper to use a pump to bring liquefied petroleum gases (LPG) or naphtha up to an elevated pressure for the reforming reaction rather than using a compressor to compress the reformed gases to the pressure of the ammonia converter. Moreover, ICI was interested in pressure reforming not only for ammonia, but also for the production of hydrogen (as a product), methanol, and "town gas," a high BTU gas that could be used to replace coal-based water gas in British residential heating and cooking installations. All of these desired products are made from mixtures of carbon monoxide and hydrogen (i.e., products of reforming).

Between 1959 and 1962, an ICI team under the leadership of Dr. T. J. J. Pearce successfully developed the pressure-reforming process (2, pp. 54–67). Much of the piloting was carried out in a single full-sized reactor tube, where the range of conditions required for different feedstocks and synthesis gas compositions could be properly simulated and which would make eminently feasible the scale-up to a commercial reactor containing hundreds or even thousands of these tubes. This required extremely detailed studies on the pressure-reforming reaction at various steam-to-hydrocarbon ratios and reformer exit temperatures, including at levels considerably higher than could be carried out with available tube materials up to that time. Primary reforming at these elevated pressures occurs at 780–850°C, while secondary reforming temperatures reach 1,000°C!

ICI's development program solved a number of very important problems along the way. Catalyst poisoning was found to be caused by sulfur in the feedstock and effective desulfurization catalysts were developed to remove this impurity by pretreatment with a hydrogen stream. It was found that carbon deposition in the reforming tubes, as first encountered under pressure, was due to the acidity of the catalyst support and this resulted in the development of a new support and catalysts containing alkalis. The development team was able to overcome the metallurgical problem associated with higher temperature operation by using reformer tubes constructed with high percentage nickel-chrome alloy steels that had just come on the market. Other developments and improvements were also made in the course of this superb development program. By 1963, four pressure reformers were operating at Billingham and ICI decided to offer the pressure reforming process to the world.

By 1970, 300 ICI reformers had been built by six engineering contractors licensed by the British firm. Of these, 200 were used to make hydrogen, 76 to make lean gas* and 24 for town gas plants. Of the 100 or so reformers built for chemical installations, 75 were for ammonia synthesis, 15 for hydrogen, 5 for carbon monoxide-hydrogen mixtures (oxo synthesis) and 4 for methanol (2, pp. 66–67).

As far as ammonia was concerned, ICI selected M. W. Kellogg as a result of a competitive tender to eventually build three large plants at Billingham. Kellogg's experience in ammonia plant design and construction was extensive. With several relatively large ammonia plant projects completed during the Second World War and thereafter, Kellogg had in the early 1950s embarked on a program to elevate the pressure in the reforming step, though on natural gas feedstock, which was the obvious choice for U.S. producers. In 1953, Kellogg designed a plant for Shell at Ventura, California, operating a reformer at 65 psig and capable of operating up to 90 psig, versus the normal 20 psig required to push the gases through to the suction of the (reciprocal) ammonia synthesis gas compressor.

During the 1950s, Kellogg and other contractors continued to improve the ammonia flowsheet. Reforming pressure was gradually raised to 200 psig. The year 1955 saw the first single train unit as large as 300 tons/day, of course still employing reciprocal compressors.

The Kellogg engineers were quick to capitalize on the break-

*A gas mixture enriched with butane and used for town gas.

through provided by ICI pressure reforming. As recounted in later papers by Len Axelrod, Tom O'Hare, Jim Finneran, and other Kellogg technical managers (3,4), the advent of the ICI pressure-reforming process, together with Kellogg's previous work on natural gas reforming under elevated pressure, opened the way for a new ammonia flowsheet that would integrate the heat and compression energy requirements of the process for the first time, so that there was no major need for an external supply of steam or electric power. This required a complete redesign of the steam generation system, recovery of waste heat at high steam pressure levels, and the use of steam turbine compressor drives. By reducing the synthesis pressure to 2,200 psig, centrifugal compressors could be used for compression for single-stream plants having outputs as low as 600 tons/day of ammonia. This was made possible because the exit pressure from the primary reformer was set around 400 pounds per square inch (psig). Below 600 tons/day, reciprocating compressors continued to be used.

Although Kellog's contribution was less fundamental than ICI's, the firm basically succeeded in tying together a number of individual steps and equipment selections that brought about the large, single-train ammonia plant. Kellogg's key contributions included: (a) the adjustment of reforming and synthesis pressure levels to allow the use of centrifugal compressors, (b) recovery of waste heat at several elevated pressure levels, (c) redesign of the steam generation system, (d) incorporation of a low temperature shift catalyst to reduce the carbon monoxide levels in the gases leaving this step (which, among other benefits, allowed the use of a wider range of hydrocarbon feedstocks), and (e) use of more efficient, lower-cost carbon dioxide scrubbing systems and solvents. The interaction of the many variables involved in the design of optimum synthesis gas and conversion sections was thoroughly evaluated and a series of designs were prepared that covered various plant sizes, feedstocks, and energy/feedstock cost situations relative to specific plant sites. Kellogg also came up with a substantially improved reforming furnace design (Fig. 11.3), although other contractors also developed successful designs for their versions of single-train plants (5). Extensive problems had to be overcome in the successful design of reforming furnaces, involving feasible tube length, tube supports, heat density criteria, etc.

Table 11.2, taken from a 1965 paper delivered by Kellogg at a fertilizer symposium at Kiev in the Ukraine, compares the eco-

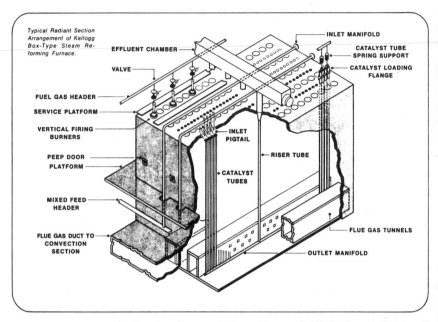

Typical Radiant Section Arrangement of Kellogg Box-Type Steam Reforming Furnace.

EFFLUENT CHAMBER

INLET MANIFOLD

CATALYST TUBE SPRING SUPPORT

VALVE

CATALYST LOADING FLANGE

FUEL GAS HEADER

SERVICE PLATFORM

VERTICAL FIRING BURNERS

INLET PIGTAIL

PEEP DOOR PLATFORM

RISER TUBE

CATALYST TUBES

MIXED FEED HEADER

FLUE GAS DUCT TO CONVECTION SECTION

FLUE GAS TUNNELS

OUTLET MANIFOLD

Figure 11.3 Typical reforming furnace design. (*Source:* A. V. Slack and G. Russell James, eds., *Ammonia,* Part I, New York, Marcel Dekker 1973, p. 239.)

nomics of a 1000-ton-per-day single-train ammonia plant to a 333-ton-per-day plant, typical of designs in the mid-1950s (3). The table shows that the large plant allowed a 22 percent reduction in the production cost. If a return on investment criterion was added,* the difference in required ammonia selling price to achieve the specified return becomes even larger.

In an article published in 1977, (6) Kellogg engineers presented recalculated numbers for this comparison, using cost figures current at that time. With natural gas at 50 cents per million BTU (a cost figure then corresponding to that prevalent in a number of Third World areas), a 400-ton-per-day ammonia plant with reciprocating compressors would give operating costs of $110 per ton, while a 1200-ton-per-day, single-train unit would reduce the cost to $75 per ton.

Figure 11.4 depicts the flow arrangement for a high capacity

*That is, the increment to be added to the manufacturing cost to give a sales price that would yield the desired return on investment.

Table 11.2 Economics of Ammonia Manufacture (high capacity versus low capacity)

Plant size	1,000 tons/day	333 tons/day
Investment	$12,700,000	$5,900,000
Operating cost	$/day	$/day
Raw material		
Naphtha @ $0.60/MM Btu	12,816	4,176
Utilities		
Fuel @ $0.60/MM Btu	6,926	1,714
Power @ $0.011/kWh	53	2,428*
Cooling water @ $0.02/1000 gal	1,112	242
Boiler Feed Water @ $0.25/1000 gal	166	58
Export steam @ $0.60/1000 lb	In balance	−(115)
Catalysts and chemicals	580	150
Labor @ $2.00/M.H. (5 men/shift)	240	240
Maintenance (%/yr)	1,085 (3%)	674 (4%)
Indirect costs @ 16.5%/yr	6,000	2,875
Total operating cost	**$28,978**	**$12,352†**
Cost per ton of ammonia	**$ 28.97**	**$37.06**

Source: See ref. 3.

Note: Investment figures do not include royalty charges.

* Electric drive on reciprocating compressors.

†Equivalent to $37,056 for 1,000 tons/day.

single-train ammonia plant, while Figure 11.5 shows the fairly complex steam system that becomes an inherent part of such a plant. The improved economics and simplicity of the new large plant designs brought about an unprecedented boom in the construction of ammonia plants, first in the United States and soon after in Canada, Europe, and other parts of the world. In early 1964, Kellogg was already working on the construction or expansion of 21 such plants, though most of these used natural gas (not naphtha) feedstock. The first of the "new breed," a 600-ton-per-day Kellogg unit, had already come on stream at Monsanto's Luling, Louisiana complex. This all-centrifugal plant operated its reforming section at 350 psig and its ammonia synthesis loop at 2200 psig. The first 1000-ton-per-day Kellogg plant was placed in operation by Mississippi Chemical at Yazoo City, Mississippi in the spring of 1966.

In May of that year, Kellogg announced that it had received orders for 23 plants with capacities ranging from 600 to 1000 tons per day, adding up to 7 million tons annually, equivalent to

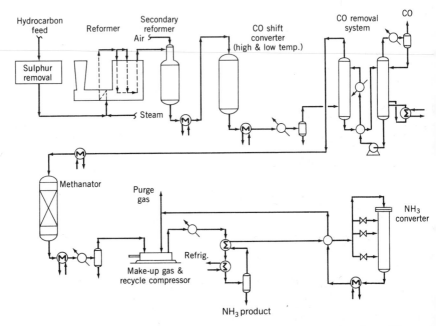

Figure 11.4 Flowsheet for high capacity single-train ammonia plant. (*Source: Encyclopedia of Chemical Processing and Design,* Vol. 3, New York, Marcel Dekker, 1977.)

about half of worldwide capacity for plants of this size. Several of the other major engineering firms were also busy building large ammonia plants, including Chemico (for Arkla Chemical, Borden, American Oil), C. F. Braun (for Grace in Trinidad and Collier Chemical), and Bechtel (for Agrico and Olin Mathieson) (7,8).

Interestingly, Kellogg now called the industry's attention to a patent that claimed pressure reforming as a Kellogg invention. Filed in 1953, long before ICI's practical development work on high pressure reforming, the patent showed that there were advantages when reforming was carried out at pressures above 50 pounds per square inch (psig). And Kellogg was able to show that it had, in fact, operated a pilot plant in the early 1950s at 32–58 psig and had designed a reformer for the Shell plant in Ventura, California that could operate at reforming pressures up to 90 psig. Competing contractors were required by Kellogg to pay a royalty for designs combining the pressure-reforming step with the steam and heat

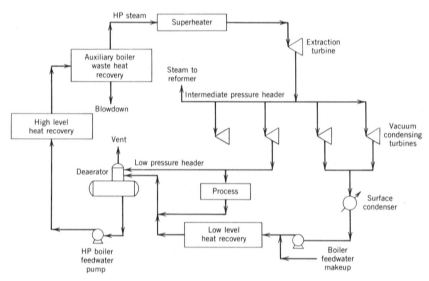

Figure 11.5 Typical ammonia plant steam system. (*Source: Encyclopedia of Chemical Processing and Design,* Vol. 3, New York, Marcel Dekker, 1977.)

balance and centrifugal compressor usage in the modern ammonia process flowsheet. Although the royalty was not particularly large, it gave Kellogg some advantage over its competitors. (Eventually, the patent was successfully contested by Fluor and others.) (9)

Not surprisingly, a number of problems were encountered in some of the early large units designed by Kellogg and the other contractors. There is usually a price to pay when a major scale-up step is taken and giant ammonia plants were no exception. Some of these problems involved mechanical design and construction materials (e.g., reformer tubes). There were also some operating problems, including reformer tube "hot-spotting," waste heat boiler fouling, and catalyst poisoning. These problems were, however, solved in a surprisingly short time, with the different contractors and operators coming up with various solutions. Ammonia producers who encountered these difficulties were also often able to exchange information at industry technical meetings.* Thus, the

---

*Such information exchanges are perfectly legal (under the antitrust laws) if pricing is not discussed.

design and operation of 1000 ton per day ammonia plants soon became routine.

Many other contractors became proficient in the design of single-train ammonia plants, including such U.S. firms as Fluor and Foster-Wheeler, as well as foreign contractors such as Humphreys and Glasgow (England), Davy McKee (England), Haldor Topsoe (Denmark), Stamicarbon (Holland), Uhde (Germany), Snamprogetti (Italy), and Toyo Engineering (Japan) to name only a few. Several of these firms also specialized in the design of large, single-train urea plants, which were frequently built next to ammonia plants to utilize the carbon dioxide by-product.

By 1975, about 80 plants with ammonia production capacities greater than 600 tons per day had been constructed in various parts of the world. This resulted in a dramatic increase in world production of ammonia, which rose from 12.5 million short tons in 1955 to 75 million short tons in 1975 (Fig. 11.6).

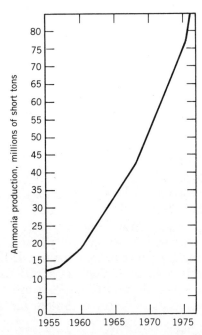

Figure 11.6 Annual world ammonia production. (*Source: Encyclopedia of Chemical Processing and Design,* New York, Marcel Dekker, 1977, p. 256ff.)

At this writing, large scale ammonia plants continue to be constructed in all parts of the world, since nitrogen fertilizers are required in increasing quantities by Third World nations. In that sense, the greatly improved economics of large-scale ammonia plants have been a boon to mankind in the poorest as well as in the wealthiest countries.

APOTHEOSIS: "WORLD SIZE" STEAM CRACKERS

Ethylene was, at an early stage, known as being a constituent of gases coming off coke ovens. At first, it was found to be useful only as an illuminant, a result of the double bond between the two carbon atoms. As a reactive chemical "building block," however, ethylene for a long time took a back seat to acetylene, which contains a triple bond and is therefore even much more reactive than ethylene. But there came a time in the late 1920s when George Curme at Union Carbide and other researchers in Germany and elsewhere began to believe that one day ethylene would be a more important, less expensive chemical building block than acetylene. Within a relatively short time, they were proved to be right. How ethylene took over most large-scale acetylene uses for chemical synthesis is covered in earlier chapters of this book. The following pages describe how the development of very large single-train steam crackers became what some believe was the crowning achievement of the engineers serving the petrochemical industry.

By the end of World War II, ethylene production via thermal steam cracking of light hydrocarbons was already well established in the United States, although a substantial proportion of the ethylene converted to derivatives at that time was recovered from refinery cracking plants. Engineering contractors, led by Stone and Webster, had learned to design plants to crack ethane or ethane-propane mixtures to obtain reasonable yields of ethylene and (when cracking LPG) propylene, and other by-products, including some butadiene for conversion to SBR rubber.

A paper published by Stone and Webster engineers in December 1945 gives an overview of the state of the art in steam cracking at that time (10). Little detail was provided on furnace design, but the tube residence times discussed in the paper were quite long. Furnace coil length was then about 400 feet, versus only 100 feet or so today and coil outlet temperature 1150°F versus 1600–1700°F presently. The cracked gases were brought up to 600 psig in three or four stages of a reciprocating compressor installation. After dehydration, there followed a methane tower, an ethylene tower, an ethane tower, and a propylene tower. The columns used conventional cross-flow layouts, with steel trays and 4-inch diameter bell type cast iron bubble caps. Ethylene itself was used as a refrigerant for the methane tower, with either propane or ammonia used for the subsequent fractionations, in line with traditional Linde technology. Centrifugal compressors were already employed for refrigerant compression service. Ethylene was produced at a purity level of 95 percent. Asked in the subsequent discussion about the economics of such a plant, one of the authors said that for a 100 ton per day unit (about 60 million pounds per year) the cost of ethylene might average 2 cents, but could be as high as 3 cents per pound.

Variations of this type of flowsheet were used by other engineering contractors and operating companies designing ethylene plants in the late 1940s and 1950s. In Europe and Japan, where light hydrocarbons such as ethane and propane were not particularly abundant, but where there was usually a surplus of light naphtha from petroleum refineries, steam crackers were based on petroleum distillates. Standard of New Jersey and others had already accumulated considerable know-how before and during World War II on cracking liquid feedstocks, so that the design and operation of so-called "heavy feedstock" crackers did not present any particular difficulties. And the advantage of cracking these distillates was that the exit gases contained even larger quantities of valuable by-products, including propylene, butylenes, butadiene and benzene. For the European and Japanese chemical firms building these heavy feedstock crackers, this was very important, since the refineries in these countries usually lacked the catalytic cracking units and reformers that provided a substantial percentage of the C_3 and higher reactive building blocks in the United States. Steam crackers in Europe and Japan thus produced much of the benzene and propylene converted to petrochemical end products in these regions.

As ethylene derivatives production increased, so did the number of steam crackers. Nevertheless, a large number of companies—particularly in Europe, but also in the United States—felt that this production technique left something to be desired. For one thing, a thermal process can never be as selective as a catalytic one and is therefore difficult to tailor so as to provide a specifically desired distribution of products. LPG or naphtha were fed in at one end of the furnace and, within limits, a certain distribution of products came out the other, regardless of what your product distribution needs might be. Also, furnace tubes, particularly in ethane cracking—which occurs at very high temperatures—gradually developed a layer of coke, so that the furnaces had to be shut down periodically for coke removal.* In addition, tube metallurgy limitations kept maximum cracking temperatures below the theoretically most efficient levels. Finally, many companies in the 1950s were still using substantial amounts of acetylene for the production of such important monomers as vinyl chloride, vinyl acetate, and acrylonitrile. These companies often felt that it would be advantageous to use a cracking process that could coproduce both ethylene and acetylene. This seemed like a reasonable objective, since George Curme and German researchers had shown that when hydrocarbon feedstocks are subjected to successively higher temperatures and shorter residence times, mixtures of ethylene and acetylene are formed. But conventional steam crackers in the 1950s could not operate at high enough temperatures to produce some acetylene.

Given this situation, it is not surprising that, in the 1950s, a number of other processes were being developed for the coproduction of ethylene and acetylene from petroleum hydrocarbons. Generally, these took one of two forms:

- Reaction systems consisting of *two vessels* and employing a heat carrier, such as sand or pebbles, which was circulated between these vessels. In one of these, the heat carrier was raised to a temperature considerably higher than that employed in conventional steam crackers (by combustion of reaction coke and externally added fuel with air) and then transported to the other vessel, where the hydrocarbon feedstock was cracked to ethylene or to mixtures of ethylene and acetylene. The BASF-Lurgi sand cracker and the Phillips Pebble Heater system (Fig. 11.7) were examples of such plants. However, very few of these units were ever built, due to their high cost and difficulty of operation (11).

*Later, on-stream decoking procedures were developed.

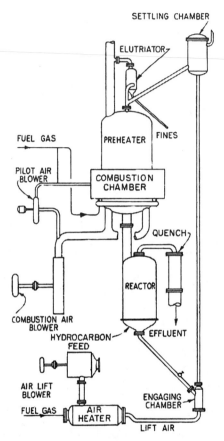

Figure 11.7 Phillips pebble heater, flow diagram. (*Source:* S. A. Miller, *Ethylene and Its Derivatives,* London, Ernest Benn, 1969.)

- A two-stage system, employing extremely hot combustion gases to crack the hydrocarbon feedstock; this operation was carried out in a *single vessel*. In the first chamber, combustible "tail gases" from the recovery section of the plant were burned with oxygen to produce combustion gases at temperatures exceeding 2,000°F. In this step, flame temperatures as high as 4,000°F were reached and a special water-jacketed design was employed to cool the refractory-lined chamber. In the second chamber, the preheated hydrocarbon feedstock was injected into the hot combustion gases leaving the first chamber and cracked to ethylene and acetylene. The HTP Process developed by Hoechst, a large user of acetylene, as well as ethylene, in the 1950s, was the prime example of such a process. Société Belge de l'Azôte also developed this type of technology. Considerably later, TRW (previously Thompson-Ramo-Wooldridge, a company named after the three CalTech professors who founded the firm) attempted unsuccessfully to develop a similar system, using a rocket engine from the U.S. space program.*

Other ethylene and acetylene production schemes were also being developed during this period. One of these, called the Wulff process after its German inventor, later became the property of Union Carbide. This process used a furnace system designed to operate at higher temperatures than in normal steam cracking furnaces through the use of regenerative brickwork and by reversing flows. One of the interesting features of the process was that by varying the temperature in the furnaces, the relative amounts of ethylene and acetylene could be varied over a wide range, as shown on the graph in Figure 11.8 (12). Several plants of this type were built, including one for Marathon Oil at Burghausen, Germany, and another for a Union Carbide subsidiary in Brazil.

Interestingly, no company was able to develop a viable *catalytic* approach to the basic steam cracking step (i.e., a cracking process that would use a catalyst inside the tubes, where the cracking reaction takes place), although such a process would have allowed the use of lower cracking temperatures and would presumably have improved the yields of ethylene. No such route was commercialized then or since that time. The probable reason is that in thermal steam cracking, essentially all of the products emanating from the reaction furnace have a use, either as feedstocks for further processing or as a plant fuel. A more selective process could never be justified, in that such a process always had lower total product and by-product revenues. This rather unusual situation for a chemical process has resulted in maintaining, up to the present time, essentially the same basic approach to ethylene production (i.e., passing a mixture of hydrocarbon feedstock and steam through

*Chem Systems, asked to evaluate this technology, could not recommend commercialization and the process work was subsequently discontinued.

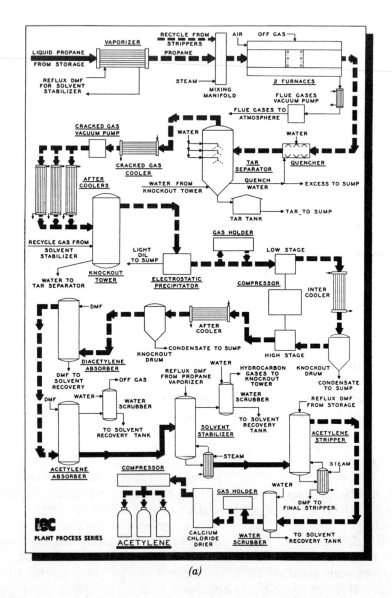

Figure 11.8 (*a*) Flowsheet for the production of acetylene by the Wulff process. (*Source:* G. H. Bixler and C. W. Coberly, Wulff process acetylene, in *Modern Chemical Processes,* Vol. 3, New York, Reinhold, 1954, pp. 260–270.)

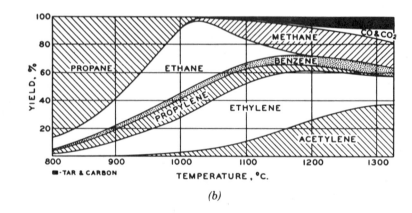

(b)

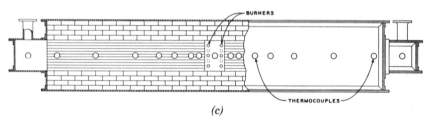

(c)

Figure 11.8 (*b*) Distribution of products using propane feed. (*c*) Wulff regenerative furnace. (*Source:* same as for Figure 11.8*a*.)

externally fired furnace tubes). Industry people concur that this system will probably continue to be employed for the foreseeable future.

In any event, the economics of the Hoechst HTP process and of the other ethylene and ethylene/acetylene production techniques were never as good as those achieved in conventional steam crackers, except for special situations, such as at Hoechst, which required large amounts of acetylene. And, as discussed in Chapter 10, the superior economics of ethylene—versus acetylene-based processes—for making vinyl chloride spelled the end of hydrocarbon cracking processes designed to produce mixtures of the two reactive hydrocarbons. Eventually, even Hoechst decided to discontinue manufacture of both building blocks and switched to ethylene as a feedstock, investing in the petrochemical refinery of Union Rheinische Braunkohlen Kraftstoff AG, which henceforth supplied ethylene to Hoechst's downstream operation.

The 1950s were therefore a period when the petrochemical industry was aware that a number of companies were interested in developing more selective technology for the production of ethylene, or ethylene and acetylene. There was also considerable hope that this would result in processes with reaction systems that could be more readily scaled up, as compared to conventional steam crackers, which required multiple cracking furnaces. The issue of scale-up had become important, since ethylene production rose from 1.5 to 5.3 billion pounds between 1950 and 1960 and was projected to rise to almost 10 billion pounds by 1965. In the early 1950s, the largest ethylene plant designed up to then had a capacity of 100 million pounds per year and utilized a number of cracking furnaces. By the end of the decade, it also became obvious to the operating companies and contractors engaged in the design and operation of ethylene plants that new technologies* would not, at least for the time being, become a factor in the design of large ethylene plants. Thus, perhaps somewhat reluctantly, the ethylene manufacturing industry decided to turn its attention to the development of a flowsheet for giant ethylene plants based on the tried and true thermal steam cracking process, but which would hopefully have higher yields and much lower fixed costs.

Although many companies played a part in this all-important program, some of the firms most closely associated with the development and commercialization of today's giant, highly economical ethylene plants were Stone and Webster, Lummus, Kellogg, Selas and Foster-Wheeler (both furnace designers), Standard Oil Development Company (Esso Chemical), and Schmidt (a German heat-exchanger manufacturer). Working partly together and partly in competition with each other, these firms came up with what would later be called the "new breed" of "world-size" steam crackers, that would start to be installed in the major countries located in the three important industrial regions, starting in the mid-1960s. Over this period, Lummus, which was selling its ethylene know-how harder and more successfully than the other firms, became the busiest ethylene contractor for a period of time, although the Stone and Webster design, using Selas furnaces, and the Kellogg design were considered comparable to that offered by Lummus. And although Esso was well ahead of both of

---

*i.e. radically new processes, such as those described earlier.

these contractors in furnace design know-how and operating experience, its own review of the Lummus, Stone and Webster, and soon thereafter, Braun and Kellogg designs convinced the oil company, which had pioneered the steam cracking of heavy liquids, that there was now going to be a new, considerably more economical generation of ethylene plants. Henceforth, Esso would rely on contractor designs rather than on Esso Engineering for its olefin units (except for furnace design). Esso's earlier successful experience with very high heat flux furnaces had, of course, been an important factor in stimulating the pilot plant programs that allowed the contractors to develop the new ethylene plant designs.

An awareness that important breakthroughs in ethylene manufacture were at hand came during the summer of 1964. The term "high severity" furnaces or cracking yields, for example, started to appear around that time. We also started to hear about "transfer line exchangers" (called "quench boilers" by Kellogg) which were used to recover high level heat by generating high pressure steam from the cracked gases leaving the furnaces. Previously, these gases had been quenched to a low temperature by direct contact with recycled fuel oil, a far less efficient technique, involving a waste of potential energy recovery. The design of the new exchangers represented a breakthrough by Schmidt and another German firm, Borsig. Units designed by these firms provided a means to rapidly cool the furnace exit gases in an exchanger configuration that precluded fouling and therefore avoided the frequent shutdowns that occurred in conventional exchangers, where polymers present in the hydrocarbon stream would condense and form coke on the tube walls. And it was also understood that centrifugal compressors were being used throughout the plant, including on the cracked gases, so that there would henceforth be only a single large (centrifugal) compressor in each of the major services, no matter what the size of the ethylene plant.

These reports and rumors came from various companies and locations. Selas had designed the furnaces for Rheinische Olefin-werke (R.O.W.), a joint venture of Shell and BASF in Wesseling, Germany, which had recently built a 600-million-pound-per-year plant, with C. F. Braun designing the fractionation and recovery section. Monsanto had just started up a new 500 million pound per year heavy liquids cracker at Chocolate Bayou, Texas, employing new Foster-Wheeler high severity furnaces. Stone and Webster had designed and placed in successful operation several high severity Selas furnaces and was now designing a cracker for Shawinigan Chemical in Varennes, Quebec, which allegedly incorporated the various design features. Kellogg, which was particularly secretive about its design, was known to have received contracts from Sinclair-Koppers and other companies that had been impressed with the operation and economics of short residence furnaces and quench boilers that Kellogg had installed in one or two existing ethylene plants. Lummus was making broad claims regarding the success of a patented new high severity furnace that had been placed in operation in several plants in the United States and in Europe, and was designing a "new breed" 750 million lbs./year cracker for DuPont in Texas. All of these new installations apparently used the new transfer-line exchangers, about which there was great speculation and secrecy.

In October 1964, at a United Nations technical conference held in Teheran, some of the mystery surrounding the allegedly fabulous economics of these large new ethylene plants was lifted with the delivery of an important paper by P. Braber of Royal Dutch Shell (13). As a part-owner of R.O.W., Shell was very close to the new developments in ethylene manufacture and the company apparently now decided that it was time to publish some of the results. In many respects, Braber's paper was a stunner. Discussing primarily the new design for naphtha-based crackers, he disclosed the following information:

- High severity naphtha cracking could give yields in the range of 30 weight percent, versus 18 percent for the older furnace designs.
- As the total yield of C_4 hydrocarbons dropped significantly, the amount of highly desirable butadiene in this fraction was nevertheless doubled.
- The cost of utilities for operating a new 200,000 ton per year plant was reduced from £19 to £7.5 per ton of ethylene.
- The total production cost for ethylene was dramatically lower. Braber produced the following comparison:

Plant Size	Manufacturing Cost
1955: 20,000 TPY	81£ per ton
1965: 100,000 TPY (new design)	32£ per ton
1975: 200,000 TPY (new design)	25£ per ton

Confidentiality agreements with his company, and with contractors who had disclosed their new design schemes to Shell, kept Braber from providing specific information on how these dramatic improvements in yield and other production costs had, in fact, been achieved. But more details emerged as the months passed and by October 1965, Don Burke and Ryle Miller of *Chemical Week* magazine published a comprehensive two-part article that provided a better understanding of what many people in the industry already largely knew (14).

The most important developments had occurred in furnace design. Careful study of both theoretical variables and actual conditions inside the cracking tubes led several of the firms designing the new heaters to the conclusion that the residence time for the reactants should be reduced from the previous range of 1–1.5 seconds to about 0.4 seconds or less. At the same time, the heat flux (radiant heat input) was increased from the previous levels of 8,000–12,000 to as high as 25,000 Btu/hr/sq ft of tube wall surface. Among other things, this required a complete redesign of the cracking furnaces, with single rows of radiant-type burners supplying this unprecedented high heat input. Tube wall temperatures would rise to 1900°F or higher, with the tubes now constructed of 25 percent chromium–20 percent nickel alloys, similar to the steels used for ammonia plant reformer tubes. Esso was said to be using even higher heat densities in its furnaces. The key point, apparently discovered independently by several developers, was that a combination of much higher heat fluxes and shorter residence times would not only give much higher ethylene yields, but would actually inhibit the coke formation that occurred at lower heat fluxes by favoring the olefin-forming reactions rather than the secondary reactions at the tube wall film. The latter evidently produced higher boiling liquids and polymers and resulted in the progressive laydown of coke experienced up to that time. It was this new aproach to furnace design that evidently gave the higher ethylene and butadiene yields reported in the Braber paper. An additional major benefit was that the furnaces could be designed to handle a much greater throughput and experienced far less coking. Thus, the same number of furnaces could be used for a plant two or three times larger than the previous typical plant, designed for low severity operation, and their on-stream time was much longer. The evolution of furnace design at the Lummus Companies is shown on Figure 11.9 (15).

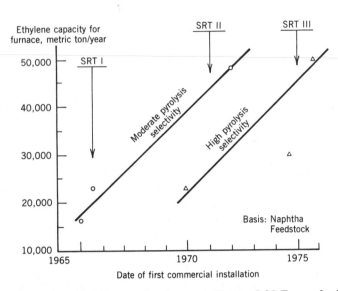

Figure 11.9 History of SRT furnace development. (*Source:* J. M. Fernandez-Baujin and A. J. Gambro, Lummus Corp. Interamerican Congress, Caracas, Venezuela, July 1975.)

Mounted directly on the outlet line from the furnaces were the new transfer-line exchangers, which were one of the main reasons for the lower utility consumption (Figs. 11.10 and 11.11) (16). The high pressure steam generated in these units could now be used in efficient turbines that would drive the cracked gas or refrigeration compressors in other parts of the plant, providing a major utility savings.

A number of important improvements were also made in the refrigeration and distillation sections, which separated the hydrogen and methane and recovered the ethylene and propylene produced in the furnaces. Greatly improved vapor-liquid equilibrium data for the separation of methane, ethylene and ethane had recently become available and the contractors used this information to modify column design (e.g., lower reflux ratios) and to reduce refrigeration horsepower. A typical flowsheet for the complex refrigeration system around the demethanizer tower is shown in Figure 11.12. New, highly efficient sieve trays were substituted for the bubble cap trays used in the earlier designs.

While none of these modifications was as dramatic as the change in furnace design, they resulted in a substantially more

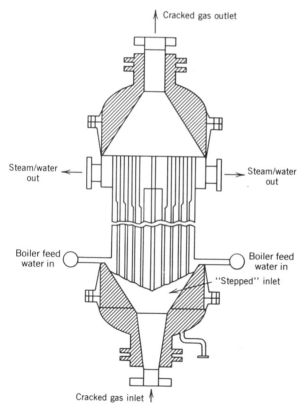

Cracked gas outlet

Steam/water out

Steam/water out

Boiler feed water in

Boiler feed water in

"Stepped" inlet

Cracked gas inlet

Figure 11.10 Transfer line exchanger (Schmidt design). (*Source:* Chem Systems.)

economical recovery and purification section for the new ethylene plants. In one comparison of which I was aware, a new Kellogg design saved approximately 5000 horsepower, in total, for the three compressors (17,800 vs. 22,800 brake horsepower), versus a more traditional recovery and purification design. Interestingly, the overall equipment arrangement had not changed appreciably from earlier designs. A current schematic flowsheet of an ethylene plant is shown as Figure 11.13.

Often, petrochemical complexes are built in locations reasonably far from frequently traveled highways. Even if one side of a production complex is adjacent to a main highway, a plant using novel technology is often placed well away from the road. It was, therefore, an exciting surprise that the new Sinclair-Koppers eth-

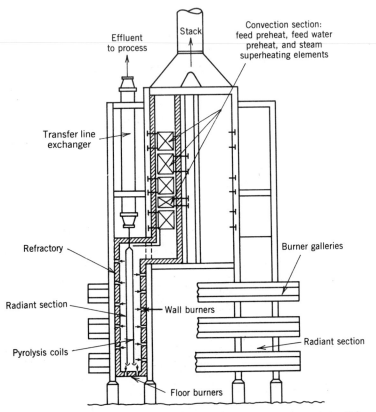

Figure 11.11 Typical ethylene plant cracking furnace arrangement. (*Source:* L. Kniel, O. Winter, and C. Tsai, the Lummus Co.)

ylene plant built on the Houston ship channel was easily visible from Texas State Route 225, going south from Houston to LaPorte. Traveling along this road, one could get a good look at this great leap forward in ethylene plant design. One of the most impressive parts of the plant was the furnace section, containing as I recall, four very large vertical furnaces with integrally mounted transfer line exchangers and with their flue gas ducts tied together in a complex arrangement that reached toward the Pasadena sky. And well behind the furnaces the large, gleaming towers, some operating at temperatures far below ambient, separating the hydrogen and methane as plant fuel and recovering the ethylene at a rate that was, in fact, larger than the entire production of this chemical during World War II. There was truly something majes-

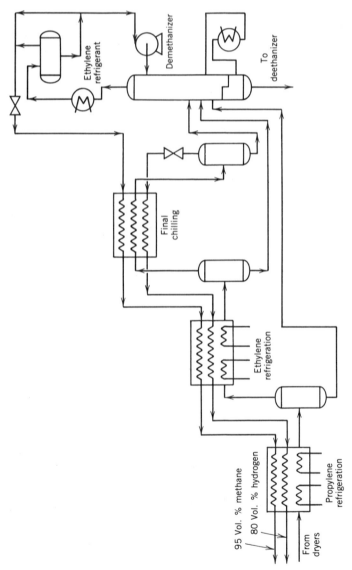

Figure 11.12 Refrigeration systems around an ethylene plant demethanizer. (*Source:* Chem Systems.)

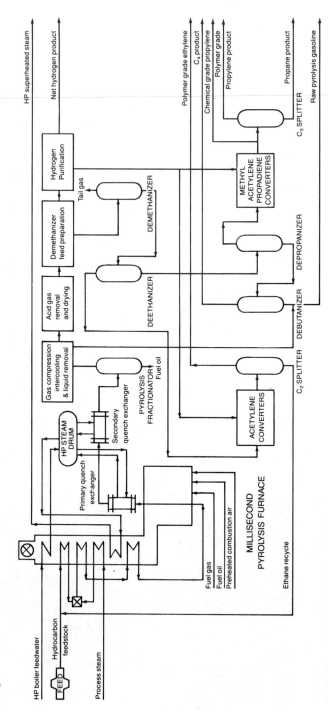

Figure 11.13 The M. W. Kellogg Co. ethylene process. (*Source:* Courtesy M. W. Kellogg Company.)

tic about such a plant—the culmination of chemical engineering achievement in an industry barely 40 years old.

The *Chemical Week* paper also provided information on the improved investment economics of the new large high severity cracking plants. Data submitted by Kellogg indicated that the capital cost of a 400–450 million pound per year cracker had dropped from $22 million in 1960 to less than $13 million as a result of the design improvements made in the period 1960–1964 (14). Braber had given even more dramatic figures in his paper, citing a decline in capital costs from $140 per 1000 pounds in 1957 to $35 in 1964 on the same basis (13).

The ethylene industry was, as usual, quick to react to these favorable economics. In 1960, ethylene sold for 5.25 cents per pound on the Gulf Coast, but by 1964 the price had dropped to 4.75 cents and in the fall of 1965 ethylene was down to 4 cents per pound. Because, at the prevalent Gulf Coast cost of light naphtha, ethylene could now be produced for only 2 cents per pound (including capital charges), if all by-products were sold at full credit; if not, the production cost on the same basis would rise to 3.4 cents per pound, according to the Burke-Miller paper. The economics of ethylene production from propane and ethane were even more favorable. Most of the ethylene in the United States was, in fact, produced from these very light feedstocks.

Over the late 1960s and early 1970s, the size of ethylene plants kept increasing (see Fig. 11.1). Soon, a number of billion pound per year plants were on the drawing boards and not long thereafter, these units went into operation in the United States and in Western Europe. Several even larger plants were built in the 1970s. Recognition then dawned that, beyond a certain size, there was no incentive to make the plants even larger. The economics of scale did not improve markedly beyond a certain size. Moreover, no further key improvements were made in ethylene plant design, and so the technology also stabilized. Typical economics for a one billion pound per year ethylene plants using various feedstocks, published by Stone & Webster in 1976 (see Table 11.3), have not been improved very much since that time (17).

Although the operation of the giant plants became routine and essentially trouble free, the operating companies became aware of certain disadvantages as the size of their plants increased. In periods of oversupply, it is more efficient to operate a somewhat smaller plant at full capacity than a very large plant at a capacity

Table 11.3 Yield Structure for One-Billion-Pound-per-Year Ethylene Plants (1976)

LPG Feedstocks

Feed:	Ethane	Ethane/Propane (30/70)	Propane
Annual Feed, Bbl/Stream Day:	28,300*	33,500	35,600
Products:			
Propylene	—	201,000	325,600
Butadiene in C_4 Mixture	—	46,800	64,600
BTX in pyrolysis gasoline	10,300	44,400	69,800
Fuel Oil	—	500	900

Naphtha Feedstocks

Feed:	Kuwait Naphtha		Heavy Kuwait Naphtha	
Cracking severity:	High	Moderate	High	Moderate
Annual Feed, Bbl/Stream Day:	37,000	43,900	38,900	45,500
Products:				
Propylene	419,800	627,000	444,600	649,500
Butadiene in C_4 mixture	141,100	171,400	151,800	179,600
BTX in pyrolysis gasoline	500,300	412,000	612,200	685,300
Fuel oil	195,400	117,500	240,600	136,700

Table 11.3 (continued)

Feed:	East Texas Gas Oil	West Texas Light Gas Oil
Cracking severity:	High	Moderate
Annual Feed, Bbl/Stream Day:	40,600	43,700
Products:		
Propylene	557,400	614,200
Butadiene in C_4 mixture	186,800	202,900
BTX in pyrolysis gasoline	409,100	450,900
Fuel oil	729,400	1,006,500

Source: See ref. 17.

*Except where noted, quantities are in thousand pounds per year.

455

well under design. Also, it became clear that, it was not always a simple matter—even for a refiner with an ethylene plant—to supply a full slate of reasonably priced feedstocks for this unit. Thus, if a company had an ethylene plant that utilized several different refinery and LPG streams to bring the total feed rate up to the required (roughly) 30,000 barrels per day, the last increment of feedstock was often quite a bit more expensive than the first increment. There often were times, in fact, when a somewhat smaller plant would have actually provided better economics by cracking only the less expensive feedstocks.

The "new breed" of ethylene plants, however, did become the standard for the industry and represented a culmination of the golden era of the petrochemical industry. The efficiency of these plants was remarkable, as contractors kept improving their flowsheets, for example reducing refrigeration/compression horsepower requirements by 50 percent between 1960 and 1975. With Gulf Coast ethane and propane priced far lower than in any other industrial region, U.S. producers were, for many years, able to export ethylene and propylene derivatives to many other parts of the world, creating a highly favorable trade balance in chemicals. To the dismay of domestic producers, however, they collectively managed to drop ethylene prices to under 3 cents per pound by the late 1960s, with one purchaser obtaining a well-publicized long-term price of only 2.6 cents per pound. With over 20 producers fighting for the merchant market, and most Gulf Coast ethylene producers tied together by a comprehensive network of pipelines, the buying power of ethylene purchasers became a permanent feature of the industry. The fact that these companies succeeded in keeping the price of ethylene well below a level that gave producers a reasonable return on investment was a bitter pill for the operators to swallow. It might well be said: seldom has such a magnificent achievement produced such a disappointing return!

LARGE PLANTS—OTHER ISSUES AND CONCLUSIONS

Although this chapter has focused only on ammonia and ethylene as good examples of processes that were scaled up to large, single-train plants, the same approach was taken for a number of other petrochemicals. Thus, vinyl chloride and styrene plants were built with capacities approaching one billion pounds per year, and methanol plants with capacities in excess of that figure. A number of other petrochemical plants were designed with capacities of at least 500 million pounds per year. What made these plant sizes even more significant, in many cases, was the fact that the product they produced often represented a relatively high share of the market. The consequence to the industry of absorbing the output of such large plants was therefore by no means inconsequential. This was not usually true in the case of ethylene, however, where each new (even one billion pound) plant corresponded to a considerably smaller share of the market into which it was selling this next "tranche" of capacity.

Similar to large ethylene plant economics, the production costs of these other large plants also did not improve markedly beyond a certain size. Thus, the fixed costs of a vinyl chloride plant designed for 800 million pounds per year were only a little lower than for a plant half that size—a savings of perhaps a 0.2 or 0.3 cents per pound. While this difference must have seemed significant to the companies deciding to build the larger plant, these firms later often found that other elements of operating costs, such as changes in raw material or utility costs, were more important and that the penalties of operating a larger plant at a lower operating rate frequently outweighed the advantages sought in building the bigger plant in the first place.

The fact that any company with enough money (and courage) could, in many cases, build the largest plant with the latest, most efficient technology also disproved to a considerable extent the "Experience Curve" concept, advanced by the Boston Consulting Group, as a strategic weapon for companies in the petrochemical industry. B.C.G. related this concept to companies that used a high market share position to maintain or increase their technological lead due to their ability to invest more money in research, allowing greater production efficiencies. While the concept was valid in some industries, such as in electronics manufacture, it was *not* particularly applicable to the petrochemical industry. In the United States, companies such as Esso Chemical, Union Carbide, Dow, and Gulf had, for a number of years, been the leaders in ethylene production. Then, engineering contractors learned how to build these plants. No doubt to the considerable chagrin of the traditional ethylene producers, such newcomers to the industry as Conoco, Arco and Amoco could now engage contractors to build ethylene plants that were bigger and at least as, or even more, efficient than those operated by the traditional producers. This was because the experience that had been gained by the contracting industry was now made available to all willing to pay the price. Table 11.4 illustrates the furious activity of contractors in the construction of ethylene plants in the late 1960s worldwide. It was hardly surprising, therefore, that the traditional producers did not enjoy any greater profitability in ethylene manufacture than their new competitors. The profitability of the ethylene industry has never really recovered since that time.

The contractors that promoted the large plant concept must also accept a certain amount of responsibility for overselling, at times, the advantages of large plant economics. Thus, a July 1968 article by Len Axelrod and two other Kellogg engineers predicted that ammonia plants would reach capacities of 3000 tons per day and ethylene plants, two billion pounds per year (18). Presenting a series of tables showing how the size of various types of process units had increased between 1940 and the late 1960s, the authors confidently extrapolated ammonia and ethylene plant sizes to emulate what had previously happened in the design of ever larger refinery pipe stills and fluid catalytic cracking units. To the Kellogg engineers, the main issue involved the feasibility of equipment scale-up, particularly rotating equipment, such as turbines and compressors. Distillation towers and reactors could certainly be made larger by known field welding techniques and most other parts of plant design would not present any particular scale up difficulties. Recognizing the unfavorable publicity that accompanied the startup of some of the early single-train ammonia plants, Axelrod cited the better experience gained in subsequent installations and cautioned operators to develop a greater understanding of new plant designs and to exert more effort on equipment knowledge, as well as on equipment care and maintenance. Given these conditions, and continued development of larger rotating equipment, he saw no difficulty in further increasing the size of single-train petrochemical plants.

Up to the present time, almost 20 years after publication of this article, not one ammonia or ethylene plant of the size visualized by Axelrod and his co-workers has been constructed to my knowledge, and it is doubtful that such plants will ever be built. Extrapolation of trends beyond a certain point is a dangerous exercise and, in this case, not justified. The large plant syndrome reached its apex in the years just before the 1973 oil shock and has been surpassed by other events since that time.

Table 11.4 Record of Four Major Ethylene Contractors (late 1960s)

Contractor	Complete Record		Plants On-Stream or Under Construction since Jan. 1966	
	No. Plants	C_2H_4 Capacity (billion lb/yr)	No. Plants	C_2H_4 Capacity (billion lb/yr)
Braun	15	3.0	5	2.20
Kellogg	24	4.4	8	2.50
Lummus	41	9.0	11	5.63
Stone & Webster	72	10.0	20	4.84

Source: Chem Systems, Multiclient Subscriber Report on Ethylene Production (1967).

REFERENCES

1. W. Tucker and M. A. Abrahams (1976). Heavier feedstock trends: The changing economics of petrochemical production, presented at the World Congress of the Société de la Chimie Industrielle, Valley Forge, PA, October 1976.

2. B. G. Achilladelis (1973). Process innovation in the chemical industry, Ph.D. thesis, University of Sussex, England, The Billingham Site.

3. L. C. Axelrod and T. E. O'Hare (1965). Aspects of large scale ammonia production, United Nations Interregional Seminar, held at Kiev, Ukranian Soviet Socialist Republic, August 24–September 13.

4. Vincent Sanchelli, ed. (1964). *Fertilizer Nitrogen,* New York, Reinhold.

5. A. V. Slack and G. R. James (1973). *Ammonia* (4 volumes), New York, Marcel Dekker.

6. *Encyclopedia of Chemical Processing and Design,* Vol. 3, New York, Marcel Dekker, 1977, pp. 256ff.

7. First of the big, big ones, *Chemical Week,* November 20, 1965.

8. Kellogg's first giant NH_3 plant, *European Chemical News,* October 22, 1965.

9. CPI resists reformer royalties, *Chemical Week,* January 23, 1965.

10. A. W. Pratt and N. L. Foskett (1945). Low temperature processing of light hydrocarbons, A.I.Ch.E. Meeting, Chicago, Illinois, December 18–19.

11. S. A. Miller (1969). *Ethylene and Its Industrial Derivatives,* London, Ernest Benn, pp. 73–74.

12. G. H. Bixler and C. W. Coberly (1954). Wulff process acetylene, *In Modern Chemical Processes,* Vol. III, Editors of *Industrial and Engineering Chemistry,* eds., New York, Reinhold, pp. 260–270.

13. P. Braber (1964). Technical and economic changes in ethylene manufacture, presented at United Nations Inter-Regional Conference on the Development of Petrochemical Industries in Developing Countries, October.

14. Donald P. Burke and Ryle Miller (1965). Ethylene, *Chemical Week,* October 23, p. 63, November 13, p. 69.

15. J. M. Fernandez-Baujin and A. J. Gambro (1975). Technology and economics for modern olefin plants, presented at Sixth Interamerican Congress of Chemical Engineering, Caracas, Venezuela, July 13–16.

16. Ludwig Kniel, Olaf Winter, and Chung-Hu Tsai (1980). The Lummus company, *Kirk-Othmer Encyclopedia of Chemical Technology,* Vol. 9, Third edition, New York, Wiley, pp. 393–431.

17. T. B. Baba and J. R. Kennedy (1976). Ethylene and its co-products, the new economics, *Chemical Engineering,* January 5.

18. L. Axelrod, R. E. Daze, and H. P. Wickham (1968). Technology: The large plant concept, *Chemical Engineering Progess,* **64**(7), July, 17–25.

ADDITIONAL READING

Brooks, M. E. and J. Newman (1971). Gas oil cracking problems that had to be solved, presented at World Petroleum Congress, Moscow, U.S.S.R., June.

Catalyst Handbook, with special reference to unit processes in ammonia and hydrogen production, New York, Springer Verlag, 1970.

Freiling, J. G., C. C. King, and J. Newman (1979). Ethylene raw materials and production economics, *Advances in Chemistry,* Series 103, Washington, DC, American Chemical Society.

Landau, R., ed. (1966). *The Chemical Plant. From Process Selection to Commercial Operation,* New York, Reinhold.

Schutt, H. C. and S. B. Zdonik (1956). What are feedstocks, yields, costs in ethylene production? *Oil and Gas Journal,* February 13, pp. 98–103.

Tucker, W. J., J. G. Freiling, and B. L. Huson (1968). *Commercial Implications of Trends in Cracker Technology,* European Petrochemical Association, 2nd meeting, Knokke, Belgium.

12 / The 1970s: Discontinuities and Uncertainties

In two important books written in the late 1960s, Alvin Toffler (1), a futurist, and Peter Drucker (2) a well-known business consultant and lecturer, warned that the world was changing rapidly and that people should understand the nature of these changes and become ready for their consequences. Toffler indicated that many aspects of our life were in a state of rapid transition, but that we were often unwilling or unable to adapt to the change. One of his major points was that the United States had advanced not only through its agricultural, but now also through its industrial labor stage and was well on its way to becoming a service economy. Drucker identified the important developments taking place in technology and in the political and economic area and, like Toffler, cautioned us to be ready for a different kind of business world.

While Drucker's and Toffler's books were widely read and discussed and, in many respects, did reflect trends of which people were becoming aware, it is now obvious that the decade we were about to enter was even more of a watershed than we had been led to expect. For the 1970s can now be seen as a time of unprecedented change and reassessment. Many of the problems confronting the United States today became sharply defined during the 1970s, even though they may have surfaced somewhat earlier. Now, from the perspective of the 1980s, we can confirm that a number of things taken largely for granted in the past are no longer true. And some of the issues and problems that came to light in the 1970s remain unresolved and worrisome to the present time.

Although major events like the Watergate scandal and the Vietnam war did not impact American industry to the same extent as they affected the country's political and social climate, they did have direct and indirect consequences for the business community. And the 1973 "oil shock," another feature of a turbulent decade, was a turning point not only for the public, in terms of long lines at the gasoline pumps, but even more for a number of industries depending on energy supplies. Before the end of the 1970s, it had become obvious that the future of oil supplies was now closely tied to our relationship with some of the Third World countries, that certain oil-rich developing nations strongly condemned our country's international policies and that they were quite willing to hold the United States and its citizens hostage to express their disapproval.

It also developed that not only Japan but a number of other countries, largely located in Southeast Asia, were becoming highly viable competitors in the manufacture of a broad variety of manufactured goods, ranging from textiles and fabricated metals to such sophisticated products as printed circuit boards for computers. These goods were entering the country in amounts large enough to cause a major negative shift in the U.S. balance of trade. By the end of the 1970s, a surprisingly large part of America's heavy manufacturing industry was being characterized as the country's "aging smokestack industry." This seemed to be an even more rapid transition than Toffler or Drucker had foreseen. And perhaps of even greater concern, the country's traditional technological lead in many areas was recognized as having been severely shortened or lost altogether.

This chapter deals with the effect on the world's petrochemical industry of some of the key events that occurred in a tumultuous decade. In the 1970s, this industry became a global entity, as the rest of the world became interested in the production of chemicals from oil and gas. Third World countries stridently claimed that they considered the petrochemical and other "downstream" industries not only as key to their industrialization process, but also as a means toward their emancipation from industrial dominance by the Organization for Economic Cooperation and Development (O.E.C.D.) countries. And, partly as a result, many of the companies that had been so eager to participate in the petrochemical miracle during its heyday, were planning their exit before the decade was over.

The 1970s were a time when the United States lost its first war and, in the process, became a nation far less sure of its role in the world. The 1970s were also a time when the country's citizens forced the resignation of a president, who left the office in disgrace. During this decade, the country realized that some of its most important raw materials resources were being rapidly depleted and that other countries, upon whose raw materials it would increasingly depend, might now start to influence its destiny in certain ways. It was also a period when industry was forced to review its responsibility to the public in the areas of toxicity and the environment. And it was the start of an era when the financial community and some of its biggest clients—the insurance companies, pension and other managed funds, and a growing group of wealthy speculators—would become a dominant force in determining the performance of the managers of Industrial America and, effectively, in deciding its future. All of these factors shaped the country's industries in different ways. In many respects, the U.S. petrochemical industry was at the center of the changes that were transforming the country's industrial landscape in an apparently irreversible manner.

At this writing, years after the second "oil shock" in 1979 and well into the second term of the Reagan administration, much of American industry is still trying to evaluate the environment in which it will be conducting business in the future. A still rising wave of imports and a resulting vast trade deficit has replaced a traditionally fairly balanced international trade picture, which was greatly helped by a very favorable balance in the chemical sector. A series of regulatory measures enacted in the late 1960s and in the 1970s resulted in vast industry expenditures to deal with past, present, and future problems involving (1) the discharge of vapor and liquid streams, as well as solid wastes, into the environment surrounding its plants and (2) the health of its workers, and of the public. In the process, the image of the chemical industry which, at an earlier time, was one of technological innovation and manufacturing supremacy, not only suffered in the perception of the public, but also in the eyes of the financial community. And as far as the issue of future crude oil availability and cost is concerned, the oil and chemical industry today can do no better than to prepare forecasts in the form of alternative scenarios. It is just too difficult to know what the future will bring.

The end of the 1960s also brought to an end the period of high growth that characterized the petrochemical industry over the first 25 years of its life. This was then followed by 10 or 12 years of discontinuities and major change. And just after the end of the decade, there came a deep economic recession that seemed a fitting conclusion to a period that shook U.S. industry to its foundations and caused its leaders to understand that they would henceforth have to live with uncertainties of various kinds. These uncertainties would likely remain a feature of their day-to-day life.

While the various effects of the long war in Vietnam and its aftermath will not be a part of this story, nor the issue of Watergate and the fall of the Nixon administration, these events did have certain consequences for the country's industrial establishment, among which the following may be the most important:

- The strong rise of environmentalism, probably long over-due, but also greatly abetted by the counterculture elements spawned by the Vietnam war.
- The negative image gained by the chemical industry due to the use of napalm and other chemicals in the defoliation programs carried out against Vietcong soldiers and their supply line through the Vietnamese mountains.
- Changes in the composition of the U.S. Congress that brought to Washington a large number of legislators with antibusiness biases and a strong mandate to make industry conform to what they saw as "the will of the people."

As an example of the latter, a number of laws were enacted that worked greatly to the detriment of U.S. companies conducting business in a rapidly changing world. Whether these restrictions were imposed to a proper degree or went beyond a reasonable point is not the issue. The fact is that, as a result of new regulations, U.S. companies often abandoned product lines and were often placed at a serious disadvantage versus their international competitors. This situation had already been recognized when chemical plant contractors had found the U.S. Export-Import Bank much less helpful than similar foreign agencies set up to finance contractors bidding on Third World plant construction projects. Now, U.S.

manufacturing companies were also becoming less competitive due to (*1*) much higher outlays on equipment for various environmental control programs, (*2*) cessation of production of a number of chemicals judged as being harmful (e.g., insecticides, detergent builders), and (*3*) proscription of fees paid to foreign agents to secure export contracts. The American chemical industry was, in effect, told to become a model of rectitude in domestic and international affairs and it had a corresponding price to pay. It would now turn more inward, at least for a time, and would work on its own problems, which seemed to be multiplying during this decade.

And, in any case, Europe and Japan had now succeeded in building up their petrochemical industries to a point where U.S. firms had little residual advantage, in terms of either technology, plant size, or even raw materials costs, in many cases. By the late 1960s, Western Europe's chemical industry had grown more rapidly than that of the United States, so that its consumption of primary petrochemicals was starting to approach U.S. levels. This is shown in the following comparison table:

Relative Consumption of Primary Petrochemicals in 1970
(Tons per year)

	United States	Western Europe
Ethylene	7,800,000	4,900,000
Propylene	3,800,000	2,800,000
Benzene	3,800,000	3,200,000

The rapid growth in European and Japanese demand for products made by the petrochemical industry is illustrated by the high per capital consumption of plastics, as shown in the next table, taken from a Monsanto paper published in 1973 (3):

Plastics Consumption in 1971 (kilograms per head)

West Germany	50
U.S.	45
Belgium	42
Japan	35
France	34
Italy	27

The rapid growth of European demand for petrochemicals spurred the construction of new capacity to a degree that matched or even surpassed the earlier surge in the United States. Figures published by Shell Chemical (4) show an average annual growth rate of 15 percent between 1960 and 1973. This exceptional rate of expansion was ascribed to a combination of (1) relatively high economic growth in general, (2) a low state of penetration of synthetics in various applications at the start of the period, and (3) a decrease in petrochemical prices during the period, while the prices of most other materials was rising (see Fig. 12.1). Annual automobile production and demand for packaging materials were increasing at a rate of 6–7 percent and fibers demand at close to 10 percent. As a result of this surge in demand for plastics, synthetic fibers, solvents, coatings, and other petrochemical products, European producers started to think of petrochemical growth rates in terms of multiples of Gross National Product growth rates (e.g., two or three times the rate of GNP growth). As it turned out, they were soon to become bitterly disappointed, as petrochemical growth rates dropped sharply in the 1970s and they found themselves with far too much petrochemical plant capacity.

By the end of the 1960s, European steam crackers and polymer plants matched in size similar units in the United States.

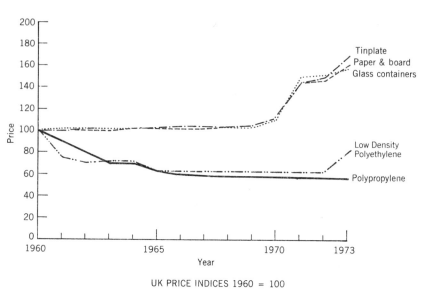

Figure 12.1 Petrochemical prices. (*Source:* Shell International Chemical Co.)

Japanese plants were generally still somewhat smaller. Licensing of petrochemical technology was essentially wide open throughout the world, thus allowing any company with enough money and courage to build a large modern plant, employing the most modern capacity. (This was not the case, of course, for certain chemicals employing closely held technology). Moreover, Europeans generally continued to build plants in their own countries, instead of engaging in joint ventures or making other arrangements with countries in the same trading area. Reasons for this were traditional nationalism, a desire to limit regional trade deficits and, to some extent, a desire to utilize local raw materials resources. Even countries such as Norway, Sweden, Finland, and Portugal, all with populations far too small to support petrochemical projects, eventually decided to build large installations, oriented largely toward major export trade. Their hopes for profitable operations were not often realized.

The rash of installations in countries with small markets had started to occur in the 1960s and was in full swing by the mid-1970s. As a result of this additional, very extensive, buildup of European petrochemical capacity, which only exacerbated an already ample supply situation in the Common Market countries, a number of American firms involved in the production of petrochemicals in Europe now decided to reduce the scope of their operations and in some cases to make a major withdrawal. Thus, Union Carbide sold its European business to British Petroleum (BP Chemicals), U.S.I. sold its polyethylene business in Antwerp, Belgium to Esso Chemical, and Gulf Oil shut down its steam cracker, styrene, and cumene plants in the Netherlands. Monsanto also started its withdrawal from Europe and Dow slowed down and later stopped completely its plans to build additional petrochemical capacity in Europe (e.g., in Yugoslavia) and soon thereafter in much of the rest of the world.

Clearly these business exits were, to a considerable extent, based on the decreased attractiveness of Europe's petrochemicals business, which had become very competitive, as supply overtook demand. But these decisions were also influenced by an increasingly jaundiced view of petrochemicals manufacture in general, held not only by these companies' managements, but to an even greater degree by the U.S. financial community. Last, but not least, these pullbacks were also closely associated with a rising concern about the future of petroleum feedstock supplies, which had now apparently passed into the hands of the oil-rich nations. This included not only the OPEC producers, but also Canada, Mexico, and other countries with abundant oil or natural gas reserves. Looming over the industry was what many felt to be the most important long term problem, one that literally shook the world in this decade—the issue of future energy and feedstock availability and cost.

This chapter, then, describes how in the 1970s the petrochemical industry in the developed countries of the world arrested its heady progress and became a somewhat mature and even embattled industry. This came about for a number of reasons, relating most importantly to the abrupt changes in the world's energy picture and to the fact that these occurred at a time when the demand growth for petrochemicals was starting a sharp decline. The highly inflationary effect of the steep rise in oil prices had a strongly negative effect on these countries' GNP growth, further aggravating the demand decline. Wall Street quickly dropped petrochemicals from its list of growth industries and became negative on their future and on the companies engaged in making the products. And when a large section of the public indicted the industry on environmental and toxicity issues, petrochemicals could be said to be in full retreat. Certainly, it was the end of an era, as many people became fond of saying by the end of the decade. How and why this happened is fairly clear. Some comments and speculations on whether the industry can overcome its problems, resume its growth, regain its standing in the financial community and, in sum, recapture its prestige are the subject of the next and final chapter.

THE U.S. ENERGY PICTURE DARKENS

Concerns about the future of U.S. hydrocarbon supplies had already begun in the late 1960s, when the demand for natural gas had started to outstrip supply. Priced at unrealistically low levels for a long time, natural gas had become the preferred fuel for almost all applications. Cheap natural gas had, in fact, been available throughout the period when the petrochemical industry was in its double digit growth phase. It had been used to provide refinery and chemical plant fuel for furnaces, steam boilers, and crackers. It had been processed in natural gas liquids plants to recover ethane and propane to feed the nation's ethylene plants. And it had been burned in the boilers and combustion turbines of huge Gulf Coast utility concerns, such as Gulf States Power and Houston Lighting and Power to generate the low cost electricity used to drive the compressors and pumps in the "spaghetti bowl" of plants reaching from Mississippi to Corpus Christi, Texas. And the gas had also been transported through a network of large interstate pipelines to many other parts of the country, where it was likewise used as an industrial and utility fuel, being generally cheaper than coal and often also cheaper than fuel oil. Natural gas had also become an important residential and commercial fuel in homes, business buildings and shopping centers across the nation, heavily advertised as the most clean-burning and desirable fuel.

And so, natural gas consumption had risen from 14 trillion cubic feet (TCF) in 1960 to over 21 TCF in 1970. It was always available, it was easy to use and the equipment used to burn the gas required the lowest installation cost. There had never been much concern about the supply of this indispensable commodity. During the early part of the 1960s, annual additions to U.S. gas reserves had averaged close to 20 TCF, a figure well above that of U.S. consumption during that period. But by the 1960s, America's oil and gas establishment could no longer add reserves to the country's supply at the same rate as these reserves were being drawn down by rising gas demand. In 1968, only 12 TCF of new gas was discovered and in the following several years this figure dropped below 10 TCF, only half of the amount consumed the same year. Whether this was due to the fact that the low gas price was making it more economical to drill for oil rather than gas or whether wildcatters were running out of promising locations was not clear. What was certain, however, was that a major national problem had surfaced.

During the cold winter months of 1976–1977, the public as well as the industrial firms that had become so dependent on what was once one of America's greatest resources found out that domestic gas supply could no longer be taken for granted. As the winter proceeded, industries and utilities with so-called "interruptible" gas supplies* were cut off in many parts of the country, while many

---

*An interruptible supply contract between a gas distributor and a gas user gives the purchaser the advantage of a lower price in return for allowing the seller to cut off the gas supply during periods of high demand or restricted supply in the supplier's system. The concept of interruptible supply contracts was not originally based on a national supply shortage, but rather to provide suppliers and users with mutually advantageous flexibility. Companies with interruptible supply contracts always have alternate fuel firing systems.

other users with firm contracts were also hit with serious supply curtailments. Interstate pipelines were unable to fulfill close to 25 percent of firm demand, on average (5). Suddenly, gas was going to be a scarcer resource and in typical American fashion a number of stratagems were conceived to deal with a problem that had resulted in shutting down four thousand manufacturing plants, with more than a million workers temporarily laid off.

Now, everybody came up with solutions. Gas could be purchased in larger quantities from gas-rich Canada, pipelines could be built from Mexico's gas fields to the Gulf Coast network, and liquefied natural gas could be produced in places such as Alaska, Algeria, and Indonesia and transported to the United States, to be regasified and fed into the distribution system. Substitute natural gas (sometimes also called synthetic natural gas or SNG) could be produced from naphtha. And there was also great interest in the production of SNG from coal or lignite, using a variety of gasification processes that, in part, hearkened back to the German coal industry of the 1930s.

It is of some interest that the technology to produce SNG from naphtha was based almost entirely on know-how that ICI and several engineering firms had developed in the early 1960s for the production of ammonia and methanol, as well as "town gas," from petroleum feedstocks. SNG can therefore be said to have strong "petrochemical" origins. Whereas British town gas contained both hydrogen and carbon monoxide, the United States had to have a synthetic gas indistinguishable from the gas flowing through the network of gas pipelines that distribute natural gas to various kinds of users. To produce methane, the gas mixture from naphtha reforming had to be "shifted" to a ratio of three mols of hydrogen to one mole of carbon monoxide. This gas mixture was then passed over a "methanation" catalyst to produce essentially pure methane.

SNG from naphtha was relatively expensive to produce, but the plants, built during this period, were meant to operate primarily during periods of peak gas demand or periods of curtailed supply. As the SNG was mixed into a much larger stream of relatively cheap gas still flowing under old gas contracts controlled at low prices, the high cost of naphtha-based SNG was not a major problem, at first. But chemical firms familiar with the economics of these plants recognized that this form of methane would certainly be too expensive to use as a feedstock for ammonia, methanol, or other natural gas derivatives.

As far as production of SNG from coal was concerned, this was limited to a great deal of study work and some government-funded pilot plants. There were a number of reasons why coal-based SNG plants were not constructed during this period, the most important being their high capital cost, particularly when the infrastructure for coal handling and waste stream treatment was considered. The fact that available gasifier technology required the use of multiple small reactors created a need for so-called "second generation" gasification technology, and there was insufficient time to develop and commercialize large gasifiers with advanced designs. Naphtha-based SNG plants could be built faster and cheaper and naphtha feedstock was still relatively inexpensive in the early 1970s, especially since the best naphtha for this purpose was the low octane material that was not particularly suitable for blending into motor gasoline.

The development of second generation coal gasification processes came into stronger consideration several years later, when oil prices had started their precipitous rise. "Synthesis gas" made via coal gasification then became of interest as an alternative feedstock for producing petrochemicals. But more about this later.

The possibility of future shortages of natural gas in the United States caused a number of industrial and utility gas users to shift from gas to oil. Although it was also a depleting domestic resource, oil had long been considered as being available in almost unlimited quantities at low prices from the Middle East, Latin America and, more recently, from African countries as well. Thus, in the early 1970s, U.S. dependence on petroleum products increased, with some shift also to coal. Nuclear energy was starting to become important, apparently presenting the United States with some options, regardless of the availability of natural gas.

Petrochemical producers were, however, becoming more dependent on oil. Steam cracking of naphtha or gas oil provides a number of useful by-products (propylene, butylenes, butadiene, BTX aromatics) all of which were in substantial demand. Also, U.S. natural gas was becoming "leaner," containing less ethane and propane, resulting in a gradual price rise for these natural gas liquids, which had been the main feedstock for ethylene production. Liquefied petroleum gas (propane and butane, primarily) were now also being used increasingly for space heating and for gasoline blending, respectively, which contributed to the price rise for these materials. "Heavy liquids" cracking therefore became relatively more attractive. Not only Exxon Chemical, but Monsanto, Shell, and Mobil were cracking substantial amounts of these heavy liquids. And in Puerto Rico, where Commonwealth Oil Refining Company had recently built an ethylene plant in joint venture with PPG Industries, inexpensive Venezuelan and Libyan naphthas were to be used as the main feedstocks.

By the mid-1970s, over 50 percent of actual or planned U.S. ethylene capacity was based partly or wholly on heavy liquids cracking, versus less than 20 percent in 1970. For petroleum refiners, naphtha and gas oil cracking made particular sense, since it was often possible for them to achieve good integration between the petrochemical (cracking) and refining parts of their operation. Exxon (when it was known as "Jersey") had, of course, found out about this many years ago. If propylenes or butylenes, made in large quantities from heavy liquids cracking, could not all be sold or converted into petrochemicals in captive derivatives plants, they could be sent over to the refinery and used as a feedstock for alkylation or polymerization units, thus ending up in gasoline. The substantial quantities of poor quality fuel oil obtained as bottoms streams in heavy liquids crackers could most easily be disposed of by blending with higher quality refinery fuel oils. And the BTX stream recovered from cracker "pyrolysis gasoline," could also be treated and blended into gasoline as an octane booster, if this was a higher value outlet, rather than running it through a Sulfolane aromatics extraction plant and then fractionating it into benzene, toluene, and xylene to sell as petrochemical feedstocks.

The synergies available to refiners when conducting refining and steam cracking operations on the same site were quite evident to chemical companies. Union Carbide, DuPont, and others were still cracking ethane-propane mixtures, while purchasing large amounts of aromatics for making styrene, phenol, and fiber intermediates. Also, several other large refining companies not yet in the petrochemical business felt that their overall economics would be improved by adding a large steam cracker and selling ethylene in the merchant market. The concept of operating a refinery and a steam cracker, including various petrochemical recovery and derivatives units, in an integrated manner became known as a "chemical refinery."

In the late 1960s and early 1970s, studies carried out by Chem Systems evaluated the subject of chemical refineries for a number of companies. Of particular interest to chemical firms was a configuration that would produce a combination of petrochemicals and fuel oils, with no production of gasoline at all. This would preclude the need for chemical companies to get into gasoline marketing and essentially allow the operator of such a refinery to use all of the products internally, perhaps including the shipment of some of the fuel products to other company sites. Since the economics of such grass roots chemical refineries did not look as attractive as these companies had hoped, none was built in the United States, although a complex of this type was eventually constructed by a joint venture of DuPont, Union Carbide, and Polysar at Sarnia, Ontario. In the United States, Dow Chemical did build a refinery adjacent to its giant petrochemical complex at Freeport, Texas, but the company later changed its mind about being in the refining business and put the plant on the market.

For chemical firms, which had often bought their light hydrocarbon cracking feedstocks directly from the gas fields, the thought of not having to rely on petroleum refiners for naphtha feedstock or aromatics was seductive. As chemical refineries were apparently not the answer, this could also be done by buying naphtha on the world market. Dow was able to pursue this policy with considerable success, particularly in Europe. Monsanto, for a period of time, did the same at its complex in Chocolate Bayou, Texas. Eventually, however, chemical companies realized that the oil companies would somehow always have better control of the heavy cracker feedstocks. Perhaps more than anything else, this signaled the start of many chemical companies' withdrawal from the manufacture of commodity petrochemicals.

In 1970, Chem Systems undertook a comprehensive study for a number of companies entitled "The Petrochemical Industry (1970–1980)." This five-volume report summarized then current technology and markets for all the important petrochemicals and projected the next 10 years, as we then saw the future. In one part of the study, we assembled a number of historical forecasts for various products to demonstrate that these projections had invariably been too conservative and had been greatly exceeded by actual consumption statistics. An example of such projections, taken from that study, is shown in Figure 12.2. History would later show, however, that this time it would have been better to be more conservative. Although previous forecasters had always felt that the high growth rates experienced up to the time of their forecast were about to decline (which they had not), we were soon to find out

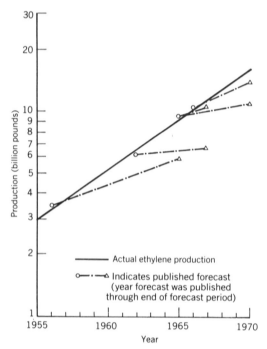

Figure 12.2 Ethylene historical projections versus actual growth. (*Source:* Chem Systems.)

that the end of high growth rates had, in fact, arrived. It turned out that the market saturation that many had been expecting was about to occur. But, more importantly, the price of petrochemicals was about to take a quantum leap.

It is hard to believe that in the early 1970s ethylene in the United States was still selling for only 3 cents per pound and benzene for 20-25 cents per gallon. Gasoline (leaded, of course, since unleaded gasoline was only sold by Amoco, as a differentiated premium product) was priced at 35 cents per gallon at the pump. U.S. crude oil was priced around $3 per barrel, slightly higher than the world oil price as a result of the oil import quota that had been established to protect U.S. oil producers from cheap foreign crude oil. Natural gas prices had started to rise as a result of shortages, but a large percentage of U.S. gas was still flowing under very low price contracts. In summary, the price of energy and feedstocks was one of the best bargains available and the price of petrochemicals produced from these inexpensive hydrocarbons reflected this situation.

THE FIRST OIL SHOCK

What should the price of world oil have been to avert the climactic price rise that was about to occur? There is obviously no simple answer to this question, since the events about to unfold were not only related to price but also to geopolitics and emotion. But if the 1972 price of oil at $3 per barrel is viewed on a constant 1950 dollar basis (i.e., corrected for inflation between 1950 and 1970), one can easily calculate that oil in 1982 was priced at less than one 1950 dollar per barrel. This is because crude oil prices actually declined in absolute terms over much of the period. For example, Venezuelan crude was priced at $2.12 in actual dollars per barrel in 1950 and at $1.82 in 1970. Middle East crudes fared even worse. The landed price of Iranian and Saudi light crudes in Germany dropped by $1 per barrel between 1959 and 1967, from the level of just under $3.00 per barrel in the earlier year to under $2.00 per barrel (6).

Much of the world's oil was, of course, very cheap to bring up from the ground, with operating costs in the Middle East as low as 5-10 cents per barrel. Thus, at the world oil price of $3 per barrel prevalent in 1972, the oil companies producing in the U.S. and purchasing crude from host countries in the Middle East and elsewhere could still make a good profit on the oil they were transferring to their refineries or selling to other refiners. But the oil producing countries were not receiving what they considered to be a fair share of these profits. Perhaps, if world crude oil prices had risen in line with inflation and if the Third World oil producing countries had received a reasonable increase in their "take" during the 1960s, the world oil crisis could have been avoided, or at least mitigated.

In any event, the ascendancy of the Organization of Petroleum Exporting Countries (OPEC) occurred almost overnight, though the group had actually been in existence since 1960. Increasingly unhappy with the oil "majors" policy of setting what OPEC members considered as unrealistically low posted price for their crude oil and also paying minimal royalties on their oil purchases, OPEC had, for a number of years, tried to influence the policies and decision of the Seven Sisters—the major world oil companies. Then, in 1970, when a pipeline break in the Middle East created a temporary shortage, Libya, whose production and sales were unaffected by the supply disruption, had taken the initiative and had obtained a considerably better deal from one of its purchasers, Occidental Petroleum Company. This then set the pattern for other agreements. Less than a year later, strong pressure from the Shah of Iran brought the host countries' "take" up another notch. Now, the oil producing countries were obtaining an amount equal to about half the price of crude oil as royalties. But the price was still far too low, in their collective judgment.

To set the stage for what happened next, it is important to understand that the United States and other major countries had come out of a recession in 1970 and that the U.S. economy was booming in 1972 and 1973. As an example, automobile production had risen from 6.5 million cars in 1970 to 9.6 million units in 1973. And GNP, which had been sluggish around the turn of the decade, grew 6.1 percent in 1972 and a further 5.9 percent in 1973. These are very high numbers. Overheating of the economy had, in fact, resulted in the imposition of government wage and price controls. Petrochemical plants, in late 1973, were operating at close to full capacity. Ethylene production, which had only increased nominally from 17.1 billion pounds in 1970 to 17.5 billion pounds in 1971, rose to 20.6 billion pounds in 1972 and 22.2 billion in 1973.

Two factors combined in late 1973 to allow the OPEC nations to succeed in wresting control of the world's crude oil supply from the major oil companies. Firstly, world petroleum products demand had been surging for several years, to the point where all oil producing countries except Saudi Arabia and Iran were essentially at the limit of their production capacities. You might say that, at that point, the valves at most of the world's wells were wide open. No longer required to protect its domestic oil industry, the United States had recently lifted its traditional oil import quotas, thus adding to the demand for Middle East crude oil. For the first time in history the two largest oil producers in that region were the key to the world's oil supply/demand balance.

What actually triggered the crisis was the other factor— America's support of Israel during its "Yom Kippur" war with Egypt and Syria. Shortly after hostilities broke out, the United States started to supply Israel with replacement arms and ammunition. Saudi Arabia warned that if this were not stopped it would take appropriate punitive action. Unwilling to let itself be intimidated and concerned about Israel, the Nixon administration continued to support that country's war against its Arab nations. King Faisal now ordered a 25 percent cutback in Saudi oil output and instituted the historic oil embargo against the United States and several other countries friendly to Israel. Most of the other Arab countries then instituted a similar embargo.

As crude oil supply started to fall short of demand, the price of oil skyrocketed. Crude oil is heavily traded on the world market and, at times of shortages (or oversupply), the spot price reflects the real condition of the market. In December, only three months after the start of the embargo, the spot price had risen from the level of $3-4 to $17 per barrel. Later that month, meeting again in Teheran under the leadership of the Shah, the OPEC countries could easily decide to raise their take on crude oil to $7 per barrel. The posted (official) price of crude now rose to around $12 per barrel. Figure 12.3 shows how host companies thus raised their take from less than one dollar per barrel in 1970 to seven dollars by early 1974 (7). By the time the embargo ended in March 1974, Saudi Arabia, Iran, and the rest of OPEC had the world oil situation under their complete control.

The price of Middle East oil had effectively quadrupled in less than a year. In the United States, price controls had been installed via a rather complex arrangement involving (*1*) *old* oil, discovered before a certain date, and (*2*) *new* oil. The price of the latter soon rose to a level close to that of Middle East crude oil. With imports accounting for almost half of U.S. petroleum consumption, the price controls on old oil only helped to a limited extent in keeping down the price of crude oil and refined products. By the end of 1974, the weighted average price of oil pumped to U.S. refineries had, in fact, tripled, in spite of price controls.

Natural gas price had also moved up sharply over this period. While federal controls had kept down the price of *old* gas flowing in the *interstate* pipeline system, which was historically under its jurisdiction, the new contract price for *intrastate* gas sold to users within gas producing states such as Texas and Louisiana rose from 29 cents per thousand cubic feet in 1970 to 45 cents in 1971, 63 cents in 1972, 80 cents in 1973 and $1.00 per thousand cubic feet in 1974. (It was to reach $1.90 by 1977.) (8)

We now come to one of the great paradoxes of that time, as far as the chemical industry was concerned. It turned out that what had happened to world oil prices became, for a short time, a major boon

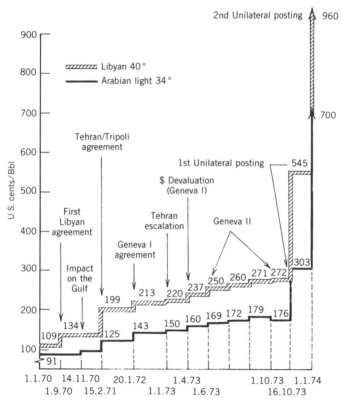

Figure 12.3 Host government take, U.S. cents per barrel. This illustrates the gradual increase of host government take arising from changes in posted price negotiated between the industry and members of OPEC and the dramatic rise resulting from the producing countries' unilateral postings. (*Source:* Geoffrey Chandler, The changing shape of the Oil Industry, *Petroleum Review,* June 1974.)

to the companies producing chemicals from petroleum. Unfortunately, it provided the petrochemical companies with the wrong signals, eventually making their situation considerably worse than it might have been. This was the sequence:

- The oil embargo created tremendous shortages for a period of time.
- Oil and chemical producers were able to push up prices in line with their raw materials cost increases, though price controls did not allow them to do this as fast as they would have liked.

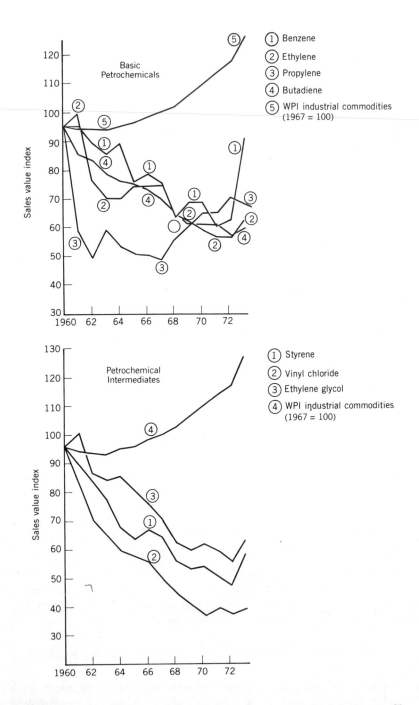

Figure 12.4 Cost index for petrochemicals before 1973 "oil shock." (*Source:* Chem Systems.)

480

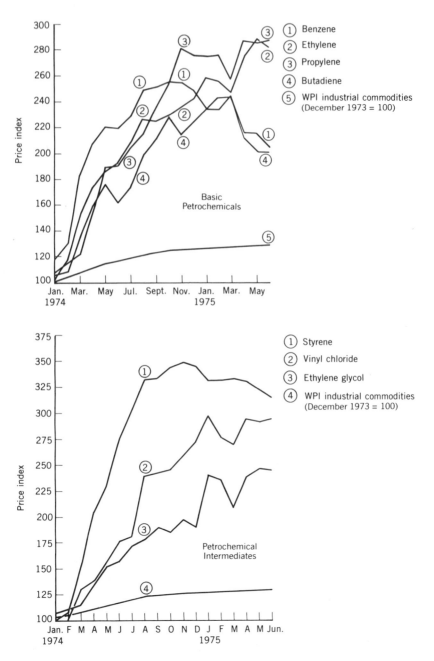

Figure 12.5 Cost index for petrochemicals after 1973 "oil shock." (*Source:* Chem Systems.)

481

Nevertheless, a lot of money was made in 1974, particularly in the export market, which was not subject to price controls.

- Operating at full capacity (except when unable to purchase the full amount of hydrocarbon feedstocks required for their plants) and now seeing cash flows two or more times higher than ever before experienced, petrochemical producers were itching to build more capacity.
- With world inflation rampant as a result of much higher oil prices, there was an urgency to build new plants before construction costs got completely out of hand.

Though 1974 was a very hectic year, with shortages, government controls, bartering for feedstocks and intermediates, and a great deal of concern about the future, 1974 was also the best, most profitable year the industry had ever seen.

The charts shown in Figures 12.4 and 12.5 illustrate two important points. The graphs for the years ending in 1972 indicate how petrochemical prices declined on a real basis in the 1960s, versus the wholesale price index, which increased by 20 percent over this period. As covered elsewhere, this had almost completely been due to the improving economics of scale of large petrochemical plants, as well as the intensely competitive nature of the industry. The dramatic price rises that took place in the period from January 1974 to May 1975 were the complete reverse of that historical trend. As shown on the charts, petrochemical prices now increased much faster than the wholesale price index, reflecting the tremendous increase in feedstock costs (9).

The poor profitability of the industry in the years from 1968 to 1972 had caused producers to postpone additions of new capacity in many cases. Thus, no new ethylene plants had been announced for some time, in spite of rapidly rising demand in 1972 and 1973. Now, Arco Chemical, Gulf, and several other companies announced new plants or expansions. A number of other new projects were approved in 1974, as company managements did not want to be left behind in the renewed game of adding petrochemical capacity, in line with rosy projections. To deal with the growing issue of natural gas shortages and price rises, a number of chemical companies also now started programs to drill for natural gas.

It was at this time, as well, that petrochemical producers started thinking about alternative feedstocks to use instead of oil or natural gas. With hydrocarbon prices now so much higher, why not consider the use of coal, which had served the industry so well in its early days? After all, coal prices had remained essentially unaffected by the oil crisis, being driven almost entirely by mining labor and by transportation costs. The government-supported synthetic fuels program had, by now, spawned a great deal of research and development work on second generation gasifiers and these were the key to relatively low-cost synthesis gas (mixtures of carbon monoxide and hydrogen) that could be converted to many of the petrochemicals produced from oil and natural gas and gas liquids. Such chemicals as ethylene glycol, acetic anhydride, vinyl acetate, styrene, and even ethylene could conceptually be produced from synthesis gas or from methanol (a product also made from synthesis gas), although at considerably higher cost than from oil or gas feedstocks at 1972 prices. With petroleum prices escalating, many companies started to step up their research work in this area. In Germany, BASF was known to be working hard at improving the yield of ethylene obtained from synthesis gas or methanol. Mobil stepped up its research and development work on the use of its patented ZSM-5 shape-selective catalysts to make aromatics, as well as olefins, from synthesis gas or methanol. An important part of Mobil's work in this area was also directed at making motor gasoline from methanol. (Ten years later, such a plant was successfully built and started up in New Zealand, with Chem Systems acting as consultants to the banks financing this $1.5 billion project.)

The newly created Government Energy Department and the Commerce Department were predictably becoming bullish on the future of synthetic fuels. As noted earlier, work on the production of SNG from coal was now in high gear at a number of company laboratories, with substantial government funding support in most cases. A number of technologies were also under development for the production of gasoline, diesel fuel, and petrochemical feedstocks from coal and from shale rock. Predictions of even much higher oil prices around the corner lent a sense of urgency to this work. Even the National Science Foundation became interested and funded a study, carried out by Chem Systems in 1975, covering the subject of producing chemicals from coal and shale (10).

In the chemical process industries (CPI), dire warnings were expressed on what would happen if the country did not proceed rapidly with a synthetic fuels industry. Clark Lattin, president of M. W. Kellogg, indicated that 60 or so synthetic fuels plants, each probably costing $1 billion or more would soon have to be built and that an extreme shortage of engineers and equipment suppliers would shortly develop. Many people agreed that only by building these plants would the United States achieve what became a favorite catch phrase, "energy independence."

It was obvious that such a major program—chemical, as well as synthetic-fuels oriented—would take a considerable amount of time and a great deal of investment. But by 1975, the next development in the topsy-turvy decade of the 1970s was taking place: the United States and the rest of the world were sliding into recession.

To economists, this hardly came as a surprise. The United States, Western Europe, and Japan were very large importers of oil, with Japan the largest, relatively speaking. With the very large increase in oil import bills, a huge amount of purchasing power was transferred to the oil export nations (and to some extent to the domestic oil producers) with a correspondingly large loss of purchasing power by consumers. The effect on the annual GNP growth in the three regions was devastating. By the end of 1974, it turned out that United States GNP, instead of growing by an expected 2.6 percent had actually declined by 2.1 percent, a net change of 4.7 percent. Western Europe fared somewhat better, but in Japan the net change was 7 percent (11). In the United States, the unemployment rate had risen by a full percentage point over the year 1974.

By the time the new chemicals plants, approved in the glory days of 1974, came on stream, it was a different picture than their builders had expected. The world oil picture had settled down for some time and crude oil prices were now actually declining somewhat, as a result of recession and corresponding lower world oil demand. There were no shortages, price controls had been lifted in 1974, and the United States and other countries were only slowly emerging from recession. And the growth rate for petrochemicals was again slowing down. Companies that had hoped to sell ethylene from plants built on the basis of favorable contracts signed in 1974 had to tear up these contracts and go back to the old basis of selling at market prices—which had again become extremely competitive. The industry had more or less adjusted itself to much higher feedstock and product prices but, in other respects, was not much different from its condition before the embargo. In 1975, ethylene demand took a steep dive and by 1976 it only recovered to a figure slightly above the 1973 level (Fig. 12.6). The bloom was definitely off the rose.

Now, another concern began to worry the industry. Would petrochemicals—synthetics, in other words—be able to hold their own against the natural materials they had been displacing over the last 20 years? Or would a major reversal take place, with petrochemicals pricing themselves out of many of their established markets and no longer continuing their penetration into markets held by traditional materials? Some thoughts about this were expressed at industry meetings and some papers were published. In general, the feeling was that things would work out all right, that after all, the production of natural materials also required energy (e.g., tractor fuel for agricultural products, electricity for sawing wood, natural gas for melting glass) so that the price of these materials would, in the future, rise as much as the synthetics made from petrochemicals. Nevertheless, there was considerable nervousness on this issue.

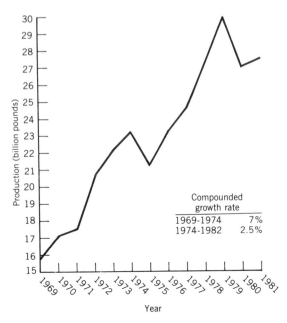

Figure 12.6 U.S. ethylene demand. (*Source:* Chem Systems.)

OIL-RICH COUNTRIES ENTER THE PETROCHEMICAL INDUSTRY

Meanwhile, it had become very clear that the oil- and gas-rich countries were in a headlong rush to build petrochemical plants. In the case of Canada, this involved principally the province of Alberta, which produces most of Canada's oil and natural gas. Recognizing that the Western world and Japan would consider Canada as a "safe" source of supply, Alberta announced its intention to sponsor and promote a major program to build plants for the production of ammonia, methanol, and various ethylene derivatives. This could be done through the use of Alberta's newly established "Heritage Fund," into which the provincial government paid much of the "windfall" profits received as a result of the dramatic escalation of crude oil prices.

The fact that Eastern Canada already had ample petrochemical capacity did not faze the Albertans, long known for their independent thinking and actions. In fact, as a result of Alberta's relatively tough bargaining stance with the Federal Canadian government, as well as with foreign firms, their oil men soon became known as "the blue-eyed Arabs of the North."

For a time, it looked like Alberta would become a major world source of petrochemicals, with products shipped from its relatively remote, landlocked plants to the Western United States, as well as to Japan and Europe. And, in fact, a number of plants were eventually built, although fewer in number and product range than originally envisaged. As it later turned out, Canadian and Albertan energy and feedstock pricing policy did not provide the substantial cost advantages that had originally been projected.

The Middle Eastern and North African countries were in a different position. In these regions of the world, a great deal of resentment over the past policies of the Western countries had spawned an aggressive stance on "industrialization" that bordered on confrontation. Although some countries, such as Kuwait and Iran, had progressed quite well in establishing locally owned and controlled refining industries, other countries had left the processing of crude oil largely in the hands of the international oil companies—either locally or in refineries in the consuming countries. Now, a pent-up desire surfaced to build local refineries and petrochemical plants and, more importantly, to get the Western countries and Japan to agree that they would take large amounts of the products from these plants into their markets. There was an implicit threat, "if you want to buy our crude oil, you will, in the future, also have to take some refined petroleum products and some petrochemicals from us."

Actually, Iran had already started to produce some chemicals before the first "oil shock." The country's desire to advance rapidly in petrochemicals manufacture had been strong and palpable under the aegis of the Shah, who considered this as "a noble use for oil." A number of foreign firms had hoped to participate in such projects in some manner, but local corruption had often made it difficult to come to acceptable terms. Nevertheless, N.I.O.C.* had formed joint ventures with Goodrich (PVC), Amoco (sulfur, LPG), and Cabot (carbon black), among others. A larger venture with Allied Chemical almost went ahead in 1971, but then Allied changed its mind. The emergence of Iran as a leader of OPEC in 1973–1974 brought a number of foreign companies to Teheran, but little progress was made for awhile. Then, a group of Japanese companies under the leadership of the Mitsui group formed a joint venture with the Iranians to build an ambitious $2.3 billion petrochemical complex at Bandar Shahpur in the rich Iranian gas fields. (When this plant was finally placed in operation, war broke out with Iraq and the complex was almost totally destroyed.)

Saudi Arabia had no petrochemical industry and, in fact, had allowed the Arabian American Oil Company (Aramco) to carry out the refining of crude in that country. Though the Ras Tanura refinery was one of the most modern in the world, it was not owned or controlled by the Saudi Government. In 1974, however, Saudi Arabia took control of Aramco. The Saudi Government then also founded a company to promote the establishment of a petrochemical industry and other industries vital to the country's industrialization program. The country's policy was to seek joint ventures with Western and Japanese firms. These would provide technology, operating experience and marketing know-how, while the Saudis would provide cheap natural (flare) gas and attractive financing.

The Saudi proposals were greeted with mixed feelings by the Western and Japanese companies producing gas-based petrochemicals. On the one hand, there was already ample petrochemical capacity in their regions, so that the prospect of being flooded with

*National Iranian Oil Company.

Middle Eastern products was not particularly attractive. On the other hand, there was the issue of future crude oil supplies and here the Saudis seemed to have a very strong card to play. By, on the one hand, tying crude oil purchasing "entitlements" into the joint venture agreements and, on the other, hinting darkly that they would take a dim view of countries that did not help Saudi Arabia to industrialize, the country was soon able to proceed with two large petrochemical complexes. Joint venture partners for several projects within these complexes included some of the international oils (Exxon, Shell, Mobil), some U.S. chemical firms (Celanese, Dow*), and some Japanese firms (e.g., Mitsubishi).

The Western producers rightly concluded, however, that countries basing their petrochemical industries on low cost gas would only succeed in capturing a somewhat limited share of the total petrochemical market (i.e., those products based on gas) rather than on oil (e.g., naphtha) feedstock. It was surmised that Saudi Arabia would not transfer its *petroleum* products into local petrochemical projects at a discount and therefore would not have a cost advantage in such products as styrene, synthetic fibers, elastomers, and so on, particularly when freight and duty were considered. In this, the West turned out to have been right.

Complexes were also built in Qatar (joint venture with CdF Chimie, a French government-owned firm) and in Algeria. These projects were less ambitious, however, than the Saudi installations. Mexico also became a large oil and gas producer during the decade, as huge new hydrocarbon reserves were discovered in the Gulf of Campeche. For a time, it appeared that Mexico, like Alberta, might become a major exporter of petrochemicals, given the very ambitious program planned by Pemex, the country's national oil company. But it soon became obvious that the rapidly growing Mexican population would absorb the output of these plants, which were also not being built as rapidly as had once been planned (or "feared", depending on the viewpoint).

Even Alaska got into the act. Large amounts of gas associated with Alaskan crude oil were being reinjected under the North Slope, since only an *oil* pipeline existed to bring Alaska's hydrocarbon riches to the lower 48 States. Now, Alaska's treasury was bulging with royalties from its suddenly very high priced crude oil.

---

*Dow later pulled out of their projects, which were taken over by SABIC, the Saudi's industrial arm.

Native tribes making up much of Alaska's population and exercising strong political control in Fairbanks, the capital, saw an opportunity for Alaska to industrialize. Make petrochemicals! In 1980, a competition was announced for a large refinery-petrochemical complex, to be built by the successful bidder with partial ownership and financing by local interests. Chem Systems was asked by a Houston group to formulate a project and to provide guidance and help in the competition. And our group, involving Alaska Interstate Pipeline Company, won out over four other contestants. There were some interesting considerations. Where should the plant be built? On the North Slope under Arctic conditions with no sea access half the year? In Fairbanks, where there was only a single-track railroad and where temperatures varied from 100 degrees in the summer to minus 50 in the winter? Or near Anchorage, requiring a very expensive new gas line from the North Slope? The project was probably not viable, unless crude oil prices would soar above $50 per barrel. Predictably, the concept was dropped when oil prices stabilized and then started to decline. Petrochemical production in Alaska would have to wait for a while.

With all of this capacity planned or threatened all over the world, it was hardly surprising that companies producing petrochemicals in the major industrial regions were becoming extremely nervous. Considering the amount of cheap flare gas available in the OPEC Countries, as indicated in Table 12.1 (12), how much capacity would actually be built and where? On the other hand, wouldn't the cost of grass roots plants built in faraway lands with hostile climates and using unskilled, imported labor be so high as to make production uneconomical? Particularly, when freight and duty were added to the F.O.B. (freight on board) price? Would the oil-rich countries really price their gas at essentially zero cost, or would some "opportunity cost" be added? Would there be some sort of retaliation if the industrial countries did not agree to absorb the petrochemicals produced in countries that were counted on to supply crude oil? It was a time when many such questions were asked, a good time also for consultants and engineering firms studying these issues.

The emergence of the Third World as a potential large new factor on the petrochemical scene thus caused a great deal of anxiety. In the United States, the problem was seen as troublesome, although probably not severe. It did, however, contribute to the general malaise that had started to envelop the petrochemical in-

Table 12.1   Flaring of Natural Gas in OPEC Nations, 1979

Nation	Billion Cubic Feet	Percentage Flared*
Abu Dhabi	293	60.9
Algeria	353	23.0
Ecuador	14	91.7
Gabon	64	92.2
Indonesia	222	22.5
Iran	558	39.8
Iraq	431	84.5
Kuwait	127	27.4
Libya	166	20.0
Nigeria	1,014	95.4
Qatar	81	34.7
Saudi Arabia	1,342	75.1
Venezuela	81	6.3
Total	4,746	

Source: Organization of the Petroleum Exporting Countries, *Annual Statistical Bulletin 1979.*

*Percentage of gross production flared (i.e. not used for industrial, commercial or residential purposes) in 1979.

dustry. Japan took a fairly rational approach to the issue, recognizing that it might ultimately be just as simple to import a certain percent of its petrochemicals as to keep importing the same amount of naphtha to convert to these products in its local factories. There would be some industry realignments, no doubt of that, but they would be managed in the Japanese manner. In sum, Japan decided that a policy of cooperation with the Middle East was preferable to one of confrontation.

Western Europe was the region that felt the most threatened, being closest to the Middle East and North Africa, where the new plants would soon start to emerge from the sand. A series of discussions that became known as the Euro-Arab dialogues were established to try and make some sort of an accommodation. These discussions, later extended to a worldwide forum called the "North-South" dialogues, did not accomplish very much, but at least prevented the adversary entities from taking rash actions. The Third World countries said that they were entitled to a certain share of the world market, including part of the market in the O.E.C.D. countries. The Europeans countered by stating that this might eventually happen, but that this would have to be a very slow process, given world overcapacity and the uncertainties surrounding the activities of the new producers.

In October 1978, the OPEC Secretariat sponsored a seminar in Vienna to discuss important issues involving the "downstream operations of OPEC member countries." Three speakers from the Western countries and Japan* presented their viewpoints, while four speakers from OPEC gave their countries' position on the construction of refineries and petrochemical plants by oil-rich nations. I was invited as the sole "neutral" speaker to give a balanced paper on the subject (13). It was a relatively friendly meeting, with both sides simply expressing their needs and concerns. There was no desire to settle any of the issues then and there, just to exchange views and to understand the position of the other side. I found Sheik Ali Khalifa al-Sabah, the oil minister of Kuwait, an urbane and extremely knowledgeable and affable person. The same could be said for many of the other attendees from Arab members of OPEC.

Only weeks after the meeting was concluded, the Shah was forced to flee from Iran and the world soon experienced the second "oil shock," which, for a time, put the downstream ambitions of the OPEC countries into the background. For the world was shortly contemplating the possibility of oil prices rising to $50–100 per barrel.

ENVIRONMENTAL AND TOXICITY CONCERNS

Energy and feedstock worries were not the only problems confronting petrochemicals producers in the 1970s. While this issue was certainly the most worrisome and perplexing concern, the rising public sentiment against the industry with respect to environmental and toxicity issues was not far behind.

A number of events had sensitized the public. Publication in 1962 of Rachel Carson's book *Silent Spring* (14) had alerted people to the fact that pesticides not only controlled destructive insects, but also killed or chased away the birds that fed on these insects. Another issue coming to light was the rapidly growing number of lakes that

---

*The paper was by Dr. Yasugi Torii, Chairman of Mitsui Petrochemical Company, with whom I had the privilege to become acquainted over the years.

could no longer support fish life, due to the growth of algae fed by the phosphate "builders" in the detergents contained in household waste water. The very visible foams building up on lakes and rivers emphasized the issue and raised people's consciousness on this chemical problem. The Thalidomide scandal showed that improper testing procedures and hasty or unwarranted government approvals of a new drug could bring terrible consequences for fetuses in pregnant women. The problem of chemical toxicity broadened from one affecting mainly pharmaceutical companies to envelop the entire chemical industry, when health problems were tied to the dumping—years earlier—of chlorinated chemicals near Love Canal in Niagara Falls, New York. When a number of health problems, including some birth defects, were soon thereafter caused by the accidental release of a cloud of dioxin-containing vapors from a chemical plant in Seveso, Italy, it had become obvious that air, water, and ground pollution from chemical plants should be subjected to more rigorous controls and that the public should receive enhanced protection from the possibly harmful effects of certain existing and newly developed chemicals and chemical applications.

A number of executive and legislative actions by federal and local government agencies resulted in stricter controls on the chemical industry. Many of these new regulations were unquestionably justified and the industry generally complied with diligence to meet the new standards and procedures. But new problems and dangers surfacing during this period kept the industry on the defensive much of the time.

In 1974, B.F. Goodrich announced that several workers in its polyvinyl chloride (PVC) plants had developed liver cancer, for which there was no known cure. Soon, other PVC manufacturers made similar determinations. The problem was traced to the long-time ingestion of vapors of vinyl chloride, the monomer that is polymerized to make PVC. Since many hundreds of plants manufactured this product worldwide, it was unthinkable to have to shut down all this capacity. Instead, determinations were made relatively to the maximum amount of free monomer vapor that workers could tolerate without incurring a risk of developing cancer. The industry then moved quickly to install equipment to limit vapor discharges to this amount. Moreover, procedures were developed to reduce to an infinitesimal percentage the amount of "free" vinyl chloride monomer in the PVC products sold to the public. All this was successfully accomplished, but at considerable expense.

New product development was also strongly impacted by the issue of potential carcinogenicity. It is hard to make judgments on whether regulatory agencies became overly strict on this matter, since most people would agree that any errors should be made on the side of protecting the public. The industry often felt, however, that the government went way overboard in its approach to testing and in the conclusions it drew from these tests. Many of these involved the exposure of test animals to a new chemical or chemical application at chemical levels thousands of times higher than those to which the public would be subjected. This then raised questions regarding the validity of the conclusions drawn from such tests.

For example, when Monsanto and Coca Cola cooperated in the development of a new plastic bottle for soft drinks, tests showed that minute levels of acrylonitrile remained associated with the resin and would therefore be ingested in the drink. This chemical, in very large doses, was shown to cause cancer in test animals. Monsanto demonstrated that the levels of acrylonitrile in its Cycle-Safe bottles was far below the danger point, but to no avail. The expensive development program therefore had to be written off. The same fate befell another Monsanto product called Cyclamate, a substitute for the sugar substitute *saccharin.* Years later, many people came around to agreeing that both Cycle-Safe and Cyclamate were as safe as many other products in general use by the public.

The discharge of hazardous liquid and solid wastes by chemical firms also became a major issue in the 1970s. The dumping of a chemical known as Kepone into the James River in Virginia by a firm associated indirectly with Allied Chemical created a furor when the toxicity of this material came to light. And the problems of Occidental Chemical Company at Love Canal were repeated at other sites, where chlorinated wastes and other hazardous chemicals had for many years been disposed of in ground fills adjacent to plants or hauled to other sites. These findings and others resulted in regulations that would require chemicals firms to be far more careful in the future disposal of their waste and to take essentially full responsibility for their past errors of omission and commission. Although justified on public grounds, these regulations caused chemical firms to spend large amounts of money, further impacting the decreasing profitability of their operations. And while the industry considered itself responsive in dealing with the large amount and variety of environmental and toxicity problems arising over this period, it received little credit for these efforts and its image deteriorated further with every revelation.

In some cases, such as certain types of solvents that were banned under California's *Rule 66,* acceptable replacements could be found, but these were also petrochemical products. In the case of well-established products with carcinogenic properties, such as vinyl chloride and benzene, the industry had to learn to deal with the issue in such a way as to fully protect its workers and the public. And in the development of new chemical applications, the industry and its regulating agencies would have to try and define an approach that would represent a reasonable balance between public protection and irrational overconservatism. The hope was that, in this manner, the industry would regain the good graces of the public and coincidentally of the financial community. Because one thing was certain. There was no way to live without the products the petrochemical industry was, by now, providing to the world.

THE SECOND OIL SHOCK

In late 1978, the Middle East literally came apart, as violence erupted in Iran and quickly spread to some of its neighboring countries. Long hated by many of his people because of his repressive regime and his support of Western values in a largely fundamentalist country, the Shah was forced to leave his throne and to escape to save his life. Fighting between various political factions soon spread to the oil fields, which had been accounting for five million barrels per day of the world's crude oil supply. Soon, Iran's oil production capacity was shut down by internal forces that were more concerned with their country's religious customs and other traditional values than with earning foreign currency to modernize the country. Shortly thereafter, Iran and Iraq were at war and the Khomeini government also threatened Kuwait and Saudi Arabia, whose rulers pursued the Sunni rather than the fundamentalist Shiite faith.

The large reduction in world oil supply now caused a second round of dramatic price increases. Where the system had, in 1977–1978, been in fairly good balance, there was now a two-million-barrel-per-day shortfall in crude oil. In December 1978, the spot price of crude jumped from $13 to $21 per barrel and OPEC members started to cancel long-term agreements by invoking "force majeure" clauses. Although some Iranian production came back on the market by March 1979, OPEC had succeeded in effecting the second round of major price increasing. Between the end of 1978 and the last quarter of 1979, the average price of crude oil imported to the United States rose by 83 percent. It increased by a further 30 percent in late 1980, by which time it had reached the level of $30 per barrel.

The petrochemical industry predictably went through another tumultuous period, as energy and feedstock price once again went through the roof. In Europe, ethylene prices quickly rose from 17 cents per pound to 28 cents per pound and low density polyethylene from 26 cents per pound to 44 cents per pound. Spot prices for benzene almost doubled, from $270 per metric ton to $510 per metric ton, corresponding to $1.83 per U.S. gallon. With U.S. natural gas and crude oil prices still under control (although also rising), an even wider gap in pricing opened up between European and U.S. petrochemical tabs. Petrochemical exports to Europe had already increased substantially after the first oil shock, as a result of U.S. price controls and the cost advantage of U.S. producers using natural gas (versus crude oil) feedstocks. Now, exports started flowing abroad in even much larger amounts. Between 1974 and early 1979, the annual rate of U.S. exports of high density polyethylene more than doubled, from 200 million pounds per year to over 500 million pounds per year and low density polyethylene exports from 400 million pounds per year to over 800 million pounds per year. Happy days were here again for the petrochemical industry!

In the United States, Europe, and Japan, chemical producers placed many products on allocation, a condition that meant that customers could only get a certain percentage of the amounts for which they had signed long-term contracts. A shortage of feedstocks, as in 1974, again prompted U.S. petrochemical producers to petition the government for favorable treatment under its petroleum products allocation program. The increase in world naphtha use for the production of olefins and aromatics affected all three major production regions, with Western Europe and Japan hit the hardest. The combination of a doubling in naphtha price, together with a world shortage, created for a number of months a chaotic marketplace for many of the chemicals derived from this all-important feedstock.

"Prices are up, profits are up, and producers are under attack. They're accused of profiteering, and their plea is 'not guilty,' " stated the first paragraph of a story in *Chemical Week* (15). Customers of chemical firms complained bitterly about big price increases and pointed to the large profits recently disclosed in oil and chemical company financial reports. But the industry and U.S. Bureau of Labor Statistics countered by showing that price increases by companies in the Chemical Process Industries (CPI) had risen at a considerably lower average rate than their costs—apparently as a result of complying with the Carter administration's voluntary guidelines on prices and wages. In August of that year, Celanese reported that, between late 1978 and the middle of 1979, its materials cost index had increased by 21 percent, while the selling price index for all its products had risen by only 5 percent (16). Competitive pressures often acted to keep prices lower than they might have been. Nevertheless, profits made on the rising value of inventories, on exports, and as a result of shortages and the generally charged atmosphere made 1979 a vintage year for the petrochemical industry, almost as good as 1974.

Now, ethylene producers were beginning to think that perhaps they had been right all along in feeling that ethylene would keep growing at a 5-8 percent annual rate. In 1979, ethylene production had finally risen to 30 billion pounds per year (see Fig. 12.6). "Ethylene Overcapacity: The End Is In View" was the headline in a lead article in *Chemical Week* (17). During the last quarter, the industry had actually been running at a rate equivalent to 32 billion pounds per year and ethylene prices had increased to 18–19 cents per pound from 13 cents per pound a year earlier. Exports contributed a part of the large production increase, with the overheated U.S. economy accounting for the rest. New ethylene units were under construction, with Shell, Exxon, and Dow adding units sized at over 1 billion pounds per year and several joint venture companies (e.g., Monsanto-Conoco and Corpus Christi Petrochemical) also building plants of this size. By early 1981, U.S. ethylene capacity would exceed 37 billion pounds per year, though as recently as 1977, ethylene demand had only been in the range of 24 to 25 billion pounds per year. Producers' hopes for not only an ebullient but also a profitable ethylene industry were vindicated when U.S. ethylene prices in late 1980 reached 25 cents per pound.

For another year or so, this euphoria continued, only to be rudely shattered 12 to 15 months later. By that time, a severe recession had hit the country, ethylene consumption had dropped to an annual rate of 22 billion pounds (about 1973 levels), and ethylene prices were back down to 17 cents per pound or lower.

IMPLICATIONS OF HIGHER ENERGY AND FEEDSTOCK COSTS

By mid-1974, it was already apparent to heavy users of petroleum and natural gas that a number of their manufacturing operations would have to be carefully reexamined to reflect the new energy economics. This involved making detailed studies of relative fuel costs and coming to a number of decisions on fuel switching or installing dual fuel-firing capabilities, as well as carrying out plantwide studies on the economic payout that could be obtained by installing additional insulation to reduce heat loss. For petrochemical companies, these studies also involved the reoptimization of heat balances, leading to the installation of additional heat exchangers, instead of losing the heat contained in process streams to cooling water. Many plants designed in the 1950s and 1960s had been based on natural gas fuel purchased at 15–20 cents per million Btu or on $3 crude oil. With such low fuel prices, plants were designed for low investment and therefore tended to be relatively inefficient energy users, in many cases. After the first oil shock, when natural gas prices had also started to rise, the balance between investment and operating costs had already changed considerably. With crude oil rising to over $30 per barrel and natural gas going to $3.00 per MCF or higher, there was every reason to make plants as energy efficient as possible. A great deal of capital was therefore spent in the general area of energy conservation, making less money available for new plant investment.

As a matter of fact, energy usage in the United States and in the rest of the O.E.C.D. countries had received a great deal of attention since the first oil shock. Energy demand growth had long been associated with economic growth, in general, and there were many questions about the possibility of maintaining adequate GNP growth at a relatively lower level of energy usage. These concerns were, however, counterbalanced by a determination to reduce the size of oil import bills and to restore a correspondingly larger degree of consumer purchasing power. There was also the hope that lower energy, and particularly lower petroleum consumption would improve the oil supply/demand balance enough to forestall even larger future increases in crude oil prices, which would presumably occur when the demand on OPEC oil would cause the cartel to reach its maximum production capacity.

Research activities and goals were also impacted by the dramatically higher energy and feedstock costs. Although there had never been a time when process developers had deliberately designed plants to have low feedstock efficiencies, there was now a new driving force to develop technology to make reaction yields as high as possible, thus reducing the amount of feedstock required to produce a given quantity of a product. If new catalysts could be developed to increase the selectivity (specific yield) of a reaction by a few percent, the benefits would be several times greater than they had been ten years earlier. The research departments of many of the large petrochemical firms were quick to respond to this challenge and put a great deal of new process research work in hand. Unfortunately, relatively little benefit seemed to have come from this effort, which was discontinued several years later, when managements became disinclined to spend big research dollars on their companies' petrochemical operations and reduced severely their companies' process research activities.

WILL PLASTICS REMAIN COMPETITIVE?

With oil prices now seemingly headed for the stratosphere, petrochemicals producers were really becoming concerned about the future position of their products in the marketplace. The price of such key products as polyethylene, PVC, synthetic fibers and other chemically derived materials was escalating in line with feedstock price increases. Where was it all going to end? Petrochemical products had made major inroads into markets that had once been held by natural fibers, natural rubber, leather, asbestos, wood, glass, and paper, among other traditional materials. Would these traditional products regain these markets now that synthetic polymer prices were escalating every month? And even if that only happened to some extent, would the demand growth for synthetics come to a halt, as these materials could no longer extend their gains in the marketplace?

Fond of making studies and publishing the results, the petro-chemical industry addressed this issue with great vigor. In addition to "White Papers" published by companies on this issue and other papers and speeches delivered at industry forums, several consultants performed multiclient studies on this subject. Predictably, the viewpoints of the various people examining the issue varied widely.

In an ICI paper (18) taking a positive view for petrochemicals, D. J. Dowrich concluded that "among the many existing applications for plastic materials, the great majority are unlikely to be affected by the increases in naphtha prices that have occurred so far." He showed that between 1973 and 1978, the price increases for LDPE film (123 percent) were less than those for Kraft wrapping paper (135 percent); those for LDPE heavy duty sacks (126 percent) less than those for paper sacks (162 percent); and those for plastic building materials (158 percent) less than those for aluminum plate (164 percent) or uncoated steel sheets (180 percent). Of course, further large price increases had occurred in late 1978, but the author expected the conclusions regarding relative price increases to remain the same. Detailed studies by ICI had shown that in most cases it actually required more oil to produce the fabricated traditional materials than to make the competing plastic products. As an example, to produce one million square meters of packaging film, it required 155 tons of "oil equivalent" versus only 110 tons for polypropylene. Also, one million one-liter bottles required only 97 tons of "oil equivalent" versus 230 tons for glass bottles. The same was true for other competitive situations, although for the production of fertilizer sacks, paper was slightly better than polyethylene and for drainage pipe, clay was considerably better than PVC.

Dowrich further showed that the effect of naphtha price increases was less and less evident as you went down the "production chain" toward the finished product. Thus, a 100 percent increase in naphtha price caused only a 65 percent rise in ethylene price, a 35 percent rise in polyethylene price and only a 10 percent increase in the price of polyethylene bags, other things being equal. In his evaluation, he particularly stressed the low manpower requirements involved in the fabrication of plastic goods, which enhanced their value relative to metals, wood, and other traditional materials.

Several other industry papers seemed to come to similar conclusions. But the Townsend update of a Springborn-Townsend study published after the first oil shock offered rather opposite findings, when it appeared in 1980. It concluded that "penetration by plastics on sheer economic grounds is considerably more difficult now than it was in 1978." Even at that time, according to the earlier study, most of the traditional materials had gained an advantage over synthetics, and this advantage had been substantially enhanced by the price rises caused by the second oil shock. Products studied included pressure pipe, shipping sacks, drinking cups, automobile bumper beams, 55 gallon drums, 5 gallon milk pails, and other items (19).

It was difficult to decide who was right or wrong. Perhaps the best analysis of the situation was in a paper published around the end of the decade by Mal Sagenkahn of Shell Chemical (20). Sagenkahn, who later left Shell to found his own consulting firm, studied this issue with his co-workers and offered the following thoughts:

- The acceptance of synthetics in the marketplace would be unlikely to change very dramatically.
- The development of differentiated synthetic products has been economically successful (and would presumably continue).
- We are running out of traditional materials (wood, high grade metal ores, etc.) so that there is a need for synthetics, regardless of small changes in the relative prices of synthetic versus natural materials.

Sagenkahn also cautioned that the "discontinuities" inherent in such trends as concern with the environment, "zero population growth" and feelings against a totally materialistic society would certainly have consequences for the petrochemical industry, in terms of lower growth rates, if nothing else.

And so, industry leaders and planners were left to wonder who, among these forecasters, had the best insight into the ultimate issue of petrochemical growth rates for the future.

DISCONTINUITIES AND UNCERTAINTIES

It should now be clear that, from a number of standpoints, the decade of the 1970s was a time of major change and uncertainty for the companies engaged in the manufacture of petrochemicals.

Among the changes and "discontinuities" that occurred during this period, the most troubling were (1) the advent of much lower growth rates for most products, (2) dramatically higher energy and feedstock costs, (3) the arrival of the oil-rich countries as petrochemical producers, and (4) a decided slowdown in the introduction of new technology, as it became more difficult to assess the need for new plants and the benefits of changes in feedstocks associated with such new technologies. Offsetting these issues, to some extent, was another change: it was effectively the end of an era when new entrants to the industry appeared with regularity, usually to the detriment of the existing producers.

As far as "uncertainties" were concerned, there was an ample supply. Of all of these, the issue of energy availability and future cost was the most perplexing and unpredictable and no good answers were available, even at the end of a roller-coaster decade. Many issues surfacing during this period made future planning extremely difficult and frustrating to company managements and consultants alike, a condition that gave rise to one of the best papers published during that period (21). Figure 12.7 is taken from that article, written by Peter Beck of Shell Chemical U.K. Some of the thornier issues: (1) the extent of government reactions to environmental and toxicity problems in the form of even stricter regulations, which would require even much larger industry expenditures for compliance, (2) estimating the likely rate of inflation, an important factor for companies attempting to decide whether to build a new plant now or in several years, when its cost might be twice as high), (3) assessing the relative competitiveness of plastics versus natural materials, in light of the much higher energy and feedstock costs, (4) likely legislation on the removal of tetraethyl lead from gasoline, which would make BTX aromatics much more valuable in gasoline and would impact the supply of these key feedstocks for the production of petrochemicals, and (5) evaluating the risks and rewards of process research expenditures, which required good forecasts of industry growth, suitable for estimating the number of future plants that might be constructed with better technology. A number of other issues of equal importance and complexity could be cited.

In the introduction to this chapter, I referred to books published at the start of the decade by Peter Drucker and Alvin Toffler, which predicted that major change was about to occur in many aspects of our personal life and in the conduct of government

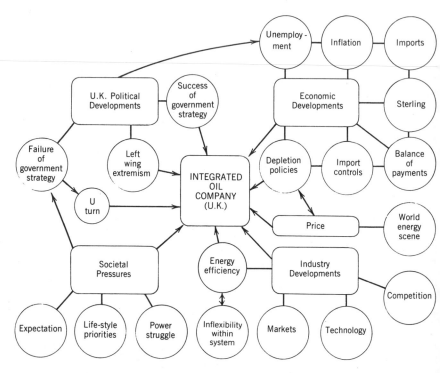

Figure 12.7 Pressures acting on an international oil company in the late 1970s (*Source:* Peter Beck, Corporate Planning for an Uncertain Future, Ref 21.)

and industry. Although not always optimistic in tone, these works offered a reasonable view of a future that would be quite different, but not necessarily unpleasant or widely limiting. The authors mainly warned their readers to prepare for change and they tried to outline what the changes might be. But in 1972, another book came out with quite a different message. In *The Limits to Growth* (22), D. H. Meadows and several coauthors reported on the results of a study carried out by The Club of Rome on "The Predicament of Mankind." Concerned with the harmful effects of exponential growth in energy demand and with the rapid depletion of the earth's raw material resources and worried also about the environmental effects of these trends, the group issued a dour forecast for the future of the world. With a continuation of current trends, the authors warned, the earth would reach the limits of its resources within 100 years, following which there would be a disastrous drop in population and industry capacity as various entities would start to compete for these scarce resources (22, pp. 23-24). This situation could only be avoided, Meadows went on, if the world started right now to curb its voracious appetite for various forms of "growth."

The Limits to Growth at first received considerable notice, since its message was very much in tune with the country's mood at the end of the Vietnam war era—as evidenced by the environmentalist movement, recognition of the need for energy conservation, etc. Within a short period of time, however, the conclusions of the Meadows book were broadly attacked as being unrealistic projections of historical exponential trends, many of which were already in transition as the book was being written.

Industry predictably did not embrace the concepts advanced by The Club of Rome. Nevertheless, there did seem to be a slight sense of relief in some quarters that chemical growth rates had apparently started to abate and that the United States would not soon be required to convert half or more of its oil and natural gas to petrochemicals. Among the people in our industry, any gloom about the future of the world engendered by the Meadows book soon faded into the background, to be replaced by the more mundane issue of the likely future health of the petrochemical industry. One of the book's warnings did, however, stay in people's minds. Even though the world's resources of coal and shale were large enough to over-come—at high cost and inconvenience, to be sure—the problems posed by oil and gas shortages, the amount of carbon oxides that would pour into the atmosphere from coal conversion plants might eventually bring about a major change in the earth's atmosphere, the kind of serious problem predicted by the authors of *The Limits to Growth*.

In any case, in the mid-1970s, it was difficult to see how the United States would be able to switch from oil and gas to coal and shale oil for some time to come, regardless of circumstances in the world oil industry. But it had become fairly obvious that, for one reason or another, the growth of the petrochemical industry would have to slow down, if it had not done so already. It simply was not realistic to expect that the developed countries would be able to secure the amounts of hydrocarbons consistent with supporting a 5 to 10 percent growth rate for petrochemicals for the next 10 to 20 years.

In March 1974, I presented a paper at an American Institute of

Chemical Engineers Meeting in Tulsa, Oklahoma (23), in which I tried to put this situation into perspective. In 1970, petrochemicals had taken slightly under 10 percent of the total amount of hydrocarbons processed by refineries and natural gasoline plants in the United States. If petrochemicals were to continue to grow at the 8–9 percent compounded annual rate of the 1960s, they would, by 1985, consume 15 percent of domestic oil and gas production. By the year 2000, this would rise to over 30 percent. Because it was reasonable to assume that people would still be driving cars and using fuel oil by that time, such an increase would require an unacceptable level of foreign oil imports, even if U.S. crude oil production did not decline very rapidly. These figures just didn't make sense. Petrochemical growth rates would undoubtedly be slowing down.

A 1973 report by Stanford Research Institute (24) projected that plastics would keep growing at 10 percent annually through 2000. I felt that the projections published in the same year by Shell Chemical (25) were more realistic. These assumed that growth rates would, by 1990, decline to 6 percent annually, dropping to 4 percent thereafter. (As it turned out, even these were too optimistic.)

Everything considered, the decade of the 1970s must be viewed as a time of hectic transition from a fairly orderly postwar world to a period of instability and change. For the United States, this was a particularly difficult time, as the nation recognized that its leadership position was eroding and that many of the advantages it had enjoyed in building up its economy were disappearing. This was especially evident with respect to the country's oil and gas reserves, which were seen as having been depleted to a greater extent than had generally been realized, as a result of uninterrupted industrial growth. The Paley Commission Report in the early 1950s (26) had warned that the United States would run short in its crude oil supplies by the 1970s and would have to depend on imports, but traditional American optimism had prevailed over the report's somber geological projections. The Paley Commission had, however, been right.

Now, even America's technological lead was being severely challenged, as Japan and other countries focused their scientists' and engineers' efforts on the development and commercialization of new processes and products that would compete successfully in the large and desirable U.S. market.

The U.S. petrochemical industry did not fare well in the 1970s, though the reasons for its many problems were more complex than such single issues as coping with changes in energy cost or dealing with foreign technology or low cost skilled foreign labor. Strongly impressed with its accomplishments of the past and at the same time weakened by excessive competition within its own ranks, the industry found it difficult to adjust to a different kind of world.

Chemicals were no longer a "glamor" product. The industry that had invented so many exciting new synthetic materials had lost much of the public's respect and a considerable amount of its own self-confidence. It was now at a crossroads. A continuation of recent trends could make the petrochemical industry one of those "smokestack" industries headed for decline and fall. But this was by no means its only possible destiny. For this was not an industry that had been technologically obsolesced by foreign countries and had therefore become hopelessly uncompetitive. It was clear that the petrochemical industry could conceivably choose to revitalize itself and regain much of its former vitality. Chapter 13 presents some views on this subject, as a final message in this historical perspective.

REFERENCES

1. Alvin Toffler (1970). *Future Shock,* New York, Random House.
2. Peter Drucker (1969). *The Age of Discontinuity; Guidelines to our Changing Society,* New York, Harper & Row.
3. J. W. Barrett (1973). Economic incentives and constraints for using plastics, paper presented at symposium entitled "Plastics Industries in a Developing World," London, Institution of Electrical Engineers.
4. Shell International Chemical Company (1978). *Substitution Revisited, A Study on Petrochemical Growth,* London, Shell International Chemical Company.
5. A. R. Tussing and Connie C. Barlow (1984). *The Natural Gas Industry: Evolution Structure and Economics,* Cambridge, MA, Ballinger, p. 113.
6. M. A. Adelman (1972). *The World Petroleum Market,* Baltimore, John Hopkins University Press, published for Resources for the Future Inc.
7. Chem Systems (1976). A study of the factors influencing the crude oil pricing and output policies of OPEC countries. Report to the Federal Energy Administration, carried out under Purchase Order P-03-76-15330-0, January.
8. Robert Stobaugh and Daniel Yergin (1979). *Energy Future.* New York, Random House, p. 63.
9. Chem Systems (1979). Structure and competition within the petrochemical industry. Report to the Federal Energy Administration, carried out under Contract CO-03-50232-00, March, pp. 86, 88, 102–103.

10. Chem Systems (1975). *Chemicals From Coal and Shale.* An R&D analysis, study for the National Science Foundation, document PB 243 393, Washington, DC, June.

11. E. R. Fried and C. L. Schulze (1975). *Higher Oil Prices and the World Economy,* Washington, DC, The Brookings Institution.

12. Organization of Petroleum Exporting Countries (1979). *Annual Statistical Bulletin.*

13. Proceedings of the OPEC Seminar on Downstream Operations in OPEC Member Countries—Prospects and Problems, Vienna, Austria, October 9-11, 1978.

14. Rachel Carson (1962). *Silent Spring.* Boston, MA, Houghton Mifflin.

15. *Chemical Week,* May 16, 1979. p. 20.

16. *Chemical Week,* August 15, 1979, p. 18.

17. *Chemical Week,* October 3, 1979.

18. D. J. Dowrich (1979). The consumer's viewpoint—What will the industry stand, paper presented at the Industry of Purchasing and Supply, May.

19. The energy impact study, Houston, TX, Philip Townsend Associates, Inc., April 1980.

20. M. L. Sagenkahn (1979). Chemical markets in the age of discontinuity, paper presented to the Chemical Marketing Research Association.

21. Peter W. Beck (1982). Corporate planning for an uncertain future, *Long Range Planning* **15,** No. 4, pp. 12-21.

22. D. H. Meadows et al. (1972). *The Limits to Growth,* New York, Universe Books.

23. Peter Spitz (1974). Petrochemical production scenarios and the limits to growth, paper presented at the A.I.Ch.E. meeting, Tulsa, Oklahoma, March 13.

24. Stanford Research (1973). The plastics industry in the year 2000, paper prepared for the Society of Plastics Engineers, April, Stanford, CA.

25. J. L. McCormick and W. W. Reynolds (1973). The future role of the petrochemical industry in a world of limited natural resources, paper presented at the MCA Plastics Group Conference, Absecon, NJ, September.

26. A report to the president by the President's Materials Policy Commission (1952).

ADDITIONAL READING

St. Pierre, L. E. and G. R. Brown, eds. (1979). *Future Sources of Organic Raw Materials—CHEMRAWN I,* New York, Pergamon Press.

Shilling, A. Gary (1986). *The World Has Definitely Changed,* New York, Lakeview Press.

Turner, Louis and James A. Bedore (1975). Middle East industrialization—a study of Saudi and Iranian downstream investments, Westmead, England, Saxon House, published for the Royal Institute of International Affairs.

Yager, Joseph A. and Eleanor B. Steinberg (1975). *Energy and U.S. Foreign Policy,* Cambridge, MA, Ballinger.

13 / The Once and Future Industry

On a bright, sunny day in early June 1984, a group of people assembled in front of a structure housing two Unipol reactors, which constituted the heart of Union Carbide's newest polyethylene plant, located at Taft, Louisiana. A number of other petrochemical production units, including two steam crackers, made the Taft complex, which the company had built in the 1960s, one of its largest production sites. The Unipol polyethylene plant was a relatively recent addition, employing a new process the company had developed to make so-called linear low density polyethylene (LLDPE). This was a tougher version of the conventional resin, which the Carbide technology could produce at considerably lower cost by using a gas-phase, fluidized-bed process in large reactors operated at low pressure instead of in a series of smaller, high-pressure reactors.

The company had previously proven out the technology in a smaller production unit and had then decided to license the process to the world. The so-called "Star Plant" at Taft was the second of two new plants it had recently built to expand its own polyethylene capacity and also to show prospective licensees how a giant Unipol plant could be built at low cost.

Within a relatively short time, Carbide had achieved astounding success with its licensing program. The improved properties of LLDPE, together with the highly publicized low investment and operating costs of the Unipol process, had led many polyethylene producers to conclude that this technology and the type of resin it could produce would soon capture a large share of the world's polyethylene market. This left them the choice of either taking a license on the Carbide process or to work on the commercialization of a similar type of technology, a step that only a few companies might willingly undertake at that point. Accordingly, many polyethylene producers in all parts of the world had taken licenses from Union Carbide to build Unipol plants in the United States, Europe, Canada, Argentina, Saudi Arabia, and elsewhere.

The company had joined forces with Shell Chemical to develop and license an analogous process for making polypropylene, using Carbide's Unipol technology and Shell's high efficiency polypropylene catalysts and market know-how. The group of people standing in front of the reactor structure comprised representatives of Union Carbide, Shell, and Chem Systems. Our firm had been engaged to assist the partners in assessing the potential of the Unipol polypropylene process.

Behind the levee in the background, tugboats were moving barges up and down the wide Mississippi River, many loaded with petrochemicals produced at other plants nearby, such as those operated by Exxon Chemical and Ethyl Corporation at Baton Rouge; Dow and Georgia Pacific at Plaquemine; Borden, BASF—Wyandotte, Borg-Warner, Cosden, ICI, and Allied Chemical at Geismar; etc. Some of the barges had come much farther, from petrochemical plants located along the Ohio River in West Virginia, Ohio, Kentucky, and Tennessee. Barge trains heading South would reach the Gulf Coast well below New Orleans. From there, these bulk chemical cargoes would then move through the inland waterway system to various points along the Gulf of Mexico and up the Atlantic Coast. In some cases, they would be terminaled and later reloaded into oceangoing tankers for export to Europe, South America, or the Pacific Rim, including California.

That morning, gazing at the newest polyethylene plant, at the gleaming distillation towers from other plants not far away and at the busy river in the background, it was hard to escape a poignant feeling that combined excitement with a strange sense of nostalgia and "déjà vu." Excitement, because the Star Plant was another achievement of the petrochemical industry, which had, over the last 50 years, become such an important contributor to the American way of life through the application of advanced technology. This compact plant, fully monitored and controlled by computers, could convert the entire ethylene output of a world-sized steam cracker into polyethylene resin. The plant took up far less space than the railroad hopper cars lined up by the hundreds to receive the polyethylene resin flowing in a continuous stream from the few small holding silos collecting material from the reactors. These resins would later be blown into film to make plastic bags in various shapes and sizes or cast into thicker sheets of transparent plastic that would be used for various construction, agricultural, and other purposes. My sense of excitement was heightened by the fact that here at Taft, we were standing in an industrial landscape created over the past 50 years by firms that had employed "the best and the brightest" chemical engineers of their time to create the U.S. petrochemical industry. Here, in Louisiana and in Texas, not far away, natural gas had been the driving force, available for many years at very low prices to serve as a fuel and feedstock for producers of ammonia, methanol, olefins, and many other chemicals and derivatives.

But the feeling of nostalgia, that registered just as strongly in that brief reflective period, was also not hard to trace. For some years, it had become clear that we had come to the end of an era. Petrochemicals no longer captured people's imagination, and the industry was now increasingly characterized as one in advanced maturity or even in decline.

Natural gas was no longer cheap on the Gulf Coast: its price had risen from 15 cents per thousand cubic feet in the 1950s and 1960s to $3 or so by 1984. And this had set in motion a number of changes. Some years ago, a substantial amount of liquid ammonia had started to be shipped to the United States from Russian plants using that country's own low-priced gas, a deal arranged by Occidental Petroleum's Armand Hammer in exchange for super-phosphoric acid shipped to Russia from his company's Florida plant.

Methanol had already been coming in for some years from gas-rich Alberta Province in Canada and now it would also be shipped to the Gulf Coast from Trinidad and Saudi Arabia. A large part of the country's synthetic alcohol (ethanol) would shortly be imported by a Shell Chemical joint venture with a government-sponsored company in Saudi Arabia, where huge new petrochemical plants were constructed in the late 1970s. Saudi plants would operate on by-product flare gas priced at a fraction of the cost of domestic natural gas. This gas had simply been burned and discharged to the atmosphere for many years, being associated with the production of vast amounts of Saudi crude oil.

Other Middle Eastern projects under construction included several Unipol LLDPE plants, which would ship much of their output to Japan, Europe, and possibly even to the United States. The Saudi projects and others in Canada and in gas-rich Third World nations established the reality that the United States would no longer be the low-cost producer of a number of high-volume commodity chemicals. Instead of exporting a large amount of petrochemicals, the United States might even become a net importer, with serious consequences for its balance of trade with the rest of the world.

The end of the era had also come due to a significant drop in the annual growth rate for the various petrochemicals, as producers found that many markets had reached saturation, including loss of exports to countries developing their own petrochemical facilities. Finally, there was also this sense of déjà vu, which had a more specific association. Union Carbide had decided that it would be far more profitable to offer its Unipol process for license, instead of keeping the new process for itself and building a series of plants as fast as the world market for Unipol LLDPE could be developed. In choosing a broad-scaled licensing strategy, Carbide had emulated what other firms had often decided to do with new technology in situations where they felt they could not hope to dominate the market with the new invention. From Carbide's standpoint, the total investment which would have been required for the company to build LLDPE capacity as fast as the worldwide market for this product would expand, would be far too high. As a result, Carbide had decided that it would build only a certain amount of new domestic capacity, and that the process would be licensed to secure as much royalty income as possible in the United States and in all other parts of the world.

Already, a number of Unipol plants were in operation or under construction around the globe. The improved characteristics of LLDPE were starting to transform the polyethylene business. Consumers would get trash bags with considerably greater resistance to puncturing. And they would probably pay less money for these higher quality bags, since Union Carbide and the new LLDPE producers cut their prices to introduce the new product. From these companies' standpoints, a low price would rapidly expand the market over a short time frame. New producers predictably cut prices to enter the business and to gain market share. The profitability of producing this outstanding new material therefore was already poor, as a result of these actions. This was totally consistent with the experience of the petrochemical industry over much of its recent history. We had seen it all so often before.

Fifty years earlier, Union Carbide had been able to take the opposite approach, when it developed the first direct oxidation process for making ethylene oxide. By building, over a period of time, a number of plants to make this intermediate for antifreeze and by promoting the product in a classical manner under the Prestone label, Carbide became the world's leading supplier of automobile engine coolant. This business area was one of the most profitable in the company's portfolio. But now the world was different. If Carbide had decided not to license its LLDPE technology, a number of competitors would have decided to develop a similar process. Several would eventually have succeeded. Nevertheless, most would have preferred to pay royalties to Carbide to obtain its technology under license. In this way, they could avoid research costs and risk and could presumably beat some of their competitors to the marketplace. For Carbide, the substantial income from licensing—which might in other cases be considerably less than that derived from exploiting the technology in its own plants—was a sure thing.

But there was nothing new in this, since the industry had, in fact, become extremely competitive during the most recent phase of its historical development. The profitability of manufacture for most of its chemicals had suffered correspondingly. Many participants began assessing their petrochemical business areas, in line with an increasingly recognized need for what came to be called industry "restructuring." This term was used to describe a process where, among other changes, the industry would be strengthened by being reshaped into a smaller number of stronger producers, with weaker players divesting their positions or shutting down uneconomical capacity. A severe recession in 1981–1982 and mounting concern over having to compete with low-priced imports from oil-rich nations had already caused some producers to start trimming their petrochemical portfolios. Much of the driving force for this development came from the financial community, which had concluded that, at least for now, the production of petrochemicals had become an unprofitable business with poor prospects, given the fierce competition in many of its product lines. This situation could only get worse with the advent of more capacity from abroad. It was up to the chemical community to take appropriate steps to deal with this problem.

Something had gone seriously wrong, but exactly when and how? This industry had been a leader in technology development and in providing the products that had created vast new markets, but some time ago the music had stopped. Was this an inevitable consequence of forces beyond its control or could things have gone differently? Could things change again for the better? There was a need to develop answers to these questions.

The 50 years or so that had elapsed between the time that Union Carbide had become the country's first petrochemical company and that day at the company's new polyethylene plant somehow took concrete form in my mind. They spanned the history of the petrochemical industry. My vivid impressions at Taft seemed somehow to symbolize both the best and the most troublesome features of the industry in which I had spent much of my professional career. And that was the origin of this book.

The petrochemical industry had come a long way in a very short time. Over the span of a few decades, it had made the production of chemicals the largest industry in the country, equal to such Commerce Department manufacturing categories as Petroleum and Coal, Motor Vehicles, and larger than Communications (1). (See Table 13.1.)

Now, serious cracks had appeared in the facade of this once golden industry and it seemed important to gauge whether the

Table 13.1   Total Shipments by U.S. Manufacturers (billions of current dollars)

Category	1983	1984
Chemical and allied products	190	216
Petroleum and coal	191	216
Motor vehicles and parts	152	195
Communications services	109	123
Communications equipment	49	62
Glass furnace and steel mills	48	55
Iron and steel foundries	12	16
Total (All US Manufacturers)	2,052*	2,360*

*Includes many categories not shown in table.

problems the industry had encountered were in the nature of a malaise associated with "growing pains," a condition that would pass as it entered a normal phase of benign maturity, or whether the illness was chronic and therefore largely irreversible. There was, in particular, a need to examine the history of the industry to obtain a better perspective on how to evaluate its future course, in terms of trends in technology, feedstocks, and in modes of behavior. Such a journey into the past would not only provide a chronology of the events that had shaped the industry, but would also be edifying and exciting. And so I turned back the clock to an earlier time and started to study the industry's beginning and I began to write. Now, at the conclusion of my journey, some perspectives have emerged.

FEEDSTOCKS: THE CONDITION PRECEDENT

It seems appropriate to begin with the name. Based on a review of the literature, it appears that the word "petrochemicals" did not come into the language until the late 1930s or the early 1940s. For some years, people in the United States and in England referred to the products involved as "petroleum chemicals" and this term continued to be used in England for some time after it was changed to the shorter form in the United States. Either way, the name of what was soon recognized as a new industry reflected the fact that a different source of feedstocks was involved. By the early 1950s, it was clear that the entire basis of the raw materials that had hitherto supported the growth of the organic chemical industry had undergone a major change.

The transition from one set of raw materials to another would seem to be an important and unusual subject, but I actually found little treatment of this in the literature. Yet, feedstocks and feedstock changes are a central theme for the history of the organic chemical industry. And there will continue to be changes. In the 1970s, when there was much concern about the future availability and price of crude oil and natural gas, study work had energetically commenced on how the petrochemical industry could be switched from these feedstocks to coal, shale, and agricultural wastes. Although the world still had ample crude oil, its supply was suddenly restricted and people began contemplating a forced change to these less desirable feedstocks, occasioned not only by economics, but also by considerations of geopolitics and national security. Such a switch in feedstocks did not occur, however—in part because Sheik Yamani, the Saudi Arabian Oil minister, wisely warned the OPEC cartel members not to price crude oil so high as to force the industrial nations into developing cost-effective substitute sources of fuels and chemical feedstocks. If history had proceeded differently, the chemical industry would, for the first time, have based itself on raw materials sources for *artificial* reasons. For in the past, the organic chemical industry had always been driven by feedstock availability, a point that became very clear as I delved into the past.

My most interesting discussion on this subject was with Prof. Dr. Carl Heinrich Krauch, head of the Vorstand (managing board) of Huels and the son of a key member of the Vorstand of I.G. Farben in the 1930s. Prof. Krauch had carried out research work at the Max Planck Institute at Muehlheim-Ruhr after receiving his doctorate in chemistry (a family tradition), and had then risen rapidly through the ranks of the German chemical industry, with a middle management assignment at BASF and a high-level supervisory post at Henkel, before attaining his present position. In addition to his management responsibilities, he had also read a number of papers on issues of the chemical industry, including past and future sources of feedstocks (2). He had discussed this subject often with his father, who was closely involved in I.G. Farben's technical exchange with Jersey Standard in the 1930s. Dr. Krauch Sr.'s "dream," put into practice by Carl Bosch of BASF, was to marry German high-pressure technology and catalyst know-how with the hydrocarbon resources of a large oil company, thus creating the conditions for producing almost unlimited amounts of light hydrocarbon fuels and chemical feedstocks from the heavy oil fractions that constituted a large percentage of most crude oils. Although coal hydrogenation was considered to be a feasible and necessary goal—in fact, it later became crucial for Germany's war effort—the elder Dr. Krauch foresaw, as early as the start of the 1930s, the development of a large petrochemical industry.

Prof. Krauch at Huels told me that in his view the organic chemical industry had always been feedstock, rather than technology or market driven. It was the availability of large quantities of relatively useless coal tars and coke oven gases in the mid- and late-1800s that had led to the recovery and purification of a number of organic chemicals present in these streams (e.g., phenol, benzene, naphthalene) and the development of technology for their transformation into dyestuffs, pharmaceuticals, and other consumer-oriented products of that time. Then, in the earlier part of this century, large amounts of agriculturally derived alcohol became available, far more than could be consumed in wines and liquors. Thus it came about that a number of chemists in different countries, starting with Ipatieff at the turn of the century, developed processes to convert ethanol to various aliphatic chemicals. This created the chemistry that would allow many other consumer products (solvents, coatings, synthetic detergents, engine coolants) to be produced in substantial quantities in plants built on the basis of the new technologies. The advent of the automobile created a huge market for chemicals of all types, but it was the availability of cheap feedstocks that allowed the chemical industry to produce, at popular prices, the products the transportation industry would need to grow and prosper.

In the 1930s, as Prof. Krauch then pointed out, it was the availability of large amounts of reactive hydrocarbons from refinery cracking units that led to the creation of what came to be called the petrochemical industry. In the United States, in the 1940s, it became the successor to a then rather fragmented bulk organic chemical industry, still based largely on coal and on agriculturally-derived ethanol. Some of the technology upon which the new industry was based had been sourced from existing chemistry, but much more was developed in the late 1930s and 1940s. It was over this period that the world became aware of synthetic rubber, synthetic fibers and commodity thermoplastics, such as the vinyls and polyethylene.

These new products soon created huge markets that allowed the petrochemical industry to grow at a rate that caught the attention of the entire world. The dimensions of this industrial accomplishment can only be captured in part by graphical illustration (Figs. 13.1, 13.2, 13.3, and 13.4). (3,4). Figure 10.1, which shows U.S. vinyl chloride monomer demand climbing from 300 million pounds in 1950 to over 4 billion pounds in 1970, gives a particularly good U.S. perspective.

DIMENSIONS OF A NEW INDUSTRY

Statistics are only one way of showing how so much of the American landscape was transformed by the many hundreds of petrochemical plants that sprang up in various parts of the country

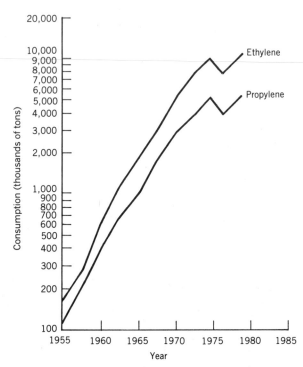

Figure 13.1 Ethylene and propylene consumption in Western Europe, 1955–1985. (*Source:* A. L. Waddams, *Chemicals from Petroleum—An Introductory Survey,* 4th ed., (1980) London, John Murray.)

over a short period of time. Although a majority of these plants were built along the Gulf Coast in Louisiana and Texas, many other petrochemical production centers were established in Oklahoma, West Texas, New Jersey, Delaware, along the Ohio River, and in the area around Chicago. Some were also built in California, although the West Coast never became an important center for the industry, partly because of more stringent environmental regulations in that part of the country.

The selection of production sites was based on availability of raw materials or on the proximity to consumer markets and sometimes on both. Important transportation channels for raw materials, particularly for intermediate products, were established through the use of the Mississippi and Ohio Rivers, the inland waterway system along the coastline, and product pipeline grids.

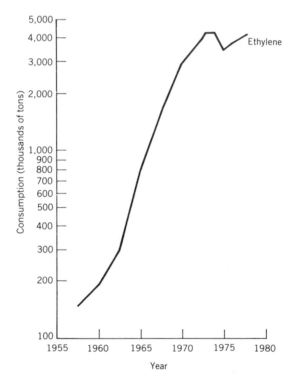

Figure 13.2 Ethylene consumption in Japan. (*Source:* A. L. Waddams, *Chemicals from Petroleum—An Introductory Survey,* 4th ed. (1980) London, John Murray.)

These grids, separately or in combination, greatly expanded the range of possible sites where petrochemical production could be carried out.

Outdoor construction techniques of the type used in petroleum refineries became the standard for petrochemical installations, even in the coldest climates. The increasing size of distillation columns and reactors in any case precluded the location of some of the equipment inside closed buildings, as was common practice until the 1930s. Besides, it was found that the open construction technique used in refineries provided much better access to equipment for maintenance. Moreover, such plants were less expensive to construct, since the cranes used to lift large equipment items could easily place these towers, reactors, and compressors on their outdoor concrete foundations.

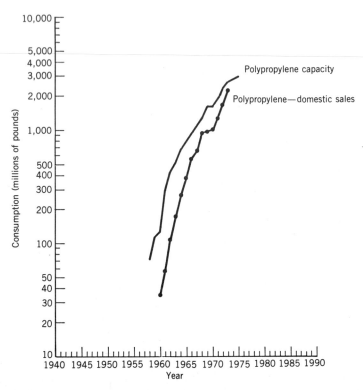

Figure 13.3 U.S. capacity and domestic sales for polypropylene resins. (*Source: Chemical Economics Handbook,* SRI International.)

The development of the petrochemical industry also spurred tremendous growth in the engineering, construction and equipment supply industries. The major *refinery* contractors could easily transfer their skills to the design and construction of *petrochemical* plants. These were generally smaller than refineries, but also more complex, frequently involving equipment that was subjected to more severe operating conditions, such as very high pressures and temperatures, and the presence of corrosive liquids. This led to the use of more sophisticated construction materials, including special stainless steels, alloys of esoteric metals (e.g., titanium), and even graphite. The use of reinforced plastics for vessels, tanks, and piping in a number of plants helped to further increase the market for polyester resins, PVC, and other petrochemical end

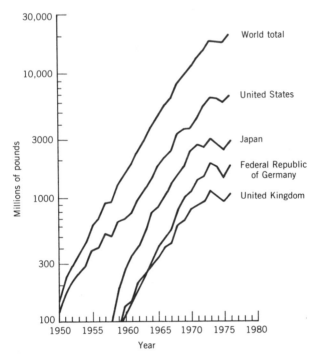

Figure 13.4 Noncellulosic fibers—world production, by country. (*Source: Chemical Economics Handbook,* SRI International.)

products. In many cases, operating companies or contractors had to experiment with different construction materials to solve corrosion problems. Then, the knowledge of what materials to use became part of these companies' proprietary know-how. But some of this information was also disseminated by equipment vendors interested in expanding the market for their products.

There was a great deal of cooperation between the engineers designing the plants and the fabricators who would build the equipment for these units, since each of these groups was dependent on the other. For example, the engineer might propose a new, specialized configuration for a heat exchanger to suit an unusual requirement, and the fabricator would then devise a useful, new design. Successful application would then lead to more sales later on, perhaps to a number of other companies licensing the new process. Operating companies and distillation column tray manufacturers worked closely together to develop more efficient, lower cost fractionation systems that could provide greater separation of components in a given height of distillation tower, thus achieving lower costs. Cooperation between chemical companies or contractors on the one hand and reactor vessel fabricators on the other, resulted in the construction of reactors with as many as 5,000 one-inch, twenty-foot long tubes (later to be filled with catalyst) welded into shells as large as 12 feet in diameter. Requirements spelled out by plant design engineers also led to the design of pumps that could better handle the presence of abrasive solids in flowing liquid streams, including the use of flushed mechanical seals on pump shafts, instead of the more conventional packing rings.

A great expansion took place in the field of chemical engineering, which came into its own in the 1940s. The number of students receiving degrees in chemical engineering from U.S. universities and colleges increased substantially in the 1950s, versus the previous two decades. Undoubtedly, this accounted for the fact that the number of engineers joining the American Institute of Chemical Engineers (A.I.Ch.E.) rose from 14,000 in 1940 to over 37,000 in 1960. The advent of the petrochemical industry was the most important single factor in this surge, though other parts of the so-called Chemical Process Industries (C.P.I.), including petroleum refining, pulp and paper, cement, nuclear, etc. enjoyed considerable growth over this period.

A perspective on the importance of chemical engineering contributions made by companies in the petrochemical industry is afforded by a review of some of the winners of the Kirkpatrick *Chemical Engineering* Achievement Award in the period from the early 1930s to the late 1960s. The jury selected to decide on this award consists of a group of distinguished professors of chemical engineering from a number of U.S. colleges and universities and their selections are published annually in *Chemical Engineering* magazine. Some of the achievements of petrochemical industry participants so honored are highlighted below (5):

- *1933—Carbide and Carbon Chemicals.* For commercially producing many synthetic organic chemicals from petroleum and natural gas.
- *1935—E.I. du Pont de Nemours & Co. Organic Chemicals Dept.* For the successful industrial development of neoprene, synthetic camphor, and certain other important chemicals and dyestuffs.

- *1939—Standard Oil Development Company.* For new chemical engineering processes and equipment to make available superfuels for aviation, plus other valuable products synthesized from oil.
- *1943—American synthetic rubber industry.* For crowding into 24 months, chemical engineering planning and construction that normally would have required many years. Awarded to 67 companies.
- *1948—Shell Development Co.* For the successful synthesis of glycerin from petroleum for the first time on a commercial scale.
- *1949—Celanese Corp. of America.* For the notable chemical engineering integration of its textile, plastics, and chemical operations.
- *1951—Phillips Petroleum Co.* For development of high abrasion carbon blacks and major contributions to the success of cold rubber.
- *1959—Texaco Inc.* For development of a route to low-cost, pure synthesis gas (hydrogen) from liquid, gas, or solid hydrocarbons.
- *1965—Monsanto Company.* For developing a process for one-step electrolytic conversion of acrylonitrile to adiponitrile.
- *1967—The M. W. Kellogg Co.* For the design and development of large capacity, single-train ammonia plants.

THE INDUSTRY BECOMES TOO ATTRACTIVE

It was a time of sustained expansion unmatched in the history of a capital-intensive industry. No wonder that this dynamic business area attracted so many companies. Some entered the production of petrochemicals with reasonable qualifications, but many others were essentially swept along by the headiness of entering an exciting new business. It was known at the time that one or two of the oil companies decided to build petrochemical plants not so much because of their raw materials position, but because outside directors asked at board meetings why their firm had not yet made its move into the petrochemical industry.

As a result, over the 1950s and 1960s, the industry grew in size and in the number of competitors for most of its products. "Double digit" annual growth* in consumption was matched and often exceeded by additions in industry production capacity, as some firms expanded and others made *de novo* entries. This included not only chemical and oil companies, but also firms engaged in such diverse industries as natural gas transmission (Tenneco, El Paso Natural Gas), textiles, (Beaunit, J.P. Stevens), and shipping (W.R. Grace). The tire companies, (Goodyear, Goodrich, Firestone, U.S. Rubber), which had built the wartime synthetic rubber plants, had stayed in the industry to produce not only elastomers and the intermediates used to make them but also plastics and other petrochemicals.

Many company decisions to add production capacity were not taken as a result of a great deal of analysis, but to capture the next slice of the expanding market. However, the penalty for building a new plant without making an extensive study to justify its construction was not too severe in the earlier years. During this period, the industry was growing rapidly enough to always require new capacity in a matter of a year or two. However, as plant sizes increased, the price that had to be paid for adding new capacity too soon began to rise. By the late 1960s, ill-advised addition of capacity—particularly by a new producer—started to be recognized as a major issue, but it took another decade before the industry finally accepted the fact that it could not continue to play the game in this manner.

As noted in the two preceding chapters, the profitability of petrochemical manufacture had actually been on the decline since the early 1960s. In an article published in *Fortune* magazine in October 1961, Perrin Stryker defined the problems of the industry as being threefold (6, p. 125):

> "First, there has been a heavy invasion of the industry by new companies. Chemical production is no longer confined to the major 'general chemical' companies . . . among these newcomers to the industry are National Distillers, W.R. Grace, the five major tire makers, and all the major oil companies . . . various producers of soap, paper, paint, metal, glass . . . have got (sic) into the chemical business on their own.

> "Second, pressure and counterpressures from the invading companies, rising costs of labor, construction, and raw materials and declining prices of chemicals (especially plastics) have combined to set up a

---

*This term is used when the compound annual growth rate is 10 percent or higher.

severe price squeeze. Overcapacities have meant low operating rates and consequently higher operating costs. . . .

"Third, the companies are facing a dilemma caused by their own recent and swift expansion abroad . . . this expansion, along with the rapid growth of European companies, has already started to reduce the flow of U.S.-made chemicals to Europe . . . more (European) capacity has already been developed in some products than the European market can absorb, and this excess production may seek U.S. markets."

Stryker's concern regarding large amounts of foreign petrochemicals entering the United States never became troublesome, though there were some exceptions (e.g., butadiene, which was often in excess supply in Western Europe). However, even small amounts of foreign products entering the industry from abroad could cause producers to cut prices to lessen or eliminate the threat of large imports and in this respect the foreign producers were, at times, a factor. The other two issues Stryker identified were very much on target.

In this article, Stryker also illustrated how the financial results of two major players, du Pont and Dow, began to be squeezed over the late 1950s. du Pont's operating profit as a percent of total capital invested, dropped from around 50 percent in 1951 to the level of 30 percent by 1960, while Dow's decreased from 30 percent to around 15 percent over the same period. During this same timeframe, petrochemical prices dropped by an average of seven percent, with plastics prices falling 23 percent. "In part," Stryker said, "price reduction is the normal and traditional passing on of technological gain to the consumer, but it also reflects new pressures" (6).

The industry participants' troublesome history covering the production of vinyl chloride is recounted in some detail in an earlier chapter of this book. Stryker illustrated this problem for another plastic product, polystyrene, as follows (6, p. 208):

"Since 1955, the industry's annual sales of this resin have risen 55 percent to about 700 million pounds . . . nevertheless, competition among sixteen producers has driven the price of polystyrene down from 27.5 cents in 1956 to less than 17 cents per pound . . . with 14 cents per pound raw materials and conversion costs there is only about a 3-cent margin to cover research and development, marketing, shipping, overhead and profit . . . last year, Dow raised the price by 1 cent per pound (but) was forced to retract its price increase when none of the other fifteen producers followed suit."

Some of the rationale that caused petrochemical industry margins to deteriorate as new companies entered the industry is well described in a recently published book by Prof. Joseph Bower who teaches at the Harvard Business School (7). He points out that some of the companies entering petrochemicals production came from industries enjoying a considerably smaller profit margin (e.g., the tire industry). The lower expectations of firms conditioned to smaller profit margins would tend to make them more competitive players. Also, some companies entering the industry could utilize a large amount of the chemicals they would produce in their own nonchemical operations (e.g., forest products companies that use adhesives, coatings, plastic liners, etc.). These firms were often willing to sell the balance of the output of these plants at lower than normal merchant market prices, as long as such sales gave some contribution to overhead costs.

As the 1960s progressed, the problems that Stryker, Bower, and many others identified then and later, became increasingly acute. The profitability of basic chemicals manufacture, which had as recently as the 1950s been relatively high, compared to other industries, now dropped below the average (Fig. 13.5), where it has largely stayed since that time.

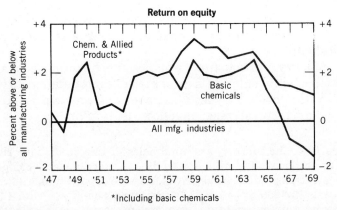

Figure 13.5 Financial performance of U.S. chemical industry versus all manufacturing industries. (*Source:* T. P. Forbath, speech made at the CCDA meeting, March 1970.)

THE 1970s—AND THEN RESTRUCTURING

The 1970s proved to be a particularly difficult period, since industry participants received a series of mixed signals. High energy and feedstock prices reduced demand growth still further and created doubts about the future availability and supply of traditional raw materials. On the other hand, 1974 and 1979 were two of the best years the petrochemical industry ever had, the result of supply shortages, upward revaluations of inventories, and increased exports, as U.S. firms derived substantial advantages from oil and gas price controls instituted by the government, which made these producers very competitive abroad.

The expected advent of petrochemicals from oil-rich nations did become a gloomy reality, and this prospect not only discouraged any potential new domestic entrants but, even more importantly, acted as one of the major factors that caused many existing producers to consider withdrawing from the industry. On balance, it was therefore hard to say whether the arrival of these new, low-cost producers represented a net positive or negative effect.

The deep recession in 1981–1982 then gave the industry another severe blow, as plants operated at rates as low as 50–60 percent of capacity, in many cases. This, of course, only confirmed the intentions of some participants to leave this cyclical, unpredictable and, much of the time, unprofitable industry as soon as they could make a graceful exit.

Some of the oil companies (e.g. Sun Company, Union Oil) had long decided against commodity petrochemicals. Other oil companies were now substantially reducing their commitment to this sector (e.g., Arco's sale of its polyethylene and polypropylene businesses (8), Gulf Oil's sale of its polypropylene business, Shell Chemical's "mothballing" of a large vinyl chloride plant and divestiture of its polystyrene business, etc.). Others decided to stay and watch guardedly for further developments.

Diversified companies that had entered the industry to broaden their business portfolios (e.g., Grace, Borden) and some of the other firms not thought of as chemical companies (e.g., Goodyear, Georgia Pacific) were exiting from some or many of their petrochemical operations, or were about to do so. This was particularly the case for several of the gas transmission companies, which for a number of reasons, were greatly de-emphasizing petrochemicals. Some were acquired (e.g., El Paso by Burlington Industries), some (e.g.,

Tenneco, Texas Eastern) decided that other parts of their diversification program apparently promised better returns, and some needed to raise cash to reduce debt due to acquisitions (e.g., Enron, the surviving combination of Houston Natural Gas and Internorth).

Even many of the chemical companies, including several that had participated broadly in the petrochemical industry, substantially decreased their commitment to this sector. These companies either diversified heavily into specialty and "performance" chemicals or embarked on major programs to acquire companies in product areas outside the traditional chemical industry, such as pharmaceuticals (Monsanto), consumer products (American Cyanamid), and aerospace components (Hercules).

The financial community generally applauded these efforts to escape what it considered the tyranny of extreme competition in the commodity end of the business, which had caused firms in the United States, and particularly in Western Europe and Japan, to incur huge losses in the early 1980s. At the depth of the 1982 recession, the move for many companies was to get out of petrochemicals production as fast as possible.

SMOKESTACK INDUSTRIES, MATURITY, AND THE GROWTH CYCLE

In this age of buzzwords and stylized planning systems, there is a tendency to simplify complicated industrial issues by applying slogans and matrices. Some of these may apply and some may not, but it is clear that an understanding of the specific characteristics of a business is the most important aspect of any analysis, and here it becomes quite plain that it is too early to write off the manufacture of petrochemicals as an industry that is now passing from "maturity" into "decline." The reasons for this seem evident when the industry is compared to others that are in considerably greater degrees of difficulty or even in mortal peril.

Some observers have stated that the oil shocks of the 1970s and the desire of Third World countries to industrialize brought about a major change in world industrial conditions that propelled a number of heavy industries in the developed countries into a dangerous state of decline. Thus, the iron and steel industries in the United States, Western Europe, and now even in Japan are in a considerably poorer competitive position than before and cannot be expected to recover their former status. Countries such as Brazil, Taiwan, and Korea have been able to install modern steel mills—often with large loans from banks in the O.E.C.D. countries—that are more efficient than most of those in the three major industrial regions. In addition, the cheap labor available in the new producing regions and the fact that coal and iron ore deposits in Germany, England, the United States, and other advanced countries are becoming more expensive and are now often of poorer quality, contributes to the greater competitiveness of the new producers. Thus, in the United States, it is no longer surprising to find diesel engine castings imported from Brazil or heavy outdoor barbecue grills from Taiwan.

The steel industry is only one example of a number of others that are suffering the same fate. In the 1970s, it became fashionable to characterize such superannuated manufacturing segments as "smokestack" industries, which were considered to be in a state of decline from which they would not recover. Special tariffs could protect such industries for a time, but sooner or later they were doomed. In the list of such "smokestack" industries, petrochemicals were often mentioned.

The 1970s were also a time when many of the current strategic planning methodologies started to be applied by several of the major consulting firms, to explain what was happening. We learned that industries go through a "life cycle," starting from an "embryonic" state and advancing through periods of first slow and then much more rapid growth, followed eventually by "maturity" and then "decline." The trick was to get into an industry at an early stage and to make heavy investments during the growth period, leading hopefully to a high market share. Then, as the industry (or product line) approached maturity, there was an opportunity to generate a great deal of cash flow, since businesses no longer required new investment nor substantial research expenses. They could, as the Boston Consulting Group said, become "cash cows" and could be "harvested" during this period. Meanwhile, investment would have already been directed to other industries or to industry sectors growing at a higher rate.

Although people have characterized the petrochemical industry as now being a "smokestack" industry in the mature or even declining part of its "life cycle," many facts do not support such a conclusion. The connotation of a "smokestack" industry is of one that has become hopelessly uncompetitive, due to either a major change in the demand for its products or because of low-cost foreign competition. The first point is obviously not applicable to an industry that produces such key products as engineering polymers and plastics, synthetic fibers, residential house siding and insulation, and automobile surface coatings, to name just a few examples. As for low-cost foreign competition, the problem is not nearly as serious as had once been anticipated. The United States is still the low-cost producer of many petrochemicals. Moreover, in petrochemicals, we are not dealing with products that have a high labor component, as is the case for textiles, computer circuit boards, or the production of certain fabricated steel products.

There is also no indication that in the petrochemical industry the industrial countries have suffered the kind of low productivity growth that has led economists such as Profesor Lester Thurow to warn about impending industrial decline and fall (9). Although there is some low-cost competition from oil-rich nations in certain sectors—mainly natural gas and ethylene derivatives—the total volume of these (less expensive) products available from these sources for the world market is a very small fraction of total world demand. Much of this material will in any case be absorbed by the growing demand represented by the population of the Third World. For all these reasons, it is quite wrong to place the petrochemical industry in the United States and even in Western Europe into the same category as such industries as steel and television sets.

Japan represents a different situation. Raw material supply has always been a cause for a less world-competitive industry there, and in the 1970s other considerations made government planners decide that the country's petrochemical industry faced major viability problems in the long term. Among these were the fact that the country was running out of land to build large plants and that pollution problems were becoming more and more severe. Documents published by Japanese government agencies now projected a dramatic decline in the size of the country's petrochemical industry. Although such forecasts were not accompanied by restrictive government actions, the Japanese companies seemed prepared to accept their fate with reasonable equanimity. The conclusion of the country's industrial leaders seemed to be that Japan could probably come out reasonably well by effectively replacing naphtha feedstock imports with petrochemical intermediates from the Middle East, Canada, and other oil-rich areas building new capacity.

Western Europe was not prepared to take such a step. This

would, in any case, have been difficult, since it is still close to impossible for this region to act in a concerted, unified manner, given the fractious state of the European Common Market as an area for the establishment of joint trade policies. Also, a substantial share of European petrochemical capacity is owned or controlled by individual country governments, a situation that makes it much more difficult to shut down plants and put people out of work. Europe is better off than Japan, since it does have a reasonable resource base in hydrocarbon feedstocks (North Sea Oil, Dutch gas) and can therefore take a somewhat more independent tack. The main problem was oversupply. There was no doubt, by the early 1980s, that a substantial amount of West European capacity was relatively inefficient and should be shut down. And there was no question that Middle Eastern petrochemicals would be entering the continent in increasing quantities, as the decade of the 1980s progressed.

At the request of a number of these firms, Chem Systems undertook a comprehensive study of some of the more important segments of the European petrochemical industry to project its future under different scenarios (10). Demand growth would be low under any circumstances and supply/demand conditions unfavorable, given the industry's overcapacity and the expected arrival of more products from the Middle East. By shutting down a considerable amount of uneconomic capacity, however, and through the withdrawal of certain firms from different business segments, a viable condition could probably be achieved.

This seemed to augur well for the European industry, provided it could bring supply in line with expected demand and product imports. The industry's profitability might then recover from the heavy losses experienced in the late 1970s and early 1980s, particularly if the industry's participants could learn lessons from the past. In fact, the profitability of European petrochemical producers has been improving markedly in recent years, though not for every product. (See Figs. 13.6 and 13.7 taken from Chem Systems International's Quarterly Business Analysis Report in 1986.) The "leader-laggard" analysis methodology created by our firm shows the cash cost margins for the best and worst performing firms, using a complex rating scheme.

Starting around 1980, many U.S. operating companies and their outside advisors started to study the same issues. In many respects, the situation in the United States was conceded to be the

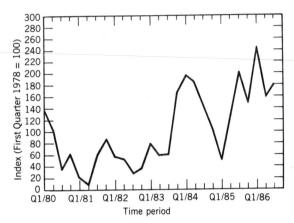

Figure 13.6 West European profitability index. Cash cost margins in Deutschmarks (1978 = 100). (*Source:* Chem Systems.)

least serious, although one could not know that from the negative image the industry had attained.

Some of the reasons for the pessimism often expressed regarding the future of the petrochemical industry do, in fact, relate to the uncomplementary terms used in strategic planning analyses to describe the latter stages of industry or sector development. According to such analysts, it is a foregone conclusion that at the end

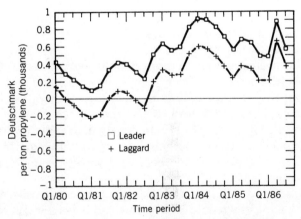

Figure 13.7 Polypropylene margins—variable cost. (*Source:* Chem Systems.)

of a "life cycle," there looms "maturity" and "decline." When the "end game" is at hand, a new set of frightening rules starts to apply. And when a "cash cow" no longer provides milk, it must be sold or killed. As alluded to earlier, however, there is some doubt as to whether these concepts really apply to the U.S. petrochemical industry at this juncture. There is, in fact, much reason to conclude that they do not properly characterize the current situation and that much harm can be done with such facile analyses.

Professor Kathryn Harrigan at the Columbia Business School has well analyzed "end-game" strategies for various industries (11), including the production of acetylene, for which such a characterization is quite applicable (Dictionary definition: *"End game 1:* the last stage (as the last three tricks) in playing a bridge hand, *2:* the final phase of a board game; specifically the stage of a chess game following serious reduction of forces"). For petrochemicals, as a whole, this description hardly seems to apply.

Professor Michael Porter at the Harvard Business School authored one of the most important books on the subject of strategic planning, in which the subject of industry maturity is discussed in considerable depth. He defines a mature industry as one in which there is slowing growth, more competition for market share, a "topping out" in industry capacity, fewer new products and product applications, more international competition, and a fall in industry profits (12). Pessimists would say that all of these characterizations apply to the petrochemical industry, but this is not really true and, in any case, the situation is far more complex than that. "Slowing growth" and "more international competition" are the only categories that apply without qualifications. But "competition for market share" and "fall in industry profits" have been with us through most of the rapid growth period and are therefore hardly new events that signal a transition to a new state of industry behavior.

It is also fair to state that many petrochemicals reached "maturity" as early as 1960 and certainly by the early 1970s, in the opinion of one Exxon Chemical executive (13). Yet, during this period many other chemicals were experiencing very high growth rates, as new markets continued to develop (Table 13.2.).

There has been some "topping out" in industry capacity, but for some products (polyethylene, for example) even relatively low demand growth means substantial capacity additions every year or two. Also, it is probably fair to state that in the 1980s, there has,

Table 13.2 U.S. Basic Chemical Industry Maturity

Petrochemical Product	Decade in Which Reached (Maturity Growth = GNP Growth)	Market Penetration in 1980, %
Ethyl alcohol	1955–1965	85*
Acetone	1970–1980	95†
Benzene	1960–1970	95
Synthetic detergents‡	1965–1975	85
Synthetic fibers‡	1970–1980	75
Synthetic elastomers‡	1970–1980	75

Source: Reprinted by permission of World Petroleum Congress from Proceedings of the Eleventh World Petroleum Congress (Volume 4), 1984, John Wiley and Sons, Ltd.

*Down from 95% in 1955–1965.

†Reached 95% by 1955.

‡Contains some coal-tar benzene.

if anything, been a surge of new products and products applications (linear low density polyethylene, new engineering polymers, structural composites, etc.) that have injected new vitality into the production of petrochemicals.

A very important point Porter made was that (12, p. 237)

"Industry maturity does not occur at any fixed point in an industry's development and it can be delayed by innovations or other events that fuel continued growth for industry participants. Moreover, in response to strategic breakthroughs, mature industries may regain their rapid growth and thereby go through more than one transition to maturity"

Why should this not be true for the petrochemical industry?

RAW MATERIALS OPTIONS AND THE ROLE OF TECHNOLOGY

The United States continues to have a substantial raw material base, a very large market for petrochemical products, and a capacity to innovate which is, in a number of areas, still unmatched by any other country. From a larger perspective, it is therefore not difficult to visualize an optimistic scenario for the industry's future. It now seems fairly clear that conventional feedstocks for petrochemical production will be around for a long time—in retrospect, there was no need to panic in the mid-1970s. While in the past, petroleum supply/demand and pricing forecasts have more often than not been wrong, projected conditions for the supply of crude oil and petroleum products are now improving, since a great deal more is now known regarding such key variables as OPEC production capacity, the long-term effects of energy conservation measures, fuel substitution, production by non-OPEC producers and other aspects of the world petroleum market. It is now considered reasonable to project that the world will have ample petroleum supplies available at least through the first half of the next century. Undoubtedly, crude oil prices will rise again, perhaps fairly sharply, in the 1990s, but we will not have to relive the energy traumas of the 1970s. Moreover, the petrochemical industry will have increasing raw material options with time.

Continued development of technology is one reason for this. As times goes by, the range of organic chemical products that can be economically made from raw materials other than oil and gas will keep broadening. Most importantly, a large amount of development work has now been carried out on what is called "C_1 chemistry," the manufacture of a variety of organic chemicals from synthesis gas (mixtures of carbon monoxide and hydrogen). New coal gasification techniques, more economical Fischer-Tropsch processing,* and a variety of new chemical reactions based on synthesis gas have demonstrated that if the price of crude oil rises to the level of $30-$40 per barrel, we can start making "petrochemicals" from coal and other such heavy fossil-derived materials. These solid sources of carbon are far more abundant than petroleum and their price is related only to mining and transportation costs, rather than to the whims of a cartel.

Tennessee Eastman's coal-based new acetic anhydride plant in Kingsport, Tennessee and the cooperative coal gasification-combined cycle power generation project in Daggett, California (sponsored by the Electric Power Research Institute), are proof that the chemical and utility industries are well on their way to demonstrating the use of coal in sophisticated applications, where oil and gas have recently been exclusively used. C_1 chemistry can, of course, be based on natural gas, as well as coal. This is important, since there is much more gas than oil under the earth's surface. The demonstration of Mobil Chemical's MTG process for the production of high octane gasoline from natural gas in New Zealand has shown that countries with large gas supplies (but little or no oil) can be independent of OPEC in this respect, should that cartel regain control of world crude oil supply and pricing.

Strides made in the field of biotechnology will also broaden the range of future chemical feedstocks. In the earlier years of this century, ethyl and butyl alcohol, acetone, and ethylene were produced from agricultural feedstocks, but in most parts of the world this became uneconomical when low-priced oil and gas became the preferred feedstocks. As the cost of crude oil again starts to rise, the older technologies, now improved through the use of more productive bioorganisms derived through genetic manipulation, will again be available as an alternative. Moreover, modern biotechnology is now also uncovering production routes to many other organic chemicals,

---

*See Chapter I. This technology was used in Germany during World War II to make fuels and chemicals from coal.

including propylene oxide, adipic acid, glycerine and methanol, though much more development work remains to be done. Well before the year 2000, as the price of oil increases and provides the incentive to substitute other feedstocks, these new routes will most likely be ready.

Opportunities for new technology development in chemistry are, in fact, prolific and they cover the full range of disciplines. This was well described in the so-called Pimentel Report, a study by the National Research Council Committee to Survey the Chemical Sciences, organized under the leadership of Professor George C. Pimentel at the University of California at Berkeley. In this report, a committee of 26 members, organized into five task forces, interviewed over 350 chemical researchers to obtain an overview of "cutting edge" research areas and opportunities and to develop a road map for research progress in a number of key areas.

The executive summary of the report set the theme:

"Fortunately, this is a time of intellectual ferment in chemistry, deriving from our increasing ability to probe and understand the elemental steps of chemical change and, at the same time, to deal with molecular complexity. Powerful instrumental techniques are a crucial dimension. We can anticipate exciting discoveries on a number of frontiers of chemistry. . . ."

And, relevant specifically to the future of petrochemical (more broadly, large scale organic chemical) technology, the Pimentel Report made some very poignant projections:

In Chemical Kinetics
"Over the next three decades, we will see advances in our understanding of chemical kinetics that will match those connected with molecular structures over the past three decades . . . lasers have spectacularly expanded experimental horizons for chemists . . . elementary reactions can (now) be dissected . . . these new avenues of study will clarify the factors that govern temporal aspects of chemical change.

In Chemical Theory
"Chemistry is on the verge of a renaissance, because of emerging ability to fold experiment and theory together to design chemical structures with properties of choice . . . computers (can) clarify transient situations not readily accessible to experimental measurements (and new) theoretical understandings are developing across chemistry. . . .

In Synthesis
"Modern instrumental techniques greatly facilitate discovery and testing of new reaction pathways and synthetic strategies . . . our accelerating progress . . . is erasing the border between inorganic and organic chemistry. . . .

In Catalysis
"Developing insights, fueled by an array of powerful instrumentation, are moving catalysis from an art to a science . . . it is now possible to see molecules as they react on catalytic surfaces . . . fundamental advances in these various facets of catalysis are forthcoming that will have great economic and technologic impact."

Does this seem like a mature industry? The catalysis area, in particular, is now experiencing a number of major advances in the development of both homogeneous and heterogenous catalysts. While much of this work is being done in universities in various countries, industry is also becoming somewhat more active. It is true that over the last several years, there has been little commercialization of new petrochemical process technology for all the reasons identified in this and the previous chapter. Nevertheless, a number of promising new catalyst systems and process routes have been researched at the pilot plant level, and they will undoubtedly lead to new processes at the industrial scale, in time. A good example is the technology known as the "functionalization of alkanes," a term used to describe the conversion of paraffins (rather than olefins) to such intermediates as vinyl chloride and acrylonitrile. It also refers to the production of aromatics from LPG, a new technology under development by BP Chemicals, Ltd, UOP, Mobil Oil, and other firms.

There has been some controversy with respect to whether scientific invention is stimulated primarily by product demand and the desire for economic gain or by technological opportunity. Although in some industries the former seems to be more important, it is not difficult to conclude that in the petrochemical industry, "perceived technological opportunity for process improvement is a major factor in determining the level of inventive activity." This statement, which is consistent with my own experience in the industry, comes from a recent study of patent filings over several decades in the area of synthetic fiber intermediates, including acrylonitrile, adipic acid, adiponitrile, terephthalic acid, p-xylene and other chemicals used in the production of synthetic fibers (15).

Although companies go through periods where low profits or changes in corporate strategy reduce funds spent on process research, there is no question that new routes, based on novel catalyst systems, will be invented as a result of the sheer excitement of making a "breakthrough" in an important area.

Therefore, it is safe to say that technological developments in industrial organic chemical synthesis will continue at a rapid rate. These advances promise the use of cheaper raw materials and the achievement of higher yields, greater productivity and/or higher purity products in many cases. Of course, the same could have been said 50 years ago, since it was just as true at that time. The question now is whether the chemical industry will have a second chance—an opportunity to implement new technologies, while achieving a more reasonable balance between (a) the benefits to society in the form of better products at lower cost and (b) the financial return to the company's shareholders.

PROBLEMS OF THE PAST

It is now timely to consider the problem of "what went wrong" in the petrochemical industry at some point along its development path. This is necessarily a complex question that defies easy answers and can stimulate controversy. Most observers will agree, however, that it is not accurate to say that the industry went into a state of decline as a result of the events of the 1970s (energy cost uncertainties, low demand growth, Third World projects, etc.). These issues affected many other industries as well, and not only those often characterized as "smokestack" industries. Moreover, there had already been warning signs by the 1960s, as far as petrochemical industry financial performance was concerned, and industry executives were quite aware of that fact. They were simply unwilling or unable to do anything meaningful about it at that time, choosing instead to build larger and larger plants to achieve incrementally lower production costs, or attempting to secure minor advantages in raw material costs. But these strategies did not deal with the problem of an excessively competitive environment and, as a result, profitability became even more unsatisfactory.

The events of the 1970s and early 1980s exacerbated the industry's problems but, in some respects, also had a salutary effect. (Several petrochemical executives were heard to say: "If only the recession had lasted a little longer, the industry 'shakeout' would have gone far enough to really do some good.") They forced companies to decide whether to stay in the business and, if they were to stay, to think about how to conduct business in the future. One of the main conclusions producers arrived at was that they were in too many diverse business segments and could not hope to compete well in all of them. This brought about "core business" definitions, divestitures, and shutdowns. Another conclusion was to differentiate products (even "commodity" products in some cases) to a greater degree, and to pursue niche, brand name and other such strategies. There was also a concerted effort to shift production to higher valued-added specialties and "performance" products, wherever possible.

All of these moves represented means to deal with the fundamental problem of extreme, sometimes irrational competition, the root cause of low profitability. To the extent that the industry restructuring process proceeds to a significant extent in reducing the number of players, industry financial performance should improve, perhaps substantially. Some positive feelings can also be derived from an examination of certain other factors that have historically caused many of the industry's problems. There is reason to believe that some of these factors will be of considerably less importance in the future.

From a historical perspective, it is relevant to ask which state of the industry (i.e., the extremely competitive conditions of the 1960s and 1970s or the more oligopolistic era of the 1930s) is the more "normal" one. We know that we cannot turn back the clock to the time of the cartels and countenance the anticompetitive market sharing and price-fixing agreements that characterized that era, but perhaps an intermediate condition can be found, where a more limited number of producers can achieve reasonable profits at product price levels that support new investment when increased demand requires the addition of capacity. If that seems like a utopian goal, it can be pointed out that even now, the manufacture of certain petrochemical products (e.g., propylene oxide) is profitable enough to fit this model. The question at hand is whether a much larger part of the industry could, in the future behave in this fashion. There are only two ways this can happen: (1) with closely controlled technology, and (2) through better management of product prices. Since both of these factors are, in large part, under the industry's control, and since some of the negative external factors that have plagued the industry in the past are abating, a road map for a better future can be drawn.

Looking at the past, it is seen that the items that exerted a negative influence on industry financial performance can be divided into those the industry could not do anything about and those over which it had some control.

THE INDUSTRY HAD NO CONTROL OVER THESE ISSUES

1. *Low "entry barriers" in most product lines over much of the time.* It was easy for firms to enter the petrochemical industry as soon as suitable technology became available. Plants were not particularly expensive in the 1950s and 1960s, particularly for companies already in capital-intensive industries.

2. *The independent actions of research and engineering firms serving the industry.* When companies like Scientific Design developed and broadly licensed process technology and to the extent engineering firms gained access to operating company design and operating experience, these firms could serve as a source of technology to new industry entrants and could therefore promote the construction of plants according to their own agendas, regardless of industry need.

3. *Government policies and actions, including social forces acting on these agencies.* Among these can be mentioned: (a) vigorous enforcement of antitrust legislation, including compulsory process licensing in the 1950s, (b) exemption of many Third World nations from import tariffs set under GATT (General Agreement on Tariffs and Trade) rules, (c) the reticence by European governments to shut down uneconomic capacity, which would aggravate already existing unemployment problems, and (d) the Canadian federal and provincial governments' energy pricing policies, as well as those of other oil-rich countries. A much larger list could easily be constructed.

4. *The aspirations of oil-rich and other Third World nations to industrialize.* Once the OPEC countries had asserted themselves in the pricing and supply of crude oil, it was only a short step for them to decide to build "downstream" refining

and petrochemical units. The only question was how many
and what kinds of units would be built and over what time
frame.

THESE ISSUES WERE UNDER THE CHEMICAL INDUSTRY'S CONTROL

1. *Management of capacity additions.* There was always too
   much enthusiasm and game playing here. Unrealistic demand growth projections, particularly in the more recent
   phase of development; unreasonable push for market share
   without the necessary means to achieve it; and poor strategic moves, in general, characterized much of the period.
   There were instances where preemptive moves to add capacity were quite successful (Rohm and Haas' strategy in methyl
   methacrylate monomer comes to mind), but, more often than
   not, there was oversupply, there were new entrants cutting
   price to gain market share and there was insufficient "signal-
   ing" by producers, which might have prevented duplication of
   new capacity.

2. *Frequent lack of pricing "discipline."* As early as 1961,
   Archie Albright of Stauffer Chemical said that price cutting in the face of rising costs was "poor economic states-
   manship" (6, p. 208). This statement was made in various
   forms throughout the 1960s and 1970s by executives of companies whose own salesmen were usually guilty of price cutting throughout the period. Of course, this practice was always blamed on the other guy. Price cutting occurred when
   new plants came onstream, when supply greatly exceeded
   demand, when companies were fighting for greater market
   share, and in the export market. Sometimes, when corporate
   executives took pricing decisions out of the hands of their
   salesmen, things got a little better, but usually the improvement did not last very long.

3. *Dissemination of proprietary technology.* Over much of the
   period, there was a strong tendency for operating companies
   to seek licensing income as an antidote to poor profits in
   their manufacturing business. In retrospect, this was a poor
   decision in many cases. For example, when Western Europe

became flooded with petrochemicals shipped from Eastern Europe as part of "compensation" agreements entered by contractors, the folly of licensing in this manner became crystal clear. Even within the home market, the policy of licensing proprietary technology was often a mistake. Good technology can and frequently will make more profit for the inventor when it is used in his own manufacturing plants than if it is licensed, but it is difficult for companies to resist the lure of licensing income, even when they realize that such a policy may backfire.

4. *Decisions to enter too many product lines.* In the 1950s and 1960s, it was common to find companies (Union Carbide and Monsanto are good examples) who had entered into the manufacture of so many organic chemicals and plastics that it became impossible for them to support the technology and market development of all of these products. Such companies became strong producers in a certain number of areas and "also-rans" in others. This proliferation of product lines made it difficult for management to have a strategic overview of the firm's entire business slate, leading to poor decisions regarding pricing, capacity additions, and industry exits. Only by the late 1970s did this fact really sink in, leading to the restructuring process still under way.

CHANGES IN INDUSTRY CONDITIONS

As mentioned earlier, there are reasons to believe that some of the problems that have plagued the industry in the past will not be as serious in the future.

The Number of Competitors Is Shrinking

Over the last five years or so, many companies have left different segments of the petrochemical industry by either shutting down uneconomical capacity or by selling it to competitors interested in building up their market share. Examples of this in two product areas are shown in Figure 13.8.

One reason why there are fewer competitors is that the Reagan administration has shown itself to be more lenient than previous administrations in its interpretation of the provisions of the

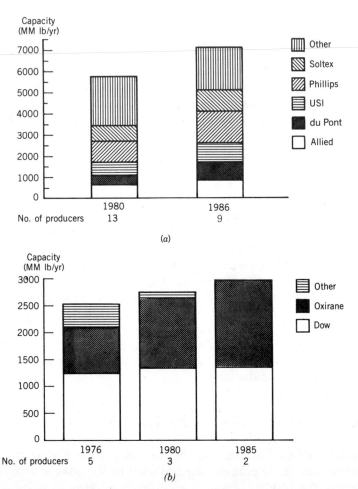

Figure 13.8 (*a*) Production of high-density polyethylene. (*b*) Production of propylene oxide. (*Source:* Chem Systems.)

Sherman and Clayton Antitrust Acts. Partly as a result of initiatives by the Commerce Department, there has been a general recognition that these venerable pieces of legislation, which were meant to protect small businesses from the predatory actions of monopolies, trusts, and "robber barons," had to be restudied in light of the many changes that have taken place in the United States and in global trade over the last several decades. In speeches and presentations by Administration officials, a new viewpoint was advanced with respect to how mergers should be evaluated and to what extent companies can cooperate in such areas as long-term research (16–19). Whereas Section 7 of the Clayton Act forbids mergers that will "tend to inhibit competition," the administration is now taking the attitude that a proposed industry consolidation may be acceptable if it leaves a sufficient number of strong competitors. Also, the market share of the proposed merged entity is now evaluated not only by looking at domestic competitors but also by adding the sales of foreign firms in the United States to the domestic market in determining the market share of domestic producers.

People outside the industry may believe that an environment of fewer competitors and higher profit margins is economically undesirable. However, if the goal is to have a strong domestic industry, then a reduction in the number of competitors and better pricing discipline will help avoid the need for protective tariffs, which are considered as being particularly undesirable by those interested in a free market system.

Capacity Additions Are Made Much More Carefully

The management of petrochemical companies has become increasingly concerned about the likely returns to be expected from a new plant, in fact about the wisdom of any new investment at all in the production of petrochemicals. In many large chemical companies, there is much greater interest in diversification through acquisitions or in entering the production of specialty and performance chemicals with higher profit margins than in producing basic petrochemicals. Where capacity additions are made, this is now done mainly in product areas that have been defined as part of the company's "core" business. And such new investments are now made only after a much more careful analysis of the industry supply/demand situation and of the likely actions of competitors.

The Large-Plant Syndrome Is No Longer An Issue

Although most new plants will still be world size, plant capacities have reached their maximum levels. There is no longer the enticement to build a larger plant than that operated by the largest competitor, a stratagem that may have provided a small advantage in production economics, while fostering capacity "overhang," leading to price cutting and poor profitability.

It is now recognized that giant plants are often too expensive, involving excessive financial risk, and that at times it makes sense to build a smaller plant, that can be kept at a higher operating rate. Also, the trend toward global product strategies often calls for building several smaller plants in different geographical areas. In the 1980s, the name of the game has actually been small incremental expansions at existing production sites, involving stepwise additions of reactor trains, distillation columns, etc. This is a beneficial regression to the earlier days of the industry.

Environmental Problems Inhibit New Construction

Public pressures have made it difficult to build "grass-roots" plants in new locations. The emission of liquid and gaseous waste streams from existing plants is carefully monitored by local government authorities so that, very often, it is difficult or impossible to build new units, even at existing sites, unless other units are put out of commission, thus keeping constant the total amount of pollutants emitted by the complex. These factors tend to act as strong entry barriers for new producers that do not operate plants at existing production sites.

Petrochemical Import Problems Are Not as Severe as Expected

While in some cases, such as for methanol, ammonia, and synthetic ethanol, the volumes of chemicals entering the United States from oil-rich and Comecon countries is substantial, the general effect of imports from oil-rich nations on the rest of the petrochemical industry is considerably less than once feared. This is not only true with respect to imports from the Middle East but also relative to Canada and Mexico, which were once considered as posing a major threat to U.S. producers.

The foreign import threat was really never as serious as it was made out to be, because it affected only a few petrochemicals made from natural gas, including gas-derived ethylene. While this included some important chemicals, many others must be made from propylene, butylene, butadiene, benzene, toluene, and xylene. Products made from these feedstocks would not be cheaper in Saudi Arabia or Canada than in the United States, because they are based on *oil* rather than *gas*. This is significant because the oil-rich nations have not been inclined to transfer oil-based feedstocks into their petrochemical operations at discount prices.

Even in the case of natural gas derivatives, the situation is much better than once projected, at least as far as U.S. and European producers are concerned. The total amount of petrochemical capacity installed in the Middle East and in Canada is quite small, relative to world demand, as was pointed out earlier in the chapter. Moreover, the landed price in the United States of materials such as Saudi polyethylene is such that it is only barely competitive with domestic material. Canadian polyethylene and styrene have also frequently not been competitive in the United States, except where Canadian producers were willing to sell at cash costs or less, providing them with little or no profit margin.

Independent Petrochemical Research Companies Have Almost Vanished

Obviously, this has some unfavorable connotations, since it has been shown that a disproportionate number of new inventions come from individual inventors and small R&D establishments. However, it is a fact that the companies that were so active in the development of chemical technology in the 1950s and 1960s are no longer a factor or have a very small role. Some, like Scientific Design, have ceased to exist, though some SD technology can still be purchased at this writing.* UOP and I.F.P. (The French Petroleum Institute) were more successful in developing petroleum refining than petrochemical technology and are not expected to provide a series of petrochemical "breakthroughs." The engineering contractors that made such major contributions in the design of petrochemical plants in the 1950–1970 period have almost all discontinued their research activities (Davy McKee is one exception). Because of the current low level of construction work, these contractors can no longer support process development efforts. They would now generally be unwilling to cooperate on development projects (which historically was done at their own cost), since the likely payout for success would be considered to be too low (slow demand growth means few new projects). The situation was quite different in the 1960s, when Badger worked with Goodrich on oxychlorination and with Sohio on acrylonitrile, in order to create opportunities for engineering-construction projects when these processes were licensed to other companies by their partners.

---

*Denka Chemical purchased certain assets of this firm in 1986.

It thus seems evident that many of the negative factors that caused problems for the industry and over which the industry had little or no control have, one way or another, taken a more favorable turn. It now remains to be seen whether the industry can do something about the other side of the equation: can industry achieve better control over its own behavior?

THE LICENSING DECISION

If one can learn anything from a study of the history of the chemical industry over the past 50 years, it is that proliferation of technology will lead to reduced operating profits. This is true not only for licensees, but also for the company that developed and licensed the technology, although this factor may be overshadowed by the income it receives from licensing.

The question of whether to license or not and, if so, to what companies, is an issue of considerable complexity for operating companies that have developed promising new technology. Although it is difficult to generalize, it is not inappropriate to suggest that companies in the past have too often taken the easy road and have licensed their new technology to competitors, rather than using it exclusively for their own benefit. As has been pointed out earlier, these companies might well have made more money by exclusively practicing the technology. Nothing in the antitrust laws denies inventors the right to monopoly control of their technology, as granted under the patent laws, provided companies behave in accordance with the rules. These make it possible for them to use the new technology to become or remain the dominant producer and to effectively cause the exit of less efficient producers. Instead, companies have often kept these companies in business by licensing the new technology to them (although the licensing firm usually tries to keep its technology slightly ahead of that made available to its licensees).

There are, of course, instances where the new invention is in a product area so large that the inventor cannot hope to dominate it—say, the production of ammonia or polyethylene. In the case of such products, no single company can build enough plants to establish a dominant market share. Even then, however, there may be a reason not to license, since the new invention may give a product that can be differentiated from the standard material produced by the rest of the industry. Dow and du Pont did this very successfully with their higher valued Dowlex and Sclair LLDPE polyethylene resins, respectively, at a time when Union Carbide was licensing dozens of companies with Unipol technology.

On the other hand, if the technology covers a "specification" product, such as ammonia or methanol, it is difficult to conclude that licensing will not be the appropriate way to recoup research costs and to make the highest profit from the invention, even if the company will have to compete with its own licensees. The proper decision in such cases, however, may still not be to license every competitor that applies. History has shown that in cases of indiscriminate licensing, the price of the product will tend to drop to unacceptably low levels. This redounds to the disadvantage of both licensor and licensees, since companies using the technology under license recognize that they cannot pay high royalties in situations where licensors will grant nonexclusive licenses to anybody in the industry. This has convinced a number of firms to adopt a selective licensing policy. It has also caused operating companies that have decided to support research programs at outside research establishments to insist on total control (essentially ownership) of the technology when it is commercialized.

A number of chemical firms have for a long time been opposed to licensing their technology to current or future competitors. Dow has hardly ever licensed and du Pont licenses very infrequently. Both companies have, in fact, said publicly on a number of occasions that they oppose licensing. A speech I gave to the Chemical Market Research Association at Pinehurst, North Carolina in 1973, also covered this ground (20):

> "... New, more economic technology offers a new producer a unique opportunity to penetrate a market dominated by other producers—or an existing producer to outdistance his competitors. Licensing such technology soon after commercialization may work in the wrong direction for little added gain in terms of royalty income and a real potential loss in terms of market share ... we strongly believe that the development of new process technology ... can ... pay off very well (when used by the operating company)".

Cogent thoughts along the same lines are expressed in an article published in 1985 in the *Journal of Business Strategy,* where the authors detail the pitfalls of licensing good technology to competitors (21). To what extent companies are likely to pursue such an exclusionary licensing policy in the future is difficult to say, but there is some reason to believe that firms will increasingly keep the best new technology for themselves. As has been discussed earlier, Halcon and Arco Chemical (in propylene oxide), du Pont, and Dow saw things this way a long time ago. Amoco Chemicals licensed its breakthrough terephthalic acid technology very selectively, eventually licensing just one domestic competitor (du Pont). Now, with little new capacity required for most petrochemicals, there is much more reason to maintain control over proprietary new processes. In applying new technology, it is easier to capture a large chunk of a market when that market is only expanding very slowly.

In the final analysis, it is up to the companies in each case to evaluate the course that will give them the highest ultimate return on their research investment. The issue here is whether these evaluations have been made correctly and which course should be taken in each situation. It is indeed a very difficult decision. Thus, with respect to polyester Terylene, Sir John Harvey-Jones, until recently chairman of ICI, has said, "we certainly gave more licenses than was wise," resulting in overcapacity in the world fiber market and excessive international competition, from which it took years for ICI to recover, yet "there was no way ICI could have kept an invention like that to itself . . . we couldn't have commanded the capital. The risk would have been enormous . . ." (22).

How great are the rewards for the development of "breakthrough" technology in petrochemicals? We have some answers for the past from several sources, including a book—scheduled for publication in 1987—entitled *Innovation and Competition,* written by Professor Robert Stobaugh at the Harvard Business School (23). He estimates that nylon earned du Pont well over $1 billion (probably over 90 percent from operating profits—P.H.S.) and that Sohio's profits on acrylonitrile reached $700 million (partly from selective worldwide licensing—P.H.S.). When a company does not license its new technology, it can usually enjoy a fairly long period of not having to deal with process imitators. Stobaugh's detailed study on nine chemicals showed that an average of 5.7 years elapsed between the time a new product and process for its manufacture appeared and the time another firm was able to imitate the invention. This is a reasonably long period, of course, and there is no reason to assume that the second firm began to engage in cutthroat competition as soon as it had developed a comparable process. In some cases, the second firm was even in another country.

Stobaugh's data should therefore be viewed in that context. Again, the experience of Halcon and Arco Chemical in propylene oxide and of Amoco in terephthalic acid, in both cases involving highly profitable ventures for 15 and 25 years, respectively, and representing more recent examples than those cited by Stobaugh, should be carefully noted.

Let's develop a very simplified scenario of how a firm currently in the styrene business might profit from developing a novel process, based on a less expensive raw material than benzene and ethylene. Assume that the firm has gained a dominant patent position, making it impossible for other firms to invent a similar process by circumventing the patents. (This does happen: Mobil Chemical has had such a position in shape-selective catalysts used for processes such as xylene isomerization, ethylbenzene, lube oil treating, and for the conversion of methanol to gasoline. The company's patents on its ZSM-5 zeolite catalysts used for these processes have, by some estimates, generated several hundred million dollars in profit for Mobil.) The firm with the new styrene process decides that it has a 5 cent per pound cost advantage over the most efficient current producer of styrene. It therefore decides to build a new styrene plant with a capacity of one billion pounds per year—about the usual size for new styrene plants. Let us now assume that the most efficient *existing* producer makes a profit of 2 cents per pound after covering his costs (including raw materials, utilities, other variable and fixed costs, depreciation—if any—and selling, general, and administrative [(S.G. and A.) expenses]. After startup, the new producer would, if he did not decide to cut the price of styrene,* be able to earn $50 million a year of additional pretax profit versus the next best producer (one billion pounds per year × $0.05 = $50 million). His total pretax profit would then be $70 million dollars per year (adding the current 2 cents per pound profit level). A couple of years later, a similar plant is started up in Western Europe to serve the EEC market. Then, a somewhat smaller joint venture plant is started up in Japan. It does not take a great deal of higher mathematics to show that such a scenario can be very profitable, since it can fairly rapidly recoup the company's research and development investment of,

---

*This is not necessarily an unrealistic situation–it might involve (a) the new producer shutting down some old, inefficient capacity and (b) a very inefficient producer finally exiting the business.

say, $30 million and can then generate a great deal of return on this investment.

If instead, a decision had been made to license the technology broadly, the price of styrene would probably have dropped to the point where very little profit would be made by the licensees as well as by the inventor-licensor. The latter would, of course, receive royalties, but based on experience, these would probably amount to less than five million dollars per year per licensee. Moreover, it is also very likely that the new producers (licensees) will cut the price of styrene to gain market share, so that the operating profit drops sharply or disappears altogether. It seems reasonable to conclude, therefore, that calculations of this kind have kept some firms from licensing their best proprietary technology to other companies.

The above example should be viewed against the experience with process licensing in the vinyl chloride industry, as recounted in Chapter 10. In this industry, little of the new technology was covered by strong patents, or in some cases, several new processes competed against each other. The patents involved were always easy to get around. Here again the experience in propylene oxide technology provides an answer. When Halcon and Arco found that they were working in the same area (i.e., use of an organic hydro-peroxide for the epoxidation of propylene), the companies decided to join forces and together build plants around the world. Reverting to vinyl chloride, we can only speculate what might have happened if Goodrich and Stauffer had decided to pool their oxychlorination technologies for ethylene dichloride production and to jointly exploit the process.

A MORE DIFFICULT RESEARCH CLIMATE

The breakup of the Conoco-Stauffer joint venture in vinyl chloride and PVC in the 1960s showed that the government was not ready for operating company joint ventures. Now, proposed legislation recommended by the Reagan Administration, including joint research programs by operating companies, indicates that we may have a new situation, though it is not yet clear that R&D joint ventures could be transformed into operating partnerships in all cases.

There are cogent reasons why government policy in this area has been under careful review and change. The odds against successful commercialization of new process technology have risen steeply over the last decade for many of the reasons elaborated previously. With few new plants needed and giant plants no longer being built in the hope of squeezing out some minor benefits of scale, operating companies have been keeping their older plants in operation. Most of them plan to keep doing that for a long time to come, if possible. In taking this position, they are supported by a new set of economics, which became a reality when companies no longer leapfrogged competitors with giant plants and when low demand growth made it more difficult to justify building new capacity. For a new producer to commercialize novel technology by shutting down an existing producer, he must be able to achieve a sales price (cost plus depreciation plus return on investment) equal to or lower than the cash cost of the existing producer. This often means that the new process must have variable costs 30 to 40 percent lower than those of the existing producers, and this is not often achieved. Moreover, if a different, cheaper raw material is used in the process, there must be reasonable certainty that its cost advantage can be maintained at least over the first several years of the plant's operation. This is difficult to project in this time of feedstock cost uncertainty.

Knowledgeable technical people in government positions recognize that technology will be invented and commercialized by somebody, somewhere, if the state of knowledge is propitious. This is why in Japan there are a number of research joint ventures in chemicals, such as in C_1 chemistry, which are not only supported but also partly funded by the government. In Europe, part of the chemical industry is under government control and this situation also allows more funds to flow to research. Many of the Comecon countries have active research and development efforts in many cases. Perhaps this is another reason why the U.S. government has apparently decided to support a policy that will spur and support research, including tax benefits, a review of antitrust legislation, and stronger enforcement of patent rights.

The barriers to new process commercialization may now actually be lower in Western Europe and Japan than in the United States. This is because there is more government support and ownership of petrochemical facilities in these areas and also because management in Europe and Japan seems to be able to take a longer range perspective. This allows companies, in some cases, to consider installing new facilities even if current economics do not fully support this step.

To summarize, the climate for process research is less favorable than in the 1950s and 1960s, the cost for process development has risen steeply, and the penalty for making wrong decisions is immeasurably higher. Yet, opportunities for new process development remain great, as the Pimentel Report suggests, and new breakthroughs will inevitably occur. Petrochemical process R&D will certainly be carried out actively in Europe and Japan. U.S. industry, which has traditionally led in this area, cannot allow itself to fall behind. With the United States losing its advantage in high technology products, there is now increasing government recognition that U.S. innovation must be fostered and facilitated. The patent laws remain in place to protect companies' rights to practice their inventions for many years, far longer than necessary to recoup their research investments. Development of excellent technology and the use of this technology to gain an advantage over domestic and international competitors remain two of the best means to achieve profitable operation. It is now up to industry to rise to this challenge.

MANAGEMENT GUIDELINES FOR THE FUTURE

If the opinions expressed in these pages are helpful in gaining a perspective on some of the problems the industry will have to solve, much will have been accomplished. One way or the other, the future is up to the industry's current and future management. Some final thoughts follow.

Getting back to Porter, his views on how to conduct business in industries reaching maturity are important reading matter (12, p. 238–240). His observations on the state of such an industry, partly covered earlier in this chapter, include:

- Slowing growth and more competition for market share
- More buyer sophistication
- Competition involving greater emphasis on cost and services
- Topping-out problem in adding industry capacity
- More international competition.

Some of Porter's recommendations on how to deal with these issues are very apt. He notes the errors of:

1. Placing too much attention on revenues and not enough on profitability
2. Hanging on too long with uneconomical capacity (in an excess capacity environment)
3. Emphasizing short-run profits at the expense of future market share, likely to be lost due to insufficient research, marketing, and other investments.

From the viewpoint of those who do not feel that the petrochemical industry is, in all respects, mature or who, like Professor Porter, believe that industries can have strategic breakthroughs where they can regain rapid growth through innovation, some of the recommendations Porter makes for mature industries would decidedly be counterproductive for petrochemical manufacturers. Thus, in mature industries, according to Porter:

- Companies should price aggressively to gain market share.
- There is too much emphasis on "creative, new" products, rather than concentrating on existing ones.
- There is also too much emphasis on product quality at the expense of aggressive pricing and marketing.

The consensus of the industry is just the opposite on the last two points and it is hard to believe that the industry is wrong in this respect. Moreover, there now seems to be a trend toward greater recognition that market share battles in this industry usually result only in losers.

As early as 1982, some strategic planners concluded that the "name of the game" in this decade would be to determine how companies finding themselves (temporarily or permanently, as the case may be) in a mature industry could become winners. An excellent Arthur D. Little paper advised companies to identify rapid growth segments or niches in their mature businesses, on the basis that (a) the potential rewards can be much greater due to the size of the (mature) industry, (b) competitors are unwilling to expend funds in industries that, on the whole, show low growth, and (c) fast footwork as a result of innovation can bring surprisingly large rewards (24). A recent, good example of this is afforded by the specialty copolymers developed by some of the high-pressure polyethylene producers during a time when others had effectively written off any attempt to do more than milk whatever cash might be available from the future operations of their conventional plants in light of the advent of linear low density polyethylene (LLDPE).

An already-referenced article (21) advises firms to refrain from concluding that the history of a product will inexorably follow conventional life-cycle concepts. With Richard Foster of McKinsey & Company (25), these authors believe that new process technology can result in renewed product growth and profitability for companies that understand the limitations of their existing processes, and are willing to invest in new technological approaches. And while Professor Lester Thurow, now head of M.I.T.'s Sloan School, has warned that "our most serious failure is in research that would lead to new processes for making old products, or to new products that are five to ten years from marketability" (26), this cautionary advice seems to apply more to the real "smokestack" industries than to petrochemicals.

Bill Reynolds of Shell Chemical who has contributed many good articles and industry association speeches over the years, recently addressed the issue of how he believed business should be conducted in the current environment. Tables 13.3 and 13.4 give his views on how players should view the quality of their business environment and what kind of checklist a petrochemical industry "survivor" should have at his fingertips, when going through the restructuring process. According to Reynolds, companies who should stay in businesses are those that, at the end of the day, will have 10 or less

Table 13.3 Quality of the Business Environment

Factors	Favorable	Unfavorable
Excess capacity		X
Ten or fewer players	X	
Low exit barrier	X	
Product differentiation		
Utility		X
Pockets of differentiated products	X	
Growth rate exceeds 2 × GNP	X	
Growth rate GNP or less		X
Reinvestment requirements high		X
Vertical integration pervasive		X
International business		X

Source: See Ref. 27. Reproduced by permission of the American Institute of Chemical Engineers.

Table 13.4 Survivor's Checklist

Factor	Essential	Desirable
Low-cost producer	X	
High-quality customer list	X	
$\dfrac{\text{Value added}}{\text{fixed cost}} = 1.2$ during economic downturn	X	
$\dfrac{\text{Value added}}{\text{fixed cost}} = 1.5$ during economic upturn		X
Program in place to lower fixed cost in real terms 1% per year or better	X	
Minimal layers of management		X
Strong technical position	X	
Some areas of differentiation		X

Source: See Ref. 27. Reproduced by permission of the American Institute of Chemical Engineers.

players due to low exit barriers (my recommended figure is lower—P.H.S.), whose growth rate is expected to be well above that of the GNP, and which allow some "pockets" of product differentiation. A contented survivor will be the low-cost producer able to enjoy a reasonable "value-added" component, which is defined as what is left over to pay the fixed costs plus a profit. Reynolds also addresses the key subjects of decentralization, new business creation, and entrepreneurism: The ability to apply creative thinking to old situations will make the difference in many cases (27).

Professor Bower at Harvard ended his book on recent petrochemical industry problems and their possible solutions with a chapter entitled "A Restructuring Agenda for Managers." (7, pp. 207–217). Here, he recommends three tasks of ultimate importance. First, it is necessary for firms to create a long-term "profit capability" through a detailed, strategic analysis of every business segment, followed by a ruthless weeding out of all parts that will not make it in the future. Second, a corporate structure must be established that treats each business in accordance with its essential qualities and its future prospects. Inevitably, this leads to a highly flexible management approach, involving major deviations from the classical type of organizational structure. Finally, management must convince its workers and staff and the outside world, including public agencies of the "legitimacy" of the company's rationalization strategy, which embodies the firm's belief that with these changes, which often require disposal of employees and businesses, there can be a viable future.

The petrochemical industry's management now appears to be coming to the same conclusions. By 1990, the restructuring process should be complete, and it will be time to get back to long-range planning. Profitability in 1986 and 1987 became much better and considerable optimism over the future of this cyclical industry was starting to be expressed. By 1990, it would also be evident whether the industry had finally learned its lessons.

THE END AND THE BEGINNING

And so we come to the end of the story, but, of course, it is not the end. In this book, now much longer than originally visualized, an attempt has been made to trace the history of modern organic and polymer chemistry and to show how the advent of petroleum feedstocks made it possible for this vigorous new industry to give the world the products it now considers indispensable. This petrochemical industry, which now accounts for close to six percent of the Gross National Product (GNP) in the industrial countries, will continue to grow and perhaps even prosper if, in the current parlance, it finally "gets its act together."

There were numerous beginnings and milestones and most of these had nothing to do with petrochemistry, as some of the earlier chapters indicate. For the most part, they were important scientific discoveries that broke new ground in man's desire to obtain a better understanding of his universe, particularly of the materials—chemists would say, the elements in the form of atoms and molecules—found on earth. It was a long, often difficult search that is far from over. But today, at least, it is largely carried out without the skepticism that once made research a lonely and frequently unrewarding task.

In many respects, the discovery that compounds containing carbon (the element) could be synthesized by man was one of the biggest chemical breakthroughs and, at the time, highly controversial. All of synthetic organic chemistry and almost all of polymer chemistry is based on carbon, which is also the "sine qua non" of life itself. In a marvelous autobiographical work, *The Periodic Table,* Primo Levi, an Italian chemist, had this to say in his chapter on *carbon* (28):

"Carbon, in fact, is a singular element: it is the only element that can bind itself in long stable chains without great expense of energy and for life on earth (the only one we know so far) precisely, long chains are required. Therefore, carbon is the key element of living substance: but its promotion, its entry into the living world, is not easy and must follow an obligatory, intricate path, which has been clarified (and not yet definitively) only in recent years. If the elaboration of carbon were not a common, daily occurrence, on the scale of billions of tons a week, wherever the green of a leaf appears, it would by full right deserve to be called a miracle."*

Sooner or later, chemists were bound to discover that carbon-containing compounds known to be associated with the life process could be produced in their laboratory by reacting simple chemicals, at least one of which contained a carbon atom. Thus, when Woehler in 1828 synthesized an animal product, urea, from ammonium cyanate, he opened the door on a new world. Now man could start to think about augmenting the supply of "organic" materials found in nature through the use of chemistry that, to that time, had been limited to producing "inorganic" chemicals (e.g., strong acids and alkalis) or to transform one organic material into another (e.g., thermal decomposition of coal into various gases, liquids, and tars). But Woehler, whose discovery was highly controversial, and to some even frightening, changed the course of chemistry forever. Together with Justus Liebig, another very famous chemist of his time, Woehler wrote (29, p. 225):

"The philosopher of chemistry will from this work draw the conclusion that the production of all organic matters in our laboratories, inasmuch as they do not belong any more to the organism, must be regarded not only as probable but as certain. Sugar, salicin and morphine will be made artificially. It is true we do not know the methods by which this final result will be reached, because the rudiments are unknown from which they are to be developed, but we shall know them in time. We have not to deal with bodies whose composition rests on assumptions, we know that with positive certainty; we know in what proportions they are combined; we know that they are products of forces of which we are cognizant."

What a magnificent statement to make in the year 1848, before the synthesis of organic dyestuffs, aspirin, and other organic chemical specialties and many decades before the development of synthetic rubber, synthetic fibers, and polyethylene!

*From *The Periodic Table* by Primo Levi, translated by Raymond Rosenthal, copyright 1984, Schocken Books, published by Pantheon Books, a Division of Random House, Inc.

Woehler's contemporaries were reluctant at the time to acknowledge his dramatic accomplishment. Wasn't the cyanide used as a reactant derived from animal materials? It was, so that for a short time it was still possible to believe that "organic" materials came only from nature, from what was then called "a vital force." Only a few years later, however, this skepticism was laid to rest through the work of Berthelot in France. Stimulated by his knowledge of fat chemistry and the reaction of glycerine and higher fatty alcohols with acids to form other carbon-containing alcohols, Berthelot became convinced that it was possible to build up such materials from simple carbon oxides. In 1855, he produced formic acid from carbon monoxide. Soon thereafter, he synthesized methane, ethylene, and acetylene. He then also produced alcohols from ethylene and benzene from acetylene. Berthelot's work "effectively broke down the barrier between organic and inorganic chemistry and presented synthesis as an attainable goal" (29).

In our time, we have lived through another great discovery—the unraveling of the puzzle represented by the genetic code. And chemists have come much further in synthesizing the substances that constitute key parts of the life process, such as the amino acids, the building blocks for proteins and enzymes. Not surprisingly, this research is again accompanied by concern, as we come another step closer in our understanding of the secret of life. Yet, in some respects, these discoveries come just in time, for in the next century we will have to become less dependent on the fossil resources left to us over millions of years by the decay of vegetable and animal matter. We are using these up too fast. At some point we will have to change our ways and become more dependent on the biomass resources around us, the forests, agricultural wastes, plants that efficiently convert sunlight into carbohydrates, etc. Our increasing understanding of biochemistry will help us in this transition.

More relevant to the subject of this book, biomass sources such as wood, the guayule and jojoba plants, starch sugar, and fats can all be used to make chemicals. In a paper I presented to the World Petroleum Congress in Houston in April 1987 covering trends in petrochemical technology (30), I referred to remarks made by Prof. Krauch of Chemische Werke Huels at a conference in Tokyo several years earlier. He said that the availability of cheap fossil fuels has led to a "destructive" chemistry of "fragmentation," whereas utilization of carbon sources based on biomass would lead to a "preserving" chemistry. This would take further development since, in nature, "synthesis reactions, rearrangement reactions and degradation reactions proceed under the mild conditions of vegetable and animal life with a level of selectivity which is beyond the reach of petrochemistry" (2). Even now, the same chemists who are advancing the art of conventional catalysis are in the early stages of identifying so-called biomimetic catalysts, materials that imitate the highly selective action of enzymes, but can perform this function at higher rates and under more severe conditions of pressure and, particularly, temperature.

And so, the search continues and we are privileged to be observers and sometimes even participants. For those of us who believe that the advancement of science and technology is an inexorable process that brings far more good than harm to mankind, the future looks bright.

REFERENCES

1. H. F. Tomfohrde III (1984). Maintaining state-of-the-art technology in a slower growth environment, paper presented to the Société de la Chimie Industrielle, Paris, France.
2. Peter Hofman and Carl Heinrich Krauch (1982, 1986). Carbon sources in the future chemical industries, lecture presented to the Annual Meeting of the Chemical Society of Japan, Tokyo; also Chemie ein Teil der Ökologie, lecture presented at Thyssen A.G., July.
3. A. L. Waddams (1980). *Chemicals From Petroleum—An Introductory Survey*, Fourth Edition, London, John Murray.
4. Stanford Research Institute (0000). *Chemical Economics Handbook*, Menlo Park, CA, Stanford Research Institute.
5. Help us choose a winner, Kirkpatrick Chemical Engineering Achievement Award, *Chemical Engineering*, February 5, 1973, p. 40.
6. Perrin Stryker (1961). Chemicals: The ball is over, *Fortune*, October.
7. Joseph L. Bower (1986). *Why Markets Quake: The Management Challenge of Restructuring Industry*, Boston, MA, Harvard Business School Press.
8. H. A. Sorgenti (1986). Restructuring towards a new age of vitality, paper presented at the Society of Chemical Industry Meeting, Madrid, Spain, October 6.
9. Lester C. Thurow (1985). *The Zero Sum Solution: Building a World Class American Economy*, New York, Simon & Schuster, p. 100.
10. Chem Systems International Ltd. (1983). *Restructuring the European Petrochemical Industry*, A Multiclient Subscriber Report, London.
11. Kathryn Harrigan and Michael E. Porter (1983). End-game strategies for declining industries, *Harvard Business Review*, July-August, pp. 111-120.

12. Michael E. Porter (1980). *Competitive Strategy,* New York, Free Press.

13. Norman Hochgraf (1983). The future technological environment, paper presented at the Eleventh World Petroleum Congress, London.

14. Opportunities in chemistry: Long-awaited report issued, *Chemical and Engineering News,* October 14, 1985, 9-22.

15. P. Wiseman (1983). Patenting and inventive activity on synthetic fibre intermediates, Research Policy No. 12, North Holland, Elsevier Science, pp. 329-339.

16. James C. Miller III (1983). Federal Trade Commission, statement on antitrust, innovation, and productivity before the Subcommittee on Monopolies and Commercial Law of the House Committee on the Judiciary, U.S. House of Representatives, September 14.

17. J. Paul McGrath (1984). Department of Justice, Remarks on Current Antitrust Enforcement Policy and the Revised Merger Guidelines, New York, June 7.

18. Malcolm Baldridge (1986). U.S. Department of Commerce, Press Conference Statement, Washington DC, February 19.

19. Department of Justice press release, February 19, 1986.

20. Peter H. Spitz (1974). Perspectives on process technology, paper presented at Chemical Marketing Research Association Meeting, Pinehurst, NC, September 8-10.

21. Robert V. Ayres and Wilbur A. Steger (1985). Rejuvenating the life cycle concept, *Journal of Business Strategy,* Vol. 6, No. 1, Summer, 66-76.

22. Carol Kennedy (1986). *ICI: The Company That Changed Our Lives,* London, Century Hutchinson, p. 180.

23. Robert B. Stobaugh (1988). *Innovation and Competition: The Global Management of Petrochemical Products,* Cambridge, MA, Harvard Business School Press.

24. Roger F. Hearne (1982). Fighting industrial senility: A system for growth in mature industries, *The Journal of Business Strategy,* Vol. 3, No. 2, 3-20.

25. Richard N. Foster (1986). *Innovation: The Attacker's Advantage,* New York, Summit Books.

26. Lester C. Thurow (1985). A world class economy: Getting back into the ring, *Technology Review,* August/September, 27-37.

27. W. W. Reynolds (1986). Strategies for survival and growth, *Chemical Engineering Progress,* June, 21-24.

28. Primo Levi (1984). *The Periodic Table,* New York, Schocken Books.

29. F. Sherwood Taylor (1922). *A History of Industrial Chemistry,* New York, Abelard-Schuman.

30. Peter H. Spitz (1987). Technology trends in petrochemicals manufacture, Twelfth World Petroleum Congress, Houston, TX, April 26-May 1, 1987.

APPENDIX: Description of Technical Terms

Readers not familiar with chemistry and with terms used in the refining and chemical industries will have difficulty in following the text of some of the chapters. The following list is not comprehensive, but may nevertheless be helpful. Some of the following definitions are purposely kept simple to avoid confusion. (To chemists: please pardon such transgressions.)

TERMS RELATING TO HYDROCARBONS

Hydrocarbons. Chemicals containing only carbon and hydrogen atoms.

Petroleum Fractions. Crude oil is a mixture of light and heavy hydrocarbons that are separated into various fractions in a refinery distillation column (pipe still) and then further processed or treated and sold as products. In progressive order, these fractions are:

	Contained Carbon Atoms (generalized)
Liquefied petroleum gas (LPG) or gas liquids	3 or 4
Light naphtha (gasoline boiling range)	5–6
Heavy naphtha (gasoline boiling range)	7–9
Light gas oil (kerosene, diesel oil range)	10–12
Heavy gas oil (lubricating oil range)	Higher
Residual oils (asphalt, heavy fuel oil)	Much higher

NOTES:
1. "Distillates" is the term generally used for naphthas and gas oils.
2. Methane (one carbon), ethane (two carbons), and propane (three carbons) are gaseous at ambient temperature.
3. Most crude oil has an average composition equivalent to gas oil. Since gasoline is usually the product desired in the largest quantity, a certain amount of the crude must be "cracked" into the naphtha boiling range.
4. Fuel oils have boiling ranges varying from light and heavy gas oils to residual oils.

Natural Gas. Found either separately or associated with crude oil; this is primarily methane, with some ethane, propane, and higher hydrocarbons. Natural gas often contains hydrogen sulfide, carbon dioxide, and other nonhydrocarbon constituents.

Alkane. A straight-chain hydrocarbon without double bonds— also called *paraffin.*

Methane, Ethane, Propane, Butane. The simplest straight-chain alkane structures, with respectively one, two, three, or four carbon atoms. Isobutane is an *isomer* of butane (i.e., same formula but with a branch.)

Olefins. A hydrocarbon containing one double bond in its structure (double bonds are much more reactive than the usual single bonds found in most fractions of crude oil and natural gas). Ethylene is the simplest olefin, with two carbon atoms. Then comes propylene (three carbon atoms, one double bond), butylene (four carbon atoms, one double bond), etc. Compounds with double (or triple) bonds are also called *unsaturates.*

Diolefins. These compounds contain two double bonds and are even more reactive than olefins. The diolefin *butadiene* has two double bonds.

Aromatics. A hydrocarbon or hydrocarbon derivative containing a ring structure. Benzene is the simplest common aromatic hydrocarbon. (The term "aromatics" is also used for ring compounds with side chains that may contain atoms other than carbon and hydrogen.)

Naphthenes or Cycloparaffins. Same as aromatics, but without double bonds in the ring structure. Cyclohexane is a simple naphthene, with a six-membered ring, like benzene.

TERMS RELATING TO HYDROCARBON DERIVATIVES

Aliphatics. Hydrocarbon derivatives that do not have a ring structure.

Aromatics. Hydrocarbon derivatives with a ring structure.

Alcohols. Organic liquids containing a hydroxyl group (-OH) attached to a carbon atom.

Oxygenates. Generally, chemicals containing carbon, hydrogen, and oxygen in their structure (e.g., alcohols, aldehydes, ketones).

Organics. Term used to cover the compounds of carbon, which may contain hydrogen, oxygen, nitrogen, sulfur and other *heteroatoms*.

TRANSFORMATIONS*

Alkylation. Usually the reaction of a hydrocarbon such as an alkane or aromatic with an olefin (double-bond-containing molecule), using an acid or other catalyst.

*Often referred to as *processes* in the text.

Isomerization. Rearrangement of a molecule to a different chemical configuration (e.g., branched versus linear), while maintaining the same atomic composition.

Dehydrogenation. The process of removing one or more hydrogen atoms from a hydrocarbon structure to form a double bond (where the hydrogen leaves), or which can produce an aromatic material from a naphthene ring compound (e.g., cyclohexane) or can form a ring compound upon removal of hydrogen. (*Hydrogenation* is, of course, the opposite process.)

Cracking. The process whereby a long-chain molecule or a complex mixture of longer chain molecules is broken into smaller molecules through the use of heat, with or without a catalyst. In the latter cases, the process is often referred to as *pyrolysis*.

Hydrocracking. Petroleum fraction cracking in the presence of hydrogen—usually under relatively high pressure—to produce smaller molecules with little or no unsaturation. (See *Other Terms*)

Steam Cracking. Used to describe the high-temperature cracking of hydrocarbons to give fairly high yields of olefins (e.g., ethylene, propylene).

Reforming. Use of heat and usually a catalyst to transform hydrocarbons into (1) other hydrocarbons (e.g., in naphtha reforming used to make aromatics from paraffins and naphthenes) or (2) mixtures of hydrocarbons and oxides of carbon, with air or steam taking part in the reaction. Reforming is used to improve the quality (octane number) of gasoline.

Polymerization. The formation of very large molecules from small molecules, a catalyst being normally employed for this purpose. The resulting material is a polymer.

Condensation reaction. The formation of a molecular that usually results from the reaction of an acid (carboxyl) group and an alcohol group, which also produces water as a by-product. This type of reaction can yield very large molecules.

Oxidation. Reaction of oxygen with a hydrocarbon molecule to produce an oxygenate or, if carried further, to produce carbon monoxide, carbon dioxide, and water.

Pyrolysis. See *Cracking,* above.

PHYSICAL SEPARATIONS

Distillation. Separation of two or more components in a column containing trays or packing, whereby, through the use of successive vaporization and condensation, the feed mixture is separated into a lighter and a heavier fraction.

Crystallization. Separation of a mixture by chilling a solution and recovering the solid crystals (e.g., in a filter or centrifuge).

Extraction. Separation of a component in a mixture, using a liquid with selective solvent characteristics.

Absorption. Contacting a gaseous stream containing a separable material with a liquid solvent flowing down a column, using trays or packing, whereby the solvent absorbs the material from the gas.

OTHER TERMS

Catalytic Process. Use of a catalyst to increase a chemical reaction to a rate that allows the design of a commercially economic plant.

Dimer, Trimer, Oligomer. These are successively formed when a molecule containing a double bond reacts with itself to start forming a longer chain molecule.

Saturation/Unsaturation. Refers to the presence (or lack of) molecules containing double bonds (see *Olefins*), above.

Elastomer. A synthetic polymer with rubberlike characteristics.

Intermediate. A chemical formed as a middle step in a series of chemical reactions. Intermediates can often be converted to different end products.

Monomer. A chemical of relatively low molecular weight that may be reacted with itself or other reactive chemicals to form various types and lengths of molecular chains termed polymers or copolymers.

Polymer. A high-molecular-weight material obtained by joining together many simple molecules (monomers), linked end to end or cross-linked.

Thermoplastics. *Polymers* that soften without chemical change when heated or cooled.

Thermosets. *Polymers* that form networks when heated, altering the structure such that they do not soften at higher temperatures.

Chemical Index

567

Subject Index